MW01104106

Hungarian Language Contact Outside Hungary

Impact: Studies in language and society

IMPACT publishes monographs, collective volumes, and text books on topics in sociolinguistics. The scope of the series is broad, with special emphasis on areas such as language planning and language policies; language conflict and language death; language standards and language change; dialectology; diglossia; discourse studies; language and social identity (gender, ethnicity, class, ideology); and history and methods of sociolinguistics.

General Editors

Annick De Houwer
University of Antwerp

Ana Deumert
Monash University

Advisory Board

Peter Auer
Uuniversity of Freiburg

Elizabeth Lanza
University of Oslo

Jan Blommaert
Ghent University

William Labov
University of Pennsylvania

Annick De Houwer
University of Antwerp

Peter H. Nelde
Catholic University Brussels

J. Joseph Errington
Yale University

Peter L. Patrick
University of Essex

Anna Maria Escobar
University of Illinois at Urbana

Jeanine Treffers-Daller
University of the West of England

Guus Extra
Tilburg University

Victor Webb
University of Pretoria

Marlis Hellinger
University of Frankfurt am Main

Volume 20

Hungarian Language Contact Outside Hungary:
Studies on Hungarian as a minority language
Edited by Anna Fenyvesi

Hungarian Language Contact Outside Hungary

Studies on Hungarian as a minority language

Edited by

Anna Fenyvesi

University of Szeged

John Benjamins Publishing Company

Amsterdam / Philadelphia

™ The paper used in this publication meets the minimum requirements
of American National Standard for Information Sciences – Permanence
of Paper for Printed Library Materials, ANSI z39.48-1984.

Library of Congress Cataloging-in-Publication Data

Hungarian Language Contact Outside Hungary : Studies on Hungarian as a
minority language / edited by Anna Fenyvesi.
        p.   cm. (Impact: Studies in language and society, ISSN 1385–7908 ; v.
20)
        Includes bibliographical references and indexes.
        1. Hungarian language--Foreign countries. 2. Hungarian language--
Social aspects. 3. Hungarian language--Political aspects. 4. Linguistic
minorities. 5. Sociolinguistics. 6. Languages in contact. I. Fenyvesi, Anna,
1964- II. Series.

        PH2700.H86 2005
        494'.511--dc22   2005040626
        ISBN 90 272 1858 7 (Eur.) / 1 58811 630 1 (US) (Hb; alk. paper)

John Benjamins Publishing Co. · P.O. Box 36224 · 1020 ME Amsterdam · The Netherlands
John Benjamins North America · P.O. Box 27519 · Philadelphia PA 19118-0519 · USA

Table of contents

List of tables

List of figures

List of maps

List of abbreviations

Abbreviations referring to languages and varieties

AH   Hungarian used in the United States
AmE   American English
AusH   Hungarian used in Australia
BLH   Hungarian used in Burgenland, Austria
BLG   German used in Burgenland, Austria, by German-only speakers
DU   Dutch
E   English
G   German
HH   Hungarian used in Hungary
HO   Hungarian used outside Hungary
HS   Hungarian used in Slovakia
OWH   Hungarian used in Oberwart, Austria
PH   Hungarian used in Prekmurje
RH   Hungarian used in Romania
R   Romanian
SuH   Hungarian used in Subcarpathia
SS   Slovak used in Slovakia
VH   Hungarian used in Vojvodina, Yugoslavia

Abbreviations used in glosses

1SG   first person singular
1PL   first person plural
2OBJ   second person object
2PL   second person plural
2SG   second person singular
3PL   third person plural
3SG   third person singular
ABL   ablative case
ACC   accusative case
ADER   suffix deriving an adjective
ALL   allative case

CAF	causal-final case
CAUS	causative suffix
CMP	comparative suffix
COND	conditional mood
DAT	dative case
DEF	definite conjugation
DEL	delative case
DIM	diminutive suffix
ELA	elative case
EMPH	emphasis marker
ESS	essive case
FUT	future tense
ILL	illative case
IMP	imperative-subjunctive mood
INDEF	indefinite conjugation
INE	inessive case
INF	infinitive
INS	instrumental case
NDER	suffix deriving a noun
NEG	negative
PART	participial form
PAST	past tense
PL	plural
POSS	personal possessive
POT	potential suffix
PVB	preverb
PX	possessive suffix
REFL	reflexive
SUB	sublative case
SUP	superessive case
TEM	temporal case
TERM	terminative case
VDER	suffix deriving a verb

About the authors

Attila Benő (b. 1968) is lecturer at the Hungarian Language and Culture Department at Babeş–Bolyai University in Cluj/Kolozsvár, Romania. He studied linguistics and literature at the same university, where he received his PhD in 2000. His dissertation addressed the semantic aspects of Romanian–Hungarian language contact. His research and publications focus on the cognitive aspects of bilingualism.

Address for correspondence: Univ. Babeş-Bolyai, Facultatea de Litere, Catedra de Limba Maghiara, 3400 Cluj-Napoca, str. Horea nr. 31, Romania; abeno@lett.ubbcluj.ro.

Csanád Bodó is assistant lecturer at the Hungarian Historical Linguistics, Sociolinguistics, and Dialectology Department at Eötvös Loránd University, Budapest, Hungary. His research interests include bilingualism and language planning, with particular reference to ethnic minorities in Hungary and Hungarian minorities in Austria and Romania.

Address for correspondence: ELTE BTK Magyar Nyelvtörténeti, Szociolingvisztikai, Dialektológiai Tanszék, 1052 Budapest, Pesti Barnabás u. 1, Hungary; csanad_bodo@ ludens.elte.hu.

István Csernicskó (b. 1973) teaches linguistics at the Subcarpathian Hungarian Teacher Training College, Berehove, Ukraine. He completed his university education at the State University of Užhorod, Ukraine, in 1995, and received his PhD in linguistics at Eötvös Loránd University in Budapest, Hungary, in 2000. His research is focused on the bilingualism of Hungarians in Ukraine, including its linguistic, educational, language planning and language policy aspects.

Address for correspondence: KMTF, Illyés Gyula sétány 1, Beregszász, 90200 Ukraine; limes@kmtf.uz.ua.

Casper de Groot is senior lecturer of theoretical linguistics and Hungarian linguistics at the University of Amsterdam. His fields of research and teaching are Functional (Discourse) Grammar, linguistic typology, morphology, and tense and aspect systems. He is one of the editors of the *Functional Grammar Series*, published by Mouton de Gruyter.

Address for correspondence: Theoretical Linguistics, Universiteit van Amsterdam, Spuistraat 210, NL-1012 VT Amsterdam, The Netherlands; C.deGroot@uva.nl.

Anna Fenyvesi is Associate Professor of Linguistics at the English and American Studies Institute at the University of Szeged, Hungary. She received her PhD in linguistics (1998) at the University of Pittsburgh. She is co-author of the first descriptive grammar of Hungarian written in English (published by Routledge in 1998). Her research interests include language contact, sociolinguistics, bilingualism, the immigrant languages of the USA, and the language of Hungarians in the USA.

Address for correspondence: SZTE BTK Angol-Amerikai Intézet, Szeged, Egyetem u. 2, 6722, Hungary; fenyvesi@lit.u-szeged.hu.

Lajos Göncz (b. 1944) is Professor and Chair of Psychology at the University of Novi Sad, Serbia and Montenegro. He received his university education in psychology at the University of Zagreb, Yugoslavia, and completed his graduate studies in psychology at the University of Belgrade. He attended further courses in Canada and Hungary. His publications include 3 monographs and about 100 articles. His area of research is the psychology of bilingualism and its developmental psychology, educational psychology, and psycholinguistic aspects.

Address for correspondence: Filozofski fakultet, Katedra za psihologiju, 21000 Novi Sad, Stevana Musića 24, Serbia and Montenegro; goencz@eunet.yu.

Miklós Kontra is Professor of Linguistics at the University of Szeged and Head of the Department of Sociolinguistics in the Linguistics Institute of the Hungarian Academy of Sciences, Budapest. His primary interests lie in variation in Hungarian; the contact varieties of Hungarian in Slovakia, Ukraine, Romania, Serbia, Slovenia and Austria; Hungarian-American bilingualism; educational linguistics and Linguistic Human Rights. He has published *Fejezetek a South Bend-i magyar nyelvhasználatból* [The Hungarian language as Spoken in South Bend, Indiana] (1990), *Túl a Kecegárdán* [Beyond Castle Garden: An American Hungarian Dictionary of the Calumet Region, co-authored with Andrew Vázsonyi] (1995), coedited *Hungarian Sociolinguistics* [=*IJSL* # 111, 1995], *Language: A Right and a Resource. Approaching Linguistic Human Rights* (1999), and edited *Language Contact in East-Central Europe* [=*Multilingua*, Volume 19-1/2, 2000].

Address for correspondence: MTA Nyelvtudományi Intézet, Budapest, Pf: 701/518, 1399, Hungary; kontra@nytud.hu.

Magdolna Kovács is Professor of Hungarian Language and Culture at the Department of Finno-Ugric Studies, University of Helsinki, Finland. She was born in Hungary where she graduated from university in 1981. Since 1987 she has lived in Finland where she received her PhD at Åbo Akademi University in 2001. Her research interests include Finno-Ugric languages, especially Finnish, Hungarian and Sámi, and sociolinguistics. Several of her recent publications deal with language change in Australian Hungarian and Australian Finnish.

Address for correspondence: Department of Finno-Ugric Studies, University of Helsinki, P.O. Box 25, 01400 Helsinki, Finland; kovacs@mappi.helsinki.fi.

István Lanstyák was born in Losonc/Lusanec, Slovakia, in 1959. He received his university degree in English and Hungarian in 1983 at Lajos Kossuth University, in Debrecen, Hungary. He has been teaching at the Hungarian Department of Comenius University, Bratislava, Slovakia, since 1989. He received his PhD at Comenius University in 1995. He carried out research in dialectology until the early 1990s. Since then his main research interest has been in the study of Hungarian-Slovak bilingualism. His publications focus on issues of bilingualism, as well as language planning, language cultivation, mother tongue education, and language policy. Recently he has started work on the theory of translation.

Address for correspondence: Nám. priateľstva 2171/36, 929 01 Dunajská Streda, Slovakia; lanstyak@fphil.uniba.sk.

Klára Sándor is Professor of Linguistics at the University of Szeged, Hungary. Her fields of interest are the theory of language change connected to evolutionary theory, the culture-specific and universal characteristics of linguistic stigmatization, folk linguistics, the history of Hungarian, and the linguistic situation of the Csángós. She also works on applying linguistic knowledge to decrease linguistic discrimination in education, and to build up inhabitant-friendly artificial intelligence systems at local governments. In 1995/1996 she served as advisor of the pilot copy of the first Csángó spelling-book that intended to introduce the Hungarian alphabet to Csángó pupils and to make the first steps towards the establishment of Csángó literacy.

Address for correspondence: SZTE JGYTFK, Department of Hungarian Linguistics, H-6725 Szeged, Boldogasszony sgt. 6, Hungary; sandor@jgytf.u-szeged.hu.

Gizella Szabómihály (b. 1956) received her university education in Hungarian and Slovak at Comenius University in Bratislava, Slovakia, in 1979. After graduation, she taught at the Hungarian Department of the same university until 1992. She is affiliated with the Gramma Language Office and works as a freelance linguist, interpreter and translator. Her research interests include Slovak-Hungarian contrastive linguistics, sociolinguistics, the theory and practice of translation, language planning, and language policy.

Address for correspondence: 930 08 Čil. Radvaň 295, Slovakia; szmihalyg@stonline. sk.

Sándor N. Szilágyi (b. 1948) is Associate Professor at the Hungarian Language and Culture Department at the Babeş–Bolyai University, Cluj/Kolozsvár, Romania. He studied linguistics and literature at the same university, where he received his PhD in 1999. His dissertation is titled *Theory and Method in Phonology*. His research focuses on general problems of cognitive linguistics based on the study of Hungarian grammar and semantics, linguistic human rights, and language contact. He participated in the Sociolinguistics of Hungarian Outside Hungary research project.

Address for correspondence: Univ. Babeş-Bolyai, Facultatea de Litere, Catedra de Limba Maghiara, 3400 Cluj-Napoca, str. Horea nr. 31, Romania; szilagyi@lett.ubbcluj.ro.

Sarah G. Thomason is the William J. Gedney Collegiate Professor of Linguistics at the University of Michigan. She is a historical linguist who specializes in contact-induced language change and related topics, including pidgin/creole genesis. Among her publications are *Language contact, creolization, and genetic linguistics* (co-authored with Terrence Kaufman, 1988) and *Language contact: An introduction (2001)*.

Address for correspondence: Department of Linguistics, Frieze Building, University of Michigan, Ann Arbor, MI 48109-1285, USA; thomason@umich.edu.

Ottó Vörös is Professor of Linguistics at the Hungarian Linguistics Department at Berzsenyi Dániel Teachers' Training College, Szombathely, Hungary. His areas of specialization and research interests are in dialectology, onomastics, minority Hungarian language use and language policy, and language contact at border areas of the Hungarian speech community. He was a visiting professor at the University of Maribor for 2 years, at the Konstantin University (Slovakia) for 5 years, and at the Comenius University in Bratislava, Slovakia, for 5 years.

Address for correspondence: 9900 Körmend, Bartók Béla utca 2., Hungary; dkati@fsd.bdtf.hu.

Acknowledgements

The idea of this volume and several of the papers contained in it grew out of the tri-lateral, Dutch–Flemish–Hungarian research project called "Study Centre on Language Contact" carried out in 1999–2000. The project was coordinated and supported by the Netherlands Institute of Advanced Study (NIAS) in Wassenaar, the Netherlands. NIAS's generous financial support of the creation of this book, without which it could not have been realized, is gratefully acknowledged.

I am thankful to Pieter Muysken for providing the impetus and conceiving the idea of the book, and for his scholarly feedback and encouragement in developing the concept behind it. I am grateful for Casper de Groot's insight, for his mediation towards NIAS as well as for his expert help in various practical issues. I thank Miklós Kontra, István Lanstyák, and Sally Thomason for their scholarly input and insight at various stages of the editorial process.

On the Hungarian end of things, I want to acknowledge assistance from Attila Kiss of the English Department, Arts Faculty, University of Szeged, Hungary, who, out of his funds as head of my department provided additional financial support for the creation of the book.

I want to thank Helga Arnold Fuszenecker, Etelka Polgár, and Eszter Szabó for providing excellent translations of the book chapters that were originally written in Hungarian. Thanks are due to Donald W. Peckham for his comments and suggestions on improving the English of chapters written by nonnative speaker contributors of this volume. My greatest appreciation goes to the editorial assistants I worked with on the editing of this book, Viktória Papp and Eszter Szabó. Their – especially Eszter's – diligence, computer skills, enthusiasm and unfaltering optimism truly contributed to the book taking shape. I thank Zoltán László for his expert technical assistance in various computer-related issues.

I am thankful for the ready cooperation and patience of the contributors to the volume during the editorial process, which took quite a bit longer than anticipated.

I thank series editor Annick De Houwer for her insight, feedback and encourage-ment throughout the creation of the book.

I am grateful for the loving support of my children, Andy and twins Julie and Emily, as well as of my family and friends, whose love has made all the difference during the time when this book was created and gained its final shape – which was also the time of the most elemental changes of my life.

Introduction*

Anna Fenyvesi

1. The aims of this volume

This volume discusses situations of community bilingualism involving Hungarian as a minority language outside of Hungary. It is the first collection of papers aiming to provide comprehensive reports on sociolinguistic research involving Hungarian minorities. While summarizing findings on some situations which are relatively well described in English – such as the Hungarian immigrant communities in Australia and the United States – this volume provides the first opportunity to survey Hungarian minority communities studies which have so far largely been published only in Hungarian.

With their specific 20th century history of large groups of population finding themselves in minority situations at the exact same time, and then living under varying sociohistorical and political conditions in each neighboring country, Hungarians provide a unique sociolinguistic case where the effects of social factors on their minority situation can be traced and compared across countries.

This book provides a great deal of information and previously unpublished data on the linguistic situation and social as well as linguistic characteristics of the language use of minority Hungarian speakers. A large part of this information and material is derived from a basically variationist sociolinguistic survey, viz., the Sociolinguistics of Hungarian Outside Hungary project (see in more detail below, as well as in Kontra, this volume), based on a uniform questionnaire and carried out in the 1990s. The relevant overall findings are set in a typological framework in order to allow the interpretation of instances of contact-induced language change from this additional point of view.

Thus, the goals of the book are complex and manifold: (i) it aims to contribute to a description of varieties of Hungarian existing outside of Hungary, (ii) it offers in-depth analyses for a better understanding of sociolinguistic variation in language contact situations, and (iii) it attempts to provide an insight into typological aspects of language change under the conditions of language contact.

2. Hungarians around the world

Hungarian, the language of altogether between 13 and 14 million people around the world today (10.2 million of these in Hungary and 12.7 million in the Carpathian Basin, cf. Gyurgyík & Sebők 2003), was spoken almost exclusively inside Hungary's borders until the end of the 19th century. Today, Hungarian is found as a minority language throughout most of Western and East Central Europe, as well as in North America, South America, Australia, South Africa, and Israel.

The origin of minority Hungarian speakers in the world is twofold. First, mass immigration, starting in the 1880s and continuing until the 1920s, took millions of Hungarians first to the United States and then to other countries. Later waves of immigration continued throughout the 20th century, first only to the United States for economic reasons, then, during and after World War II, and again after the 1956 Hungarian revolution, for political as well as economic reasons, and to other destinations as well.

The second source of minority Hungarians was the partition of Austria-Hungary under the Treaty of Trianon after World War I, in 1920, which placed two-thirds of Hungary's territory as well as almost 3 million ethnic Hungarians (approximately one-third of the total ethnic Hungarian population of Hungary at the time) in neighboring countries such as the newly formed Czechoslovakia and Yugoslavia, as well as Romania and Austria. Even though a few hundred thousand ethnic Hungarians re-migrated into Hungary after the treaty went into effect and the borders were redrawn, most of them remained in their new respective home countries. These Hungarians constitute the largest groups of minority Hungarians today – autochthonous minorities living outside of Hungary's political borders but inside the Carpathian Basin, i.e., the area surrounded by the Alps and Carpathian Mountains where Hungarians have lived since the 9th century.

The Budapest-based World Federation of Hungarians estimates the number of Hungarians living around the world as reflected in the figures in Table 0.1 (A. Kovács 1999).

Table 0.1. The estimated number of Hungarians in the world*

Region	Number of Hungarians
Carpathian Basin (including Hungary)	13,000,000
Europe (without the Carpathian Basin)	360,000
Africa	30,000
Asia	230,000
Australia	55,000
North America	1,930,000
South America	130,000

* Based on the estimates of the World Federation of Hungarians, A. Kovács (1999).

Table 0.2. Estimated numbers of Hungarians living in Europe outside the Carpathian Basin in the late 1990s*

Coutry	Number of Hungarians
Austria	44,000 – 51,000
Belgium	14,000 – 15,000
Denmark	4,000
France	40,000 – 45,000
Germany	120,000
Great Britain	25,000 – 30,000
Italy	9,000 – 10,000
Netherlands	11,000 – 12,000
Norway	4,000
Spain and Portugal	2,000
Sweden	25,000 – 27,000
Switzerland	18,000 – 19,000
Other	27,000 – 33,000
Total	343,000 – 371,000

* Source: A. Kovács (1999:49).

Figures on Africa and Asia refer mostly to Hungarians living in South Africa and Israel, respectively. Some of the figures – especially those about Hungarians in North America – are inflated due to the way they are calculated. For instance, the United States Census 2000 (http://www.census.gov/) reported only 900 thousand Hungarians in the United States according to first ancestry (people who indicated *Hungarian* either as their sole ancestry or the first of their multiple ancestries such as *Hungarian and Polish*), which only together with the Hungarians of second ancestry (500 thousand) yields a figure closer to the World Federation's estimate (the number of Hungarian immigrants in Canada has been estimated at 140,000 by Szántó 2001:115). At the same time, the number of actual speakers of Hungarian in the United States is better estimated at around 130,000 to 140,000 at present (calculated on the basis of 1990 United States Census results on Hungarian speakers and the decrease of Hungarians in the United States in the past decade; for details see Fenyvesi, this volume).

The most recent estimates of the number of Hungarians living in Europe outside the Carpathian basin are from A. Kovács (1999:49), based on reports of Hungarian organizations in the Western, Northern and Southern European countries in question made in the late 1990's (see Table 0.2).

3. Sociolinguistic research on Hungarians outside Hungary

This volume presents the most comprehensive collection of studies in English on Hungarian as a minority language available to date, and includes papers on all language contact situations involving Hungarian outside Hungary that have so far been studied in detail. Even though a large body of historical linguistic research focuses on the lexical results of language contact of Hungarian with other languages in Hungary, work with its main focus on synchronic linguistic situations of bilingualism involving Hungarian did not start until the 1980s.

Until 1989, the subject of Hungarians living outside Hungary, especially in countries surrounding Hungary, was considered taboo in Hungary and the other European communist countries. This is one reason why sociolinguistic research on Hungarians living outside Hungary started so comparatively late. Another reason is the fact that because of various political and ideological reasons, it was nearly impossible to carry out sociolinguistic research in general in countries of the former Eastern Bloc. (For an insightful analysis of the effects of politics and communist ideology on scientific research, see Harlig 1995a and 1995b.)

Because the bilingualism of Hungarians in neighboring countries inevitably tied into political issues involving the Hungarian minorities in these countries, research on them, especially by Hungarian linguists, was not possible in communist times. The only exception is Gal's classic 1979 book on Hungarian–German bilingualism in Austria. The first substantive investigation of Hungarian bilingualism by a Hungarian linguist from Hungary, Miklós Kontra, focused on Hungarians overseas, namely those living in South Bend, Indiana (for a comprehensive overview in Hungarian, see Kontra 1990; cf. Kontra 1993a and 1993b for reports in English), and was later followed by research on Hungarians elsewhere in the United States and Australia (in English, see Bartha 1995/1996; Bartha & Sydorenko 2000; Fenyvesi 1995a, 1995/1996, 2000; M. Kovács 2001a, 2001b, 2001c). Following the collapse of communism, scholars started linguistic research on Hungarian minorities in countries neighboring Hungary as well. The results of this by now considerable amount of research have largely been unavailable in English until now (exceptions are, e.g. Beregszászi 1995/1996; Csernicskó & Fenyvesi 2000; Kontra 1999, 2001a, 2003; Langman & Lanstyák 2000; Lanstyák 1999/2000, 2000c; Lanstyák & Szabómihály 1996a; Sándor 1999, 2000; Simon & Kontra 2000).

There are a number of Hungarian minority communities that have not been studied to date. For instance, there are no sociolinguistic studies on Hungarians in Canada, South America, South Africa, or in most Western European countries. There are, though, a few smaller scale, partial descriptions of linguistic aspects of these communities or their members' bilingualism and Hungarian use (see, e.g. Csapo 1983 on language shift and maintenance among Hungarians in Canada, Vago 1991 on one Israeli Hungarian's first language attrition, A. Benkő 2000 on morphological change in the Hungarian of London speakers, or Tátrai 2000 on aspects of code-switching by Hungarians in Switzerland).

4.   The broader theoretical framework of this volume

Following the tradition of sociolinguistic studies on languages in contact and their speakers established by Weinreich's classic 1968 work, the bilingual Hungarian communities discussed in this book are investigated in a sociolinguistic framework that incorporates the dual focus of describing the large scale macro-sociolinguistic facts characteristic of the communities, as well as the micro-sociolinguistic level of the linguistic results of contact-induced language change.

Since the situations in question involve minority language use in majority language environments, discussions of the macro-sociolinguistic aspects focus primarily on issues of language maintenance and shift, and the various factors (demographic, economic, historical, factors relating to policy and institutional support and the like) affecting these. The overall picture that unfolds shows the continuing bilingualism and Hungarian language maintenance of the autochthonous Hungarian communities neighboring Hungary, with some signs of language shift (of greater or lesser extent in the various groups), and clear language shift in the case of the Hungarian immigrant communities overseas. In the case of the Hungarians in the neighboring countries, there is a more language maintenance and less language shift in the bigger regions with greater numbers of Hungarians (in Slovakia, the Ukraine, Transylvania and Vojvodina) than in the smaller regions with fewer Hungarians (in Prekmurje, Burgenland and Csángó Moldavia).

At the micro-sociolinguistic level, the linguistic results of language contact observable in the varieties of Hungarian under discussion are viewed throughout this book in the context of historical and social forces (Thomason & Kaufman 1988; Thomason 2001). Of the two kinds of contact-induced change identified by Thomason and Kaufman (1988: 37–57) and Thomason (2001: 59–95), namely borrowing and shift-induced interference, the linguistic changes under discussion fall under borrowing, as they are the results of the influence of the dominant majority language present in the bilingual Hungarian communities' life rather than features carried over from the bilingual speakers' L1 into their L2 (i.e. the majority language) in the course of language shift. Following Thomason and Kaufman (1988: 37), borrowing is defined broadly as "the incorporation of foreign features into a group's native language by speakers of that language", including both lexical and structural (i.e. phonological and grammatical) borrowing, and occurring as a correlate of sociohistorical factors at play in the language contact situation. As predicted by the Thomason and Kaufman framework, in the minority Hungarian situations of the countries neighboring Hungary where language contact with the majority language is less intense than in the immigrant communities overseas, extensive lexical borrowing is coupled with less structural borrowing and results in only minor typologically relevant change.

The linguistic analyses applied in this book are based on two different methods. The first is the contrastive method and the second is the method of linguistic typology. In using the first method, data from one language is contrasted to similar data from one or more other languages. In this contrastive method, structural features of the language systems form the standard of comparison, where structural features relate to phonological, morphological and syntactical properties of languages such as syllable structure, affixation, and order of constituents. In using the second, typological method, (a part of) the grammar of a language is evaluated against linguistic universals, which are derived on the basis of a large number of languages in the world. Linguistic universals are statements which hold for all natural languages. Since Greenberg (1963), four main types of universals have been distinguished on the basis of the parameters: absolute and statistical on the one hand, and unconditional and implicational on the other (see De Groot, this volume).

The contrastive method which is used almost throughout the entire book is particularly useful in the study of language change and language contact. Thomason presents a typological survey in which some salient Hungarian structural features are compared systematically to the main relevant Indo-European (IE) languages. She argues that the typological differences and similarities between Hungarian and the relevant IE languages permit us to make limited predictions about the kinds of changes that are likely to take place under different contact conditions. The most general and most obvious prediction is this: if Hungarian is under the strong influence of one (or more) of the IE languages, it is likely to retain structural features that are typologically similar to the corresponding features in the other language(s) but to simplify or lose structural features that it does not share with the other language(s).

The method of linguistic typology is applied in the last chapter, where De Groot evaluates a number of apparently unrelated differences between Hungarian used in Hungary (HH) and Hungarian used outside of Hungary (HO) from a linguistic-typological point of view. He shows that changes in the HO varieties follow and do not violate linguistic universals and implicational hierarchies, and that co-occurrences of changes can indeed be explained in terms of universals or hierarchies. The observation, for example, that the category of Noun as a 'set noun' – type in HH changes into a 'singular object noun' – type in HO neatly account for three different phenomena: the plural marking of nouns after a numeral, the use of plural forms of the noun in some other cases, and plural agreement with the verb in a number of cases.

5.   The studies of this volume

This volume contains eight chapters, each providing a case study and covering a situation where Hungarian is a minority language, as well as three other chapters whose aim is to contextualize these case studies from various perspectives.

In Chapter 1, Sarah G. Thomason surveys typological and structural aspects of Hungarian in contact with other languages and their theoretical implications. Hungarian, which is a Finno-Ugric and agglutinative language, has been in contact with Indo-European inflectional languages throughout its entire history of language contact both in the Carpathian Basin and outside it. Considering the typological aspects of Hungarian and the languages it is in contact with as well as the social contexts in which they have occurred, Thomason discusses the probabilities of various kinds of contact induced change that Hungarian is likely to undergo.

Chapter 2, by Miklós Kontra, discusses the socio-historical background of linguistic research on minority Hungarians in general, and the Sociolinguistics of Hungarian Outside Hungary (SHOH) project in particular. This project, which was carried out in 1995–1996, was the first large-scale sociolinguistic study of contact varieties of Hungarian spoken in the countries neighboring Hungary. It provided a great amount of sociolinguistic and linguistic data about the stratification of the Hungarian language use of minority Hungarians in these countries, as well as in-depth information about their use of their respective languages in their everyday lives. Several of the case studies in subsequent chapters present detailed findings of this project (see the chapters by Lanstyák and Szabómihály, Csernicskó, Benő and Szilágyi N., and Göncz and Vörös) or rely in part on findings obtained with slightly modified versions of the project's questionnaire (see chapters by Sándor and Fenyvesi).

After Thomason's and Kontra's articles, Chapters 3 through 10 provide comprehensive analyses of the Hungarian minorities in the countries under discussion. They describe macro-sociolinguistic aspects of these minorities as well as provide overviews of the linguistic aspects of language contact effects on the Hungarian used in them. In the first part of each chapter, the authors discuss the historical background of the contact situation in question, the demographic, economic, and language policy aspects of the Hungarian minority communities. The domains of Hungarian language use in the communities are also described, and they are characterized from the point of view of language maintenance vs. language shift. The second and more extensive parts of these chapters are devoted to discussions of the linguistic aspects of Hungarian language use in the minority communities. They describe the lexical and structural borrowing in the variety of Hungarian in question, and, where relevant and where findings are available, they also discuss the code-switching practices of the community and the presence or absence of any language attrition related linguistic phenomena.

In Chapter 3, István Lanstyák and Gizella Szabómihály provide a comprehensive description of the Hungarian language as used in Slovakia. Slovakia has the second biggest minority of Hungarians (after Romania) of the countries neighboring Hungary. In 2001 Slovakia totaled 520,000 Hungarians, or almost 10% of the total population of the country. In Section 3.1.2 on the linguistic behavior of bilinguals, in addition to talking about the role and effect of L2 elements and of transfer, Lanstyák and Szabómihály discuss phenomena such as linguistic insecurity, overfulfilment of the norm, language lapses and language gaps. Section 3.2.1 presents a typology of lexical borrowings in Hungarian as used in Slovakia. The chapter provides a wealth of examples, drawing on the over one decade long research of the authors. This chapter is one of a total of two chapters in the book (together with the one on American Hungarian) that discusses pragmatic borrowing, and specifically issues relating to address systems.

Chapter 4, by István Csernicskó, discusses Hungarian in Subcarpathia, the region of Ukraine southwest of the Carpathian Mountains where Ukraine's Hungarian minority lives. Subcarpathia Hungarians numbered 151,000 in 2001 (or 12% of the population of the country). This chapter describes the highly unique details of language use in post-Soviet Ukraine, where the new official language, Ukrainian, is struggling for dominance, since it was long overshadowed by Russian, while Hungarian, Ukraine's largest minority language, is relatively more established.

In Chapter 5, Attila Benő and Sándor Szilágyi N. describe the situation of the largest Hungarian minority of East Central Europe, that of Romania. In 2002, 1,434,000 Hungarians lived in Romania, or almost 10% of all Hungarians in the world. The majority of the Hungarians in Romania live in Transylvania, in the northwestern quarter of the country. Transylvania's Hungarian minority has been decreasing steadily in the past decades due to emigration from an oppressive dictatorial regime until 1989, and from an economic situation riddled with difficulties since then. Nevertheless, Transylvania's Hungarian minority is still characterized by language maintenance for the most part, due to the high level of loyalty to the mother tongue among these minority Hungarians, as well as the high cultural prestige they ascribe to it.

Klára Sándor's Chapter 6 on the Csángós, a community of Hungarians in Romania's northeastern region of Moldavia, discusses the unique historical and linguistic characteristics of this people. She also analyzes the components of the complex Csángó identity. The chapter provides a glimpse into the controversial history of how Hungary has been trying to support the Csángó minority in past decades, often in ways directly opposed to the interests of the minority community itself.

Chapter 7, by Lajos Göncz and Ottó Vörös, provides an overview of the situation of Hungarians in two different regions of the former Yugoslavia, namely in Vojvodina and Prekmurje. These two regions are now found in separate states – i.e. in Serbia and Montenegro and in Slovenia – but are discussed in the same chapter because of their joint modern history in pre-1991 Yugoslavia. The number of Hungarians in Vojvodina was 290,000 in 2002 – which makes it the third biggest Hungarian minority of the Carpathian Basin. This constituted 3.91% of the total population of Serbia. In 2002, Hungarians totaled 6,200 by nationality and 7,700 by mother tongue (constituting 0.31% or 0.39% of the country's total, respectively). The chapter provides in-depth analyses of linguistic features studied in the SHOH project, offering comparisons between Vojvodina and Prekmurje Hungarian language use as well as between these varieties and Hungarian language use in Hungary.

In Chapter 8, Csanád Bodó discusses the Hungarian minority in Austria – probably the best known case of Hungarian minority bilingualism since Gal's 1979 book on language shift in this community. According to 2001 census results, 40,000 people (or 0.5% of the total population of the country) used Hungarian on a day-to-day basis in Austria. Bodó provides an up-to-date picture of the sociolinguistic aspects of the Hungarian communities of Austria in his chapter, discussing both the autochthonous community of Oberwart /Felsőőr, in the Burgenland province of the country, and immigrant Hungarians living mostly in Vienna. In the second part of his chapter, Bodó outlines the main linguistic aspects affected in Oberwart /Felsőőr Hungarian. He also presents some preliminary findings of the Austrian part of the SHOH study (the study itself was carried out by the late István Szépfalusi).

In Chapter 9, on Hungarian in the United States, I attempt to provide a current sociolinguistic characterization of Hungarian Americans, whose number, according to ancestry, totaled about 900,000 people in the year 2000 (but only about 130,000 of whom can be estimated to actually be Hungarian speakers). In the part of the chapter dealing with the linguistic characteristics of American Hungarian I summarize the findings of the main studies by Kontra (1990), Bartha (1993), and myself (Fenyvesi 1995). I also provide a discussion of the adaptation of loanwords and of pragmatic borrowing in this variety.

In Chapter 10, Magdolna Kovács discusses the Hungarians of Australia, a community estimated to comprise between 55,000 and 75,000 people of Hungarian descent, of whom about 30,000 were home users of Hungarian in 1991. Drawing on her recent dissertation work, she presents a detailed picture of code-switching practices among Australian Hungarians, as well as of other characteristics of their Hungarian language use.

Finally in Chapter 11, "The grammars of Hungarian outside Hungary from a linguistic-typological perspective", reflecting on the descriptions of the varieties of Hungarian outside Hungary in previous chapters, Casper de Groot identifies instances of typological change observable in these varieties. His analysis connects the study of linguistic typology with the research of linguistic outcomes of language contact in an innovative way, and presents an insightful picture of contact induced typological change in contact varieties of Hungarian.

The range of studies presented in this book is much narrower than the range of minority Hungarian communities around the world. It is basically limited to studies on communities in countries neighboring Hungary, and on two overseas communities living in great geographical isolation from Hungary and from each other. It is my sincere hope that the present collection of studies will stimulate work on other, so far undescribed communities and their Hungarian varieties, especially from parts of the world such as Western Europe, South America, South Africa and Israel. Work on these communities would, most probably, uncover cases very different from those described in this volume, thereby certainly broadening our knowledge and understanding of minority Hungarian communities as well as describing situations where Hungarian is in contact with languages other than Indo-European ones.

Note

* I'd like to thank Annick De Houwer, Casper de Groot and István Lanstyák for their meticulous comments on an earlier draft of this introduction. I owe special thanks to Casper regarding the section discussing linguistic typology.

CHAPTER 1

Typological and theoretical aspects
of Hungarian in contact with other languages

Sarah Grey Thomason

1. Introduction

This chapter surveys broad typological similarities and differences between Hungarian and relevant Indo-European (IE) languages, and considers some theoretical implications of this survey for contact-induced language change, especially in Hungarian. In historical times, Hungarian speakers have come into close contact with speakers of numerous other languages, primarily IE languages belonging to the Slavic, Romance, and Germanic branches of the family. Comparing the typological profiles of these languages will highlight structural similarities and differences that may help predict contact-induced changes in Hungarian and the other languages.

Hungarian is one of the three members of the Ugric branch of Finno-Ugric, itself the larger of the two branches of the Uralic language family. According to the on-line *Ethnologue* (Grimes 2002), there are about 14,500,000 Hungarian speakers in all, over four million of them outside Hungary. Aside from Hungary itself, the only country in which Hungarian is designated as an official language in a national constitution is Slovenia, where there are 9,240 Hungarian speakers.

The social circumstances of contacts between Hungarian and other languages vary widely. Some contacts are within Hungary itself, others are in neighboring countries with significant Hungarian-speaking minorities, and still others are in countries with large numbers of Hungarian immigrants. The chapters in this book focus on contacts outside Hungary, but the history of Hungarian within Hungary also offers opportunities to study contact-induced change. Many or most Hungarian-speaking communities outside Hungary have experienced language loss to a greater or lesser degree, as community members acculturate and shift to the dominant language of their environment. Contact-induced changes that can be observed in Hungarian cover a range of possibilities. Some, especially within Hungary, may reflect shift-induced interference, as speakers of IE languages shift to Hungarian; others, both within and outside Hungary, are due to borrowing, where native (or at least fluent) speakers of Hungarian adopt vocabulary and structural features from another language. Still other changes represent attrition, the loss of structure and vocabulary during a slow process of language death.

Section 2 below presents broad typological profiles of Hungarian and the major languages with which its speakers have been in contact, to set the stage for a consideration in Section 3 of the probabilities for types and degrees of contact-induced change in Hungarian (and, to a lesser extent, in the other languages), given the kinds of social contexts in which these contacts have occurred. Although the emphasis is on external contacts, Section 3 also gives a sketch of Hungarian in contact with other languages, in order to show how the in-country contacts compare with the external contact situations. The chapter ends with a brief conclusion (Section 4).

2.   Typological aspects of contacts between Hungarian and other languages

Speakers of Hungarian have of course come into contact with a wide variety of languages, but in considering structural typological issues I will discuss only those languages with which Hungarian has been in most intense contact. First, there are the IE languages spoken in countries that share borders with Hungary, most notably the following: the West Slavic language Slovak in Slovakia; the East Slavic language Ukrainian in Ukraine; the South Slavic languages Slovenian, Croatian, and Serbian in Slovenia, Croatia, and Serbia, respectively; the Romance language Romanian in Romania; and the West Germanic language German in Austria. Second, there are the languages of countries with sizable Hungarian immigrant communities – the United States, Canada, and Australia, all predominantly Anglophone nations, and also Israel (where there are 70,000 Hungarian speakers, according to Grimes 2002).

In a full-scale study of this topic, significant linguistic minorities within Hungary should also be taken into account. Fenyvesi (1998b: 150), drawing on 1990 census figures, lists six languages (in addition to Hungarian) that are spoken natively in Hungary by more than 5,000 speakers; all of them are Indo-European. In descending order of speaker numbers, they are Lovári (or Romani, but called Gypsy in the census report; 48,172), German (37,511), Croatian (17,577), Slovak (12,745), Polish (10,000), and Romanian (8,730). Six (or seven) languages are mentioned in the census but with fewer speakers: Bulgarian (3,000), Greek (2,500–3,000), Serbian (2,953), Slovenian (2,627), Armenian (1,500), and Ruthenian and Ukrainian (1,000). Grimes 2002 has three other languages in her list of minority languages of Hungary – Macedonian, Ossetic, and Yiddish – and she gives a figure of 150,000 for the number of Lovári speakers, the biggest linguistic minority in Hungary. In any case, I have little information about the nature of contacts between Hungarian and Lovári, so I will mostly ignore them here (but see Hutterer & Mészáros 1967). And I will say nothing about contacts between Hungarian and Israeli Hebrew, because I have no data on those contacts.

This section presents a typological survey in which some salient Hungarian structural features are compared systematically to the main relevant Indo-European languages. Because Serbian and Croatian, which are mutually intelligible in their stan-

Table 1.1. The Hungarian phoneme inventory

p	t	ts	tʃ	c	k	
b	d	(dz)	(dʒ)	ɟ	g	
f	s	ʃ				h
v	z	ʒ				
m	n			ɲ		
	l					
	r			j		
i	y	iː	yː		u	uː
ɛ	ø	eː	øː		o	oː
				aː	ɑ	

dard forms (at least), are identical in the typological features covered here, I will use the formerly standard language name Serbo-Croatian (which is interchangeable with Croato-Serbian) in discussing their features.

Let's begin with the phonology. Table 1.1 gives the Hungarian phonemic inventories for consonants and vowels (Vago 1998: 382ff.).

The Hungarian inventory of consonant phonemes, like Uralic consonant inventories generally, is not strikingly different from typical European IE phonemic inventories. Both have voiced vs. voiceless stops and fricatives, labiodental fricatives, alveopalatal obstruents, and similar arrays of sonorant consonants, for instance. But Uralic languages typically have a larger number of palatal consonants than IE languages have, including not only alveopalatals (which are also common in IE) but also palatalized apicals and dorso-palatals (both of which are rare in IE).[1] Hungarian has two sets of palatal consonants, the typologically common alveopalatals and also a set which is variously described as palatalized apical or dorso-palatal. Some descriptions of the Hungarian consonants spelled *ty*, *gy*, and *ny* specify palatalization in the phonetic realization of the three phonemes. But Vago (1998: 382–383, 384) describes them as dorso-palatal stops (or affricates) and nasal, respectively. Although both these types of consonant are rare in IE, they do occur in Slavic. In some Slavic languages, for instance Serbo-Croatian, palatalization is distinctive only in apicals, as in Uralic generally; and in fact Serbo-Croatian, like Hungarian according to some experts, has voiced and voiceless palatalized apical affricates as well as alveopalatal affricates. Elsewhere in Slavic, notably Russian, the opposition *plain : palatalized* is also found in other places of articulation, especially labials. The opposition is not inherited in Slavic, and may ultimately be due to shift-induced interference from Uralic (see e.g. Thomason & Kaufman 1988: 247). It is an old distinction in Uralic; Campbell (1989, citing Sammallahti 1988: 481–482) lists a series of dorso-palatal consonants for the Proto-Uralic inventory.

The Hungarian vowel system comprises seven sets of short and long vowel phonemes: two sets of unrounded front vowels and two of rounded front vowels, two sets of rounded back vowels, and a long unrounded low central vowel contrasting with a short rounded low back vowel. This inventory contrasts significantly with the vowel inventories of most of the relevant Indo-European languages. Some Slavic languages (including Slovak, Slovenian, and Serbo-Croatian) have distinctive vowel length, but they generally lack rounded front vowels; and English has neither distinctively long vowels nor front rounded vowels. Only German, of the major languages with which Hungarian is in contact, has both short vs. long vowel phonemes and front rounded vowel phonemes.

One salient phonological feature sets Hungarian apart from all the other relevant languages: its vowel harmony system. In this feature too Hungarian is a typical Uralic language. The most general Hungarian vowel harmony process restricts the vowels in a word to all back or all front vowels; the four front unrounded vowels are neutral in this system. Short mid vowels also exhibit roundedness harmony (Vago 1998:419ff.). Vowel harmony is absent from Slavic, Germanic, and Romance languages, with a few minor exceptions. In particular, there's the historical sound change and persisting morphophonemic pattern of Germanic umlaut, a right-to-left process (contrasting with the left-to-right word-level Hungarian harmony processes) in which a high front vocoid /i/ or /j/ fronts a vowel in the preceding syllable. Old Church Slavic (and therefore potentially all of Common Slavic) has been claimed to have a vowel harmony system affecting only the two extra-short front and back 'jer' vowels, perhaps as a result of Uralic or Altaic influence (see Menges 1945); but modern Slavic languages generally lack vowel harmony altogether.

Canonical syllable structure is extremely diverse in Indo-European languages, some of which, including Germanic and Slavic, have highly marked syllable-initial and syllable-final consonant clusters, while others, e.g. Romance, have very limited possibilities. English, for instance, has as many as three consonants in syllable onsets and as many as four or five in codas, in words like *stroll* and *sixths* (/siksθs/); Spanish, a typical Romance language in this respect, has only two-consonant syllable-initial clusters (in e.g. *plano* 'flat') and no syllable-final clusters at all. Uralic, in sharp contrast, permits few or no syllable-initial consonant clusters and relatively few syllable-final clusters in native words. The Proto-Uralic canonical syllable structure was (C)V(C), although the glides /j/ and /w/ could form part of the V syllable nucleus (Janhunen 1981:25). Hungarian is a typical Uralic language with respect to consonant clusters, but only in native vocabulary. Initial clusters occur only in loanwords (Vago 1998:386ff.; citing Törkenczy 1994, the source of all the examples here); they may consist of two or three consonants, e.g. /sm/ in *szmoking* 'tuxedo' and /ʃtr/ in *strand* 'beach'. Two-consonant clusters, including geminates, occur finally in native vocabulary as well as in loanwords. Examples are /dv/ in *nedv* 'moisture', /ps/ in the loanword *bicepsz* 'biceps', and /tt/ in *ott* 'there'. Final three-consonant clusters occur only in loanwords, e.g. /nks/ in *szfinx* 'sphinx'.

Stress is predictable and therefore not phonemic in Hungarian: it occurs on the first syllable of a word. This fixed word-initial stress pattern is very old, dating back to Proto-Uralic (Janhunen 1981:27). Germanic languages like English and German inherited word-initial stress from Proto-Germanic (though not from Proto-Indo-European), but loanwords – especially in English – have completely disrupted the inherited pattern, so that stress is now phonemic and may occur on any syllable in the word. Proto-Slavic had phonemic stress, and most of the modern Slavic languages preserve this feature. (Polish, with fixed penultimate stress, is a prominent exception to this generalization; Czech, with fixed initial stress, is another prominent exception. Czech may owe its fixed stress pattern to contact with German and/or Hungarian.) Stress is also phonemic in some, but not all, Romance languages.

Morphologically, too, Hungarian is a typical Uralic language in most respects. Like other Uralic languages, it makes extensive use of morphological processes. Its morphological type is agglutinative – that is, it tends to use a separate affix for each morpheme. So, for instance, case and plural number are expressed by separate suffixes. Indo-European languages, by contrast, are primarily flexional in type: in a Slavic language like Russian, for instance, the combination of a case morpheme and a number morpheme is expressed in a single suffix.

Hungarian is almost exclusively suffixing; suffixes are used both in derivation and in the elaborate inflectional systems for nouns and verbs. The exception to the typical Uralic suffix-only pattern is the Hungarian system of verbal preverbs, often called prefixes, which primarily express aspectual and adverbial meanings. However, the behavior of the preverbs is clitic-like rather than affix-like in that they occur after the verb 'when there is a preverbal focus constituent or a negative particle' (Fenyvesi 1998c:329), so they constitute only a partial exception to the otherwise exclusively suffixing morphology. (Hungarian shares the preverb system with the other two Ugric languages, though the actual preverbs in the three languages are not etymologically connected; Kiefer 1997:323.) IE languages are primarily suffixing, and in the modern languages almost all inflection is suffixal. But there are several highly productive derivational prefixes in Indo-European, and Slavic languages have a well-developed system of aspectual prefixes that are, according to some analyses, inflectional. In fact, the Hungarian adverbial and aspectual preverbs resemble the Slavic aspectual prefixes in certain salient respects; they may also be compared with the so-called separable prefixes of German, which also display clitic-like behavior (though under morphosyntactic conditions that differ sharply from the syntactic positioning of the Hungarian preverbs).

Hungarian nominals inflect for number, case, and person – the person of a possessor. Proto-Uralic apparently had a dual number as well as a singular and a plural, but most of the modern languages, including Hungarian, have only singular and plural in their inflectional number category. The same is true of IE: Proto-Indo-European had a dual as well as singular and plural numbers, but most modern IE languages have lost the dual. (Of the IE languages with which Hungarian is in contact, only Slovenian retains the dual.) Hungarian has one morphosyntactic feature that sets its number-marking system apart from English and the other relevant IE languages: whereas IE nouns following a numeral or other quantifier are morphologically plural, Hungarian nouns are singular in this context. Compare, for instance, English *two/some books* with the Hungarian equivalent *két/néhány könyv* (lit. 'two/some book') (Fenyvesi 1998c:255).

Finno-Ugric languages are famous for their rich case systems, and Hungarian is no exception. There is some controversy about the total number of Hungarian cases; analyses range from 17–27, the variation depending on whether certain putative cases are analyzed instead as derivational formations (see Fenyvesi 1998c: 191 for discussion). Even 17 cases, of course, would more than double the number of cases in the most elaborate IE system, and no modern IE system has more than seven cases. Serbo-Croatian arguably has seven of the inherited eight IE cases (though the distinction between dative and locative is shaky in many Serbo-Croatian dialects); other Slavic languages have at most six: nominative, accusative, genitive, dative, instrumental, and locative. All these cases except the genitive are also found in Hungarian, in which possession is expressed inflectionally, but not with a specifically genitive case suffix. Hungarian has in addition several semantically diverse cases such as the comitative, but the main elaboration of case distinctions is in the locative category, with at least nine different locative cases (e.g. inessive, elative, illative, and superessive; see Fenyvesi 1998c: 192ff. for details). Aside from (most) Slavic languages, modern IE languages generally have few case distinctions. English has none in noun inflection, for instance (unless one considers the possessive suffix -s in e.g. *John's book* a case suffix), though a distinction between nominative and non-nominative remains in personal pronouns. German has four cases, expressed primarily through inflection of articles and other modifiers: nominative, accusative, genitive, and dative. Romance languages are generally similar to English in case morphology, but with three rather than two cases in personal pronominal inflection.

The personal possessive suffixes on Hungarian (and other Uralic) nouns have no analogue in IE. Constructions expressed in English by possessive pronouns in noun phrases like *my book* and *his book* are expressed in Hungarian by suffixes, e.g. *könyv-em* 'my book' and *könyv-e* 'his book'. This is a striking typological difference between Hungarian and all the IE languages with which it is in contact. The existence of the pronominal possessive suffixes on nouns is linked to another typological feature that distinguishes Hungarian sharply from IE languages. Whereas in IE there is no overlap between nominal and verbal inflection, in Hungarian the personal suffixes on nouns and verbs may be identical. Compare, for instance, *kert-em* 'my garden' with *kér-em* 'I ask for', and similarly *kert-ed* 'your garden' and *kér-ed* 'you ask for', *kert-ünk* 'our garden' and *kér-ünk* 'we ask for', *kert-etek* 'your (pl.) garden' and *kér-tek* 'you (pl.) ask for'.

Another striking typological difference is in the category of gender, or noun classification: Hungarian lacks grammatical gender entirely, while IE languages have well-established gender systems. Slavic languages in fact have two systems of noun classification, one contrasting masculine, feminine, and neuter and the other contrasting animate and inanimate. German has masculine, feminine, and neuter genders, again expressed primarily in articles and other modifiers; Romance languages generally have only masculine and feminine. English lacks gender distinctions in nouns entirely, distinguishing the three Germanic genders only in third person singular personal pronouns (*he* vs. *she* vs. *it*).

Hungarian verbs inflect through the grammatical dimensions of person, number, tense, and mood. The person categories are the same as in IE – first, second, and third – and the number categories are the same as in nouns. Hungarian has present, past, and future tenses, but the future is analytic, not agglutinative; this too is similar to IE. The language has also sometimes been claimed to have a very restricted passive voice construction (see Fenyvesi 1998c: 282 for discussion) but this is probably best considered a functional equivalent to a passive construction rather than an inflectional category (Anna Fenyvesi, p.c. 2002). Perfective aspect is expressed by preverbs, which may or may not be true prefixes and may or may not be inflectional (see above, and see ibid., pp. 299ff.). In these categories there are no striking typological differences between Hungarian and the relevant IE languages. As in IE, other distinctions (especially aspectual or quasi-aspectual distinctions) are expressed in Hungarian by derivational rather than inflectional formations. However, Hungarian makes more use of morphological derivation, whereas IE languages use more analytic constructions in expressing similar distinctions.

In the grammatical dimension of mood, most Uralic languages differ significantly from IE. IE languages typically have at most two or three moods – indicative, imperative, and perhaps subjunctive – and some, like modern English, lack morphological mood distinctions altogether. The average number of moods in Uralic languages is four or five. But here Hungarian differs from other Uralic languages and resembles IE languages typologically, because it has only three morphological moods: the indicative, the conditional, and the imperative (Fenyvesi 1998c: 308).

One other inflectional category in the Hungarian verb system does differ markedly from IE verbal inflection. This is a distinction between transitive verbs with a definite direct object (the so-called 'objective' or definite conjugation) and verbs without a definite direct object, i.e. intransitive verbs and verbs with an indefinite object (the so-called 'subjective' or indefinite conjugation) (Fenyvesi 1998c: 321). The relevant IE languages have no comparable construction; IE verbs inflect for the person and number of the subject, but not for the object.

It's difficult to compare typological features of Hungarian syntax systematically with those of the relevant IE languages, both because the IE languages differ so much among themselves and because syntactic structures that are superficially similar may actually be radically different. (Of course the latter problem also arises in comparisons of morphology and even phonology, but it isn't as acute there.) I'll make just a few comparative comments about syntactic features.

First, Hungarian sentential word order, like Proto-Uralic, is basically Subject – Object – Verb, SOV. The major relevant IE languages have unmarked surface SVO word order in simple declarative sentences, though German at least, is generally analyzed by modern syntacticians with underlying SOV order. The surface order is likely to be crucially relevant in contact situations, however, so it is important to note the difference.

Other ordering features that tend to cluster with basic sentential word order are mixed in Hungarian. Relative clauses, for instance, may either precede the noun they modify, as expected in an SOV language, or follow the noun (Kenesei 1998a: 38). Some ordering features do follow the expected pattern for an SOV language: adjectives precede the head noun in a noun phrase (ibid., p. 92), and the language has only postpositions, no prepositions (ibid., p. 336). In typical SVO languages, including the major ones in contact with Hungarian, relative clauses follow the head noun, adjectives precede the head noun, and prepositions are used instead of postpositions.

Second, Hungarian agreement patterns are partly similar and partly quite different from IE patterns. Verbal agreement is in general similar to IE verbal agreement: the verb agrees with its subject in person and number. The major difference here is that the Hungarian transitive verb, unlike the IE transitive verb, also agrees with its object in one feature, definiteness. Agreement patterns differ sharply in noun phrases. In IE languages that still have quite a bit of inflectional morphology (not including English, with its poverty-stricken inflectional morphology) an adjective agrees with the noun it modifies in gender, number, and case. In Hungarian, by contrast, attributive adjectives receive number and case marking only when they are pro-forms – that is, when they are not in construction with an overt head noun (this analysis and the following example are from Fenyvesi 1998c: 331). An example is *kék-et* 'the blue one' (lit. 'blue-ACC') in the sentence *A fehér ing-et vesz-ed fel vagy a kék-et?* 'Are you going to wear the white shirt or the blue one?' (lit. 'the white shirt-ACC put-DEF.2SG up or the blue-ACC').

Before turning to a consideration of the implications of this typological survey for the study of contact-induced changes, let's summarize the most striking typological differences we've identified between Hungarian and the IE languages with which it has been in close contact. In contrast to the IE languages, Hungarian has vowel harmony, a total lack of syllable-initial consonant clusters in native words, few syllable-final consonant clusters, agglutinative morphology (vs. flexional morphology in IE), 17–27 cases (vs. at most 7 in modern IE), possessive pronominal suffixes, overlap (because of the possessive pronominal suffixes) in noun and verb affixes, singular nouns after quantifiers, a total lack of gender/noun classes, verb agreement distinguishing a definite from an indefinite object, surface and underlying SOV word order (vs. at least surface SVO word order in the IE languages), postpositions (vs. prepositions in IE), and optionally preposed relative clauses. Unlike most of the relevant IE languages, Hungarian also has front rounded vowel phonemes, long vs. short vowel phonemes, more palatal consonants than most IE languages have, and fixed word-initial stress.

3. What kinds of contact-induced changes are probable?

The typological differences and similarities between Hungarian and the relevant IE languages permit us to make limited predictions about the kinds of changes that are likely to take place under different contact conditions. The most general and most obvious prediction is this: if Hungarian is under the strong influence of one (or more) of the IE languages, it is likely to retain structural features that are typologically similar to the corresponding features in the other language(s) but to simplify or lose structural features that it does not share with the other language(s). The converse should also hold: if one of the IE languages is under the strong influence of Hungarian, it is likely to retain or abandon structural features according to their typological fit with the features of Hungarian. As we will see in this section, though, the actual situation isn't quite so simple. In particular, under sufficiently intense contact conditions, a language may also acquire new structural features that alter its typological profile significantly. Typologically-based predictions about types of change are most likely to be relevant in relatively less intense contact situations.

Predicting language change is at best a chancy enterprise. In the area of contact-induced linguistic change, social factors turn out to be even more important (if this is possible) than in the innovation and especially the spread of internally-motivated changes. The difference is that an internal linguistic innovation might arise from purely structural pattern pressures, while every contact-induced change inevitably has a social component. (In the most trivial case, there can't be any contact-induced change unless there is direct or indirect contact between two languages.) Aspects of linguistic structure are certainly relevant for contact phenomena too – hence the typological survey above – but no language will adopt any features from another language unless the social circumstances are right. We know very little, unfortunately, about the social circumstances of language contact. Or, rather, we know quite a bit about the general and particular social circumstances of particular contact situations, but we cannot correlate specific social factors with specific linguistic changes with any confidence. It is possible, however, to characterize a few very general social factors that are relevant for predicting contact-induced changes. I'll start with some general remarks and then focus on Hungarian contacts.

First, a broad distinction can be drawn between contact-induced changes that are effected by people who are fluent speakers of both the source language and the receiving language, on the one hand, and on the other hand contact-induced changes in which the people primarily responsible for the transfer of features are not fluent speakers of the receiving language. Typically, bilinguals borrow material from a second language into their first language, whereas in the other case the changes are brought about as a result of imperfect learning of a target language by a group of people. Because it typically happens as a direct result of language shift, this second type of change may be called shift-induced interference; in this section I'll use this term for the second type of interference, and restrict my usage of the term 'borrowing' to situations involving full, or at least fluent, bilingualism.

It's important to keep in mind that the typical cases are not the only possibilities. For instance, a native speaker of English who is very fluent in Hungarian might borrow words or even structures from English into his or her variety of Hungarian. And the type of interference that is characteristic of language shift situations also occurs frequently when no actual language shift takes place; this is the major way in which many distinct varieties of English have arisen around the world, usually among educated people who use English for economic, political, and/or academic purposes – people who, in their private lives, stick to their native languages and do not shift to English.

Borrowing, in my narrow sense, is a fairly straightforward process (relatively speaking): a person who speaks two languages fluently simply incorporates material from one of the languages into the other. There are in principle no linguistic barriers to this type of interference – anything a speaker is aware of can be transferred to her/his other language – but there are certainly social barriers that block the most extreme kinds of borrowing in the great majority of cases. Distorting one's language drastically through borrowing requires powerful social motives, and the motives must of course be shared by other speakers of the receiving language; if they aren't, only a single speaker's speech will change, not the language as a whole.

Shift-induced interference is a more complicated process. If we assume a situation of language shift by speakers who haven't learned the target language well, it involves at least two different things: shifting speakers may fail to learn some features that the target language (TL) has, and they may also carry over features from their native language into their version of the TL. If they eventually amalgamate with the TL speech community, a third thing may happen: TL speakers will adopt – by borrowing – a subset of the initial interference features into the emerging new variety of the TL.

The two basic kinds of interference yield different predictions about the linguistic results. In borrowing, lexicon is (almost?) invariably borrowed first; under more intense contact, structure may also be borrowed, but there will still be more lexical than structural interference. In shift-induced interference, by contrast, lexicon may or may not be transferred at all; phonological and syntactic features are most prominent among the interference features, with lexicon and (for different reasons) morphology lagging behind. In both borrowing and shift-induced interference, the typological fit between the source and receiving languages is relevant in predicting the interference features, except in the most extreme cases involving the most intense contact. In borrowing situations, features are more readily transferred if they do not disrupt the typological structure of the receiving language. And in shift-induced interference, universally marked (harder to learn) TL features are less likely to be learned by shifting speakers, and universally marked source-language features are less likely to be adopted by original TL speakers from the shifting group's version of the TL.

Aside from the broad social factors that determine the presence or absence of imperfect learning of a TL, we can point to other social factors that are likely to be relevant for predicting the amount of contact-induced change. Intensity of contact is always important, but it's a hard-to-define notion. In borrowing situations, intensity is usually (though not always) connected with duration of the contact – longer contact generally means more bilingualism and therefore more possibilities for the adoption of interference features. In shift situations, intensity is usually correlated with the relative sizes of the shifting and TL speech communities: a smaller TL community provides fewer native-speaker models for shifting speakers to learn from, so more interference is likely when the speaker numbers are skewed in favor of the shifting group.

But of course other factors are also crucial, sometimes even more so. Prestige is often relevant, though not as universally relevant as one might infer from much of the language-contact literature. In all contact situations, probably, speakers' attitudes are extremely important. Of course, the sense of what counts as prestigious is ultimately an attitudinal factor, but there are other relevant attitudes too. Some shifting speakers, for instance, refuse to learn the TL "properly", i.e. to speak it the way original native speakers speak it; and in some quite intense contact situations involving high levels of bilingualism, speakers of a pressured language refuse to borrow material from the language of a sociopolitically dominant group. Sociolinguistic predictors of change that have been investigated systematically, in both bilingual and monolingual contexts, include gender, age, urban vs. rural residence, level of education, and so forth; these are surely also relevant for predicting contact-induced changes, though few if any generalizations can be drawn at present about their interaction with other social factors and with linguistic factors in efforts to make such predictions.

One final social factor is relevant only for some contact situations, but it is especially important for the study of Hungarian outside Hungary. This is the phenomenon of language death, brought about by social factors and often manifested linguistically by a combination of attrition (the loss of lexicon and structure without replacement by foreign material) and assimilation to a "conquering" language through borrowing. As we will see, distinguishing between these two processes is by no means always possible or desirable in a language death situation, because many changes that occur in a dying language seem to be produced by both of them.

Now, what about Hungarian? Its linguistic behavior under contact conditions is almost certain to vary depending on whether we look at its contacts within Hungary or its contacts outside Hungary – especially in immigrant Hungarian communities on other continents, where direct contacts with Hungary are likely to be quite limited.

Within Hungary, Hungarian has been the major language for over a thousand years. This is not to say that Hungarians have tended to be monolingual; in particular, many, most, or all educated Hungarians were bilingual in German during the Habsburg Empire (starting in the 17th century) and its successor state, the Austro-Hungarian Empire (1867–1918). If the Hungarian of Hungary has been influenced by other languages, then, there are three major possible sources of influence. First, Hungarian might have been influenced by minority languages spoken within Hungary, through borrowing by either native speakers of Hungarian or bilingual native speakers of the minority languages. Lexical borrowing, at least, has occurred: there are, for instance, loanwords from Lovári in Hungarian, many of them slang terms (Fenyvesi 1995c). Second, the minority languages might have influenced Hungarian through shift-induced interference, if members of minority groups shifted to Hungarian in sufficient numbers; in this case, the expected interference features would be primarily phonological and syntactic. The question of major structural influence from either of these sources has been the subject of much debate. A striking fact is that non-standard varieties of Hungarian in Hungary display some features that are attributed to neighboring languages when they appear in Hungarian as spoken in neighboring countries (see e.g. Csernicskó and Fenyvesi 2000). It may well be, therefore, that minority languages within Hungary have also influenced Hungarian (and see comments below about possible influence from German, a minority language with special historical status).

Meanwhile, the minority languages themselves may well have undergone structural as well as lexical borrowing from Hungarian. I have little information about such changes in most of these languages, but Kiefer (1997) discusses several structural borrowings from Hungarian in Lovári. Lovári has apparently developed verbal prefixes – converting native adverbs to prefixes – under Hungarian influence, though in Lovári the prefixes are inseparable; this change, Kiefer argues, must have happened after Habsburg wrote his Lovári grammar (1888), because he makes no mention of verbal prefixes (pp. 329, 333–334, 339). (By contrast, Lovári in northern Slavic -speaking contexts developed a functionally equivalent verbal prefixing system by borrowing Slavic prefixes – same structural borrowing phenomenon, different strategy.) Typologically, Lovári has changed in this respect to match Hungarian rather closely, in spite of the fact that the Lovári prefixes are inseparable and the Hungarian preverbs are separable. That is, Lovári has adopted a foreign morphological feature that complicates its morphology and alters its typological profile significantly. This is one of the most important lessons to be learned from language contact studies: given sufficient intensity of contact, typological mismatches are no barrier to structural borrowing. Hungarian influence is also responsible for the restructuring of the Lovári tense system, including its simplification from five to three tenses, a set of changes that also post-dates Habsburg 1888 (pp. 329–330, 333). This change, because it simplifies the tense system, is less surprising than the development of prefixes. But it also underlines the point that borrowings can have significant typological effects.

Third, and perhaps most promising as a source of structural interference in Hungarian, bilingual Hungarian speakers might have borrowed words and even structure from German, and these borrowings could have spread to Hungarian as a whole – especially Standard Hungarian, given its link to the more highly educated segment of the population. There was certainly a high level of bilingualism in German, among educated Hungarians in particular; knowing German would have been socially, politically, and economically important under German-speaking rulers, and the prestige of German would have provided a motivation for adopting some of its features. There's no question about lexical borrowing from German; examples like *smaragd* 'emerald', *knédli* 'Czech bread-like dumplings', *treff* 'club (card)', and *strand* 'beach' are easy to find. Structural borrowing is harder to find and may not exist. Some of the salient features that Hungarian shares with German, for instance the fixed initial stress pattern, are ancient in Uralic and therefore cannot be due to German (or other recent foreign) influence; others, in particular the Hungarian preverbs – which, in their movement possibilities, are reminiscent of German separable prefixes – cannot easily be traced to German influence. In fact, Kiefer asserts flatly that the mobility of the Hungarian preverbs is 'definitely not' a result of German influence (1997:337). I've seen no discussion of shared Hungarian and German typological features that points uncontroversially to mutual or one-way influence on their development. Although the possibility of German structural interference in Hungarian was present for some centuries, then, it may never have happened.

Outside Hungary, interference in Hungarian is almost sure to be the result of borrowing. The only possible exception would be in a community where speakers of another language shifted in sizable numbers to Hungarian; there could be such cases, especially in countries that share borders with Hungary, but if so I haven't heard of them. The borrowings into Hungarian in neighboring countries and in distant immigrant communities comprise both lexical and structural features. Here are two examples from neighboring countries. In Subcarpathia (southwestern Ukraine) and in Slovakia, some Hungarian speakers use IE-style plural number of nouns, e.g. in reference to body parts that occur in pairs or to a group of identical items, instead of the singular expected in Standard Hungarian (Csernicskó & Fenyvesi 2000: 107ff.; Lanstyák & Szabómihály 1996a: 119, 1997: 80–84). In Subcarpathia, some Hungarian speakers also use an IE-like analytic construction in verb phrases instead of the expected Standard Hungarian agglutinative construction. For instance, for 'traveling by bus' in a sentence like 'I'm very tired of all this traveling by bus', they'll use *utazás-t busz-szal* (lit. 'travel-ACC bus-INS]') instead of *busz-oz-ás-t* (lit. 'bus-VDER-NDER-ACC', a derived denominal verb form) (Csernicskó & Fenyvesi 2000: 105). Similarly, the Standard Hungarian inflectional suffix *-hat/het* 'potential' (i.e. 'having the ability, opportunity, etc., to act') is often replaced in Subcarpathia by an analytic construction using the auxiliary verb *tud* 'be able to', as in e.g. *Ki tud-ok men-ni?* 'May I go out?' (lit. 'PVB be.able-INDEF.1SG go-INF') instead of Standard Hungarian *Ki-me-het-ek?* (lit. 'PVB-go-POT-INDEF.1SG') (Csernicskó & Fenyvesi 2000: 106). In these examples, the innovative Subcarpathia and Slovakia Hungarian constructions are the result of borrowing from Ukrainian and Slovak, respectively. Some apparent structural interference features are also found in nonstandard varieties of Hungarian within Hungary, but others – for instance the analytic 'potential' construction – are not found in any variety of Hungarian spoken in Hungary.

All these examples fit the general typological prediction made at the beginning of this section: Hungarian has abandoned certain morphosyntactic features that are not shared with the relevant IE languages – or rather, the features are replaced by constructions that fit the typology of the functionally equivalent IE constructions.

The situation is more complicated when we consider immigrant Hungarian communities in distant places like North America and Australia. As noted above, these Hungarian speech communities are very likely to experience some degree of language loss, as their members shift to the sociopolitically dominant language of their new country – usually English. They might or might not conform to the 'three-generation shift' pattern that is said to be typical of immigrant communities in the U.S.: the original immigrants are monolingual in their home-country language, their offspring are bilingual in (in this case) Hungarian and English, and the third generation of children will be monolingual English speakers. But even if they don't fit this rapid-shift pattern, the pressure to shift to English is powerful.

If language loss does occur, it is likely – though not inevitable (see Section 4 below) – that its effects on the language itself will be of several different kinds. First, as in any bilingual context where one language is clearly dominant in the larger community, the immigrant language is likely to borrow words and structure from the dominant language. These borrowings are not different in kind from ordinary lexical and structural borrowing in contact situations that don't involve language loss, but they may be more extensive. Second, the immigrant language is likely to lose material without replacing it: this is what is known as attrition, the loss of lexicon and structure. Attrition occurs primarily because, as the original ethnic-group language is used less and less in day-to-day communication, less frequent constructions and stylistic options will be forgotten by older community members and never learned by younger ones. The dominant language to which the group is shifting will, in effect, take up the slack: if you can't remember how to say something in your native (ethnic-heritage) language, you can always say it in your new country's dominant language instead. Or, of course, you might know perfectly well how to say it in your native language but simply prefer to say it in your new language.

The third possibility for linguistic results was mentioned earlier in this section: some changes undergone by the immigrant group's language will be a combination of borrowing and attrition. Any change that both simplifies the group's language and brings it closer to the structure of the dominant language belongs to this category.

This three-way categorization of changes in a dying immigrant language is spelled out in Fenyvesi (1995a), a systematic study of changes in all the major grammatical components of a variety of Hungarian spoken in McKeesport, Pennsylvania. Fenyvesi's three categories are (a) borrowing alone, changes that brought the language closer to English but did not obviously simplify it overall; (b) attrition alone, changes that were simplificatory but did not bring the language closer to English; and (c) both borrowing and attrition. It's difficult to be certain in every instance which category a change belongs in, but overall her results were clear. Changes in category (b) were the least common; categories (a) and (c) were numerically close, but category (c) changes were the most frequent.

Here are a few examples of the changes Fenyvesi found. In category (a), borrowing from English, she found a partial shift of stress from the beginning of a verb to the verb's root (arguably an actual complication in the language's structure), allophonic aspiration of voiceless stops, a retroflex vocoid pronunciation of /r/, a partial change from dominant SOV to dominant SVO word order, and a change from quantifier word (e.g. a numeral) plus singular noun to quantifier plus plural noun. (This last change is akin to the partial replacements of singular by plural nouns in the Hungarian spoken in Ukraine and Slovakia.) Category (b) changes – changes that simplified McKeesport Hungarian structure but did not make it more like English – included the regularization of inflection in irregular verbs and the replacement of one preverb by another. And a few category (c) changes, the largest category, were degemination of consonants between vowels, the partial loss of certain case suffixes, the partial collapse of the distinction between definite and indefinite conjugations, and the loss of semantically redundant possessive suffixes in dative possessive constructions. It should be emphasized that all the changes in categories (a) and (c) are typical structural borrowings; there is nothing that makes them specific to language death situations. And the changes in category (b), though not borrowing, are typical internally-motivated linguistic changes – although in a thriving language lost material is likely to be replaced by structures elsewhere in the language. That is, there is nothing about the changes themselves in (some) dying languages that sets them apart from changes in other social contexts; what is peculiar to the language death situation is the degree of overall attrition and often (though not always) the degree of borrowing.

Not all these changes affect the typological profile of Hungarian; the regularization of inflection and the replacement of one preverb by another, for instance, are typologically inert. The changes that are typologically important fit the general typological prediction at the end of Section 2. Hungarian features like fixed word-initial stress, SOV word order, and definite vs. indefinite conjugations, which are absent in English, are (partially) abandoned; but typological features that are shared with English, including for instance much (though not all) of the Hungarian inventory of consonant phonemes, are retained. In addition, however, some features of English that are typologically marked cross-linguistically are adopted by McKeesport Hungarian speakers; examples are the vocoid English /r/ pronunciation and allophonic aspiration of voiceless stops. So loss and retention are not the only options for typological change in a pressured language; addition of new features also occurs, not only in this case but fairly often elsewhere in intense contact situations.

Language death and its frequent linguistic concomitants, attrition and extensive structural borrowing, are not confined to immigrant communities. It is quite possible that some (varieties of) minority languages within Hungary present the same profile as McKeesport Hungarian and other immigrant varieties of Hungarian, with both borrowing and attrition.

Similarly, the languages with which Hungarian speakers have been in contact outside Hungary may undergo the various types of change discussed above. In particular, shift-induced interference from Hungarian has been identified in dialects of neighboring Slavic languages. One especially interesting example is the stress pattern of a dialect of Serbo-Croatian spoken near the Hungarian border. The area originally had a sizable population of Hungarian speakers, all of whom eventually shifted to Serbo-Croatian. But the shifting group left its mark on the local Serbo-Croatian dialect, in at least one salient feature: the stress system. Serbo-Croatian has free (phonemic) stress – depending on the dialect, the stress may fall on any syllable or on any but the final syllable of a word. Hungarian, as we saw in Section 2, has fixed initial stress. After the local Hungarian speakers shifted to Serbo-Croatian, the dialect had fixed stress – but on the penult (the second syllable from the end) rather than on the initial syllable. Apparently the shifting speakers recognized that Serbo-Croatian didn't have initial stress but assumed that it had fixed stress somewhere, and settled on the penult as a kind of average place of stress. (The source of this example is Ivić 1964.) What is striking about the example is that the resulting stress pattern is not identical either to the original shifting group's pattern or to the original target language pattern; this is quite typical of shift-induced interference. It's also important to note that stress in this Serbo-Croatian dialect has changed typologically to resemble Hungarian, moving from free stress to fixed stress; the fact that the actual position of the fixed stress differs does not change the typological picture appreciably. Other possible interference features from Hungarian in neighboring Slavic languages (or dialects of those languages) are discussed in Greenberg 1999; one example is the development of front rounded vowels in some Kajkavian and Štokavian dialects of Serbo-Croatian and in Slovenian.

4. Conclusion

As we've seen, Hungarian in immigrant communities can be expected to undergo borrowing and, if the variety is dying, attrition as well. This pattern holds, as far as I know, for all Hungarian immigrant communities in North America and Australia. Borrowing has also affected Hungarian in speech communities in countries bordering Hungary itself, and lexical borrowing, at least, can be found in Hungarian within Hungary. Shift-induced interference might possibly be present in Hungarian within Hungary; it's improbable in Hungarian speech communities beyond the country's borders. Typologically-based predictions about the linguistic results of intense contacts generally seem to hold for Hungarian contacts, though typological changes through added foreign features have also occurred and can be expected to occur in other intense contact situations as well. It's vital to keep in mind, however, that predictions based on structural typology are always secondary to predictions based on social circumstances. To take the most obvious example, casual borrowing contexts will never lead to typological changes in the borrowing language; for typological disruption, intense contact, including much bilingualism among borrowing-language speakers, is needed.

Conversely, minority languages within Hungary are likely to have borrowed words and even structure from Hungarian. Outside Hungary, at least a few varieties of neighboring languages have undergone shift-induced interference from Hungarian. But overall, our expectations about interference both in Hungarian from other languages and in other languages from Hungarian mainly concern borrowing.

In spite of these reasonable expectations about borrowing – and, in Hungarian speech communities outside Hungary, language death – this chapter must close with a caveat. It is this: reasonable expectations about contact-induced language change are not always met. Sometimes, even in intense contact situations where one would predict extensive interference, no such interference takes place. Some cultures, for instance, borrow little or no lexicon from dominant groups' languages; instead, they construct new words for borrowed cultural items out of native linguistic material. Another example: a language or dialect that dies rapidly may never undergo either borrowing or attrition before it is abandoned by its speakers. Of course some predictions will certainly hold, especially negative ones – for instance, you can't borrow what you don't know, so the borrowing of linguistic structure requires a rather high level of bilingualism on the part of the borrowing speakers; and there will be no shift-induced interference unless there is imperfect learning of a target language by a group of speakers.

But positive predictions, predictions about what features will be transferred under what specific social conditions, won't always be accurate. In other words, although general predictions can be made about the probable types of contact-induced change to be found in a particular social situation, the actual results are subject to the influence of social factors that are not, to put it mildly, well understood.

Note

1. I'm using the term 'apical' here to designate the category of consonants pronounced with the tip or the blade of the tongue as the lower articulator; it corresponds to the category [+coronal] in distinctive feature terminology.

Chapter 2

Contextualizing the Sociolinguistics
of Hungarian Outside Hungary project

Miklós Kontra

1. Introduction

At the turn of the 21st century at least one in four, and perhaps as many as one in three
native speakers of Hungarian live outside the Hungarian Republic. Genetically a Uralic
language, Hungarian is unrelated to German, Romanian, and the Slavic languages that
it has been in contact with since the Hungarian Conquest of the Carpathian Basin in
895. For a millennium prior to World War I, historical Hungary extended over the
entire central Danubian Basin, with a largely multilingual and multiethnic population. Following the dissolution of the Austro-Hungarian Empire and the Peace Treaty
of Trianon in 1920, Hungary lost about two-thirds of her territory and population to
Czechoslovakia, Romania, Yugoslavia and Austria. Millions of ethnic Hungarians became citizens of another country overnight, in a similar fashion to "members of the
Spanish culture" who "woke up one morning to find themselves citizens of the Unites
States" (Marshall 1986:40) when the US annexed New Mexico following the Treaty of
Guadalupe Hidalgo in 1848.

At the time of this writing in 2004, Hungarians are a nation in eight countries.
Slightly over 10 million Hungarians live in the Hungarian Republic, about 520,000
live in Slovakia, 157,000 in Subcarpathia, Ukraine, over 1.4 million in Romania, about
290,000 in Vojvodina, Serbia, 17,000 in Croatia, and a few thousand each in Slovenia
and Austria. These indigenous Hungarians belong to one cultural nation and eight
political nations (see Map 2.1).

According to the theory of *political nation*, national identity is defined on the basis
of citizenship. According to the theory of *cultural nation*, it is defined on the basis of
language and culture. Hungarians define themselves as a cultural nation. Many American, British, French and other readers who define national identity on the basis of
citizenship, find this difficult to understand. For instance, in a Council of Europe
monograph, the French geography professor Michel Foucher (1994:45) writes that
"The 1920 Trianon Treaty is still considered in Hungary as an 'unjust' treaty." Foucher
seems to be suggesting here that the treaty which dismembered the Kingdom of Hungary and put millions of indigenous Hungarians into foreign states was not unjust, but

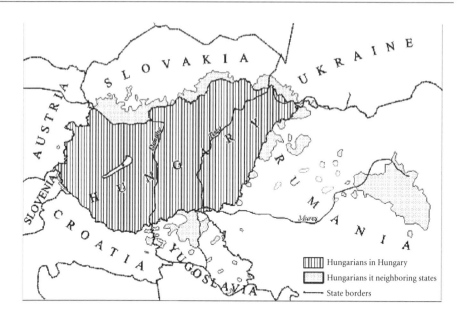

Map 2.1. Hungarians in the Carpathian Basin

even if it could have been seen as unjust after World War I, by now it should have been reevaluated as a just treaty. This may perhaps be a legitimate expectation under the theory of political nation, but it is simply nonsensical for a nation which is constituted as a cultural nation.

This fundamental difference in how a nation defines itself is usually concealed in English academic prose when authors use phrases like *Hungarian Slovaks, Hungarian Romanians* etc. Rather than follow the typical English usage, which reflects the theory of political nation, I will be using phrases like *Hungarians in Slovakia* or *Slovakia-Hungarians*, which are in harmony with how the large majority of Hungarians view themselves.[1] The cultural nation vs. political nation difference and the way it is or is not reflected in how we write can determine the success of our communication. For instance, what one author intends as new information for readers may look like stating the obvious to some of them. Suppose an article in an encyclopedia has something like "Hungarians are an important minority in Romania, and they perceive themselves as Hungarians rather than Romanians." This statement about self-perception is probably newsworthy to readers who believe in the political nation, but it is quite vacuous to those believing in the cultural nation and may well be offensive to Hungarians in Romania.[2]

One more terminological problem should be mentioned right at the beginning, namely the curious distinction between *ethnic minorities* and *national minorities*. Oftentimes these two terms are used as (near)synonyms, but sometimes they denote different kinds of communities.[3] The definition of *ethnic* in The American Heritage Dictionary of the English Language (3rd ed.)[4] is broad enough to include immigrant communities such as Hungarian-Americans, indigenous communities like the Spanish in New Mexico, or stateless nations like the Gypsies/Roma or the Kurds. The term *national minority* has received political significance in the Organization for Security and Cooperation in Europe when the OSCE created its Office of the High Commissioner for National Minorities in 1992, a diplomatic instrument to prevent inter-ethnic conflicts. The first High Commissioner, Max Van der Stoel was engaged in a number of conflicts where language issues figured prominently, and this prompted him to request internationally recognized experts to create documents such as *The Hague Recommendations Regarding the Education Rights of National Minorities* (1996) and *The Oslo Recommendations Regarding the Linguistic Rights of National Minorities* (1998), which should serve as guidelines for an appropriate and coherent application of minority language rights in the OSCE area (see Kemp 2001). Among others, Max Van der Stoel was successful in reducing serious language-related conflicts between Hungarians and Slovaks in Slovakia and Hungarians and Romanians in Romania in the 1990s. Although his mandate from the OSCE does not define the term *national minority*, Max van der Stoel's pragmatic diplomatic approach was based on human rights, and regarding some language rights as part of human rights was certainly not alien to him. This international political context has been playing a significant role in influencing the fate of bilingual Hungarians in the Carpathian Basin in the last decade, and for this reason considering the human rights and language rights situation of the Hungarian national minorities is essential for any understanding or analysis of Hungarian language contacts today.

The language rights situation of the bilingual Hungarians has a clear effect on their contact-induced changes, which can be shown, for instance, by grammaticality judgments of an object *pro*-drop sentence as in (1b):

(1) a. *Találkoz-t-am   Hedvig-gel   s   megkér-t-em   ő-t,*
         meet-PAST-1SG.IND Hedwig-INS and ask-PAST-1SG.IND s/he-ACC
         hogy ve-gy-en   nek-em egy kifli-t.
         that buy-IMP-3SG.IND DAT-1SG a   croissant-ACC
         'I met Hedwig and asked her to buy me a croissant.'
     b. *Találkoz-t-am   Hedvig-gel   s   megkér-t-em   0, hogy*
         meet-PAST-1SG.IND Hedwig-INS and ask-PAST-1SG.IND 0 that
         ve-gy-en   nek-em egy kifli-t.
         buy-IMP-3SG.IND DAT-1SG a   croissant-ACC
         'I met Hedwig and asked her to buy me a croissant.'

Lanstyák and Szabómihály (1997: 90–91) report that the medium of instruction (Hungarian or Slovak) significantly influenced which of the two sentences, (1a) or (1b), Hungarian high school students in Slovakia chose as more natural. Hungarian being an object *pro*-drop language,[5] it was expected that Hungarians in Hungary would favor (1b), but that Hungarians in Slovakia, who are bilingual in Hungarian and Slovak, a language with overt object, would favor (1a). Lanstyák and Szabómihály's expectations proved essentially correct. As shown in Figure 2.1, monolingual Hungarian

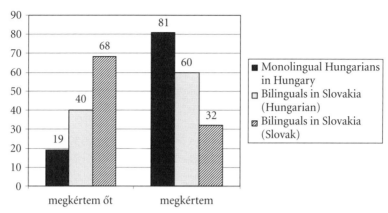

* Based on Lanstyák and Szabómihály (1997:90–91).
N = 798

Figure 2.1. The effect of the medium of instruction on choosing a Hungarian object *pro*-drop sentence (*megkértem*) as more natural than an overt object sentence (*megkértem őt*) by three groups of high school students in percentages*

students favored object *pro*-drop more than bilinguals, and the Hungarian-Slovak bilingual students who studied in a Hungarian-language school in Slovakia favored it more than those who studied in a Slovak-language school. A similar implicational relationship was found for sentence (4a) (discussed in Subsection 3.2.3 below) which was chosen as more natural by 91% of the monolingual Hungarian students in Hungary, by 86% of the bilinguals in Slovakia who study in a school with Hungarian as the medium of instruction, and by 69% of the bilinguals who study in a school with Slovak as the medium of instruction. Thus the medium of instruction has a significant effect on the judgments of contact-induced sentences. The choice of the language of teaching can be either free or enforced. If it is enforced, there is linguistic genocide in education (see Skutnabb-Kangas 2000a). In Slovakia, one in five Hungarian pupils go to Slovak-language schools, and at least part of them study through the medium of Slovak as a result of force rather than free will (see, for instance, Kontra 1995/1996; Lanstyák 2000c).

A great deal of the research on contact-induced changes that I am familiar with pays less than adequate attention to the language rights situation of the bilingual speakers undergoing linguistic change. It is one of the characteristics of Hungarian bilingualism research in the Carpathian Basin that we are accumulating more and more information on both the structural changes of the languages in contact and the social situation of the speakers.

2. Hungarian contact linguistics

Although the history of Hungarian is also a history of Hungarian language contacts, Hungarian contact linguistics in the modern sense of the word is very young. Language contact research as pioneered by Haugen and Weinreich had no impact whatsoever on Hungarian linguistics until about the 1980s. Hungarian historical linguists wrote excellent monographs on, for instance, Turkic loanwords in Hungarian (e.g. Ligeti 1986), Slavic influence on Hungarian (e.g. Kniezsa 1955; Kiss 1976), Hungarian-Romanian language contacts (e.g. Gáldi 1947; Bakos 1982), German-Hungarian contacts (e.g. Mollay 1982) or the Hungarian influence on Serbo-Croatian (e.g. Hadrovics 1985), but all of them analyzed contacts of olden times with the apparatus of the language historian-etymologist. In these studies etymology was all important but any other contact effects, especially grammatical borrowing, was almost totally disregarded (see K. Sándor 1998).

Modern studies of bilingualism with the linguist using a tape-recorder and doing participant observation of bilingual communities began with Réger (see, for instance, 1979) in Hungary. In neighboring Yugoslavia, Mikeš (1974) and Göncz (1985) did pioneering psycholinguistic work with Hungarian-Serbian bilinguals. The indigenous Hungarians in Burgenland, Austria were studied by the American linguist Gal in her classic book on language shift in Oberwart/Felsőőr (1979), and the immigrant Hungarian-Americans by Kontra (1985, 1990, 1993a), Bartha (1993), and Fenyvesi (1995a), but the large indigenous Hungarian minorities behind the Iron Curtain remained *terra incognita* for language contact research up till the fall of communism. This was mainly due to the making taboo of all minority issues in the communist countries, but partly it was also a consequence of the state of Hungarian linguistics, most of whose prominent figures were unaware of Labov's credo that the present is a laboratory to study the past.

When communism collapsed and Hungarian bilingualism began to be studied by Lanstyák (1991) in Slovakia and by others elsewhere, bilingual Hungarians with their contact dialects rapidly came to center stage in Hungarian linguistics, so much so that the loudest and most agitated polemic among linguists in the 1990s filled hundreds of pages in linguistic journals, literary monthlies and daily newspapers in and outside Hungary (see Kontra & Saly 1998 for a rich selection). The idea that bilingual Hungarians speak Hungarian somewhat differently from monolingual Hungarians in Hungary seemed to be untenable to the old guard of Hungarian linguists, who feared that such a recognition of linguistic differences by professional linguists may lead to the fragmentation of the nation (see Fenyvesi 1995b; Kontra 1997). Meanwhile the younger linguists in Hungary and her neighboring countries were conducting empirical research projects on variation in Hungarian in growing numbers, held conferences, and published articles and books in Hungarian, Romanian, Slovak and English. This coming of age of Hungarian bilingualism research has recently led to a well-argued proposal from a Hungarian linguist in Romania, Sándor Szilágyi N., to revise the periodization of Hungarian linguistics. In a lecture delivered at the Hungarian Academy of

Sciences in Budapest on 2 May 2002, he suggested that the *modern Hungarian period*, which is held to begin in 1772 and last up to the present day, should end in 1918, and the period following World War I should be regarded as the *latest period* (*legújabb kor* in Hungarian) because it is since the end of World War I that Hungarian has been spoken as a native language not only in Hungary but in several other states as well. This change in the political conditions under which native speakers of Hungarian live, says Szilágyi N., warrants recognition by linguists as well.

3.   The Sociolinguistics of Hungarian Outside Hungary project

When in the mid-1990s The Sociolinguistics of Hungarian Outside Hungary project (SHOH for short) was launched,[6] members of the research team[7] set out to systematically gather data in a replicable fashion, which would allow us to answer, or begin to answer, such questions as the following:

a.   In what domains are Hungarian and the majority languages used?
b.   What is the de jure and de facto situation of Hungarian in the neighboring countries?
c.   What are the attitudes to Hungarian used in Hungary, to Hungarian used in the neighboring countries, and to the majority languages therein?
d.   What roles do Hungarian and the minority languages play in education and in government?
e.   Are the contact varieties diverging from the Hungarian of Hungary?
f.   How could L1 teaching for minority Hungarians be improved?
g.   In order to help minority Hungarians to maintain their mother tongue, what should and what should not be done with regard to language policy, linguistic ideology etc.?
h.   What is the social and geographic distribution of important linguistic variables, i.e. what makes the contact varieties of Hungarian similar to and different from Hungarian in Hungary?

Before this project, most of these questions were not even asked by linguists, let alone answered. Nearly all of the information concerning bilingual Hungarian language use in the neighboring countries was anecdotal or consisted of purists' lamentations of the use of contact-induced lexical and grammatical items. If Hungarian linguists knew little about their own minorities' bilingualism, it is no wonder that the international encyclopedia of contact linguistics (Goebl et al. 1997) did not even mention the existence of Hungarians in Subcarpathia, Ukraine. But this volume served our research team well by providing guidelines for its authors, which our team also used when designing the research that is producing historical sociolinguistic portraits of the minorities from 1920 through the mid-1990s and the empirical survey which we conducted in 1996 to study the social context of language use and the contact phenomena in the Hungarian spoken by the minorities in the neighboring countries.[8]

3.1 The respondents of the SHOH project[9]

A quota sample was used, which was stratified for age, education, and settlement type. (In addition, field workers made an attempt to interview about as many men as women.) The three age groups are 13–32-year-olds, 33–53-year-olds, and 54–85-year-olds. Two educational groups were predefined: those without tertiary education and those with a college- or university-degree. Settlement type breaks down into two oppositions: city vs. village, and local majority vs. local minority. A local-majority settlement was defined as one where Hungarians constitute at least 70% of the local population, while in a local-minority settlement they constitute less than 30%. In addition, in the case of Romania, another criterion, proximity to the Hungarian border, was also used (a factor irrelevant in all other countries, where most Hungarians live near the border).

With six respondents each in the 3 age groups by 2 education groups, we get 36 respondents in a settlement. With 4 settlements we get $4 \times 36 = 144$ respondents for a project country, but for various reasons in only two countries is the number of respondents 144 (Ukraine and Yugoslavia[10]). In the case of Slovakia, where Hungarians live in densely Hungarian-populated areas, the category of "local-minority village" is rather atypical, therefore the number of respondents in Slovakia is $144 - 36 = 108$. In Romania the use of the "proximity to the Hungarian border" variable increased the number of respondents by 2×36, yielding a total of 216. Due to the small number of Hungarians in Slovenia and Austria, the sampling method for countries with large Hungarian national minorities could not be used. In Slovenia 67 respondents were surveyed while in Austria 60 questionnaires were administered. An important difference between Austria and all other countries is that most Hungarians there are immigrants scattered across the country, rather than indigenous Hungarians. Thus in Austria the respondents are geographically stratified into 20 people in Vienna, 20 elsewhere in Austria, and 20 in Burgenland (10 of whom are autochthonous to the region and 10 are immigrants). A control group of Hungarians in Hungary (N = 107) was also surveyed. The survey studied people who identified themselves as Hungarian in answer to the question "Are you Hungarian? I mean by nationality, not by citizenship."

Table 2.1 shows the respondents by education. The Chi-square test is not significant ($\chi^2 = 9.386[df = 6], p = n.s.$), which is to say that the sample is homogeneous with regard to the educational level of the respondents.

Comparisons of the aggregate data of the six project countries with Hungary show that the sample is also homogeneous with regard to the age and sex of the respondents, but a country by country comparison has revealed some significant differences at the $p < .05$ level; for instance, the sex distribution is nearly equal in all countries, but in Yugoslavia it is 34.7% males vs. 65.3% females.

Table 2.1. The educational attainment of the respondents of the SHOH survey

Count Column %	Slovakia	Ukraine	Romania	Yugoslavia	Slovenia	Austria	Hungary	Row total
No tertiary education	63	76	132	84	48	37	55	495
	58.3%	52.8%	61.1%	58.3%	72.7%	61.7%	53.4%	58.9%
Tertiary education	45	68	84	60	18	23	48	346
	41.7%	47.2%	38.9%	41.7%	27.3%	38.3%	46.6%	41.1%
Column total	108	144	216	144	66	60	103	841
	12.8%	17.1%	25.7%	17.1%	7.8%	7.1%	12.1%	100.0%

Number of missing observations: 5

3.2 Towards a linguistic description of the contact varieties of Hungarian

Fifty-nine linguistic tasks were used in the 1996 survey with the respondents mentioned above (N = 846, of whom 107 were Hungarians in Hungary). The variables were selected on the basis of previous work (e.g. Lanstyák & Szabómihály 1996a; Kontra 1995b) and as a result of project meetings.

Our variables fall into two broad categories: Universal Hungarian variables and Contact variables. To the former belong items which are used across the entire Hungarian-speaking area in the Carpathian Basin (such as *t*-final verbs [see Váradi & Kontra 1995], the (bV) and (bVn) variables [see Váradi 1995–1996] etc.). Contact variables show the effect of bilingualism in either of two ways.

First, a feature can vary both in Hungary and her neighboring countries but there may be significant differences in terms of frequency. One such example is furnished by nouns denoting professions. Since Hungarian does not have grammatical gender, a profession noun like *fodrász* 'hairdresser' is usually used for males and females alike in standard (monolingual) Hungarian. However, if there is some pressing communicative need to mark gender, femaleness can be expressed by compounding: *fodrász+nő* 'haidresser+woman, that is female hairdresser'. Because in the Slavic contact languages and Romanian gender is marked obligatorily,[11] we hypothesized that the contact languages of the bilingual Hungarians will exert grammatical and lexical influence on their use of L1. In the example here, it was hypothesized that *fodrásznő* will be used by a greater proportion of bilingual Hungarians than monolingual Hungarians.

Second, some contact features vary with Standard Hungarian forms in the speech of minority Hungarians but such variation is unknown in Hungary. For instance, as Lanstyák and Szabómihály (1996a: 124) show, under Slavic influence (2) may vary with the Standard Hungarian (3).

(2) *Nek-em   et-től   a   szobá-tól   nincs   kulcs-om.*
DAT-1SG this-ABL the room-ABL be.3SG.NEG key-PX1SG
'I don't have a key to this room'

(3) *Nek-em   eh-hez   a   szobá-hoz   nincs   kulcs-om.*
DAT-1SG this-ALL the room-ALL be.3SG.NEG key-PX1SG
'I don't have a key to this room'

In the questionnaire, a variety of tasks was used. (For a translated version of the part of the questionnaire containing linguistic tasks, see the Appendix.) In one type of task, respondents had to "choose the more natural" of two sentences provided. Another type required them to "judge the correctness of a sentence and correct it in writing if need be". Yet another type of task asked respondents to "choose either of two alternatives provided" for a blank in a sentence. In the fourth major type of task "blanks in a sentence had to be filled with a word-ending or a full word in writing".

Several research questions were asked, the most important from a linguistic ideological point of view being whether contact varieties of Hungarian are diverging from Hungarian in Hungary (see e.g. Kontra 1997). Put simply, what differences, if any, are there between Hungarian in Hungary and in the neighboring countries? A related question concerns differences between the various contact varieties of Hungarian, e.g. Hungarian used in Slovakia and Yugoslavia. The effect of age, education, sex and settlement type are obvious factors to study. Of the many analyses carried out so far, only a few will be presented here for illustrative purposes.

3.2.1   Analytic constructions

In contact varieties of Hungarian, analytic constructions may be used where monolingual Hungarians use a more synthetic form, e.g. Standard Hungarian uses the compound *tag-díj* (member-fee) 'membership fee' vs. the Contact Hungarian two-word phrase *tag-ság-i díj* (member-NDER-ADER fee). Table 2.2 shows that the distribution of the two variants in Hungary and abroad is significantly different. (The sentences were (i) *Befizetted már az idei tagsági díjat?* and (ii) *Befizetted már az idei tagdíjat?* 'Have you paid this year's membership fee yet?')

Table 2.2. Judging an analytic vs. synthetic construction more natural by Hungarians in Hungary and in the neighboring countries

	Abroad	Hungary	Total
Contact Hungarian *tagsági díjat*	502 (68.9%)	30 (28.6%)	532 (63.8%)
Standard Hungarian *tagdíjat*	227 (31.1%)	75 (71.4%)	302 (36.2%)
Total	729 (100.0%)	105 (100.0%)	834 (100.0%)

$\chi^2 = 64.500$ $(df = 1)$ $p < .001$ Number of missing observations: 12

3.2.2   Mental maps and morphology

The majority of Hungarian city and village names take the surface cases (e.g. *Budapest-en* 'in Budapest') whereas some names denoting Hungarian settlements and all names of foreign cities take the interior cases (e.g. *Tihany-ban* 'in Tihany' and *Boston-ban* 'in Boston'). The role of the semantic feature 'foreign' in suffix-choice can be illustrated by such minimal pairs as *Velencé-n* 'in Velence, a village in Hungary' vs. *Velencé-ben* 'in Velence [=Venice], a city in Italy', and *Pécs-en* 'in Pécs, a city in Hungary' vs. *Bécs-ben* 'in Bécs, i.e. Vienna'. The Hungarian vs. foreign distinction is often interpreted as "belonging to historical (pre-1920) Hungary" vs. "outside historical Hungary" (see,

Table 2.3. Choice of the Standard Hungarian inessive suffix *-ban* vs. the superessive suffix *-n* by Hungarians in Hungary and abroad (in the neighboring countries)

Count Column %	Abroad	Hungary	Row Total
Craiován	353	34	387
Contact Hungarian	49.6	32.1	47.3
Craiовában	359	72	431
Standard Hungarian	50.4	67.9	52.7
Column Total	712	106	818
	87.0	13.0	100.0

$\chi^2 = 11.339$ ($df = 1$) $p < .001$ Number of missing observations: 28

e.g., Bartha 1997; Fenyvesi 1998c: 236, 241). The distinction is also expressed in the dichotomy "home" vs. "abroad". There is considerable variation in the use of the interior cases (e.g. the inessive *-bVn* suffix) and the surface cases (e.g. the superessive *-Vn* suffix). Purely phonological factors interact with the "home vs. abroad" rule (see Bartha 1997) but the interaction is not yet sufficiently understood. Nevertheless, on the basis of sporadic data gathered earlier from Hungarian newspapers and conversations in neighboring countries, we formulated the following hypothesis:

> The 1920 border changes have an impact on both majority and minority Hungarians' mental maps which govern the choice of surface vs. interior cases with placenames. As there is a growing divergence between the mental maps of majority and minority Hungarians, so there will be a growing divergence in their use of the placename suffixes.

Two placenames were chosen to scratch the surface of this highly complex problem: *Craiova* (a city in Oltenia, Romania) and *Kosovo* (Hungarian *Koszovó*, an autonomous region in southeast Yugoslavia). The assumption to be tested was that both placenames would be used with the inessive suffix categorically by Hungarians in Hungary, but the superessive suffix (showing "home") would be used near-categorically by Hungarians in Romania and Yugoslavia (Vojvodina) respectively. Minority Hungarians in countries other than Romania and Yugoslavia (Vojvodina) would show no difference from majority Hungarians in Hungary. Table 2.3 shows the result of a suffix-choosing task. (Respondents were instructed as follows: Choose the word that best fits into the sentence *Az egyik ismerősöm fia ... volt katona.* 'The son of an acquaintance of mine was a soldier in....')

The data show that, contrary to expectations, there is considerable variation within Hungary. Usage is even more divided abroad, but this cannot be solely attributed to Hungarians in Romania (to whom *Craiova* would be "home" under the hypothesis tested) since 353 respondents chose the "home" suffix *-n* but only 216 of them are from Romania.[12]

3.2.3   *Number of source-language speakers*

Among the factors that increase intensity of contact and hence borrowing, Thomason and Kaufman (1988:72) mention "many more source-language speakers than borrowing-language speakers." In the SHOH study one of the stratifying variables is directly relevant to this: an equal number of local-minority subjects and local-majority subjects were selected. We hypothesized that source-language influence will be greater among local-minority Hungarians.

In Kontra (2001a) the effect of this social variable was measured by analyzing 24 linguistic tasks in four countries: Slovakia, Ukraine, Romania and Yugoslavia (N = 536). On 16 out of the 24 tasks statistically significant differences were found at the .05 or .01 level. For instance, on an object *pro*-drop task (given in (4) below), 28% of the local-majority Hungarians abroad chose the contact-induced nonstandard overt-object sentence (b) as opposed to 38% of the local-minority Hungarians (see Figure 2.2). On this task, respondents were instructed to choose the sentence which was more natural. (Possible models for (4b) include, e.g., Slovak *Včera som videl v televízii* teba. and Serbian *Juče sam video* tebe *na televiziji.* The object pronouns are de-italicized.)

(4)   a.   *Tegnap   lát-t-alak   a   tévé-ben.*
           yesterday see-PAST-1SG.2OBJ the TV-INE
           'I saw you on TV yesterday.'

     b.   *Tegnap   lát-t-alak   téged   a   tévé-ben.*
           yesterday see-PAST-1SG.2OBJ you.SG.ACC the TV-INE
           'I saw you on TV yesterday.'

It is noteworthy that in all 16 cases where a statistically significant difference has been found, it is the local-minority subjects who favor the contact-induced variants. The

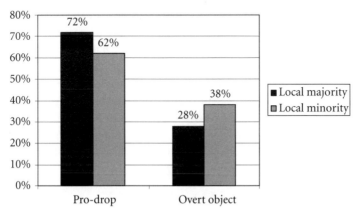

* Hungarians in Slovakia, Ukraine, Romania and Yugoslavia, N = 536, $\chi^2(df = 1) = 6.056$, $p < .05$

Figure 2.2. The effect of source-language speaker number on borrowing-language speakers' grammatical judgments*

16 variable tokens include several instances of number concord, object *pro*-drop, analytic forms, a contact-induced diminutive noun and a contact-induced "feminine noun." This finding gives solid empirical support to Thomason and Kaufman's factor "number of source-language speakers" as an important component of intensity of contact.

3.2.4   *An important caveat*
From a methodological point of view the SHOH project differs in important ways from most western sociolinguistic research on bilingualism. Our survey used various grammaticality judgment tasks (with or without an added written correction task) and written gap-filling tasks. The use of tape-recorders during interviews was encouraged but not required, hence we do not have comparable speech data from the project countries. From this it follows that while in most western research phrases like "bilinguals use more contact-induced variants" describe the differences, in our research "a greater proportion of bilinguals used the contact-induced variants" is the appropriate description. Western research, which is primarily based on speech data, usually analyzes many tokens of a type (variable), but the SHOH project, which used questionnaires, analyzes only one, two, maybe three tokens of a type, as will be seen in chapters by Csernicskó, Benő and Szilágyi N., Göncz and Vörös, and Lanstyák and Szabómihály in this volume.

3.2.5   *Language-in-society questions*
In addition to the linguistic data, we gathered a considerable amount of data concerning language use and attitudes. Questions were asked, for instance, about the medium of instruction in schools, the choice of languages in conversation with various interlocutors, the use of languages in various domains such as home, government offices, police stations etc. Attitudes were investigated by tasks in which respondents rated their attachment to their hometown, to Hungary, to the state they live in etc. In a folk linguistic spirit (see Niedzielski & Preston 2000) we asked questions concerning the beauty of various varieties of Hungarian, gathered data on the mutual intelligibility or its lack between minority Hungarians and metropolitan Hungarians, and also probed into folk linguistic rights, that is folk perceptions of language rights (see Kontra 1999). Thus in many a chapter written by SHOH project members conclusions and the interpretations of findings will be based on data like in Figure 2.3, which shows the choice of languages by Hungarians in Slovenia. (The question here was *Which of the languages do you usually use to communicate with the people listed in the table?*, and more than one language could be indicated.)

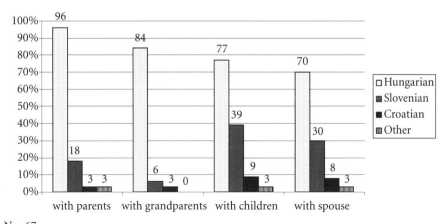

N = 67

Figure 2.3. The choice of languages in Hungarian families in Slovenia

4. New perspectives

In a sense, all the chapters on Hungarian in the neighboring countries in this book must provide new information to readers who do not read Hungarian, unless they have happened to read one or more of the following papers: Lanstyák and Szabómihály (1996a), Jordan (1998), Votruba (1998), K. Sándor (1999, 2000), Kontra (1999, 2001a, 2003), Csernicskó and Fenyvesi (2000), Simon and Kontra (2000), Langman and Lanstyák (2000) or Langman (2002).[13] While I realize the risk in my assessment of what may provide new perspectives on international bilingualism research in our SHOH project, I will nevertheless suggest a few topics where I believe Hungarian contact research may furnish new insights.

One such area concerns linguicism, that is discrimination between groups of people defined on the basis of language (see Skutnabb-Kangas 2000a). The provision of mother-tongue-medium education for national minorities is usually adequate for pupils in elementary schools but tends to decrease in high schools and is oftentimes non-existent for students in tertiary education. The Hungarian research reveals the magnitude of such language-based educational discrimination in several countries. For instance, Benő and Szilágyi N. provide statistical data on Romania, where in the 1970s the proportion of Hungarian university students studying in either Romanian or Hungarian was 5.53%, much lower than the proportion of Hungarians in Romania (7.9%). In 1992 only 3.57% of the Hungarians in Romania had higher degrees, while among Romanians the ratio was 5.34% (see Tables 5.5 and 5.6 in Benő and Szilágyi N.'s chapter). What such data show is that linguicism in Central Europe can deprive minorities not only of mother-tongue-medium education but of education in any language, the state language included.[14]

The Hungarian research also highlights the importance of the right to learn an L2 as an L2. In most if not all neighboring countries, Hungarians are taught the state languages as if those were their mother tongues. What usually happens is that a school subject like "Romanian language and literature" is identical in the curriculum for Romanian pupils and minority pupils, although the teaching should serve radically different purposes. For Romanians the goal is to educate mother-tongue (L1) speakers of Romanian in Romanian language and literature, but for Hungarians and other minorities in Romania the goal is to enable minorities to acquire Romanian as a second language (L2). If the same methods and teaching materials are used to teach the state language as an L1 and an L2, the result can only be that Hungarians do not acquire Romanian well enough in school, which later renders them disadvantaged (see Szilágyi N. 1998). Such practice constitutes educational malpractice (see Baugh 1999) and generates social conflicts, also in Subcarpathia, Ukraine, where government pressure on Hungarians to learn the state language Ukrainian is increasing at a time when the Ukrainian educational authorities have not yet trained teachers in sufficient numbers who are bilingual in Ukrainian and Hungarian, nor has there been a Ukrainian–Hungarian dictionary published for their minority citizens. What such cases make abundantly clear is that the responsibility to acquire the state language by national minorities[15] should be matched by the right and possibility to learn it as a second language.

A third avenue of research, pioneered in the Carpathian Basin by István Lanstyák, concerns what he and Szabómihály (this volume) call language lapses and language gaps. The former denote cases when a speaker is temporarily unable to recall a word or a grammatical structure s/he is otherwise familiar with. By the latter the authors mean cases when a required word or structure is not part of the speaker's linguistic system at all. These phenomena contribute a great deal to bilingual Hungarians' linguistic insecurity and may lead to register attrition. For instance, Hungarians in Romania often find it hard or impossible to write an official letter in Hungarian since they have hardly any opportunity to write them in their mother tongue. Language gaps have also become evident recently to Hungarian school teachers in Slovakia, who find it difficult to write class registers and school reports in Hungarian now that it has become legally possible. Earlier this was not a problem because in Czechoslovak times whatever Hungarian was used in school documents was officially translated from Slovak and digressions were not allowed, even if the translations smacked of calquing. What Lanstyák has called our attention to is that extensive research into lapses and gaps is an important prerequisite for what Szilágyi N. (2002a) calls *linguistic rehabilitation* for minority Hungarians, that is language planning efforts to stop and reverse the effects of register attrition. The challenge is enormous, says Szilágyi N., because the only thing we know is how one must *not* go about linguistic rehabilitation: anything that resembles traditional Hungarian language cultivation is doomed to failure.

Finally, I would like to call readers' attention to a unique case of language contact in Europe, that of the Csángós in Moldavia, Romania. "The Csángós are a non-homogeneous group of Roman Catholic people of Hungarian origin," says the first sentence of a recent Committee on Culture, Science and Education report of the Parliamentary Assembly of the Council of Europe.[16] All three adjectives in the quoted sentence (*non-homogeneous, Roman Catholic,* and *Hungarian*) are highly important for the understanding of the linguistic situation of "one of Europe's most enigmatic and least known ethnic minorities" (Baker 1997). The Csángó Hungarians migrated beyond the Carpathian Mountains, into Moldavia in several waves between the 14th and 18th centuries. To this day they live in a pre-industrialized rural society which harmonizes with their medieval-like world view. Most of them have assimilated to Romanians, mostly as a result of force used by the Roman Catholic church and the Romanian state, but about 64,000 of them still speak dialects of Hungarian that contain many archaic features. There is a great deal of variation among Csángó dialects, all of which show heavy contact effects from Romanian. Mutual intelligibility between Csángós and Hungarians in the Carpathian Basin can be far from satisfactory. In her chapter in this book, Sándor provides an illuminating analysis of the complex interrelationships of the ethnic, religious and linguistic identities of the Csángós, and summarizes nearly everything linguists know about them today. From a contact linguistic point of view, Csángós present a number of intriguing problems, both theoretical and practical. One contentious issue is how far varieties of Csángó can still be considered varieties of Hungarian. K. Sándor argues for the position that Csángó dialects form a roofless and diffuse Ausbau-language which is very close to Hungarian. Contrary to Sándor, Szilágyi N. (2002b) claims that "Csángó is one of the dialects of Hungarian, and not a self-standing language, because Csángós believe they speak Hungarian when they speak their mother tongue." The Csángó issue is fraught with international (Romanian vs. Hungarian) historical and political polemic, linguistic human rights violations, and insufficient sociolinguistic research. As a result of the Council of Europe's recommendations to the government of Romania, as of September 2002, mother-tongue-medium education has begun in a few classes. The applied sociolinguistic challenge for the school teachers is enormous, and it remains to be seen whether this last-minute introduction of mother-tongue education can influence the fate of this highly endangered language.

5.   What the future holds in store

The study of contact varieties of Hungarian in Hungary's neighboring countries was taboo until 1989. When serious research began after the fall of communism, a host of new data and analyses became available and several linguistic and other polemics ensued. For the first time after World War II, contacts between Hungarians across the borders became intensive with the result of growing awareness of linguistic differences between bilingual and monolingual Hungarians. Although there is hardly any research to show that convergence of the contact varieties to the Hungarian in Hungary has been taking place, there is good reason to believe it is happening. However, this convergence may soon be slowed down or even thwarted by Hungary's accession to the European Union in 2004 while other countries such as Ukraine, Romania, Serbia or Croatia are likely to gain accession later. When Hungary is in the EU but some of her neighbors are not, a reseparation of Hungarians will occur as a result of the creation of the Schengen borders around Hungary. Visiting relatives or taking temporary jobs in Hungary will be much more difficult than during the decade and a half after communism. Thus, when increasing mobility and international migration are becoming a major sociolinguistic factor worldwide,[17] lack of mobility among Hungarians across the EU borders will provide a laboratory to study the contact linguistic consequences of the opposite trend.

Notes

1. The Hungarian word *nemzet* 'nation' denotes the community of a people with the same language and cultural traditions, regardless of what state they live in; in other words it is an ethnonym. The Romanian word *naţiune* 'nation' denotes the community of those people who have the same citizenship; in other words it is a politonym. English blurs this distinction. On the role of such a linguistic difference in interethnic conflicts as analyzed by Sándor Szilágyi N., see Kontra 2000: 168–170.

2. I realize that this in an uphill battle. When I edited a paper by my colleague Anna Borbély (1995–1996) some years ago, I suggested that she use the phrase *Romanian-Hungarians* with reference to the indigenous Romanians who live in today's Hungary. I did it in compliance with English as used by its native speakers.

3. One example is the Hungarian Act about the Rights of the National and Ethnic Minorities (*1993. évi LXVII. törvény*), which terms the Slovak, Romanian, Serbian etc. minorities in Hungary "national minorities" but the Gypsies an "ethnic minority". The distinction rests on whether or not a minority has a kin-State or "mother country".

4. 'Of or relating to sizable groups of people sharing a common and distinctive racial, national, religious, linguistic, or cultural heritage'.

5. Hungarian is also a subject *pro*-drop language, of course, as are the surrounding languages described, so there would be no major contact-induced phenomena to observe in the main type of *pro*-drop constructions.

6. Thanks are due to the Research Support Scheme of the Higher Education Support Program, Prague, for its grant No. 582/1995. Throughout the project we benefited greatly from Peter Trudgill, who helped us in many ways, which include delivering the plenary lecture at our yearly conference held in Užhorod/Ungvár, Ukraine in 1995 (see Trudgill 1996), lecturing to teachers of Hungarian from Hungary's neighboring countries in Miercurea Ciuc/Csíkszereda, Romania in 1996, and visiting the Csángó-Hungarians in Moldavia, Romania the same year.

7. The team included István Lanstyák (Slovakia), István Csernicskó (Ukraine), János Péntek and Sándor Szilágyi N. (Romania), Lajos Göncz (Yugoslavia), the late István Szépfalusi (Austria), Ottó Vörös (Hungary) and was directed by myself. We also enjoyed the help of uncontracted linguists in the team such as Anikó Beregszászi (Ukraine), Csilla Bartha, Anna Borbély and Klára Sándor (all in Hungary).

8. See the series *A magyar nyelv a Kárpát-medencében a XX. század végén* [The Hungarian Language in the Carpathian Basin at the End of the 20th Century], in which the volumes on Ukraine

(Csernicskó 1998), Yugoslavia (Göncz 1999) and Slovakia (Lanstyák 2000a) have already been published.

9. Unfortunately, the war in the former Yugoslavia made it impossible to carry out research in Eastern Slavonia, Croatia in 1996.

10. In the rest of this paper the name *Yugoslavia* will be used because that was the name of the country when our fieldwork was conducted in 1996. As of 2003 Vojvodina belongs to *Serbia and Montenegro*.

11. About two decades ago German used masculine nouns but recently masculine and feminine nouns have been used variably in order to avoid sex bias.

12. For a detailed analysis of how the 1920 international border changes have triggered morphological change in Hungarian see Kontra 2003.

13. As discussed in Section 2 above, the study of Hungarian bilingualism in Hungary and her neighboring countries was minimal until the fall of communism in 1989. The various chapters in Harlig and Pléh (1995) show that minority languages were badly underresearched or totally neglected also in Poland, Czechoslovakia, Romania and Bulgaria.

14. See also Kontra et al. (1999: 13–14) for how denial of the right to mother-tongue-medium education results in lifelong unemployment for many Gypsies in Hungary.

15. In *The Hague Recommendations Regarding the Education Rights of National Minorities & Explanatory Note* it is stated that "persons belonging to national minorities have a responsibility to integrate into the wider national society through the acquisition of a proper knowledge of the State language."

16. See *Csango minority culture in Romania*.

17. As Jack Chambers showed in a series of lectures in the University of Szeged in April 2002. See also Chambers 2003.

CHAPTER 3

Hungarian in Slovakia*

István Lanstyák and Gizella Szabómihály

1. Introduction

In this chapter we describe the sociolinguistic and linguistic aspects of the Hungarian
language use of the Hungarian minority in Slovakia.

The overview of the sociolinguistic situation of Hungarians in Slovakia in Section
2 is based on census data as well as a wide range of studies describing the historical and
social side of this minority community.

The description of the linguistic characteristics of the Slovakia Hungarians in
Section 3 is based, primarily, on the findings of the Slovakia-Hungary High School
(SHHS) project, as well as the Sociolinguistics of Hungarian Outside Hungary
(SHOH) project (for details, see Kontra, this volume) and several other studies by
the present authors.

The variety of Hungarian used by Hungarians in Slovakia bears the effects of
what Thomason and Kaufman (1988: 74–76) define as casual to slightly more intense
language contact. On their borrowing scale, one extreme of which represents simple
lexical borrowing induced by casual language contact (category one) and the other extreme being large-scale structural borrowing as a consequence of very strong cultural
influence (category five), *spoken* HS contact varieties could be placed somewhere in
between categories one and two, probably closer to the latter. This category is characterized by a fair amount of lexical borrowing which, in addition to involving content
words, also affects function words, and slight structural borrowing (i.e. phonetic, syntactic and semantic borrowing) which does not affect the typological features of the
recipient language – as we will show in detail throughout Section 3.

2. Sociolinguistic aspects

2.1 The development of the contact situation

Slovak-Hungarian contacts first occurred in the 9th and 10th centuries when Hungarians (the "Magyars") gradually invaded the northern regions of the Carpathian Basin.

The territory of what is Slovakia today was integrated into the Hungarian state between the 11th and the 13th centuries. The independent Czechoslovak state was proclaimed on October 28, 1918, and hailed by the Slovak political elite, which had been struggling for autonomy since the 19th century. There had never been any kind of separate Slovak administrative region in Hungary, and the Paris Peace Conference (Treaty of Trianon, June 11, 1919) marked the southern border of the new Czechoslovak state – satisfying Czech demands – due to strategic and economic reasons much further south than the Slovak-Hungarian language border. Consequently, fully Hungarian-populated areas were annexed to the newly created state.[1]

The Vienna Award of 1938 returned 4,600 square miles of Czechoslovak land to Hungary. According to Hungarian records, 84.5% of the total 1,027,450 inhabitants were native speakers of Hungarian (Kocsis & Kocsis-Hodosi 1998:64; Szarka 1998:36–39). Slovakia became autonomous on March 14, 1939, and 67,502 Hungarians remained in and around Bratislava/Pozsony and Nitra/Nyitra, which continued to be part of Czechoslovakia.

The victorious allies of World War II invalidated the Vienna Awards, so the borders established after World War I were restored. Czechoslovakia was declared a federation on January 1, 1969, and, as a result of the growing struggle for Slovak autonomy after the 1989 political changes, the sovereign Slovak Republic was formed on January 1, 1993.

2.2 Demographic data

2.2.1 *Variation and the reasons for variation in the number of Hungarians in Slovakia*

Table 3.1 shows the variation within the composition of national groups of Slovakia between 1910 and 2001.[2] Slovak historians and demographers question the 1910 data (see, for instance, Očovský 1992), since they believe that these numbers reflect the Magyarization of the 19th century. Besides the reasons to be discussed below, they explain the enormous decrease in the number of Hungarians between 1921 and 1930 directly with the idea that Slovaks who had previously conceded to being Hungarian now dared to stand up for their original nationality again. However, the ethnic processes preceding the 20th century could not be clearly defined as one-way processes, since within the area of what Slovakia is today, after the expulsion of the Ottoman Turks (in the 17th century), the Slovak-Hungarian ethnic border gradually shifted south due to the more and more southward expansion of the settlement of the Slovak population (Kocsis & Kocsis-Hodosi 1998:49). The ethnic border became basically settled during the course of the 18th and 19th centuries, and both the Slovak and Hungarian linguistic areas became homogeneous. The Magyarization and assimilation procedures after the Austrian-Hungarian Compromise in 1867 mainly affected the urban population.

The number of Hungarians greatly decreased between 1910 and 1930 (Gyönyör 1994:59) with 106,000 people, mostly civil servants and other officials fleeing to Hun-

Table 3.1. The minorities of Slovakia between 1910 and 2001*

Year	Czech (%)	Slovak (%)	Hungarian (%)	German (%)	Ukrainian (%)	Other and unknown (%)	Total (%)
1910	7,489 (0.26)	1,688,155 (57.82)	884,309 (30.29)	198,304 (6.79)	97,162 (3.33)	44,375 (1.52)	2,919,794 (100.00)
1921	72,635 (2.42)	1,952,368 (65.06)	650,597 (21.68)	145,844 (4.86)	88,970 (2.96)	90,456 (3.02)	3,000,870 (100.00)
1930	121,696 (3.65)	2,251,358 (67.61)	592,337 (17.79)	154,821 (4.65)	95,359 (2.86)	114,222 (3.43)	3,329,793 (100.00)
1950	40,365 (1.17)	2,982,524 (86.64)	354,532 (10.30)	5,179 (0.15)	48,231 (1.40)	11,486 (0.33)	3,442,317 (100.00)
1961	45,721 (1.10)	3,560,216 (85.29)	518,782 (12.43)	6,259 (0.15)	35,435 (0.85)	7,633 (0.18)	4,174,046 (100.00)
1970	47,402 (1.04)	3,878,904 (85.49)	552,006 (12.17)	4,760 (1.10)	42,238 (0.93)	11,980 (0.26)	4,537,290 100.00)
1980	57,197 (1.15)	4,317,008 (86.49)	559,490 (11.21)	2,918 (0.06)	39,260 (0.79)	15,295 (0.31)	4,991,168 (100.00)
1991	52,884 (1.00)	4,519,328 (85.69)	567,296 (10.76)	5,414 (0.10)	30,478 (0.58)	98,935 (1.88)	5,274,335 (100.00)
2001	44,884 (0.83)	4,614,854 (85.79)	520,528 (9.67)	5,405 (0.10)	35,015 (0.65)	159,033 (2.96)	5,379,455 (100.00)

* Based on Gyurgyík (1994:85) for 1910–1991; and on http://www.statistics.sk/webdata/english/census2001/ for 2001.
Explanation: The 1910 data are the results of the last census within Austria-Hungary, and minorities are indicated on the basis of mother tongue. The 1921, 1930, and 1950 data refer to the population present (including, e.g. army personnel stationed at the given locality), whereas 1961, 1970, 1980, 1991 and 2001 data to the permanently resident population. The category *other* includes Polish (each census), Jewish (1921, 1930), Moravian (1991), Silesian (1991), Romani (1991, 2001), Croatian and Serbian (2001) minorities. The category "Ukrainian" includes both Ruthenians and Ukrainians in the 1991 and 2001 data. According to the Census 2001 the Number of Romani is 89,920 (1.67%), Ruthenian 24,201 (0.45%), Ukrainian 10,814 (0.20%).

gary after World War I (because they refused to sign a declaration of allegiance de-manded by the Czechoslovak authorities). The authorities denied granting Czechoslo-vak citizenship to a disproportionately great number of Hungarians;[3] for instance, in 1931, 27% of all stateless persons in Slovakia were Hungarian (Gyönyör 1993:97). In the course of time, 'Jewish' was introduced as a separate nationality in the census questionnaire, which led to a further decrease in the number of Hungarians (Gyönyör 1994:48; Kocsis & Kocsis-Hodosi 1998:61–62).

Among the aims of the reorganized state after 1945 was to completely eradicate the so-called "war criminal" German and Hungarian minorities. In his decree #33, in 1945, President E. Beneš stripped all people of German and Hungarian nation-ality of their Czechoslovak citizenship, except those with an active anti-fascist past (for more details see http://www.cla.sk/projects/TheBeneš Decrees). Since the allies did not allow a unilateral expulsion of Hungarians, the authorities tried to diminish the number of Hungarians in another way. Between 1945 and 1948, 44,129 Hungari-ans (whole families) were deported to Bohemia for forced labor, of whom 24,000 were able to return after 1949. At the same time, the so-called re-Slovakization effectively targeted Hungarians living in Slovakia by granting Czechoslovak citizenship to those abiding by certain requirements. Re-Slovakization applications were sent in on behalf of 423,264 people, and by 1948, the committees accepted 193,415 of them.[4] In accor-dance with the Slovak-Hungarian population resettlement agreement (on February 27, 1946) enforced by the Czechoslovak side, 89,660 people were expelled to Hungary and replaced by volunteer ethnic Slovaks (73,273 people altogether) from Hungary (Vad-kerty 1994).[5] The effect of these measures became apparent in the results of the 1950 census, since the number of Hungarians in Slovakia decreased by 240,000 compared to 1930 figures. The population growth observed in later census results can primarily be explained by the fact that a great number of the coercively re-Slovakized Hungarians now dared to admit their nationality again. Actually, the number of Hungarians has practically stagnated since the 1970s.

There has been no major and observable emigration abroad within the Hungarian community of Slovakia besides the greater migration waves due to the world wars and some smaller ones after 1968. In-migration has primarily targeted the large industrial centers and big cities of the Czech Republic.[6]

2.2.2   *Further demographic characteristics of Hungarians in Slovakia*
The population of Slovakia has shown the signs of aging in recent decades, although the demographic figures of Hungarians show greater scale aging than those of the en-tire population. The age composition of the Hungarians is more unfavorable than that of Slovaks (see Table 3.2). The significant decrease of natural increase in Slo-vakia started in the 1980s, and came to a mere −0.2‰ by the year 2001. In the case of Hungarians, however, natural increase fell in 1990 to 1.5‰, and in 1995 it took a negative value, −0.8‰ (Gyurgyík 1999:32). Hungarian minorities are characterized by endogamous marriages within the community, i.e. in 1991 only 17.8% of married Hungarians lived in exogamous marriages, usually with a Slovak partner. The pro-

portion of mixed marriages of Hungarians is higher than this: for instance, 27.7% of Hungarian marriages registered in 1990 were exogamous.

2.2.3   *The settlement structure of the Hungarian population*
The mostly contiguous area of Hungarian settlements is situated along the Slovak-Hungarian political border, with most Hungarians (about 60%) living in the southwest of Slovakia. The homogeneity and the extent of the Hungarian linguistic area drastically decreased in the beginning of the 1920s and during the 1940s. Besides the reasons mentioned in Section 2.2.1, this can be accounted for by inner Slovak resettlements. In the beginning of the 1920s, Czech, Moravian, and Slovak villages were established in the previously Hungarian-owned latifundia (with an approximate number of 14,000 new settlers), and Slovaks occupied the land of the displaced Hungarian population after World War II. During the era of the first republic, officials, police, and military people were mostly of Czech nationalities, whereas immediately after 1945, mostly Slovaks.

Between 1910 and 1930, 117 Hungarian majority settlements became Slovak majority settlements (Kocsis & Kocsis-Hodosi 1998:61), and the urban areas with sporadic Hungarian population almost completely disappeared. The size of the Hungarian linguistic area did not change between 1950 and 2001, but the ethnic composition did considerably (see Table 3.3).[7] The rate of Hungarians living within the Hungarian linguistic area is gradually decreasing (in 1991 61.5%, in 2001 56,8%; Gyurgyík 2002:11), but still, more than 90% of Hungarians live there, and 76.1% live in Hungarian majority settlements. However, these settlements, again, have a decreasing Hungarian population. In 2001, 38,887 (7.5%) lived outside the Hungarian linguistic area, and only the big cities on the outskirts of the linguistic area, Bratislava/Pozsony, Košice/Kassa, and Nitra/Nyitra have considerable numbers of Hungarians.

2.3   Economic and social characteristics of Hungarians in Slovakia

Presently, most of the Hungarian population lives in rural settlements. In 2001, 55.6% of the whole population and 40.8% of Hungarians lived in settlements having more than 5,000 inhabitants (urban settlements), but this rate is even more disproportionate in the case of bigger cities (of over 50,000 inhabitants): 24.4% of the whole population and 5.5% of Hungarians live there. At the same time, all settlements having more than 90% of Hungarians have fewer than 5,000 inhabitants. There are four towns in which the number of Hungarians is over 10,000 (Hungarian population given in brackets): Komárno/Komárom (pop. 22,452), Bratislava/Pozsony (pop. 16,451), Dunajská Streda/Dunaszerdahely (pop. 18,753), and Nové Zámky/Érsekújvár (pop. 11,653). In 1921, 18.1% of Hungarians lived in settlements with over 5,000 inhabitants, whereas the rate of Slovaks was 17.8% (Gyönyör 1994:59, 352). In the 1930s and after the 1945 resettlements, there was a radical decrease in the number of urban Hungarians. The centrally administered and forcible one-sided industrialization and urbanization of the 1960s focused on Bratislava/Pozsony, Košice/Kassa, and the cen-

Table 3.2. The age distribution of Slovaks and Hungarians in Slovakia between 1970 and 2001*

Age	1970		1980		1991		2001	
	Slovaks (%)	Hungarians (%)	Slovaks (%)	Hungarians (%)	Slovaks (%)	Hungarians (%)	Slovaks (%)	Hungarians (%)
0–14	1,078,396 (27.8)	134,205 (24.3)	1,161,797 (26.9)	123,908 (22.1)	1,153,276 (25.5)	116,117 (20.5)	885,273 (19.3)	77,943 (15.0)
15–59	2,276,554 (58.7)	323,396 (58.6)	2,591,591 (60.0)	343,365 (61.4)	2,711,773 (60.0)	348,805 (61.5)	2,997,959 (65.5)	339,062 (65.4)
Over 60	523,944 (13.5)	94,405 (17.1)	563,620 (13.1)	92,217 (16.5)	654,279 (14.5)	102,374 (18.0)	693,651 (15.2)	101,462 (19.6)
Total	3,878,904 (100.0)	552,006 (100.0)	4,317,008 (100.0)	559490 (100.0)	4,519,328 (100.0)	567,296 (100.0)	4,576,883 (100,)	518,467 (100.0)

* Based on Gyurgyík (1994:10) and http://www.statistics.sk/webdata/slov/scitanie/

Table 3.3. The division of Hungarians in Slovakia and their settlements between 1970 and 2001

The rate of Hung. inhabit. in settlem.	1970			1980			1991			2001		
	Number of settlements	Number of Hungarian inhabitants	Rate within the Hungarian population	Number of settlements	Number of Hungarian inhabitants	Rate within the Hungarian population	Number of settlements	Number of Hungarian inhabitants	Rate within the Hungarian population	Number of settlements	Number of Hungarian inhabitants	Rate within the Hungarian population
10–100%	534	528,548	95.8%	486**	518,973	92.8%	523	520,968	91.8%	526	481,631	92.2%
20–100%	513	517,606	93.8%	464	504,685	90.2%	503	508,948	89.6%	501	466,042	89.5%
50–100%	442	460,488	83.4%	421	443,522	79.3%	432	437,788	77.2%	410	396,214	76.1%
80–100%	286	289,327	52.4%	257	264,473	46.9%	169	252,296	44.5%	216	178,111	34.2%

* Based on Gyurgyík (1994:87) and http://www.statistics.sk/webdata/slov/scitanie/
** In the 1970s, several smaller settlements were administratively merged. Many of these later became individual settlements again, which is why the number of settlements is lower in 1980 than in 1970 and 1991.

tral regions of the country, so the southern, mostly Hungarian-populated regions kept their agricultural profile.

In 2001, 10.0% of the Hungarian working population were employed in the agricultural sector, and 17.4% worked in industry (while 4.9% of Slovaks worked in agriculture, and 20.8% in industry). Most of the Hungarians who worked in the industry had to commute due to the lack of local employment. The educational profile of Hungarians in Slovakia is also worse than that of Slovaks, for instance, the rate of college educated Hungarians is steadily low: in 2001, 8.2% of Slovaks, and only 4.5% of Hungarians had a college degree (http://www.statistics.sk/webdata/slov/scitanie/).

The post-1989 economic changes (especially an agricultural crisis) deeply affected the Hungarian population. Considerably more Hungarians got involved in private enterprises than Slovaks, but they were almost completely forced out of the privatization process of previously state-owned possessions. As a result of the economic policies of preceding decades, Hungarian-populated areas have the worst demographic, economic, and social indices in Slovakia and are, therefore, defined as underdeveloped regions (see Gajdoš & Pašiak 1995), where unemployment rates have been much above the national average for years, and GDP per person and earnings are below average (*The Hungarians in Slovakia* 1997:15). In addition, due to the lack of proper infrastructure, foreign capital investments are few (for further details, see *The Situation* 2002).

2.4 Domains of minority language use in the Hungarian speech community of Slovakia

2.4.1 *The Hungarian speech community of Slovakia and the number of minority language speakers*

The ethnic composition of Slovakia is determined on the basis of self-report nationality status surveyed in censuses. In addition to nationality, mother tongue was also surveyed in 1970, 1991 and 2001. In 2001, 572,929 people (10.7%) stated that their mother tongue was Hungarian, of which 88.5% were of Hungarian and 9.6% of Slovak nationality. So 97.4% of the Hungarians in Slovakia report Hungarian as mother tongue (http://www.statistics.sk/webdata/slov/scitanie/). We define the Hungarian speech community of Slovakia as the population (primarily persons of Hungarian nationality with Hungarian as mother tongue) with traditionally strong national bonds (Lanstyák 2000a:68). Of the 89,920 people who declare themselves to be Romani, 9.9% claim Hungarian as their mother tongue.[8] Census questions are not concerned about the knowledge of other languages, so it is not known how many more people speak Hungarian, for instance, as a second language. Research conducted in the late 1980s showed that at least half of those defining themselves as Slovaks living in the Hungarian linguistic area speak Hungarian at some level (Zel'ová 1992:157).

2.4.2   *Domains of minority language use*

After Hungarians became a minority in 1920, they became severely restricted in the places and opportunities for the use of their mother tongue. Moreover, between 1945 and 1948, it was practically forbidden to speak Hungarian in public. After 1948, the Slovak language has become more and more dominant in public life and, even more prominently, in government offices. Outside the private domains (and depending on their type of residence), Hungarians in Slovakia presently use their mother tongue in a variety of places, as described in detail below.

Hungarians living within the Hungarian linguistic area have the opportunity to have their children educated in Hungarian primary schools, although the number and situation of Hungarian high schools does not satisfy the demands. Around 20% of all Hungarian students attend primary and high schools with Slovak as the medium of instruction, and approximately 50% are involved in secondary technical education. There is no public Hungarian higher education, so teachers are trained only partly in Hungarian. There are some branches of universities from Hungary operating in Slovakia where it is possible to study in Hungarian. Slovak is taught as a subject in Hungarian schools, and in secondary technical schools technical subjects are taught either partly or totally in Slovak. Hungarian is not taught at all in schools with Slovak as medium of instruction.

The denominational distribution of Hungarians and Slovaks (regarding only the major denominations) was the following in 1991: Roman Catholic 64.9% of Hungarians vs. 60.8% of Slovaks, Calvinist 11.4% of Hungarians vs. 0.4% of Slovaks, Lutheran 2.2% of Hungarians vs. 6.9% of Slovaks. Of all Calvinists in Slovakia 78.2% are Hungarian, whereas in case of the other religions, the rate of Hungarian members is 15% at most. Although Czechoslovak and Slovak authorities have always tried to restrict the religious practices in Hungarian, most of the Hungarian believers still have the opportunity to attend religious services in Hungarian. The lack of Hungarian priests causes problems within the Roman Catholic Church along with the politics and attitude of the Slovak church leaders (who, for instance, reject the establishment of a Hungarian bishopric). Several Hungarian church primary and high schools have been established since 1989, and it is possible to attend religious education classes according to the language of the given public school.

One Hungarian daily paper, *Új Szó*, was published in Slovakia in 2002.[9] The number of Hungarian weeklies is 2, and in addition, 8 monthlies and 24 regional papers are published. The public state radio has been broadcasting in Hungarian since 1928, with its present broadcasting time being 45 hours a week.[10] The state television has been broadcasting Hungarian news programs since 1983. In the year 2002, news programs were broadcast for 5 minutes 5 times a week, and magazine programs for 30 minutes twice a week.[11] After 1990 many places have launched a local cable television channel, and some of these broadcast also in Hungarian. It is possible to receive radio and television programs from Hungary in the Hungarian linguistic area, and these are traditionally preferred by the Hungarians of Slovakia (see Lampl & Sorbán 1999).

After the termination of centralized cultural and educational policies in 1989, the cultural life of Hungarians in Slovakia has become richer, however, it is still characterized by the rural qualities of this minority society, that is, by the predominance of amateur groups (folk-dancing ensembles, drama groups, and choirs). High culture is traditionally represented by literature. There are two professional Hungarian theaters and many private and state publishers in Slovakia at present. The Hungarian folk-dancing and music ensemble "Young Hearts" functions on a semi-professional basis. The Museum of Hungarians Culture in Slovakia (as a department of Slovak National Museum) was founded in 2002. The Hungarian academic life in Slovakia is almost completely restricted to the social sciences and humanities (literary studies, linguistics, history, and sociology) and to minority studies. Natural sciences are only present at the level of popular science.

Theoretically, Hungarian could be used in any domain within the Hungarian linguistic area. However, in villages and cities of Slovak majority, the (sometimes exclusive) use of Slovak is rather prominent as well. The use of Slovak as the language of communication is most prominent in offices, workplaces, and the field of health care (Lanstyák 2000a: 125). Written communication in Hungarian is minimal.

2.5 Bilingualism, language maintenance, and language shift

About 90% of the Hungarians in Slovakia speak Slovak (Zeľová 1992: 156; Csepeli et al. 2000: 55). Directed second language acquisition characterizes the children of endogamous Hungarian families who live in Hungarian-majority settlements and acquire Slovak in school. Most of the members of the Hungarian speech community can be defined as Hungarian-dominant bilinguals (Lanstyák 2000a: 149). The following factors are significant in terms of language maintenance and language shift: family, school, and the ethnic make-up of the given settlement. Most of the parents living in endogamous Hungarian marriages socialize their children as Hungarian (as far as language and national identity are concerned), while most of the parents living in Slovak-Hungarian marriages have their children socialized to be of Slovak nationality (Csepeli et al. 2000: 50). In Slovak-majority settlements children of the latter type of families do not even learn the minority language (see A. Sándor 2000: 134), whereas in a Hungarian-majority settlement they learn both languages. However, since these children usually attend Slovak schools, they become Slovak-dominant bilinguals just like children from endogamous Hungarian families attending Slovak schools (for details see Part 2, on the SHHS Project). In addition, since the rate of exogamous marriages is affected by the given type of settlement, mass language shift takes place in villages and cities on the edges of the Hungarian linguistic area, and in sporadically Hungarian-populated settlements (Lanstyák 2000a: 228). Language shift is also facilitated by an unsatisfactory network of minority schools in these areas.

2.6 Attitudes towards nationalities and languages

2.6.1 *Attitudes of Hungarians and Slovaks towards each other*

In the early 1990s, there were many public opinion polls targeting Hungarian-Slovak relations. According to the results of these polls, Hungarians had a somewhat more positive attitude towards Slovaks than vice versa, although those Slovaks who were living in mostly Hungarian-populated areas had the most positive attitude towards Hungarians (Rosová & Bútorová 1992:178–179). The majority of Hungarian-Slovak conflicts arose in connection with language. The above mentioned public opinion polls have also shown that although the majority of Hungarians (63%) admit that knowledge of Slovak is necessary to get ahead socially, they also expect the opportunity to use their mother tongue besides Slovak in various official places (Zel'ová 1992:157). At least 60% of Slovaks, however, refused to accept the bilingual marking of public places and buildings of mainly Hungarian-populated areas. This rejection in the behavior of Slovaks towards the Hungarian language is apparently promoted by myths reinforced and amplified by some of the media as well (Langman & Lanstyák 2000) and supported by the opinions of the Slovak political elite (see Section 2.7).

2.6.2 *Attitudes of the Hungarian speech community of Slovakia towards Hungarian language varieties*

Several empirical studies have proven that the members of the Hungarian community of Slovakia have strong ties with the Hungarian nation and the Hungarian minority of Slovakia (Zel'ová 1992:156), and, within these national ties, mother tongue and national culture play an important role (Gereben 1999). Although the Hungarian language has a lower prestige in Slovakia than the Slovak language (due to the lower educational and social indices of the Hungarian population), it cannot be claimed that Hungarians regard their mother tongue as having become depreciated, for the Hungarian language has maintained its positions in the cultural sphere (Lanstyák 2000a:145).

Primarily Hungarian language varieties of Hungary, especially the Standard Hungarian variety has high cultural prestige. Within this context, the Hungarian language varieties of Slovakia have low prestige, which is most probably related to the vernacular of the speakers, and the contact-induced features characterizing their speech (Lanstyák 2000a:148). The Hungarians of Slovakia (especially teachers and professionals) usually have a negative evaluation of the contact-induced features of Slovak origin, the most stigmatized features being loanwords proper. However, most of the more "hidden" types of borrowing, such as semantic loans, are not even noticed by the speakers (see Section 3 for more details).

2.7 Language policy

2.7.1   *The status of languages and the legislative regulation of language use*

The status and use of languages spoken in Slovakia are currently determined by the constitution, by international agreements ratified by the Slovak Republic, and by several national laws. In 1992, the constitution (http://www.concourt.sk) adopted the regulations of the Charter of Fundamental and Freedom Rights concerning the language rights of minorities, stating that minorities have the right to provide and receive information, and to be educated in their mother tongue, as well as to use their language in official contexts. Of the international treaties, the most prominent are the Framework Convention for the Protection of National Minorities (1995; http://www.coe.int/T/E/human_rights/minorities), the Slovak-Hungarian Basic Treaty (operative since 1997; http://www.htmh.hu), and the European Charter for Regional or Minority Languages (operative since 2002; http://www.coe.int/minlang). Two of the national laws are the most significant, one of them is the Law on the State Language[12] passed in 1995, and the other one is the Law on Minority Language Use, in force since September 1, 1999 (http://www.culture.gov.sk/english; see Šutaj & Olejník 1998 for more details).

Slovakia is the republic of the Slovak nation, and its official language is Slovak, as stated in the constitution and the Law on the State Language. Minority languages may be used for the following purposes and in the following places. It is possible to register names (first names and family names) in their minority language forms (Law on Names and Surnames, 1993; Registers Act, 1994). The name of a town or village can only be indicated in the minority language form on the road signs at the settlement boundaries in places where the given minority constitutes at least 20% of the total population (1994). In court procedures (according to international regulations) the client who does not speak the official language (regardless of mother tongue and citizenship) may have access to the help of a court interpreter. According to the laws on public education, the language of the elementary and secondary education may be a minority language as well, and these schools issue bilingual official documents (for instance, certificates). The Law on the Slovak Radio and Slovak Television allows these public stations to broadcast programs in the minority languages.

According to the Law on the Use of Languages of National Minorities, in those settlements where the given minority constitutes at least 20% of the total population, private individuals of the minority may use the minority language in some of the administrative offices (in writing as well), and the office is required to reply in the minority language. The administrative offices and public places of these settlements may also be marked with signs in the minority language, and the sessions of the local government may be conducted in the minority language, provided all persons present (including guests) give their consent (see Daftary & Gál 2000 for more details).

2.7.2 *Practical application of measures*

The Slovak political elite (regardless of party affiliation) rejects the collective rights of minorities and defines language rights as private rights (Šutaj & Olejník 1998:285), regarding them as the private affairs of the individual. In addition, the Slovak government also rejects the idea of the positive discrimination of minorities. Moreover, they regard as the discrimination of majority speakers the request of minority communities to require proficiency in the given minority language for certain positions, or at least to consider the applicants' language proficiency. The laws broadening the possibilities of minority language use have been passed and adopted by the Slovak government and parliament upon international pressure (they were tied to Slovakia's admittance into the Council of Europe, for instance, and part of the negotiations concerning its accession to the European Union), so there is no adequate attention given to their practical enforcement.

The following facts should be emphasized concerning the present situation. Theoretically, the Law on Minority Language Use makes the use of minority languages only possible at the local and district levels, since none of the minorities reach a 20% rate in the centers of higher-level administrative and self-government units.[13] Official data can usually be turned in only on Slovak application forms, and since the law does not specifically address the issue of forms, minority clients have practically no opportunity to turn in their applications in their mother tongue. The number of decisions and resolutions which can be published in a minority language is also few. Although according to the international contracts ratified by Slovakia, the general use of traditional settlement names in the minority language should be made possible, the Slovak government restricts this right to the use of road signs, so, for instance, the name of a settlement can only be indicated in Slovak in offices. The recently accepted Language Charter differentiates between minority languages spoken in Slovakia and extends the opportunities of minority language use (especially the use of Hungarian), but presently, it has no visible results in practice yet.

3. Linguistic aspects

The description of the linguistic aspects of the Hungarian language use of the Hungarians in Slovakia in this section is based mostly on the results of the Slovakia-Hungary High School (SHHS) Project and Sociolinguistics of Hungarian Outside Hungary (SHOH) project (for details of the entire project, see Kontra, this volume).

The SHHS project was carried out between 1991 and 1993 and comprises the findings of 1,602 sociolinguistic questionnaires. The aim of the study was basically twofold: on the one hand to compare monolingual and bilingual speakers' language use, and on the other hand to compare the language use of students receiving instruction in their mother tongue and those instructed in their L2. Our informants were secondary school students living in three HS towns and students living in three HH towns. The western region was represented by Šamorín/Somorja and Csorna, the central region by Fiľakovo/Fülek and Bátonyterenye, and the eastern by Kráľovský Chlmec/Királyhelmec and Tokaj. In the towns in Slovakia, students who reported speaking Hungarian and attended either schools with Hungarian as language of instruction or schools with Slovak as language of instruction filled in the questionnaires. (For details of the study, see Lanstyák & Szabómihály 1996a, 1997.)

The SHOH study was carried out between 1995 and 1996 in three sites in Slovakia: in Dunajská Streda/Dunaszerdahely (chosen as a town in Western Slovakia with an overwhelmingly Hungarian population), in Tešedíkovo/Pered (a village in Western Slovakia with an overwhelmingly Hungarian population) and in Lučenec/Losonc (a town in Central Slovakia with an overwhelmingly Slovak population). (For details of the Slovakia part of the project, see Lanstyák 2000a.)

In this section of the paper, first we discuss contact-induced features of Hungarian in Slovakia, and then provide an overview of the most salient kind of the contact-induced features, namely borrowing (both lexical and structural), illustrating it with a great range of examples. Due to limitations of space in this chapter, we do not address issues of the establishment of borrowed forms into the system of the recipient language.

3.1 Contact-induced features of Hungarian in Slovakia

3.1.1 *Two layers of contact-induced features*
If we do not take into consideration the linguistic consequences of the influence that Western Slavic languages and Slovak have had on Hungarian as a whole, we need to differentiate two layers of contact-induced features of Western Slavic and Slovak origin in the varieties of Hungarian as spoken in Slovakia (henceforth HS varieties). One of the layers consists of those contact-induced features that Northern Hungarian dialects took over from Western Slavic and Slovak dialects, while the second layer is comprised of contact-induced features of Slovak (and partly of Czech) origin in the language of Hungarian speakers in Slovakia, who have lived as a minority since the formation of Czechoslovakia in 1918.

These two layers of contact-induced features differ greatly from each other. The older layer, which has been present for centuries, exists on a regional level and is the spontaneous, natural result of prolonged group bilingualism, that is, of different ethnic groups' cohabitation in a region. This layer comprises dialect words, phonetic, morphological and syntactic dialectal features present in Hungarian-speaking areas of Slovakia and oftentimes forming a continuum with those on the other side of the Trianon border, that is, in parts of what is present day Hungary. Among these features, there are borrowings as well as shift-induced interference[14] resulting from the language shift under way among the Western Slavic and Slovak population of the area. The majority of loanwords are part of the colloquial language of the dialects in question and of the vocabulary of traditional crafts. Logically, present day large-scale Hungarian-Slovak bilingualism has not played a role in the formation of the elements of this layer. Some of these elements are even receding, moribund and archaic ones, which are used

by elderly monolingual dialect speakers and which are not part of the Hungarian vocabulary of Hungarian-Slovak bilinguals. Although other elements are strengthened
by the present Hungarian-Slovak bilingualism (which may slow down their disappearance from the dialects or even contribute to their spread),[15] this layer is essentially
a closed set of elements. Even if the number of these elements changes, it tends to
decrease rather than increase.

As opposed to this, the other, more recent layer of contact-induced features has
been formed in the past decades since 1918 through an artificial, that is, officially ini-
tiated and promoted bilingualism. Like the pre-1918 layer, this layer consists partly of
elements of the colloquial language which speakers of Hungarian adopted through
the direct contact with Slovak speakers, but it also contains a large number of elements systematically spread by Hungarian speaking government officials, schools,
work places, the Hungarian printed media in Slovakia and commerce. Their use is
largely restricted to what is today Slovakia, although a number of them have been
adopted by some speakers of Hungarian living in Hungary (HH speakers) as a result of
contact between people residing close to the Hungarian-Slovak border. The majority of
elements adopted through direct contact are in use in the whole of the Hungarian area
of Slovakia, not only in specific regions. This layer consists solely of borrowings and
completely lacks instances of shift-induced interference.[16] Here we have an ever-open
set which is continually enriched through large-scale and vigorous Hungarian-Slovak
bilingualism, although we cannot rule out the possibility that some borrowings are
becoming marginal. This latter claim is, however, only based on our observations and
needs to be empirically proven.

The present section only surveys borrowings that belong to the post-1918 layer
of contact-induced features (for a description of the older layer, see Lanstyák 1994a).
Even so, space limitations do not allow a detailed description of each type of contact-
induced features, so we discuss most of them very briefly and analyze only borrowings
in considerable detail.

3.1.2   *The linguistic behavior of bilinguals*

3.1.2.1 *The overall effects of the bilingual situation.* The linguistic behavior of
speakers living in bilingual speech communities is affected by the very fact that, on
the one hand, in bilingual situations, speakers use their first language less often, irrespective of their proficiency in the L2. The resulting characteristic features of their
language use are, thus, L2-independent, that is, they depend neither on what language
the speakers speak as their L2 nor on the degree of speakers' proficiency in the L2. On
the other hand, in shaping the other group of specific characteristics of the language
use of bilinguals, it is their bilingualism that plays a crucial role. In this subsection, we
do not deal with the influence of the specific elements and features of the L2 but with
that of bilingualism in general. The global effect of the bilingual situation may be called
the situation effect of bilingualism. Such bilingualism-specific effects arise with any
combination of two languages, although their nature and degree obviously depend on
the type of speakers' bilingualism and on the actual combination of languages. As L2-

independent characteristic features of language use (that is, those resulting from less exposure to the L1) and bilingualism-specific features are not always unambiguously distinguishable, we discuss them jointly in the subsections below.

3.1.2.1.1 Manifestations of linguistic insecurity.   By linguistic insecurity we mean the phenomenon when speakers demonstrate an insufficient proficiency in one or more fields of their linguistic competence. If a speaker does not have enough opportunity to use their language in a number of domains, or, in a situation of language shift, in all domains, they will have difficulty in recalling some, mainly the seldom used structures and vocabulary items and may become insecure about the normative use of these items. Besides less exposure to L1, bilingualism itself can also cause linguistic insecurity and not only because bilinguals need to divide their time between their L1 and L2, and, consequently, do not have the opportunity to use their L1 as often as monolinguals, but also because access to two linguistic systems can make speakers insecure as to which of their languages a particular element or phenomenon belongs to, or, even if they are able to assign the element to either language, they may not be able to decide whether it is an established element of that language or merely an instance of L2-influenced interference.

We believe that linguistic insecurity can manifest itself in errors, slower speech rate, hesitations, false starts, pauses and, in writing, stylistic errors, slower writing, greater reliance on outside sources such as dictionaries etc. The occurrence of these in bilinguals is more likely, more frequent than in monolinguals. In addition to all these, linguistic insecurity can trigger instances of overgeneralization, simplification, hypercorrection, hyperpurism, overfulfilment of the norm, and speakers' preference for analytical structures over synthetic ones. These phenomena are well-known, so, except for the last two, their relevance to the present discussion needs no further explanation. As for the last two concepts in the list, the entire next subsection of our paper is devoted to the phenomenon of overfulfilment of the norm. Examples of speakers' preference for analytical structures over synthetic ones are HS *tagok létszáma* vs. SS *taglétszám* 'number of members [of a group]', HS *légi tér* 'air [adj] space' vs. HH *légtér* 'air space' and HS *szolgáltatási ház* 'house of services' vs. HH *szolgáltatóház* 'service house'. Using analytical structures instead of synthetic ones can indicate linguistic insecurity because when using analytical structures, the odds of making an error are smaller and the errors are less conspicuous since the analytical structures are grammatically well-formed in the target language and easy to produce with the help of grammatical rules, whereas their synthetic counterparts are often idiosyncratic and therefore harder to remember.

A "milder" form of linguistic insecurity is linguistic precaution. This makes some bilinguals speak less spontaneously, produce fewer individual, ad hoc linguistic forms, and makes speakers less creative even in familiar registers than monolingual speakers (at least, this is the case in some sections of such puristic bilingual communities like the HS language community). It would be difficult to empirically test linguistic precaution; however, even laymen have already realized the lack of linguistic creativity in minority Hungarian newspapers compared to newspapers produced in Hungary. In personal communication, we were also told that the journalists in question attribute their relatively uncreative language to their increased linguistic precaution: they are often inhibited from using more daring structures, fearing that their linguistic instinct, "impaired" by their bilingualism, would not "alert" them if they were to use inappropriate structures.

3.1.2.1.2 Overfulfilment of the norm.

In the bilingualism literature, overfulfilment of the norm is a little studied field, although it is a highly significant – though less salient – feature of bilingual language varieties spoken in minority situations in general and not only of HS varieties. However, even the relatively restricted space that is at our disposal should not prevent us from discussing this phenomenon in some detail as our empirical data on borrowing (see Section 3.2 below) would be impossible to interpret without a reference to this concept.

In overfulfilling the norm, speakers' motivation is the same as in the case of hypercorrection and hyperpurism. Unlike the latter two, however, overfulfilment of the norm does not involve using forms that are not part of the language variety in question, but rather, it manifests itself in the unusually frequent occurrence of a number of features in the speech of a whole group (for example, of a social class). In a bilingual situation, overfulfilment of the norm means that the bilingual group observes the rules of the prestige norm more closely than monolingual speakers with roughly the same social characteristics. In a monolingual environment, the phenomenon is called Labovian hypercorrection. In Labov's classic 1966 study, the second highest social group, the lower middle class, was found to use the prestige variants with a higher frequency in formal styles than members of the highest social group themselves. Besides the differences of the groups involved, a further difference between overfulfilment of the norm in bilingual situations and in Labovian hypercorrection is that, in bilingual situations, "the highest status social group" (i.e. the monolingual group) and "the second highest status social group" (i.e. the bilingual group) do not belong to the same speech community (not only do they not live in the same cities but they even live in different countries).

In the SHHS Project, overfulfilment of the norm manifested itself in the fact that, in the test situation, Hungarian-Slovak bilingual speakers outperformed their reference group, Hungarian grammar school students living in Hungary, in the use of standard variants of a number of sociolinguistic variables, although HS speakers are widely known to use more non-standard (substandard) variants in informal situations than the HH reference group. The Hungarian language is of central importance for the identity of Hungarians in Slovakia (see, for instance, Gereben 1999:76; Lampl 1999:15). Since, for Hungarians in Slovakia it is the standard dialect of Hungarian that outwardly represents Hungarian to the outside (see Lanstyák 2000a:148), rigorous observation of the norms of the standard by HS students attending schools with Hungarian as language of instruction can be interpreted as their symbolic identification with the Hungarian nation.[17] Students living in Slovakia and attending schools

with Slovak as language of instruction, in some cases, demonstrated greater norm ob-
servance, too, albeit to a considerably lesser extent. One of the reasons for that is that
only 50% of these students were born in endogamous Hungarian marriages,[18] thus,
only a part of them felt the urge to identify themselves with the Hungarian nation this
way. The other reason is that in schools with Slovak as language of instruction, Hungarian is not taught in any form (not even as an optional subject, see Section 1.4.2),
which leaves those students without the chance to acquire standard Hungarian in an
academic context.

Figure 3.1 below shows examples of overfulfilment of the norm taken from the
Slovakia-Hungary High School Project. Four verbs (*alszik* 'to sleep', *vitatkozik* 'to argue', *iszik* 'to drink' and *elkésik* 'to be late') conjugated in first person singular declarative general conjugation take either *-m* or *-k* as their ending, where *-m* is the prestige
variant and *-k* is the one used in informal, colloquial contexts. The latter ending,
however, is only very slightly stigmatized probably because it is widely in use among
educated speakers, too. Figure 3.1 shows that HS students attending schools with Hungarian as language of instruction (group BH) conjugated all four verbs following the
prestige norm in the greatest proportion, students living in Hungary (group HH) fell
behind them, and students living in Slovakia and attending schools with Slovak as
language of instruction (group BS) followed the prestige norm the least.[19]

Figure 3.1 shows that HS students attending schools with Hungarian as language
of instruction used the prestige form in a higher proportion than students of the control group in Hungary. The difference was highly significant in the case of three verbs
(*alszik, iszik, elkésik*), and not significant in the case of the fourth verb (*vitatkozik*).[20]
Hungarian students in Slovakia are, at least passively, fairly familiar with Standard
Hungarian as spoken in Slovakia and, as "good Hungarians", they wanted to demonstrate their "correct Hungarian" in this test situation. Their behavior, we believe, also
stemmed from their wish to compensate for their linguistic insecurity described above.
HH students do not have such a need to demonstrate correctness. Students attending
schools with Slovak as language of instruction in Slovakia did not overfulfill the norm

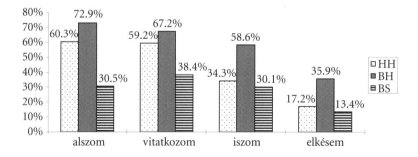

Figure 3.1. The choice of the *-m* ending for the verbs *alszik* 'to sleep', *vitatkozik* 'to argue',
iszik 'to drink' and *elkésik* 'be late' for first person singular declarative general conjugation
by the three groups of the SHHS Project

in the case of these four verbs: they used with each verb fewer prestige forms than HH students, although the differences were significant only in two cases out of four (for *al-szik* and *vitatkozik*), but then in both cases they were highly significant. The differences between the choices of students living in Slovakia and having Hungarian as language of instruction and those attending schools with Slovak as language of instruction were in all four cases highly significant.

3.1.2.1.3 Language lapses and language gaps.

Restricted exposure to the L1 results invariably in lapses and language gaps, among other things. We consider it a case of "language lapse" when a speaker is temporarily unable to recall a word or grammatical structure he or she is otherwise familiar with. A "language gap", in our usage, is a case when a required word or structure is not part of the speaker's linguistic system at all (if lexical items are missing, it is a case of lexical gap). To avoid language lapses and gaps – or, at least to conceal them, – speakers may choose to stick to their first language and replace a missing word with, for example, its hyperonym or synonym, or they may paraphrase the word, substitute it with a word of related meaning etc. Furthermore, in order to avoid language gaps, bilingual speakers may fall back on their second language and take over elements from that. To eliminate communicative failures resulting from language gaps, speakers may also resort to extra- and paralinguistic means (pointing at objects, imitating sounds, drawing pictures etc.), and of course, they may choose to leave the lexical gap unfilled. Such compensatory procedures and other symptoms of linguistic insecurity may impair text cohesion (for a more detailed discussion of the concept of language gap, see Lanstyák 2000a: 176–184).

On the level of language varieties, language gaps may manifest themselves in a lower level of proficiency in some language varieties, especially in the standard dialect and in the use of technical jargon. In their mildest form, language gaps on the level of language varieties manifest themselves in increased permeability of different varieties (e.g. use of more regional elements in the standard, less "technical" technical jargons, milder slang). This in practice means greater variability within bilingual language varieties compared to their monolingual counterparts. Thus, HS varieties are more diffuse than monolingual HH varieties, which are characteristically more focused (for the terms, cf. Trudgill 1992).

When speakers are exposed to some varieties of their first language to an extremely small extent, their language gaps may grow to lead to code attrition (dialect attrition or register attrition). In such situations, lapses and signs of linguistic insecurity may occur in a drastically increased number. In the case of speakers with relatively high proficiency in their L2, code attrition may reach all varieties of L1 as they have another language at their disposal. This phenomenon is called language attrition or, in its more dramatic form, language loss. (Language loss affecting an entire community is labeled language shift.)

3.1.2.1.4 Base language switching.

One of the characteristic features of language use in bilingual situations is that of code-switching between languages. Code-switching is a way of speaking in which, within a single stretch of discourse, more than one language (or more broadly speaking, more than one language variety) plays an active role. (With the use of the adjective "active", we mean to differentiate one-word switches from borrowings, because with borrowings, the role that source languages play is not an active one any more.) Code-switching has essentially two basic types: base language switching and transfer (cf. Auer 1998a: 200). The former one can be considered a situation effect of bilingualism, whereas the latter is a type effect of bilingualism and will therefore be discussed below. In base language switching, the language which determines the grammatical structure of a longer utterance (one that consists of at least one clause), that is, the base language, gets switched once or several times, either temporarily or permanently. The following examples have been taken from a data base comprising conversations among four young women (Németh 2002).[21]

In (1), both speakers switch to Slovak as soon as their Slovak friend, Martina is mentioned: B provides information about Martina in Slovak and A asks back in Slovak, even though she spoke Hungarian before B mentioned Martina. B switches back to Hungarian too when speaking about herself and not about Martina. The clause with Slovak as its base language uttered by B is separated by a medium long pause from the clause with Hungarian as its base language. (Here and in other examples of utterances, P, PP and PPP indicate short, medium, and long pauses.)

(1) A: *Hallod PP, ki fogja eztët csináni?*
     B: *Čo, **Martina tam pôjde**, PP én nem mëgyëk, szabadságon lëszëk.*
     A: ***Martina pôjde?***

     A: Listen PP, who's going to do this?
     B: *Well, Martina is going there, PP I'm not going there, I'll be on holiday.*
     A: *Is Martina going?*

In (2) Lívia, the colleague of the speaker, was about to sign an official form for her director, which the speaker apparently finds inappropriate. The initial clause is in Hungarian, while the second one is in Slovak. The code-switching in this case was obviously triggered by the fact that the language of official administration is Slovak, which the speaker indirectly refers to by her switch.

(2) *No, de Lívi, de hogy írhatod te alá, **ty si zamestnávatel**'?*
     Well, but Lívi, how can you sign it, *are you the employer?*

The speaker in (3) relates how a police officer stopped her when she was driving her car. She quotes both herself and the officer in the language they spoke during their conversation, that is, in Slovak, while narrating the story itself in Hungarian. The expression she used for 'turn on the light', *fölnyitja a villanyt* lit. 'to open up the light' is probably not an indirect loanword but a dialectal feature (we are not familiar with any corresponding SS expression that would literally mean 'to open up the light').

(3) *Odaadtam a autópapírokot, mondom nëki: **aj vodičák?** [nevet] No, **však ano!** Mondom nëki,* [nevet]: ***musím to pohl'adat'.*** [nevet] *Fölnyitottam a villanyt.*

I gave him the car documents and asked him, *driver's licence, too?* [laughs]
Well, *obviously yes!* I say to him, [laughs]: *I need to find it.* [laughs] I turned
on the light.

Even in this single group of speakers, base language switching has various causes and
goals (for details see Németh 2002). Speakers belonging to different segments of the
HS community make use of code-switching in different ways and to different degrees. Members of homogeneous, that is, all-Hungarian, groups use code-switching
as a communicative strategy less often than members of heterogeneous groups (those
consisting of bilingual Hungarians and bilingual Slovaks). The most trivial occurrence
of base language switching in homogeneous groups is like the one in the last example: speakers quote utterances in the language that they were originally uttered in. (For
a more detailed discussion of the issue see Lanstyák & Szabómihály 1996b; Lanstyák
2000a: 158–168, 2000b.)

3.1.2.2 *The effects of L2 elements and features.* When considering the effects of bilingualism it is usually the effect the very elements and features of the speaker's L2 have
on the elements and features they use in their L1 that first come to mind. This phenomenon can be called the type effect of bilingualism. The language use characteristics
due to the type effect of bilingualism are unquestionably L2-specific.

The effect the elements and features of one of the bilingual speaker's languages
have on the elements and features of his or her other language is called interference and
the features resulting from interference are called interference features (see Lanstyák
1999/2000: 22–24). One of the possible linguistic results of language interference is
borrowing at all levels of L1, predominantly at the level of vocabulary, less in syntax,
and even less in morphology and phonology. The question of borrowing is addressed
later on in this chapter.

An L2 may have both "hidden", that is, indirect or salient, and direct effects on an
L1. Indirect L2-effects are manifested through elements of the L1. This is called substitution by Haugen (1949: 288, 1972: 82). To take just two examples,[22] HS *munkatöltet*
(lit. "filling of work") 'sphere of work' (cf. HH *munkakör*, "circle of work") or HS
délután majd hívok neked ("I will call you.DAT in the afternoon") 'I will give you a
ring in the afternoon' (cf. HH *délután majd felhívlak* "I will call you.ACC in the afternoon") do not contain any free or bound morphemes unknown in HH but their
combination follows SS rules; compare SS *pracovná náplň* ("filling of work"), and
SS *zavolám ti* ("I will call you.DAT"), respectively. Similarly, HS *névhasználat*, pronounced as ['neːvhasnaːlat], contains phonemes that all belong to the HH phoneme
inventory, but its HS pronunciation reflects SS influence, namely that /h/ fails to devoice /v/, producing a HS pronunciation ['neːvhasnaːlat], which is different from HH
pronunciation ['neːfhasnaːlat].[23]

Direct L2-effects are manifested in the form of the very elements and features
of the L2 occurring in the L1, which, of course, does not necessarily leave them unchanged by the phonological, morphological and syntactic system of the recipient

language, that is, they may be subject to partial substitution. Direct L2 effects are called importation by Haugen (ibid.). An example of importation is HS *hranolki* 'French fries', where both the pronunciation and the meaning have been directly imported from Slovak (cf. SS *hranolky* 'French fries'). Importation, however, can go alongside with modified form on the phonetic level: through substitution, the word can be pronounced in HS with a voiceless initial [h] and a rounded [ɑ] as well.[24] In HS varieties as a whole where the fairly short history of bilingualism and the peculiarities of the HS speech community have prevented SS from having a great impact on them, borrowing proper is present only on the level of vocabulary, leaving the syntax, morphology and phonology of HS largely affected by loanshifting only.

A marginal, less definite type of borrowing that is often difficult to differentiate from interference and even less conspicuous than loanshifting is convergence, more specifically, one-way convergence. In a case of one-way convergence, fixed differences in the frequency of occurrence of specific features are observable: bilingual speakers (both individually and at the group level) use the same features that are also used by monolinguals, but they use them with a considerably greater or smaller frequency. Convergence (differences in frequency of occurrence) comprises a significant proportion of the differences between bilingual and monolingual language varieties. As Section 3.2 on borrowing will show, absolute differences are found mainly in vocabulary and phonology (but differences in the latter are very few in number anyway); while contact-induced features at the level of morphology are all cases of convergence, and so are the majority of features on the level of syntax.

3.1.2.2.1 Transfer.   The second major type of code-switching, transfer, demonstrates the type effect of L2. With transfer, the base language does not change, and it is only units of different sizes, embedded language islands (mostly isolated words and phrases) that are adopted from the embedded language. Elements of the source language that get integrated into the system of L1 become borrowings. In the examples below (taken from the above mentioned corpus), the embedded language islands are single words.

In (4), two embedded language islands are subjects (*majitel'ka* '(female) owner' and *podnikatel'ka* '(female) entrepreneur'), and one is an adverb of place (*firmá-ba*, 'at the firm'), with a suffix attached to in the base language. HS *Szilvinek hívtam* 'I called Szilvi.DAT' is a case of borrowing of argument from Slovak (see above and Section 3.2), its HH equivalent being *fölhívtam Szilvit* ('I called Szilvi.ACC'). In fact, the speaker here quotes in Slovak the key words associated with the Slovak-language world of Bratislava. On retelling her own sentence from the phone conversation, she switches to Slovak, but it is a case of base language switching, as described earlier.

(4)   *Mondom, úr isten, mondom, biztos a Szilvinek hívtam a **firmá**-ba Pozsonyba, és biztos a P **majitel'ka** vagy valami **podnikatel'ka** fölvëtte P, és mondom P, mondom, hogy* [kedvesen kezd beszélni] **dobrý deň** P, **Silviu Vargovú hl'adám** [...]

I say, oh, my God, I say, I think I called Szilvi at the *firm* in Bratislava, and P *the owner* or some kind of *entrepreneur* must have answered the phone P, and I say P, I say, [starts speaking in a very friendly way] *good afternoon P, I'd like to speak to Szilvia Varga, please* [...]

In (5), the embedded language islands are a dative case marked possessor phrase (*Ivan-nak*) and a comitative adverbial bearing instrumental case (*Ivan-nal*), respectively. In this case, code-switching indicates the Slovak ethnicity of the person in question: the use of the Hungarian equivalent of this given name, *Iván*, would imply that he is Hungarian. The quote starts with a complex sentence with Slovak as its base language.

(5)   *No PPP, **ale nie s Ivanom, ale** [nyomatékkal] **s Vilom**. [nevet] Az a **Ivan-nak** a legjobb barátja. **Ivan-nal** tëgnap PP, tëgnapelőtt összeveszëtt.*
Well, PPP, *but not with Ivan, but* [emphatically] *with Vilo*. [laughs] He is *Ivan's* best friend. She broke up with *Ivan* yesterday PP, the day before yesterday.

In (6), the speaker informs her colleague about the regulation that on quitting a job after signing a document saying that she did so in full agreement with her employer, she will not even be eligible for unemployment benefit. However, if her employer lays her off without such an agreement, the employer would be liable to pay her severance pay. The three key terms are said in Slovak, and the Hungarian accusative case marker is added to two of them (*odstupné-t, dohodá-t*). Because of its topicality, the noun *podpora* is on the brink of becoming a borrowing into several HS varieties. If the word-final <a> was pronounced as a non-rounded vowel, the word should possibly be regarded as an embedded language island, but if it was pronounced as a rounded vowel – which would be a sign of assimilation into the base language – it would instead count as a case of borrowing. In the workplace situation described above, the other two technical terms may also count as cases of borrowing.

(6)   *Mer, ha aláírod, akkor még a **podpora** së jár. Ő csak úgy kűdhet el, ha ad **odstupné-t** is. És **odstupné-t** biztos nem hajlandó, úgyhogy ad nëkëd **dohodá-t**, és azt ha aláírod, akkor a **podpora** is rövidül a felére.*
Because if you sign it, you won't even be eligible for [*unemployment*] *benefit*. She cannot lay you off unless she pays you *severance pay*. And she is surely not prepared to give you *severance pay,* so she'll give you an "*agreement*", and if you sign that, your *benefit* will be cut by half, too.

Let us now turn to examples where the units from the embedded language are multi-word phrases.

In (7), the embedded language island is an attributive structure. As it is, in fact, the name of an institution, which can, in some cases, get borrowed, too (for this, see Section 3.2 on Borrowing), this instance of code-switching may alternatively be regarded as an example of the rare case of phrase borrowing.

(7)   *Láttad, hogy ki van világítva a **Národná banka**?*
Did you see how the *National Bank* is all lit up?

In (8), speaker B refers back to the key words of the previous base language switching (*pánske návštevy*), which has the role of strengthening text cohesion. This phrase receives the Hungarian accusative case marker *-t* (*pánske návštevy-t*). On its second occurrence, it has a metalinguistic function, that is why we left it uchanged in the translation. Speaker B talks about the fact that by spelling *návštevy* with an <i> rather than a final <y>, the Slovak shop-assistant in question had made a grave spelling mistake (**návštevi*). This example dialog ends in a base language switching serving as a quotation.

(8) A: *Mi van a izébe, Sellyén, Kati?*

B: *Hun, Angi? Üzletünkbe? Nagy sëmmi PP, **už ani návštevy nám nechodia**, van ëgy füzetünk, amibe írjuk a **pánske návštevy**-t. És a hülye Vigi P, [. . .], és leírja **a pánske návštevy**-t P **mäkké i**-vē. Mëg, mëg olyanokot beír abba a füzetbe, hogy javítom ki utána.*[nevet] *Mondom, **do frasa, Maď'arka to má opravovať'!** [nevet]*

A: What's up in what-do-you-call-it, in Šaľa, Kati?

B: Where, Angi? In our shop? Nothing at all PP, *not even male visitors come to us any more*, we have a notebook we put down *male visitors* in. And stupid Vigi P, [. . .], and she writes *pánske návštevy* P with *a soft i*. And she writes such things in that notebook, and I just go through it and correct them afterwards. [laughs] I say, *what the heck, a Hungarian needs to correct her*! [laughs]

In (9), the embedded language unit is a phrase that is part of the official register, which the informant probably does not even know in Hungarian. Thus, the switch also serves to fill the language gap. The structure may even have for some groups of speakers the status of a borrowing (see Section 3.2).

(9) ***Dohoda o vykonaní práce*** *van, az lëhet, száz órát dógozhat le ëgy évbe . . .*
She has a *contract of agency*, that's possible, she can work a hundred hours a year . . .

In (10), the speaker uses a unit from Slovak (*krém na nohy*) as well as from English (*present*) because the person she is talking about is an Arab man with whom she speaks English. The phrase *krém na nohy* 'foot lotion' (lit. 'lotion for the feet') could be interpreted as a kind of quotation if this is what it read on the label. Here we have a prepositional phrase, the Hungarian equivalent of which is a compound noun (*lábkrém*), but which is a word not yet registered in dictionaries of the Hungarian language. The marginal currency of *lábkrém*, the power of the experience, the great difference between the forms in the two languages and the great phonetic similarity of the analog *krém* 'lotion' in Hungarian and in Slovak may have triggered the switch.[25] The accusative case marker (*-t*) is missing, probably because it was problematic for the speaker whether to attach it to the stem (to the word *krém*, as "*krém*-et *na nohy*"), or to the unit as a whole ("*krém na nohy*-t").

(10) *És akkor kimënt PP, és ëgyszër csak gyün vissza, és hozott nëkëm ëgy KRÉM na*
      nohy P, mint hogy present.
      And then he left PP, and then suddenly returned, and brought *a foot lotion* for
      me P, as a present.

3.2 Borrowing

3.2.1 *Lexical borrowing*

We start our discussion of borrowing with the types of lexical borrowing first, lexical
borrowing being the only real type of borrowing in the sense that it is only words
and phrases that are directly taken over from one language into the other, whereas
sounds, patterns of intonation, and affixes follow a "secondary route" and get into the
recipient language through words. (Shift-induced interference is an exception in this
regard, but we do not expect such to be present in the more recent, post-1918 layer
of contact-induced features.) For this reason, a familiarity with lexical borrowing is
required for a full understanding of all other types of borrowing.

On the level of the lexicon, borrowing produces loanwords proper and loanforms,
while loanshifting produces calques and semantic loans. These four are the basic types
of lexical borrowing. Both loanshifting and borrowing is involved in the production of
loanblends, a special subcategory of calques.[26] It is important to note about the examples of lexical borrowing cited below that in the majority of cases, their HH equivalents
are also widely in use: some segments of the speech community use the HH variants of
these words, others alternate between the HH and HS forms according to the speech
situation, while the rest of the population are familiar with the HS forms only.[27]

3.2.1.1 *Loanwords proper.* Historically, loanwords proper are words and phrases that
were transferred from the source language with no or minimal morphemic substitution. To begin with, it is advisable to differentiate between proper nouns and common
nouns within the category of loanwords proper, as these differ in several respects.
Examples of directly borrowed common nouns (cases of importation, in Haugen's
terms) are (a) items of clearly Slovak origin (e.g. HS *horcsica* 'mustard', cf. SS *horčica*;
HS *nanuk* 'ice cream bar', cf. SS *nanuk*; HS *vlecska* ~ *lecska* 'trailer', cf. SS *vlečka*;
HS *szporozsíró* 'checking account', cf. SS *sporožíro*); (b) foreign words – i.e. words of
clearly non-Slovak origin – in Slovak (e.g. HS *deratizáció* 'rat extermination', cf. SS
deratizácia; HS *inventúra* 'inventory', cf. SS. *inventúra*; HS *szkripta* ~ *szkriptum* '(distributed) lecture notes', cf. SS *skriptá;* HS *tunel* 'tunnel', cf. SS *tunel*); (c) acronyms
(HS *eszenesz* 'Slovak National Party', cf. SS *esenes* (SNS) ~ *eseneska*; HS *véúbé* 'General
Credit Bank', cf. SS *véúbé* ~ *véúbéčko* (VÚB); HS *dépéhá* 'value added tax', cf. SS *dépéhá*
~ *dépéháčko* (DPH)).

Another group of common nouns comprises phrases which may contain both
groups of Slovak origin and foreign words, e.g. *výpis z registra trestov* 'good-conduct
certificate'; *rodné číslo* 'personal identification number'; *rodný list* 'birth certificate'; *by-
tové družstvo* 'building and loan association'; *daňový úrad* 'revenue office'. It is dubious

whether they may be considered established loans for any segments of the population. However, they are definitely cases of code-switching for many.

Based on semantic criteria, the group of various types of proper nouns may be identified, the most important of them being personal names (e.g. first names like *Slavomír, Zuzana*; nicknames like *Slavo, Zuzka*; surnames like *Ondrejovič, Drábeková*; full names like *Slavomír Ondrejovič, Zuzana Drábeková*), placenames (e.g. *Prešov, Nové Mesto nad Váhom*) and the names of institutions (e.g. *Jednota* 'Unity' [a co-op and its chain of stores]; *Slovenská sporiteľňa* 'Slovak Savings Bank'). Their status is, similarly to that of phrases, dubious. Some of them may be considered established loans, others are, instead, instances of code-switching.

3.2.1.2 *Loanforms.* Historically, a loanform is a word in the recipient language the phonemic shape of which has been modified under the influence of the analog's phonemic shape in the source language. Here are some examples: HS *prax* 'practice', cf. SS *prax*, but HH *praxis*; HS *diplom* 'certificate, diploma', cf. SS *diplom*, but HH *diploma*; HS *notorikus* ~ *notórikus* 'notorious', cf. SS *notorický*, but HH *notórius*; HS *kontrola* 'check-up', cf. SS *kontrola*, but HH *kontroll*; HS *dezert* 'bonbons', cf. SS *dezert*, but HH *desszert*; HS *buldozér* 'bulldozer', cf. SS *buldozér*, but HH *buldózer*.

The process of adjusting the Latinate endings to the Slovak pattern has evoked a process in the opposite direction, i.e. the relatinization of the words on the basis of their HH equivalents. Since these equivalents are not always known (indeed, they are sometimes unknown to most HH speakers as well), the result of the "relatinization" is not always identical with the HH (and the one-time Latin) sound shape, e.g. HS *evidenció* 'registry', cf. SS *evidencia* and HH *evidencia*; HS *prémió* 'bonus', cf. SS *prémia*, but HH *prémium*; HS *antikvariátus* 'second-hand bookshop', cf. SS *antikvariát*, but HH *antikvárium*. These hypercorrect forms are, strictly speaking, not cases of borrowing, though they are certainly by-products of the borrowing process.

3.2.1.3 *Calques.* Historically, lexical calques as well as their special type, loanblends, are words created in the recipient language under the influence of the words of the source language; they more or less closely follow the morphemic structure of the model words or at least are semantically motivated in a similar way as their models. While calques, in a narrower sense of the word, are created solely by morphemes belonging to the recipient language, loanblends as a special type of calques contain at least one morpheme imported from the source language.

Calques may consist of one word only (most of the examples are compounds or derivatives) or they may be formed by a group of words. Examples of simple word calques are HS *távoktatás* 'correspondence course' ("distance education"), cf. SS *diaľkové štúdium* ("distance education"), but HH *levelező oktatás* ("correspondence education"); HS *minőséges* 'good quality [adj]' ("quality"), cf. SS *kvalitný*, but HH *jó minőségű* ("good quality"); HS *kenő* 'spread (made from various kinds of food, like meat, fish, cheese, eggs, etc.)', cf. SS *nátierka*, but no HH form; HS *kitárcsáz* 'dial a phone number' ("dial out"), cf. SS *vytočiť* ("dial out"), but HH *tárcsáz* ("dial"). Examples of blended words are HS *víberliszt* 'pastry flour' ("víber flour"), cf. SS *výberová múka* ("selected flour"), but HH *rétesliszt* ("strudel flour"); HS *konyhalinka* 'kitchen units' ("kitchen linka"), cf. SS *kuchynská linka* ("kitchen line"), but HH *konyhabútor* ("kitchen furniture"); HS *kipratál* 'take/carry out' ("to take/carry out"), cf. SS *vypratať* ("to take/carry out"), but HH *kirak* ("to put out"), *kihord* ("to carry out").

The calqued phrases are structurally either verbal or nominal. Semantically a special subtype may be identified, that of translated idiomatic expressions (Ligeti 1976: 134–135; Grosjean 1982: 319). Examples of simple calqued verbal phrases are the following: HS *javaslatot ad* 'make a proposal' ("give a proposal"), cf. SS *podať návrh* ("give a proposal"), but HH *javaslatot tesz* ("do a proposal"); HS *vizsgán van* 'take an exam' ("be at an exam"), cf. SS *byť na skúške* ("be at an exam"), but HH *vizsgázik* ("sit for an exam"); *csúszást kap* 'skid' ("get a slip"), cf. SS *dostať šmyk* ("get a slip"), but HH *megcsúszik* ("slide") or *farol* ("tail skid"). There is one example of a loanblend belonging to this category, a phrase that is a synonym of the above mentioned *csúszást kap*, namely *balancot kap* 'skid' ("get a balance"), cf. SS *dostať balanc* ('get a balance'), but HH *megcsúszik* ("skid") or *farol* ("tail skid").

There are many simple calqued nominal phrases in HS, e.g. HS *egészségügyi központ* 'polyclinic' ("health center"), cf. SS *zdravotné stredisko* ("health center"), but HH *rendelőintézet* ("ambulatory institute"); HS *városi hivatal* 'town council' ("town office"), cf. SS *mestský úrad* ("town office"), but HH *polgármesteri hivatal* ("mayor's office"); HS *szociális biztosítás* 'social security' ("social insurance"), cf. SS *sociálne poistenie* ("social insurance"), but HH *társadalombiztosítás* ("society insurance"); HS *fehér jogurt* ~ *joghurt* 'plain yogurt (without fruit, syrup etc.)' ("white yogurt"), cf. SS *biely jogurt* ("white yogurt"), but HH *natúr joghurt* ("natural yogurt"). Among the nominal phrases we can find proper names of various institutions, e.g. HS *Szlovák Nemzeti Párt* 'Slovak National Party', cf. SS *Slovenská národná strana*; HS *Általános Hitelbank* 'General Credit Bank', cf. SS *Všeobecná úverová banka*.

Finally, let us see some examples of calqued idioms: HS *kockában mondja el* 'tell in a nutshell' ("tell in a cube"), cf. SS *povedať v kocke* ("tell in a cube"), but HH *dióhéjban mondja el* ("tell in a nutshell"); HS *kéztől van* 'lie far from' ("be off-hand"), cf. SS *byť od ruky* ("be off-hand"), but HH *félre esik* 'fall aside'; HS *benne van az ujja* 'have a finger in it' ("have a finger in it"), cf. SS *mať v tom prsty* '~' ("have fingers in it"), but HH *benne van a keze* ("have a hand in it").

3.2.1.4 *Semantic loans.* Historically, semantic loans (extensions) are words and phrases that have acquired at least one of their meanings under the influence of their source language equivalent. Semantic extension presupposes that the source language lexeme and its recipient language equivalent have something in common: their phonemic shapes, or their semantic structures, or both are similar in the two languages. This serves as a basis for a finer classification of semantic loans by distinguishing homophones, homologs and analogs (Haugen 1949: 283, 1972: 92).

Interlingual homophones are words with identical or similar phonemic shape but completely different semantic structure in the two languages. For example, HS *galan-*

téria 'haberdasher's', cf. SS *galantéria*, but HH *galantéria*: '1. faultless politeness, 2. courting, 3. generosity'; HS *fix* [n] 'felt pen', cf. SS *fixka*, but HH and HS *fix* [adj] 'fixed'; HS *protektor* 'tyre tread', cf. SS *protektor* '~' but HH *protektor* 'patron, protector'. This may be regarded a case of borrowing proper (3.2.1.1.) producing homonyms in the target language (loan homonyms).

Interlingual homologs are words with completely different phonemic shapes but identical or similar semantic structures in the two languages. "Similarity" in meaning usually means at least a certain overlap in the meanings of the homologs in the two languages. For example, HS *fal* 1. 'wall', 2. 'cabinet units', cf. SS *stena* 1. '~', 2. '~', but HH *fal* only 'wall'; HS *ül* 1. 'sit', 2. 'be OK, agree with something', cf. SS *sediet'* 1. '~', 2. '~', but HH *ül* only 'sit'; HS *fizet* 1. 'pay', 2. 'be valid', cf. SS *platit'* 1. '~', 2. '~', but HH *fizet* only 'pay'; HS *hártya* 1. 'pellicle, film', 2. 'mimeograph copy', cf. SS *blana* 1. '~', 2. '~', but HH *hártya* only 'pellicle, film'. Beside single words, phrases may also extend their meaning to include that of the SS model. For example, HS *ebéden van* 'have lunch' is used for any occasion when somebody is not having his/her lunch at home or directly at his or her workplace, but e.g. in a cafeteria. This is in line with the use of its SS model, *byt' na obede*. However, in HH this phrase is used only to denote special occasions when somebody is invited for a formal lunch.

Interlingual analogs are words with both similar phonemic shape and similar semantic structure in the two languages. Among our examples are the following: HS *szemafor* 1. 'traffic lights', 2. 'railway stoplight', cf. SS *semafor* 1. '~', 2. '~', but HH *szemafor* only 'railway stoplight'; HS *iskola* 'any type of school, including university', cf. SS *škola* '~', but HH *iskola* 'elementary or secondary school'; HS *akció* 1. 'sale', 2. 'cultural programme', cf. SS *akcia* 1. '~', 2. '~', but HH only 'sale'; HS *szirup* 1. 'syrup as a soft drink', 2. 'syrup as medicine', cf. SS *sirup* 1. '~', 2. '~', but HH *szirup* only 'syrup as medicine'; HS *pohár* 1. 'drinking glass', 2. 'fruit jar (made of glass)', 3. 'cup given as a prize in competitions', cf. SS *pohár* 1. '~', 2. '~', 3. '~', but HH *pohár* only 'drinking-glass'; HS *spirál* 1. 'spiral', 2. 'immersion heater', cf. SS *špirála* 1. '~', 2. '~', but HH *spirál* only 'spiral'.

Stylistic loans are a special subtype of semantic loans. There are many analogs in SS and HH which have roughly the same denotative meanings, but their stylistic value differs considerably (e.g. HS *novella* 'amendment act' (neutral), cf. SS *novela* (neutral), but HH *novella* (technical, obsolete); HS *restitúció* 'restitution' (neutral), cf. SS *reštitúcia* (neutral), but HH *restitúció* (formal); HS *certifikátum* 'certificate' (formal), cf. SS *certifikát* (neutral), but HH *certifikátum* (obsolete); HS *katedra* 'university department' (colloquial), cf. SS *katedra* (neutral), but HH *katedra* (obsolete); HS *szvetter* 'sweater' (colloquial, almost neutral), cf. SS *sveter* (neutral), but HH *szvetter* (obsolete)). Stylistic loans are a borderline case of borrowing, as the stylistic value of the HS words is often not identical with that of the SS models. However, it may also be considered as a special way of semantic integration of these loans into the system of HS, and this justifies the use of the term "loan".

3.2.2   *Phonetic and phonological borrowing*

On the level of phonetics, borrowing produces borrowing of subphonemic features and, on the level of phonology, a borrowing of phonemes. Borrowing of phonological rules is a type of indirect form of phonological borrowing.

No cases of phonetic borrowing characteristic of the whole HS speech community are known to us. Obviously, different groups of speakers demonstrate effects of the phonetics of SS, but these are mostly cases of interference. According to our observations, for example, in some border areas of the northern, Palóc dialect region of Hungarian (most notably in a number of towns with overwhelmingly Slovak populations) what one can hear is, contrary to our expectations, not a Palóc accent (unrounded /a/ and slightly higher /ɛ/, /e/ and /aː/) but Slovak-colored subphonemic features (the unrounded /a/ is higher than is usual in Palóc; like in Slovak and unlike in Palóc dialects, /aː/ is not rounded, only higher than in Standard Hungarian; and /ɛ/ is also higher than its usual Palóc counterpart.)

Similarly, we have not found any instances of borrowing of phonemes from SS language varieties. The diagraph <ch> is pronounced as /x/ in international words (e.g. *mechanika* 'mechanics', *pszichológia* 'psychology') and in loanwords from Slovak (e.g. *chata* 'weekend cottage', *chripka* 'flu'), which seems to be a case of borrowing of a phoneme. However, this is not an unambiguous case of phoneme borrowing, since the voiceless velar fricative as an allophone of /h/ exists in HH too (cf. *doh* [dox] 'must [n]', but *dohos* [dohoʃ] 'musty'), and HH speakers pronounce a [x]-like sound in international words if the phonological environment allows it (e.g. *archaikus* [arxaikuʃ] 'archaic', *jacht* [jaxt] 'jacht', *Allah* [allax] 'Allah').

The phenomenon we illustrated with the word *névhasználat* in Section 3.1.2.2 above is a case of borrowing of phonological rules. Here, the devoicing capacity of /h/ does not take effect after /v/, eg. HS *nyelvhelyesség* [ɲɛlvɦɛjɛʃʃeːg] 'linguistic correctness', *nyelvhez* [ɲɛlvɦɛz] 'to language [language.ALL]', *távhívás* [taːvɦiːvaːʃ] 'long distance call' vs. HH *nyelvhelyesség* [ɲɛlfɦɛjɛʃʃeːg] 'linguistic correctness', *nyelvhez* [ɲɛlfɦɛz] 'to language [language.ALL]', *távhívás* [taːfɦiːvaːʃ] 'long distance call'. Also, providing that we do not label pronouncing [x] in international words as borrowing of a phoneme, we can state that [x] in HS can occur, under Slovak influence, in such phononological environments where this is unusual in HH. The phonological environments in question are primarily in word-initial position where in HH [k] is pronounced, or, intervocalically where HH speakers pronounce [h] (e.g. HS *charta* [xarta] 'charter', but HH *charta* [karta]; HS *szacharin* [saxarin], 'saccharin' but HH [saharin]). Thus, this can also be interpreted as a case of borrowing of a phonological rule. Haugen (1972:99) calls the phenomenon just described 'phonemic redistribution'.

3.2.3   *Morphological borrowing*

On the level of morphology, no full-fledged examples of borrowing (of derivational or inflectional suffixes from Slovak) can be found in our data base, which is not surprising, given the nature of Hungarian-Slovak bilingualism and the period of time it has existed in the area as a whole. Still, it is worth pointing out that we have a num-

ber of tokens of a noun (HS *mamuszki* 'felt boots') in which the stem is part of both
the HH and HS lexicons (HH and HS *mamusz* 'felt slippers'), while the derivational
suffix-like second part (-*ki*) is clearly of SS origin. Numerous words denoting types
of footwear have been taken over from SS into HS with the same second part, eg. HS
teniszki 'tennis shoes' vs. SS *tenisky* (plural); HS *botaszki* 'Botas shoes', vs. SS *botasky*
(plural); HS *tramki* 'ankle-height linen tennis shoes', vs. SS *trampky* (plural) etc. As the
HS suffix -*ki* could be attached to a word of Hungarian origin too, thus a new derivational suffix from SS was adopted into HS. However, we have to admit the fact that
in the Csallóköz dialect area (along the Danube, stretching from Bratislava/Pozsony
to Komárno/Komárom) and also in other dialects which are not only spoken in what
is today Slovakia (in the dialect of the Kőszeg area in western Hungary, for example), the word *mamuszka* ('little mamusz'), a variant of *mamusz* 'felt slippers' plus the
diminutive suffix -*ka* does exist. Consequently, this might actually be a replacement of
derivational suffixes. Providing we are able to detect the derivative -*ki* in more words
of non-SS origin which are not in use in HH and HS with the diminutive suffix -*ka*,
we will reclassify HS -*ki* as a derivational suffix directly borrowed from SS.

As for loanshifting, although we cannot report cases of borrowing of the denotative meaning of suffixes, there are examples of stylistic borrowing. A typical example of stylistic borrowing is the unusually high frequency of diminutive forms in
the speech of bilinguals whose dominant language is Slovak. Clearly, the reason for
this phenomenon is that the use of diminutive forms is far more characteristic of SS
than of HH. However, as HS diminutive forms do exist in Hungarian, and it is usually their higher frequency in HS varieties that is salient, we have a case of one-way
convergence here.

In the SHOH study, informants were asked to choose the more natural of two
sentences which were identical except for one word (for the task in question, see the
translated version of the questionnaire in the Appendix): one of them contained *kenyér*
'bread' and the other *kenyérke*, a diminutive form of *kenyér*. For 37.0% (40 out of 108)
of HS informants the sentence with the diminutive form sounded more natural, while
only 16.0% (17 out of 106) of HH informants chose this as the more natural one (see
Figure 3.2). The difference is highly significant (p < 0.01).

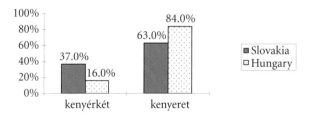

Figure 3.2. The choice of *kenyérke* vs. *kenyér* in the SHOH Project in Slovakia and in
Hungary, respectively

It might also be due to Slovak influence that, within the sample from Slovakia, young people tended to choose the diminutive form in the greatest proportion. The difference was, however, not significant. (It was, though, in the case of another sentence of the questionnaire containing a similar diminutive form).

3.2.4   *Syntactic borrowing*

Elements of syntax are almost exclusively subject to loanshifting. We have no knowledge of borrowed morphemes with a grammatical function, although conjunctions may occur in the Hungarian language use of HS speakers who are exposed to Slovak to a great extent, but these are probably instances of interference or code-switching. The HS question word *mire* 'for what', 'why' (literally "to what"), could count as an example of borrowing of meaning (cf. HH *minek* 'for what', 'why', but *mire* 'to what'), as it closely resembles in its form and meaning Slovak *načo* 'for what', 'why', literally "to what". For example, HS *Mire jöttél ide?* vs. HH *Minek jöttél ide?* 'Why did you come here?' and HS *Mire kell annyit nyafognod?* vs. HH *Miért kell annyit nyafognod?* ' Why do you have to whine so much?'.

3.2.4.1 *Borrowing of arguments.* The effect of SS on the syntax of HS varieties does not usually manifest itself in forms that are absolutely different from those in monolingual varieties. One of the few examples of this, however, is that of borrowing of arguments. By borrowing of arguments, we mean cases where the noun phrase governed by the verb, adjective or noun functioning as the basic constituent of the syntagm in the recipient language takes a new inflectional suffix the meaning of which resembles more closely the meaning of the corresponding suffix in the source language than that of the original suffix in the recipient language. Borrowed arguments in the HS varieties are, for example, HS *operál/műt vkit vmire*, 'operate on somebody's something' (involving the sublative case), ("operate on somebody to something"), e.g. HS *epéjére operálták*, 'his bile has been operated on' cf. SS *operovali ho na žlčník* 'he has been operated on his bile' vs. HH *epéjével operálták* 'he has been operated with his bile' (involving the instrumental case); HS *kulcs vmitől*, 'a key to something' (involving the ablative case), ("a key from something") e.g. HS *ettől a szekrénytől nincs kulcsom* 'I don't have a key from this closet' cf. SS *od tejto skrine nemám kľúč*, 'I don't have a key from this closet' vs. HH *ehhez a szekrényhez nincs kulcsom* 'I don't have a key to this closet' (involving the allative case); HS *vki után jön* ~ *megy* 'come to see somebody' ("come ~ go after somebody"), e.g. HS *a főnök után jöttem*, 'I have come after the boss' cf. SS *prišiel som za šéfom*, 'I have come after the boss' vs. HH *a főnökhöz jöttem* 'I have come to see the boss'. Foreign words may also assume a new argument under Slovak influence, e.g. *interpellál* 'interpellate' is used in the HS printed media as a transitive verb governing accusative case, e.g. HS *interpellálja a minisztert* 'he interpellates the minister' cf. SS *interpelovat' ministra*, 'to interpellate the minister' whereas in HH it is intransitive, governing the allative case, HH *interpellál a miniszterhez* "to interpellate to the minister".

The influence of SS on HS syntax, just like on morphology, is largely a matter of statistical differences. Thus, these are again cases of convergence rather than of borrowing in a stricter sense of the word: under L2 influence, the proportion of contact variants used in HS increases. In the majority of the examples below, only differences in frequency are demonstrable between HS and HH varieties.

3.2.4.2 *Word order.* Most differences between the word order of HS varieties and that of HH are solely differences in frequency, that is, the word order used in the contact varieties of Hungarian spoken in Slovakia exists in Standard Hungarian, too. A well-known exception is the HS expression *Mit én tudom!* 'How should I know!', (literally "What I know!") which is used by HS speakers in this fossilized form, as an idiom, obviously under SS influence (SS *Čo ja viem!* 'How should I know!'). (The corresponding HH expression is *Mit tudom én!*) In some regions, the expression may be rooted in the older, pre-1918 layer of contact-induced features.

As for the differences in frequency, although we targeted a number of issues related to word order in both the SHHS and SHOH projects, we were not able to convincingly demonstrate the contact effect: in the speech communities we investigated, the differences between HS and HH speakers were not significant. Again, we should not rule out the possibility that the mechanism we called overfulfilment of the norm above concealed the contact effect. The constructions involving alternation of attributive adjectival phrases and postposed adjectival phrases (e.g. *Péterrel való találkozás* lit. 'Peter-with be.PART meeting' vs. *találkozás Péterrel* lit. 'meeting Peter-with', both meaning 'meeting with Peter') are an exception, though. Of the two possible word orders, the first one is considered "traditional" and "better Hungarian", while the second one, well-known from Indo-European languages, does exist in HH and is further reinforced by HS speakers' L2, Slovak. In the Slovakia-Hungary High School Project, informants attending schools with Slovak as medium of instruction (group BS) chose constructions involving postposed adjectival phrases in two sentences in significantly higher proportions than HH speakers (group HH), and, with one of the example sentences, we found a significant difference between the two groups from Slovakia (BH and BS); see Figure 3.3.[28] The bilingual students attending schools with Hungarian as medium of instruction used the Indo-European word order to a far lesser extent than HH monolingual students did. It seems to be plausible to assume that their overful-

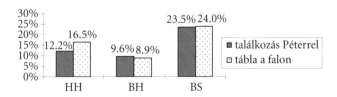

Figure 3.3. The choice of constructions involving attributive adjectival phrases by the three groups of the SHHS Project

filment of the norm neutralized the contact effect (in one case, the difference was not significant, but in the other, it was highly significant).

3.2.4.3 *Reference to one item out of several of the same kind.* In Standard Hungarian, things consisting of several similar or identical items are usually referred to in the singular, as opposed to Slovak and other Indo-European languages, where the plural form is far more usual. This fact may have an influence on the frequency of occurrence of plural forms in HS varieties. For example, with paired parts of the body and the corresponding pieces of clothing, singular forms (like *fáj a lábam* lit. "my leg is aching" for "my legs are aching"; *szorít a cipőm* lit. "my shoe is too tight" for "my shoes are too tight") count as "better Hungarian" than plural forms (*fájnak a lábaim* 'my legs are aching'; *szorítanak a cipőim* 'my shoes are too tight'). Also, names of fruits, vegetables, flowers and a number of other things consisting of far more than two items, are supposed to be used in the singular (*krumplit ültet* 'plant potato' and *almát szed* 'pick apple', is considered more correct than *krumplikat ültet* 'plant potatoes' and *almákat szed* 'pick apples'). Other cases are less clear-cut and ambiguous. For example, in the case of *Ez a szerelő nemcsak tévét, hanem magnót is javít* vs. *Ez a szerelő nemcsak tévéket, hanem magnókat is javít* 'This mechanic repairs not just tv sets but also cassette recorders', it is not clear which variant is "more correct" and "better Hungarian", the first one using singular, or the second using plural forms.

In the Slovakia-Hungary High School Project, a significantly smaller proportion of HS students attending schools with Hungarian as language of instruction than HH students inserted plural forms into the sentence *Kati néninek már rég kihullottak a fogai, és újabban gyakran fáj… a láb… is* 'Aunt Kati lost her teeth long ago and nowadays her leg/legs is/are aching, too'. However, HS students not receiving any kind of formal education in Hungarian filled in the gap with the plural form (*fájnak a lábai* 'her legs are aching') in a considerably higher proportion than either HH students or HS students attending schools with instruction in Hungarian, the difference between the two HS groups being statistically highly significant. Similarly, for the choice in the sentence *Nézd, milyen szép banánt/banánokat árulnak az üzletben* 'Look, what beautiful bananas are sold in the store' (with either 'banana' or 'bananas' in the original), HS students attending schools with Hungarian as language of instruction chose the plural form in a smaller proportion than HH students (although the difference was not significant), while HS students not receiving any kind of formal education in Hungarian opted for the plural form (*banánokat* 'bananas') in a higher proportion than either HH students or HS students attending Hungarian schools, the difference being statistically highly significant compared to both groups (see Figure 3.4). The question of plural versus singular forms of this type of nouns (especially in relation to paired body parts) is fairly widely known because it is part of the school grammar curriculum and is a question of "correct usage" widely discussed by language cultivators. Thus, the apparent lack of contact effect in the BH group is, again, probably due to the overfulfilment of the norm.

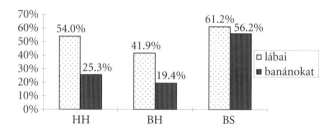

Figure 3.4. The usage of plural forms by the three groups of the SHHS Project

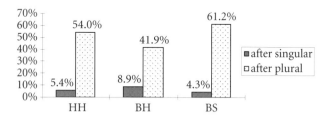

Figure 3.5. The usage of plural forms following singular vs. plural antecedents by the three groups of the SHHS Project

A further factor influencing the occurrence of the plural form is context. In the Slovakia-Hungary High School Project, we elicited the forms *fáj a lába* vs. *fájnak a lábai* in two contexts: in one of them, the informants were asked to use either the singular or the plural form preceded by a phrase in the singular, while in the other sentence, the phrase in question was preceded by one in the plural. The differences between the forms chosen for the gaps in the different contexts were striking for each of the three groups (Figure 3.5).

In the psycholinguistics literature, this phenomenon is called priming and basically means that in the mental lexicon, elements of language affect the access to other, identical or similar, elements in their proximity (cf. Kontra et al. 1990:450).

3.2.4.4 *Number concord.* It is one of the special typological features of Hungarian that nouns following a quantifier are usually in the singular. Exceptions to this rule also exist, though (e.g. *összes művei* or *műve* '(an author's) complete works'). Sporadically, as slips of the tongue, in child language and in some regional dialects, a plural form may occur after other quantifiers in HH too (e.g. *sok házak* 'many houses'), but they do not correspond to the standard norm. As opposed to this, in Slovakia, nonstandard plural forms can sporadically be detected even in the HS printed media (e.g. *sok más irodalmi művek szerzőjéről* 'about the author of many other literary works', *számos olyan létesítményeik vannak...* 'they have several facilities of the kind ...', *az önök számtalan leveleiből* 'from your countless letters', plural morphemes in bold). This kind of concord should, however, be better regarded as an instance of interference rather than

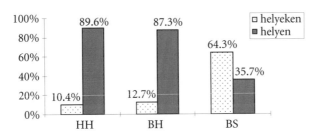

Figure 3.6. The usage of plural vs. singular concord by the three groups of the SHHS Project

of borrowing. The findings of the SHHS Project also seem to justify this claim: HS students attending Slovak schools used the plural *helyeken* 'places' after *számos* 'many, a great number of' as often as students in the other two groups. HH students used the plural form in 10.4% of the cases, HS students attending Hungarian schools did so in 12.7% of the cases, whereas 64.3% of HS students attending Slovak schools did so. While the difference between the answers of HH and HS students was not nearly significant, the difference between those of HS students going to Slovak schools and the other two groups was highly significant; see Figure 3.6 (cf. Lanstyák & Szabómihály 1997:84).

3.2.4.5 *Redundancy induced by obligatory L2-categories.* A possible manifestation of bilingualism is the omission of elements which are a part of L1 but are absent in L2. However, the opposite is also possible: under the influence of L2, categories which are not or not usually marked with a separate morpheme in L1 get increasingly marked.

A salient example of this phenomenon is what in the SHOH study we called feminization. In Hungarian, some occupations, namely, those traditionally associated with women, get the *-nő* '-woman' ending (e.g. *mosónő* 'washerwoman', *óvónő* 'preschool teacher', *varrónő* 'dressmaker'), while others are mostly used in their generic form (that is, without the ending *-nő*), especially if the context or the speech situation make it clear that a woman is being referred to (e.g. *kalauz* 'conductor', *sportoló* 'sportsperson', *egyetemi hallgató* 'university student', *tolvaj* 'thief'). In addition to these, cases in between exist, too; then both forms are equally natural (e.g. *Marika énekes/színész/fodrász* 'Marika is a singer/actor/hairdresser' or *Marika énekesnő/színésznő/fodrásznő* 'Marika is a (female) singer/actress/(woman) hairdresser'). As opposed to this, in Slovak, which makes use of three grammatical genders, it is obligatory to explicitly express the gender of the noun. This fact may influence the frequency of occurrence of nouns with *-nő* ending in the HS varieties.

The subjects of the SHHS Project were asked to insert four names of occupations (*fodrász* 'hairdresser', *tanár* 'teacher', *orvos* 'doctor', and *vegyész* 'chemist') into four sentences, each of which in the context referred unambiguously to a woman. Figure 3.7 shows that the three groups of students in the study chose the nouns with the *-nő* ending in very different proportions. For the HH group, a marked difference

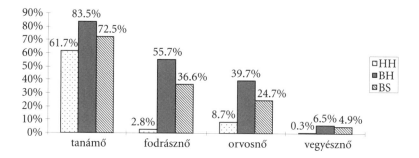

Figure 3.7. The choice of names of occupations with the *-nő* ending by the three groups of the SHHS project

emerged between the use of *vegyésznő* 'female chemist', *fodrásznő* 'female hairdresser' and *orvosnő/doktornő* 'female doctor' on the one hand, and *tanárnő/tanítónő* 'female teacher' on the other hand: while only a few percent of informants used the first three, *tanárnő/tanítónő* 'female teacher' was chosen far more often than its generic counterpart. HS students attending Hungarian schools chose the forms with the *-nő* ending in a considerably higher proportion than HH students, the difference between the two groups being statistically significant for each word (Figure 3.7).

Such extensive usage of femininizing forms is not necessarily only due to the contact situation. Again, overfulfilment of the norm could be at play here, too. This would also account for the fact that HS students attending Hungarian schools by far outperformed HS students going to Slovak schools in the case of each of the four nouns: the former group used the forms with the *-nő* ending far more often than the latter group. Were only the contact effect at play here, exactly the opposite finding would be expected. Names of occupations explicitly marked for gender are more specific and seem therefore "more correct". (The difference between the two HS groups was in one case highly significant, in another slightly significant, and in two cases not significant.)

Another attested case of redundancy induced by obligatory L2 categories is the increasingly frequent use of overt personal pronoun objects. Namely, in Hungarian, it is not obligatory to overtly state the pronominal object because the definite conjugation already expresses the definite object. The SHHS Project provided data on this question through two pairs of sentences: *Tegnap láttalak a tévében* vs. *Tegnap láttalak téged a tévében* 'I saw you on TV yesterday'; and *Találkoztam Hedviggel, és megkértem, hogy vegyen nekem egy kiflit* vs. *Találkoztam Hedviggel, és megkértem őt, hogy vegyen nekem egy kiflit* 'I met Hedvig and asked her to buy a croissant for me'. HH students felt the sentences containing personal pronominal objects more natural in the smallest proportion, HS students going to Hungarian schools did so in a somewhat greater proportion, and HS students attending Slovak schools found those sentences natural most often. The differences between the choices of the three groups were in all but one case highly significant: for the sentence containing the overt second person singular object, no significant difference between HH students and HS students attending Hungar-

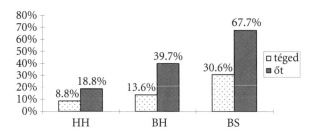

Figure 3.8. The choice of sentences containing overt second (*téged*) and third (*őt*) person personal pronominal objects by the three groups of the SHHS Project

ian schools could be demonstrated (see Figure 3.8). These are textbook examples of contact-induced features indeed.

On comparing the two examples above, it emerges that the occurrence of the overt, theoretically redundant pronominal objects is highly dependent on whether the object is of second or third person. Of course, the discrepancy may be due to yet other factors as well.

3.3 Pragmatic borrowing

In HS, several instances of the borrowing of rules of pragmatics are related to the *tu/vous* issue and the address and greeting terms that go with it. The present situation has predominantly been shaped by the strong rural traditions (the majority of Hungarians in Slovakia live in villages, see Section 1.3 of this chapter) and, of course, by the contact situation. Both in terms of the *tu/vous* issue and that of address terms, HS speakers seem to occupy an intermediate position between HH and SS speakers.

As for addressing one another with "*tu*" forms (H *tegezés*), we can state that HS speakers, primarily young ones, initiate it more easily than Slovaks and without any rituals, even if the interlocutor is of the opposite sex. However, among the older age groups or when the speech situation is of a kind that participants do not have very much in common, it seems to be less usual to use the T-form than in Hungary. As for greeting forms, most HS men greet women according to the time of day, while *csókolom* (literally "I kiss (your hand)", a greeting form used by men to greet women and by children to greet adults, regardless of the time of day) is not as widespread as in Hungary. HS children use *csókolom* all the more often: they greet and take leave from every adult (including preschool teachers) with *csókolom*, while Slovak children greet adults with forms appropriate for the time of day (e.g. *Dobré ráno!* 'Good morning!') and take leave saying *Do videnia!* 'Good-bye'.

Our observations suggest that there are no substantial differences in the use of informal address terms between HS and HH speakers. Addressing somebody with *öregem*-style ('old boy') forms seems, however, to be less widespread than in Hungary, and so are probably forms involving diminutives of the *Sanyikám*-type ('my Sanyi'). The fact that Hungarian formal address terms are often clumsy, unsystematic and, therefore, difficult to use, provides a favorable precondition for L2 influence. As it is almost impossible to appropriately address, say, a bus driver or a conductor in Hungarian (one has at best the indirect option *Legyen szíves* 'Please' plus infinitive or imperative), people sometimes address them in Slovak even in conversations the base language of which is otherwise Hungarian. Alternatively, speakers have the almost universally applicable Hungarian *Főnök úr*, approximately 'Mr. Boss' at their disposal. Addressing women by men is also problematic in Hungarian, which could be the reason for adopting HS *panyika, panyikám* from Slovak (see SS *pani, panika* 'Miss' and 'Ma'am').

The "Hungarian tradition" seems to prevail in the fact that HS teachers tend to call HS students by their first names, whereas it is considered absolutely normal for Slovak teachers to call Slovak students by their family names. Paradoxically, in this case, the contact situation favors the "Hungarian tradition", too: as HS speakers instinctively feel the need to express the natural gender of nouns more often than HH speakers, they are averse to calling women by their family names, which is quite impolite in Hungary. Thus, HS speakers prefer to use the first names of women. On reference to a woman, however, if the speaker does not know the first name of the person in question, and she is an unmarried woman, HS speakers often resort to using forms with the SS *-ová* suffix, such as *Pólyová* and *Ráczová* even if she is Hungarian (to a married woman, HS speakers can refer with *Pólyáné* or *Ráczné*, which neatly solves the problem of expressing the gender of the person, too). For a discussion of the use of *Pólyová* and *Ráczová*-like forms in the interwar period, see Arany's work (Arany 1998:19).

Before 1989, the address terms officially required at school were as follows: *tanító/tanár/igazgató elvtárs* 'comrade teacher'/'director' and *tanító/tanár/igazgató elvtársnő* '(woman) comrade teacher'/'director'. Additionally, the forms *tanító néni* and *tanárnő* both meaning 'school mistress' were also in use. The staff of the Department of Hungarian Studies at Comenius University expected students to use *tanár úr* 'Mr Teacher' in addressing them, and quickly trained freshmen to do so. Also, it is worth noting that Hungarians in Slovakia were under no circumstances willing to use HS *tanító elvtársnő* '(woman) comrade teacher', the required terms of address in preschools in Slovakia, while in Slovak kindergartens its equivalent SS *súdružka učiteľka* was probably entirely general.

The discourse strategies of HH speakers, HS speakers and of other bilingual Hungarians would also be worth studying. So, we would only like to point out a single difference between HS and HH discourse strategies. The usual HH answer to the phone 'I'd like to talk to so and so', in case the person in question answers the phone the answer is *XY vagyok* 'I am so and so', whereas HS speakers say *a telefonnál* 'at the phone', in accordance with the Slovak rule of the same meaning, *Pri telefóne*.

4.   Conclusion

The present state of HS varieties has been an inevitable consequence of the changes that took place in the life of Hungarians of the northern territories of Hungary after the formation of the Czechoslovak Republic in 1918. As our survey only contains a selection of examples, it cannot really reveal how extensive the changes are that have taken place in the past eighty or so years. It is hard to make any generalizations about the extent of the changes, as HS speech communities consist of a number of highly different groups rather than a single homogeneous community (Lampl 1999), whose language habits and, therefore, the language varieties they speak, are also fairly different. Still, it is safe to claim that disregarding the linguistic processes under way in the speech communities currently undergoing language shift and the language use of individuals experiencing language loss, Slovak has had a relatively minor influence on HS varieties so far. Our research has shown that SS can substantially influence HS varieties only where Slovak corresponds to the tendencies of development in the Hungarian language or seems to be in line with their extension or further development. The contact-induced features integrated into the system of language remain relatively isolated that is, they do not affect entire linguistic categories or subsystems (Lanstyák & Szabómihály 1997: 141).

The relatively small impact of SS on HS varieties is mainly due to the nature of the contact situation: its relative shortness in time, (cca. eighty years, disregarding what had happened before 1918 on the regional level);[29] the highly developed sense of ethnicity of the HS community, which lived for a thousand years in a dominant or at least equal position with the Slovaks in the area; and the fact that after 1918, the HS community was able to preserve a part of their existing institutions and organize themselves as a relatively independent community. In this respect, the role of primary and secondary education should be emphasized, which, although it does not completely meet the expectations of the HS community, plays a crucial role both in counterbalancing the efforts of the Slovak state to assimilate the Hungarian minority and in slowing down the divergent linguistic development of the HS community (for empirical evidence, see Lanstyák & Szabómihály 1996a, 1997). Finally, a linguistic factor contributing to the relative unaffectedness of HS varieties by SS is worth mentioning here, even though it is of a lesser importance than the extralinguistic factors discussed above. Namely, the fact that Hungarian widely differs from Slovak may prevent large-scale linguistic interaction between the two languages.

Translated by Helga Arnold F. and Etelka Polgár

Notes

* This paper is based on the research carried out in the Mercurius Research Group and the Gramma Language Office with the support of the Illyés Public Foundation, Zsigmond Telegdi Foundation, Domus Hungarica and János Arany Public Foundation.

1. Following the decision of the peace treaties concluding World War I, the partly Hungarian-populated Subcarpathian territories of today's Ukraine were annexed to Czechoslovakia. We do not discuss this region in this chapter since it is the subject of a separate chapter within this book.

2. We provide census data concerning exclusively the area of what Slovakia is today.

3. According to article 62 of the peace treaty, those who were registered after January 1, 1910, in any of the areas that were annexed to Czechoslovakia could only acquire Czechoslovak citizenship with the consent of the Czechoslovak state (Gyönyör 1993:92).

4. Besides these, 89,179 applications were automatically accepted, since they came from people who declared their nationality Slovak in 1930 as well.

5. The ancestors of Slovaks living in present-day Hungary left the Slovak ethnic region mostly in the 17th and 18th centuries during the inner migration following the expulsion of the Turks, and they moved to southern Hungarian regions depopulated during the wars, mainly to the Great Hungarian Plain.

6. Approximately 15,000 Hungarians lived in the Czech Republic in 2001.

7. Slovak statistics define a settlement heterogeneous in terms of ethnicity in which the rate of a minority population is either above 10% or above 100 people (Gyurgyík 1994:17). This paper, however, regards those settlements as belonging to the Hungarian linguistic area that have at least 10% of Hungarian population (Gyurgyík 1994:17).

8. Experts believe that the approximate number of the Roma is around 250,000–300,000. Gypsies usually declare themselves of Slovak nationality in a Slovak environment, and of Hungarian nationality in a Hungarian environment.

9. *Új Szó* has been published since 1948 and its readership is 3% nationally, whereas the most widely read Slovak language daily has a readership of 12% (source: *Új Szó*, September, 2001).

10. Its national listening rate is 4% (source: the Public Opinion Poll Institution of the Slovak Radio, September, 2001).

11. This totals approximately 0.04% of the Slovak state television's 2 channels' average weekly broadcast time.

12. The Law on the State Language made only the use of the Slovak language possible under official circumstances, and it also restricted the use of minority languages in other fields. It also mandated serious fines for the breach of the law. This law generated international protests (Simon & Kontra 2000). Although some of the measures of the law were repealed by the Constitutional Court and the minority language use law accepted in 1999, most of them are still operative.

13. The needs and demands of minorities (especially those of the Hungarian minority) were completely disregarded in the regional-administrative division of Slovakia (see Hungarians in Slovakia 1997).

14. For the differences between borrowing and shift-induced interference, see Thomason and Kaufman (1988:37–45 and passim).

15. For empirical evidence supporting this claim, see Lanstyák and Szabómihály (1997:92, 96, and 117–118).

16. Although we have knowledge of a number of villages where the language shift from Slovak to Hungarian was completed probably after 1918 (see Liszka 1996:203–204), possible instances of shift-induced interference in their dialects date back to the pre-1918 layer. (These features have, however, not been studied yet.)

17. Over 95% of the 493 informants attending schools with Hungarian as language of instruction reported being of Hungarian nationality. What is more, 21 of the 22 students born in mixed marriages (they made up 4.5% of the entire sample) claimed that Hungarian was their mother tongue and 19 of them reported being of Hungarian nationality as well.

18. Only 80% of these 141 students claimed to be of Hungarian nationality.

19. Informants were asked to fill in the gaps with appropriately conjugated forms of the verbs given in brackets. *Én ritkán ... reggel hétnél tovább (aludni)* 'I rarely ... longer than 7 A.M.' (to sleep); *A főnökkel én is ..., amikor kell. (vitatkozni, jelen idő)* 'I also ... with the boss when I have to.' (to argue, Present Tense); *Nem baj, ha te nem iszol kólát, én azért... (inni, jelen idő)* 'It's fine if you don't drink Coke, but I will...' (to drink, Present Tense). *Ha még egyszer..., nagyon megszidnak (elkésni)* 'If I ... one more time, I'll be told off.' (to be late).

20. Throughout this paper, differences between the answers of two groups are considered highly significant if $p < 0.01$ (i.e. the probability of differences being merely accidental is less than 1 percent), and slightly significant if $0.01 < p < 0.05$ (i.e. the probability of differences being merely accidental is between 1 percent and 5 percent). If $p > 0.05$ (the probability of differences being merely accidental is over 5 percent), the differences are regarded not significant.

21. The example dialogs are presented as follows. Readers find the phonemic transcription of the original conversations first, and then their English translations. In the text of the original, bolded stretches indicate Slovak (the corresponding English translation is given in italics). Analogs (words that are similar in form and meaning in Hungarian and Slovak) are capitalized.

22. Throughout the paper, if the SS or HH equivalents of HS words are not given, those HS words have the same meaning in HS and SS or HH. The translation of HS words is given between single quotation marks, while literal meanings are given in double quotation marks.

23. Slovak has /ɦ/, a voiced glottal, which obviously does not devoice the preceding /v/ (or any other consonant). In both HH and HS, /h/ is voiceless, and devoices the preceding consonant. HS /v/ is an exception in this regard, however, because /h/ may fail to devoice it. The voicing of /h/ that accompanies it does not cause a phonological change because [+/− voiced] is not a distinctive feature of /h/ in Hungarian.

24. In SS, the phoneme /ɦ/ is voiced, in HH (and in HS) it is voiceless. In SS, /a/ is unrounded, in standard HH (and standard HS) it is rounded. (Word-final <y> is merely an orthographic convention, its pronunciation is [i], just like that of HH and HS <i>).

25. On being asked about the sentence she had said, the informant herself explained it as follows: "*Krém* came to my mind first and then I couldn't finish it like *krémláb* ['lotion foot'] but had to say *krém na nohy*." (Némethová 2001:25)

26. For the details of this classification see Lanstyák (2001), and for a shorter English version, see Lanstyák (1999/2000).

27. We have studied the vocabulary of HS varieties in a number of research projects employing various research methodologies (e.g. Lanstyák 1999/2000:18–19 and 2001). Our continu-

ally growing database (the Database of Lexical Contact Phenomena) draws on these research projects.

28. Informants were asked to choose the "more naturally sounding" of the two options. The first sentence of each pair contained a construction involving a postposed adjectival phrase, the second an attributive adjectival phrase, more usual in HH.

29. In the pre-1918 layer of contact-induced features, stronger Slovak and Western Slavic dialectal influence can be demonstrated (Lanstyák 1994a).

CHAPTER 4

Hungarian in Ukraine

István Csernicskó

1. Introduction

The present chapter describes the status and language use of the Hungarian community living in Subcarpathia, Ukraine. The term 'Subcarpathian Hungarians' describes the autochthonous community of Subcarpathia, which is made up of people of Hungarian nationality and/or people whose mother tongue is Hungarian. Subcarpathia is a region of present-day Ukraine. Its territory is 4,942 square miles (roughly the size of Connecticut), and it borders on Poland and the Lviv region in the north, the Ivano-Frankivsk region of Ukraine in the east, Romania in the south, Hungary in the southwest, and Slovakia in the west. It is embraced by the Carpathian Mountains as a natural boundary in the east and the Tisza river winding along the frontier in the south.

2. Sociolinguistic aspects

2.1 The origin of the contact situation

Hungarians have been living in the territory of what is Subcarpathia today since the 9th century. This region was part of Hungary until 1919, and after several 20th century territorial and governmental changes, it is now one of Ukraine's 25 counties (Magocsi 1996:525) (see Map 4.1).

The region was part of the border areas of Hungary, where a wide variety of minorities lived together, thus providing minority contacts of several hundreds of years of history. Language and minority contacts were burdened by differences in religion and ways of life up to the 20th century. Roman Catholic Hungarians and, from the 16th century on, also a gradually increasing number of Protestant Hungarians, inhabited the flatlands of present-day Subcarpathia, while Eastern Orthodox Slavs and Romanians inhabited the highlands. Hungarians primarily lived off agriculture, while the Slavs raised livestock and did lumbering. Until the 20th century, language contacts were mainly characterized by Hungarian having a greater influence on the local Slavic dialects. However, after the post-World War I division of Hungary in 1919 under the Treaty of Trianon, the territory of present-day Subcarpathia was annexed to

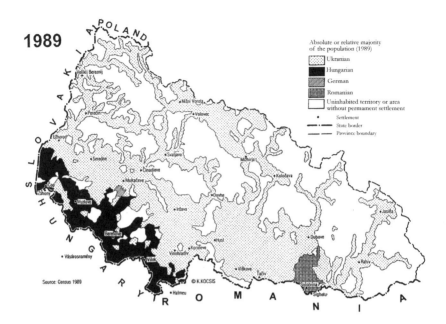

Map 4.1. The ethnic composition of Subcarpathia in 1989. (Source: Kocsis & Kocsis-Hodosi 1998:95)

Czechoslovakia, re-attached to Hungary for a short period in 1938, and then became part of the Soviet Union in 1944. Since the fall of the Soviet Union, it has been part of the sovereign Ukraine, formed in 1991. When Hungarians found themselves in a minority position in their ancestral land, the characteristics of language contact also changed: Slavic language influence on Hungarian became more intensive than before.

2.2 Geography and demographics

Subcarpathia has been an independent geographical and political entity since December, 1918, when the Ruska Kraina autonomous region was formed combining the territories of Bereg, Máramaros, Ung and Ugocsa Counties of Austria-Hungary (cf. *Magyar törvénytár. 1918. évi törvénycikkek*, 396–398).

After World War I, in September, 1919, the Saint Germain Convention declared Subcarpathia's annexation to the newly formed Czechoslovak Republic under the name Podkarpatska Rus'. In November, 1938, in accordance with the Vienna Award of 1938, returning much of the land lost by Hungary under the Treaty of Trianon, the area of Subcarpathia inhabited by Hungarians was annexed to Hungary again.

In 1944 the Allies invalidated the territorial changes brought about between 1938 and 1940 under the auspices of Germany and Italy, and the Soviet army liberated Subcarpathia as part of Czechoslovakia. On November 19, 1944, the Subcarpathian

Ukrainian Communist Party was founded in Mukačevo, and its members passed a resolution about Subcarpathian Ukraine's reunion with the Soviet Ukraine.

On June 29, 1945, the Soviet Union and Czechoslovakia signed a treaty concerning the Soviet annexation of Subcarpathia. On January 22, 1946, the Presidium of the Supreme Council of the Soviet Union rearranged Subcarpathian Ukraine to be the Subcarpathian Region of the Ukrainian Soviet Socialist Republic. Administratively, it has since then consisted of thirteen districts (*rajon* in Ukrainian): the districts of Berehove/Beregszász, Xust/Huszt, Iršava/Ilosva, Mukačevo/Munkács, Velyka Berezna/Nagyberezna, Vinohradiv/Nagyszőlős, Mižhirya/Ökörmező, Perečen'/Perecseny, Raxiv/Rahó, Svaljava/Szolyva, T'ačiv/Técső, Volovec/Volóc and Užhorod/Ungvár, and the regional center, the city of Užhorod/Ungvár.[1]

When Ukraine became independent in 1991, Subcarpathia remained one of the administrative regions of Ukraine called *Zakarpatska oblast'*.

There are no exact and reliable retrospective data about the minorities living in the territory of today's Subcarpathia. Some of the reasons for this are as follows. Subcarpathia as an independent geographical and political entity was formed only in 1918, therefore statistical and demographic surveys concerning this region do not exist from before. Subcarpathia's population experienced several changes of government of various states between 1918 and 1991, and the census data of certain states – because of their different methods – are not always comparable. Due to the changes of state boundaries within the region, the territory of Subcarpathia was also altered, although only to a lesser extent. Some states manipulated the demographic data in their own interests, therefore such data do not always show the real situation. In the former Soviet Union, the statistical data concerning minorities were kept secret.

Although it is very difficult to compare the different census data (because of the different methods, questions etc.), Tables 4.1, 4.2 and Figure 4.1 show that the censuses carried out after changes in Subcarpathia's state affiliation display great differences compared to the previous ones, showing that the political changes greatly influenced the region's minority composition. (In 1880 and 1910, figures are according to mother tongue, after 1921, according to nationality. Census data before 1959 are calculated for the territory of present-day Subcarpathia. 1880, 1910, and 1941 figures are based on Hungarian census results, 1921 and 1930 on Czechoslovak census results, and 1959, 1970, 1979, and 1989 on Soviet census results. Calculations are based on the following works: *Kárpátalja...* 1996; Botlik & Dupka 1993:286; Kocsis & Kocsis-Hodosi 1998.)

In both 1880 and 1910 Hungarian statistics, mother tongue data are given. At the time the Jewish population is believed to have been mainly of either German or Hungarian mother tongue.

According to the 1921 and 1930 census data, the ratio of Hungarians in Subcarpathia decreased, which can be explained by the migration of people due to the post-Trianon political changes (on the one hand, Hungarian civil servants and professionals emigrated to Hungary, while, on the other hand, Czech and Slovak officials settled down in Subcarpathia). When referring to minorities, the Czechoslovak censuses stated that Jews and Gypsies whose mother tongue was mainly Hungarian form

Table 4.1. The population of Subcarpathia 1880–2001, according to mother tongue in 1880 and 1910 and according to nationality since 1921 (in absolute numbers)*

	1880	1910	1921	1930	1941	1959	1970	1979	1989	2001**
Hungarian	102,219	184,789	111,052	116,975	233,111	146,247	151,949	158,446	155,711	151.5
Ruthenian***	239,975	334,755	372,278	446,478	500,264	–	–	–	–	–
Russian	–	–	–	–	–	29,599	35,189	41,713	49,458	31.0
Ukrainian	–	–	–	–	–	686,464	808,131	898,606	976,749	1,010.1
German	30,474	63,561	9,591	12,778	13,222	3,504	4,230	3,746	3,478	3.5
Romanian	–	–	–	–	–	18,346	23,454	27,155	29,485	32.1
Slovak****	7,849	6,344	19,632	34,700	6,847	12,289	10,294	8,914	7,329	5.6
Jewish	–	–	80,117	91,845	–	12,169	10,857	3,848	2,639	no data
Romani	–	–	–	–	–	4,970	5,902	5,586	12,131	14.0
Other	20,763	13,325	19,772	31,531	97,145	6,585	7,515	7,745	8,638	6.8
Total	401,280	602,774	612,442	734,315	850,589	920,173	1,056,799	1,155,759	1,245,618	1,245.6

* Sources: *Kárpátalja ...* (1996), Botlik and Dupka (1993:286), Kocsis and Kocsis-Hodosi (1998), and *Pro kilkist'* (2003).
** 2001 figures are given in thousands.
*** Between 1880–1941 together with Russians and Ukrainians.
**** Between 1921–1930 and between 1959–1979 together with Czechs.

Table 4.2. The population of Subcarpathia 1880–2001, according to mother tongue in 1880 and 1910 and according to nationality since 1921 (in percentages)*

	1880	1910	1921	1930	1941	1959	1970	1979	1989	2001
Hungarian	25.47	30.66	18.13	15.93	27.41	15.9	14.4	13.70	12.50	12.1
Ruthenian**	59.80	55.54	60.79	60.80	58.81	–	–	–	–	–
Russian	–	–	–	–	–	3.2	3.3	3.60	3.97	2.5
Ukrainian	–	–	–	–	–	74.7	76.5	77.75	78.41	80.5
German	7.59	10.54	1.57	1.74	1.550	0.4	0.4	0.32	0.27	0.3
Romanian	1.86	1.90	–	–	1.83	2.0	2.2	2.34	2.36	2.6
Slovak***	1.96	1.05	3.21	4.73	0.80	1.4	1.0	0.76	0.58	0.5
Jewish	–	–	13.08	12.51	9.25	1.3	1.0	0.33	0.21	no data
Romani	–	–	–	–	0.14	0.5	0.5	0.48	0.98	1.1
Other	3.32	0.31	3.23	4.29	0.19	0.6	0.7	0.66	0.69	0.4
Total	100	100	100	100	100	100	100	100	100	100

* Sources: *Kárpátalja* … (1996), Botlik and Dupka (1993:286), Kocsis and Kocsis-Hodosi (1998), and *Pro kilkist'* (2003).
** Between 1880–1941 together with Russians and Ukrainians.
*** Between 1921–1930 and between 1959–1979 together with Czechs.

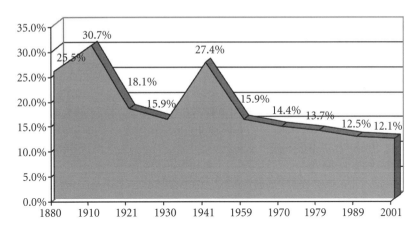

Figure 4.1. Changes in the ratio of the Hungarian population in Subcarpathia between 1880 and 2001

separate minorities. Besides, in this period, several Slavic settlements were formed within the homogeneous Hungarian settlement area near the Trianon frontier, as a result of the agrarian reform of the 1920s when Czechs and Ruthenians were given land nearby Hungarian villages if they moved to the area.

The, again Hungarian, census of 1941 showed new changes in the minority ratios. Hungarian-speaking Jews and Gypsies again were categorized as Hungarians, and Czech civil servants left the area and were replaced by Hungarians.

The first Soviet census in Subcarpathia was carried out in 1959, in which the minority composition of the population was examined. The census data greatly disguised the real situation. The Soviet army occupying Subcarpathia had taken 40 to 60 thousand Hungarian and German males between the ages of 18 and 50 to what was called *malenkij robot* ('little work', i.e. forced labor) to the inner territories of the Soviet Union in accordance with Decree No. 0036 of November 13, 1944 (cf. Dupka 1994: 167).

It is not surprising that we do not have exact data about the number of those taken to forced labor and of those who perished, because these events were kept strictly secret (Dupka 1993: 202, 1994: 167). However, it is true that these deportations influenced the results of later censuses because people were persecuted for their nationality, and many Hungarians, therefore, declared themselves to be Slovaks, Ukrainians, etc. in order to escape deportation (Dupka 1993: 202, 1994: 167).

The 1970 and 1979 censuses indicate a growth in the Hungarian population, but the 1989 census registers a decrease. The decline can be explained by the emigration of Hungarians, on the one hand, while, on the other hand, it is due to the fact that the Gypsies, who had declared themselves to be Hungarians before, admitted their real nationality in 1989 (Jemec & Djačenko 1993: 9; Myhovyč 1997: 47). This is also the reason why the number of Gypsies doubled between 1979 and 1989, while the number of Hungarians showed a relative decrease.

From the census data on mother tongue, we see that mother tongue and nationality are not always identical in Subcarpathia. The majority of those whose mother tongue is not identical with their nationality consider the Hungarian language to be their mother tongue. Thus the number and ratio of people whose mother tongue is Hungarian is higher than the number of people of Hungarian nationality. According to the 1989 census data, based on self-report, the number of people in Subcarpathia whose mother tongue was Hungarian was 166,700, that is 13.3% of the entire population of the region, as opposed to the 12.5% of people of Hungarian nationality. Mother tongue and nationality are identical for 97.2% of Subcarpathian Hungarians. (The modification of nationality composition in the territory of today's Ukraine is summarized in Table 4.3.) The same is true for 98.4% of the Ukrainians, 98.2% of Romanians, and 95.7% of Russians (Botlik & Dupka 1993: 284).

Table 4.3. The ethnic composition of Ukraine (in a thousand people and percentages in 1930, calculated for the territory of present-day Ukraine)*

	1930		1959		1979		1989		2001	
Ukrainian	31,317	(75.0%)	32,158	(76.8%)	36,489	(73.6%)	37,419	(72.7%)	37,541.7	(77.8%)
Russian	3,331	(8.0%)	7,091	(16.9%)	10,472	(21.1%)	11,355	(22.1%)	8,334.1	(17.3%)
Jewish	2,710	(6.5%)	839	(2.0%)	634	(1.3%)	486	(0.9%)	103.6	(0.2%)
Byelorussian	143	(0.3%)	291	(0.7%)	406	(0.8%)	440	(0.9%)	275.8	(0.6%)
Moldavian	327	(0.8%)	242	(0.6%)	294	(0.6%)	324	(0.6%)	258.6	(0.5%)
Hungarian	112	(0.2%)	149	(0.4%)	164	(0.3%)	163	(0.3%)	156.6	(0.3%)
Other	3,846	(9.2%)	1,099	(2.6%)	1,150	(2.3%)	1,263	(2.5%)	1,786.6	(3.3%)
Total	41,776	(100%)	41,869	(100%)	49,609	(100%)	51,452	(100%)	47,457.0	(100%)

* Sources: Botlik and Dupka (1993: 283), Brunner (1995: 85), Dupka (1994: 173), *Bjulleten' Statistiki* 1990(10): 76–79, and *Pro kilkist'* (2003).

Table 4.4. The rate of larger nationalities in Subcarpathia in 1989 and 2001*

Nationality	In Ukraine		In Subcarpathia		Proportion living in Subcarpathia	
	1989	2001	1989	2001**	1989	2001
Ukrainian	37,419,053	37,541,700	976,749	1010.1	2.6%	2.7%
Hungarian	163,111	156,600	155,711	151.5	95.4%	96.8%
Russian	11,355,582	8334,100	49,458	31.0	0.4%	0.4%
Romani	47,917	47,600	12,131	14.0	25.3%	29.2%
Romanian	134,825	151,000	29,485	32.1	21.0%	21.2%
German	37,849	33,300	3,478	3.5	9.2%	12.5%
Total	51,452,034	4,8457,000	1,245,618	1258.3	2.4%	2.6%

  * Sources: Tur (1996), Maco and Luc (1997: 233), and *Pro kilkist'* (2003).
 ** 2001 figures are given in thousands.

It is worth observing the 1989 and 2001 census data separately with respect to Subcarpathia and Ukraine (Table 4.4).

Examining the Subcarpathian data, one can see that the Hungarian minority is the largest one in the region. 22.2% of Ukraine's population was not of Ukrainian nationality in 2001. If we take into account the mother tongue data, we see that only 64.6% of Ukraine's population (33,271,865 people) had Ukrainian as their mother tongue in 1989. The rate of Hungarians within Ukraine was 0.3%. Nationally, 98.4% of the Russian population, 95.6% of the Hungarian population, and 87.8% of the Ukrainian population had their mother tongue and nationality identical.

According to the 2001 census data, of the 156,600 Hungarians living in Ukraine 151,500 (96.7%) live in Subcarpathia (*Pro kilkist'* 2003). Though there are some smaller colonies of Hungarians in L'viv or Dnipropetrovsk, for instance, there are no significant Hungarian communities of more than 1,000 members outside Subcarpathia in Ukraine.

Subcarpathia is linguistically and ethnically heterogeneous. The Hungarians living in Subcarpathia formed a relatively homogeneous block until the end of the 20th century, and the contiguous settlement area has not been completely broken yet (see Maps 4.2 and 4.3). Before the 20th century, due to the different way of life of the Hungarian and Slavic ethnic groups, the Hungarian and Slavic settlement areas overlapped only in a narrow band. The contiguous settlement structure of the Hungarians living in the southern plain of the region started to become more heterogeneous through the settling of the Slavic population.

Though the Hungarian settlement area is a relatively precisely definable unit even today, we can find a number of settlements with mixed populations in Subcarpathia, not only among towns but the villages as well. However, segregation is very much characteristic of cohabitating minorities. This was also demonstrated in the investigation of a Soviet ethnographer, Grozdova (1971: 458) as well.

There are ten settlements of town status in present day Subcarpathia: Užhorod/Ungvár, Mukačevo/Munkács, Xust/Huszt, Berehove/Beregszász, Vinohradiv/Nagy-

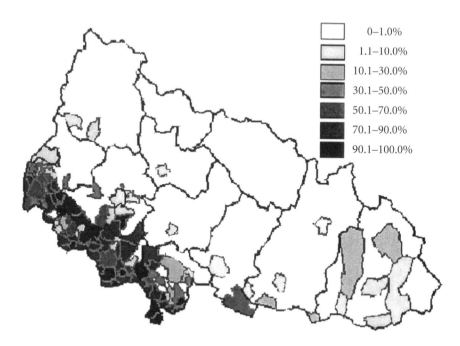

Map 4.2. The ethnic geography of Hungarians in Subcarpathia in 1989. (Source: http://www.htmh.hu/)

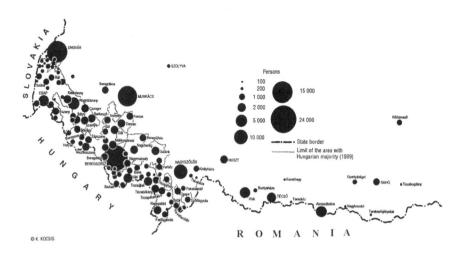

Map 4.3. Hungarian communities in Subcarpathia in 1989. (Source: Kocsis & Kocsis-Hodosi 1998:97)

Table 4.5. The ethnic composition of Subcarpathia according to settlement types in 1989

	In villages		In towns	
Hungarian	111,731	(71.7%)	43,980	(28.2%)
Ukrainian	732,640	(75.0%)	244,109	(25.0%)
Russian	10,714	(21.6%)	38,744	(78.4%)
Other	43,742	(68.6%)	19,958	(31.4%)
Total	898,827	(72.2%)	346,791	(27.8%)

szőlős, Svaljava/Szolyva, Raxiv/Rahó, T'ačiv/Técső, Iršava/Ilosva, and Čop/Csap. In these ten towns Hungarians constituted the largest group in 1900–1920.

If we examine the ratio of town and village inhabitants within certain minorities, we see that the characteristic settlement type of the Subcarpathian Hungarians is the village, and the case is the same with the Ukrainians, while the majority of the Russians live in towns (see Table 4.5).

The Soviet census data broken down according to settlements are inaccessible even now, that is why we can only examine (through the indices of the 1989 census) how Subcarpathian Hungarians are distributed between certain districts.

89% of the Subcarpathian Hungarians live in four districts: the Užhorod, Mukačevo, Berehove, and Vinohradiv districts. These four adjacent districts are situated next to the Ukrainian-Hungarian border, and 85.3% of the Hungarians of Ukraine reside in these. The only district of the region where Hungarians are in a majority is the Berehove District, while in the Vinohradiv District every fourth person is Hungarian, and in the Užhorod District every fifth is. The total population of the four above mentioned districts is 575,267, of whom 139,197 (24.2%) are Hungarians.

The total number of inhabitants of the Užhorod, Mukačevo, Berehove, and Vinohradiv districts without the towns (i.e. Užhorod and Mukačevo) is 375,858 people, of whom 123,305 (32.8%) people are Hungarians. About one third of the total population of the four districts of Subcarpathia (without the two biggest towns) is Hungarian. These 123,305 Hungarians make up 75.6% of the Hungarians living in Ukraine, and 79.2% of the Hungarians living in Subcarpathia. Thus, three-quarters of the Hungarians living in Ukraine and almost four-fifths of the Subcarpathian Hungarians live in a contiguous settlement area.

Nearly half of those recorded as Hungarians in the census live in settlements with 1,000–2,000 inhabitants (24%) or 2,000–5,000 (23%) inhabitants. Only one quarter of Hungarians live in settlements with more than 10 thousand inhabitants and 5.6% in towns over 100 thousand people. In 1989, 71.8% of Hungarians lived in settlements where they formed an absolute majority. In the maintenance of their ethnic awareness, this may be a positive factor: 46.8% of them live in settlements where they constitute over 75% of the population and only 16.1% of them live in places where the Hungarian population makes up less than 25% (Kocsis & Kocsis-Hodosi 1998: 95).

2.3 Policy[2]

2.3.1   *Legal status*

In Ukraine at present, the legal status of the minorities is regulated by the following legal documents: The Constitution of Ukraine (1996), Ukraine's Declaration of Nationality Rights (1991), The Law of Ukraine about National Minorities (1992), and a great number of decrees. Statements concerning only the Hungarian community can be found in various international treaties between Ukraine and Hungary (e.g. the Treaty Between the Hungarian Republic and Ukraine About the Basis of Good Neighborhood and Cooperation, 1991, Declaration of the Principles of Cooperation Between the Republic of Hungary and the Ukrainian Soviet Socialist Republic in Guaranteeing the Rights of National Minorities, 1991) and in the Suggestions of the Ukrainian–Hungarian Between-State Joint Commission.

Articles 11, 24 and 92 of the Ukrainian Constitution touch upon the question of the legal status of national minorities. Article 11 proclaims that the state guarantees "the ethnic, cultural, language and religious development of Ukraine's indigenous peoples and national minorities" (p. 6). Article 24 prohibits discrimination based on race, ethnicity, nationality, and language etc. According to the wording of the text, positive discrimination cannot be implied, either: "There shall be no privileges or restrictions based on race, color of skin, political, religious and other beliefs, sex, ethnic and social origin, property status, place of residence, linguistic or other characteristics" (ibid., p. 12). Article 92 proclaims that the human and civil rights and freedoms of indigenous peoples and national minorities are defined exclusively by the laws of Ukraine.

Article 1 of Ukraine's Declaration of Nationality Rights guarantees equal rights for the national minorities and forbids discrimination based on nationality. Article 2 says that the state takes on itself the creation of circumstances necessary for the development of the language and culture of national minorities. Article 4 permits the use of national symbols.

The Nationality Law of Ukraine declares that human rights and nationality rights are inseparable notions. Article 1 of the Law admits citizens to be equal irrespective of their nationality, and states that the rights of people belonging to national minorities are part of generally accepted human rights. According to Article 3, "Those citizens of Ukraine who are not of Ukrainian nationality and declare their national identity belong to national minorities". Article 11 makes it possible for citizens to freely choose or re-establish their nationality. The Law forbids discrimination on the basis of nationality (Article 18), provides the right of nominating candidates for Parliament and for national organizations (Article 14), and states that separate funds are allocated in the state budget for assisting national minorities.

In the Ukrainian–Hungarian Between-State Basic Treaty signed in 1991, there is only one paragraph, Paragraph 17, that deals directly with the minorities. Without reference to specific documents, the contracting parties proclaim the necessity of the defense of the ethnic, linguistic and religious identity of the national minorities. The text contains a reference to a document signed by the two states before, under the title "Declaration of the Principles of Cooperation Between the Republic of Hungary and the Ukrainian Soviet Socialist Republic in Guaranteeing of the Rights of National Minorities". Four items of the treaty deal indirectly with the minorities. These are about border cooperation, the widening of contacts between citizens and organizations across the border, and about cultural cooperation (*Kárpátaljai Szemle* 1995(8–9): 24–25).

The introductory part of the Basic Treaty states that national minorities live in Ukraine and Hungary, declares their rights on a personal and also on a community level, and considers nationality rights to be a part of human rights. The document names the national minorities as a state-forming element (Paragraph 1). It declares respect for openly admitting and choice of nationality (Paragraph 2). The signing parties take responsibility on themselves for creating conditions for national minorities which provide the right to participate effectively in public affairs (Paragraph 5). The parties promise not to strive for the assimilation of national minorities but create conditions for preserving the identity of the minorities, and admit that the minority organizations express the opinion of minority communities.

In sum, the above mentioned documents declare the existence of national minorities living in Ukraine, they see minority rights as part of human rights, and consider minorities to be a state-forming element. They also forbid discrimination based on nationality, and one document (the Declaration signed by Hungary and Ukraine) mentions not only the individual, but the collective minority rights, too.

Besides the above mentioned documents (in force since 1991), there is a valid resolution (Resolution No. 52 of November 26, 1944, adopted at the first congress of People's Committees of Subcarpathian Ukraine) which declares the collective guilt of the Hungarians, saying that the Hungarians and Germans are eternal enemies of the Ukrainian nation. This resolution served as the ideological basis for the deportation of the Hungarian adult male population in late 1944. A group of Subcarpathian Hungarian intellectuals addressed petitions to the Soviet government in 1971 and 1972, in which they asked for the abrogation of this document (cf. Botlik & Dupka 1991), but the writers of the petitions were called to account, and the resolution remains in force even today. The Subcarpathian Hungarian Cultural Association have asked for the resolution's abrogation several times, but the authorities have not yet taken any steps concerning the matter. Thus, in spite of the above mentioned more recent documents, in Ukraine, Hungarians are still theoretically the enemies of the Ukrainian nation and a collectively guilty people.

2.3.2   *The status of the languages used in present-day Ukraine*

In the independent Ukraine, the following documents concern the status of languages: The Constitution of Ukraine (1996), The Law of the Ukrainian Soviet Socialist Republic About the Languages of the Ukrainian SSR (1989), Ukraine's Declaration of Nationality Rights (1991), The Law of Ukraine about National Minorities (1992), The Law of Ukraine about Local Municipalities (1997) and several resolutions.

Articles 10, 11, 12, 24, 53, 92, 103, 127 and 148 of the Constitution of Ukraine contain paragraphs concerning languages. Article 10 declares that "The state language of Ukraine is the Ukrainian language", and that the state ensures the functioning of Ukrainian in all spheres of social life throughout the entire territory of Ukraine. According to the next paragraph, "In Ukraine, the free development, use and protection of Russian, and other languages of national minorities of Ukraine, are guaranteed". But, in accordance with the last sentence of the Article, "The use of languages in Ukraine is guaranteed by the Constitution of Ukraine and is determined by law". Article 92 says, also, that it is Ukraine's laws exclusively that determine the procedure for the use of languages.

Article 11 contains general declarations about the protection of all nationalities and languages of Ukraine, whereas Article 24 prohibits discrimination based on linguistic characteristics. Article 12 guarantees to meet the requirements of Ukrainians living beyond the borders of Ukraine. Article 53 states that citizens who belong to national minorities are guaranteed, in accordance with the law, the right to receive instruction in their native language, or to study their native language in state or community educational establishments. Articles 103, 127 and 148 say that knowledge of the state language is required for occupying a governmental position (e.g. President of the republic, membership in the Constitutional Court, or office of judge).

According to Articles 10 and 92, with respect to the status of languages, the Language Law passed in 1989 – during the Soviet era – is in force. The Language Law defines Ukrainian as the state language (Article 2), but at the same time Russian remains the language of communication between peoples (Article 4). According to Article 5, the use of the native language or any other language is guaranteed for the citizens of Ukraine; they have the right to conduct their affairs with state or societal organizations and associations, etc. in Ukrainian, in another language used by these organizations, in Russian, or in another language acceptable for both parties. The law does not only prohibit discrimination based on linguistic characteristics (Article 8), but puts forth sanctions for limitations in the use of minority languages. According to regulations, a civil servant who refuses to take an application written in a nationality language with reference to his/her lack of proficiency in that language can be called to account (Article 5).

The law makes it possible to use minority languages equally to and together with the Ukrainian language in the functioning of state authorities, enterprises, and institutions on the territories of administrative units (e.g. villages, towns, districts, and regions) where a greater part of the population belongs to national minorities (Article 3).

State documents are accepted and published in Ukrainian, on lower levels, too, but if need be, they are also published in minority languages. Official forms have to be printed in Ukrainian and Russian (Article 10). The language of office administration is Ukrainian, but it is possible to use a minority language as well as Ukrainian in those areas where a greater part of the population belongs to national minorities (Article 11).

Official personal documents (identity cards, work records, certificates of education, and birth, marriage and death certificates) have to be bilingual in Ukrainian and Russian (Article 14).

The language of services is Ukrainian, or another language chosen by the two parties involved (Article 17). The language of court procedures is Ukrainian, but the use of minority languages is possible in areas where a greater part of the population belongs to a national minority; the person who does not understand the language of the court has the right to request a court interpreter and to give evidence in his/her own native language (Article 18).

The language of services provided by solicitors and prosecutors and that of legal guidance is Ukrainian or another language which is the most appropriate for both parties (Article 23).

The choice of language of education is an indefeasible right (Article 25). But minority citizens can assert this at most up to the end of their secondary school studies. According to Article 25, applicants to institutions of higher and vocational education take their entrance examinations in Ukrainian, and only those applicants are allowed to take an entrance examination in their native language who apply to institutions training minority educators.

The language of official mass media is Ukrainian or other languages of Ukraine (Article 33). The language of address of telegrams, letters, and parcels is Ukrainian or Russian (Article 34).

The language of official announcements, advertisements, and posters is Ukrainian; along with the Ukrainian text there can be translations in other languages, too (Article 35).

The language of labels of goods produced in Ukraine is Ukrainian and those cannot be translated into other languages (Article 36).

The official names of institutions, social and political organizations, and businesses, etc. are in Ukrainian; they can be translated into other languages, and the translation must be placed either under the Ukrainian inscription or to the right of it (Article 37).

Ukraine's geographical names are in Ukrainian. It is also possible to display or indicate them in the language of the national minority (Article 38).

Ukrainian citizens have the right to choose a name appropriate to their national traditions which can be rendered into Ukrainian by means of transliteration (Article 39).

Ukraine's Declaration of Nationality Rights guarantees the right of use of the mother tongue in all spheres of social life for all its peoples and nationalities (Article 3).

According to the Law of Ukraine about its National Minorities, the use of the language of the minority is possible parallel with the official language in the functioning of state and social organizations, enterprises, and institutions in the areas where the national minority makes up a greater part of the population (Article 8). It also guarantees for minorities the use of personal names according to their national traditions (Article 12).

Article 26 Item 1 Paragraph 50 of the Law of Ukraine about Local Municipalities provides the opportunity to local municipalities to choose the language they conduct their work in (*Kárpáti Igaz Szó*, July 3, 1997).

Thus, the state language of Ukraine is Ukrainian, according to the official documents in force. Russian functions as an official language, parallel with Ukrainian throughout Ukraine, and as a language of communication between nations, while the use of the minority languages is allowed in the areas where a greater part of the population belongs to national minorities. But none of the documents contain items where the conditions under which minority languages can be used on a par with the state language would be explicitly determined. However, besides the documents of legal force, there are a number of state and regional decrees regulating the use of language which prove that the rights declared by the law work differently in practice or do not work at all.

Ukrainian has gradually become the state language since the time Ukraine became independent, but Russian – in spite of its being mentioned in the Constitution and the Language Law as a language which can be used in official functions – is declining in the state and official sphere alongside with the expansion of Ukrainian. Thus, disagreements frequently arise between the Russian minority (making up almost one third of the country's population) and the government, which gives preference to a national language policy. The idea of passing a new language law has been formed by both the government and the opposition.

Theoretically, besides the Ukrainian state language or parallel with it, it is possible for Russian and other minority languages to function in the status of an official language (in areas where a greater part of the population belongs to minorities), but this is not the case in reality. We can state that, *de jure* and *de facto* Ukrainian is Ukraine's state language, Russian is of official language status, and people speaking minority languages have the possibility to use their mother tongue in all spheres of social life in those areas where they form a majority according to their nationality. *De facto*, however, despite the administrative prohibitions, Russian is used as an official language in the eastern territories, which are densely inhabited by Russians. Nevertheless, minority languages are only used in education, the minority media (press, radio and television programs), minority public life, church life and the private sphere. Thus, the status of the Hungarian language has not changed much even after Ukraine proclaimed its independence.

On December 9, 1997, the Ukrainian Parliament ratified the Framework Convention about the protection of national minorities. The parts of the Convention about the minority languages practically coincide with the legal documents in force in Ukraine. Item 1 of Article 10, for instance, guarantees the right of native language use for the minorities in private and public spheres of life, in oral and written forms. But Item 2 defines the conditions of the permission of official use of minority languages (Convention 1997).

2.3.3 *Differences of status between the languages*

Kloss (1967:15) distinguishes five different statuses languages can have in society: (1) the language is official in country-wide measures; (2) it is the official language of a larger regional unit (area, district, etc.); (3) minority language use is permitted by authority in public education, public advertisements, although the minority language does not have an official status; (4) there is tolerance towards the language in the private sphere (in the press, church and private schools, etc.); and (5) the language is prohibited from use.

Today in Ukraine the status of Ukrainian has Status One. The status of Russian within certain administrative units *de facto* and *de jure* is close to Status Two, with the restriction that there is no official governmental admission of this, even though it would be legally possible. The status of the Hungarian language can only be examined within Subcarpathia, as it is the only region where a considerable number of inhabitants are Hungarian. In Subcarpathia, the status of the Hungarian language, *de facto*, is at Status Three. Even though its use is somewhat limited, closer to Status Two, but the negative political attitude of the state towards the Russian language's becoming official, and efforts made towards the limiting of mother tongue education of minorities, make it clear that under the present conditions there is not much hope for advance.

The Hungarian language for Subcarpathian Hungarians is mainly the means of communication within their own group, while the Ukrainian and Russian languages are mainly used in communication between different groups.

2.3.4 *Public bilingualism*

According to Article 11 of the Ukrainian Language Law passed in 1989, the language of administration and documentation is Ukrainian, but in those territories (districts, towns, villages, etc.) where minorities form a numerical majority, besides Ukrainian the use of the minority languages is also allowed. Article 5 guarantees for every Ukrainian citizen the right to apply to state, political or social organizations in Ukrainian, Russian or a third language acceptable for both parties. The resolutions of these organizations are written in Ukrainian or another language used by the organization, but if necessary, they can be translated into Russian. According to Article 17, the language of the services is Ukrainian or any language acceptable for the parties involved.

Thus, under legal regulations, theoretically, Subcarpathian Hungarians can use their mother tongue in official functions. Yet, the declared rights and the real situation do not always coincide. It is because the Language Law does not require that the official organizations use the languages of minorities, it simply does not prohibit it. This use is dependent on conditions the explicit explanation of which can be found nowhere in the Law. For instance, it is unclear what the law understands by the term 'nationality majority area', as it is not defined in the Law.

The possibilities provided by the Language Law are made use of in the Berehove District where 67% of the population is Hungarian. Administration is conducted in

Hungarian only in this district, but mainly only orally, and written official communication in Hungarian is not common or general even in this district.

In other districts of Subcarpathia, Hungarian written official documents (e.g. form registers, minutes of staff meetings, etc.) are produced only in schools with Hungarian as the language of instruction. In villages with a Hungarian majority, in state offices and village councils, it is only oral communication that is carried out in Hungarian.

The lack of Hungarian or bilingual Ukrainian–Hungarian forms makes official written management or documentation in Hungarian impossible (*Kárpáti Igaz Szó*, October 24, 1996:4).

2.4   Economic standing

Agriculture is the dominant sector of the economy of Subcarpathia, which, considering all sectors, is of low efficiency and characterized by outdated technical standards and poor organization. The existing urban industry has deteriorated and been cut back in recent years. Per capita production in the region is less than half of the national average. A decline in production, which lasted until 1999, affected 70.5% of the country's enterprises and had a negative effect on the population's income. A revival of the economy began in 2000, the decline in agricultural production was arrested, and industrial production rose by 12% compared to the previous year.

Due to a lack of a suitable business environment and capital, privatization mainly involves small and medium size enterprises. According to local figures from July 1, 1997, foreign capital of over $40 million has been invested in the region, a mere 2.5% of the foreign capital invested in the whole of Ukraine. One out of three companies operates currently with foreign capital. Investors and company shareholders from Hungary are in the first place, with over 110 Ukrainian–Hungarian joint ventures in Subcarpathia.

71.7% of the Hungarian minority lives in small villages and is engaged in jobs of lower social prestige due to a lack of schooling in the mother tongue. Hungarians are threatened by unemployment more than Ukrainians or Russians. Official figures show a rather favorable situation of unemployment: they demonstrate that the rate of unemployment was 1.4% in 1996 and 2.49% in 1997. The figures, however, fail to reflect a realistic number of the unemployed, as only one in ten unemployed persons seeks assistance from job centers (i.e. the actual rate of unemployment is at least ten times higher). Regarding the rate of unemployment, Subcarpathia is 9th of the 24 Ukrainian counties. As the number of the jobless increases, fewer and fewer people are entitled to unemployment benefits, since companies have been freed of the obligation to contribute to employment funds. Social problems are further aggravated by hidden unemployment (forced leaves, shortened shifts, and shortened working hours) and by often several-month-long delays in the payment of salaries, caused by a continuous decline of production.

The average salary in Subcarpathia is 180 Hrivnja (about $40) a month, lower than the national average. Most food products are imported by entrepreneurs from Hungary and Slovakia and are sold from privately owned outlets or markets (the average price of a pound of pork is $1.25, while a quart of milk costs $0.25, and a quart of cooking oil is between $1 and $1.5).

A revival of agriculture and the development of private farms is hindered by the fact that the ownership of land has not been solved. If a land act makes it possible, co-operative farms based on real ownership may emerge relying on farmers' groups that have formed in the villages of the Hungarian minority over the past few years to replace state farms.

Setting up a special economic region in Subcarpathia could favorably affect the social and economic situation of the population. The standard of living could increase, which would slow down a trend of emigration of the Hungarian minority (more on which see, for instance, the *Report on the Situation of Hungarians in Ukraine*).

2.5 Identity awareness

A sociological investigation carried out in 22 Subcarpathian settlements with the participation of 300 subjects (E. Kovács 1996) has arrived at the conclusion that the image of the native land in the case of Subcarpathian Hungarians is quite contradictory. According to the investigation, the subjects believed that Ukrainian independence has brought more bad than good so far. Only 1.4% of those asked accepted Ukraine as their native land, 1.4% accepted Europe as their native land, and only 1% would have preferred to live in the Soviet Union again. According to the survey, 5.2% of the subjects feel at home in the whole of the Hungarian-speaking territory. 8.2% of the people surveyed view Hungary as their native land. The fact that 10.7% of the subjects feel they have no native land demonstrates the feeling of uncertainty and the foreignness of the environment. Analyzing the image of native land of Subcarpathian Hungarians, E. Kovács (1996) comes to the conclusion that the population of the region has created its own, narrowed notion of native land, "according to which the motherland is not a country but a broken piece of the real native land that once existed, a narrower region: that territory where one lives according to one's own traditions, where one uses one's own mother tongue and forms a community with the representatives of one's own nation" (my translation). It is that image of native land, according to the analyst, which 71.8% of the subjects accepted. At the same time, it seems to be a contradiction that 53% of the subjects reported that they or their relatives were or had been thinking about emigrating to Hungary (p. 18).

A similar study was carried out as part of the Sociolinguistics of Hungarian Outside Hungary (SHOH) project (see the description in Kontra, this volume), where 144 Subcarpathian Hungarian subjects were asked to answer the following question: "How much are you attached to the following places: your native village or town; Subcarpathia; Ukraine; the former Soviet Union; Hungary; Europe; and nowhere. By

Table 4.6. The attachment of Subcarpathia Hungarians to various places

	1		2		3		4		5	
	N	%	N	%	N	%	N	%	N	%
Own town/village	1	(0.7%)	2	(1.4%)	16	(11.1%)	39	(27.1%)	86	(59.7%)
Subcarpathia	–	–	–	–	12	(8.3%)	42	(29.2%)	90	(62.5%)
Ukraine	82	(56.9%)	28	(19.4%)	23	(16.0%)	6	(4.2%)	5	(3.5%)
Soviet Union	65	(45.1%)	34	(23.6%)	35	(24.3%)	6	(4.2%)	4	(2.8%)
Hungary	4	(2.8%)	5	(3.5%)	42	(29.4%)	53	(37.1%)	39	(27.3%)
Europe	14	(9.9%)	9	(6.3%)	30	(2.1%)	40	(28.2%)	49	(34.5%)
Nowhere	140	(97.9%)	1	(0.7%)	1	(0.7%)	1	(0.7%)	1	(0.7%)

(N=144)

Table 4.7. The national attachment of Subcarpathia Hungarians

	1		2		3		4		5	
To the Subcarpathian Hungarians	–		1	(0.7%)	15	(10.4%)	35	(24.3%)	93	(64.6%)
To the Hungarian Nation	1	(0.7%)	2	(1.4%)	12	(8.3%)	22	(15.3%)	107	(74.3%)
Not attached to any place	139	(96.5%)	1	(0.7%)	1	(0.7%)	2	(1.4%)	1	(0.7%)

(N=144)

circling the appropriate numbers, rate the following on a 1–5 scale (where 1 = I am not attached to it at all; 5 = I am very much attached to it)." (See Table 4.6.)

Other questions in the questionnaire asked subjects to define in the same way how much they are attached to the Subcarpathian Hungarian community, to the Hungarian nation, and how much they feel they do not belong anywhere. The answers demonstrate that the awareness of belonging to the Hungarian nation is very strong (cf. Table 4.7), but this feeling is not necessarily accompanied by a close attachment to Hungary as a state.

The results of the two investigations briefly described above are almost exactly the same. The minor differences can be explained by the time difference between the two studies and the different ways of sampling. According to the investigations, the image of the native land of Subcarpathian Hungarians is connected to the native geographical region and not to the state. Hungary occupies a particular place, but the attachment to it as to a symbol of the Hungarian nation is rated higher than to that of Hungary as a state. The uncomplying separation from the new Ukrainian statehood is the direct result of the despair caused by the country's appalling economic state.

2.6 Language attitudes

In the SHOH questionnaire there were six questions directly or indirectly targeting language attitudes. Question 62 has inquired about whether Subcarpathia Hungarians have a positive or negative opinion on their own language variety, while question 71 about whether or not the speakers had an experience of facing the differences between the language variety spoken in Subcarpathia and in Hungary. Questions 72 and 73–75 have directly asked about linguistic features in which, according to the speakers, there is a difference between local language use and language use in Hungary.

The responses show that Subcarpathia Hungarians have a positive attitude towards their own language varieties. We received 136 responses to the question "where do you think is the most beautiful Hungarian spoken?", of which 76 speakers (that is, 55.9%) chose Subcarpathia out of the indicated areas as the place where Hungarian is spoken most beautifully. 53 speakers (39%) claimed that the most beautiful Hungarian is spoken in Hungary, and out of these 53 speakers, 33 (24.3% of speakers) stated that within Hungary, the most beautiful Hungarian is spoken in Budapest. 7 speakers (5.1%) claimed that Hungarian is spoken most beautifully in Transylvania.

The majority of the speakers, therefore, have a positive attitude towards their own language variety, for more than half of the interviewed speakers claimed that the most beautiful Hungarian was spoken in Subcarpathia. This result proves to be positive for the linguistic future of the community, since one of the reasons of language shift may be the negative attitude of speakers towards their own language variety (see, for instance, Gal 1979, 1987).

Subcarpathia Hungarians have a positive attitude towards the Hungarian language and its varieties spoken in Subcarpathia. In the spring of 2000, 595 Hungarian high school students in Subcarpathia were asked in a questionnaire survey to decide which language was more beautiful, the Hungarian or the Ukrainian language. 69% regarded Hungarian as more beautiful, 2% found Ukrainian more beautiful, and 29% claimed to find both languages equally beautiful. At the same time, 84% of the speakers stated that it was easier to function in Ukrainian than in Hungarian in Subcarpathia. 92.8% of the 595 subjects believed that the teaching of the Ukrainian language was necessary in Hungarian schools, although only 22.6% of them thought that it was possible to learn Ukrainian in school, while 38% thought it was possible to learn only to some extent.

In the survey, 88.1% of the speakers said they would like to learn Ukrainian, 10.8% would not really like to learn Ukrainian, and only 1% of the speakers claim that they do not wish to learn Ukrainian at all.

The overwhelming majority, 84.7%, of Hungarian high school students in Subcarpathia believe that the Hungarian language should be taught in Ukrainian schools in Subcarpathia, and only 15.3% think that it should not. 29.1% of those supporting the teaching of Hungarian claim that it is important to have Hungarian taught in Ukrainian schools because "we are the autochthonous people here", whereas 55.6% would like to have Hungarian taught on a mutual basis, that is, because "we are learning their language, too".

60.3% of our high school students agree that Hungarians living in Ukraine have to learn Ukrainian. In addition, 70.6% of the speakers agree that it would be appropriate for Ukrainians in Subcarpathia to learn Hungarian.

Motivation has a major role in the acquisition of a foreign language, so our subjects were asked why it was necessary to study Ukrainian. According to the answers, good grades in school only motivate 2.3% of the subjects and 20.2% think Ukrainian should be studied because it is the official language of Ukraine. The majority, 77.2%, study Ukrainian in order to have better opportunities in their lives after high school.

We were also interested in the surveyed students' parents' attitude towards their children being taught Ukrainian in school. The overwhelming majority, 91.3%, of the parents believed that it was essential to acquire the Ukrainian language in order to have better opportunities later on, and only 3.4% thought that their children should not be required to study Ukrainian.

2.7 Domains of language use

Studying the organizing principles behind language use according to domains of language use provides valuable insight into the functions and status of a given language, and the relationship of the language within a bilingual or multilingual setting.

2.7.1   *The private sphere*

The answers given by a sample of 144 persons in the SHOH project indicate that Subcarpathia Hungarians use almost exclusively the Hungarian language in communication with family members. Besides Hungarian, Russian and Ukrainian are also used with friends and neighbors. However, the common language has an essential role in selecting the circle of friends (see Table 4.8).

The majority of the speakers, 96%, use Hungarian for writing private letters, however, 14% and 10% of speakers also write private letters in Russian and Ukrainian, respectively.

Newspapers and magazines are generally read in Hungarian by almost all of the speakers (that is, 94%), whereas about one-third of the speakers also read Russian and Ukrainian papers (34% in each case). Literature is read primarily in Hungarian (that is, by 85% of speakers), although one-fourth of the speakers (that is, 24%) read poems and novels in Russian, while 16% in Ukrainian as well.

Table 4.8. Languages used in informal encounters by Subcarpathia Hungarians*

	Hungarian		Russian		Ukrainian		Other	
with parents	144	(100%)	3	(2%)	3	(2%)	–	–
with grandparents	142	(99%)	3	(2%)	–	–	–	–
with children	92	(94%)	4	(4%)	5	(5%)	–	–
with partner	100	(93%)	6	(6%)	4	(4%)	–	–
with friends	139	(97%)	65	(45%)	63	(44%)	2	(1%)
with neighbors	132	(92%)	40	(28%)	67	(47%)	–	–

(N = 144)

* Some of the lines here and in other tables as well have a sum exceeding 100%, because if speakers used more than one language in a given domain, they were instructed to put an X in more than one box.

Table 4.9. The language of radio programs listened to and television programs watched by Subcarpathia Hungarians

	Hungarian		Russian		Ukrainian		Other	
	N	%	N	%	N	%	N	%
Films	140	(97%)	98	(68%)	85	(59%)	8	(6%)
Entertainment programs	139	(97%)	66	(46%)	53	(37%)	3	(2%)
Sports	120	(89%)	70	(52%)	72	(53%)	9	(7%)
News	135	(94%)	41	(29%)	55	(39%)	1	(1%)
Weather forecast	136	(95%)	18	(13%)	52	(36%)	2	(1%)

(N=144)

Table 4.10. The language use of Subcarpathia Hungarians in the inner domain

	Hungarian		Russian		Ukrainian		None	
Praying	130	(90%)	1	(1%)	–	–	14	(10%)
Counting	144	(100%)	12	(8%)	8	(6%)	–	–
Swearing	81	(56%)	51	(35%)	35	(24%)	63	(44%)
Thinking	144	(100%)	10	(7%)	6	(4%)	–	–
Talking to animals	141	(98%)	13	(9%)	12	(8%)	–	–

(N=144)

Practically all speakers watch Hungarian programs on television, although many claimed to watch films, entertainment programs, news, etc. in Russian and Ukrainian as well, as is shown in Table 4.9.

Subcarpathia Hungarians use almost exclusively the Hungarian language in what could be called the inner domains of language use (praying, thinking, counting, talking to animals, and swearing). The only exception is swearing, as 56% of the speakers swear in Hungarian, and besides Hungarian, 35% of them also swear in Russian, and 24% in Ukrainian as well (see Table 4.10).[3]

2.7.2 The public sphere

Among public domains, language use in church has a very important role in the life of minorities. An overwhelming 88% of speakers read the Bible and other religious texts in Hungarian, while only few read these in Russian (4%) and Ukrainian (3%) as well (and 12% of speakers do not read religious literature at all).

Half of the speakers (that is, 49%) use Hungarian in cultural organizations, while 18% use Russian, and 15% Ukrainian as well. This rate is somewhat different in restaurants, where slightly over one-third of the speakers (38%) claimed to use the Hungarian language, approximately half of them (54%) use Russian, and, 39% use Ukrainian as well (see Table 4.11).

21% of speakers use the Hungarian language in banks, whereas 62% and 42% choose Russian and Ukrainian, respectively.

Table 4.11. The language use of Subcarpathia Hungarians in entertainment places, restaurants, and cultural organizations

	Hungarian		Russian		Ukrainian		None	
In restaurants	55	(38%)	77	(54%)	56	(39%)	30	(21%)
In other places of entertainment	49	(34%)	63	(44%)	50	(35%)	45	(31%)
In cultural organizations	71	(49%)	26	(18%)	22	(15%)	61	(42%)

(N = 144)

Table 4.12. The language use of Subcarpathia Hungarians at the workplace

	Hungarian		Russian		Ukrainian		Other	
hardly ever or never	23	(16%)	27	(19%)	59	(42%)	138	(99%)
sometimes	27	(19%)	69	(49%)	22	(15%)	–	–
often	92	(65%)	46	(32%)	61	(43%)	2	(1%)

(N = 144)

In case of language use at the workplace, Hungarian is often used by 65% of the speakers, sometimes used by 19%, and 16% of the speakers hardly or never use it (see Table 4.12).

One-third (that is, 33%) of the speakers write letters and do other writing in connection with their profession in Hungarian, 49% claimed to plan these writings in Russian and 29% in Ukrainian. The language of professional literature is Hungarian in the case of 46%, although half of the speakers read it in Russian, 40% in Ukrainian, and 4% read professional literature in other languages as well.

2.7.3 Administrative venues

Nearly a quarter, 24%, of the speakers write official letters and applications in Hungarian, although the majority, that is, 56% and 41% use Russian and Ukrainian, respectively, as well.

The language of administrative venues (government and town hall offices etc.) is Russian and Ukrainian according to the majority, that is 58% and 52% of the speakers, respectively, although there are speakers (19%) conducting their official affairs in Hungarian.

A quarter (that is, 26%) of the speakers stated that they have never had any encounter with the police. 45% use the Russian language and 43% the Ukrainian language with the police. Hungarian is only used by a mere 7% of the speakers in contacting the police. 79% of the speakers have no personal experience concerning language use in court. 12% of the speakers use Russian, 8% Ukrainian, whereas 7% use Hungarian there as well.

2.7.4 Summary of domains of language use

Language use in the family is dominated by the use of the Hungarian language, and this dominance is also a characteristic of the whole private sphere, although Russian and

Ukrainian do have an important role in communication with neighbors and friends, in reading newspapers, listening to radio, and watching television programs. These three languages are almost equally used in public domains. It is interesting to note that while in villages the use of the Ukrainian language is more frequent than the use of the Russian language, this distribution is reversed in cities. This can be explained with the fact that, first, in Subcarpathia, as in the whole of the former Soviet Union, people of Russian nationality comprise the most urbanized population, and second, resettlement policies in the Soviet era were targeted towards towns. Mainly Russian-speaking people and other nonautochthonous minorities were brought to the towns who did not speak the local languages, i.e. Ukrainian and Hungarian in this case.

The use of the Hungarian language is the least prominent at administrative venues. According to data presented above, there are three main groups of domains within the Hungarian community in Subcarpathia. The first group includes domains in which the great majority (at least 60%) of speakers use the Hungarian language exclusively. These include the following domains: communication and contact with family (parents, grandparents, children, partners), private correspondence, cultural life (participation in cultural organizations, reading literature and newspapers), religious life, and, out of what has been labeled inner domains of language use, counting, thinking, and talking to animals.

The second group includes domains in which the majority (at least half) of the speakers indicated a mixed use of the Hungarian language and the majority languages (i.e. Russian and Ukrainian). Communication and contact with friends and neighbors, watching television (primarily movies and sports programs), language use in sports activities, at shops, the post office, and the doctor's office are all included in this group, along with language use at professional venues, at the workplace, and in swearing.

The third group of domains involves those in which the speakers mainly use the majority languages. Restaurants, banks, offices, the police, and the court belong to this category. Such organization of language use domains also indicates that the Hungarian language is primarily dominant in the private sphere, whereas majority languages are mainly used in domains related to the state and offices. Mixed language use is shown in domains outside the private sphere and that part of the public sphere where no official rules and regulations determine the use of a given language in a specific situation, and so, on-the-spot norms of language choice determine the use of one language or the other (for instance, language use between a Hungarian shop assistant and a Hungarian customer).

2.8 Language proficiency

The area of what Subcarpathia is today has been a multi-nationality area since early times, and, thus, bilingualism has a strong tradition in the region. We know little about the linguistic situation before the 20th century, however, some earlier written documents show that bilingualism was present in the region even, for instance, in the 17th century.

Besides mother tongue, question 9 of the questionnaire used in the 1989 (Soviet era) census conducted in the territory of Ukraine asked about fluency in any language of the (former) Soviet Union.[4]

In 1989, according to the census results, 976,749 of the total 1,245,618 inhabitants of Subcarpathia regarded themselves of Ukrainian nationality and 961,489 of them claimed Ukrainian as mother tongue. 11,338 others also chose Ukrainian as mother tongue, so altogether 972,827 persons stated in the census questionnaire that their mother tongue was Ukrainian. 48,106 speakers (that is, 17.6%) of the 272,791 non-Ukrainian mother tongue inhabitants of Subcarpathia stated that they spoke Ukrainian fluently. In 1989, together with Ukrainian mother tongue speakers, 1,020,933 persons, that is, 81.9% of the population of Subcarpathia claimed to speak Ukrainian. On the other hand, together with the native speakers of Russian, 732,556 persons, that is, 58.8% of the total population spoke the Russian language fluently in Subcarpathia in 1989, and, based on self-evaluation, 53.7% (more than half!) of the non-native speakers of Russian spoke Russian (while 514,516 persons, that is, 41.3% of the total population believed that they did not speak any language besides their mother tongue). Out of the 155,711 Hungarian nationality inhabitants of Subcarpathia, 65,718 (that is, 42.2%) stated that they spoke the Russian language. Despite the fact that Ukrainians constitute the majority in the region, only 17,723 Hungarians (that is, 11.3%) stated that they spoke Ukrainian fluently, so a lot more Hungarians indicated a proficiency in Russian than a proficiency in Ukrainian. This is most probably due to the fact that during the Soviet era the Russian language was mandatory at every educational level, while the teaching of the Ukrainian language was required only in Ukrainian schools and practically not taught at all in Hungarian schools. 72,178 Subcarpathia Hungarians claimed that they spoke only Hungarian (see Table 4.13).

Table 4.13. Subcarpathia residents' fluent proficiency in another language of the former Soviet Union in addition to mother tongue*

Nationality	Number	Speak Russian as well	%	Speak Ukrainian as well	%	Only speaks mother tongue	%
Ukrainian	976,749	575,627	(58.9%)	–	–	392,031	(40.1%)
Hungarian	155,711	65,718	(42.2%)	17,723	(11.3%)	72,178	(46.3%)
Russian	49,458	–	–	21,813	(44.1%)	26,125	(52.8%)
Romani	12,131	3,440	(28.3%)	1,265	(10.2%)	7,412	(61.0%)
Romanian	29,485	15,056	(51.0%)	994	(3.3%)	11,809	(40.0%)
Slovak	7,329	3,781	(51.5%)	2,081	(28.3%)	1,457	(19.8%)
German	3,478	1,333	(38.3%)	1,580	(45.4%)	560	(16.1%)
Jewish	2,639	853	(32.3%)	1,079	(40.8%)	669	(25.3%)
Other	8,638	4,239	(49.0%)	1,571	(18.1%)	1,275	(14.7%)
Total	1,245,618	670,046	(53.7%)	48,106	(3.0%)	514,516	(41.3%)

* Source: 1989 census data.

Table 4.14. The self-reported language proficiency of Subcarpathia Hungarians

	Hungarian		Russian		Ukrainian		Other	
native level	127	(88.2%)	3	(2.1%)	–	–	–	–
very well	10	(6.9%)	23	(16.0%)	10	(6.9%)	–	–
well	6	(4.2%)	62	(43.1%)	48	(33.3%)	4	(2.8%)
not very well	1	(0.7%)	47	(32.6%)	39	(27.1%)	5	(3.5%)
a few words	–	–	5	(3.5%)	27	(18.8%)	4	(2.8%)
don't speak only understand	–	–	2	(1.4%)	11	(7.6%)	1	(0.7%)
don't speak it at all	–	–	2	(1.4%)	9	(6.3%)	130	(90.3%)

(N = 144)

According to the self-report figures of the 1989 census, more than half (53.3%) of Subcarpathia Hungarians speak at least one majority language fluently (Table 4.13). If we take into account that these figures include the elderly and the children living in these Hungarian-majority settlements, this rate is not low at all. It is also important to note that in the box of the census questionnaire asking about language spoken fluently besides mother tongue, only one other language could be indicated, so those speakers who believed they spoke more than one language besides their mother tongue could only mark one of them.

7 years after the 1989 census, in the course of the Sociolinguistics of Hungarian Outside Hungary project conducted in the summer of 1996, the language proficiency of the population of Subcarpathia was also surveyed. Altogether 144 speakers from four different types of settlements answered the question inquiring about what level they thought they spoke Hungarian, Russian, and Ukrainian at, 95% of the speakers claimed that their knowledge of Hungarian was either very good, or native level. An overwhelming majority of the speakers (91%) indicated their knowledge of Russian between the levels not very good and very good, however, only two-thirds of the speakers (67%) claimed to have a similar level of proficiency in Ukrainian. In case of Hungarian speakers, the lower level knowledge of Ukrainian compared with the knowledge of Russian is also indicated by 6.3% of the speakers stating that they spoke a few words in Russian, whereas 32.7% of the speakers marked the same level proficiency in Ukrainian (see Table 4.14).

In their answers to the question regarding the ability to read and write in Hungarian, Russian, and Ukrainian, 97% of the speakers claimed being able to read and write in Hungarian, and 3% claimed they could only read in Hungarian. The rate of speakers who can read and write in Russian is almost the same as the rate of speakers who are able to read and write in Hungarian (95.8%), but considerably fewer speakers, 56%, can read and write in Ukrainian as well, 30% of speakers can only read Ukrainian, and 14% are illiterate in Ukrainian.

2.8.1 *Language proficiency and social variables*

The Chi-square test did not show a significant relation between language proficiency and the sex of the speakers. Age showed a significant relation with the self-assessed level of Ukrainian language proficiency by indicating that the middle-aged speak Ukrainian significantly (at the $p<0.05$ level) better than the young and the elderly. The educational level has an effect on proficiency in both Russian and Ukrainian (significant at the $p<0.01$ and $p<0.05$ levels, respectively). The college-educated speak both languages significantly better than those with primary and secondary education. Settlement type influences proficiency in Russian (significant at the $p<0.05$ level), that is, speakers living in cities speak Russian better than those living in villages. The ethnic composition of the given place of residence has a significant effect (at a $p<0.01$ level) on both Russian and Ukrainian proficiency, which means that speakers living in Hungarian-majority settlements regarded their knowledge of Russian and Ukrainian lower than speakers living in a Hungarian-minority settlements.

2.8.2   Language proficiency and dominance

It is difficult to define language proficiency with the closed questions of a questionnaire used in a research study. It is highly possible, for instance, that a speaker who has claimed to have a *very good* knowledge of the Russian language would also claim to have problems with using it in situations where s/he generally uses Hungarian (for instance, when speaking about one of the most intimate topics, that is, his/her own health), as is demonstrated by the following conversation, recorded as part of the project:

(1)   Fieldworker (FW): *Tehát ott tartottunk, hogy orvosnál, bár sose kelljen, de milyen nyelvet használnál?*
Subject (Su): *Nagyon kevés a magyar orvos. Lényegében mindenki kiment. Nem tudom, az orosz orvosok talán azér nem mennek ki, mer ugye elkerülhetetlen, hogy tudják a nyelvet, de, de hát tényleg nézz körül, akikhez jártál eddig Beregszászba vagy Ungvárra, vagy akárhol. Senki, egy orvos nincs a régiek közül. És nem a jók maradnak itt.*
FW: *És a régiek? Azokkal milyen nyelven?...*
Su: *Magyarul. Persze, hogy magyarul.*
FW: *És ez hol?*
Su: *Beregszászba.*
FW: *Beregszászba. És mondjuk, ha oroszul, oroszul el tudod mondani, hogy mi a bajod, ez nem okoz nehézséget?*
Su: *Hát látod, ha ilyen területekre kerül a társalgás, akkor már nagyon nehéz megfogalmazni, hogy, hogy mit akarsz, vagy hogy mi fáj, vagy... Elmutogatja az ember, hát ezér van a keze. Vagy ha végigtapogat, akkor jajgatsz nagyokat, és akkor úgyis észreveszi.*
"Fieldworker (Fw): So, I hope you never have to go to the doctor's, but in case you do, what language would you use there?
Subject (Su): There are few Hungarian doctors. Actually, everybody has emigrated. I don't know, maybe the Russian doctors don't emigrate because it is unavoidable for them to know the language, but, but really, look around

those to whom you have been going to in Berehove and Užhorod, or anywhere. Nobody, there is not a single doctor there out of those who had been there earlier. And it is not the good ones who stay here.

Fw: And what about the earlier ones? What language did you use with them?…

Su: Hungarian. Of course, Hungarian.

Fw: And this was where?

Su: In Berehove.

Fw: In Berehove. And, let's say, if Russian, in Russian you could tell what your problem is, wouldn't that be hard for you?

Su: Well, you see, if the conversation gets to a topic like this, it becomes very difficult to say what you want, or to express what hurts, or… One can use gestures to express this, since this is what hands are for. Or if the doctor examines you with the hand, you may say 'ouch', and they will notice it anyway."

This can happen the other way around as well, that is, communication problems may arise in situations where the speaker generally uses the second language, so it is hard for him/her to use the mother tongue. The excerpt below serves as an example of this.

(2) Subject: *Egy nyelv inkább szokás, mint tudás. És a szakmai szinten ez megjelentkezik. Mondjuk hit terén, vallásos, vallás terén, vallási szférába jobb a magyar. Ööö … ilyen hétköznapi szférába, mondjuk filológiai szférába, de mondjuk zenei, a zenei szakmát ukránul sajátítottam el, így mondjuk ott, mondjuk a szakterminusokat… Mer magyarul nem kicsinyített szeptakor, hanem szűkített szeptakor, oroszul viszont kicsinyített, tehát gondolkodnom kell, hogy nehogy tükörfordítást alkalmazzunk, és ilyen téren néha az ember megáll, hogy elgondolkozzon, hogy mit használjon. Ez, ez előáll.*

Subject: "Language is more of a habit than knowledge. And this is apparent on a professional level. For instance, in case of faith, religious, religion, in the religious sphere, Hungarian is better. Erm … in an everyday sphere, let's say, in the philological sphere, or for instance, in music, I acquired the musical profession in Ukrainian, so let's say there, let's say the professional terms… Because in Hungarian it is not a "reduced septet chord", but a "diminished septet chord", however, it is called a "reduced septet chord" in Russian, so I have to think not to use a calque, and so in such a domain, one stops to think what to use. This, this happens."

Therefore, it is possible that a speaker may communicate in a given language more easily in one situation, whereas s/he would prefer the use of another language in another situation.

3.   Linguistic aspects[5]

3.1   Code-switching

Code-switching is defined as "the process whereby bilingual or bidialectal speakers switch back and forth between one language or dialect and another within the same conversation" (Trudgill 1992:16). Grosjean's definition is similar, he defines code-switching as "the alternate use of two or more languages in the same utterance or conversation" (Grosjean 1982:145). In this paper, I define code-switching as switching between two languages.

In the bilingualism literature, code-switching is discussed as one of the characteristics of bilingualism, and it is often referred to as the means for expressing identity, defining roles in a given group, or indicating a situational change. For instance, Gumperz (1982:70) states the following: "code-switching occurs in conditions of change, where group boundaries are diffuse, norms and standards of evaluation vary, and where speakers' ethnic identities and social backgrounds are not matters of common agreement." Gal (1988:247) gives this definition: "code-switching is a conversational strategy used to establish, cross or destroy group boundaries; to create, evoke or change interpersonal relations with their accompanying rights and obligations".

According to personal observations and tape recorded interview sessions, code-switching is not a characteristic feature of a situation in which a Hungarian person is talking to another Hungarian in the Hungarian speech community in Subcarpathia.[6] This is most probably due to the fact that most Subcarpathia Hungarians live in a homogeneous block, have a steady sense of identity, and use exclusively the Hungarian language in communication within the group. Therefore, in an interaction between two Hungarians in Subcarpathia, context and change in roles are not primarily indicated by code-switching between languages.

The interviews show that in an interaction between two Hungarians in Subcarpathia, out of the many types of code-switching, quotation occurs most frequently in the Hungarian community.

Some examples are as follows, with code-switching into Russian in (3) and (4), and into Ukrainian in (5):[7]

(3)   Subject: *Egyszer a vonaton jöttünk Ungvárról és a provodnyiknak feljebb állt, kérdezte, van-e jegyem, én meg magyarul mondtam, erre rámszólt, és mondtam:* **jeszty, forma.**
"Once we were traveling by train from Užhorod, and the provodnik [conductor] was all worked up, and he asked me if I had a ticket, and I answered in Hungarian, and then he snapped at me, and I replied: **jest', forma** ['I do, I'm uniformed.' = 'I work for the railway.']."

(4)   Subject: *Orosz osztályban tanítok. Valamit magyaráztam, magyar gyerekek is vannak az osztályban, annak mondtam magyarul, rámszóltak:* **Tak eto russzkij klassz.**

Subject: "I teach in a Russian class. I was explaining something; there are some Hungarian children in the class, so I gave an explanation to them in Hungarian. The children commented on this and said: **Tak ètò russkij klass** ['This is a Russian class']."

(5)   Fieldworker: *Rászóltak-e Önre, hogy ne beszéljen magyarul?*
      Subject: *Ilyen még nem volt, de azt már mondták, hogy ne beszéljek oroszul, mert **vi zsivete na Ukrajini, a ne u Rossziji.***
      Fieldworker: "Have you ever been told not to speak in Hungarian?
      Subject: This has not happened before, but I have been told not to speak in Russian, because **vy živete na Ukrajini, a ne u Rossiji** ['you live in Ukraine, not in Russia']."

It is important to note that in the above quoted examples the subjects mentioned two instances of situations where communication was not between Subcarpathia Hungarians. In these examples, code-switching can be interpreted as the expression of identity, where besides support and making the message of the given utterance more authentic, code-switching also expresses an "us vs. them" relationship, that is, "we are using Hungarian within the group, but it is impossible to speak in Hungarian with people outside the group." This indicates that in other situations, for instance, in a linguistically heterogeneous company, code-switching is a more frequent phenomenon than in a linguistically homogeneous one.

The examples below contain instances of code-switching within the category of quotations, although they can be interpreted as repetitions as well.

(6)   Fieldworker: *Hogy szerepel a neved a személyigazolványodban?*
      Subject: *Oroszul mondjam?*
      Fieldworker: *Ahogy a személyigazolványodban szerepel.*
      Subject: *Nagy Melinda. **Nagy Melinda.***
      Fieldworker: "How is your name written in your identity card?
      Subject: Should I say it in Russian?
      Fieldworker: As it is written in your identity card.
      Subject: Nagy Melinda. **Nad' Melinda.**"

(7)   Fieldworker: *És melyik iskolában tanítasz?*
      Subject: *Ungvári Gyermekművészeti Iskola. Ez a címe. Ungvári Gyermekművészeti Iskola. **Uzshorodszkaja gyetszkaja skola iskussztv** orosz nyelven.*
      Fieldworker: "And what school do you teach at?
      Subject: Užhorod Children's Art School. The name is: Užhorod Children's Art School, **Užhorodskaja detskaja škola iskusstv** in Russian."

(8)   Fieldworker: *A neved a személyi igazolványodba hogy szerepel?*
      Subject: *Mármint az orosz változatát?*
      Fieldworker: *Igen.*
      Subject: ***Tovt Szilvija Zoltanova.***
      Fieldworker: "How is your name written in your identity card?

Subject: You mean the Russian form?
Fieldworker: Yes.
Subject: **Tovt Sil'vija Zoltanova.**"

In these examples the speakers repeated the Russian and/or Ukrainian official name or entry in Russian and/or Ukrainian, respectively, during a conversation in Hungarian.

In the course of the statistical analysis, due to the relatively small number of elements, I could not apply the Chi-square test to see whether or not there was a correlation between the code-switching occurrences during the interviews and social variables. (However, without statistics I can state that in the data, there were no recorded occurrences of code-switching in case of elderly speakers living in Hungarian-majority settlements.) This, of course, does not mean that code-switching does not involve any kind of social stratification within the Hungarian community in Subcarpathia. It can only be stated that due to various reasons (for instance, the research method chosen was not the most appropriate for the study of code-switching), the present research could not indicate the factors influencing code-switching. This can probably be explained by the fact that these interviews do not contain instances other than interactions between two Subcarpathia Hungarians. Further research is needed to study the frequency of code-switching occurrences in other speech situations, and what types of code-switching can be observed, etc.

3.2 Linguistic characteristics[8]

3.2.1 *Lexical borrowing*

Lexical borrowing is practically the only contact-induced feature that has been investigated in connection with the Hungarian language varieties in Subcarpathia. Several vocabulary lists have been compiled and published which contained Russian and Ukrainian words that the authors believed were used among Subcarpathia Hungarians (for instance, Drávai 1969; Horváth 1991, 1998; Csernicskó 1995). In addition, we encounter loanwords discussed in many papers on dialects (for instance, Fodó 1973; Kótyuk 1973). Kótyuk (1973) is the first and only work that gives a monographic analysis of the Ukrainian loanwords in a dialect of Hungarian in Subcarpathia. Monographs by Rot (1968:255–256) and Lizanec (1970:38–39) also contain lists of loanwords, and the volumes of the dialect atlas of Subcarpathian Hungarian dialects (Lizanec 1992, 1996) also include some borrowed elements. However, besides registering the words, these sources do not provide any information on, for instance, the use and the frequency of occurrence of these loanwords. Moreover, the majority of the authors condemn loanwords and label them as unnecessary and needless elements.

According to the present stage of research, I cannot state that we know considerably more about the borrowed elements of Hungarian language varieties in Subcarpathia now than we knew before, because the systematic and methodologically well-established studies targeting them are yet to be carried out.

In connection with Hungarian language varieties in Subcarpathia, Kótyuk (1973) carried out a classification of Ukrainian loanwords of a Hungarian dialect in Subcarpathia according to semantic fields. He found 247 loanwords he qualified as of Ukrainian origin and grouped them into 21 semantic fields. The interesting part of his classification is that he put only 2 words into his category of "state, social, and political life", whereas he put 64 words into the category of "people, their description, and characteristics." This is most probably because he registered the Ukrainian loanwords of village communities, which mostly belong to the category of old Ukrainian (Ruthenian) loanwords according to Lizanec (1993a, 1993b), who also provides a further explanation, namely: "The number of new [i.e. post-1945] Ukrainian elements in Hungarian dialects in Subcarpathia is very small. This is because the Russian language was dominant compared to Ukrainian in both schools and workplaces" (Lizanec 1993b: 54, my translation). This paper, therefore, simply cannot include the grouping of loanwords used in the Hungarian community of Subcarpathia according to semantic fields. I only intend to bring examples for the several types of loanwords from the SHOH project corpus.

In the language contact literature, it is considered a language universal that in a language contact situation, characterized by borrowing rather than by shift-induced interference, the elements most easily borrowed from one language to the other are nouns, verbs, and adjectives. The overwhelming majority of lexical borrowings in Hungarian language varieties in Subcarpathia are also nouns and adjectives (see Kótyuk 1973, 1995: 8–9, and see further below).

3.2.2 Loanwords proper

The most generally encountered elements in the vocabulary lists of linguistic works concerning the issue of lexical borrowings of Subcarpathia Hungarians are loanwords proper.

As part of the SHOH project, speakers mentioned the following loanwords characterizing Hungarian language use in Subcarpathia: SuH *bánka* 'fruit jar' (vs. HH *befőttes üveg*), SuH *batri* 'battery' (from Russian *batarejka* 'dry battery'; vs. HH *elem*), SuH *blánka* '(printed) form' (vs. HH *űrlap*), SuH *bulocska* 'pastry' (vs. HH *péksütemény*), SuH *dogovor* 'contract' (vs. HH *szerződés*), SuH *dovidka* '(e.g. doctor's) certificate' (vs. HH *igazolás*), SuH *elektricska* 'commuter train' (vs. HH *HÉV*), SuH *gorszovet* 'city council' (vs. HH *önkormányzat*), SuH *grecska* 'buckwheat' (vs. HH *hajdinakása*), SuH *gripp* 'flu' (vs. HH *influenza*), SuH *jászli* 'nursery school' (vs. HH *bölcsőde*), SuH *kocsegár* 'heater [person]' (vs. HH *fűtő*), SuH *kraszovki* 'sneakers' (vs. HH *edzőcipő*), SuH *kriska* 'jar lid' (vs. HH *fedél*), SuH *májka* 'T-shirt' (vs. HH *pólóing*), SuH *obsi* 'dormitory' (from the Russian word *obščežitije* 'student's or worker's dormitory'; vs. HH *kollégium*), SuH *ocsered'* 'line, standing in line' (vs. HH *sor*), SuH *pácska* 'package' (vs. HH *csomag*), SuH *paszport* 'identification card' (vs. HH *személyi igazolvány*), SuH *pedszovet* 'faculty meeting' (vs. HH *tanszéki értekezlet*), SuH *práva* 'driver's licence' (vs. HH *jogosítvány*), SuH *prokuror* 'prosecutor' (vs. HH *ügyész*), SuH *provodnyik* 'conductor' (vs. HH *kalauz*), SuH *szágyik* 'kindergarten' (vs. HH *óvoda*), SuH *(med)szesztra* '(medical) nurse' (vs. HH *nővér*), SuH *szok* 'fruit juice' (vs. HH *gyümölcslé*), SuH *szoljárka* 'diesel oil' (vs. HH *gázolaj*), SuH *szosziszki* 'wiener' (vs. HH *virsli*), SuH *szprávka* '(e.g. doctor's) certificate' (vs. HH *igazolás*), SuH *sztolova* 'cafeteria' (vs. HH *menza*), SuH *ucsi* 'technical or vocational school' (from the Russian word *učilišče* of the same meaning; vs. HH *szakiskola*)), SuH *váfli* 'wafer biscuit' (vs. HH *nápolyi*), etc. These words are generally well-known in the Hungarian community in Subcarpathia and occur frequently in the spoken language. They hardly ever occur in the written language, or if they do, they are merely used for stylistic purposes, for they are strongly stigmatized in the language cultivation literature (see Kótyuk 1995: 8–9; Horváth 1991, 1998, etc.). Moreover, they are also stigmatized by the speakers themselves, who are trying to avoid using them in more formal styles.

It is interesting that speakers only mentioned words of Russian origin and words that can be attributed to Russian. The only word of obviously Ukrainian origin is *dovidka* '(e.g. doctor's) certificate', whose counterpart of Russian origin of the exact same meaning, *szpravka*, however, also sometimes occurs. The explanation lies in the fact that similarly to Hungarian, the Ukrainian language was practically considered a minority language in Subcarpathia until the declaration of independence of Ukraine in 1991. The Ukrainian language has legally been the official language since the passing of the 1989 Law on Language and the Constitution, but established Russian loanwords have remained in use. It is likely, however, that the change in the status of languages is going to be reflected in the lexicon as well, that is, the number of Ukrainian loanwords might increase in the Hungarian language use in Subcarpathia.

3.2.3   *Loanforms*
Loanforms are considerably less stigmatized in Subcarpathia Hungarian than direct borrowings. Generally well-known loanforms in the Hungarian community in Subcarpathia include, for instance, SuH *agronóm* 'agronomist' (vs. HH *agronómus*), SuH *archív* 'archive' (vs. HH *archívum*), SuH *bufet* 'buffet' (vs. HH *büfé*), SuH *diplom* 'university degree' (vs. HH *diploma*), SuH *dokument* 'document' (vs. HH *dokumentum*), SuH *gruzin* 'Georgian person' (vs. HH *grúz*), SuH *infarkt* 'heart attack' (vs. HH *infarktus*), SuH *internát* 'boarding-school' (vs. HH *internátus*), SuH *invalid* 'physically disabled person' (vs. HH *rokkant, invalidus*), SuH *konzerva* 'canned food' (vs. HH *konzerv*), SuH *referát* 'presentation' (vs. HH *referátum*), SuH *sláng* 'sprinkling hose' (vs. HH *slag*), etc.

3.2.4   *Loanblends*
The are also very few loanblends, for instance, SuH *főszesztra* 'head nurse' (vs. HH *főnővér*), SuH *kibrakkol* 'throw out' (vs. HH *kidob*), SuH *povorotnyiklámpa* 'turn signal' (vs. HH *indexlámpa*), etc. in the Hungarian language varieties in Subcarpathia.

3.2.5   *Borrowing of meaning*
Some examples of borrowing of meaning in the language of the Hungarian community in Subcarpathia are the following: SuH *csenget* 'ring, phone [vb]' (vs. HH 'ring

(bell)'), SuH *deficit* 'shortage' (vs. HH 'deficit'), SuH *dolgozik* 'work [with inanimate subject]' (vs. HH 'work [with animate subject]', SuH *fal* '1. wall; 2. wardrobe' (vs. HH 'wall'), SuH *egyedül* 'you [V-address]' (vs. HH 'by oneself'; *maga* 'you [V-address]'), SuH *emelet* 'level' (vs. HH 'floor, except ground floor'; *szint* 'level'), SuH *kiírat* 'subscribe' (vs. HH 'have somebody put on medical leave'; *előfizet* 'subscribe'), SuH *kimenő* 'day off' (vs. HH 'servant's day off'; *szabadnap* 'day off'), SuH *metodista* 'methodologist' (vs. HH 'Methodist'; *módszertanos* 'methodologist'), etc. All of these have one or more common meanings in Hungarian, Russian and/or Ukrainian, in addition, Subcarpathia Hungarians use these words in a given meaning of a word's equivalent in the second language, which is unknown in the standard variety of Hungarian spoken in Hungary.

An interesting example of borrowing of meaning is the word *szoknya* 'skirt', which is, influenced by the Russian word *jubka* 'skirt' used in Subcarpathia Hungarian in sports to describe the passing of the ball between soccer players in a way that one player kicks the ball further between another player's legs. In Hungarian as spoken in Hungary, the word *kötény* 'apron' is used to describe the same thing. See the excerpt illustrating this below in (9).

(9)   Fieldworker: *Mit mondanak másképpen Kárpátalján, mint Magyarországon?*
      Subject: *Én focizok Magyarba egy csapatba, oszt mondom egyszer, amikor átvittem a labdát a védő lába között, hogy na, haver, kaptál egy szoknyát. Erre az nevetett, azt mondja, az nem szoknya, hanem kötény. Mink meg itthol szoknyának mondjuk, mer azoktul a srácoktul, oroszoktul tanultam, hogy **jubka**, akikkel együtt fociztam az ungvári csapatba.*
      Fieldworker: "What is said differently in Subcarpathia than in Hungary?
      Subject: I play soccer on a team in Hungary, and I said once, when I passed the ball between the defender's legs, that, well, buddy, you got a skirt. And the player was laughing and said that it was not a skirt but an apron. And we call it a skirt here at home, because I learned it from those guys, those Russians, that it was **jubka**, those guys I played soccer with on the Užhorod team."

The use of the word *tanító* with the meaning of 'educator' is very particular in Subcarpathia. In standard Hungarian, the word *tanító* means 'primary school teacher', but in Subcarpathia, secondary school teachers are often called *tanító*, too, because neither Russian, nor Ukrainian differentiates between primary and secondary school teachers, for both are named with the word *učitel'* (for a similar phenomenon in the Hungarian language varieties in Slovakia, for instance, see Lanstyák 1998:43). In question 631 of the SHOH project questionnaire, the speakers had to complete the following sentence with a name of an occupation: *Anyám egy középiskolában tanít, ő tehát …* 'My mother teaches in a secondary school, so she is a…..' (for a translated version of the part of the questionnaire containing the language tasks, see the Appendix). 49% of the 144 speakers in Subcarpathia completed this sentence with the words *tanár/tanárnő* 'teacher [male]/teacher [female]', 2.8% of the speakers used the word *pedagógus* 'educator', and 48.2% of speakers used the words *tanító/tanítónő* 'primary school teacher [male]/primary school teacher [female]'.

Some of the borrowings of meaning are used as standard elements in Subcarpathia (for instance, they are used in the local papers as well) and most probably some of them are going to be included in the lexical material representing the variety of standard Hungarian in Subcarpathia in the revised edition of the Explanatory Dictionary of Hungarian to be published (see Beregszászi 1997; Csernicskó 1997).

3.2.6   Calques and calqued expressions

The following words are examples of calques and calqued expressions occurring in the Hungarian language used in Subcarpathia: SuH *átfordít* 'translate' (lit. 'turn over'; from Russian *perevesti* 'translate', lit. 'take over'; vs. HH *lefordít* 'translate', lit. 'turn down'), SuH *(pénzt) cserél* 'exchange (money)' (lit. 'change (money)'; from Russian *menjat'* (*dengi*) 'change (money)'; vs. HH *(pénzt) vált* 'exchange (money)'), SuH *(kérdést) felad* 'ask (a question)' (lit. 'give up a question', from Russian *zadat' vopros* 'give up a question'; vs. HH *(kérdést) feltesz* 'ask (a question)', lit. 'put up a question'), SuH *(vizsgát) lead* 'pass (an exam)' (lit. 'give down an exam', from Russian *sdat' èkzamen* 'pass an exam', lit. 'give down an exam'; vs. HH *(vizsgát) letesz* 'pass (an exam)', lit. 'put down an exam'), and SuH *leesik* 'fall' (lit. 'fall down', from Russian *upast'* 'fall down'; vs. HH *elesik* 'fall', lit. 'fall over'), etc. (see Kótyuk 1995:10–11 as well).

3.2.7   Phonological borrowing

The contact induced features on the level of phonology and phonological borrowing are probably the least investigated part of Subcarpathia Hungarian. Due to the lack of experimental phonetic measurements and detailed investigations, I can only summarize the scarce relevant discussions of the issue in the literature.

The shortening of long vowels and consonants in the Hungarian dialects in Subcarpathia is considered a contact-induced feature by Rot (1967:190, 1968:256), Horváth (1976), and Horváth and Lizanec (1993:57). Rot (1968:263) and Kótyuk (1995:8) describe phonemic borrowing, although both authors agree that borrowed phonemes only occur in loanwords. According to Rot, the Russian and Ukrainian /x/, whereas according to Kótyuk the palatalized /ʎ/ and the unrounded /a/, occur in the pronunciation of "mostly those who did not go to Hungarian schools or grew up in heterogeneous families" (Kótyuk 1995:8, my translation) in loanwords like, for instance, *xozjajstvo* 'farmstead', *pel'meni* 'pelmeni, i.e. beef dumplings', *zaj a va* 'application', etc.

3.2.8   Grammatical features

The influence of the Russian and Ukrainian languages on the morphology and syntax of the varieties of Hungarian in Subcarpathia is mainly a statistical issue (see Lanstyák 1998:61), that is, a matter of difference in frequency of use of various features. Therefore, I discuss this separately as differences in frequency of occurrence in the next subsection.

3.2.9   Differences in frequency of occurrence

Code-switching and borrowing belong to the most apparent effects of bilingualism. However, differences in frequency of occurrence are much more hidden. Differences in frequency of occurrence mean that, under the influence of their second language, bilingual speakers use certain linguistic elements significantly more frequently (or, sometimes, less frequently) than monolingual speakers.

3.2.10   Analytical vs. synthetic constructions

During the course of its history in the Carpathian Basin, the Hungarian language has had immediate contact with analytical Indo-European languages, which entails the past and present effects of the tendency towards the preference for analytical constructions over synthetic ones in the Hungarian language variety, even in the standard spoken in Hungary (see Kossa 1978:5–6; Herman & Imre 1987:524; Szathmári 1988:40–41). Moreover, there are analytical structures in Hungarian that can be regarded as the result of internal development (see Grétsy & Kovalovszky 1983:1247). As part of the SHOH project, we supposed that the frequency of occurrence of analytical structures is higher in the Hungarian language varieties in Subcarpathia which have close contact with two Indo-European languages (namely Russian and Ukrainian) than in case of Hungarian spoken in Hungary. Russian and Ukrainian are analytical languages, while the agglutinative Hungarian language belongs among synthetic languages. The literature on Hungarian mentions analytical structures as a phenomenon closely related to bilingualism or at least some kind and degree of language contact (see Lanstyák & Szabómihály 1997:78; Lanstyák 1998:7). The Hungarian language cultivation literature in Subcarpathia also discusses analytical constructions as contact induced features (Kótyuk 1991:69, 1995:11).

In the SHOH questionnaire, sentences 532 and 603 compare compounds, while sentences 507 and 613 compare derived words with analytical structures. In sentences 514 and 536 we investigated the replacement of the derivational suffix -hat/-het with auxiliaries, that is analytical structures (Table 4.15).[9]

Out of the six investigated variable types, sentence 536 showed a higher rate of standard answers in Subcarpathia (although this difference was not significant), while in case of the others, the rate of standard answers was higher in Hungary. The difference between the two samples is significant at the $p < 0.05$ level.

3.2.11   The singular and plural forms of nouns

The differences between the use of the singular and plural forms of nouns is considered one of the most typical differences between the Hungarian and the Slavic languages of neighboring countries (Grétsy & Kovalovszky 1985:295).

In standard Hungarian, paired body parts and classes of identical or similar objects are usually named in the singular (Tompa 1969:516; Grétsy & Kovalovszky 1985:295), while in Russian and Ukrainian, the plural is used in similar cases (see P. Csige 1993:381).[10] Paired body parts are usually referred to in plural form in Subcarpathian Hungarian dialects (Horváth & Lizanec 1993:72). We investigated the use of the sin-

Table 4.15. Subcarpathia Hungarians' versus Hungary Hungarians' responses to analytical versus synthetic structures

		Subcarpathia (N = 144)		Hungary (N = 107)		p <
532	standard *bankszámláján*	37	(25.9%)	39	(36.4%)	–
	nonstandard *banki számláján*	106	(74.1%)	68	(63.6%)	
603	standard *légterét*	71	(49.3%)	97	(90.7%)	0.01
	nonstandard *légi terét*	73	(50.7%)	10	(9.3%)	
507	standard *buszozást*	89	(62.2%)	86	(80.4%)	0.01
	nonstandard *utazást busszal*	54	(37.8%)	21	(19.6%)	
613	standard *szépítkezett*	91	(63.2%)	84	(80.0%)	0.01
	nonstandard *szépítette magát*	53	(36.8%)	21	(20.0%)	
514	standard *kimehetek*	136	(94.4%)	104	(97.2%)	–
	nonstandard *ki tudok menni*	8	(5.6%)	3	(2.8%)	
536	standard *kinyithatom*	123	(85.4%)	87	(81.3%)	–
	nonstandard *ki tudom nyitni*	21	(14.6%)	20	(18.7%)	
The average of standard answers		547	(63.4%)	497	(77.6%)	0.05

Table 4.16. Subcarpathia Hungarians' versus Hungary Hungarians' responses to the singular versus plural forms of nouns

		Subcarpathia (N = 144)		Hungary (N = 107)		p <
		N	%	N	%	
505	standard *banánt*	90	(62.9%)	94	(87.9%)	0.01
	nonstandard *banánokat*	53	(37.1%)	13	(12.1%)	
604	standard *autóban*	85	(59.4%)	93	(86.9%)	0.01
	nonstandard *autókban*	58	(40.6%)	14	(13.1%)	
626	standard *fáj a lába*	97	(67.8%)	93	(94.9%)	0.01
	nonstandard *fájnak a lábai*	46	(32.2%)	5	(5.1%)	
The average of standard answers		272	(63.4%)	280	(89.7%)	0.01

gular and plural forms of nouns with three variable tokens, with sentences 505, 604, and 626 in the SHOH questionnaire (Table 4.16).

The rate of standard answers in case of all three variables was significantly higher in the sample from Hungary. (The difference between the two samples is significant at the p<0.01 level.) Lanstyák and Szabómihály (1996a: 119) and Szabómihály (1997: 81) had similar results from their comparative study concerning the language use of high school students in Slovakia and Hungary.

3.2.12 *Number agreement*
The verb-governed adjectival complements of plural subjects or objects may be in either singular or plural form in the Hungarian language, although Hungarian language cultivators prefer the singular form, as it is regarded the traditional form (Grétsy &

Table 4.17. Subcarpathia Hungarians' versus Hungary Hungarians' responses to number agreement

		Subcarpathia (N = 144)		Hungary (N = 107)		p <
		N	%	N	%	
506	standard *önzővé*	58	(40.3%)	75	(70.1%)	0.01
	nonstandard *önzőkké*	86	(59.7%)	32	(29.9%)	
601	standard *komolynak*	66	(45.8%)	75	(70.1%)	0.01
	nonstandard *komolyaknak*	78	(54.2%)	32	(29.9%)	
The average of standard answers		124	(43.0%)	150	(70.1%)	0.01

Kovalovszky 1983:815–816). Therefore, in the SHOH study we also regard this as the primary variant. However, in Eastern Slavic languages plural agreement is obligatory in this case. This phenomenon was studied through two sentences, 506 and 601, in the SHOH project (Table 4.17).

The rate of the plural agreement variant was significantly lower in both sentences in the sample from Hungary than in the Subcarpathian one. The difference between the occurrence of standard answers is significant in both cases.

3.2.13 *Feminization*

Unlike Russian and Ukrainian with which Hungarian is in contact in Subcarpathia, the Hungarian language does not differentiate between grammatical genders. In Hungarian, the suffix *-nő* has to be added to the name of an occupation if it describes the occupation of a woman (Grétsy & Kovalovszky 1985:324). In the two Slavic languages, however, gender reference is obligatory. In each investigated sentence, 631, 632, and 633, the gender of the person the sentence referred to was clearly female, therefore, the use of the suffix *-nő* was redundant.

The investigation of feminization is also relevant because, as Rot described it in several of his works: "If we consider that there is no grammatical gender in Hungarian-Ukrainian bilingualism, the possibility of differentiation between males and females in primarily nouns describing occupations has still emerged." (Rot 1968:265, and see 1967:191 as well; my translation).

In Hungary, the frequency of occurrence of feminized variants was lower in case of all three variables, although the difference in the case of sentence 632 was not significant (Table 4.18). In addition, sentence 631 stands out in both samples with a significantly lower rate in standard answers. Similar results were registered in a study conducted in Slovakia as well (Lanstyák & Szabómihály 1996a:122–123, 1997:72–74). The higher frequency of occurrence of the variants of *tanárnő* '[female] teacher' compared to those of *igazgatónő* 'head mistress' and *fodrásznő* '[female] hairdresser' can be explained with the fact that even though the hairdresser profession is supposedly more feminine than the teacher profession, *tanárnő* is also used as a form of address, while *fodrásznő* is not, and the position of headmaster is still more frequently filled by males

Table 4.18. Subcarpathia Hungarians' versus Hungary Hungarians' responses to feminization

		Subcarpathia (N = 144)		Hungary (N = 107)		p <
631	standard *tanár*	44	(30.8%)	61	(58.7%)	0.01
	nonstandard *tanárnő*	99	(69.2%)	43	(41.3%)	
632	standard *igazgató*	110	(77.5%)	85	(82.5%)	–
	nonstandard *igazgatónő*	32	(22.5%)	18	(17.5%)	
633	standard *fodrász*	104	(72.7%)	94	(89.5%)	0.01
	nonstandard *fodrásznő*	39	(27.3%)	11	(10.5%)	
The average of standard answers		258	(60.3%)	240	(76.9%)	0.05

than females (see Lanstyák & Szabómihály 1997:73). The difference between the two samples is significant at the p<0.05 level.

3.2.14 *The use of borrowing of meaning in test situations*

Lexical borrowings are heavily stigmatized in the Hungarian language cultivation literature in Subcarpathia. We investigated the attitude of speakers towards borrowings of meaning in test situations with the help of two test sentences. In sentence 701, the word *kiírat* (in the SuH meaning of 'subscribe') is used as the equivalent of the Russian word *vypisat'*, while in sentence 702, the word *becsenget* 'call, phone' is used with the same meaning as the Russian word *pozvonit'* in Subcarpathia. In Hungarian as spoken in Hungary, *kiírat* means 'have somebody put on medical leave', while *becsenget* is 'ring the doorbell'. Both of these borrowings of meaning have been the subject of local language cultivation literature several times, stigmatizing their use (Horváth 1991; Kótyuk 1995:63–64). The phenomenon was targeted with two sentences, 701 (given as 10 below) and 702 (given as 11):

(10) *Péter erre az évre is kiíratta a Kárpáti Igaz Szót.*
      'Peter subscribed to Kárpáti Igaz Szó for this year as well.'

(11) *Edit tegnap becsengetett a vasútra, hogy megkérdezze, késik-e a vonat.*
      'Yesterday Edith called the railway station to ask whether the train was late.'

There is a considerable difference between the average of the two samples. The rate of acceptance of the borrowings of meaning was significantly higher in the Subcarpathian sample than in the Hungarian control group (Table 4.19). It is surprising, however, that many speakers in Hungary accepted the sentence containing the borrowing of meaning as being correct. This is, on the one hand, due to the fact that borrowings of meaning are much less conspicuous than loanwords proper, and, therefore, they are less stigmatized, and on the other hand, because of the productive nature of the sentence correction task, which task type has an effect on the results. At the same time, it has to be taken into consideration that in sentence 702, the word *becsenget* could have been understood by the subjects in Hungary as having the meaning of 'Yesterday

Table 4.19. Subcarpathia Hungarians' versus Hungary Hungarians' responses to borrowing of meaning in test situations

		Subcarpathia (N = 144)		Hungary (N = 107)		p <
701	standard *előfizette*	25	(17.4%)	62	(64.6%)	0.01
	nonstandard *kiíratta*	119	(82.6%)	34	(35.4%)	
702	standard *telefonált*	42	(29.2%)	61	(58.7%)	0.01
	nonstandard *becsengetett*	102	(70.8%)	43	(41.3%)	
The average of standard answers		67	(23.3%)	123	(61.5%)	0.01

Edith rang the doorbell at the railway station...', so this might also have had an effect on the results.

In accordance with the sentence correction type of task, which has a favorable effect on the acceptance of nonstandard answers, the frequency of occurrence of nonstandard borrowings of meaning is rather high in the Subcarpathian sample. This can be accounted for with the following.

3.2.15   The use of a redundant pronominal object

A traditional Hungarian descriptive grammar (Tompa 1970:150) and the language cultivation literature (for instance, Grétsy & Kovalovszky 1985:975–976; Grétsy 1976:52–53) agree that the use of object personal pronouns is only necessary if the object is emphasized, since otherwise the pronominal object is redundant due to the definite conjugation of the verb already signaling the object. In equivalent cases in Russian and Ukrainian, the personal pronoun cannot be left out of the sentence. Therefore, in the SHOH project we supposed that under the influence of the second language(s), the pronominal object occurs more frequently in case of Hungarian speakers in Subcarpathia than in Hungary. Our hypothesis had been supported by the fact that several authors also discuss the use of pronominal objects in similar cases of language contact. According to Kontra, for instance, "based on the structural differences between the agglutinative Hungarian and the analytical English language, American-Hungarians (and native speakers of English who speak Hungarian as a foreign language) presumably sometimes use more personal pronouns than SH [=Standard Hungarian] speakers" (1990:82, my translation). Bartha (1993:137, 1995/1996:426–427, 1996:280) also discusses the use of redundant pronouns as a phenomenon related to language contact in American Hungarian. Moreover, Lanstyák (1998:69) sees the manifestation of "redundancy [to be] due to obligatory second language categories" in the use of pronominal objects. Kótyuk (1995:11) also mentions the use of redundant pronouns as a contact induced feature. The phenomenon was investigated with sentences 510, 515 and 615 in the SHOH questionnaire (Table 4.20).

Table 4.18 shows that the rate of standard answers was higher in Hungary in case of all three variable tokens. The difference between the two samples is significant in all three cases, and there is a considerable difference between the averages as well.

Table 4.20. Subcarpathia Hungarians' versus Hungary Hungarians' responses to redundant pronominal objects

		Subcarpathia (N = 144)		Hungary (N = 107)		p <
510	standard *látsz*	32	(22.2%)	36	(33.6%)	0.05
	nonstandard *látsz engem*	112	(77.8%)	71	(66.4%)	
515	standard *láttalak*	56	(38.9%)	82	(78.1%)	0.01
	nonstandard *láttalak téged*	88	(61.1%)	23	(21.9%)	
615	standard *megkértem*	65	(45.1%)	77	(72.6%)	0.01
	nonstandard *megkértem őt*	79	(54.9%)	29	(27.4%)	
The average of standard answers		153	(35.4%)	195	(61.3%)	0.01

Table 4.21. Subcarpathia Hungarians' versus Hungary Hungarians' responses to the frequency of use of diminutive derivational suffixes

		Subcarpathia (N = 144)		Hungary (N = 107)		p <
504	standard *kenyeret*	87	(60.4%)	89	(84.0%)	0.01
	nonstandard *kenyérkét*	57	(39.6%)	17	(16.0%)	
538	standard *bankkönyveket*	30	(20.8%)	54	(52.4%)	0.01
	nonstandard *bankkönyvecskéket*	114	(79.2%)	49	(47.6%)	
602	standard *kis kezedet*	83	(57.6%)	71	(66.4%)	–
	nonstandard *kezecskédet*	61	(42.4%)	36	(33.6%)	
612	standard *kávé*	130	(90.3%)	105	(98.1%)	0.01
	nonstandard *kávécska*	14	(9.7%)	2	(1.9%)	
The average of standard answers		330	(57.3%)	319	(75.4%)	0.01

The frequency of occurrence of the pronominal object is the highest in case of the sentence 510 variant in both samples. This is most probably because of the possibility of interpreting the indefinite conjugation verb *látsz* 'see (have the ability to see)' as having no object, therefore, being a context-dependent verb (see Lanstyák 1998:70).

3.2.16 *The frequency of use of diminutive derivational suffixes*
Discussing the characteristics of Hungarian language varieties in Slovakia, Lanstyák (1993:93, 1998:59–60) suggests that the unusually frequent use of diminutive derivational suffix forms (especially among non-Hungarian dominant speakers) is probably due to language contact. The Subcarpathian Hungarian dialects "considerably favor diminutive derivational suffix forms" (Horváth & Lizanec 1993:72, my translation; and see Rot 1968:257 as well). The frequency of use of diminutive derivational suffixes was investigated with four sentences in our questionnaire, sentences 504, 538, 602, and 612.

Table 4.21 shows that in case of all investigated variable tokens, the frequency of use of diminutive derivational suffix variants is higher in Subcarpathia, and the difference between the averages of the two samples is also significant.

The difference between the Subcarpathian and Hungarian samples is significant in case of three variable tokens. The highest frequency of use of the diminutive derivational suffix variant occurred in sentence 538 in both samples. This is most probably due to the fact that this variable was investigated with the sentence correction task, which as has been mentioned above, has an effect on the results.

3.2.17 Summary of structural borrowing
The rate of the frequency of occurrence of standard answers was higher in case of the Hungarian sample in 27 out of the investigated 30 variable tokens, and in only 3 cases (622, 536, 513) were standard answers more frequent in case of the Subcarpathian sample. The difference between the two samples is significant at the $p < 0.01$ level in 19 cases, and at the $p < 0.05$ level in 3 cases (625, 535, 510). In case of seven variable tokens (622, 532, 536, 632, 537, 513, 602) there is no significant difference between the two samples, and in case of 514, the use of the Chi-square test is problematic.

According to the total average of the 30 investigated variable tokens, the rate of standard answers is 51.6% in Subcarpathia and 75.2% in Hungary. The difference between the two samples is significant at the $p < 0.01$ level. Figure 4.2 shows the summary of the average of the frequency of standard answers according to variable types, which are referred to as follows: (a) analytical structures; (b) the singular and plural forms of nouns; (c) number agreement; (d) feminization; (e) borrowing of meaning; (f) redundant pronominal object; and (g) diminutive derivational suffixes.

All this seems to support the claim accepted in the Hungarian linguistics literature, namely that minority Hungarian language varieties in the Carpathian Basin are generally more dialectal, that is, they are less standard than corresponding language varieties in Hungary (see Deme 1970:39; Lanstyák 1994b:64; Kiss 1994:94–100; Sándor 1995:132-133; and see Horváth 1991; Kótyuk 1995:7 for reference to Hungarian in Subcarpathia). So far, this statement has been verified by empirical sociolinguistic re-

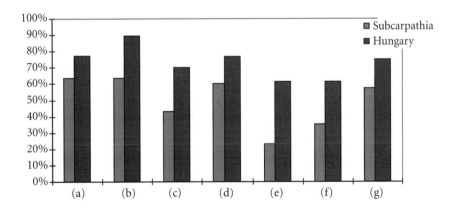

Figure 4.2. The average of standard answers according to variable types in Subcarpathia versus Hungary

search and statistical methods only in case of Hungarian language varieties in Slovakia (cf. Szabómihály 1993; Lanstyák & Szabómihály 1996a, 1997).

4. Conclusion

The present situation of Subcarpathia Hungarians is best summarized as controversial. In Subcarpathia Hungarians live in one contiguous area close to the Hungarian border, but their numbers and ratio in the total population are continuously decreasing. The political situation of Subcarpathia Hungarians is favorable at present, but the most recent political developments are pointing towards a narrowing of minority rights.

Ukraine's disadvantageous economic situation is raising the prestige of the Hungarian language in the eyes of the Hungarian minority, but, at the same time, hundreds of Subcarpathia Hungarians emigrate to Hungary every year.

The linguistic analysis shows that, among Subcarpathia Hungarians, in formal domains the use of Ukrainian and Russian is predominant, while in informal domains Hungarian is used almost exclusively.

The varieties of Hungarian used in Subcarpathia show some effects of language contact (such as code-switching, borrowing, and subtle differences in the use of universal Hungarian sociolinguistic variables), but these do not threaten mutual intelligibility, and the separate development of Subcarpathia Hungarian varieties or a formation of a separate language are not issues whose probability would seriously arise.

Translated by Etelka Polgár

Notes

1. Throughout this paper, names of Subcarpathian towns and villages are given first transliterated, in their official Russian or Ukrainian versions, and second, in their traditional Hungarian forms.

2. For more details of Ukraine's minority and language policy, see the following works: Arel (1995), Csernicskó (1998), Orosz and Csernicskó (1998), Solchanyk (1993), Stewart (1993), Várdy (1989a), and Beregszászi et al. (2001). On the situation of other minorities, see *Etnići menšćini v Ukraini* [Ethnic Minorities in Ukraine]. Kiiv: Institut sociologii NAN Ukraini, Ministerstvo Ukraini u spravax nacional'nostej ta migracii.

3. Knowing these results, it would not be irrelevant to investigate whether or not this habit could be explained similarly to the case of German speakers in Romania, who generally use Romanian when telling jokes or in drunk arguments (see Gal 1987).

4. The original question was worded as follows: "(9) Mother tongue. Indicate also any other language of the USSR that you speak fluently" (my translation). Cf. *Census questionnaire, USSR Census of Population*, 1989, The State Committee on Statistics of the USSR. Censuses (both in 1970 and 1989) did not take into account the language knowledge of those who did not speak

another language fluently, that is, who believed they "could not communicate fluently in this language", but could read and understand that language.

5. On the Hungarian language use of Subcarpathia Hungarians also see Csernicskó (1998:217–220) and Csernicskó and Fenyvesi (2000).

6. Only 71 instances of code-switching were identified in the analysed 36 hours of tape recorded interviews (with 31 people). These included one-word switches as well as sentence-long ones. The ones quoted below are typical instances of code-switching from the interviews.

7. The personal data of the speakers were modified in the quotations from the interviews.

8. In addition, see Csernicskó (1998:217–220) and Csernicskó and Fenyvesi (2000) on Hungarian language use in Subcarpathia.

9. Traditional Hungarian descriptive grammars consider -*hat/-het* as derivational affixes (see, for instance, Rácz 1971:128–129), however, theoretical linguists regard them as inflectional affixes (see, for instance, Kiefer 1998:228). The debate in connection with this issue (see, for instance, Keszler 1997; Kenesei 1996, 1998b) has not been concluded yet, although the outcome has no direct impact on our results.

10. In Hungarian, the singular variant is considered "more correct" (Grétsy & Kovalovszky 1985:296).

CHAPTER 5

Hungarian in Romania

Attila Benő and Sándor Szilágyi N.

1. Introduction

The vitality of a minority language in a country is manifested in its usage. The usage and the social value of the language depends on the legal status of the language, on the number of its speakers, as well as the attitude of speakers towards their mother tongue and towards the language of the majority group. In order to present a general overview on the Hungarian language in Romania, we first describe the Hungarian community in Romania through demographic data and by referring to its economic, religious and educational situation. The language policy of the Romanian state is then analyzed in the context of the linguistic rights of the ethnic minorities in another subsection of the paper. The focal topics of the chapter are the sociolinguistic characteristics of the Hungarian speakers in Romania as well as language contact issues. One of the main sources of sociolinguistic and linguistic data we use in this chapter is part of the Sociolinguistics of Hungarian Outside Hungary project conducted in Romania (see Kontra, this volume). The chapter does not discuss the Csángós, a special group of Hungarian speakers living in Romania, since a separate chapter by Sándor is devoted to them in this volume.

2. Sociolinguistic aspects

2.1 Origin of the contact situation

Most of the Hungarians in Romania live in Transylvania. Today Transylvania conventionally includes not only the historical Transylvania, which was the eastern part of the Hungarian Kingdom up to the mid-19th century, but also the provinces of Banat/Bánát (in western Romania, bordering Serbia), Crişana/Körösök vidéke (north of Banat and bordering Hungary), and Maramureş/Máramaros (in northern Romania, bordering Hungary and Ukraine). We use the term 'Transylvania' in this broader sense. This area comprises a territory of 38,548 square miles.

In the Middle Ages, Transylvania was a part of the Hungarian Kingdom. Then starting from 1526, as a consequence of the disintegration of Hungary, it became an independent Principality. From 1867 until 1920 Transylvania belonged to Austria-Hungary, and, after World War I, in 1920, it was ceded to Romania. Thus, in Romania a Hungarian minority was created by the 1920 borders. As a consequence of the change of the borders, more than 200,000 Hungarians left Romania and moved to Hungary (Köpeczi 1994:673–674).

The Vienna Award of 1940 gave to Hungary the northern and eastern parts of Transylvania (16,792 square miles), which made the situation more confused. A considerable number of Romanians once again became ethnic minorities in the Hungarian State. In 1944, the 1920 borders were reinstated and have remained unchanged since.

2.2 Demographics

Hungarians constitute the largest ethnic and linguistic minority group in Romania. It is a minority group which actually lives in Romania as a consequence of the change of the state borders in 1918–20 as part of the Treaty of Trianon. According to the latest, 2002, census, the entire population of Romania is 21,680,974, of which 1,431,807 (6.60%) are Hungarians.[1] The number of people who declared Hungarian as their mother tongue is 1,443,970, that is 6.66% of the whole population. The percentage of groups other than Romanian or Hungarian is 3.8% (Roma 2.5%, Germans 0.3%, Ukrainians 0.3%, Russians 0.2%, Serbs 0.1%, Turks 0.2%, Tatars 0.1%, Slovaks 0.1% etc.) Thus, 10.5% of the population, that is 2,281,377 people, are members of ethnic minority groups. In 1930, at the time of the first post-Trianon census, the proportion of nationalities other than Romanian was 22.15%. The percentage of ethnic minorities decreased steadily between 1930 and 2002 (see Table 5.1).

In 2002, Transylvania's total population was 7,221,733, and the number of Hungarians in Transylvania was 1,415,718.[2] That means that 98.87% of the Hungarians in Romania live in Transylvania. Hungarians represent 19.60% of the total population of Transylvania. Comparing this figure with data from previous censuses, we can see that since 1956 the percentage of Hungarians in Transylvania has been decreasing ev-

Table 5.1. The number and percentage of Romanians and other ethnic groups in Romania between 1930 and 2002

Year	Total population	Romanians		Others	
1930	14,280,729	11,118,170	(77.85%)	3,163,181	(22.15%)
1956	17,489,450	14,996,114	(85.74%)	2,493,995	(14.26%)
1966	19,103,163	16,746,510	(87.66%)	2,357,330	(12.34%)
1977	21,559,910	18,999,565	(88.12%)	2,561,317	(11.88%)
1992	22,810,035	20,408,542	(89.47%)	2,401,896	(10.53%)
2002	21,680,947	19,399,597	(89.48%)	2,281,377	(10.52%)

Table 5.2. The number and percentage of Romanians and Hungarians in Romania and Transylvania between 1930 and 2002

Year	Total population of Romania	Total population of Transylvania	Romanians in Romania	Romanians in Transylvania	Hungarians in Romania	Hungarians in Transylvania
1930	14,280,729	5,520,086	11,118,170 (77.85%)	3,189,537 (57.78%)	1,423,459 (9.96%)	1,349,563 (24.44%)
1956	17,489,450	6,218,427	14,996,114 (85.74%)	4,041,156 (64.98%)	1,587,675 (9.07%)	1,558,254 (25.05%)
1966	19,103,163	6,719,555	16,746,510 (87.66%)	4,559,432 (67.85%)	1,619,592 (8.47%)	1,597,438 (23.77%)
1977	21,559,910	7,500,229	18,999,565 (88.12%)	5,203,846 (69.38%)	1,713,928 (7.95%)	1,691,048 (22.54%)
1992	22,810,035	7,723,313	20,408,542 (89.47%)	5,684,142 (73.59%)	1,624,959 (7.12%)	1,603,923 (20.76%)
2002	21,680,974	7,221,733	19,399,597 (89.5%)	5,393,552 (74.69%)	1,431,807 (6.60%)	1,415,718 (19.60%)

Table 5.3. The growth of the number of Romanians and Hungarians in Romania between 1930 and 2002

Period	National growth		Growth of Romanians		Growth of Hungarians	
	N	%	N	%	N	%
1930–1956	3,208,721	22.47	3,877,944	34.88	164,216	11.54
1956–1966	1,613,713	9.23	1,750,396	11.67	31,917	2.01
1966–1977	2,456,747	12.86	2,253,055	13.45	94,336	5.82
1977–1992	1,250,125	5.80	1,408,977	7.42	−88,969	−5.19
1992–2002	−1,129,061	−4.95	−1,008,945	-4.94	−193,152	−11.89
1930–2002	7,400,245	51.82	8,281,427	74.49	8,348	0.59

ery decade: 25.05% in 1956, 23.77% in 1966, 22.54% in 1977, 20.76% in 1992, and 19.60% in 2002 (see Table 5.2). The tendency can also be noticed if we look at the proportion of Hungarians at the national level: 9.96% in 1930, 9.07% in 1956, 8.47% in 1966, 7.95% 1977, 7.12% in 1992, and 6.60% in 2002.

Since 1930, the increase of Hungarians has been permanently lower than that of Romanians. Thus, between 1930 and 2002 the growth of the number of Hungarians was 0.59%, while that of Romanians was 74.49%. It is important to point out that between 1992 and 2002 the number of Hungarians decreased by 193,152 (11.89%), while that of Romanians increased continuously. Table 5.3 and Figure 5.1 show that the growth of Hungarians in different periods between 1930 and 2002 was below the average national growth in terms of percentages.

In Transylvania, the average growth was continuously lower than the national growth (see Table 5.4), and that of the minorities was also lower than the growth of the majority population. The growth of the number of Romanians in Transylvania

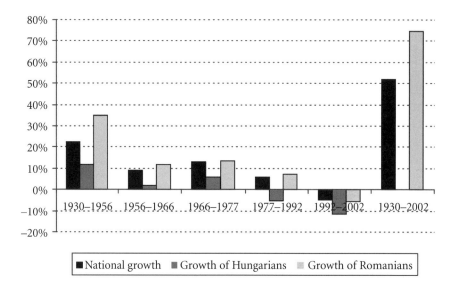

Figure 5.1. The growth of Romania's total, Hungarian and Romanian populations between 1930 and 2002

between 1930 and 2002 was well above the average growth in Transylvania and even above the national growth.

The decrease in the number of Hungarians between 1977 and 2002 might be due to three factors: a low birth rate, emigration, and assimilation.

The data of the 1992 census show that the percentage of the children between ages 0–4 and 5–9 was 7.07% and 7.25% at the national level.[3] Among Hungarians these percentages were only 5.74%, and 5.96% respectively. These data confirm that the decrease in the number and ratio of Hungarians in Romania is continuing.

In the period between 1977 and 1992 the emigration among Hungarians was relatively greater than in the whole population. The percentage of Hungarians among the emigrants was 12% in this period, which means a total of 66,950 legal Hungarian emigrants (*Anuarul Statistic al României* 1993, 141–143.). There are no data available

Table 5.4. The growth, in percentages, of the number of Romanians and Hungarians in Transylvania between 1930 and 2002

Period	National growth	Total growth in Transylvania	Growth of Romanians	Growth of Hungarians
1930–1956	22.47	12.65	26.70	15.46
1956–1966	9.22	8.06	12.82	2.51
1966–1977	12.86	11.62	14.14	5.86
1977–1992	5.80	2.97	9.23	−5.15
1992–2002	−4.87	−6.44	−5.11	−11.66
1930–2002	51.94	30.89	69.09	4.98

about the number of illegal emigrants, but it is well known that, especially starting in 1988–1989, a great number of Hungarians emigrated illegally.

Assimilation and a subsequent change of ethnic identity is determined by several factors. One of them is the great number of ethnically mixed marriages. The data of the 1993 census show that ethnically mixed families increase the majority group and, thus, directly influence the decrease of Hungarians. In the 1992 census, 94,413 Romanian–Hungarian mixed families were recorded. Specifically, out of all 407,509 married Hungarian males, 45,444 (11.15%) had Romanian wives, while out of all 411,973 married Hungarian females, 48,969 (11.89%) had Romanian husbands. The statistical data show that if the husband is Romanian and the wife Hungarian, the children are declared Romanian in 82.28% of the families, while if the husband is Hungarian and the wife Romanian, 63.31% of the families declare the children are Romanian. (These data concern only those families with children where all the children's ethnic identity is declared according either to that of the father's or that of the mother's.)

Another factor in assimilation is the structure of the settlement where people live. According to the 1992 census 56% of the Hungarians in Romania live in settlements where they are in absolute majority, i.e. constitute over 50% of the population. If the type of settlement, urban vs. rural, is taken into consideration, there is a great difference: 79.05% of the Hungarian rural population (561,926 persons) live in villages where they are in absolute majority, while only 38.42% of the urban population (349,591 persons) live in towns and cities where they are in absolute majority. These differences between urban and rural settlements are a consequence of the industrialization and urbanization which took place between 1950 and 1989, since the increase in the number of townspeople led to the change in the ethnic structure in the towns and cities in Transylvania (Figure 5.2): in the communist period there was an enhanced industrial migration of Romanians from regions outside Transylvania to Transylvania. This process was politically organized and stimulated.

These demographic data are also important in terms of the linguistic environment. As much as 44% of the Hungarians in Romania are numerically in a minority in their

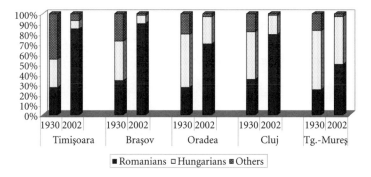

Figure 5.2. The ethnic composition of Transylvania's major towns in 1930 and 2002

locality. In such environments the use of the Hungarian language is also limited. It is to be expected that in these localities the influence of Romanian is more intensive, and the domains of usage of Hungarian are more restricted since Hungarian is not an official language in Romania.

A third factor of assimilation is the insufficiency of the educational system in mother tongue education. This topic is discussed in detail below.

2.3 Economic structure, education and religion

2.3.1 *Economic structure*
In the interwar period Romania was an underdeveloped agricultural country. According to the 1930 census, almost 80% of the active population was working in agriculture. The percentage of people working in industry was under 10%. As a result of the forced industrialization during the communist regime, the social and economic structure radically changed. In 1992 only 22.25% of the active population worked in agriculture and 42.90% in industry.

Concerning occupation and the representation of Hungarians in certain branches of the economy in 1992, one can easily notice that Hungarians in Romania are underrepresented (that is their percentage in the active population at the national level is below 6.67%) in professional and administrative occupations. Here are the most important occupations where the Hungarians are underrepresented: high civil servants in public administration, directors of social institutions and managers (5.56%), intellectuals (5.03%, specifically lawyers 3.12%, professors and instructors in higher education 2.96%, secondary school teachers 6.47%, medical researchers 3.22%, financial, bank, administration and trade specialists, 2.25%, economists, experts in economy and social sciences 2.39%, researchers in economy, social sciences, and humanities 1.84%), army personnel 5.15%, police officers and detectives 1.09%, secretarial staff 6.55%, farmers and skilled workers in agriculture, forestry and fishing 4.03%.

Hungarians in Romania are overrepresented among blue collar workers and handicraftsmen, their proportion in this category is 8.72%. Their representation in certain occupations is illustrative in this respect: construction workers 10.23%, miners and stone-cutters 8.64%, house-painters 10.64%, wood workers 17.26%, textile industry workers 9.93%, leather-workers 14.72%. Hungarians are also slightly overrepresented among unskilled laborers, their proportion being 7.65% there. (This percentage is higher, 7.87%, among Hungarian town dwellers.)

2.3.2 *Education*
As is well known, employment is directly tied to education. The employment situation of Hungarians presented above is partly a result of the policy affecting the Hungarian minority in the field of education. Before presenting the contemporary situation, it is necessary to refer to its recent history in order to get a full picture of the minority education.

The educational system created in the years immediately following World War II, between 1945 and 1948, in principle, ensured education in Hungarian at all levels. In 1948 the all-Hungarian Bolyai University was founded in Cluj/Kolozsvár, in addition to the Romanian university which had already existed there since 1919, when the Hungarian university established in 1872 was appropriated by the Romanian state. As a branch of the university, in Târgu Mureş/Marosvásárhely, a medical-pharmaceutical faculty was founded, which later on became independent. During the same period the Hungarian academic educational system was supplemented with an agricultural college, an academy of fine arts and a conservatory, all in Cluj/Kolozsvár, and with an academy of dramatic art in Târgu Mureş/Marosvásárhely.

Beginning with the 1960s there was already discrimination concerning the education opportunities in mother tongue for ethnic minorities in Romania. In 1959, the Hungarian Bolyai University in Cluj was merged with the Romanian Babeş University under the name of Babeş–Bolyai University. The institution thus became bilingual, but this bilingualism, in most fields of study, was gradually replaced with all-Romanian language instruction. After the merger, the number of Hungarian students and instructors decreased. Thus, in the academic year 1970/1971, the proportion of the Hungarian faculty members was only 23.68% and in 1980/1981 only 18% (Antal 1993:17). The medical-pharmaceutical faculty in Târgu Mureş/Marosvásárhely, which in 1946 was a Hungarian university, underwent similar changes. In the academic year 1970/1971, the proportion of the Hungarian faculty members in this institution was 60.66% and in 1982/1983 only 49.81%. The 1966 census shows that 219 in every 10,000 Romanians had a university diploma, while this ratio was 150 in every 10,000 Hungarians (Antal 1993:15–16). In the 1970s the discrimination became even more intense. The proportion of Hungarian students became much lower (5.53%) than their proportion in the total population (7.9%) (see Table 5.5).

In the 1960s the formerly Hungarian high schools became, similarly, Hungarian sections of Romanian schools, and later, within these institutions, many Hungarian classes were gradually eliminated, especially intensively in the 1980s.

After 1989, the educational system in Romania underwent a change, which had a favorable influence on minority education. The possibilities of receiving education in the mother tongue increased on all levels of the educational system, including higher education. Some of the Hungarian schools with long traditions were re-established in those cities in Transylvania where the number of Hungarians is considerable. (There

Table 5.5. The number and proportion of Romanian and Hungarian university students in the 1970s*

	1970/1971	1976/1977	1977/1978	1978/1979	1979/1980
Romanian university students	96,900 (91.59%)	110,807 (91.91%)	118,385 (91.67%)	125,696 (91.66%)	132,137 (91.91%)
Hungarian university students	5,694 (5.38%)	6,813 (5.65%)	7,497 (5.80%)	7,869 (5.73%)	7,956 (5.53%)

* Sources: Telscu (1972:355–56), Anuarul Statistic al R.S.R. (1977, 1978, 1979, 1980).

is just one exception in this respect: Târgu Mureş/Marosvásárhely. There is no state school providing education exclusively in Hungarian in this city, although Hungarians are in a majority, in 1992 their proportion was 52%).[4] At a national level, the number of students in state universities doubled, and many Romanian private universities were established. But the demand of the Hungarian minority for a Hungarian language state university has not been met up to now, although 500,000 Hungarians signed a petition to this effect in the early 1990s. The Hungarians' consistent request for a Hungarian language state university is caused by the discrimination of ethnic minorities, which still exists in the Romanian education system, especially in higher education. The latest census shows that Hungarians continue to be underrepresented in higher education. Analyzing the Hungarians' participation in different types of higher education, one can easily notice that Hungarians are represented to a lesser degree. Thus, in 1992, their participation in the whole of higher education (universities, colleges, technical education, etc.) was just 5.18%.

Hungarians face problems in their mother tongue education at lower levels, too. In 1994/1995, 18.8% of the Romanian population was enrolled in primary and secondary education. In the same period only 12.8% of Hungarians studied in school in their mother tongue (Murvai 1996: 132). This disproportion can be seen every school year starting from 1989. According to data from the National Statistics Office, in the period between 1989 and 1999, the number of primary school students studying in Hungarian was under 5% every school year, which is, again, lower than their proportion in the whole number of students in Romania (Murvai 2000: 126).

Due to the fact that Hungarians in Romania have been underrepresented in higher education for decades, the 1992 census presents a very unfavorable image about Hungarians' qualifications: only 49,592 (3.57%) of the Hungarians have higher education degrees, while among Romanians the ratio is 5.34% (Table 5.6). If the presence of Hungarians in higher education had been proportional to the ratio of those with higher education in the population (5.15%), the number of Hungarians with higher education degrees would have been 71,483, the difference being 21,891.

A favorable change after 1989 has been the fact that the number of students in higher education has increased considerably: 164,507 in 1990 vs. 407,613 in 1999. But the participation of Hungarian students in higher education is still disproportionate: their number was 7,091 (4.31%) in 1990, and 16,122 (3.96%) in 1999 (Murvai 2000: 127).

Table 5.6. The distribution of Hungarians in Romania by level of education in 1992 in comparison to Romanians and the national average

	Total population (12 years and older)	%	With higher education	%	Additional studies after high school	%	High school	%
Total	18,801,610	100.00	967,570	5.15	373,553	1.99	3,468,577	18.45
Romanians	16,825,925	89.49	898,829	5.34	344,788	2.05	3,154,680	18.75
Hungarians	1,389,042	7.39	49,592	3.57	23,449	1.69	257,930	18.57

2.3.3   Religion

The denominational distribution of the various ethnic groups in Romania is very different: some are denominationally very homogeneous (such as the Romanians or the Tatars), others are heterogeneous (such as the Hungarians). According to the 1992 census, 94.68% of the Romanians are Eastern Orthodox Christians, and the Romanian ethnic group is characterized by a lesser denominational diversity. The highest denominational diversity can be found among Hungarians. 47.10% of the Hungarians are Reformed Christians, 41.20% are Roman Catholics, and 4.55% belong to the Unitarian church. In fact, Hungarians can be found in all officially recognized denominations (see Table 5.7). Hungarians belonging to the Orthodox church are most likely persons who live in ethnically mixed marriages, since there is a correlation between the members of Orthodox Hungarians and of Hungarians living in ethnically mixed marriages.

Table 5.7. The denominational distribution of the population of Romania and the Hungarians' denominational diversity in 1992

Denomination	Total	Ratio in the population (%)	Hungarians belonging to that denomination	Ratio of Hungarians in that denomination (%)	Ratio of that denomination among Hungarians (%)
Eastern Orthodox	19,802,389	86.81	27,828	0.14	1.71
Roman Catholic	1,161,942	5.09	669,420	57.61	41.20
Reformed	802,454	3.52	765,370	95.38	47.10
Greek Catholic	223,327	0.98	23,393	10.47	1.44
Pentecostal	220,824	0.97	4,339	1.96	0.27
Baptist	109,462	0.48	12,845	11.73	0.79
Adventist	77,546	0.34	8,280	10.68	0.51
Unitarian	76,708	0.34	74,021	96.50	4.55
Muslim	55,928	0.24	35	0.06	0.002
Evangelical Christian	49,963	0.22	2,393	4.79	0.15
Evangelic Augustan	39,119	0.17	7,201	18.41	0.44
Christian Old Style	28,141	0.12	98	0.35	0.006
Orthodox Old Believer	32,228	0.14	59	0.18	0.004
Presbiterian Evangelical	21,221	0.09	12,842	60.52	0.79
Jewish	9,670	0.04	193	2.00	0.01
Other	56,329	0.25	11,924	21.17	0.73
Atheists	10,331	0.04	616	5.96	0.04
No religion	24,314	0.11	3,277	13.48	0.20
Undeclared	8,139	0.04	825	10.14	0.05

The denominational difference of Hungarians and Romanians, in general, is favorable for the maintenance of their mother tongue, even if a connection between the ethnic identity and the denominational affiliation might favor language shift in certain cases. Such a situation might appear in ethnically mixed Hungarian-Romanian marriages, when the Hungarian spouse adopts the Romanian spouse's religion, Eastern Orthodoxy. This denominational shift might affect ethnic identity, too, since the Orthodox religion is strongly linked to Romanian identity in Romania.

The Orthodox church is seen by most Romanian politicians as the national church. Although this attitude is not officially declared, it manifests itself in public life. It is well known that since 1990 the Protestant and Catholic churches have received proportionally less financial support from the Romanian state than have Orthodox churches. "This discrepancy is in part the result of the ambiguous relationship between church and state in Romania" (Horváth & Scacco 2001:246).

2.4 Language policy

The language policy of a state manifests itself most clearly in the laws which legally codify the inalienable human right of the usage of mother tongue. In this subsection we present three of the most important documents in this respect: the Romanian Constitution, the Law on Education, and the Public Administration Law.

The Constitution of Romania (1991) declares that "Romania is a sovereign, independent, unitary and indivisible National State" (Article 1), and states that "in Romania, the official language is Romanian" (Article 13). (According to Article 148, dispositions of the constitution concerning the official language "shall not be subject to revision".) The language of education is also Romanian: "(2) Education of all grades shall be in Romanian. [...]" (Article 32), although the next paragraph of this article states that "(3) the right of persons belonging to national minorities to learn their mother tongue, and their right to be educated in this language are guaranteed; the ways to exercise these rights shall be regulated by law."

There are no explicit provisions about the status of minority languages, although Article 6 states that "the State recognizes and guarantees the rights of persons belonging to national minorities, to the preservation, development and expression of their ethnic, cultural, linguistic and religious identity".

Legal procedures are to be conducted in Romanian (Article 127), and court interpreters are provided for those who cannot speak Romanian.

These articles of the Constitution create disadvantaged situations for the linguistic minorities, since the usage of their mother tongue is permitted only in certain fields and not guaranteed in all cases, in formal and informal situations, in all forms, spoken or written. In institutions, all official documents must be written in Romanian, even if all of the employees belong to a linguistic minority. In education, abuses can be justified by declaring that the official language is Romanian. For instance, according to the law, classes with Romanian as the language of instruction must be running in all localities, whereas classes with minority language instruction can be formed on request: so, even if all students request minority language instruction classes, these may be formed only after a Romanian language class is filled.

Sometimes the term *official language* is extended to *public language*, and on this basis certain modes of the public usage of Hungarian and other minority languages is forbidden in some localities. Such a case is Cluj/Kolozsvár, where the mayor of the city was against all kinds of monolingual Hungarian and bilingual inscriptions and forbade the use of posters written in Hungarian. His main argument was that Romanian is the official language in Romania. Especially before 1989, special restrictions of minority language use were applied in the army and in prisons, both in inmates' personal correspondence and in their contacts with visitors. In the questionnaire of the Sociolinguistics of Hungarian Outside Hungary project there was a question referring to the behavior of the majority group: we asked our subjects whether they were ever rebuked for speaking Hungarian. Some of those subjects who said they had been rebuked declared that it had happened in the army.

The Law on Education legislated in 1995 and modified in 1999 is, in general, tolerating education in the mother tongue of ethnic minorities, although one can find restrictions which trespass certain human and minority rights. Such a restriction is the obligation to study certain subjects such as "The history of Romanians" and "The geography of Romania" in Romanian in grades 5 through 8 and in high schools even if the students are receiving their education in a minority language in classes where the language of instruction is the native language of the minority students. Article 120, paragraph 2 of the law states that in grades 5 through 8 and in high school these subjects must be taught in Romanian, using the curriculum and textbooks prepared for students whose mother tongue is Romanian. The examinations in these subjects must be taken in Romanian.[5] All official documents issued by the Ministry of Education must be written in Romanian (Article 8, paragraph 4). This direction keeps within limits the usage of mother tongue in formal situations.

Studying Romanian language and literature is compulsory in all schools. According to the law, it is not the *right* of citizens belonging to ethnic minorities to study the Romanian language but their *duty* (Article 8, paragraph 3). But the Law on Education itself raises obstacles in fulfilling this duty, since the prescribed way of teaching Romanian to students belonging to ethnic minorities is not adequate: Article 120 states that in grades 5 through 8 Romanian language and literature must be taught to students belonging to ethnic minorities following the curriculum for students whose mother tongue is Romanian, and, what is more, in high schools not only the curriculum must be identical, but the textbooks too. The law prescribes a special language learning curriculum only for the first four years of school, but this is not enough to learn the Romanian language so as students would be able to use it as native speakers do. Since school curricula expect the students to possess that ability from the age of 10, the deficiencies in the language proficiency accumulate, and the final result is that after 12 years of learning Romanian, Hungarians cannot speak Romanian as correctly and fluently as they are expected. A solution for the problem might be the teaching of the Romanian language to students whose mother tongue is not Romanian with a special methodology, without nursing the illusion that they can learn Romanian language and literature as easily as native speakers can.

The Public Administration Law for Local Authorities, which was passed by the Romanian Parliament in 2001, provides in certain respects a big step forward in enforcing the linguistic rights of ethnic minorities.[6] The law states that in administrative units where the percentage of citizens belonging to ethnic minorities is above 20% the authorities in the local public administration shall ensure the usage of ethnic minorities' mother tongues in their relationship with them (Article 17). According to the law, local authorities have to ensure the inscription of placenames and names of public institutions as well as the signs and announcements of general interest in the native language of the citizens belonging to ethnic minorities, if the percentage of the given ethnic minority is above 20% in that locality (Article 90). These favorable steps do not eliminate the status of asymmetry between the official language (Romanian) and the mother tongues of the ethnic minorities. These measures do not make the Hungarian language official in the localities where the number of Hungarians is significant, they just increase its sphere of usage. Thus, it becomes possible to use a minority language in the meetings of local councils, if the number of the council members belonging to that minority is equal to or greater than one-third of all council members (Article 43). According to Article 43, all official documents concerning the council meetings must be written in Romanian. This measure points to the fact that the minority languages are subordinated to Romanian, and these languages by no means have acquired an official status, as some Romanian political parties declare. The documents addressed to individuals belonging to minorities can be written in their mother tongue, if they request it (Article 51). In fact, Article 90 declares that all official documents are to be written obligatorily in Romanian. Thus, one cannot speak at all about an equal administrative status of widely used languages in Romania. Such kind of policy, considered *linguicist* in the language rights literature, inevitably leads to the situation when some registers of the minority languages are never used by a great part of their speakers, which results in the gradual decay of these registers. This is confirmed by Skutnabb-Kangas (2000b: 123), according to whom, if the authorities do not ensure official rights for a language, that language is indirectly destroyed.

2.5   Macrolinguistic characteristics of Hungarian use in Romania

2.5.1   *The status and functions of languages involved*
There is a strong connection between the status of languages in any given sociolinguistic situation and the functions they can have in a given society. The legal status of a language determines those functional levels at which the language is used, as well as the degree of usage at different levels.

In order to get an idea about the functions of a certain language, one has to analyze to what extent it is used at the everyday, the professional and the literary level. The Romanian language is used without any restriction on all of these levels. Hungarian and the other minority languages in Romania differ from the official language both in their status and the function they have in social interactions. Hungarian is present on everyday and literary levels, but is scarcely used on the professional level. It is less used in the public sphere (it is present only in the institutions of local administration if the ratio of the minority is over 20% at the given place, in the churches and civil organizations of the Hungarians). It is considerably restricted in this sphere, in city squares, in various signs and forms and at the workplace, especially in Hungarian-minority localities. This functional decrease is a consequence of the expansion of the official language in certain fields of communication. As, in general, Hungarian is not used, or very rarely used in certain situations (in administration, in professional discussions), in most of the cases some registers in the bilingual Hungarians' vocabulary are wanting. Restrictions of the mother tongue usage in Hungarian-minority localities may affect negatively the linguistic competence of the speakers. The privileged legal status of the only official language creates prestige and promises a chance for success, which is reflected, for example, in the Hungarians' choice of language education.

Hungarian-Romanian bilingualism is very much asymmetrical. This asymmetry is manifested in the fact that, in communication between Hungarians and Romanians, the common code is mainly Romanian, since most Hungarians in Romania are bilingual, while most Romanians cannot speak Hungarian. It is also asymmetrical because very often Hungarian speakers know and use only their local variety of Hungarian but not Standard Hungarian, but the standard variety of Romanian, which latter variety is considered by minority language speakers as a code of social success and prestige. This phenomenon also favors the loss of the native language in the case of Hungarians living in dispersed ethnic communities where their proportion in the total population is very low (Péntek 1999:45).

Since the above mentioned sociolinguistic conditions have been present for decades and in the public usage of Hungarian there are lexical uncertainties and inconsistencies due to the strong influence of Romanian, actually one of the main tasks of minority language planning is the elaboration and codification of the administrative and legal terminology which fits with Romanian administration, and the standardization of technical terminology as much as possible in accordance with that used in Hungary. Some efforts along these lines have already been made by linguists working on Hungarian–Romanian language contact and minority language planning.

2.5.2   *The prestige of the languages and of the linguistic variants*

The prestige of languages is a complex phenomenon: it may depend on the social status of its speakers, and it has social and cultural aspects as well. Therefore, one must distinguish between the social and cultural prestige of languages, since these two aspects may differ even in case of the same language (Lanstyák 2000a:145). The social prestige of a language depends on the beliefs of the speakers about the social success and advantages which can be reached by the use of a given language. Our data show that among Hungarians, in general, the social prestige of Romanian is quite high. As has already been mentioned, Romanian is used without any restriction in all social and institutional interactions, which increases its social prestige. In the Sociolinguistics of

Hungarian Outside Hungary (SHOH) project we asked our subjects how somebody can get on in Transylvania if s/he knows only Hungarian or Romanian.[7] If somebody can speak only Romanian in Transylvania, s/he can succeed *easily*, according to 45.52% of the subjects and *with difficulty* according to only 7.94%. Those who can speak only Hungarian can succeed *easily* in the opinion of only 6.1% of the subjects and *with difficulty* according to 46%. These data suggest that, in the perception of the subjects, monolingual Romanians can be far more successful in Transylvania than monolingual Hungarians.

The social prestige of Romanian can be seen also in the fact that many Hungarian schoolchildren study in classes where the medium of education is Romanian. In some parents' opinion children can get along more easily in life if they study in Romanian. According to some recent research, 75% of the mixed families choose schools with Romanian as the medium of instruction (Sorbán 2000: 167). But even in Hungarian families, i.e. in families where both parents are Hungarian, that ratio is quite high. According to statistics, about 25% of Hungarian children are educated in the Romanian language. Of course, there are differences among localities. As can be expected, there is a positive correlation between the proportion of the Romanian population in a locality and that of Hungarian families choosing Romanian schools for their children (Sorbán 2000: 168).

The cultural prestige of Hungarian seems to be quite high among Hungarian speakers. As much as 95.2% of our subjects declared that they read literature in Hungarian (and 33.17% do so in Romanian, too). 95.45% read the Bible and other religious books and 96.27% read newspapers and periodicals in Hungarian.

The cultural prestige of the local varieties of Hungarian is present in the subjects' answers to our question "where is the most beautiful Hungarian spoken?". The answers suggest that the prestige of the Transylvanian variety of Hungarian is very high not only among Hungarians in Romania, but in all areas of the Carpathian Basin where Hungarian is spoken. The overall results from the seven investigated countries of the SHOH project (Hungary and the countries neighboring it) show that the Transylvanian variety of Hungarian was given the highest rating (31.3%), higher even than the Hungarian spoken in Budapest (26.4%). Three-quarters (75.7%) of the Transylvanian subjects believed that the most beautiful Hungarian was spoken in Transylvania. It is worth mentioning that the tradition of the Hungarian literature and folklore in Transylvania as well as the myth about the expressivity and poetic character of the Szekler dialect play an important role in the high cultural prestige of the Transylvanian variety of Hungarian.

2.5.3   *Loyalty to the community and to the region*

The sense of identity of the Hungarian community in Romania is an important factor in Hungarian speakers' attitude towards their ethnic community and to the majority group, the Romanians. It is also important because there is a strong connection between language shift and a sense of ethnic identity, and also because language is very often an essential component of a sense of identity.

Table 5.8. Transylvania Hungarians' attachment to different Hungarian communities on a five-point scale

	1	2	3	4	5	Average value
Attachment to the Transylvanian Hungarian community	7 (3.3%)	4 (1.9%)	9 (4.2%)	23 (10.8%)	169 (79.7%)	4.63
Attachment to the Hungarian community in Romania	6 (2.8%)	6 (2.8%)	12 (5.6%)	32 (15%)	157 (73.7%)	4.53
Attachment to the Hungarian nation	4 (1.89%)	1 (0.47%)	14 (6.63%)	29 (13.74%)	163 (77.25%)	4.63
No attachment to any group	59 (95.16%)	0 (0%)	1 (1.61%)	1 (1.61%)	1 (1.61%)	1.14

Our question in the SHOH project questionnaire referring to the community was the following: "To what extent do you feel attached to: (a) the Transylvanian Hungarian community, (b) the Hungarian community in Romania, (c) the Hungarian nation, (d) nowhere?" The subjects had to rate their attachment to the mentioned groups on a five-grade scale, where number 1 meant *not attached at all*, and number 5 *very strongly attached*. The results show that around 90% of the subjects consider that they are *strongly* (4) and *very strongly* (5) attached to Hungarian communities (*a, b,* and *c*). The greatest value, 5, was chosen by most subjects to describe their attachment to the Transylvanian Hungarian community (79.7%). But considering the distribution of the subjects' opinion for the given categories, there is just a very slight difference between the subjects attachment to the Transylvanian Hungarian community and to the Hungarian nation, as can be seen by the fact that the average value for these communities is the same: 4.63 (see Table 5.8). It is noteworthy that the average value for the attachment to the Hungarian nation is the highest for the subjects from Romania compared to the other countries where Hungarian minority communities live and which were studied as part of the SHOH project: Romania 4.63, Subcarpathia 4.62, Slovakia 4.48, Austria 4.32, Slovenia 4.25, and Vojvodina 4.16 (Göncz 1999:82).

Concerning the subjects' loyalty to the region, we asked the following question: "To what extent are you attached to the following places: (a) your own village or town, (b) Transylvania, (c) Szekler Land (in eastern Transylvania), (d) Romania, outside Transylvania, (e) Hungary, (f) Europe, (g) nowhere?" The same five-grade scale was used in order to evaluate the degree of the subjects' attitude. The answers show that the great majority of the subjects (88.3%) are *strongly* (4) or *very strongly* (5) attached to Transylvania, and of these 74.2% feel *very strongly* (5) attached to Transylvania, and 14.1% *strongly* (4). The subjects' option for their own village or town indicates that their attachment to the place they live in is very strong: these ratings are very close to

Table 5.9. Transylvania Hungarians' attachment to different regions on a five-point scale

	1		2		3		4		5		Average value
	N	%	N	%	N	%	N	%	N	%	
Your own village or town	2	(0.93%)	4	(1.86%)	21	(9.76%)	33	(1.34%)	155	(72.09%)	4.55
Transylvania	4	(1.9%)	4	(1.9%)	17	(8%)	30	(14.1%)	158	(74.2%)	4.56
Szekler Land	31	(14.9%)	27	(13.0%)	33	(15.9%)	36	(17.3%)	81	(38.9%)	3.52
Romania, outside Transylvania	91	(44.8%)	32	(15.8%)	44	(21.7%)	17	(8.4%)	19	(9.4%)	2.36
Hungary	23	(10.84%)	23	(10.84%)	60	(28.30%)	40	(18.67%)	66	(31.13%)	3.48
Europe	18	(8.5%)	29	(13.6%)	55	(25.8%)	34	(16%)	77	(36.2%)	3.57
Nowhere	57	(98.27%)	0	(0%)	0	(0%)	0	(0%)	1	(1.73%)	1.06

their ratings of Transylvania (see Table 5.9). Overall the subjects' attachment to Szekler Land is lower than to Transylvania or their own village or town. But there is a significant difference in the ratings of those subjects who live in Szekler Land and the others. The former are naturally more attached to Szekler Land, their native region, than the others. The lowest attachment of the subjects is to other regions of Romania, while they declare themselves attached to Hungary and to Europe almost to the same extent. Only one subject claimed definitely that he did not belong anywhere.

Comparing these values to the results of other investigated countries in the Carpathian Basin as part of the SHOH project, it is clear that in the case of Hungarians in Romania, the average value concerning their attachment to their own localities (4.55) is higher than that for the whole Carpathian Basin (4.40) (Göncz 1999: 78–85). The intensity of the attachment to the community and the territory might be a source of power for the Hungarians in Romania in the maintenance of their language and culture, and thus it may work, to a certain extent, against the assimilation processes.

2.6 Language use in the minority context

The results of the SHOH project in certain aspects confirmed previous knowledge about the conditions of mother tongue use in minority situations.

In our research, speakers were asked about the domains of their Hungarian and Romanian language use. Concerning the frequency of the use of a certain language, we observe that the type of settlement (urban vs. rural) is a relevant factor. Hungarian subjects living in towns declared more use of Romanian in various situations. Thus, 68% of the urban and 43% of the rural subjects said that they used Romanian when shopping. In the case of doctors' offices, the proportion of those who declared that they spoke Romanian is 62.9% in towns and 42.1% in villages. From these data we infer that the use of Romanian is more intense in towns than in villages. This conclusion is also supported by those demographic data which show that 61.58% of the Hungarian town

Table 5.10. The use of Hungarian at the workplace by subjects' occupation, among Hungarians in Romania

Occupation	Almost never		Seldom		Often		Total	
	N	%	N	%	N	%	N	%
Farmers	1	(7.1%)	1	(7.1%)	12	(85.7%)	14	(100%)
Workers	0		7	(21.9%)	25	(78.1%)	32	(100%)
Skilled workers	0		8	(28.6%)	20	(71.4%)	28	(100%)
Office workers	2	(20%)	3	(30%)	5	(50%)	10	(100%)
Liberal arts professionals	0		3	(10.3%)	26	(89.7%)	29	(100%)
Science professionals	0		4	(11.1%)	32	(88.9%)	36	(100%)
Doctors, pharmacists	0		3	(30%)	7	(70%)	10	(100%)
Agricultural professionals	0		0		6	(100%)	6	(100%)
Others	2	(6.5%)	12	(38.7%)	17	(54.8%)	31	(100%)
TOTAL	5	(2.6%)	41	(20.9%)	150	(76.5%)	196	(100%)

dwellers live in towns where they are in minority, and 79.05% of the Hungarian rural population live in villages where they are in absolute (over 50%) majority.

71.56% of the subjects declared that they used Romanian (or Romanian, too) in administrative offices, while 37.73% used Hungarian; 80.60% used Romanian at the police, while 10.37% used Hungarian; and 61.61% used Romanian at courts of law while 18.48% used Hungarian. These data illustrate the well-known status of the languages under discussion: in Romania, Hungarian and the other minority languages in general are less used and tolerated in formal situations and in administrative contexts.

At the workplace, the usage of the two languages under discussion seems to be more balanced: 76.5% of the subjects claimed that they often spoke Hungarian at their workplace, and 64% that they often spoke Romanian. But there is a significant difference if we take into consideration the occupation of the subjects: 50% of the office workers declared that they almost never or seldom spoke Hungarian at the workplace, while almost 90% of the liberal arts professionals said that they often used Hungarian in the same situation (see Table 5.10).

The use of Romanian at the workplace shows the same differentiation: all the office workers declared that they often spoke Romanian, and only 39.3% of the subjects from the liberal arts professionals' group said the same (see Table 5.11). It is important to mention that representatives of certain occupations declared almost in the same proportion that they often spoke Romanian or Hungarian. Thus, 70% of the doctors and pharmacists said that they often used Hungarian at the workplace, and they chose the same rating, *often*, to the same extent for Romanian. A similar balance for the extent of the use of the two languages can be found in the science professionals' opinions: they declared in 88.95% of the cases that they often used Hungarian at the workplace and in 80% of the cases that they often used Romanian, too.

On the other hand, according to the subjects' opinions, Hungarian is used in most of the cases in private, informal situations. The following percentages refer to subjects who declared that they spoke Hungarian in different relationships: 99.5% with their

Table 5.11. The use of Romanian at the workplace by the subjects' occupation, among Hungarians in Romania

Occupation	Almost never		Seldom		Often		Total	
	N	%	N	%	N	%	N	%
Farmers	5	(35.7%)	3	(21.4%)	6	(42.9%)	14	(100%)
Workers	3	(9.7%)	6	(19.4%)	22	(71.0%)	31	(100%)
Skilled workers	4	(14.3%)	9	(32.1%)	15	(53.6%)	28	(100%)
Office workers	0	0	0	0	10	(100%)	10	(100%)
Liberal arts professionals	2	(7.1%)	11	(53.6%)	15	(39.3%)	28	(100%)
Science professionals	0	0	7	(20%)	28	(80%)	35	(100%)
Doctors, pharmacists	1	(10%)	2	(20%)	7	(70%)	10	(100%)
Agricultural professionals	0	0	2	(33.3%)	4	(66.7%)	6	(100%)
Others	5	(16.7%)	5	(16.7%)	20	(66.7%)	30	(100%)
TOTAL	20	(10.4%)	49	(25.5%)	123	(64.1%)	192	(100%)

parents, 99.7% with their grandparents, 97.94% with their children, 97.4% with their spouses, 99.51% with friends (67.1% of the latter also spoke Romanian with friends).

In verbal activities in the mental sphere (thinking, counting etc.) the usage of Hungarian among native speakers clearly dominates. The ratio of subjects who declared that they used Hungarian in various mental activities is high: 98.04% think in Hungarian (13.17% also in Romanian), 95.07% pray in Hungarian, 96.11% count in Hungarian, and among those who admitted that they did swear (78%), 92% swear in Hungarian (and 31.51% of these swear in Romanian, too).

When asked about their language usage in writing, 83.7% of the subjects declared that they used Romanian when writing a document addressed to the authorities, and 67.3% when writing in their profession, while only 42.8% said that they used Hungarian when they wrote about a subject connected to their profession.

As far as the subjects' self-reported data about their proficiency in languages is concerned, the majority of the subjects (65%) declared that they spoke Romanian *well* or *very well*, and 7.9% said that they had a *native-like* command of Romanian. 94.7% of the subjects expressed the opinion that they had a *native-like* command of Hungarian.

All these results suggest that the bilingualism of the Hungarians in Romania is an unbalanced one, it is characterized by the dominance of their mother tongue, i.e. Hungarian.

A discussion of Hungarians in Romania in general may hide important differences that exist between the Hungarians living in localities where they form the majority group and those who live in dispersed communities. The differences between these two minority situations are so great that sometimes the term 'Hungarians in Romania' feels very much like an abstraction which hides important aspects of reality. Sometimes the overall results about Hungarians in Romania are not representative either of the Hungarians in a majority situation in their localities, or of those living in dispersed communities. In order to get a more refined image about the Hungarian language in Romania, we will now focus on these differences.

Table 5.12. The frequency of Hungarian and Romanian use at the workplace by the type of locality, among Hungarians in Romania

Informants living in	Hungarian						Romanian					
	Almost never		Seldom		Often		Almost never		Seldom		Often	
	N	%	N	%	N	%	N	%	N	%	N	%
Hungarian-majority localities	0	(0%)	2	(2%)	98	(98%)	20	(20.4%)	42	(42.9%)	36	(36.7%)
Hungarian-minority localities	5	(4.9%)	41	(39.8%)	57	(55.3%)	1	(1%)	9	(8.9%)	91	(90.1%)

As we mentioned above, 83.7% of the subjects declared that they used Romanian (or Romanian, too) when writing an official letter addressed to the authorities. If we take into account whether the subjects' community forms the majority or the minority in that locality, it is clear that the above mentioned 83.7% does not mirror the situation of either group: only 66.2% of the subjects living in a majority at their locality said that they wrote in Romanian (or in Romanian, too), when writing to the authorities, while 91.9% of Hungarians living in dispersed communities said the same.

The differences are also considerable in workplace language use. While 98% of the subjects living in Hungarian-majority towns or villages declared that they often used Hungarian (or Hungarian, too) at their workplace, among the dispersed Hungarian subjects this ratio is just 55.3%. No subjects living in Hungarian-majority town or village said that they almost never used Hungarian at the workplace, while 4.9% of those living in Hungarian-minority localities said the same which means that they worked in a completely Romanian-speaking environment. For the other categories of frequency (*seldom* and *often*) the differences between the subjects living in minority and majority conditions are also notable (see Table 5.12 and Figure 5.3).

There are also considerable differences between subjects living in Hungarian-majority localities and those in dispersed communities in the usage of Hungarian in verbal activities in the mental sphere. In Hungarian-majority localities the percentage of those subjects who declared that they used Romanian or Romanian, too, when thinking is 5.6%, and the proportion of those who admitted that they used Romanian (or Romanian, too) when counting is 3.7%. The same percentages in Hungarian-minority localities are 22.6% and 30.4% respectively, and, thus, the differences are not negligible.

Taking into consideration whether the subject lives in a Hungarian-minority or in a Hungarian-majority town or village, one can form a more refined image about the domains of the use of Hungarian and Romanian, too. The differences are obvious in this case. For example, 96.2% of subjects living in Hungarian-minority towns or villages declared that they spoke Romanian in doctors' offices and at the post office. In

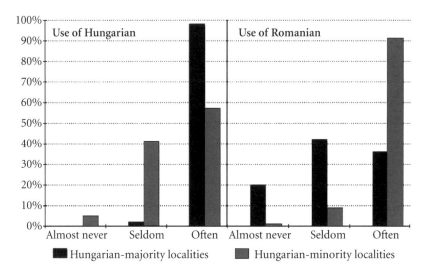

Figure 5.3. The frequency of Hungarian and Romanian use at the workplace by the type of locality among Hungarians in Romania

Hungarian-majority localities 31.5% said that they used Romanian in doctors' offices and 44.4% at the post office. In Hungarian-minority localities, 90.4% used Romanian when addressing foreigners, whereas in Hungarian-majority localities only 44.4% did. These results confirm the claim that the domains of Romanian language use are more numerous in Hungarian-minority localities, and the use of Hungarian is marginal in that social context.

As can be presumed, the official language, Romanian, is better known by Hungarians in Hungarian-minority localities. Analyzing the subjects' estimation of their Romanian proficiency, we found that those living in Hungarian-minority towns and villages claimed to a greater degree that they had a *native-like* command of Romanian or that they spoke it *very well*: their ratio, 10.3%, is almost double that of subjects in Hungarian-majority localities (5.6%). In Hungarian-majority localities 10.2% of the subjects declared that they could speak Romanian *very well*, whereas in Hungarian-minority localities 38.3% did the same.

3. Linguistic aspects

The locus of language contact and of borrowing is the bilingual individual. But the consequences of language contact go beyond bilingual speakers, and some of the borrowed lexical elements and grammatical structures may become widely used among monolingual speakers of the borrowing language, too. Below we analyze both the lexical and structural aspects of the influence of Romanian on the Hungarian spoken in Romania.

The research of Romanian-Hungarian language contact has a tradition of several decades. Important studies have been published about the linguistic influence of Romanian on the Hungarian language (Bakos 1982; Márton 1972; Péntek 1981; Szabó T. 1962; Szabó 1968, 1975; Zsemlyei 1979, 1995), as well as about the Hungarian influence on Romanian (Kis 1975; Rosetti 1964; Tamás 1966), although the socio- and psycholinguistic aspects of the contact were mostly neglected in them since they mostly focused on phonological, morphological and, to a certain extent, the semantic integration of loanwords. In the 1960s and 1970s, an intensive collection of dialectal lexical data took place in the Hungarian regional and social dialects. In 1977 Márton et al.'s dictionary of Romanian borrowings in the Transylvanian Hungarian regional and social dialects was published. Based on this lexical data, we created a computerized database of Romanian loanwords used by Hungarian speakers and, of course, later on new data were added to the database from our own research and from other sources (e.g. Bakos 1982, 1984; Murádin 1995). At present, the database of Romanian origin elements contains 2,714 lexical items used in different varieties of Hungarian in Transylvania. Most of these lexical elements are not loanwords in the sense of phonologically and morphologically integrated elements widely used by monolinguals as well. A significant part of them are products of lexical interference or code-switching, and idiosyncratic loans, lexical items which have not (yet) become part of the speech community's vocabulary (which is why they are also sometimes called speech borrowings, cf. Grosjean 1995:5), and which are sometimes interpreted as mistakes made by bilingual speakers.

3.1 Lexical borrowing

In this subsection we want to answer the following questions: What kind of words are borrowed from Romanian into the Hungarian spoken in Romania? Which are the semantic fields they refer to? And which registers of the vocabulary are influenced by the borrowing?

The Romanian borrowings originating from the administrative language are the most widely and most often used. (In our database the number of such borrowings is 201.) They do not usually designate concepts which cannot be expressed in Hungarian but, in most cases, have equivalents in Hungarian, although this fact does not rule out the possibility that these borrowings are filling gaps in the speakers' vocabulary.[8] Loanwords from the Romanian administrative language often designate the names of official documents (R *abonament* 'season-ticket' > RH *abonament,* vs. HH *bérlet*; R *certificat* 'certificate' > RH *csertifikát,* vs. HH *bizonyítvány*; R *decizie* 'order, decree' > RH *decsizió,* vs. HH *végzés*; R *chitanţă* 'acknowledgment' > RH *kitánca,* vs. HH *elismervény*), administrative notions (R *a angaja* 'employ' > RH *ángázsál,* vs. HH *alkalmaz*; R *a aproba* 'approve' > RH *aprobál,* vs. HH *jóváhagy*; R *vechime* 'period of service' > RH *vékimé,* vs. HH *szolgálati idő*) and function names of administrative positions (R *notar* 'town-clerk' > RH *notár,* vs. HH *jegyző*; R *primar* 'mayor' > RH *primár,* vs. HH *polgármester*; R *secretar* 'secretary' > RH *szekretár,* vs. HH *titkár*).

Such borrowings are used especially in informal speech; in the mass media and in formal situations in general their standard, HH variants are used. Another area of the vocabulary where Romanian borrowings can be found in great numbers is the technical language. There are 171 such borrowed lexical elements of Romanian origin in our database. These borrowings designate work processes, tools, basic materials and are present mostly in the speech of workers who learned the technical language in Romanian at school or at the workplace. Here are a few examples for this type of loanwords: R *aparat* 'machine' > RH *ápárát*, vs. HH *készülék*; R *a monta* 'assemble' > RH *montál*, vs. HH *összeszerel*; R *lichid* 'brake fluid' > RH *likid*, vs. HH *fékfolyadék*.

Loanwords originating from the language used in commercial activities are also numerous. These lexical items are names of goods or designate different aspects of selling and buying. Since minority speakers come to know many names of goods in Romanian during everyday shopping, it is natural that they name these objects using borrowings.

These layers of loanwords also indicate the registers of the mother tongue vocabulary where Hungarians in Romania have gaps and uncertainty. If we had no other data about the speech of ethnic Hungarians in Romania, we might infer from these loanwords some aspects of the lexical competence of the minority Hungarian population.

The visual environment might have an important role in the borrowing process of certain words. If there is a tendency in the bilingual speaker to name an object using its "official" name, the visual stimulus might strengthen that willingness. Many Romanian loanwords used by Hungarian speakers are found in written form on billboards, advertising pillars, building facades, packaging and official bills and documents. The frequent appearance of these visual linguistic signs favors their fixation in the memory and might make it easier to retrieve them. We marked in our database those lexical items which are very often seen in written form in the visual environment (on notices, labels, advertisements, institution names etc.), and we found that the visual environment must be taken into account as a factor which might favor the general acceptance of certain borrowings. In our database we have 461 loanwords which are very widespread and are used in the regional standard, in everyday speech. Of these 461 lexical items, 248 are connected in some respect to the visual representations. Thus the visual environment probably favors the acceptance and use of 53.7% of the most generally occurring loanwords (while its effect is not relevant in the remaining 46.3%) (Benő 1999:273).

In our Romanian loanword database, one can find many borrowings which are used not because there is a gap in the minority speakers' vocabulary, but for other reasons.

One factor which seems to play an important role among the causes of borrowing is the expressivity of the phonological form. In the case of Romanian loanwords the number of onomatopoetic words is considerable. Here we use the term 'onomatopoetic' both for words that imitate sounds, and for words which are not in fact sound imitative but whose form is felt to be expressive, such as, for example, the English *hurly-burly, walkie-talkie* or *zigzag*. The proportion of onomatopoetic loanwords is different according to their parts of speech. It is quite high in case of interjections (10 out of 25, or 40%) and verbs (107 out of 283, or 37.74%), considerable in case of the adjectives (70 out of 258, or 27.13%), and quite low, but not negligible, in the case of nouns (103 out of 2,080, or 4.95%.). If we examine how widely these onomatopoetic words are used, we observe that they are not less widespread than other loanwords, so a considerable part of them is widely used in informal speech. For illustration, here are the etymons of a few borrowings with sound expressivity. Verbs: *bîlbîi* 'stammer' (RH *bîl-bîjál*), *bîzîi* 'buzz' (RH *bîzajál*), *ciocăni, ciocni* 'knock' (RH *csokonyál*), *fluiera* 'whistle' (RH *flujerál*), *fornăi* 'snare' (RH *fornojál*), *hondrăni* 'jabber (away)' (RH *hondronyál*), *hîrcîi, horcăi* 'snare' (RH *horkojál*), *hăucăi* 'howl' (RH *haukál*), *hîrîi* 'growl' (RH *hîrăjál*) etc.; adjectives: *băbălău* 'clumsy' (RH *babaló*), *buiguit* 'cracked' (RH *bujgujit*), *bulbucat* 'goggle/pop-eyed' (RH *bulbukát*), *gîngăit* 'stutterer' (RH *gîngîjit*), *tanda-manda* 'fiddlesticks!' (RH *tándá-mándá*), *treanca-flanca* 'gibberish' (RH *tránká-flánká*) etc., nouns: *buhună* 'owl; unkempt person' (RH *buhuna*), *burbună* 'whirlpool' (RH *burbuna*), *băbălău* 'coward' (RH *babaló*), *hala-bala* 'loud speech' (RH *hálábálá*), and *pupui* 'kiss' (RH *pupuj*).

Among Romanian borrowings the proportion of words with negative (pejorative, or ironic) connotation is also considerable. They designate negative human and animal characteristics (mental or physical deficiencies, lack of fertility, clumsiness, laziness, talkativeness, defective speech, etc.). In the Transylvanian regional and social dialects the number and the proportion of loanwords with negative, pejorative connotation in part of speech breakdown is the following: 206 (79.84%) adjectives; 94 (30.51%) verbs; 171 (8.23%) nouns. Although the phenomenon is well-known in the literature (cf. Weinreich 1953:58–59; Bakos 1982:101), there is no generally accepted explanation for it. Our opinion is that ethnocentricity as a socio-psychological motivation should be taken into consideration in this respect (Szilágyi N. 1994). Ethnocentricity is a general characteristic of ethnic groups. In an ethnocentric view (which is spontaneous and unconscious behavior), values are organized in a bipolar way, based on the duality of *we* and *them*. The asymmetry of ethnocentricity is manifested in the fact that the positive features are connected to the group labeled *we* and the negative, unpleasant features to *them*. The borrowing of pejorative words could be explained by their folk perception, in the sense that people seem to believe that negative features, characteristic mainly of *them*, are named more authentically in the language of those *them*, therefore they are felt to be much more evocative.

Taking into consideration the semantic characteristics of the notions designated by the loanwords, important semantic aspects of the borrowing and integration process are revealed. In the hierarchy of concepts (categories), not all levels of abstraction are equally important for human categorization. According to findings of cognitive psychology, there is a preferred level for categorization: that of the basic level categories (Eysenck & Keane 1990; Kellogg 1995; Mervis & Rosch 1981; Soslo 1995). The superordinate and subordinate categories are compared with this level. Main characteristics of the basic level categories are the following: (1) they are expressed by simple words,

(2) the words belonging to basic level categories are the most frequent in speech, (3) in childhood they are first learnt in comparison with super- and subordinate categories, (4) basic level categories can be defined ostensively, and (5) they are the most abstract categories which can be correlated with specific physical forms (Mervis & Rosch 1981). In this context, *apple* designates a basic level category, *fruit* a superordinate and *Jonathan* a subordinate one. Most loanwords of Romanian origin refer to subordinate categories and make the taxonomy of certain semantic fields more subtle. Here are a few examples: RH *fisza* 'untidy woman' (R *fiţă*), RH *sivoja* 'thin, runny mud' (R *şivoi*), RH *mator* 'old ram' (R *mator*), RH *tálánka* 'cow bell with cracked voice' (R *talancă*), RH *sztárpa* 'barren cow' (R *stearpă*), RH *bába zile* 'spring snow-storm' (R *babă zile*), RH *guruj* 'low hill' (R *grui*).

We also examined if the basic level categories have any effect on the semantic change of the borrowings, and we found that most of the cases of narrowing of meaning can be described as changes from the basic level category to the subordinate category: a lexeme which in Romanian signifies a basic level category, turns into one in a subordinate category in Hungarian (Benő 2000: 121–132). In this way we can show more accurately the level at which the word meaning is the most often restricted: R *broască* 'frog' > RH *braszka* 'big frog', R *oală* 'pot' > RH *óla* 'earthen pot', R *ceaun* 'cauldron' > RH *csaun* 'cauldron for distilling brandy', R *căruţă* 'cart' > RH *karuca* 'oxen-cart', R *topor* 'ax' > RH *topor* 'little ax', R *toşcă* 'bag' > RH *cóska* 'linen bag'.

Analyzing the integration process of the loanwords, we find that the analogous grammatical structures of the two languages in contact may favor the integration of the borrowing. For example, the Romanian diminutive suffix *-că*, *-ţă* accidentally has a similar Hungarian equivalent (which, however, is of different origin): *-ka*, *-ca*. (Taking into consideration that the vowel *ă* in Romanian loanwords is substituted by *a* in Hungarian, the similarity of the suffixes is more evident.) The influence of the similar morphological structures is clear in the cases when the final syllables *-că*, *-ţă* in Romanian loanwords were interpreted as being diminutive suffixes even in those words where they do not have this function in Romanian but are part of the stem, as it can be seen in the following examples: R *gîlcă* 'knot'> RH *gilka* 'little knot'; R *cîrtiţă* 'fistula' > RH *kertica* 'little wound'; R *roşeaţă* 'rash, spot' > RH *rosáca* 'little blister'.

As is well known, the integration process of the borrowings is also an adaptation to the semantic structure of the language. This phenomenon is obvious in synonymity-based differentiation of loanwords, which is remarkable not only in the change of denotative meaning (e.g. restriction of meaning), but also in acquiring new stylistic values. We found that many loanwords, especially those denoting human features are stylistically marked in the speech of Hungarian speakers: they are considered pejorative, ironic, derogatory or humorous, although the etymons in themselves are stylistically neutral in the Romanian language. Because of this change in the stylistic value, loanwords become different from their Hungarian lexical equivalents and, thus, their semantic integration is facilitated: R *ciordi* 'steal' > RH *csurgyál* 'filch, pilfer' (humorous), R *doamna* 'lady' > RH *doamna* 'lady' (ironic), R *dumnezeu* 'God' > RH *dumnyező* 'god' (pejorative, used especially in curses), R *gîrtan* 'Adam's apple' > RH *gírtány* 'Adam's apple' (humorous), R *cîcăi* 'stammer' > RH *kikijál* 'stammer' (ironic).

3.2 Structural borrowing

The results of the SHOH project make it possible now to analyze some aspects of the Romanian-Hungarian interference at the structural level. The questionnaire used in that project also focused on some differences that might exist between the Hungarian spoken in Hungary and the Hungarian used in Romania. (For a translated version of the parts of the questionnaire that contained the language tasks, see the Appendix.) We now present those results where Romanian influence is very likely.

3.2.1   *Synthetic vs. analytical constructions*
As is well known, typologically Hungarian is language which is more synthetic than analytical. While analytical languages in order to express certain notions very often use phrases consisting of 2 or 3 lexical elements, Hungarian usually makes use of compounds and derived words. Analytical characteristics can be found in Hungarian too, partly due to the influence of the Indo-European languages, but they are less frequent. According to psycho- and sociolinguistic research, bilingual Hungarian speakers (i.e. those living in minority situations outside Hungary) in many cases prefer analytical variants (Göncz 1999:151). Using questions where one of the variants is a compound or a derived word and the other is a phrase consisting of several elements, one finds differences in frequency in the use of the two variants by monolingual Hungarians in Hungary vs. bilingual minority Hungarians outside Hungary. We had nine such questions in our questionnaire. In five of the nine questions involving the use of synthetic vs. analytical structures, significant differences can be found between Romania and Hungary. Since in all of the cases the average result of the analytical usage in the six Carpathian Basin countries of the SHOH project is higher than in Hungary, we can safely claim that bilingual Hungarian speakers use the analytical (nonstandard) variants in their speech more often, probably as a result of the second language influence (Table 5.13). Observing the social variables correlated with these analytical structures, it is found that the educational level and occupation of the speakers is a determining factor in six of the nine cases. In general the following correlation can be pointed out for Romania Hungarians: the higher the speakers' educational level, the fewer analytical variants occur in their speech. The age of the speaker and the type of the settlement (Hungarian-minority vs. Hungarian-majority locality) also influence the choice of the variants: we found significant differences in four cases in this respect, namely, that the young subjects and those living in dispersed Hungarian communities chose analytical variants more often. It seems that the speakers' gender is less of an influential factor here: only in one case did we find a statistically significant difference between the answers of men and women (sentence 607 of the SHOH questionnaire, see in the Appendix, $\chi^2 = 3.264$, p<.10).

Table 5.13. The acceptance of synthetic (standard) vs. analytical (nonstandard) variants by Hungarians in Romania (R), Hungary (H), and the Carpathian Basin (C)

Variables		Acceptance of the standard variant			Acceptance of the nonstandard variant		
		R	H	C	R	H	C
Q. 503	N	78	77	302	137	30	532
	%	36.3	71.4	36.2	63.7	28.6	63.8
Q. 507	N	103	86	504	113	21	335
	%	47.7	80.4	60.1	52.3	19.6	39.9
Q. 514	N	198	104	805	17	3	35
	%	92.1	97.2	95.8	7.9	2.8	4.2
Q. 532	N	135	68	485	76	39	326
	%	64	63.6	59.8	36	36.4	40.2
Q. 536	N	60	20	160	151	20	160
	%	28.4	18.7	9.7	71.6	81.3	80,3
Q. 603	N	153	97	592	60	10	238
	%	71.5	90.7	71.3	28.5	9.3	28.7
Q. 605	N	181	90	663	35	17	173
	%	83.8	84.1	79.3	16.2	15.9	20.7
Q. 607	N	126	61	450	87	45	379
	%	59.2	57.5	54.3	40.8	42.5	45,7
Q. 613	N	134	84	511	78	21	316
	%	63.2	80	61.8	36.8	20	38.2
Average	%	60.7	71.5	59.8	39.3	28.5	40.2

3.2.2   The use of redundant personal pronouns

The use of the redundant overt personal pronoun is also an analytical tendency in Hungarian speech. Since the personal pronoun as a direct object is coded in the definite conjugation of the verb following the agglutinative features of Hungarian (e.g. *láttalak* 'I saw you'), it is redundant to include the pronoun as a direct object (*láttalak téged*). However, it can be heard in everyday speech, and one might suppose that its use is more frequent in the speech of bilingual Hungarians. The Romanian results of the research point to the fact that there is such a tendency (in Romania the use of redundant pronouns is more frequent), but this tendency is not strong (and we should also bear in mind that these results reflect the judgement of respondents to language tasks rather than describe their actual use). The ratio of the general acceptance of redundant pronouns in test sentences of the SHOH questionnaire is 38.7% in Hungary and 40.37% in Romania.

3.2.3   Singular vs. plural

In Hungarian, the plural form is used less than in Indo-European languages. It is not used in noun phrases after numerals, before nouns designating paired body parts, or when speaking about identical or similar things belonging to one category (e.g. *Almát vásároltam* 'I bought apples', and not *almákat*, in the plural). We had nine items in our questionnaire for testing the subjects' choice between singular and plural forms in different syntactic contexts. The results we found confirmed the hypothesis that Hungarian speakers living outside Hungary, in bilingual situations, might use plurals in sentences where the speakers of Hungarian in Hungary would use singular forms. In Romania, our subjects accepted the nonstandard plural variant in 37.47% of the cases, on average. This ratio is higher than that for the subjects in Hungary (31.8%). In almost all cases, the subjects living in Hungary chose in greater proportion the standard (singular) variant than Hungarians in Romania did. The answers to three questions pointed to significant differences between Hungarian speakers in the two countries. The results show that social variables such as level of education and occupation have a strong positive correlation with the choice of the standard variant in this case, too. The type of the locality (minority- or majority-Hungarians) also has a considerable impact on the choice of singular vs. plural. The Hungarians living in dispersed communities chose the nonstandard, plural forms significantly more often than those living in Hungarian-majority localities. This points to the fact that this phenomenon is in correlation with the degree of the influence of the second language. The usage of the nonstandard plural is less influenced by the speakers' gender and age.

3.2.4 *Feminization*

In Hungarian there is no grammatical gender. Most nouns can be used both for referring to males and females. Like in English, nouns as *tanár* 'teacher', *orvos* 'doctor', *könyvelő* 'bookkeeper' are used in a gender-neutral sense without any specification of the grammatical gender. There are just a few exceptions in Hungarian, as the case of the nouns denoting occupations which are considered to be feminine: e.g. *mosónő* 'washerwoman' or those instances where the female characteristics are emphasized: *táncosnő* 'female dancer' (Göncz 1999: 156). To emphasize that the person we are referring to is a woman, in Hungarian a compound can be used: N + *nő* ('woman'), as in *tanárnő* ('female teacher') or *doktornő* ('female doctor'). (It is a linguistic universal that, in general, the feminine gender is marked with an extra grammatical or lexical marker, while the masculine gender has a morphologically simple form.) If the linguistic context makes it clear that the person we are talking about is a woman, in Hungarian the simple generic form is used. Since in Romanian it is obligatory to mark the gender of nouns, it is hypothesized that in the case of a strong Romanian influence, the bilingual speaker may use the feminine compound form of the nouns more often in situations where the monolingual speaker of standard Hungarian would use a generic form. Four of our questions in the questionnaire referred to the use of feminine compound forms in sentences where, in the standard, generic forms occur (questions 631 through 634, see in the Appendix). A statistical analysis of the answers reveals that the subjects in Romania chose the standard variant less often. The differences between the subjects from Hungary and those from Romania are very significant in each of the four cases. The average ratio of the former group of subjects' acceptance of the standard variable is 79.8%, while for the Transylvanian subjects that ratio is just 46.22%. This percentage is lower than the average ratio in the answers of Hungarian speakers in the Carpathian

Basin (59.5%). The cause of the differences is probably the influence of Romanian. Three social variables might be influential in this respect: level of education, occupation and the age of the subjects. We found significant differences between various occupations. Agricultural, manual and skilled workers chose the nonstandard feminine variant more often. As far as education is concerned, speakers with university and high school degrees use the standard variant more often. In two of the four instances we found significant differences between the answers of the subjects of different age: a greater proportion of young speakers use the nonstandard feminine variant than the older subjects.

3.2.5   The use of the diminutive

The use of the diminutive suffix is not as general in Hungarian as in Romanian or in Slavic languages. But frequency of this use might be influenced by these languages. Indeed, the results from Romania show that the acceptance of forms with the diminutive suffix in most of the questions is significantly higher than in Hungary. The influence of the Romanian language can be shown by the fact that subjects living in dispersed Hungarian communities accepted significantly more often the variant with the diminutive suffix than other subjects from Romania, probably as a result of the stronger Romanian influence (in questions 504 and 538, see in the Appendix).

3.3   Summary of the linguistic findings

The variety of Hungarian spoken in Romania differs from the Hungarian used in Hungary as a result of Romanian-Hungarian language contact and, as previous research (Péntek 2001a, b) has shown, also as a consequence of the stronger dialectal characteristics of the everyday variety of Hungarian used in Romania. We also investigated in our project the influence of the dialectal, everyday language on the subjects' linguistic competence. The results show that a strong dialectal background influences a subject's judgments about the standard character of certain grammatical structures and lexical items such that they tend to consider dialectal forms as standard.

In conclusion it can be pointed out that the intensity of the Romanian influence depends on two main factors: the type of locality and level of education. Romanian influence is strongest in the case of Hungarians living in dispersed communities, as well as in those with a lower level of education. We can also state that the differences between the regional varieties of Hungarian in Hungary and in the neighboring countries are minor in general, and the Hungarian language has maintained its relative organic unity, although in case of the minority varieties of Hungarian, the influences of bilingualism and of the legal conditions of minority language use are evident.

4. Conclusion

The use of Hungarian as a minority language is directly influenced by its social status in Romania, which is determined, to a great extent, by its legal status, that is, by the linguistic rights of the people belonging to the minority group. The use of and loyalty to the mother tongue is most likely a determining factor in avoiding assimilation and the change of ethnic identity. A decrease in the number of Hungarian speakers is determined by several factors, the most important of which are emigration, a low birth rate, assimilation, the ethnic composition of the settlement in question, a great number of ethnically mixed marriages (which favor the majority group), and an insufficient system of education in the minority language.

In the perception of the Hungarian speakers in Romania, the cultural prestige of Hungarian seems to be quite high. According to the findings of recent sociolinguistic research, loyalty to the community and to the region is also high among Hungarians in Romania.

As far as the domains of Hungarian and Romanian language use among the Hungarians of Romania are concerned, the type (urban vs. rural) and the ethnic structure of the settlement are relevant factors in this respect.

Linguistic borrowing between the minority and majority language affects especially the lexicon, but, to some extent, it can be traced in the grammatical structure also. Besides the well known causes of lexical borrowing, there are also others which favor this process: the insufficiency in the language of administration in the minority group, the influence of the visual environment, the expressivity of the phonetic form of the loanword, and ethnocentricity as a factor of socio-psychological motivation, as well as certain cognitive semantic and grammatical aspects of the languages in contact.

Notes

1. All data concerning demographics are from the 1992 and 2002 census, unless otherwise indicated. For 1992 census figures, see *Recensămîntul... 1992*, for 2002 census figures, see *Recensămîntul... 2002*, and http://www.recensama.ro/

2. The term Transylvania also includes reference to the regions of Partium and Bánát, which were not part of the historical principality.

3. Corresponding data from the 2002 census are not available yet.

4. It is worth mentioning that education issues were an important part of the ethnic conflicts which transformed a mass meeting into a street fighting between Hungarians and Romanian peasants (bussed in specially for this occasion) in Târgu Mureş/Marosvásárhely on March 19th, 1990.

5. Legea nr. 84 din 24 iulie 1995, republicată. Monitorul Oficial nr. 606 din 10 decembrie 1999.

6. Lege nr. 215 din 23 aprilie 2001 administraţiei publice locale, Monitorul Oficial al României nr. 204 din 23 aprilie 2001.

7. In the sociolinguistic research carried out in Romania as part of the SHOH study, 216 Hungarian subjects were asked about the scenes of their mother tongue usage, as well as about certain aspects of the verbal repertoire and the varieties of Hungarian in actual use. The composition of the sample was as follows: 111 rural (51.38%) vs. 105 (48.2%) urban subjects; 111 (51.38%) men vs. 105 (48.2%) women, 108 (50%) persons living in Hungarian majority localities vs. 108 (50%) living in dispersed Hungarian communities; and 73 (33.79%) older, 75 (34.73) middle-aged, vs. 68 (31.48%) young subjects. The educational level of the subjects was as follows: 85 (39.4%) university or college graduates, 39 (18.1%) high school graduates, 6 (2%) specialized secondary school graduates, 43 (19.9%) studied in technical schools, 36 (16.7%) with 5 to 8 years of education, and 7 (3.2%) with 1 to 4 years of education.

8. RH forms, used by Hungarians in Romania in everyday spoken colloquial discourse, are usually considered nonstandard Hungarian in Romania.

CHAPTER 6

The Csángós of Romania

Klára Sándor

1. Introduction

The Csángós are "one of Europe's most enigmatic and least known ethnic minorities" according to Baker (1997:658), writing on the origins of the Csángós (*Csángó* [tʃaːngoː] in singular), an originally Hungarian speaking minority in Romanian Moldavia.[1] I agree with Baker's phrasing: although those who read Hungarian have access to considerable literature about the Csángós, including valuable historical sources and great ethnographic corpora, there are only very few works available in English (besides Baker 1997; see K. Sándor 1999, 2000).

But, in a way, the Csángós stay "enigmatic" even to those who want to study their culture, their present life, and, especially, their language. For hundreds of years, the Romanian state, together with the Roman Catholic Church in Moldavia, have kept the Csángó minority under strong political repression, and this policy has been "successful": most Csángós are afraid of accentuating their own identity, many of them dislike the idea that they are related to Hungarian culture, and especially that their original mother tongue is related to Hungarian. In addition, until very recently, and at the level of local political life surely still today, the Romanian state and its representatives have never favored these ideas either. So scholars, even after the collapse of the Ceauşescu era, could be arrested for gathering ethnographic data in the Csángó villages.[2]

This twofold reason for the Csángós staying "enigmatic" until today causes this chapter to be somewhat different from the other chapters of this book. Unfortunately, although there have been some attempts to gather sociolinguistic data based on a modified version of the questionnaire used in the Sociolinguistics of Hungarian Outside Hungary project, because of the above mentioned reasons, it was only possible to carry out a pilot study. This also means that the linguistic data available is not as fresh, comprehensive or well-organized as the data on the other contact varieties of Hungarian.

In addition to various other works, I use primary data collected by myself and others as sources of information on the sociolinguistic and linguistic aspects of Csángó language use (for details on the data, see Section 3 below). In my discussion of the Csángó identity, I also rely on compositions written on my request by 19 13-year-old

Csángó students in Miercurea-Ciuc/Csíkszereda on the topic of "What it means for me to be a Csángó".

2. Sociolinguistic aspects

2.1 The origins of the contact situation

The forefathers of the Csángós migrated in two larger waves to Moldavia from Hungary. The first wave arrived in Moldavia in the 14th and 15th centuries. In the beginning, the settlement pattern was part of the strategy for the defense of Hungary's eastern borders against nomadic tribes attacking from the direction of the south Russian steppe: in the middle of the 14th century the Hungarian King Louis the Great (1342–1382) defeated the Mongols of the Golden Horde (Lükő 1935:96; Baker 1997:667), pushed them back to the east of the Dniester, and aimed to establish a buffer state between his kingdom and theirs.[3] With the agreement of King Louis, Dragoş, the *Voivode* (ruler) of the Romanians in Maramureş, moved to Moldavia and founded the Moldavian Principality in the 1350s. As research into dialect history (L. Benkő 1989) and ethnography (Lükő 1936) demonstrates, at the same time a large group of Hungarians moved to Moldavia from Mezőség, the northern part of Transylvania, neighboring Maramureş. These Hungarians settled in northwestern Moldavia (Lükő 1936:33–36; L. Benkő 1989:405). Soon they also populated the lower Siret/Szeret area, their villages forming a continuous chain from Suceava down to the Trotuş/Tatros river (Benda 1989:24, 29; for the toponymic data, see L. Benkő 1989:279–283).

From 14th to the 16th centuries, Hungarians played an important role in the life of the court of the Moldavian Voivode and also took a significant part in the social and economic life of Moldavia (L. Benkő 1989:287). Several Hungarian noblemen are mentioned in Moldavian historical sources, and some of the voivodes had Hungarian wives (Benda 1989:35–37). The evidence of the Hungarian loanwords in Romanian shows a strong Hungarian influence also in urban life. Most loanwords are semantically connected to the administration of the court, legal system, military, and urban life, e.g. the words for 'brave warrior', 'sword', '(soldier's) pay', 'page', 'judge', 'inheritance', 'master craftsman', 'burgess', 'lay clerk', etc. (see Mikecs 1989:156–157; L. Benkő 1989:287). The forefathers of the Csángós founded the town of Bacău/Bákó which, not much later, became an important trading center (Baker 1997:677). They built flowering trading connections with Transylvanian and Polish towns and controlled the handicraft industry (Benda 1989:35–37) together with the Saxons who migrated with the Hungarians to Moldavia from Transylvania (Benda 1989:10; Domokos 1987:48), and played an important role in the urban life of Moldavia, both in industry and trading until the end of the 17th century, by which time they assimilated either to the Romanians or to the Hungarians (Benda 1989:35). However, most of the Hungarians lived in villages, doing agricultural work (Benda 1989:35–37; Lükő 1936:14–15). Their communities were independent from anyone but the Voivode, they owned their fields, and selected their judges for themselves (Mikecs 1989:160–161; Benda 1989:38–39). Up to the end of the 16th century the number of Moldavia Hungarians increased, and they founded new villages also east of the Siret and around Bacău/Bákó (Benda 1989:30–31; Lükő 1936:37).

The Hungarian Kingdom had significant military and religious influence in the area until the 16th century. Until this time, there were two Hungarian episcopates in Moldavia. Their function had been slowly taken over by a new one in Bacău/Bákó, and, at the same time, a Franciscan monastery was founded there as an affiliate of the Franciscan province in Transylvania. During this period the Catholic priests in Moldavia were Hungarians.

The 17th century saw a dramatic turn in the life of Moldavia Hungarians. By the end of the 16th century, western and central Hungary was occupied by the Habsburg and the Ottoman Empires, respectively, and the Hungarian Kingdom lost its political influence in Moldavia. At the same time, Moldavia became a seat of war of Ottoman (Crimean Tatar), Transylvanian and Wallachian troops. Towns were demolished, poverty and disease killed thousands of people, and as a consequence of the permanent wars and epidemics of plague, many of the Moldavian Catholic communities remained without a priest. By that time the Reformation had spread across Hungary and Transylvania, creating a need for Catholic priests even there: Transylvanian Franciscans could not send enough monks to Moldavia anymore. At this point, Moldavia Hungarians became permanently isolated from the Hungarian language and culture of the Carpathian Basin, especially because in 1622 the Vatican took over all the Roman Catholic activities in Moldavia and sent Italian and Polish priests to Moldavia Hungarian villages (Benda 1989:42).

The sense of isolation continued to be strong during the following centuries, in spite of the fact that a new, second wave of the Csángó migration arrived in Moldavia from the other side of the Carpathian Mountains. These were Hungarian refugees of Szekler (in Hungarian, *székely*) origin, members of a strong Hungarian speaking community living in Eastern Transylvania. The Szeklers enjoyed the privileges of collective nobility, they had their own autonomous military system and areas of jurisdiction, and were exempt from paying taxes either to the royal court or to the Voivode of Transylvania. The notion of collective nobility, however, did not mean equal rights and equal prosperity within the community, and from the 18th century on the Habsburg rulers tried to integrate the Szeklers into the Empire and deprive them of their privileges. So both economic and political factors motivated the migration to the east, sporadically from the 16th century on. However, the bulk of the Csángós of Szekler origin fled to Moldavia after the "Disaster of Madéfalva", in 1764.[4] The Szekler groups settled in a large eastern and southern strip around Bacău/Bákó, either in newly founded villages, or in the villages of the earlier Hungarian settlers.

In the 19th century, the isolation was completed by a conscious assimilation policy on the part of the new Romanian nation state. From this time on, the history of the contact situation is painfully equal with this assimilationist approach.

2.2 Demographics

The Csángós live in Romanian Moldavia at the foothills of the Eastern Carpathian Mountains in about 90 villages scattered in small river valleys. Today, there are two large towns in this area, Roman/Románvásár and Bacău/Bákó. The great mass of the first wave of settlers populated the area surrounding Roman/Románvásár: these subgroups are called the Northern Csángós. As the population grew constantly, new villages were settled in a southerly direction, along the river Siret, in the area which surrounds Bacău/Bákó: these are now called the Southern Csángós. The Szekler groups that arrived in the second wave of Csángó migration settled down in a large western and southern strip around Bacău/Bákó: these are the Szekler Csángós. The population of the two waves of migration mixed with each other in the Bacău/Bákó area, where the newcomers often settled in or very close to the villages of the first settlers.

Because of political reasons and the special "national" identity of the Csángós (I will return to both issues below), there are no clear demographic data on the number of the Csángós. The method with which the data of the 1992 Romanian census were gathered makes these data rather unreliable. Although in order to answer the question "What is your nationality?" the census questionnaire contained several options, including both "Hungarian" and "Csángó", in many cases none of these were offered by the census workers except for "Romanian" (saying "You are Romanian, aren't you?"), or, the census workers marked "Romanian" without even asking the question (Csoma & Bogdánfalvy 1993). However, the number of the Csángó population can be reliably estimated based on the number of Roman Catholics in Moldavia, since all the Csángós are Roman Catholics, and they are the only Roman Catholic inhabitants in Moldavia. According to these widely accepted estimates, the number of Csángós is about 240,000. Most of them have undergone language shift and are monolingual in Romanian, however, about 50,500 of them still speak vernacular dialects of Hungarian origin at different levels of proficiency (Tánczos 1999).

From the 17th century on, the population of Northern Csángó villages (around Roman/Románvásár) has slowly shifted from Hungarian to Romanian. In this area today there are only a very few villages where the Csángó vernacular is still spoken; the most well-known are Săbăoani/Szabófalva, Pildeşti/Kelgyeszt, Iugani/Jugán, and Ploscuţeni/Ploszkucény. According to Tánczos (1999:17), the number of Csángós who still know their original vernacular can be put at about 9,600 in this area.

According to the same source, Tánczos (1999:17–18), there are about 6,700 Southern Csángós who still speak a Csángó dialect, living in the villages near Bacău/Bákó, e.g. in Valea Seacă/Bogdánfalva, Galbeni/Trunk, Valea Mare/Nagypatak, and Gioseni/Gyoszény. The rest of the Csángó speaking population, about 34,000 people, live in Szekler Csángó villages, at least according to Tánczos's description. However, from a linguistic point of view, it should be noted that such a calculation merges the ethnically and linguistically mixed villages such as Cleja/Klézse and Luizi-Călugăra/Lujzikalagor that alone have about 8,500 Csángó vernacular speaking inhabitants with the villages that are of clearly Szekler origin, such as Lespezi/Lészped and Pustiana/Pusztina.

The Csángó settlements are quite isolated from each other. The Csángós' way of life and the geographical location of the villages exclude everyday contact between the Csángó communities.

2.3 Economic standing and culture

The strong sense of isolation of Csángó groups both from Hungary and from each other has conserved a medieval-like culture. According to the anthropologist Benedek (1997a: 195), the frame of the Csángó society remains up until today a pre-industrialized rural society which harmonizes with the medieval-like world view of the Csángós. The great majority of the Csángó population are peasants who own and cultivate their own lands. The methods of agricultural production are rather undeveloped by modern standards, lacking almost any mechanization. Until very recently, the Csángós had an almost complete subsistence economy; so their handicraft industry could not develop further. Actually, they still identify subsistence with independence today, and look upon it as the ideal model of living (Benedek 1997b: 220). The Csángós have no handicraft industry, manufacturing exists only as part of the completion of agricultural work (Benedek 1997a: 205, 208; Halász 1994: 21). Certain agricultural work (like, for instance, corn-husking, spinning, and weaving) are still done communally, at special places or at the house of a member of the community.

The basis of the organization of the Csángó society is kinship (Halász 1994: 27). Stratification does not exist in the Csángó communities in the Western European sense of the word. The lack of towns and any urban spirit or urban way of life has also prevented the spread of bourgeois customs. There is no nobility, there are no craftsmen, merchants, civil servants, and there are no intellectuals. People differ from each other according to their relationships and wealth.

The present-day life of the Csángós seems very archaic to outsiders, not only in respect to their economy but as a whole. Theirs is a way of life in which economy, daily life, material and spiritual culture cannot be separated from each other but constitute an integral, organic unit harmonized by their religion. Even the most secular aspects of Csángó life are permeated by their faith (Tánczos 1995a: 20–21; Magyar 1994: 77), and communication with the metaphysical world is as natural a part of this life as is mysticism and the daily practice of folk beliefs (cf. e.g. Virt 1994; Nyisztor 1997; Pozsony 1997b). Religion, indeed, is not only a component or a part of the Csángó culture, but a way of life which determines morality, and which influences very strongly, and, at the same time, very naturally every particular activity in life. For example, the most important holidays for the Csángó communities are the annual feasts on the day of the patron saint of the local church and pilgrimages to other churches. Even today, the community turns out the person who does not follow the strict religious prescriptions (Kotics 1997). Disrespect of religious morals is severely punished by the priest with the means of public humiliation, as the priest can even excommunicate the person who does or says something against him (Kallós 1993:101). Normally, it is the priests who have social control in the Csángó communities as individuals (Kotics 1997:49–50), otherwise social control is practiced by the community itself. As all activities and symbols have metaphysical meaning, tradition has conserved an archaic rural culture. Folk art and folklore are not ancient relics but an integral part of the everyday life of the Csángós.

The economy as well as the culture of the Csángós has been shaped and preserved by their isolated life: they are segregated from their Orthodox Moldavian neighbors because of their religion, and they are also isolated from the Carpathian Basin Hungarians geographically and politically. Their isolation started to loosen in the 1960s, when urbanization reached Moldavia as well. From this time on, Csángó men, and especially the young (both men and women) have tried to find jobs in a nearby town (Pozsony 1997b:248). This fact, however, has not changed the structure of Csángó economy. Women have stayed in the villages, and, as mentioned above, the Csángós still keep to agricultural work as the basis of their existence (Benedek 1997a:197–198).

At the same time, urbanization has caused more significant changes in the culture. A respect for traditional values and morality is still predominant in the elder generations (Tánczos 1995a:286), but among the younger ones a mixing of traditional and "modern" values can be detected (Kotics 1997:47). The co-existence of the traditional and the "civilized" worlds is characteristic of almost all aspects of life (cf. e.g. Pozsony 1997a:246–247; Tánczos 1996:106, 118, 151). However, some young people working or studying in the towns do not respect the old traditions (Seres 1994:113). According to Magyar (1994:87), the traditional spiritual and material culture of the Csángós is beginning to crumble; urbanization and modernization are causing a crisis of values and social friction in Moldavia (Bihari 1994). Recently Hungary has become a somewhat popular place for attracting guest workers from among the Csángós, and although the Csángó culture has begun to change in the last few decades, it is very distant from the Transylvanian and especially from the Hungarian way of life. The differences are so remarkable that the Csángós arriving in Hungary experience the deepest culture shock, since the new environment is seen by them as "highly developed" and "modern", and in the "splendor" of "civilization", their own culture, values and morals seem to be backward, old-fashioned, and out of date. As a consequence, they are entirely defenseless against the symptoms of civilization. In addition, the financial differences between their home and the new environment strengthen their well established inferiority complex (see below), and removing them appears to them to be a prerequisite for integration. To achieve this financial goal is so important for them that in the worst cases, especially in Budapest, they even get involved in the criminal underworld (Bihari 1994).

2.4 Social integration and the Csángó identity

As historical data show, in the early centuries of their life in Moldavia, the forefathers of the Csángós were well-integrated into the Moldavian society: there were even noblemen among them. However, since their fate turned in the 17th century, they have become more and more isolated not only from the Hungarian culture and language, but from their Romanian neighbors as well. Since the Csángó villages were never a cohesive unit during their history, their ethnic identity lacked not only a common endo-ethnonym for themselves, but also a "we-consciousness" and a sense of common origin. This identity is very fragile between the strong Romanian and Hungarian national identities and lacking the element of national identity completely.

The Csángós certainly did not participate in the formation of the Hungarian nation that happened in the first half of the 19th century, long after the last Csángó migration to Moldavia. As a consequence, they do not know the elements which constitute the core of Hungarian national feeling, such as knowledge of and respect for a shared language and history; or the great personalities of the national pantheon; or a knowledge of and pride in the canon of Hungarian literature, arts and sciences. They also do not know the symbols that represent these elements, even the most basic ones such as the national anthem, the coat of arms of Hungary, and the national holidays, etc. The Csángós know very little about Hungarian history, no more than they can learn in the Romanian schools. If they learn about their own history at all, it is according to the official concept of the Romanian state, in which the Csángós are "Hungarianized Romanians". Only very few Csángós know from their grandparents that the Csángós had some connections with the Hungarians.

At the same time, the Csángós do not identify themselves with the Romanian nation, either, although they are taught to do this at school and are politically quite often forced to do it. For long centuries, the only difference between the Csángós and their Romanian neighbors has been their religion, since the Romanians are Orthodox, and the Csángós are Roman Catholic – their way of existence and economy was very similar, and there were no remarkable differences in their level of wealth, either. But after the creation of the Romanian nation state in the 19th century, Moldavia Romanians were offered a new ground with which they could link their identity and a new structure in which they could define themselves. The Csángós did not participate in this process, either, for two main reasons. One, because it contained the element that Romanian, being the national language, is the mother tongue of people of Romanian identity as well. And two – and it seems to be a much stronger force that has kept the Csángós from defining themselves as Romanian – because the religion connected to the Romanian national identity is Eastern Orthodoxy.

Since the Csángós did not take part in the formation of any nation, the Csángó ethnic identity differs not only in particular elements from the Hungarian and Romanian national identities, but also in its structure. First of all, there is the peculiarity that the Csángó ethnic identity does not have separable elements which can readily replace other elements (e.g. "religion" for "language" or "home village" for "history"). The ethnic identity of the Csángós is an organic aspect of their traditional mode of existence, as is their spiritual and material culture and their economic system. From this point of view, it is clear that the Csángós' Catholicism is not simply the "base component" of their identity but the projection of their religion that organizes and governs the whole of Csángó life and appears also in their ethnic identity. (Indisputably so, because it is also an appropriate tool for opposing themselves to the neighboring Orthodox culture.) Another characteristic of the Csángó ethnic identity, besides their Catholicism, is the loyalty to the territory where they live. A third characteristic is that it is essentially not an adapted but an inherited kind of identity. It is "God's will" if someone is born to be Csángó or not. Csángó children do not learn from their parents or at school how to be proper Csángós or what it means to be a Csángó, they have simply "found themselves like this" as they often phrase it, adding that this is their fate, as are the conditions of their life.

Moreover, many of the Csángós learn only as teenagers or young adults that they are actually Csángós. This may seem odd, but the Csángós are loath to transmit their ethnonym to their children for well-established historical reasons. The Csángós' lack of a common "we-consciousness" is due primarily to the fact that their ancestors arrived in Moldavia at different periods and with different cultural and dialectal backgrounds. Integration was then hindered by the geographical location of the villages, as they did not form a cohesive unit, and by the political and economic autonomy of the villages as well. For a long time Moldavia Hungarians of Szekler and non-Szekler origin sharply differentiated themselves from each other (for the main features of the differences, see Lükő 1936). This differentiation is loosening up in our days, the division according to origin and culture being replaced by a division according to the geography of the Csángó villages (Halász 1997). However, because this process is a consequence of the weakening of traditional rules and, thus, also a cause of cultural assimilation, the only factor on which the newly developing Csángó we-consciousness can be established is solidarity based on the shared experience of segregation from Romanian society (see also Tánczos 1996: 155–156).

In accordance with their lack of we-consciousness, the Csángós as a group do not have a self-selected endo-ethnonym. The name *Csángó* was given to the first Hungarian groups in Moldavia by their Hungarian and Romanian neighbors, and referred only to Moldavia Hungarians of non-Szekler origin for centuries, signifying the differences between the dialects and culture of the populations of the two large waves of Hungarian migration to Moldavia. By now these differences have lost a lot of their earlier weight, and as part of the cultural and linguistic leveling, Moldavia Hungarians of Szekler origin have also accepted the name *Csángó* (Tánczos 1996: 155–156), but the name itself still has a pejorative element. The Csángós evaluate it as being a nickname which points to the "deficiencies" of their mother tongue (see below). Due to this belief, the Csángós feel ashamed of their own name.

All this does not mean that the Csángós do not identify themselves at all: when Csángós are asked about their nationality, the most likely answer is "I'm Catholic". Religion is the main opposition which defines Csángó ethnic identity, because this is the only major feature that has distinguished them from their Orthodox Romanian neighbors who have been living in a very similar way, and this is especially apparent in those areas where the Csángós have shifted to Romanian, and where, thus, Csángós and Romanians even speak the same language. The roots of this identification reach back to the 17th century, when, after the assimilation of the German communities, all the Catholics in Moldavia were Hungarians (Benda 1989:24). At that time the Romanian words for 'Hungarian' and 'Catholic' became synonymous, as did the respective Hungarian words as well. Catholic priests were called 'Hungarian priests' both by the Csángós and their Romanian neighbors, even if the priests were Italian, German or Polish. This is the reason why Catholics are sometimes called *ungur* 'Hungarian' in Romanian even in villages where no one speaks Hungarian anymore. Later the Csángós accepted Hungarian *csángó* and Romanian *ceangău* as their names, and these words displaced the Hungarian designation *magyar* 'Moldavian Catholic' and the Romanian word *ungur* 'Moldavia Hungarian'. In the meantime, most of the Csángós have undergone language shift to Romanian, and *csángó* and *ceangău* today mean 'Moldavian Catholic', irrespective of mother tongue.

The identification of *Csángó* with 'Moldavian Catholic' has two results that strongly influence Csángó identity. One is that the attachment to Moldavia and especially to the home village is much more important than in the more abstract Hungarian or Romanian national identity. Through their loyalty to Moldavia, the Csángó ethnic identity is certainly connected also to the Romanian environment (as their culture interacts with Moldavia Romanian culture as well). This attribute is almost always disregarded in discussions about the Csángós, though some scholars have pointed out its relevance (Lükő 1936:18 and recently Kapaló 1994:31; Fodor 1995:124). In addition, because of the effective assimilation policy of the Romanian state and the Catholic Church (see below), the Csángós began learning about themselves that they were not Moldavian, not even Roman but Romanian Catholics. Undoubtedly, the replacement of the word *Roman* (Romanian *romano*) with *Romanian* (Romanian *român*) is not the Csángós' invention but an obligatory assimilation forced both by the Romanian state and the Roman Catholic Church. However, since it is this notion that the Csángós learn from the priests whose prestige is unquestionable for them, one should reckon with the possibility that there are Csángós in whose identity the doctrine of being Romanian Catholics plays an important role.

The other result of the identification of *Csángó* with 'Moldavian Catholic' is that the language of the community is not and cannot be a part of Csángó ethnic identity, since, after most of them had undergone language shift, the Moldavian Catholics do not share a common language anymore. The local dialects, of course, symbolize local culture and the village community (cf. Sándor 1996b), and through this role they are relevant at a certain level of identity, namely they can order the relationships between the Csángó groups, but they are not suitable for opposing Csángós to non-Csángós.

2.5 Domains of minority language use, language maintenance and shift, and language attitudes

Today only about 20% of the Csángós can speak a Csángó dialect, while the remaining 80% have become Romanian monolinguals. In the well known sense of the term, minority language use has actually only one domain among the Csángós, the one that could be labeled "village life". However, because of the special cultural and economic characteristics of the Csángó communities, it covers the complex of family, neighborhood, agricultural and handicraft work within the village, and all traditional cultural events except the religious ones. The language of the church, offices, school, and work outside the home village (including agricultural work as well) is exclusively Romanian. Language shift, it seems, is in its final phase even in those villages where most of the inhabitants are bilingual (e.g. in Lespezi/Lészped, Pustiana/Pusztina, Luizi-Călugăra/Lujzikalagor). In these villages, the main language of communication between siblings under the age of about 35 is Romanian even if both are bilingual; and it is not uncommon that older siblings simply cannot speak in Csángó with their younger sisters and brothers since the younger ones are monolingual in Romanian.[5] In other, less bilingual villages the average age of shift in the dominance of the two languages is even higher.

Processes of minority language shift in modern Europe are normally governed by economic and cultural factors with or without different assimilating techniques of the state (see, for instance, the language shift of the Hungarians in Burgenland, Austria, Gal 1979). However, as until very recently the Csángós kept their ancient culture and economy (which lacked industry and urbanization), as well as their relatively closed communities, one can suspect that the process of language shift must be ruled by other factors here. This suspicion is supported by the finding that in opposition to other language shifting communities, religion is not the last but the first domain where language shift has taken place (Sándor 1996b). Considering the fact that 'Catholic' and 'Hungarian' are synonyms in Moldavia, this phenomenon seems to be a rather strange one. The explanation lies in history.

In 1622, a missionary organization named *De Propaganda Fide* took over the spiritual care of the Moldavian Catholics. It sent mostly Italian, sometimes Bosnian and Croatian priests to Moldavia, although from time to time the people asked for Hungarian priests. In the 17th century the Jesuits also appeared in Moldavia, not so much in order to serve, but rather to make their order stronger. Many of the documents complain of the scandalous life of both the Italian monks and the Jesuits, claiming, for instance, that they steal ecclesiastical objects, live together with women, and have no contact with their flock, as they do not speak their language. In the meantime, the episcopate in Bacău/Bákó was taken from Hungary and given to Poland. However, the Polish bishops did not live in their Moldavian residence, going there only to collect taxes. So, in this unhappy period, four different organizations of the Catholic Church were present in the area: the priests under Polish control, the Jesuits, the Italian missionaries (who belonged to one branch of the Franciscan order, the Fratres Minorum Conventualium), and the Bosnian missionaries together with the Hungarian monks who belonged to another branch of the Franciscan order, to the Fratres Strictioris Observantiae. To make the situation even more troubled, the four parties were much busier fighting each other than serving their people. Under these circumstances, the institution of folk religion developed to such an extent that it became the main scene of religious life, led by the deacons who were members of the communities and fulfilled almost all functions of the priests, including baptisms and funerals, in the mother tongue of the community. However, the language of the liturgies remained Latin, and the people did not have any way to communicate with the foreign priests.

In the beginning of the 19th century the situation changed, but by no means in the desired direction. In fact, if possible, it became even worse. This was the time when, similarly to so many other nations in Europe, the Romanian nation state was born. National feelings became stronger, and consequently, the indolent behavior of The Holy See which led to language shift among the Csángós was replaced by an overt assimilation policy. The Romanian Orthodox Church found it humiliating that on the territory of the Romanian state Rome pursued missionary activity as if it was not a Christian area, so Rome called back the monks. In 1884 the episcopate of Bacău/Bákó was revoked, and an archbishopric was founded in Bucharest and a bishopric in Iaşi, the capital of Moldavia. At the same time Catholic seminaries were also founded at these places, so the need for priests was partly satisfied and decreased. However, both the Romanian Catholic Church and the young Romanian Catholic priests proved to be much more demanding in questions of language than their predecessors.

In the last decades of the century, Austria took over the control of the area. In the meantime, the Vatican introduced an order that church services must be celebrated in the mother tongue of the flock, but the reports of the Austrian consuls misinformed Rome claiming that the Moldavian Catholics do not need Hungarian priests. When, in spite of this hindrance, complaints of the Csángós arrived in Rome, the Pope's answer to their letters was that the priests sent to them speak the language of their country. This, in fact, was more or less true: due to their mother tongue, the Italian priests learned Romanian quite easily.

In addition, towards the end of the 19th century schooling became widespread in Moldavia. The language of instruction was exclusively Romanian but as religion was taught at church and not at school, bilingual catechisms could be used. In 1895 a law prohibited this practice, however, and religion taught in Romanian became a compulsory subject at school, and the bilingual catechisms were replaced by mono-lingual Romanian ones. Although in the church the use of Csángó was forbidden by the priests, the local religious leaders, the deacons, used it until the 1930s. At that time the prohibition of Csángó was made official by a bishop's order affecting not only the liturgies but also the service of the deacon. In order to change the language of the folk religious practices, a school for deacon training was founded already in 1923; the old Hungarian prayers and songs were translated into and printed in Romanian; the prayer-books written in Hungarian were collected and burned (Tánczos 1995b: 57, 1996: 220–221), and the deacons who did not serve in Romanian were dismissed. In the 1930s young couples who did not know the catechism in Romanian were not al-lowed to be married in the church; a priest could excommunicate people who spoke Csángó during communal work at their homes; later on the Securitate, the Communist Romanian secret police could accuse old deacons of being spies if printed Hungar-ian or handwritten Csángó prayers were found at their houses (Tánczos 1995b: 57, 1996: 220–221).

Thus, one reason for the bilingual Csángós' negative attitude towards their own vernacular is the assimilationist policy of the Romanian state and of the Roman Catholic church in Moldavia. As the priest has the absolute social control in the Csángó communities (Kotics 1997:49–50), on the grounds of their deeply religious world view, people accept whatever the priest says, even if he says – as it has often happened – that their mother tongue is "the tongue of the devil". But these negative feelings are reinforced by mockeries of their (native Hungarian) Transylvanian Szekler neighbors living on the other side of the Carpathians, and recently by the Hungarians of Hungary as well.

Although it is less known in Hungary, the Szeklers hold very strong prejudices against the Csángós.[6] For centuries, they have ridiculed the "mongrel" language the Csángós speak.[7] The popular folk etymology of the name *Csángó* is wide-spread among the Szeklers, namely, that the name refers to those people whose speech sounds unpleasant, and who cannot speak proper Hungarian.[8]

The belief that the Csángós "deserve" their name is so deeply established that even the Csángós have taken it over from the Szeklers. Csángós differentiate their own dialects from Hungarian: they usually call their own dialect *Csángó*, and although in some villages the vernacular dialect is also called *magyar* 'Hungarian', the perceived difference between the Csángó dialects and the Hungarian varieties is expressed in these villages as well by opposing the "Csángó-way Hungarian" and "pure Hungarian" (Sándor 1996a:55, 1996b:61, 1996c). Today the Csángós evaluate the differences between their own dialects and the Szekler dialects as deficiencies, and they are ashamed of using a "corrupted" mother tongue. Thus, to avoid mockery, they switch to Romanian in the presence of Szeklers (cf. Bihari 1994). The Csángós' inferiority complex towards the Szeklers is as strong as are the Szeklers' prejudices against the Csángós.

Csángó students and guest workers living in Hungary experience a very strange attitude towards themselves and the way they speak – an attitude which is totally incomprehensible to them. According to a folk myth widely held in Hungary, Csángó is supposed to be the "most beautiful ancient", or "medieval" form of Hungarian. People often praise "the taste of old times" in them, but in a normative country like Hungary, dialects are tolerated only in theory, meaning that although theoretically, traditional dialects are welcomed, as soon as they are actually spoken, they are stigmatized. So, for the same people, Csángó is also an "undeveloped" version of Hungarian, which, in addition, is "strongly corrupted" by Romanian. Also, believing that the Csángós speak a Hungarian dialect (and the "most ancient" one at that), Hungarians, including teachers, are often annoyed by the ignorance the Csángós show about the Hungarian language, history, and national symbols. This ignorance may even be misunderstood as a sign of their corrupted morality and not as a natural result of their history.

So there is nothing surprising in the fact that the Csángós value their own dialects at an extremely low level. As "the devil's tongue", it is forbidden in the church and as a "birds' tongue" (that is, not a real human language), it is forbidden in the school. It is "useless" in any official domain of language use, and even the Csángós themselves can have difficulties with the comprehension of another Csángó dialect. The traditional culture and values whose symbol is the vernacular dialect of the village might be important for the elderly and the middle aged, but this attachment is not strong enough for them to support the passing on of dialects which are associated with a feeling of being despised and threatened. Thus, these older generations align themselves with the younger ones, who prefer to speak Romanian, for whom the traditional culture is associated with the backwardness of an old rural culture and poverty, and who want to step out of this culture, feeling ashamed because of it and rejecting its symbols as well.

Today, the Csángós only use their minority language in their own villages or in domains connected strongly to their villages (e.g. a group of elderly women traveling to the nearby town would in certain cases speak in Csángó). If two Csángós originating from different Csángó villages meet, they choose to speak Romanian. One reason for this is that many Csángó varieties are not mutually intelligible (see below), but even if they are, people choose to speak Romanian because of the extremely low prestige of the Csángó dialects. The Csángós feel ashamed to use their own dialects, because, for decades, they have been hearing from their priests and from their teachers that their language was a "mongrel", and because the myth of the deficiencies of their varieties is reinforced by the Hungarians in Transylvania and in Hungary as well.[9]

2.6 Language policy

The language policy of the Romanian state towards the Csángós is strongly assimilationist. Based on the idea that the Csángós are "Hungarianized Romanians" who must re-assimilate to their original language and culture, the Romanian state does not accept the Csángós as a minority, so they are excluded from all rights other minorities enjoy in Romania, e.g. the right to have education in the mother tongue or even classes in that language. Thus, until now there has not been even a single attempt to take the opportunity that governmental decree 5023/24.05.1993 of the Romanian Ministry of Education allows minorities in Romania, to teach their mother tongues in 4 and 3 classes per week in elementary and high-schools, respectively (Borbáth 1994:219). The Csángós are afraid of using their vernacular dialects, and they have a good reasons to do so.

In the words of a Csángó teacher who lives in Transylvania today, the assimilating process which is being carried out in Moldavia is "a terrible psychological and spiritual genocide" (quoted by Borbáth 1996:217). The Moldavian Catholic priests humiliate those who preserve any connections with Transylvania or Hungary (see Sándor 1999). In the Csángó villages teachers forbid the use of Csángó dialects, arguing that if the pupils live in Romania, they must speak Romanian and that their vernacular is deficient. People teaching children Hungarian in their own houses can be accused of having violated the constitution (cf. Csapó 1994; Pálffy M. 1997:68).

The assimilationist policy of the Romanian state is based on firm grounds since the interest the Vatican has had in Moldavia for centuries coincides with the interests of the modern Romanian nation state. So most of the Csángós do not even realize what is happening to them, since the state uses the Church, the most respectable authority in the eyes of the Csángós, as a means of assimilation.

Before the 1992 census in Romania, a bishop's encyclical letter ordered the priests to call the attention of their flocks to what they should answer when they are asked about their nationality (Csoma & Bogdánfalvy 1993: 165). According to this order, priests told the Csángós not to choose Csángó, which was one of the options, but Romanian, as they are Roman Catholics (Csoma & Bogdánfalvy 1993: 165; Tánczos 1996: 115), these two words sounding almost the same in Romanian. This "merging" can be interpreted as a symbol of the interpenetration of the Vatican's and the Romanian state's interests in assimilating the Csángós. This subterfuge had been practiced by the Vatican already in the mid-19th century (Lükő 1936: 16) with the aim of acquiring also a Romanian flock. One argument supporting a reunification with the Orthodox Church (meaning, actually, its Catholicization) was that all Romanians were Catholics, as they took their faith with them from the Roman Empire, but only those Romanians could keep the ancient faith who were Hungarianized by the Catholic Hungarian kings in Moldavia – namely the Csángós. As they return to their ancient language, that is, as they shift to Romanian, so should the Orthodox Romanians return to the Catholic Church (Lükő 1936: 16; Mikecs 1989: 434). This ambition has been maintained until today (Tánczos 1996: 187), and can serve also the interests of the homogenizing intentions of the Romanian nation state.[10] This policy continues to be extremely powerful and has significantly accelerated the language shift of the Csángós (Sándor 1996b).

The assimilating force of the Catholic Church has been strengthened also by the schools. Since the end of the 19th century, when schooling became widespread in Moldavia, the language of education has been Romanian at all times (except for a short period between 1947 and the 1950s when Hungarian could also be used as the language of instruction). In most schools, speaking Csángó has always been forbidden even in recess; pupils switching to Csángó while playing could and still can be publicly humiliated or even punished. It also means that, for the Csángós, the exclusive language of literacy is Romanian.

The Csángós as a group do not have real political representation. Although the Association of Csángó-Hungarians was founded in 1989, it means no real political representation for the Csángós, partly because it has only very few members, most of them born in Moldavia but now living in Transylvania, and partly because it works as a part of the Democratic Alliance of Hungarians in Romania and thus is influenced by its goals, which do not always serve the interests of the Csángós.

And there is yet another factor that makes the situation even harder for the Csángós, namely, that from time to time the "Csángó problem" becomes the subject of Hungarian political life. Their culture is reminiscent of the 17th and 18th centuries, and in periods when the question of the "nation" is the focus of Hungarian political ideology, this archaic culture and language fascinates politicians and laymen alike.[11] In these periods politicians try to convince the public that they are, in case they are right wing, "better Hungarians than", or, in case they are left wing, "at least as good Hungarians as" their rivals. Although this form of enthusiastic interest has always produced negative results, politicians in Hungary and in Transylvania do not seem to have learned from their failures in this respect.[12] In addition, many scholars dealing with the Csángós have acted on the basis of their emotions rather than their knowledge in attempting to "rescue" the Csángós.[13]

The most recent "rescue of the Csángós" is actually a network based on the notion that the Csángós belong to the Hungarian nation, but, due to unfortunate historical processes, they have forgotten about or do not dare to admit their Hungarian national identity (for an example of this phrasing, see Pávai 1995). So, the main goal of all the "rescue operations" should be to make the Csángós aware of the fact that they are part of the Hungarian nation. Although the idea of a resettlement in Transylvania or Hungary has also sporadically occurred recently, especially dominant forms of late 20th century migration such as temporary or long term guest working by the Csángós in Hungary are welcomed by the "rescuers" (Sándor in press).

One form of the "rescue" is a rather strange form of tourism with the aim of the "awakening" of a Hungarian national feeling in the Csángós. This tourism has included taking Csángó folkgroups and village football teams, etc. to Hungary, as well as taking Csángós to a conference organized in honor of the Csángó researcher Pál Péter Domokos, to the visit of the Pope to Hungary, and to the Csíksomlyó feast (in Transylvania), as well as organizing summer vacationing of Csángó children in Hungary (Szőcs 1993:164), or even taking them to the funeral of the Hungarian prime minister, the late József Antall, in 1992. This kind of tourism goes both ways. Not only was the hosting football team taken to Moldavia for a return game, but recently it has become a kind of fashion to travel for short folkart-hunting expeditions to Moldavia.

Another form of the "rescue" involves the introduction of Csángó culture to Transylvania and especially to Hungary: in the electronic media, in special summer camps for primary and secondary school students, and folk festivals. The idea of learning more about the Csángós is of course desirable and important. There is a danger, however, in the way the introduction is conducted, namely, that people are offered an idealized picture of the Csángós.[14] And there is also a danger in the fact that this is strongly connected to politics.

But one of the most controversial "rescue operations " was the one which can be labeled as an attempt to revitalize the Csángós' language. In 1990, in the euphoric atmosphere of political changes in both Hungary and Romania, as part of an initiative by the Democratic Alliance of Hungarians in Romania, Csángó primary school students were brought to Hungarian schools in Transylvania, and Csángó young adults were sent to Hungary to get their education there. This program aimed at educating a first generation of Csángó intellectuals and was based on the presupposition that the Csángós belonged to the body of the Hungarian nation, so that it was a great opportunity that, after centuries of subjugation of their mother tongue, they can now be educated in Hungarian. The operation was supposed to be the first step towards the mother tongue education of the Csángós, and its organizers hoped that it would stop language shift among them. So, the operation had ambitions similar to those of language revitalization programs. However, since it lacked any economic, pedagogical, social, cultural and linguistic planning, it resulted in fiascos which were necessary consequences of ideological and political interference and neglect of linguistic, cultural-historical, and anthropological arguments. Most if not all of the students who participated in the operation gained bitter experiences about the intolerance of the Transylvanian and Hungarian communities that they were taken to towards their culture, and towards the "strange" and "mixed" dialects they spoke.[15]

Hungarian governments have never had a responsibly planned and carefully considered strategy for supporting the Csángó minority in Moldavia. With this, the initiators of the "rescue operations " only make the defenselessness of the Csángós even more hopeless. True enough, the assimilation policy of the Romanian state is highly sophisticated. No sober analysis can deny that the Csángós are afraid of using their vernacular dialects and to identify themselves as Csángós. But this is only one side of the coin. No actions related to the Csángós can be planned without regard to the fact that the assimilation policy does exist, and that, moreover, this policy prevails. Many Csángós are afraid of anything associated with Hungarians, and this was obviously one of the reasons why parents did not want to let their children go to Transylvanian schools (cf. Borbáth 1993:93). Many Csángós are also convinced that they do not need to maintain contacts with Hungarians either in Transylvania or in Hungary, and ostracize those who do.[16] Whatever the reasons, it is a fact that there are many Csángós who have anti-Hungarian feelings (about their manifestations, see Tánczos 1995a:155, 1996:102–105, 113, 137, 255), strongly suggesting that the strategy of the support should avoid nationalistic ideology and be, first of all, economic and legal aid.

3.   Linguistic aspects

3.1   The difficulties of linguistic description

Because of the reasons discussed in previous section – the Csángós feeling ashamed speaking their own vernacular and being afraid of getting involved in anything associated with Hungarians, and the political repression still being obvious – fieldworkers face conditions that severely hinder the collection of linguistic data in Moldavia. As a consequence, current descriptions of the status and, especially, of the corpus of Csángó dialects, including contact induced phenomena as well as the characteristics of their language shift, are remarkably inadequate.

Previous studies are of little help as well. They concentrate more or less only on those features of the Csángó dialects which are different from standard Hungarian or which differentiate between the "Hungarian Csángó" and the "Szekler Csángó" (see below) varieties but are not contact phenomena. That is, the "archaic" characteristics of the Csángó dialects are in focus that can be of great interest for language historians, but they obviously fail to show a comprehensive picture. Subjects were selected and data were gathered using traditional methods in these studies.[17] As data were specifically selected to show clear differences, they seem not only insufficient but somewhat unreliable, too. This seems to be true of the *Atlas of the Moldavian Csángó Dialect* (Gálffy et al. 1991) as well.

In addition to secondary sources of linguistic data, I rely on data collected by myself and a student of mine of Csángó background in the description of the linguistic characteristics of Csángó varieties.

In 1995 8 interviews were tape-recorded in Cleja/Klézse, a village in the Southern Csángó area with a mixed Székely and non-Székely population. The fieldworker was one of my Csángó students who was born in the same village. The questionnaire he used during the interviews was based on the questionnaire of the Sociolinguistics of Hungarian Outside Hungary project (see Kontra 1998 and this volume) and modified by myself. In addition to these interviews, in 1996 I also carried out interviews with 4 Csángó college students from the Csángó villages Săbăoani/Szabófalva, Valea Scacă/Bogdánfalva, Pustiana/Pusztina, and Lespezi/Lészped, studying in Szeged, Hungary, as well as field interviews with middle-aged and older subjects in Săbăoani/Szabófalva, Valea Scacă/Bogdánfalva, Pustiana/Pusztina, and Cleja/Klézse. I also use material from 4 interviews recorded in Pildeşti/Kelgyeszt by a former Csángó student in Szeged. All these interviews total approximately 14 hours of recordings. I have relied on all of these interviews as sources of information on the sociolinguistic aspects of the Csángó situation, and use my field interviews for the linguistic characterization of the Csángó varieties.

In my own interviews, I used my informal standard Hungarian vernacular to communicate with my subjects, who used their own approximations of Hungary Hungarian (in the case of the students studying in Hungary) or their local Csángó variety (in the case of the subjects in Csángó villages).

3.2 Differences between the "Hungarian" and the "Szekler" Csángó dialects

The dialects and the sociolinguistic situation of the Csángós are characterized by the same attributes as their culture and social situation. Csángó villages were originally easily distinguishable according to their Szekler or non-Szekler dialects. As mentioned above, in the 14th and 15th centuries, settlers from the Mezőség populated the area which surrounds the town of Roman/Románvásár, and as the population grew, new villages were settled along the river Siret in the area which surrounds the town Bacău/Bákó. Dialects spoken by the descendants of these earlier settlers are usually called *Northern Hungarian Csángó*, around Roman/Románvásár, and *Southern Hungarian Csángó* settlers, around Bacău/Bákó, and often labeled with a collective name *Hungarian-Csángó*. At the same time, dialects spoken by the descendants of the second, Szekler, wave of migration are called *Szekler-Csángó*. There are significant phonetic, syntactic, and lexical differences between Hungarian Csángó and Szekler Csángó dialects. Table 6.1 shows some of the most characteristic features, based on various sources as well as my own fieldwork.

However, in the Southern-Csángó area, where the Szekler and non-Szekler populations have mixed, their dialects have also interacted with each other. In this area

Table 6.1. The most characteristic differences between the Hungarian-Csángó and the Szekler-Csángó dialects

Hungarian-Csángó	Szekler-Csángó
phonological differences	
/s/ and /ʃ/ merge into palatalized /ç/	/s/ and /ʃ/ are opposing phonemes
/tʃ/ is palatalized	/tʃ/ is not palatalized
/ɟ/ and /c/ become [dʒ] and [tʃ], respectively	/ɟ/ and /c/ remain stops
/ʎ/ and /j/ are opposing phonemes	/ʎ/ and /j/ merge into /j/
/e/ and /ɛ/ merge into /ɛ/	/e/ and /ɛ/ are separate phonemes
/o/ and /ɒ/ merges into /ɔ/	/o/ and /ɒ/ are separate phonemes
the long upper-mid vowels are diphthongs	the long upper-mid vowels are monophthongs
morphosyntactic differences	
the instrumental suffix *-vAl* does not assimilate (*ember* 'man' + *-vel* 'with' → *embervel*)	the instrumental suffix *-vAl* assimilates to the final consonant of the stem (*ember* + *-vel* → *emberrel*)
the auxiliary for conditional is *lenne*	the auxiliary for conditional is *volna*
lexical differences, e.g.	
filesz 'rabbit'	*nyúl* 'rabbit'
fel 'fat [n.]'	*zsír* 'fat [n.]'
tyukmon 'egg'	*tojás* 'egg'

the classical features of Hungarian and Szekler Csángó dialects do not form bundles of isoglosses, that is, no sharp distinctions can be made regarding all the features at the same time. As, for historical reasons, the Szekler Csángó dialects are more prestigious, it is quite predictable that some of the features of Hungarian Csángó, like the so-called "lisping" (the result of the merger of /s/ and /ʃ/) may be stigmatized. Lükő (1936: 53–54), for one, reports on the stigmatization of the non-Szekler features and mentions clear cases of hypercorrection to avoid stigmatized "lisping" in the speech of villages with a mixed population. Still, because of the lack of reliable data, it is not known where certain features are stigmatized or even where specific features do not even exist anymore. Interviews made in Csángó villages prove that "lisping", for instance, sometimes totally disappears, while other features which seem to go together with "lisping" on a phonological basis, like the palatalization of [tʃ], are preserved. In other villages this can vary according to different rules, and other variables are governed by yet other rules. As the Csángó villages are still rather isolated from each other, practically all of them have their own, significantly distinct dialects.

3.3   Contact-induced features, lexical and structural borrowings; degrees of bilingualism

The diversity of the Csángó dialects is even more complicated by the fact that they are differently influenced by Romanian, i.e. they differ from each other also on the basis of the number and distribution of contact induced forms.

Márton (1972) and Murádin (1994) separate three groups of Csángó dialects based on the extent of the influence of Romanian on them. The borders of these groups are approximately the same as the borders of the traditional classification of the Csángó dialects, namely Northern, Southern and Szekler Csángó. Their grouping is based on data from Gálffy et al. (1991), so it relies only on the number of loans in the wordlist of the atlas, and lacks any information on non-lexical borrowing.

A lack of reliable data does not allow us to arrange the varying influence of Romanian on the Csángó dialects on a borrowing scale, for instance, like the one Thomason and Kaufman (1988) proposed. However, based on my personal field experiences and tape-recorded interviews, an unrefined picture can be presented. Dialects of the Northern Csángó area seem to show effects between moderate and heavy structural borrowing: not only their phonetics is reminiscent more of Romanian than Hungarian (for example, in the speech of a middle-aged woman code-switching was hardly recognizable on this basis), but there are important changes also in the morphosyntax (auxiliaries are used instead of suffixes) and word order. Dialects of the Southern and Szekler Csángó area show features of slight structural borrowing (a significant number of loanwords, including function words, changes in the prosody and the phonological pattern, etc.).

According to different indices of bilingualism (i.e. the percent of bilingual individuals in the community, the distribution of the two languages in domains of language use, etc.), the Csángó villages differ from each other. Dialects of the Northern Csángó area show the heaviest influence, while dialects of the Southern Csángó area showing less, and dialects of the Szekler Csángó villages the least impact of Romanian.

Historical sources prove that in the Northern Csángó area only about 25–30% of the population spoke Hungarian dialects in the mid-19th century. In bilingual Northern Csángó villages, bilingualism strongly tends towards monolingualism. Language shift is probably in its last stage in the area. The Southern Csángó and the Szekler Csángó dialects were maintained relatively successfully until about the 1930s when language shift accelerated also in these areas (for reasons see above and Sándor 1996b). Community bilingualism is still characteristic of the Southern Csángó villages. Moreover, in some Szekler Csángó villages even monolingual Csángó speakers can be found among elderly women, but today there are only very few Szekler Csángó villages (Tánczos 1995b: 62 mentions only four) where the mother tongue of the youngest generation is Csángó and not Romanian.

3.4 The status of Csángó dialects

The Csángó dialects have always been roofless dialects (cf. Trudgill 1992) staying unaffected by standard Hungarian, which had been developed in the 19th century, and have no standard variety in our days either. The diversity of the Csángó dialects has produced such a situation that there is no mutual intelligibility between some of the dialects. Nevertheless, all Csángó dialects have some common features which differentiate them from dialects of Hungarian in the Carpathian Basin. Such features are, for instance, the attributes of all peripheral dialects, i.e. the maintenance of archaic gram-matical forms and words, and the development of new forms, independently of the central dialects, as well as the bulk of contact phenomena as a natural consequence of the widespread bilingualism. From a linguistic point of view, the 200–500 years of iso-lation and contact with Romanian explain the divergence of Csángó and Carpathian Basin Hungarian. In addition, the process of natural divergence was very much rein-forced by the Hungarian language modernization movement of the 19th century, when thousands of new words were created in the Hungarian language.[18]

The Csángós themselves differentiate their mother tongue from "pure Hungarian" as they call it.[19] Csángó dialects are not heteronomous in respect to standard Hun-garian, and, apart from some handwritten collections of prayers, there has been no Hungarian literacy in Moldavia for centuries. For speakers of Hungarian, intelligibility of Csángó dialects varies from village to village; most of them are hardly or not at all understandable to them. Csángós do not understand or understand only with great difficulties the Hungarian varieties.

In traditional Hungarian linguistics, Csángó is considered to be a dialect (*one* dialect) of Hungarian. In discussions of the problem, however, the main argument dialectologists and historical linguists normally have is that "it has always been seen as a dialect of Hungarian". No question that from a historical point of view, Csángó dialects are of Hungarian origin. Still, considering the above mentioned arguments, from a sociolinguistic point of view the Csángó dialects seem to form a roofless and diffuse Ausbau-language[20] which is very close to Hungarian. However, Csángó dialects are not dialects of Hungarian (and, especially, are not one dialect of Hungarian) (Sán-dor 1996a). And, unfortunately, it should be added that this least known language of the "most enigmatic ethnic minority in Europe" has a very firm foothold in the Red book of European endangered languages.[21]

Notes

1. In popular Hungarian usage, the name *Csángó* refers not only to these groups, but also to others, e.g. to Hungarians in Bukovina (Northern Moldavia), in the Gyimes (Romanian *Ghimeş*, the valleys in the Carpathians around the Gyimes pass) or in the Hétfalu ('seven villages'), near Brassó (Romanian Braşov). Literature on the Csángós, however, differentiates these other groups from the Moldavian Csángós on the ground of the latter's significantly dissimilar history, culture and dialects.

2. In 1995 an ethnographer collecting archaic prayers in Moldavia was arrested and kept by the police for a day because the priest of the village he visited found him "suspicious" (Tánczos 1996: 159–173).

3. There are several other ideas about the origins of the Csángós which are summarized and convincingly refuted by Baker 1997.

4. Maria Teresa, the Empress of the Austro-Hungarian Empire decreed conscription among the Szeklers who at that time still enjoyed their privileges and were free, among other things, from conscription to the Austrian army. To demonstrate their protest, on January 7, 1764, thousands of Szeklers gathered at a field near the village of Madéfalva. The Austrian army fired into the crowd, and more than 4,000 people were killed that day (Domokos 1987:89).

5. This information is based on my own field experiences and on the interviews tape-recorded in 1996 with my Csángó students originating from the above mentioned villages.

6. Romanian propaganda is only one source of the anti-Hungarian feelings of the Csángós. The other source is what Tánczos (1996:184) calls "the Szekler nationalism that disdains the Csángós". This can be illustrated, among other things, with the saying "not a human being, just a Csángó".

7. "Mongrel" means that the Szeklers – as well as the Romanians – share the well-known idea that the "natural" form of language is its "pure" form, i.e. the monolingual varieties in which contact-induced phenomena are not as easily recognizable as in the contact varieties under heavy influence of another language.

8. Although this explanation seems to be folk etymological, one of the most respected Hungarian language historians asserted it as the valid etymology of the name (Horger 1913). There are two other etymologies of the name *Csángó*, neither of which is unproblematic (L. Benkő 1989; Alexics 1913). All the possible etymologies presume the name to be of Hungarian origin. The name itself definitely can be dated back to the 15th century when it first appeared in historical sources.

9. The shame is so deep that those Csángó students who come from neighboring villages whose dialects are very close to each other and are certainly mutually understandable, when studying in Hungary, used the standard Hungarian variety as a lingua franca even when speaking about topics connected to family and home, and even when no one else could hear them. They needed a lingua franca obviously because of attitudinal reasons and not for comprehension reasons.

10. The use of Csángó or Hungarian has been forbidden in the Catholic churches of Moldavia since the 19th century (see above). About the Vatican's assimilating policy in connection with the Csángós, its purposes, forms, historical aspects, and close connections with the interest of the Romanian state, see Sándor 1999.

11. The "rescue of the Csángós" became one of the most popular pieces of political rhetoric first in the 1830s and 1840s, in the period when the Hungarian nation state established its new symbols and national ideology. Then it appeared around what was called "Millennium", a series of acts to celebrate the Hungarian conquest of the Carpathian Basin; all the acts were strongly associated with the Hungarian national feeling. (The year of the Hungarian Millennium was 1886, but there were several events before and after it dedicated to it.) The "rescue of the Csángós" became the focus of the political life again in the deeply nationalistic era of the 1930s and 1940s; and again, when the official communist ideology ceased in the end of the 1980s, and political pluralism reopened a gate for the nationalistic political rhetoric.

12. In 1883, the Bukovina Csángós (settling northwest of the Moldavian Csángós, the people of five Szekler Csángó villages) were settled in southern Hungary. The process itself was rather a national show full with operetta-like elements (cf. Mikecs 1989:307), and it was carried out without any responsible consideration to where these people were settled. As their new lands were in a flood area, in 1888 their five years' work and houses were demolished, and they settled back to Bukovina in great poverty. In 1941 the people of the same five villages were settled again in Vojvodina, which at the time was again part of southern Hungary. However, in 1944, during World War II, the Bukovina Csángós had to escape again, leaving their houses and belongings. In the end they settled down in southwest Hungary, spread around about 30 villages (Forrai 1987:27).

13. Strangely enough, many of those ethnographers who otherwise publish valuable ethnographic corpora and studies about the Csángós, support the politically motivated "rescue". Tánczos suggested resettling the Csángós in Hungary as he considers it the only way to "rescue" them (Fekete 2000:7). Pozsony (1994:11) welcomes the Csángós' as guest workers in Hungary, although it does not change the Csángós' political status and linguistic human right conditions, does not improve their economy and does not decrease their poverty, either. Halász (1993:172) shares this feeling, and he organized many "rescue operations" as well. Domokos (1987) was one of the first ones who, in the late 1980s, again drew attention to the importance of the "rescue". In these cases one may suspect that a respect for the Csángós' culture and the solidarity with them is penetrated not only with nationalistic political ideology but with the hidden idea of "saving" (rather than "rescuing") their culture as well. (In Hungarian both 'save' and 'rescue' is expressed by the same verb, [*meg*]*ment*.)

14. It was Tánczos (1996:174–189) who first called attention to the fact that the Hungarian mass media paints a rosy picture of the Csángós and that this is harmful especially to the Csángós. The idealized picture of the Csángós is so strong and uniform that it can safely be called a myth. Although the media can indeed be accused of publicizing the Csángó myth, the responsibility lies with Hungarian scholarship dealing with the Csángós. Lay opinions are often hard to separate from the ones of professional scholars, who make the Csángó myth even more well-established, either on the basis of their convictions (i.e. partiality, see the previous note) or because of carelessness (i.e. through ambiguous phrasing).

15. About the Csángó schooling operation, see Pálffy M. 1997, and K. Sándor 2000.

16. Children who studied in Transylvania felt excommunicated from their own community (Pálffy M. 1997:67, 70); in one case a girl who had studied in Transylvania did not speak Csángó anymore in her village because she did not want to be mocked by other children (Gazda 1994:278). An elderly woman was humiliated and spat on by her fellow villagers because she suggested to ask for optional Hungarian classes and alternative Hungarian mass at the church (Pozsony 1994:10).

17. These studies used NORM subjects (for the term, see Chambers & Trudgill 1998:29) and asked, through questionnaires, mostly about traditional (agricultural) vocabulary.

18. The Hungarian language modernization movement, connected strongly to the effort to achieve the right of using Hungarian (and not German) in schools, academic and political life, aimed to make the Hungarian language suitable for being used in all domains of language use, and concentrated especially on the modernization of the vocabulary of the special registers in which Latin and German had been used before, as well as on the literary language. The modernization movement was lead by writers and poets, who first applied the new words, very often "translating" them in a vocabulary list attached to their books to enable the readers to comprehend the texts. Many of the new words had only ephemeral life, but still, more than a thousand survived and are used in all dialects of present Carpathian Basin Hungarian.

19. On the Csángós' opinion of lack of intelligibility between the Csángó and "pure Hungarian" dialects, see Sándor 1996c and also cf. Tánczos 1995a:153, 1995b:64–65, 1996:253–254.

20. On the term "diffuse", see Le Page and Tabouret-Keller 1985; on "roofless dialects" and "Ausbau-language", see Trudgill 1992.

21. The red book of European threatened languages is at http: //www.helsinki.fi/~tasalmin/ europe_index.html

CHAPTER 7

Hungarian in the former Yugoslavia (Vojvodina and Prekmurje)

Lajos Göncz and Ottó Vörös*

1. Introduction

The unified state of South Slavic peoples was formed in late 1918 and existed until 1991. The new state was called the Kingdom of Serbs, Croats, and Slovenes until 1929; afterwards it was Yugoslavia. There are two periods separated in its history: the first, inter-war Yugoslavia, and the second, Tito's Yugoslavia from World War II until 1991.

In 1918, 7.4% of historical Hungary's territory and 8.3% of its population (or about one and a half million people) became part of the Kingdom of Serbs, Croats, and Slovenes. In those days the area's population was 31% (580,000) Hungarian, 25.6% (384,000) Serbian, 21.6% (324,000) German, 3.8% (57,000) Slovak, 4.9%, (74,000) Romanian and 0.9% (13,000) Ruthenian.

The geographic regions from east to the west are Banat, Bačka, Baranja, Međimurje, and Prekmurje. Hungarians constitute a majority in Banat and Bačka, which, together with another area, the Srem, constitutes the territory called Vojvodina. In this chapter we discuss native language contact varieties of Hungarian in Vojvodina and in Prekmurje. The Croatian part of the study and its fieldwork could not be carried out because of the Yugoslav war.

Since 1991 Vojvodina and Prekmurje have been parts of different states. When the second Yugoslavia ceased to exist, four of its member republics, Slovenia, Croatia, Bosnia-Herzegovina, and Macedonia became independent states. At the same time Serbia and Montenegro allied in 1992 to form the third Yugoslavia, officially called the Federal Republic of Yugoslavia, and renamed in 2003 as 'the State Union of Serbia and Montenegro'. Since 1991 Prekmurje Hungarians have been living in Slovenia, while Vojvodina Hungarians in the third Yugoslavia, and, since 2003, in Serbia and Montenegro.

In Section 2 of this chapter we briefly outline historical, demographic, economic, cultural, political and other factors which have determined in recent decades and which still influence the present situation of Hungarian in Vojvodina and Prekmurje, pointing out some sociolinguistically relevant characteristics of the Hungarian speech communities (for instance, their identity, language use, and linguistic attitudes). Section 3 of the chapter examines the characteristics of Vojvodina and Prekmurje contact varieties of Hungarian, to a great extent, based on the results of the Sociolinguistics of Hungarian Outside Hungary (SHOH) project (see Kontra, this volume).

2.   Sociolinguistic aspects

2.1   Hungarian in Vojvodina

2.1.1   *The origins of the contact situation*
There are two clearly distinguishable periods in the history of Hungarians in Vojvodina. The first period started at the end of the 9th century when Hungarians came to settle the Pannonian Plain, including present-day Vojvodina as well. Hungarians living in this area played a major role in the culture of medieval Hungarian state due to Humanist centers in the region. After the 1526 division of the Hungarian state, Serbs were moved to the area, as Vojvodina Hungarians either died in the wars against the Ottoman Turks or fled elsewhere.

The second period began in 1730 and extends up to the present. In the 18th century Hungarians, Germans, Slovaks, and Ruthenians moved to the area. But the intellectual life of the 18th century was not based on the rich medieval traditions of the region, therefore Vojvodina Hungarians could only play a peripheral role in the formation of the Hungarian nation and were on the periphery of the dynamic development of Hungarian civic culture in the 19th century.

Vojvodina was ceded from Hungary in 1918 under the Treaty of Trianon, so Vojvodina Hungarians became a minority in the newly formed Kingdom of Serbs, Croats and Slovenes, and with the exception of a short, three and a half year long interval for Bačka (between 1941 and 1944 when it was re-annexed to Hungary) they have been living as such for over eight decades now. They lived in the first Yugoslavia until World War II, in the second, Tito's Yugoslavia, between 1945 and 1991, and in the third Yugoslavia between 1992 and 2003. Vojvodina is a part of Serbia, which (except for the years of World War II) was constituted a part of the South Slavs' state from 1918 to 1992, a part of the third Yugoslavia from 1992 to 2003, and the state union with Montenegro since 2003. Depending on the different period, Vojvodina had different statuses within Serbia, ranging from autonomy of a greater or smaller extent to the complete lack of it.

For many centuries Vojvodina has had a very heterogeneous community as far as ethnicity and nationality, culture, languages and religions are concerned. As a general tendency, it is important to note that the centuries-long cohabitation of peoples of different religious, linguistic, and cultural backgrounds has developed in most people a respect for one another, a recognition of others, and a high level of tolerance. At the same time, hierarchized ethnic, cultural, and linguistic minority and majority groups have appeared as a result of the politics of various elites, and various forms of discrimination disfavoring minorities have emerged. Throughout history, none of the ethnic groups living here have been an exception to this. Ethnicism and linguicism (i.e. the ideologies for ethnic, cultural and linguistic discrimination) influenced in a more or less subtle way the life of Hungarians as well, especially in the last eight decades.

2.1.2   Geography and demographics

The State Union of Serbia and Montenegro, declared in 2003, is formed of the two member states indicated in its name. Its area is 39,449 square miles, and it has a 1,789 mile long border, 180 miles of which is the Adriatic coast. Compared to neighboring countries (clockwise from the north, they are Hungary, Romania, Bulgaria, Macedonia, Albania, Bosnia-Herzegovina, and Croatia), Serbia is smaller than Romania and Bulgaria, and bigger than all the others. Its density of population is 39 people per square mile, somewhat less dense than Hungary and Albania, but denser than all the other surrounding countries.

There are two autonomous provinces within Serbia and Montenegro: Kosovo and Metohija in the southeast and Vojvodina in the north. The smaller administrative units are districts (*okrug* in Serbian), which are county-like municipalities that have local social and administrative governments and are composed of nearby towns (giving their names to their districts) and villages.

Serbia and Montenegro is a truly multiethnic state. The percentages of nationalities in the population according to the figures of the latest, 2002 census are represented in Figure 7.1 (source: *Popis* 2002). The geographic location of the various nationalities is given, according to the 1981 census, in Map 7.1. (The 2002 census was not carried out in Kosovo, only in the rest of the country, and figures on the ethnic composition are only available for Serbia, not for Montenegro.)

According to the figures of the 2002 census, Serbia and Montenegro has a population of 8,148,576 (without Kosovo). After Albanians (whose number is unavailable

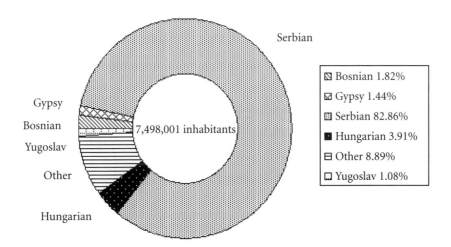

Figure 7.1. The ethnic composition of Serbia in 2002

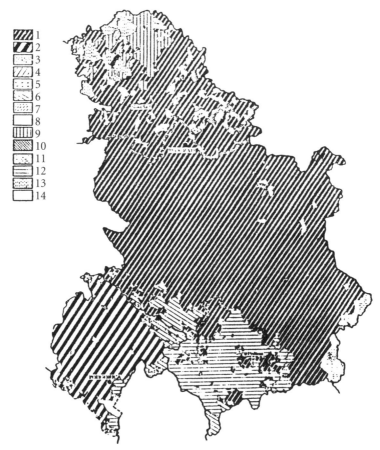

1 Serbians 2 Montenegrins 3 Yugoslavs 4 Croats 5 Macedonians 6 Muslims 7 Slovaks 8 Wallachians 9 Hungarians 10 Romanians 11 Bulgarians 12 Albanians 13 No majority present 14 Unknown

Map 7.1. The geographic distribution of ethnic groups in Yugoslavia in 1981. (Source: Spasovski 1994:53)

for 2002, but who constituted 12.3% of the poplulation of the country in 1991), Hungarians are the second biggest minority (3.6%) with a population of 293,299, which is 50 thousand people less than at the time of the 1991 census. Muslims (Bosnians), Gypsies, Croats and people declaring themselves Yugoslavs exceed 1% each, Slovaks, Romanians, Ruthenians, Macedonians, Turks, Slovenians and other ethnic minorities are below 1% each.

Of the Hungarians living in Serbia and Montenegro, 99.9% live in Serbia, and 98.9% of these in Vojvodina.

Vojvodina comprises 20% of Serbia and Montenegro's area and population. Romania, Hungary, Croatia and the Sava and Danube rivers border its territory. It has

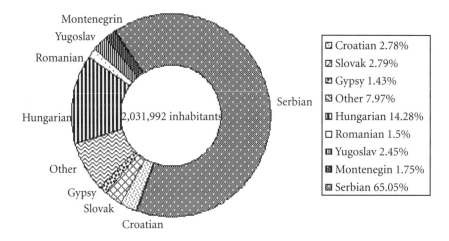

Croatian 2.78%
Slovak 2.79%
Gypsy 1.43%
Other 7.97%
Hungarian 14.28%
Romanian 1.5%
Yugoslav 2.45%
Montenegin 1.75%
Serbian 65.05%

Figure 7.2. The ethnic composition of Vojvodina in 2002

three geographical units: the biggest is Banat (the area between the Tisza river and the Hungarian and Romanian borders), the most densely populated is Bačka (the area between the Tisza, the Danube, and the Hungarian border), and Srem is in the South, between the Danube, the Sava, and the Croatian border. Vojvodina is made up of 45 districts, and of 464 towns and villages.

According to the figures of the 2002 census, Vojvodina has a population of 2,031,992. The larger ethnic groups are represented in Figure 7.2.

Considering the whole of Vojvodina, it is Serbs who constitute the biggest group (65.05%), after them come Hungarians (14.28%), then those claiming to be of Yugoslav nationality (2.45%), Croats (2.75%), Slovaks (2.79%), Montenegrins (1.75%), Romanians (1.50%), Gypsies (1.43%), while others such as the Bunyevatz, Ruthenians, and Macedonians etc. constitute 7.97%.

Serbs form an absolute (over 50%) majority in 31 of the 45 districts, and a relative (37–48%) majority in 4 districts. In 317 of the 464 settlements of Vojvodina, Serbs represent a majority (Spasovski 1994: 40), just like in each of the three parts (Banat, Bačka, and Srem). According to the figures of the 1985 Yugoslav Encyclopedia, 43.7% of the population of Bačka, 65.4% of Banat, and 75.3% of Srem was of Serbian nationality then. In Srem and Central Banat they populate large contiguous areas, in other regions they intercalate in other ethnic groups (Hódi 1989: 562).

Croats in Vojvodina are a majority in 13 villages and towns (in north Bačka), Slovaks in 18 (in Banat and Bačka), Montenegrins in 2 (in Bačka) and Romanians in 20 (in Banat). According to the figures of the 1991 census (Mirnics 1994: 152), Hungarians formed a majority in 81 villages and towns in Vojvodina (totaling 55% of Vojvodina's Hungarians), and in 47 of these districts Hungarians were in absolute or relative majority (6 in Bačka: Ada/Ada, Topola/Topolya, Beče/Becse, Senta/Zenta, Kanjiža/Kanizsa, Mali Iđoš/Kishegyes, 1 in Banat: Čoka/Csóka).[1] In Subotica/Szabadka Hungarians form a relative majority with 43%. By regions, according to the 1981 cen-

Table 7.1. Census data on the population of Vojvodina and the number of Hungarians there between 1881 and 2002*

	Total population	Hungarians	
1880	1,169,883	268,300	(22.9%)
1900	...**	378,634	...
1910	1,501,050	415,475	(27.7%)
1921	...**	371,006	...
1931	1 628,708	362,993	(22.3%)
1941	1,609,528	456,770	(28.4%)
1948	1,630,968	418,180	(25.6%)
1953	1,687,712	438,636	(26.0%)
1961	1,854,585	442,560	(23.8%)
1971	1,952,533	423,866	(21.7%)
1981	2,034,772	385,356	(18.9%)
1991	2,013,889	339,491	(16.9%)
2002	2,031,992	290,207	(14.5%)

* Sources: Mirnics 1994a: 28; Mirnics 1990b: 183; Biacsi 1994: 14, and Popis 2002.
** Data missing in the original sources.

sus, 73.8% of the Hungarians live in Bačka, 24.3% in Banat, and 1.9% in Srem (Hódi 1989: 562). In 1981, 42% of the Hungarians lived in villages and 58% in towns (Mirnics 1990b: 184).

The changes in the population of Vojvodina and the number of Hungarians between 1881 and 2002 are represented in Table 7.1.

The number of Hungarians in Vojvodina has been rapidly decreasing since the 1960s: between 1961 and 1991 it decreased by more than 100,000. Other groups, like Croats, Slovaks, Romanians, and Ruthenians are also diminishing. Figure 7.3 shows the changes of the biggest ethnic groups in Vojvodina between 1961 and 1991.

Migrations of the ethnic groups characterized Vojvodina's history in both earlier and modern times. Several tens of thousands of Hungarians moved or were forced to move to Hungary after World War I. There was continuous emigration between the two world wars to North and South America, Western Europe, Australia, and recently to South Africa as well. Thousands of Vojvodina Hungarians have been employed in Western Europe as guest workers in the past decades. In the 1990s many people fled the country because of the ethnic war, some 50,000 of them moved to Hungary. There are no reliable data on the number of emigrants, refugees, and guest workers.

Hódi (1989, 1990a) analyses questions concerning immigration, relocation into and out of Vojvodina, emphasizing the fact that nearly half of Vojvodina's population are in-migrants due to planned relocations after the World Wars from other parts of the Serb Republic, from Bosnia-Herzegovina, Croatia, and Montenegro. "They had privileges in every sphere of life. First, they received property, houses, and land for free, but even later they had better chances for jobs and progress" (Hódi 1990a: 28, our translation). During World War II as post-World War I settlers were forced away and fled, the Hungarian government relocated 22,000 persons in the area (Vinnai

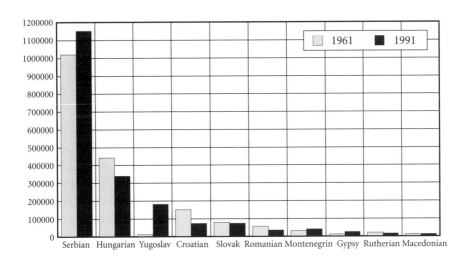

Figure 7.3. Changes in the populations of major ethnic groups in Vojvodina between 1961 and 1991

1995:409). But after the war, following party directives, 246,000 South Slavs were relocated into Vojvodina, though, at the same time, Vojvodina's German population (332,220 strong in 1941) was forcibly removed or forced away from Vojvodina (Mirnics 1990b:183). Hundreds of thousands of refugees arrived in the 1990s in Vojvodina when the second Yugoslavia fell apart and many people left the country. Due to these and other ethnic movements, the ethnic situation as a whole and the relative proportion of ethnic groups have changed considerably.

The majority of Vojvodina Hungarians live close to the Hungarian border. This geographic proximity helps maintain and intensify relations with Hungary (e.g. through frequent trips to Hungary, listening to Hungarian radio and watching Hungarian TV regularly). Studies show, though, that most Vojvodina Hungarians have no intention of leaving Vojvodina.

2.1.3   *Political, economic, cultural, and religious factors*
We will now discuss political, economic, cultural, religious and other factors of the Vojvodina Hungarians' lives that most likely affect their linguistic behavior. The nature of these factors has been determined by the relations between Hungarians and South Slavs. These relations have had a several centuries long history, but they only became relevant around 1848 and, especially, at the beginning of the 20th century.

We know from several sources (Mesaroš 1981, 1989; Domonkos 1992; Botlik et al. 1994; Vinnai 1995) that Vojvodina Hungarians had an extremely difficult situation in the first Yugoslavia, i.e. between the two world wars. Although the Yugoslav state finally provided guarantees for the protection of minorities, in practice its discriminating and violent assimilatory policies did not fulfill its duties required by the Treaty of Trianon, that is, it did not create conditions for protecting fundamental minority rights (like those of first language education, first language use, and equality regardless of ethnicity). Vojvodina Hungarians were affected by a whole range of harmful actions, and a great number of measures were introduced to severely limit the rights of Hungarians (e.g. total lack of rights between 1919 and 1922, land distribution exclusively for settlers, dismissal of state employees, discriminatory tax policies, shrinking the Hungarian school system) and frequently accompanied by severe transgressions (Domonkos 1992: 55–57; Tóth 1994: 9–12).

Hungarian political and cultural life had a slow start after the 1918 changes. In 1922 the National Hungarian Party was formed, but in 1929 it ceased to exist because of the introduction of a political dictatorship. At that time Vojvodina was annexed to the Danube Banovina, one of the nine new administrative units of the country, where the ratio of Hungarian residents in the population decreased dramatically. The Vojvodina Hungarian press was quite well developed, but it also was reduced in the 1920s. The intellectual values of Vojvodina Hungarians – since due to a strong dependence on Budapest, Vojvodina did not have its own intellectual traditions – were only preserved in frail literary attempts, strongly attached to the region. Some high quality journals existed, and several renowned writers discussed minority life.

After the 1918 annexation, the influence of Hungarian churches was reduced as well: church lands were confiscated, there was no possibility for theological education, and church schools were closed.

During World War II, Bačka was reannexed to Hungary (1941–1944), Banat was under German rule, and after the war both were annexed to the second, Tito's Yugoslavia.

In the second Yugoslavia, the situation of Vojvodina Hungarians radically changed. In the beginning, during the cleansing actions of the military administration, several thousand Hungarians were killed, their population decimated in some places. Afterwards, however, more favorable times came and Vojvodina Hungarians could live a slightly better life. A Yugoslav version of socialism was developed, i.e. a system of self-governed socialism, a kind of one-party system (with the Communist Party, or Communist Association as the ruling party) that made it possible for people to lead a more acceptable life than in other communist countries. However distorted the system was, it could somehow handle multicultural cohabitation in order to maintain a fragile ethnic balance. The second Yugoslavia acted as a state unifying different peoples, cultures, and languages, as it was in the ruling party's interest to maintain the balance through cultural pluralism. At the same time it was the state's responsibility to recognize and address wrongs committed against ethnic groups, but minorities were forbidden to organize themselves on an ethnic basis. Economic, cultural, and linguistic equality was proclaimed by the Communist Party at congresses, documents declaring equal rights were drawn up to emphasize it. The first years were quite reassuring, and in the 1950s a Hungarian system of cultural institutions emerged (judged by some to be highly centered around literature) in Vojvodina. Soon, however, no more institutions were to be established, and many of the already existing ones were closed down as well. That was the time when the government introduced a new principle, namely that culture should be cultivated jointly and not in isolation, fighting markedly Hungarian tendencies, and unifying the ethnic associations of the Hungarians, of other ethnic minorities, and of the Serbs in order to create a shared cultural life. In many cases, unification resulted in the decay of minority associations, with the majority forcing its ideas on the minorities, in the name of equality.

Similar ideas gained grounds and spread throughout the whole of society, creating a situation where Hungarians were overshadowed in every sphere of social life. Hungarians were considerably underrepresented among economic leaders, in party and youth organizations, in banks and insurance companies, in research and health institutions, in joint worker councils, in the executive branch, in the army, and in the national security service. Also, fewer of them were employed at all. It is also reflected in figures that from the early 1960s Vojvodina Hungarians shifted towards occupations not requiring secondary or higher education. In 1969, for example, the ratio of Hungarians in Serbia was 4.8%, and only 2.4% of these held university or college degrees. Also in the 1960s 12.6% of the Hungarians were employed in the village administration, 4.5% in province level administrative occupations, 10.5% as managers of economic companies, all falling behind the ratio of Hungarians in the population (23.8% in 1961, and 21.7% in 1971) (for a detailed analysis, see Göncz 1999: 56–57).

After World War II, religion was banned from every sphere of life.

With the formation of the third Yugoslavia and then of Serbia and Montenegro, the situation of Vojvodina Hungarians radically changed again. They have decreased in numbers significantly, living under difficult financial and uncertain social and political conditions in the last ten years, and subjected to numerous unfavorable situations resulting from their minority status and defenselessness (e.g. violent mobilizations, measures serving assimilation, etc.). It is hard to predict the future of Vojvodina Hungarians. The political parties formed within the multi-party system and other organizations fight for the cultural autonomy of Vojvodina Hungarians. The most important problems are the decrease of the Hungarian population, the decay of the educational system, the Hungarians' lower and lower level of education, increasing emigration and limited language use.

2.1.4   *Languages and ethnic groups in contact*

A multifaceted culture has been a characteristic of all three Yugoslav states and of Serbia and Montenegro. Ethnic groups in the south of the country have always been affected by Hellenic, Roman, Byzantine, and Ottoman Turkish influences. Central-European cultural influences were most prevailing in Vojvodina, where the mixing of peoples, languages, and customs formed perhaps one of Europe's most interesting ethnic mosaics. The biggest ethnic group of Serbia and Montenegro, the Serbs, have been under the influence of Byzantine culture, Ottoman Turkish civilization, and Central European culture for centuries. Serbs use the Cyrillic alphabet to write their language, and generally belong to the Orthodox Church. In Vojvodina, in the coastal municipalities, in the Sandžak, in Kosovo and Metohija, Catholicism and Islam are co-present. As for the culture of the Vojvodina Hungarians, it has not reached a similarly flourishing stage as, for example, that of Transylvania or other minority Hungarian regions.

Under the more than 150-year Ottoman Turkish occupation in the 16th and 17th centuries, flourishing feudal Hungarian settlements and the civilization of the Middle Ages disappeared, and afterwards new settlers came to repopulate the area. They shaped the region into a special amalgam of ethnic, linguistic, cultural, and religious features, though elements both of the original cultures of 'mother nations' and of the historical cohabitation can still be recognized. The multifaceted cultures and the wide historic orientation influenced the contents, the level and the nature of the civilization of Vojvodina Hungarians (Szeli 1983:35–136).

The majority of Vojvodina Hungarians are Roman Catholics, but 25,000 Hungarians (or about 8.5%) are members of the Reformed Church. There are Roman Catholic bishoprics today in Bačka and Banat. The number of believers is estimated to be 280,000 in Bačka. During services the Hungarian language is used. There is still no Hungarian language seminary, and there is only one church high school and one theological college. The Roman Catholic Church publishes books and periodicals.

Due to their peripherial situation, Vojvodina Hungarians have had contacts with several linguistic groups throughout their history. The change of states after World War I amplified these contacts as there were several languages spoken in the new South Slavic state. According to Škiljan (1992:32), in 1981 the larger speech communities were the Serbo-Croats (16,400,000), Slovenes (1,760,000), Albanians (1,750,000), Macedonians (1,350,000), Hungarians (410,000), Gypsies (140,000), Turks (82,000), Slovaks (74,000), Romanians (90,000), Ruthenians (19,000), Italians (19,000), Czechs (16,000), and Ukrainians (7,000). This varied linguistic picture was characteristic of the first Yugoslavia as well as the third, although the size of the various communities has changed considerably. The languages listed represent a great genetic and typological diversity. Apart from South Slavic languages (Serbo-Croatian, that is Serbian and Croatian today, Slovenian, and Macedonian), there are other Slavic languages as well (Ruthenian, Slovak, and Ukrainian), non-Slavic Indo-European languages (Albanian, Romani, Romanian, and Italian), and non-Indo-European languages (Hungarian, and Turkish) spoken in the country.

The Hungarian-Serbian language contact under scrutiny here is a genetically distant relationship, as the Hungarian language is a non-Indo-European, Uralic (more closely, Finno-Ugric) language, while Serbian is an Indo-European, South Slavic language.

One of the most important features of Vojvodina Hungarians is their numerical decrease in the past decades. Their population has been diminishing since 1960 very rapidly, over 30 years by 100,000 persons. According to Hódi (1989, 1990a, 1990b and 1992), the factors influencing this process are low increase rate in the population, self-destructive behaviors, emigration, the dominance of in-migrated Slavs, mixed marriages, the social declassing of the Hungarians, and the requirement of following the national ideal during the second Yugoslavia and the identity crisis resulting from it.

The tradition of mixed marriages is very much characteristic of Vojvodina. In 1956, the ratio of mixed marriages within all marriages was 17.3%, in 1978 it was 27.2%, and in 1980 it was 30.7%, so every third or fourth marriage is between partners of different ethnic origins. (This ratio is between 20 and 25% among Hungarians.) In 1981, 31,155 Hungarians lived in mixed marriages, and among women in Vojvodina who lived in mixed marriages the number of Hungarian women was the highest (Hódi 1990a: 29; Biacsi 1994: 19–27). Children from mixed marriages of Vojvodina Hungarians usually attend Serbian schools, and, as far as their "nationality" is concerned, they usually belong to the group declaring themselves Yugoslav: in Vojvodina, a high number of people, insecure about their own nationality, declare themselves Yugoslavs. In 1991 they constituted 8.7%, and between 1961 and 1991 their number had increased by a factor of 50, from 3,174 to 174,295. Taking into account the Vojvodina figures of the 1981 census, the number of Hungarians within the "Yugoslav" group was estimated to be 27,000 (Mirnics 1990a: 20), but as for today's situation, no reliable data are available.

2.1.5 *Sociolinguistic and psycholinguistic aspects*

Compared to the second Yugoslavia, in the third Yugoslavia and in Serbia and Montenegro rights have been restricted especially in terms of language use and education, the official argument behind it being that the previous system had given excessive rights to minorities, thereby damaging majority rights.

In 1991 the Serbian Parliament passed a law on the official and public use of Serbo-Croatian and the ethnic languages, which limited equality in language use to a greater extent than previous measures because its aim was to create grounds for the preponderance of Serbian in official and public language use, and to maintain the primary status of the Cyrillic alphabet over the Latin one. Formal use of minority languages is only allowed as an exception (in court for example, with interpretation), and the responsibility of their use is transferred to district councils and local governments as an alternative official variety with a limited scope. But even in these cases proper names (e.g. the names of towns) are not regarded as a part of the Hungarian language, and only their Serbian forms can be used. At the same time, the requirement of bilingualism has been abolished in certain occupations (e.g. in administrative offices and courts) (Papp 1992; Molnár Csikós 1993). Thus, the legal statuses of Serbian and Hungarian (and other ethnic languages) are different.

The situation of the Hungarian language is also influenced by educational laws through the following restrictions (Tóth 1994: 123; Molnár Csikós 1993: 480): elementary school classes can only be organized on an ethnic basis on at least 15 students' request; first language education is equated with bilingual education; knowledge of Hungarian is not obligatory for those teaching in Hungarian sections of schools (thus, claims about a lack of teachers can be used as grounds to shifting from first language education to state language education); on the secondary level whether a Hungarian section is open is decided on a year-by-year basis, inducing insecurity among students and their parents. Although existing measures are implemented flexibly (e.g. as far as the 15 student minimum requirement is concerned), insecurity and defenselessness constitute a constant threat to the contemporary situation of minority education and to first language use in schools.

In our case, the languages in contact differ in their functions as well. Serbian in Vojvodina is present at all three levels of language use (the familial-colloquial level, public and professional level, and the level of journalism and literature). This is not true for Hungarian.

The range of functions of Hungarian is restricted and reduced. The use of Vojvodina Hungarian is present (though not to a full extent) at the familial-colloquial level and that of journalism and literature, but at the public and professional level it has a very partial presence. As a result of an impoverishment of functions, the state language takes over certain areas from the minority language (e.g. in official governmental vocabulary, specialized vocabulary, the vocabulary of administrative and cultural life, public education, commerce, and health care, etc.). Fewer and fewer people speak the Hungarian language, in fewer and fewer communicative situations.

In terms of its functions, a language can be used for intragroup and intergroup communication in gaining information, that is, in gaining higher level knowledge and learning. From this point of view, in Vojvodina, Hungarian is used for intragroup communication. Intergroup communication in Hungarian is very rare, and its use is restricted in gaining higher level specialized knowledge and learning.

Since the community's self-identification and attitudes towards the state they live in and towards the language or variety they speak can be very telling about the language in question and about its speakers, as part of the Sociolinguistics of Hungarian Outside Hungary project we gathered information about the territorial and ethnic attitudes of Vojvodina Hungarians. We also elicited data about their attitudes towards the Hungarians of their regions and towards the Hungarian nation (see Tables 7.2 and 7.3). Subjects had to rate on a five-point scale how attached they were to certain places (ranging from their own settlement to Europe), to Hungarians in their regions, and to the Hungarian nation. Tables 7.2 and 7.3 show the results for Vojvodina and Prekmurje (see Göncz 2000b for details).

Table 7.2. The attachment of Hungarian speakers to various places, in Hungary, Vojvodina and Prekmurje*

Place	Vojvodina	Prekmurje	Hungary
a. own village or town	4.3	4.5	4.3
b. own region	4.2	4.4	–
c. the state before 1991**	3.9	4.2***	–
d. today's state	2.3	3.4	–
e. Hungary	2.7	1.8***	4.6***
f. Europe	3.3	3.5***	4.2***
g. nowhere	1.5	1.4	–

* Answers to the question: 'How much are you attached to these places?' 1= I am not attached to it at all, 5 = I am very much attached to it. Source: Göncz (2000b: 81)
** former Yugoslavia
*** the results are significantly different from those of Vojvodina Hungarians

Table 7.3. The national attachment of Hungarian speech communities in Vojvodina and Prekmurje*

How much do you feel that you belong to …?	Vojvodina	Prekmurje
a. the Hungarians of the region	4.4	4.4
b. the Hungarian nation	4.2	4.3
c. nowhere	1.9	1.8

* Answers to the question: 'How much do you feel that you belong to …?' 1 = not at all, 5= very strongly. Source: Göncz (2000b:82)

The following conclusions can be drawn from the data:

1. Subjects in Vojvodina rank their territorial attachment in the following way: 1st and 2nd, their own settlement and Vojvodina; 3rd, pre-1991 Yugoslavia; 4th, Europe; 5th, Hungary; 6th, today's Yugoslavia; and 7th, lack of territorial attachment. The samples in Vojvodina and Hungary show a similar intensity in their attachment to their own towns and villages, but Vojvodina subjects are attached less to Hungary and to Europe than subjects in Hungary. Compared to the average of the other studied regions, Vojvodina subjects' attachment to their towns and region, and to Europe, does not differ substantially, but (just like Prekmurje subjects) they have a weaker attachment to Hungary, and a stronger one to the pre-1991 state than other Hungarian subjects living in the former unions (Göncz 2000b).
2. Vojvodina subjects feel equally attached to Vojvodina Hungarians and to the Hungarian nation. As Göncz (2000b) has shown, their attachment to their minority is just as strong as the average of Hungarian minority groups living in the Carpathian Basin, and although Vojvodina Hungarians clearly regard themselves as part of the Hungarian nation, their affiliation with it is less strong than that of Transylvania and Subcarpathia Hungarians. Compared to the other regions, the differences are not substantial.
3. As for the samples of Vojvodina and Prekmurje, a lack of regional and national attachment is more obvious than in the case of other subjects in the regions studied.

Linguistic affiliation is an important factor of national identity, that is why evaluating opinions on language and dialect (i.e. linguistic attitudes) can present important information about the self-identity of the speech community. One of its possible aspects, linguistic stereotypes about varieties of Hungarian, was one of the topics of our project. Different answers came from all the different regions responding to the question about where the most beautiful variety of Hungarian was spoken. Results for Vojvodina, Prekmurje and Hungary are summarized in Table 7.4.

The figures show that for Vojvodina Hungarians, Budapest, Hungarian country towns and Vojvodina are statistically more frequent answers than other places are. Our Vojvodina subjects do not seem to depreciate their own variety. As Göncz (2000a) has shown, Hungarians in Austria, Slovakia and Prekmurje depreciate their own variety compared to other contact varieties spoken in the other regions, while subjects

Table 7.4. First language stereotypes of Hungarian speech communities in Vojvodina, Prekmurje and Hungary*

Setting	Vojvodina	Prekmurje	Hungary
1. in Budapest	37 (31.9%)	29 (56.9%)	20 (19.6%)
2. in Hungary, in the country towns	31 (26.7%)	10 (19.6%)	34 (33.3%)
3. in Hungary, in the villages	4 (3.4%)	1 (2%)	29 (28.4%)
4. in Subcarpathia (Ukraine)	0	0	0
5. in Transylvania (Romania)	12 (10.3%)	7 (13.7%)	19 (18.6%)
6. in Slovakia	2 (1.7%)	0	0
7. in Vojvodina	30 (25.9%)	0	0
8. in Burgenland (Austria)	0	0	0
9. in Prekmurje	0	4 (7.8%)	0

* Answers to the question: Where do you think is the most beautiful Hungarian spoken? Source: Göncz (2000a:49)

in Subcarpathia and especially those in Transylvania appreciate theirs. At the same time, according to subjects from Hungary, the most beautiful Hungarian is spoken in Hungarian country towns, while Budapest and Transylvania are isolated, and none of the other regions are marked. Taking into account the results of all Hungarian speech communities (answers from the control group in Hungary as well) the rank of settings is the following: 1st, Transylvania (31.3%); 2nd, Budapest (26.4%); 3rd, Hungarian country towns (19.5%); 4th, Subcarpathia (10.08%); 5th, Hungarian villages (6.9%); 6th, Vojvodina (4.1%); 7th, Slovakia (1.2%); 8th, Prekmurje (0.5%); and 9th, Burgenland (0%) (Göncz 2000a). The size of the groups and their percentage of the total sample highly influence the ranking.

Some aspects of the linguistic situation of Vojvodina Hungarians can be analyzed in terms of diglossia and bidilectism. As for the Vojvodina Hungarians' linguistic situation, the cohabitation of Standard Hungarian as a high (H) variety and the Vojvodina Hungarian contact variety as a low (L) variety is a major characteristic trait. In line with classic diglossia (Ferguson 1959), the two varieties are used in different functions; L is acquired in the family, H at school. Knowledge of Standard Hungarian is passive and only partial for most speakers, and only the small group of intellectuals in humanities uses it actively. Few can speak a 'cultivated standard' in domains (everyday life, the profession, and sciences) where its use is expected. Therefore, apart from the classic Fergusonian diglossia, Fishman's diglossia (Fishman 1967) is present as well, according to which the H and L varieties can belong to different languages, and poliglossia and bidilectism also describe part of the linguistic situation. In the speech of Vojvodina Hungarians, Standard Hungarian is the H variety, and the contact varieties of Hungarian are the L variety, while another code, Serbian, plays an ever increasing role. In different layers of society and in different regions one can find these first language varieties in different distribution. South, east and west of northeastern-Bačka, the number of speakers capable of using the national standard in formal situations is decreasing, as Serbian influences to an ever greater extent the bilingual first language varieties, and occupies more and more the place of the H variety.

The SHOH project provides information on language proficiency and language acquisition as well. Subjects had to mark on a 7-point scale their first language, majority language and other language proficiency levels. The following categories were used: 0 = I don't speak it at all; 1 = I don't speak it but understand it; 2 = I hardly know a few words; 3 = not very well; 4 = well; 5 = very well; 6 = native level. Our Vojvodina subjects gave 141 responses. According to their self-evaluation, 128 of them (90.8%) speak Hungarian natively, 4 speak it very well (2.8%) and 9 speak it well (6.4%). These figures are the following for Serbian: 12 (8.5%), 48 (34%), and 50 (35.5%), respectively, adding up to 78% of the sample, so the rest (22%) rate their Serbian proficiency to be on a lower level. Therefore, the sample can be categorized into a Hungarian dominant bilingual group, as approximately 20% of them speak Serbian not very well or know only few words of it, and only 2% of them understand but do not speak it. At the same time, 18% of the sample acknowledge knowing other languages, and if less strict criteria are used, almost half of them can be considered multilingual (Göncz 1999: 89).

If the different language proficiency levels are arranged in an increasing order, then, on this seven-point scale (0–6), proficiency in Hungarian is rated with an average of 5.83, whereas Serbian has an average of 4.21 (t = 16.93, proving that the subjects are Hungarian-dominant). Results are similar in other regions: in every region between 80 and 90% of the subjects speak Hungarian on a native level, with the exception of Prekmurje, where the corresponding rate is lower, at 64.2%. The first language proficiency of Vojvodina Hungarians does not differ from Slovakia, Subcarpathia and Transylvania Hungarians, but it is better than that of Prekmurje and Austria Hungarians. As for majority language proficiency, Vojvodina Hungarians are behind Prekmurje and Austria Hungarians, but Hungarians in Subcarpathia and in Transylvania evaluate their majority language proficiency lower (Göncz 2001b).

As for venues of language acquisition, the results clearly show that parents play the most important role in first language acquisition (with 100% of Vojvodina subjects mentioning them), but grandparents (52.5%) as well as preschools and schools (39.6% and 38.3%, respectively) are also important, with the immediate environment (friends and neighbors, 35.5%; playmates, 34%) being influential, too. The workplace has some role (21.3%), but less than 10% of the subjects mentioned higher education and language courses, military service or residence in other regions as venues of language acquisition. Contrasted with the other average results of minority Hungarian speech communities, it seems that the sources are very similar, but in the other minority regions grandparents and playmates play, on the average, a more important role (65.8% and 44%, respectively) (Göncz 1999: 92).

As for language acquisition venues for Serbian, we find the school in first place (66%), but local friends (49.6%), playmates (48.2%), and the workplace (40.4%) constitute major language acquisition venues, too. Higher education (25.5%) and preschool (20.6%) play a much less substantial role, similarly to military service (14.9%) and time spent in Serbian areas (12.8%).

In Vojvodina, other languages are mainly acquired by Hungarians in school (21.3%), but language courses, continuing education, higher education, and life in a different region can also be important.

If we analyze Vojvodina Hungarians' bilingualism in the light of different bilingualism types (Göncz 1999:97), it can be characterized as primarily one-sided and folk bilingualism. It is folk bilingualism, because they have no choice between monolingualism and bilingualism; in order to survive they have to learn the majority language. It is one-sided as well, because only the Hungarians are bilingual, while the Serbian speaking community is mainly monolingual. During their eighty years of minority life, Vojvodina Hungarians have seen periods of subtractive bilingualism (when the languages and cultures of a heterogeneous community were being hierarchized, their statuses not equal) to a lesser or greater extent. Therefore, the features of subtractive and additive bilingualism have been alternating. It was in the second Yugoslavia, in the 1970s, when several traits of additive bilingualism could be found, that is, the ideologies underlying linguicism and ethnicism were less dominant. Thus, in the 1970s in Vojvodina, for example, the number of Serbian students learning Hungarian as a second language was close to the number of students learning Hungarian as a first language. In the 1980s, their number decreased. Although legislation in the third Yugoslavia did not raise insurmountable obstacles to realizing certain ethnic rights, it is a fact that laws passed on language use and educational possibilities were well below the level of those accomplished in the 1970s. As for the time of the acquisition of bilingual abilities, for those living in communities where Hungarians are in the minority, it is early (preschool) parallel bilingual language acquisition, for those living in Hungarian majority communities it is later (school age) that is more typical. Most Vojvodina Hungarians are Hungarian-dominant bilinguals, while balanced bilinguals are more common in communities with Hungarians in the minority. Characteristics of coordinate bilingualism are more pronounced in the case of those who use the two languages in separate domains: e.g. those who attend Hungarian language schools, so their use of Hungarian is centered around school and family, but otherwise, especially in Hungarian minority communities, people use the majority language more. Naturalistic second language acquisition (when the second language is acquired in direct communication with the speakers of the other language) is more typical in Hungarian minority communities, whereas controlled (classroom) acquisition has a more important role in Hungarian majority communities.

2.1.6   *Language policy*

In this section we discuss language policy and one of the relevant settings of language use, namely language use in schools, and its effects. We will also briefly deal with the question of languages used in other linguistic settings.

Either implicitly or explicitly, it is often an ambition of states to make political borders into linguistic and ethnic borders as well. Vojvodina Hungarians have also been touched by such an ambition. But depending on the political system and historical situation, there have been differences in the harshness of its execution. Details of the behavior of states in this respect were analyzed by Lanstyák (1991:60–61).

It is a well-known fact that schools are the keystone to survival, especially to the linguistic survival of minorities. That is why we consider it important to discuss some details that have highly influenced Hungarian minority education in Vojvodina during the last eighty years.

The peace treaties after World War I defined only partially the protection of the southern Hungarians as a new minority. The right to first language education in 4 or 6 year schools obliged the state in loose terms to open minority schools in those areas where there were a large number of minority residents. In Hungarian majority settlements the new administrative authorities let elementary schools function under the condition that they have at least 30 students in the Hungarian section and the teachers had to prove through a state language exam their proficiency in Serbian, or else they were not allowed to teach. Students with non-Hungarian sounding names were not allowed to enroll in the Hungarian sections even if they claimed to be Hungarian. In fifth and sixth grades, the language of instruction was usually Serbian. In the first Yugoslavia, the number of Hungarian sections was continuously diminishing: in 1930 there were 528, in 1939 452 of them. But as for secondary education, which used to be quite well developed previously, problems were a lot more severe. By 1930 Hungarian high schools had declined, and Hungarian sections of high schools gradually ceased to exist. Therefore, by World War II, there were only 337 Hungarian high school students studying in the two surviving high schools in Vojvodina, where several subjects were taught in Serbian. The Primary School Teacher Training College functioned in Belgrade with a small number of students who could study only the Hungarian language, pedagogical courses and agriculture in Hungarian. The number of Hungarian students studying in colleges or universities was very low, so there was only a very thin layer of Hungarians trained professionally.

In the second Yugoslavia, constitutional and legal measures regulating minority rights provided relatively favorable conditions for the creation of a legal basis for the early development of Hungarian education. In the 1950s, a system of Hungarian education developed that gave Hungarian students the possibility to study in their first language: at the elementary level it was possible for a great number of students, at the secondary level for a smaller number, and at the higher educational level for a very small number. This early, dynamic development was followed by halts. In the mid-1950s regional schools were introduced (unifying minority language and Serbian schools), and in the late 1970s, specialized schools appeared (the first two years were the same for all, but then very specialized courses were taught). Both of these measures made it very difficult for Hungarians to continue studying in their first language. (High schools were restored in 1990.) In the first two decades after World War II, the number of Hungarian students increased considerably (to more than 40,000), but in the next twenty years it decreased by 32%, at the same rate as the number of teachers (Botlik et al. 1994:285–286; Tóth 1994). The decrease continued, so in the 1990s there were only 23,000 students in the Hungarian sections. This is 80% of all Hungarian students, while the others attend Serbian sections. In the case of secondary students this ratio is 35–40%, but their number has decreased as well. Furthermore, half of all the Hungarian secondary students attend vocational schools, while for Serbians the ratio is one third. The number of Hungarian students in higher education has been painfully low for decades. In 1992, for example, in colleges and universities of Vojvodina, 6.9% of the students were Hungarian, although Hungarians constituted 17% of its total population. Only 59% of them studied in their first language.

If we analyze first language education in Vojvodina in terms of typologies designed for heterogeneous communities, regarding the role of both the majority and minority language in education (see, for instance, Skutnabb-Kangas 1984; Lanstyák 1994c, 1995), we see that at the elementary level, on average, 80% of the students receive first language education, and study Serbian as one of the subjects. This mother tongue maintenance program, if it is well organized, can have satisfactory effects on general intellectual, linguistic, and socio-emotional development and on the success of education. There are problems, however, with curricula, textbooks, and a lack and inappropriate training of teachers. Humanities subject curricula lack Hungarian cultural elements, and most of the textbooks are bad translations from Serbian (the use of textbooks from Hungary is prohibited). As there is a great shortage of teachers, some subjects are taught by teachers who do not speak Hungarian but use Serbian instead. Consequently, usually we can only speak about partial and not full first language education. This is especially true at the secondary level. Thus, in many elementary and secondary schools first language education is turning into bilingual education, that is, some of the subjects are taught in one language, others in the other language. This practice gives rise to the decay of specialized first language proficiency and induces code-switching. This more and more dominant tendency goes parallel with transitional programs which do not aim at the maintenance of the native language but at a transition to majority language education. Serbian is used in teacher education in the case of many subjects, which results in problems with Hungarian technical language proficiency among Hungarians. We have already mentioned that 20% of Hungarian primary school students, and 35–40% of secondary students are educated in their second language, and their form of education can be either full second language education, first language cultivation, or language teaching as a school subject. Full second language education means submersion, promoting, on the long run, the exchange of the first language with the majority language, especially in communities where Hungarians are in the minority. In the case of students studying in the second language, the development of the first language is interrupted, and such students often retain only limited usage of it. At the same time, the language of the school is not reinforced at home as in the case of other students who grow up in their families with the culture and language of the school. As long as they do not master the school language as a tool of reflective thinking, they will underachieve in school. Submersion programs communicate to children the message that they had better renounce their language and culture because it is less valuable (which is why education is not organized in their native language), or the parents suggest this through their choice of a majority school, even if there would be a possibility for a native language school. These factors create unsatisfactory conditions for the socio-emotional development of the children; their self-confidence and self-esteem can be greatly damaged. Failures at school make them feel ashamed. Those who can overcome the linguistic obstacles usually renounce their language and culture, taking up the norms and values of the group governing the school. For those studying in Serbian language programs, sometimes there is a possibility for extra classes in language cultivation when they study the grammar of their first language and their national literature, balancing out to some extent the effects of the submersion programs. Language teaching schools function usually on the secondary level, where majority language instruction is used, but, children also study their native language as an obligatory subject; the effects are better in these schools than in those with language cultivation lessons, their long-term results are, however, similar to those of submersion programs.

All in all, Hungarian language education in Vojvodina has many problems, the greatest ones being the submersion programs and the increasing number of transitional programs, which amplify the effects of subtractive bilingualism. Possible consequences of these have been described in detail elsewhere (Göncz 1998:39–53, 1999:115–117). We can clearly state that the education in Vojvodina does not make use of the results of bilingualism research, and its methods do not encourage practices in favor of minority students.

Results of the SHOH project give insight into the language choice of the Vojvodina subjects in other domains of life, as summarized in Table 7.5.

It is obvious from the figures of Table 7.5 that in everyday language use, the Vojvodina subjects, in addition to their native language, use Serbian to some extent, depending on the different domains and have, thus, developed functional bilingualism. In writing and at the workplace the frequency of the use of the two languages is the same ($\chi^2 = .22$, df = 1, not significant, and $\chi^2 = .10$, df = 1, not significant, respectively), but in other domains first language use is more frequent. In villages native language use is more frequent than in towns because in villages Hungarians tend to be in a majority. In the table pluses indicate significant differences in the frequency of use of the two languages in the different domains; see, for example, the language of radio and television programs ($\chi^2 = 27.42$, df = 1, p < .00, that is, highly significant). More detailed analyses of the various domains show, however, that first language use tends to be very limited in official and formal situations. Thus, 76.6% of our subjects write their private letters in Hungarian, but only 41.5% of the letters connected to their work and 33.5% of the documents they address to administrative offices. Similar ratios are found in terms of reading: 65.5% of our subjects read newspapers and literature, 55% read professional literature, and 47% read official documents in Hungarian. In church Hungarian is almost exclusively used (95%), in shops, at the post office and at doctors' offices use of Hungarian is frequent (55%), but in banks, courts, administrative offices and the police, majority language communication is dominant (for instance, at the police first language use is at 32%). These figures prove that second language use is less

Table 7.5. The language use in Vojvodina in the most important domains of life (in percentages)*

	Hungarian	Serbian	Other (other language or missing data)
Private conversations (with parents, grandparents, children, partner, friends, neighbors)	75.2$^+$	23.1	1.7
Writing (private letters, official letters, in connection with the profession)	47.9	45.9	6.2
Reading (newspapers, magazines, religious scripts, poems, novels, professional literature, brochures, questionnaires, official papers)	54.5$^+$	33.6	11.9
Radio and TV programs (films, shows, sports, news)	51.3$^+$	37.1	11.6
Miscellaneous language use (e.g. in church, in shops, at the doctor's, at the post office, in offices)			
In villages:	64.3$^+$	26.5	9.2
In towns:	45	43.5	11.3
Other language use (prayer, counting, thinking, swearing, etc.)	81$^+$	13	6
Language use at the workplace	46	43	11

* Source: Göncz (1998: 126)
$^+$ Significant difference in the frequency of the use of the two languages in the different domains.

frequent in the private domain and more frequent in the domains of administration and profession.

If these figures are analyzed in detail and compared to results from other studied regions, we can state (cf. Göncz 1999: 123–132) the following. In the limited private domain (with family, friends, and neighbors) 75.2% of our subjects communicate in Hungarian, 23.1% in Serbian and 1.7% in other languages. If we only take into consideration spoken communication in the family (with parents, grandparents, children, and partners), 90.7% of the communication is in Hungarian, 7.7% in Serbian, and 1.6% in other languages. With friends and neighbors, Hungarian usage is less frequent (59%). The proportions are similar in case of other Hungarian minorities in the Carpathian Basin, but in Transylvania, Subcarpathia, and Slovakia, Hungarian is used somewhat more frequently in communicating with children, grandparents and partners than in Vojvodina.

Among Vojvodina Hungarians, 47.9% of all written communication is in Hungarian, and 45.9% in Serbian. Private letters are usually written in Hungarian, but letters addressed to administrative offices and work-related documents are written in Serbian more often. On average, Vojvodina Hungarians use Hungarian in writing more than Hungarian minorities in other countries. At the same time, 54.5% of the subjects read in Hungarian, 33.6% in Serbian, 4.2% in other languages, and 7.7% in none. Especially newspapers, magazines, poems and novels are read in Hungarian, but professional literature and newspapers are also read in Serbian, while other documents are only read in Serbian. These findings correlate highly with global results of Hungarian minorities in the Carpathian Basin. Among TV channels, the local Hungarian channel is the most popular, followed by TV channels from Hungary, and finally by Serbian channels. As for radio stations, the order is similar, although more people watch TV than listen to radio. On average, Vojvodina Hungarians watch Hungarian channels more than do Hungarian minorities in other countries, local Hungarian programs are more popular in Vojvodina than in other regions, but Vojvodina Hungarians listen to radio broadcasts from Hungary less. As for the language of radio and TV broadcasts, Hungarian is first (51.3%), Serbian is second (37.1%), and other languages are last (11.6%). Average results of Hungarian minorities in other countries are similar. According to our figures, the language of 49.5% of all studied domains is Hungarian, 39.5% is Serbian, but proportions in villages are different from those in towns. In villages 64.3% of all language use is in Hungarian, and 26.5% is in Serbian, while in towns it is 45% and 43.5% respectively. In villages, Hungarian is dominant in all domains, but in towns subjects use Serbian more frequently than Hungarian at the police, in administrative offices, at courts and at the post office. Compared to the sum of results from other minority Hungarian regions, Hungarian is used 9% more in Vojvodina, both in towns and villages. Vojvodina Hungarians use Hungarian more when counting, swearing, and thinking than in other regions, but they pray less in Hungarian (and they pray less in general). As for workplace language use in Vojvodina, in 24% of the cases Hungarian is used rarely or never, in 76% it is often used; in other regions these ratios are 30% and 70%, respectively. The differences are not significant statistically. According to the results of our study, Vojvodina Hungarians had fewer experiences of being told not to speak their native language than Hungarians in other regions, whereas it is a common belief among Vojvodina and other Hungarians that it is only proficiency in the majority language that enables them to succeed, while knowledge of Hungarian only does not allow one to get by properly.

2.2 Hungarian in Prekmurje

2.2.1 *Geography and demographics*
Slovenia is one of the small states resulting from the recent political changes that affected the contiguous territory of the western Carpathian Basin. For 70 years it had been an independently named part of Yugoslavia, that is, first of the Kingdom of Serbs, Croats, and Slovenes (later, the Yugoslav Kingdom) and then one of the Socialist Republics of Yugoslavia. Its current area has also been formed during Yugoslav times, since from the formation of the medieval Hungarian Kingdom until 1920, the territories lying west of the Mura river constituted a part of Austria, those lying east of it a part of Hungary. As a result, the Mura and the former borderline plays an important role for Slovenian people. The territories east of the Mura are distinguished by Slovenian

scholarship and dialectal and ethnographic points of view using the separate name of Prekmurje, 'beyond the Mura' (*Muravidék* in Hungarian) (*Slovenija* 1990).

At the time of the 2002 census, there were 5,445 persons of Hungarian nationality residents living here (Gyurgyík & Sebők 2003:217). The total population of the territory at that time was 120,875, so the proportion of the Hungarian-speaking minority was 4.5%. According to the census, the overall population of Slovenia was 1,964,036, that of all Hungarians in Slovenia 6,243, so the proportion of the Hungarian minority was 0.31%. Another constitutionally recognized national minority in Slovenia are the 2,258 Italians living on the northern coastal municipalities of the Istrian peninsula in Koper and in villages close to Trieste, Italy. Their number is low not because of assimilation, but because of a forced repatriation of ethnic Italians in the 1950s. There used to be a sizable German-speaking minority in Slovenia until World War II, but they fled, were forcibly moved, or assimilated during the war and post-war events. After the disintegration of the second Yugoslavia, many people from other southern republics (who had been migrant workers before) came to the area.

As is often the case with census data, the above census figures do not show the exact number of mother tongue speakers of Hungarian. This is due to the fact that in recent censuses it was possible for Yugoslav citizens to declare themselves to be of 'Yugoslav nationality'. As far as we know, a lot of people living in mixed marriages used this option. They rarely used the designation for themselves, rather it was their children who did, since for them it was almost fashionable to declare to be 'Yugoslav' instead of Serbian, Croatian, Slovenian, or Hungarian, etc. Although this fact had no impact on their language use, in certain cases it might have changed statistics by as much as 10%.

As the above mentioned geographical and historical data clearly indicate, most of the Hungarian minority in Slovenia, with the exception of the two small towns (Lendava/Alsólendva and Murska Sobota/Muraszombat), live near the Hungarian border. Here they form a linguistic majority, despite the fact that after 1920 the Yugoslav Kingdom carried out a massive internal population movement from neighboring Slovenian villages and from the coastal municipalities into the area on the pretext of land distribution. The locals still call these Slovenian settlements *colonies*. The Hungarian population of Slovenia has been decreasing ever since World War I. In the Lendava/Alsólendva region, the 1921 census counted 10,702 Hungarians, while the 1960 census registered 8,115, the 1971 census 7,432, the 1981 census 7,069 and the 2002 census 3,917.[2] So, in 80 years the Hungarian minority did not only lose their natural population growth but 63% of the original population as well. During the same time, the majority population grew. The tendency was similar in the Murska Sobota/Muraszombat district as well. The loss is even more conspicuous if compared to the population of 20,000 at the 1910 census. Hungarians are in the majority in settlements where they form a geographical, settlement-historical, ethnographic and dialectal unity with the neighboring territories in Hungary.

The linguistic borderline between Slovenian- and Hungarian-speaking areas had formed by the turn of the 19th century. Mixed language settlements were quite rare, bilingualism was not characteristic of the locals, as it was not necessary because of territorially bound agriculture (Kerecsényi 1994; Pivar 1994). People experienced linguistic and cultural diversity at fairs and markets, or in neighboring villages when they wanted to buy crops or animals, but these rare occasions did not create a need for acquiring another linguistic code. This was mainly a characteristic of Hungarians as their territory formed an integral part with Hungary's Vas and Zala counties. Their cultural and economic centers (Körmend, Szombathely, Lenti, Zalaegerszeg, etc.) were found in that area as well. In the larger, western part of the region up to the river Mura, a similarly contiguous monolingual Slovenian community was formed, which maintained economic and cultural relations not with other Slovenes in what was then Austria, but with Hungarians in Vas and Zala counties since the Austria-Hungary border separated them. That is why the development of Prekmurje Slovenians (also sometimes called Vends) from linguistic, cultural and communal mentality perspectives differs considerably from Slovenes in other geographic regions in Slovenia and displays a strong Hungarian influence (Novak 1985). The political and economic focal point of this area was Murska Sobota/Muraszombat, the district center and the biggest settlement in the region with a population of 10,000 people (the same number as today). A great number of its population was bilingual, especially the educated small town elite and the shopkeepers.

Overpopulation due to a relative lack of land presented a problem for the population of Prekmurje, regardless of nationality, beginning with the second half of the 19th century. That is why many people left the area with the first wave of emigration to the United States. Some wanted to return rich, others fled from hunger. Some succeeded in coming back, others became attached to their new life and created a new lifestyle and a new home in America.

Many people, especially the Goričko Slovenians of the hilly areas, but other groups from the overpopulated areas as well, were employed further east on Hungarian farms and manors as seasonal workers in the summer (usually at harvest time) in order to earn at least their minimally sufficient livelihood money for the winter.

Apart from this, the area was not affected by other important migrations. Wars had little impact on this area, so traditions of folk culture were successfully preserved.

2.2.2   *Historical background*

The area was part of the western no man's land when the Hungarian Kingdom was formed in the year 1000 and served as a natural protecting border of the country: its rivers and streams with their marshy streambed areas and the hills with their forests helped protect the border. That is why in early times this particular area was probably sparsely inhabited. Only guards with special privileges were moved here by monarchs in order to keep an eye on the crossings. Most authentic documents in support of this fact are connected to the area still called Őrség ('guarding area'), close to the Zala and Kerka rivers. The first inhabitants must have belonged to the conquering Hungarians. When attacks from the west, common in the 11th century, were not a problem any more, and the no man's land was no longer in use, the area was populated, the land was reclaimed and made cultivable. That is why progeny of the guards from the east and immigrants from the Holy Roman Empire from the west were welcome. Most of them were Slavs, some Bavarians. It is their descendants that inhabit present-day Prekmurje and Pomurje (beyond and around the Mura river). Apart from natural assimilation – which assimilated absolute linguistic minorities through ways mentioned before – there were no other changes amongst them during the centuries (*Zgodovina Slovencev* 1979). On the basis of facts of regional dialects we can conclude that the Hungarian minority had moved in earlier times from west to the east. It is possible that Slavs became a majority of the population. But, as we have noted before, due to the two-way assimilation, the linguistic border was sharp and clear.

We have already mentioned that the Hungarian population of Slovenia plays an important role in three Hungarian ethnographic regions, maintaining cultural, personal, and familial relationships across borders whenever possible. The first Yugoslav state attempted but did not succeed in changing this with its relocation policy. Signs of ethnic mixing have only been seen for the last few decades, but this is the result of changes in economy (including a movement toward industry).

The relationship between the ethnic groups of the region was determined by the fact that they constituted one single economic community in both the Hungarian Kingdom and the Kingdom of Serbs, Croats and Slovenes. There has never been ethnic disagreement between Hungarians and Slovenes. The only exception was a short period of time when during the distribution of land in order to create *colonies* the Hungarian penniless peasants did not receive any land (Pivar 1994). As far as we know, however, cohabitation disarmed antagonisms, and the Slovene populations of the *colonies* lived together in peace with the autochthonous Hungarian community. This was probably aided by the fact that the majority of families do not earn their living through the land.

December 1, 1918, can be regarded as the date when Hungarians in Slovenia became a minority. On that day Prince Regent Alexander announced in Belgrade the formation of the Kingdom of Serbs, Croats, and Slovenes, although at that time the new power, supported mostly by the Serbian Army, could control neither Medjumurje nor Prekmurje. Therefore, *de jure*, the Hungarians of the western parts of Vas and Zala counties became a minority then, but *de facto* they did so only on August 12, 1919, after the occupation by Serbian troops. We do not know how many Hungarians lived in this area of the kingdom after the change of regimes, as data from different sources vary, but politically motivated migration was important as well. In 1910 there were 20,737 Hungarians, that is 23% of the population, 14,065 (17.7%) in 1921, 15,050 in 1931, and 16,510 (20.1%) in 1941.

On October 3, 1929, the new name of the state became the Yugoslav Kingdom, on November 29, 1945, the People's Republic of Yugoslavia, and in 1963 the Federal Republic of Yugoslavia. In 1991, after the secession of Slovenia from Yugoslavia, the new state became the Republic of Slovenia.

At the time of the kingdom, there was no policy on minorities, as their conscious suppression and assimilation cannot be called a policy. A good example of economic subjugation is the measure by the Minister of Agriculture on land distribution in 1921–1922, proclaiming that residents of foreign nationality could not acquire land. It was at this time that 278 Slovene families from coastal municipalities were moved to the former Esterházy estate.

The Hungarian community could not defend itself from the political authorities even through self-organization. There were no political organizations in the 1920s to represent the interests of the minority, and after the extreme right turn of 1929, this would not have even been possible. In the 1930s, Hungarian teachers were laid off and replaced by teachers of other ethnicities who were placed there against their will, usually as a form of punishment. In little villages with populations of a few hundred, classes of at least 30 students were made compulsory, citing economic reasons. In most cases there were not enough Hungarian students to satisfy this requirement.

The situation was no better in other aspects of life either. In 1925 the outspoken weekly *Szabadság* and, later, every Hungarian newspaper was banned. This situation remained the same until 1941 when Prekmurje was annexed to Hungary for a short period of time.

After Prekmurje became part of Yugoslavia again, until 1949 the ethnic cultural needs of minorities were not even taken into consideration, the leaders of the new political power were preoccupied with retaliation. This is when the Committee on Hungarian Culture was set up on central, state initiative. In 1950, in Lendava/Alsólendva, during the conference on minorities, its statutes listing not the interests of minorities but rather the expectations of the authorities were adopted. We do not have any accounts of its success until the end of the decade.

The 1959 assembly of the Central Committee of the Alliance of Yugoslav Communists started a new period in minority policies. The minority question was raised again and a measure was passed according to which in 'ethnically mixed' regions ethnic committees would be set up. That marks the beginning of official Slovenian minority policy. A government level ethnic committee with Slovene, Hungarian and Italian members was established to implement an integration of the minorities. Linguistic equality, bilingual administration in bilingual areas, first language information and a right to maintain relations with the mother nation were the objectives declared through the committee by the government. From 1962 on, bilingual signs appeared in offices and marking settlement boundaries, and new checkpoints were opened on the Hungarian border. The committee took an active part in planning and writing the 1974 Constitution of the Socialist Republic of Slovenia.

Unlike the earlier, Yugoslav constitution, the current Slovene constitution starts by defining in the introduction the Slovene state as the democratic community of the Slovene people and the cohabiting Hungarian and Italian minorities. Passages 250 and 251 describe in detail the rights of these two minority communities. They legalize linguistic equality, the free usage of national symbols, the possibility of establishing contacts with the mother nations, and define it as the duty of the state to create and develop means for ethnic education, press, other information sources, and maintaining native language culture. It provides the possibility of the Hungarian and Italian minorities founding educational and cultural associations at their place of residence. According to the constitution, these rights of associations extend to deciding on and even vetoing issues concerning their education, mass information, press, and even in establishing contacts with their mother nations.

Because of their smaller number, Hungarians in Slovenia were not able to have their own independent political party influencing national politics. In certain periods (for instance, in the 1920s) Slovene parties declared their support and representation of Hungarians, but after elections they usually did not implement the campaign promises. The only association that proved able to survive is the above mentioned and described Hungarian Ethnic Educational and Cultural Self-Governing Community. It does not have registered members, since all citizens declaring themselves to be Hungarian in the census become part of it automatically. The election of its leaders is similar to parliamentary elections. After the political changes in 1991, three of their representatives became members of the Slovene parliament in Ljubljana. Since then, a law passed by the Slovene parliament has guaranteed the automatic appointment of one representative for the Hungarian community even if none is elected.

2.2.3   *Economy, culture, and religion*

2.2.3.1 *Economy.* Within Yugoslavia, Slovenia always constituted the most developed part of the country. It had a well-functioning industry and commerce, so its gross national product was higher than the national average, and therefore, the standard of living of the population was higher, too. (This was one of the reasons why Slovenia was the first to declare its independence in 1991). But within the country, Prekmurje was a much less developed region. Compared to other regions of Slovenia, its industry was scarce, and although its agriculture was said to be the stockroom of the country, it still suffered from high unemployment.

Some of the economic problems were relieved already in Yugoslav times when the Tito regime made westward labor force export (to Austria and Germany) possible. Great numbers of people migrated in many cases, like earlier to the United States, now to these countries. Whole families became guest workers. They maintained their relationship with their home, and what is more, they brought home their savings and deposited them in banks, invested them in western-like enterprises, or built new homes for themselves buying building materials abroad as well. It was common that in a family the two active wage earners left, and the children were brought up by the grandparents. Holidays and weekends were often spent at home together. Their way of life was similar to that of commuters inside the country. These prospects made it possible for this region to live under better financial conditions, to help general development. Hungarians in Slovenia never possessed an independent economic force, as primarily they were farmers. Working as guest workers, though, made it possible for several families to modernize their farms, and to live on higher standards even off agriculture. After the fall of communism in 1991, several enterprises were formed among the Hungarian minority that had contacts with Hungary. Many technical professionals started businesses using their language proficiency and family relations; numerous commercial businesses were started up as well.

Political disadvantages struck the region after the war when the relationship between Hungary and Yugoslavia had deteriorated due to Russian political influence. Borders were practically impossible to cross, the railway was disassembled first on the Körmend – Murska Sobota/Muraszombat line and later on the Rédics – Lendava/Alsólendva line as well, making eastward traffic impossible. The effects of this can still be felt today (though the development of roads helped the situation), especially after the break-up of Yugoslavia, as Slovenia became the only state neighboring Hungary which does not have a direct railroad connection with Hungary, only via Croatia.

2.2.3.2 *Culture.* The area called 'Vend-country' was a Slovene-speaking region on the eastern borderline of Slovenia, stretching from the Hungarian linguistic border to the Mura river. It was connected to the neighboring Hungarian area culturally, and in Slovenia it has constituted a separate dialectal, ethnological, and cultural region. Its unique dialect used to be the language of church, writing and literature (not limited to folk genres). In connection with this, the so-called 'Vend debate' has to be mentioned here. It was mainly generated by politics through scholarly circles. Essentially, the issue was that Slovene political groups within Yugoslavia interpreted the term Vend, previously used to designate the eastern Slovene population, as the manifestation of the desire to divide and separate this community from the Slovene nation. Therefore, to reestablish explicit unity, they suggested the elimination of the term designating the separate geographic unit of 'Vend-country'. As after World War I there were new borders instituted, the ethnic group was divided. Since then, the group remaining in Slovenia has been called *prekmurci* ("those beyond the Mura river") and the group in Hungary *porabski* ("those around the Rába river").

The formation of Yugoslavia, and later that of the Republic of Slovenia, changed considerably the cultural bonds of Prekmurje Slovenes. They became separated from Hungary in terms of economic and cultural orientation (especially after World War II), so they turned towards west, to Slovenia.

The bilingual territory described in earlier sections where the majority of Hungarians in Slovenia live plays an important role in the general cultural life of Prekmurje (cf. Section 2.1.3). As we have already mentioned, practically homogeneous Hungarian villages were formed during the centuries through continuous and slow natural assimilation as they were spared from mass migration. Being so close to and maintaining natural economic and cultural relations with the Hungarian community in Hungary, they did not need widespread bilingualism. Slovenian was learned by those who worked in neighboring villages as clerks, shop assistants, or teachers. The majority did not even have experience concerning the linguistic practices of bilingual communities. To a limited extent, they could experience it in Murska Sobota/Muraszombat, Lendava/Alsólendva, or Čakovec/Csáktornya (this latter town is now in Croatia). They could become familiar with linguistic differences in neighboring villages (on the other side of the 'linguistic' border) if occasionally they went there for fairs or markets for example, but they did not have any experience of bilingualism as a special means serving a community. Becoming part of the Kingdom of Serbs, Croats and Slovenes did not change this situation: it created the now truly bilingual regions, the *colonies*, through forced relocations.

It is possible that the above described circumstances played an important role in this small group of Hungarians near the border having such a hard time adapting to the disappearance of monolingualism, their sole method of communication. That is why there was a linguistic crisis, during which they gave up monolingual (first language) schools, where it became impossible to teach the language of the environment, the state language of the majority Hungarians at a satisfactorily high level due to lack of practice, methodological skills, and underdeveloped primary school foreign language teaching methods. The regional culture of the uniform Hungarian territory survived through natural family transmission, from parents to their children. At the same time, the transmission of Slovenian cultural influences increased, mainly through schooling.

The increase in the intensity of the new cultural influence was further facilitated not only by spiritual and school organizational problems described earlier, but also by the new situation induced by the new Yugoslavia after World War II. Hungarian agricultural villages were not left untouched by economic and political changes. Relations with neighboring villages in Hungary were completely cut. Growing migration as a result of industrialization and commuting to nearby areas increased the need to learn the Slovenian language. Moreover, from the 1940s on this tendency was amplified because of the international political fact that the prestige of Hungary considerably diminished in Hungarian-speaking and bilingual areas of Slovenia. Therefore, parents started to enroll their children in monolingual Slovenian schools instead of monolingual Hungarian schools. A proportionally small group of professionals assumed the internal (and mainly not political) fight for developing a bilingual educational plan that could stop this process, otherwise assimilation was soon going to become widespread. A drastic change had thus taken place in the education supporting the Hungarian culture.

The point of changing the school system was to create new 'bilingual schools' with the participation of Slovenian children on the designated bilingual areas where monolingual schools were lost due to depopulation. All-Slovenian schools did not remain untouched either. A political basis was furnished by Tito's ethnic policies that preached a 'fraternal cohabitation of Yugoslav nations and ethnic groups'. Political principles of bilingualism and bilingual education were determined by measures in 1959 by the Central Committee of the Alliance of Yugoslav Communists. The legal bases were created by the 1963 Constitution. In 1972, the law was passed that still determined the general principles and practices of the system. According to it, the principles of bilingual education were the following: the "guaranteeing of the basis for equal development of the Hungarian minority; the development of ethnic identity; becoming familiar with the culture, history, and geography of Hungary; deepening the creative cohabitation of the Hungarian and Slovene nationalities; the further development of bilingualism in ethnically mixed regions; and the creation of such conditions under which friendly relations between the Hungarian minority and the neighboring Hungary continue" (Székely 1983:55, our translation).

As the bilingual educational model planned by the Slovenia Hungarians was unique in its kind, it is important to describe some theoretical and practical components of it. The fundamental standpoint of the planners was to achieve a good level of proficiency both in Hungarian and in Slovenian in every domain of life, as every school-age child in the 'bilingual area' was to attend these schools. At the time, in the late 1950s and early 1960s, there was no model at hand for the planners to apply to their situation. Since they did not have international contacts, they worked out their educational system without any familiarity with other models. As our experience shows though, even if there had been a model they could have used, they would have probably wanted to create an independent system, since Yugoslavia was the 'engine' of the nonalignment movement in the UN and aimed to maintain a distance in terms of economy both from the Soviet Block and from the West as well.

Planning the educational model was conducted under the direction and control of the Murska Sobota/Muraszombat school board. The three questions to be answered were as follows: (1) At what age should education begin? (2) How should groups be organized? and (3) What should the expected proportion of the two languages be in the teaching process?

As for the first question, bilingual education seemed necessary at the preschool age (3–6 years). So employment of two preschool teachers, one with Hungarian, one with Slovenian as their first language, seemed necessary in every preschool class. Group education seemed the best solution from the beginning, as the language choice of the children was not influenced by the teachers. It was assumed that in-group communication and spontaneous bilingualism would thus be omnipresent, providing every speaker with the necessary linguistic proficiency.

The third question seems to be a methodological one but is of major importance in terms of active adult language use. The school board preferred a 80%: 20%, or at most a 70%: 30% ratio of Slovene vs. Hungarian as far as the proportion of classroom language use was concerned (although the possibility of code-switching was always present). In practice it was to be realized in the following way: oral reports by the children could be given in either language, according to individual choice, but presenting new material would be in Slovenian, whereas revisions in Hungarian, in order to familiarize students with the necessary terminology in the latter as well. In the first four years of school, minority language use was to be more frequent but would gradually decrease in grades 5 through 8 of the primary school.

Although there have been no reliable studies conducted, in recent years many teachers, linguists and psychologists noticed that children taking part in this type of education do not have satisfying proficiency in either language. Thus, the program, especially its methodology, has been reformed. Now parents have to declare whether they wish to enroll their children in Hungarian or Slovenian "first language" classes. Education goes on mainly in the first language of the class in the beginning. The designation is not always clear, since the first language of the children in question is not decided through professional assessment but through their parents' choice. We know from personal communication that the favorable effects of this policy are diminished by the underinformed choice of Hungarian parents who – with the good intention of letting their children learn Slovenian better – do not enroll them according to their real first language. Therefore, these children find themselves in a linguistically disadvantageous situation.

All in all, in evaluation of these objectives today, we can say that although we do not see any better alternatives to mother tongue education, the implementation of the new school system resulted in the slowing down of assimilation. Also, as a political effect, it attenuated conflicts resulting from ethnic cohabitation, as members of both ethnic groups learned much about the other one in school with the help of their language proficiency. But still, this system only presents a solution for or attempt at survival of quite small groups, and, thus, it cannot be followed by other ethnic or linguistic communities. A deficiency of the system is perhaps the difference in the level of education between Hungarians and Slovenes, to the disadvantage of the former. These differences were found by a representative study of the Geography Institute at the University of Ljubljana in the 1970s, according to which in this region 41.6% of the Slovenes and 57.6% of the Hungarians did not finish primary school. 47.6% of the Slovenes and 37% of the Hungarians completed primary school, and 9.8% of the Slovenes and 6.1% of the Hungarians completed secondary school. As for completed higher education, the percentages are 1.1% and 0.3% for Slovenes and Hungarians, respectively. Prekmurje Slovenes are below the national average, but Prekmurje Hungarians are below even the Prekmurje Slovenes' level (Székely 1983: 55).

In other areas of culture, public institutions are sufficient. Nationally, an academic research institute carries out research regarding the minorities. The Pedagogical Faculty of the University of Maribor trains teachers for bilingual schools. Those not majoring in Hungarian language and literature have been receiving Hungarian language teaching from native speaker teachers from Hungary for 30 years. Since 1980, a Department of Hungarian Language and Literature has functioned at the University of Maribor as well. According to Slovenian law, bilingualism should be present in every domain of life. As the Hungarian language teachers from Hungary are supposed to serve the bilingualism of Prekmurje Hungarian professionals, their lessons are attended not only by students from the Pedagogical Faculty, but by future lawyers, economists and engineers as well. There are 30 students studying Hungarian in these classes annually. On average, 3 to 4 students are admitted to major in Hungarian, but fewer graduate, as the need for such professionals is low, too. Hungarian journalists of the region are graduates of this university as well.

As for book publishing, the possibilities of the Hungarian community are manifold. In Murska Sobota/Muraszombat, Pomurska založba Publishing House publishes Hungarian books regularly. It publishes a wide range of scholarly, popular science (mainly language cultivation) works, Slovenian literature in Hungarian, Hungarian literature on Slovenian, literary works of Slovenia Hungarian authors (essays, short stories, poems, etc.) and school textbooks. Limits are of a financial nature as a result of small editions. Almost all publications require state or other funding. The situation is similar for the press. Because the border is near, Prekmurje Hungarians can get hold of Hungarian newspapers without a problem, but only one Hungarian language weekly, *Népújság* ('People's paper') is published in Slovenia. Recently a literary periodical has also been published. These publications exist in electronic versions as well. All TV and radio programs from Hungary are also broadcast across the border.

The library network is good. The public library of Lendava/Alsólendva has 20,000 Hungarian volumes, its stock is being constantly increased through assistance from Hungary and through donations. The Hungarian documents of the Murska Sobota/Muraszombat library are also important and valuable, in size coming close to the Lendava/Alsólendva collection. Even in villages one can find public and school libraries of a few thousand books.

In other areas of cultural life Prekmurje Hungarians work in associations, subsidized by the Slovenian state. There are drama associations, dance groups, choirs, orchestras, and also clubs of amateur filmmaking, philately and puppetry. Programs of high culture (e.g. professional theatrical performances) are organized with the participation of artists from Hungary. The closest theater in Hungary is in Zalaegerszeg, a half an hour drive from Lendava/Alsólendva. From time to time theater visiting trips to Budapest are organized. In Lendava/Alsólendva there is also an arts workshop of long standing traditions of bilingual culture.

2.2.3.3 *Religion.* The population of Slovenia is quite homogeneously Roman Catholic. Prekmurje, however, is different in this respect as well. One can find all denominations that have ever been present in the western part of Hungary. Slovenes living here are usually Roman Catholic, but there is a Lutheran community of 20,000, with about half a dozen congregations. Hungarians of the Őrség are mainly Protestant, either Reformed Calvinist or Lutheran. The southern part, which used to belong to Hungary's Zala county is mostly Roman Catholic, but there is a Lutheran congregation in Lendava/Alsólendva. In terms of religion, only the Reformed Calvinists are ethnically homogeneous: they are all Hungarians.

As far as we know, no linguistic or ethnic considerations played a role in church policy decisions. Priests in the region spoke Hungarian, even if they were of a different ethnicity. It is important to mention though that in Yugoslavia churches had very restricted possibilities. Even Christmas day was a workday.

Churches could not play an important role in the maintenance of the Hungarian language because of the small size of congregations and low number of priests. In Yugoslavia there were no Hungarian language church schools after the secularization of all schools in 1945.

2.2.3.4 *Language policy.* Among the language policy measures, there are two that are important to mention. The 1921, the first constitution of the Kingdom regulated the first language education of minorities, probably because the right of mother tongue language use had been mentioned in the Trianon peace treaty. This right, however, was not recognized in official language use and administration. The language of administration was Serbian at all levels. The linguistic rights of Hungarians in Slovenia were first spelled out in the 1974 Yugoslav constitution. These are the rights still in effect today. Their implementation is the only debated issue.

After 1921 Hungarian schools functioned for a few years just like before because the educational policy makers were preoccupied with the problem of Prekmurje Slovenian language use and the variety to be used in education. This constituted a problematic issue because this dialect, then called Vend, was so different from other dialects of Slovenian, including the standard, that it presented comprehension problems. What is more, this dialect was also written, and thus was also used in church (Bencze 1994: 40–41). Later, former Hungarian schools were reorganized as Hungarian sections of majority language schools on the order of Chief advisor on Education. Then the game of figures started. According to the June 18, 1925, educational law a minimum of 30 students was needed to open a section, and later, for merged grades, the number was 70. Small villages usually could not satisfy this requirement. Students from closing Hungarian sections were automatically registered in classes with Slovenian as the language of instruction. There were Slovenian classes where Hungarian students were actually in majority.

The first, 1929, census after the creation of the Yugoslav Kingdom had even more serious consequences. The census made it possible to declare oneself to be of Yugoslav nationality. Many Hungarians of low socioeconomic status used this possibility as they had been excluded of land distribution before exactly on grounds of their Hungarian nationality. They interpreted the Yugoslav label as citizenship and did not consider themselves as denying their ethnic background. But the government made it compulsory for 'Yugoslav' parents to enroll their children in majority language classes.

Table 7.6 demonstrates well the tragic effects of the measure. In the late 1930s, following the initiative of Vojvodina Hungarians, the reestablishment of minority schools was requested in Prekmurje as well. Parents had to enclose a copy of their children's birth certificate and their school report from the previous year to their request. The official response was that since there was no proof of the student's ethnicity, it was not possible to restart Hungarian schools: birth certificates and school reports did not contain information on ethnicity.

Since from April 1941 to 1945 Prekmurje became part of Hungary again, Hungarians living there no longer formed a minority and got their schools back.

Table 7.6. The number of Hungarian students and Hungarian sections in schools in Slovenia between 1925/26 and 1940/41*

	1925/26	1930/31	1935/36	1940/41
Number of Hungarian students	1,365	415	189	37
Number of Hungarian sections	30	6	4	1

* Source: Bencze (1994)

Table 7.7. The number of school-age children in Slovenia in 1958/59*

		School-age children
Hungarian ethnicity	1,206	39.32%
Slovene ethnicity	1,861	60.68%
Attends Hungarian section	825	26.89%
Attends Slovene section	2,262	73.11%
Total of school–age children	3,067	100%

* Source: Bencze (1994)

After the 1945 change of regimes, Yugoslavia could not continue the Kingdom's minority policy. The measure of August 10, 1945, of the new Ministry of Public Education stated that minority schools should be opened for minority students where the number of enrolled students was at least 20. Opening and maintaining the schools was the duty of member republics where the minority was autochthonous. According to this measure, in Slovenia, Hungarian schools and sections of schools, again in a minority, started to function again, but their situation was disadvantageous compared to the parallel Slovenian sections. Their most visible problem was the lack of teachers, as teachers posted here under Hungarian control were either sent back or voluntarily fled to Hungary. Anyone with secondary education could work as a teacher. In very small villages the required number of students was only reached in joint grades: in some cases 8 grades were joined to achieve the required number. In addition to this, financial possibilities of minority classes were limited.

Globally, it was easy to conclude that minority education was a cul-de-sac for students, because, on the one hand, even at the secondary level, it was not possible for them to continue their studies. On the other hand, Slovenian high schools were not prepared to accept students with a low language proficiency as a result of their educational circumstances. Thus, parents considered enrolling their children in Slovenian schools as more useful, and minority classes became gradually depopulated.

Independent minority classes in their last school year, 1958/59, had the number of students given in Table 7.7. It is clear from the figurers that around one third (31%) of the Hungarian students living in a minority area did not choose first language education. According to contemporary news, the situation in and around Lendava/Alsólendva was even more serious: only 7 students were enrolled in the Hungarian class of the town's school.

Because of these tendencies, from the 1959/60 academic year, the bilingual educational model described in Section 2.3.2 was introduced. This was in every respect a victory for the students of the region. The possibilities and technical equipment of bilingual schools were better than those of average monolingual Slovenian schools. As a result of the small number of students, school district boundaries were established, which resulted in financial possibilities to be concentrated better this way as well. That is why today there are four complete, 8-grade primary schools functioning in the bilingual community, with small village schools of 4 grades connected to each of them. The four school centers are Lendava/Alsólendva, Genterovci/Göntérháza,

Dobrovnik/Dobronak, and Prosenjakovci/Pártosfalva. Since the 1980s a bilingual high school has also been functioning in Lendava/Alsólendva.

3.   Linguistic aspects

3.1   Characteristics of Hungarian in Vojvodina

The native language of Vojvodina Hungarians today is a contact variety of Hungarian. There have been several empirical research projects investigating its characteristic traits, and comprehensive studies have also been published on its differences with Hungarian used in Hungary (HH). We are going to discuss a few recent findings that tackle phonological, morphological, lexical, syntactic, and pragmatic aspects of the contact situation.

Molnár Csikós (1989) mentions that in compounds stress is often not on the first syllable like in Hungarian spoken in Hungary, but on the first syllable of the second part of the compound (e.g. Vojvodina Hungarian (VH) *ugyan'akkor* vs. HH *'ugyanakkor* 'at the same time', VH *közép'iskola* vs. HH *'középiskola* 'secondary school'), and usage of plural forms is more frequent as a result of contact (e.g. VH *Feri és Zita sétálni mennek* ('go.3PL') vs. HH *Feri és Zita sétálni megy* ('go.3SG') 'Feri and Zita are going for a walk', or VH *nem találja a kesztyűit* (kesztyű-i-t glove-Px3SG.PL-ACC) vs. HH *nem találja a kesztyűjét* (kesztyű-jé-t glove-Px3SG-ACC) 's/he can't find his/her gloves'). Under Serbian influence, non-HH complements appear: VH *örül valamiért* (causal-final) vs. HH *örül valaminek* (dative) 'be happy about something', VH *meggyőződik valamiben* (inessive) vs. HH *meggyőződik valamiről* (delative) 'be convinced about something', or VH *szimpatizál valakit* (accusative) vs. HH *szimpatizál valakivel* (instrumental) 'sympathize with somebody'). Calques modeled on Serbian show contact influence as well: VH *jog-alany* (law+subject) for HH *jog-birtokos* (law+owner) 'obligee of right' as a calque of Serbian *nosilac prava* (subject+law), or VH *vert pénz* (minted money) for HH *pénzérme* (money+coin) 'coin' as a calque of *kovani novac* (minted money). Words borrowed from Serbian are also used, e.g. VH *gúzsva* 'throng', *szmena* 'work shift' (vs. HH *műszak*), VS *szmétál* 'disturb' (vs. HH *zavar*), VH *plakár* 'cupboard' (vs. HH *faliszekrény*), VH *flomaszter* 'felt pen, marker' (vs. HH *filctoll)*, and VH *pincetta* 'pincers' (vs. HH *csipesz)*. Serbian influence is present in the word order, namely in the pre-posing of the adverb: VH *eltérően a többitől* vs. HH *a többitől eltérően* (cf. Serbian *za razliku od ostalih*) 'different from the others', or VH *függetlenül a véleményektől* vs. HH *a véleményektől függetlenül* (cf. Serbian *nezavisno od mišljenja*) 'independent of opinions'.

Katona (1995) defines interference phenomena as deviation from the norm caused by elements of another language and categorizes them into types of grammatical, content, and structural calquing. She found no differences among professionals of various occupations and educational levels in their judgments of these. Her subjects accepted structural calques most and lexical borrowings least, and noticed grammatical borrowing best.

Andrić (1995) also studied the influence of Serbian on Vojvodina Hungarian. She drew attention to the fact that in some cases /ɟ/ is pronounced as [dʒ], and /c/ as [tʃ] (VH *dzserek* 'child' and VH *kucsa* 'dog' for HH *gyerek* and HH *kutya*, respectively), because in Serbian the borders of these sounds are quite indistinct. Serbian influence can be observed in the non-standard pronunciation and spelling of certain foreign words (e.g. VH *hémia* for HH *kémia* 'chemistry', VH *akreditál* for HH *akkreditál* 'accredit', VH *rentabilis* for HH *rentábilis* 'profitable'). It is also common to leave out endings in case of foreign words to parallel the Serbian equivalent (VH *delegát* for HH *delegátus* 'delegate [n]', VH *honorár* for HH *honorárium* 'honorarium'). Because of Serbian influence, the verb ending *-iroz* is often used (VH *citiroz* and *blokiroz* for HH *citál* 'cite' and *blokkol* 'block', respectively). Passive and impersonal structures are also features of Serbian and are present in the Vojvodina Hungarian contact variety, e.g. VH *távozás nincs megengedve* 'leaving is not allowed' vs. HH *távozni tilos* 'no leaving', or VH *meg lett határozva a védőár* 'the fixed price has been determined' vs. HH *a bizottság meghatározta a védőárat* 'the committee has determined the fixed price'.

Papp (1995) studied situational lexical borrowings and communicative interference. Situational lexical borrowings are in connection with official and political situations (e.g. VH *szkupstina* vs. HH *képviselőház* 'Parliament', VH *carina* vs. HH *vám* 'customs'), with internal affairs (VH *pukovnik* vs. HH *ezredes* 'colonel', VH *predvojnicska* vs. HH *katonai előképzés* 'military education'), with university life (VH *brúcos* vs. HH *gólya* 'freshman', VH *fakultét* vs. HH *kar* 'faculty'), with health care (VH *boloványe* vs. HH *betegszabadság* 'sick leave', VH *primáriusz* vs. HH *főorvos* 'head doctor'), with sports (VH *odbojka* vs. HH *röplabda* 'volleyball', VH *trénerka* vs. HH *melegítő* 'tracksuit'), with the workplace (VH *séf* vs. HH *főnök* 'boss', VH *terénszki* vs. HH *pótlék* 'supplement'), and with colloquial speech (VH *duduk* vs. HH *buta* 'stupid', VH *tezgázik* vs. HH *haknizik* 'do weekend performances'). As for pragmatic interference, he mentions expanding the use of T-address where it is not usual in Hungarian; another contact feature is to stick nicknames to first and last names (e.g. VH *Kovács Péter-Mufurc* 'Peter-Morose Kovács').

Ágoston gives a comprehensive picture of Vojvodina Hungarian in several studies (1990a, 1990b, and 1994), discussing contact phenomena as well. He emphasizes the effect of Serbian on the first language capacities of the Hungarian-speaking population. In Vojvodina, Hungarians living in villages and on farms, especially in northern Vojvodina, speak with regional dialectal features, they only have a passive knowledge of the spoken standard of Hungarian. In northeast-Bačka the spoken standard is used by most speakers, in other parts of Vojvodina only those speak it who work with language professionally. The majority of Vojvodina Hungarians speak what Ágoston terms "a foreign sounding variety that is underdeveloped in terms of vocabulary and expressions", and in terms of styles it is "painfully poor and flat". Ad hoc calques are frequent (e.g. VH *előlát*, lit. 'foresee' for HH *előirányoz* lit. 'preset', or VH *dolgozók és polgárok* 'workers and citizens' vs. HH *lakosság* 'population'), forms non-existent in

HH are often used (e.g. VH *tendenció* vs. HH *tendencia* 'tendency', VH *konzultáció* vs. HH *konzultáció* 'consultation'), forms borrowed from Serbian are frequent (e.g. VH *komitét* vs. HH *bizottság* 'committee', VH *rezimé* vs. HH *összefoglalás* 'abstract, summary'). According to Ágoston, in the provincial dialect, used as the spoken standard, Serbian expressions abound, there are word order problems, the system of definite and indefinite conjugations is breaking up, non-HH complements appear (e.g. VH *Nem zavarok neked?*, with dative for HH *Nem zavarlak téged?*, with accusative 'Am I disturbing you?'), and proverbs are often used incorrectly. These differences can result in communicational problems with Hungarians from Hungary.

3.2 The characteristics of Hungarian language use in Prekmurje

As we have outlined above, Slovenia Hungarians live along the Slovene-Hungarian border in villages with populations under 500. The only town and cultural center of the region is Lendava/Alsólendva, where Hungarians now constitute less than 50% of the total population of only 3,000 people. For this reason, the Hungarian used by Prekmurje Hungarians, even that used outside the family domain, is characterized by the use of the local dialect features to a great extent even in such speech situations when, being bidialectal, most speakers switch to the standard variety. Thus, the formal monolingual Hungarian language use is becoming gradually narrower. Speakers tend to be able to carry out undisturbed Hungarian language communication only on the topics of traditional village life and peasant economy. In other topics, the effect of language contact with the majority language can be so strong that it excludes mutual intelligibility between the locals and nonlocal Hungarians. As Varga (1990:160) writes:

> More and more foreign (i.e. Serbian and Slovenian) words become part of the dialectal and everyday vocabulary of the Hungarians living here. Not only words that do not have Hungarian equivalents, but also words used in the local administration, state bureaucracy, and in economic, industrial, social and political organizations. These are either literal mirror translations or, simply, Slovene words, which cause the attrition of especially technical vocabulary among Hungarian minority professionals to such an extent that minority Hungarian doctors, engineers, lawyers etc. with degrees from either Zagreb or Ljubljana can use their mother tongue only in "everyday conversation", because they are almost "speech illiterate" in their own field as far as Hungarian is concerned. The common use of foreign languages in everyday life affects the morphology and syntax as well. [Our translation]

In the same work Varga (1990) also publishes such a mixed language dialogue excerpt, which clearly exemplifies both the highly dialectal nature of Slovenia Hungarian speech and the substitution of words used only in the standard by contact induced lexical items:

(1) *A nyugdijjam ügyibe jártom a szociálnán. Hiábo mutattam mëg a betegkönyve-met mëg hogy a 35 év alatt csak kíccë vótam orvosná, ís **bolniskun** se vótam.*

*Potrdilut së attak, pedig a **tájnica** szerint jár.* (Varga 1990: 160)
'I went to the social services division of the town hall about my pension. It was no use showing my medical records and telling them that I had to see a doctor only twice during the 35 years and that I've never been *on sick leave*. They didn't even give me a *certificate*, even though the *secretary* says they should have.'

This example shows that the speaker uses contact language words (in bold in the Hungarian, and in italics in the English translation above) in the phonetically heavily dialectal text.

Bokor (1990) points out the unchanged dialectal nature of Slovenia Hungarians' speech, demonstrating that, despite claims to the opposite by researchers from Hungary, in the vicinity of Lendava/Alsólendva, the language use of various generations within the family domain does not show a change from dialectal features towards the spoken standard. Instead, he argues, the speech of all generations, from the young to the middle-aged to the elderly (over 60) speakers is similarly and homogeneously dialectal, resulting in speakers naming everyday objects with dialectal vocabulary, for example: PH *fészkelüdik* 'squirm in one's seat' (vs. HH *fészkelődik*), PH *rëdli* 'oven' (vs. HH *sütő*), PH *sindü* 'roof tile' (vs. HH *tetőfedő cserép*), PH *tekenyü* 'hutch' (vs. HH *teknő*), PH *traccsul* 'chat' (vs. HH *traccsol*).

Thus, the most characteristic feature of Prekmurje Hungarian is the predominance of regional dialectal features. This regional linguistic system works smoothly only in limited, familial language use and shows characteristics of a limited code as soon as the topic to be discussed includes notions and terms of modern life. This is how, through Slovenian loanwords, the local (regional) self-government gets to be called PH *obcsina* (vs. HH *önkormányzat*), the plastic floor PH *toplipod* (vs. HH *bélelt műanyagpadló*), the secretary PH *tájnik* (male) and *tájnica* (female) (vs. HH *titkár* and *titkárnő*, respectively), the director PH *direktor* (vs. HH *igazgató*), the gas station PH *pumpa* (vs. HH *benzinkút*), the head doctor PH *primár* (vs. HH *főorvos*), and the university student PH *student* (vs. HH *egyetemi hallgató*). These borrowings appear in those speech situations where the familial register should be complemented by the standardized vocabulary of Hungarian. We consider this a limited code because contact induced vocabulary is not of any use when the speakers of this new, less than six thousand strong Slovenia Hungarian speech community interact with members of the Hungarian speech community from outside Prekmurje. As we have claimed above, in the case of Vojvodina Hungarian, the realization of the limited nature of this code is what leads, among Prekmurje Hungarians, to a complete abandonment of the original first language, that is, to language shift.

3.3 Language use of Vojvodina and Prekmurje Hungarians based on the SHOH study

In this section of our paper, we discuss some of the findings of the Sociolinguistics of Hungarian Outside Hungary (SHOH) project. For more details on the project, see Kontra, this volume. The findings we discuss are almost exclusively those where, according to our initial hypothesis, we had expected to find the effects of language contact, specifically, the influence of the majority languages, Serbian and Slovenian, on the Hungarian of Hungarians in Vojvodina and Prekmurje, respectively.

The SHOH project targeted three kinds of linguistic variables, called, in the project, "universal variables", "universal contact variables", and "contact variables". The first was a label used for such sociolinguistic variables that occur in the speech of all Hungarians and are not due to language contact effects but solely to socially stratified language use. Universal contact variables are those features that are due to language contact but also occur in the Hungarian of all Hungarians: due to centuries' long contact with neighboring Indo-European languages in the case of Hungarians in Hungary, and to more intense contact with the same languages in the case of bilingual Hungarians in countries neighboring Hungary. (The third kind, contact variables, that we studied is a small group of features which occur only in the Hungarian of Hungarians in the various individual countries neighboring Hungary and which are due to contact effects of the specific majority language spoken there. These were only studied in Slovakia and Ukraine.) In this section we discuss results concerning the universal contact variables targeted in the SHOH project.

3.3.1 *Universal contact variables*
We get the following distribution if we compare the results of all the universal contact variables targeted in the study. The rate of nonstandard answers is 31.6% in Prekmurje, and 26.2% in Vojvodina, compared to 22.6% in Hungary. As the frequency of standard answers for Hungary is 10.6% higher than the average for all bilingual regions together (33.2%) ($\chi^2 = 178.71$, df = 1, p < .001), our hypothesis that the Hungarian language use of bilingual Hungarians is less standard than that of monolinguals proves to be right at this level. Vojvodina differs least from Hungary, by 3.6%, though this is a statistically significant difference ($\chi^2 = 14.82$, df = 1, p < .001). This also shows that other regions shift towards nonstandard answers, so the hypothesized effect is present everywhere. The differences are not strong to the same extent though. Both Prekmurje and Vojvodina significantly differ from Hungary. So, regularities predicted on the basis of universal contact variable answers that language use is less normative in bilingual areas than for monolingual Hungarians is proved for the southern regions, though they diverge in different proportions: Vojvodina differs from the monolingual Hungarian control group by 3.6%, Prekmurje by 9%. The 5.4% difference between Vojvodina and Prekmurje is statistically significant ($\chi^2 = 23.88$, df = 1, p < .001).

These results show that contact influence can be demonstrated at the most general level. Its validity with regard to all studied variables is analyzed in the following section.

3.3.1.1 *Analytical constructions.* Hungarian, an agglutinative language, tends to use more synthetic structures (derived words and compounds) where many Indo-European languages use more analytical structures. The tendency to make synthetic structures more analytical, however, is present in Hungarian as used in Hungary as well, under the influence of neighboring Indo-European languages. In such cases the newer analytical structures are not ungrammatical but are considered "foreign" and "less Hungarian-like" by language cultivators.

In the SHOH project we studied the tendency to use analytical forms through nine tokens of the variable. Sentences were the following (see the SHOH questionnaire in the Appendix): 503, 507, 532, 603, 605, 607, and 613.

Results were discussed in detail in a separate study (Göncz 2000c). Since figures show a strong effect of language contact, in Table 7.8 we present results from Vojvodina, Prekmurje, and Hungary. The upper numbers show the number of subjects in the given region who favor the analytical (nonstandard, Nst) and the synthetic (standard, St) forms, and the lower numbers stand for the ratio of these in the total. Missing answers were not taken into consideration, therefore the size of samples was reduced by their number.

Table 7.8. The choice of synthetic (St) and analytical (Nst) forms in Prekmurje, Vojvodina, and Hungary*

Tasks	Vojvodina		Prekmurje		Hungary	
	St	Nst	St	Nst	St	Nst
503	39	101	16	49	75	30
	27.9%	72.1%	24.6%	75.4%	71.4%	28.6%
507	102	39	21	44	86	21
	72.3%	27.7%	32.3%	67.7%	80.4%	19.6%
514	138	3	64	1	104	3
	97.9%	2.1%	98.5%	1.5%	97.2%	2.8%
532	72	52	17	45	39	68
	58.1%	41.9%	27.4%	72.6%	36.4%	63.6%
536	98	25	52	11	87	20
	79.7%	20.3%	82.5%	17.5%	81.3%	18.7%
603	102	34	44	18	97	10
	75.0%	25.0%	71.0%	29.0%	90.7%	9.3%
605	113	23	51	14	90	17
	83.1%	16.9%	78.5%	21.5%	84.1%	15.9%
607	90	47	27	38	61	45
	65.7%	34.3%	41.5%	58.5%	57.5%	42.5%
613	113	24	25	37	84	21
	82.5%	17.5%	40.3%	59.7%	80.0%	20.0%
Total	867	348	317	257	723	235
	71.4%	28.6%	55.2%	44.8%	75.5%	24.5%

* Source: Göncz (2000c: 6)

Table 7.9. The choice of analytical versus synthetic forms in Vojvodina and Prekmurje vs. in Hungary*

Regions	D	χ^2	df	p
Hungary vs. Prekmurje	20.3	67.47	1	.001
Hungary vs. Vojvodina	4.1	4.62	1	.05

D = difference between regions in %
* Source: Göncz (2000c: 8)

The following conclusions can be drawn on the basis of these results and the results of other regions studied in the SHOH project:

1. The studied Hungarian speech communities in the Carpathian Basin choose the analytical forms in 36% and the synthetic forms in 64% of the cases on the basis of the nine variables (Göncz 2000c: 6).

2. In the case of bilingual Hungarians, the tendency towards analytical forms is stronger than for monolingual Hungarians in Hungary: in bilingual regions, Vojvodina and Prekmurje among them, analytical linguistic forms are more frequent than in Hungary, see Table 7.9.

3. Bilingual Hungarian speech communities rank in the following way in terms of choice of analytical forms (Göncz 2000c): Prekmurje (44.8%), Subcarpathia (41.7%), Transylvania (40.4%), Austria (38.8%), Slovakia (30%), and Vojvodina (28.6%). The corresponding figure is 24.5% in the case of monolingual Hungarians in Hungary. There are two groups among bilingual regions in terms of choice of the analytical form: in Prekmurje, Subcarpathia, Transylvania, and Austria the tendency towards these forms is stronger than in Slovakia and Vojvodina, though even in the latter two it is stronger than in the case of Hungarian monolinguals.

4. The analytical tendency is stronger for Hungarians living in bilingual settings compared to speakers living in a monolingual situation in case of the following variables: *tagsági díj* (*tag-ság-i díj* member-NDER-ADER fee) vs. *tagdíj* (*tag-díj* member-fee) 'membership fee' (503),[3] *utazás busszal* (*utaz-ás busz-szal*, travel-NDER bus-INS) vs. *buszozás* (*busz-oz-ás* bus-VDER-NDER) 'traveling by bus' (507), and *légi tér* (*lég-i tér* air-ADER space) vs. *légtér* (*lég-tér* air-space) 'air space' (603). The variants *tagsági díj* and *légi tér* are analytical forms which distinguish clearly bilingual and monolingual Hungarian speakers (being much more common with bilingual speakers). This is the case also for *utazás busszal*, with the exception of Vojvodina, where speakers favor this form at the same rate (i.e. similarly rarely) as monolingual Hungarians do in Hungary.

3.3.1.2 *Word order.* Word order features were studied through two variable types in the study. One was the adjectival use of preposed adverbs (e.g. *a falon lévő kép* lit. 'the on-the-wall being picture', meaning 'the picture on the wall', a structure preferred in Hungarian to postposed adverbs (e.g. *a kép a falon* 'the picture on the wall'), which are considered "foreign". Both variants occur in Hungary and in Vojvodina and Prek-

Table 7.10. The choice of standard (St) versus nonstandard (Nst) word order in Vojvodina, Prekmurje, and in Hungary

Tasks	Vojvodina		Prekmurje		Hungary	
	St	Nst	St	Nst	St	Nst
501	118	20	55	11	77	28
	85.5%	14.5%	83.3%	16.7%	73.3%	26.7%
509	139	2	59	7	91	15
	98.6%	1.4%	89.4%	10.6%	85.8%	14.2%
502	133	7	48	16	95	10
	95%	5%	75%	25%	90.5%	9.5%
508	133	7	62	3	95	12
	95%	5%	95.4%	4.6%	88.8%	11.2%
608	123	13	58	6	98	9
	90.4%	9.6%	90.6%	9.4%	91.6%	8.4%
Total:	646	49	282	43	456	74
	92.9%	7.1%	86.8%	13.2%	86%	14%

murje as well – in the latter two regions the postposed variant was hypothesized to be more frequent due to its reinforcement by the equivalent constructions in Serbian and Slovenian, where it is the only possible way to express this meaning.

The other word order feature we studied is the ordering of auxiliary and main verb: in Hungarian, the neutral ordering is main verb plus auxiliary, while in Serbian and Slovenian it is the other way around. The auxiliary plus main verb order occurs in Hungarian in nonneutral, emphatic sentences. The adjectival use of preposed adverbs was targeted by sentences 501 and 509, whereas the word order of the auxiliary and the main verb in sentences 502, 508, and 608. The results are summarized in Table 7.10. The choice of word order variants differs largely in the studied regions. The average figures of the nonstandard variant rank the regions in the following order (Göncz 2000c): Subcarpathia (34.6%), Austria (20.8%), Transylvania (20.5%), Slovakia (14.4%), Hungary (14%), Prekmurje (13.2%), and Vojvodina (7.1%). This means that in Vojvodina and Prekmurje subjects favored the standard word order more. The monolingual group cannot be clearly distinguished from the bilingual groups, disproving our hypothesis that language use of subjects from Hungary in terms of the studied variables is closer to the standard than that of bilinguals. It is interesting to note that although the groups of Vojvodina and Prekmurje Hungarians favored the standard variants more, there is a considerable difference between the groups to the advantage of Vojvodina Hungarians ($\chi^2 = 9.57$, df = 1, p < .001). At the same time, Vojvodina subjects favored more standard forms than Hungarians in Hungary ($\chi^2 = 15.31$, df = 1, p < .001) and than the subjects from all the other regions, whereas the difference between Prekmurje and Hungarian subjects is not significant ($\chi^2 = .04$, df = 1). We cannot find reasons for the most standard results from Vojvodina and the more standard (compared to other regions) results from Prekmurje: it is possible that they show a dialectal effect or are due to hypercorrection (as for its reasons see Section 3.3.1.5 on redundant pronouns),

Table 7.11. The choice of standard (St) versus nonstandard (Nst) forms of adjectival use of postposed adverbs in Vojvodina, Prekmurje, and in Hungary

Tasks	Vojvodina		Prekmurje		Hungary	
	St	Nst	St	Nst	St	Nst
501	118	20	55	11	77	28
	85.5%	14.5%	83.3%	16.7%	73.3%	26.3%
508	133	7	62	3	95	12
	95%	5%	95.4%	4.6%	88.8%	11.2%
Total:	251	27	117	14	172	40
	90.3%	9.7%	89.3%	10.7%	81.1%	18.9%

Table 7.12. The choice of standard versus nonstandard forms of auxiliary and main verb word order in Vojvodina, Prekmurje, and Hungary

Tasks	Vojvodina		Prekmurje		Hungary	
	St	Nst	St	Nst	St	Nst
509	139	2	59	7	91	15
	98.6%	1.4%	89.4%	10.6%	85.8%	14.2 %
502	133	7	48	16	95	10
	95%	5%	75%	25%	90.5%	9.5%
608	123	13	58	6	98	9
	90.4%	9.6%	90.6%	9.4%	91.6%	8.4%
Total:	395	22	165	29	284	34
	94.7%	5.3%	85.1%	14.9%	89.3%	10.7%

or differences in the levels of education of the communities. At the same time, subjects from Hungary with their higher level of language proficiency had to choose from two neutral (and unstigmatized) forms, therefore their results have a higher dispersion from the standard than those of subjects from Vojvodina.

The word order preferences in the two word order phenomena separately also prove that the hypothesized influence of Indo-European languages is less strong for Vojvodina Hungarians. Both the use of adverbs and the word order of auxiliary and main verb show results closer to the standard in Vojvodina subjects (see Tables 7.11 and 7.12).

As for the use of adverbs, subjects in Vojvodina are more standard than Hungarians in Hungary ($\chi^2 = 7.78$, df = 1, p < .01), and a similar tendency is true for Prekmurje Hungarians ($\chi^2 = 3.49$, df = 1, p < .06).

In terms of the word order of auxiliary and main verb, the Vojvodina sample differs considerably from all the studied regions, from the Prekmurje and Hungary samples as well. (The values for differences between Vojvodina and Prekmurje, on the one hand, and Vojvodina and Hungary, on the other, are $\chi^2 = 6.77$, df = 1, p < .001 and $\chi^2 = 14.95$, df = 1, p < .001, respectively). Answers of Prekmurje and Hungary subjects do not differ significantly ($\chi^2 = 1.65$, df = 1).

Table 7.13. The choice of generic (St) versus feminine (Nst) professions nouns in speech communities of Vojvodina, Prekmurje, and Hungary*

Tasks	Vojvodina		Prekmurje		Hungary	
	St	Nst	St	Nst	St	Nst
631	46	82	15	45	61	43
	35.9%	64.1%	25.0%	75.0%	58.7%	41.3%
632	107	22	44	12	85	18
	82.9%	17.1%	78.6%	21.4%	82.5%	17.5%
633	89	37	48	11	94	11
	70.6%	29.4%	81.4%	18.6%	89.5%	10.5%
634	82	11	32	10	91	12
	88.2%	11.8%	76.2%	23.8%	88.3%	11.7%
Total*	324	152	139	78	331	84
	68.1%	31.9%	64.1%	35.9%	79.8%	20.2%

* Source: Göncz and Kontra (2000: 86)

All this proves that the alleged contact effect does not prevail, moreover, results for Vojvodina (and partly for Prekmurje) show a regularity contradicting the hypothesis.

3.3.1.3 *Feminine forms of profession nouns.* As is well known, Hungarian lacks grammatical gender marking. In names of professions reference to women can be done through generic terms (e.g. *tanár* 'teacher') or, when the referent's gender is not known from the context, through compounds with *nő* 'woman' as the second part (e.g. *tanárnő* 'female teacher'). In the Indo-European languages in contact with Hungarian in countries neighboring Hungary, feminine forms of profession names are more common, so our hypothesis was that this would affect the varieties spoken in these countries, increasing the use of compounded, "feminized" profession names. We used four sentences (631 through 634, see in the Appendix), where reference to females was clearly established in the context and would, in standard usage, call for generic rather than compounded profession names. As results were already discussed in detail by Göncz and Kontra (2000), we only present the most important findings here.

Table 7.13 shows the frequency of feminine and generic forms in Vojvodina, Prekmurje and Hungary. The following regularities appear in the results of all studied regions:

1. The Hungarian speech communities of the Carpathian Basin give a greater (18.8%) preference to standard (generic) forms (such as 631 *tanár* 'teacher', 632 *igazgató* 'headmaster', 633 *fodrász* 'hairdresser', and 634 *polgármester* 'mayor') than to nonstandard feminized forms (such as *tanárnő* 'female teacher', *igazgatónő* 'headmistress', *fodrásznő* 'female hairdresser', and *polgármesternő* 'female mayor'), whose rate is 59.4% and 40.6% respectively. The difference is statistically significant ($\chi^2 = 112.03$, df = 1, p < .001) (Göncz & Kontra 2000:86).

2. There are considerable differences between the different regions in accepting feminine forms. Compared to other bilingual regions, the tendency to use feminine

forms is not very widespread in Prekmurje (35.9%) and in Vojvodina (31.9%), and is significantly less for monolingual Hungarians in Hungary (20.2%). Compared to the studied regions, the latter accept feminine forms statistically significantly more rarely. Data from our studies in Vojvodina and Prekmurje also prove our hypothesis that in every bilingual region feminine forms are more frequent than in the case of monolingual Hungarians. Figures in Table 7.14 show this pattern, too.

3. It was the *tanár* 'teacher' (standard) vs. *tanárnő* 'female teacher' (nonstandard) variable where feminization appeared most saliently. In every bilingual region *tanárnő* is the prestige form and in Hungary the feminine form is as frequently favored as the standard one (41.3% and 58.7%, respectively) even in those cases where the profession noun refers unambiguously to a woman.

3.3.1.4 *The use of the diminutive suffix.* The use of diminutive suffixes is present in Hungarian but is less common than in Slavic languages. This made us hypothesize that in the Vojvodina and Prekmurje varieties of Hungarian they would be used more often than in Hungarian used in Hungary. Sentences 504, 538, 602, and 612 in the SHOH questionnaire target the refusal or acceptance of forms with the diminutive suffix. As Table 7.15 shows, in every region the standard form is favored. As for the choice of diminutive forms, the results are the following: Prekmurje 34.9%, Vojvodina 34.8%, and Hungary 23.6%. In accordance with our hypothesis, the monolingual group in

Table 7.14. Differences (D) of acceptance of feminine forms, in Hungary, vs. Prekmurje and Vojvodina

Regions	D(%)	χ^2	Df	p
Hungary vs. Vojvodina	11.7	15.56	1	.00
Hungary vs. Prekmurje	15.7	18.43	1	.00

Table 7.15. The refusal (St) versus acceptance (Nst) of diminutive forms in Vojvodina, Prekmurje, and Hungary

Tasks	Vojvodina		Prekmurje		Hungary	
	St	Nst	St	Nst	St	Nst
504	120	18	55	10	87	17
	87%	13%	84.6%	15.4%	84%	16%
538	15	108	8	51	54	49
	12.2%	87.8%	13.6%	86.4%	52.4%	47.6%
602	82	54	37	27	71	36
	60.3%	39.7%	57.8%	42.2%	66.4%	33.6%
612	132	6	64	0	104	2
	95.7%	4.3%	100%	0%	98.1%	1.9%
Total	349	186	163	88	319	104
	65.2%	34.8%	65.1%	34.9%	76.4%	23.6%

Hungary differs from the bilingual groups and favors diminutive forms rarely. Prekmurje and Vojvodina are practically the same in terms of the sum of answers of the four sentences. Vojvodina subjects' preference of diminutive forms is 11.2% higher while Prekmurje subjects' preference is 11.3% higher than that of monolingual subjects in Hungary. Both differences are statistically significant (the values are $\chi^2 = 11.12$, df = 1, p < .001 and $\chi^2 = 7.79$, df = 1, p < .01, respectively).

The overall results of the seven regions show the effects of contact. In every region subjected to the effects of Slavic languages, diminutive forms are used more frequently than in Hungary. In Austria, however, as German does not often use diminutive suffixes, the results are similar to those of monolingual Hungarians. For instance, the results of Vojvodina Hungarians in the case of sentence 538 (see SHOH questionnaire in the Appendix), where *bankkönyvecske* (*bank-könyv-ecske* 'bank-book-DIM') 'bank booklet' is favored because of the parallel Serbian *zdravstvena knjižica* of the same meaning. Sentences 502 and 602 (*Éhes vagy, kis bogaram? Adjak egy kis kenyeret* (bread-ACC)/*kenyér-ké-t* (bread-DIM-ACC)? 'Are you hungry, my sweetie? Shall I give you a little bread?' and *Miért sírsz, kis bogaram? Megütötted a kez-ecské-d-et* (hand-DIM-Px2SG-ACC) /*kis kez-ed-et* (hand-Px2SG-ACC)? 'Why are you crying, sweetie? Have you hurt you little hand?') might possibly trigger diminutive forms from subjects, which can be an explanation for its preponderance in the results of every region. While speaking to adults, diminutive forms are probably less frequent.

3.3.1.5 *Redundant pronouns.* In Hungarian, object pronouns appear overtly only if they are emphasized, otherwise they are considered redundant. The use of such redundant pronouns does, however, occur in Hungarian as used in Hungary as well. In Serbian and Slovenian the grammatical object has to be overtly expressed. This led us to hypothesize that in Vojvodina and Prekmurje Hungarian the use of redundant overt object pronouns would be more frequent than in the Hungarian of monolingual Hungarians. The following sentences were used to test this variable: 510, 515, and 615 (see SHOH questionnaire in the Appendix). The results are summarized in Table 7.16.

Table 7.16. The absence (St) and presence (Nst) of redundant pronouns in Vojvodina, Prekmurje, and Hungary

Tasks	Vojvodina		Prekmurje		Hungary	
	St	Nst	St	Nst	St	Nst
510	55	83	27	38	36	71
	40.3%	59.7%	41.5%	58.5%	33.6%	66.4%
515	127	14	58	6	82	23
	90.1%	9.9%	90.8%	9.2%	78.1%	21.9%
615	127	9	54	10	77	29
	93.4%	6.6%	84.4%	15.6%	72.6%	27.4%
Total:	310	106	140	54	195	123
	74.5%	25.5%	72.2%	27.8%	61.3%	38.7%

As for the acceptance of redundant pronouns, we get the following results: Hungary 38.7%, Prekmurje 27.8% and Vojvodina 25.5%. Redundant pronouns are used less frequently in Prekmurje and Vojvodina than in Hungary. Results from Vojvodina and Prekmurje subjects differ, on the one hand, from the monolingual group in Hungary (redundant pronouns are refused 13.2% more frequently in Vojvodina, and 10.9% more frequently in Prekmurje than in Hungary) and, on the other hand, from all the other bilingual regions which, with the exception of Subcarpathia, do not differ significantly from the monolingual group. Therefore, differences are probably not due to language contact.

These results are not in line with our expectations. Moreover, answers from Prekmurje and Vojvodina contradict the hypothesis and general expectation that the language use of monolingual Hungarians is more standard than that of bilinguals. One possible sociopsychological explanation comes from Lanstyák and Szabómihály (1997:124–127). According to them, indigenous minority Hungarians often feel that their Hungarian identity is discredited by the majority and by Hungarians in Hungary usually because 'they don't speak refined Hungarian' (i.e. like Hungarians in Hungary). That is why they want to cover linguistic differences with a 'more standard' language use proving their national identity. This phenomenon is often called Labovian hyper-correction or overfulfilment of the norm . It refers to the fact that "speakers of a given speech community favor more the standard variant of a sociolinguistic variable than speakers of another community which is sociolinguistically identical or similar with it" (Lanstyák & Szabómihály 1997:126, our translation). Monolingual Hungarians do not feel the same urge to prove this, that is why they undertake deviating from the standard and take it more loosely unless it is stigmatized or taken as a sign of lack of education. This interpretation is not, however, fully satisfying, as it does not explain why other bilingual groups did not show the same tendency. Dialectal influence may be another explanation. We may also take into account that these two groups lived together for 70 years in the same state and under similar circumstances that could play a role in unifying linguistic practices. A psychological phenomenon may also play a partial role: a greater metalinguistic awareness, i.e. a greater awareness of different linguistic occurrences, disregarding the content which is expressed through a linguistic form. Distinct metalinguistic abilities of bilingual groups are more completely fulfilled compared to monolingual groups (cf. Göncz & Kodžopeljić 1991), and so is syntactic awareness, that is, the ability to judge the grammaticality of sentences. It may also be possible that bilingual Hungarian groups take more care of linguistic norms, which helps them to define precisely if the utterance is in line with the norm. Of course, a prerequisite to this is the knowledge of the codified norm. We do not know if in our case this factor had any effect (i.e. if, for instance, in the education in Vojvodina and Prekmurje any attention was paid to variants of a foreign nature, and no attention like this was paid in other regions), as we do not have any information on how well our subjects know the codified norm. Whatever the explanation may be, the empirical fact is unchanged, namely that figures on redundant pronouns do not confirm our hypothesis.

Table 7.17. The choice of standard versus nonstandard comparatives in Vojvodina, Prekmurje, and Hungary

Tasks	Vojvodina		Prekmurje		Hungary	
	St	Nst	St	Nst	St	Nst
610	113	23	58	6	87	18
	83.2%	16.8%	90.6%	9.4%	83.2%	16.8%
621	105	25	52	11	104	3
	80.8%	19.2%	82.5%	17.5%	97.2%	2.8%
Total	219	48	110	17	193	21
	82%	18%	86.6%	13.4%	90.2%	9.8%

3.3.1.6 *Comparatives.* In Standard Hungarian and in most Hungarian dialects the adessive case (*-nál/-nél*) is used to express comparison (e.g. Standard Hungarian *Júlia magasabb Márknál* 'Julia is taller than Mark'), although some regional dialects, those spoken in Vojvodina and Prekmurje among them, use the ablative case (*-tól/-től*) for the same (e.g. *Júlia magasabb Márktól* 'Julia is taller than Mark'). The use of the ablative for expressing comparison is further reinforced in Vojvodina by the Serbian language, where the preposition *od* is used for comparison, which preposition has the same primary meaning, 'from', as the Hungarian ablative case. Thus, we hypothesized that Vojvodina Hungarian would show the effect of language contact in this structure. The targeted variable appeared in sentences 610 and 621, and the results are summarized in Table 7.17.

Acceptance of the nonstandard variants is as follows: Vojvodina 18%, Prekmurje 13.4%, and Hungary 9.8%. In Vojvodina nonstandard variants are more favored than in Hungary ($\chi^2 = 5.80$, p < .02). At the same time, there is no significant difference between Prekmurje and Hungary, and the difference of 4.6% between Vojvodina and Prekmurje is also due to chance ($\chi^2 = 1.0$, not significant). Subcarpathia (35.5%) and Transylvania (20.9%) differ significantly from Hungary, but Slovakia (12%) and Austria (9.2%) do not (Göncz 2000c). This proves that results do not confirm the hypothesis that the monolingual group compared to bilingual groups would favor more standard forms of these variables. In Vojvodina, and perhaps to a lesser extent in Prekmurje, the results might be due to dialectal influence.

3.3.1.7 *Case usage with placenames.* To express local semantic functions, in Hungarian, placenames of towns and geographical regions receive either surface cases (the superessive case, *-n/-on/-en/-ön* for expressing 'at rest', the delative, *-ról/-ről*, for expressing 'motion from', and the sublative, *-ra/-re*, for expressing 'motion to') or interior cases (the inessive case, *-ban/-ben*, for 'at rest', the elative, *-ból/-ből*, for 'motion from', and the illative, *-ba/-be*, for 'motion to'). Every placename receives either surface cases or interior cases, and, historically places inside Hungary tend to receive the former to a much greater extent than the latter, whereas foreign placenames almost always receive the latter. Both sentences used to test case use with placenames in the SHOH questionnaire had a placename each which refers to places outside Hungary's pre-Trianon

Table 7.18. The choice of standard versus nonstandard suffixes on place names in Vojvodina, Prekmurje and Hungary

	Vojvodina		Prekmurje		Hungary	
Tasks	St	Nst	St	Nst	St	Nst
512	53	83	14	51	86	21
	39%	61%	21.5%	78.5%	80.4%	19.6%
609	65	68	27	32	71	34
	48.9%	51.1%	45.8%	54.2%	67.9%	32.1%
Total	118	151	41	83	156	55
	43.9%	56.1%	33.1%	66.9%	74.2%	25.8%

borders (one, *Kosovo*, in the former Yugoslavia, the other, *Craiova*, in Romania), and which would require internal cases in standard Hungarian. We hypothesized, however, that Vojvodina Hungarians might treat the placename *Kosovo* as nonforeign and use surface cases with it (just like Transylvania Hungarians would treat the placename *Craiova*). Also, in the case of Vojvodina Hungarians, the use of the surface case would be reinforced by the equivalent Serbian preposition *na*, which has the same primary meaning as the Hungarian superessive case. Sentences 512 and 609 were used to test subjects' case usage with placenames. Results are summarized in Table 7.18.

When we analyze the answers of the two sentences jointly, the rate of standard answers is as follows: Prekmurje 66.9%, Vojvodina 56.1%, and Hungary 25.8%. These figures show that, in line with the hypothesis, the results of Vojvodina differ significantly from those in Hungary ($\chi^2 = 43.40$, df = 1, p < .001). The fact that in Prekmurje the tendency to favor the nonstandard form is somewhat stronger than in Vojvodina ($\chi^2 = 3.67$, df = 1, p < .10) does not seem to be unusual if we know that until recent times Vojvodina and Prekmurje belonged to the same state (the second Yugoslavia), to which people from Prekmurje were strongly attached, and Kosovo is, thus, still perceived by people in Prekmurje as home territory.

The distribution of answers to sentence 512 is in line with our expectation. Because of the above mentioned reasons, Vojvodina and Prekmurje subjects favored the surface case suffix with *Kosovo*, while results of other regions do not show any significant difference. Frequency of the external case suffix is 78.5% in Prekmurje, 61% in Vojvodina, and 19.6% in Hungary. The difference between Vojvodina and Prekmurje is significant at the p < .05 level ($\chi^2 = 5.26$, df = 1) and both differ significantly from Hungary ($\chi^2 = 40.26$ and 55.12, df = 1, p < .001).

The results confirm our hypothesis: the change of borders in 1920 transformed the mental map of our subjects as well, and this change is mirrored in their language use. We would like to emphasize, however, that favoring the nonstandard surface case suffix may have been induced by the majority language in case of Vojvodina Hungarians. That is, borrowing from Serbian could also be the motivation, and not only deeper, extralinguistic reasons, or changes in perceptual or cognitive functions are mirrored in the language. Surely, contact-induced change is co-present with socially induced aspectual changes (this could be crucial in case of Prekmurje subjects; the same effect is present in answers of Transylvania Hungarians who used the external case suffix only with the Romanian geographical name, and results of other regions are similar to the ones from Hungary), and this is expressed in language use. Thomason and Kaufman (1988:35) say that 'it is the sociolinguistic history of the speakers, and not the structure of their language, that is the primary determinant of the linguistic outcome of language contact' and claim that at least two factors are needed for structural change in the borrowing language: several hundred years of language contact and widespread bilingualism. The results are in line with Thomason and Kaufman's claim and complement the causes of linguistic change: apart from structural and social reasons, changes in psychological, that is, cognitive, functions can also explain it on a more molecular level. Psychological changes are, of course, the results of social changes and show that people's speech can be determined by their perception of the world.

3.3.1.8 *Number concord.* All in all, Hungarian uses singular number concord very often in cases where Indo-European languages use plural: in referring to paired body parts, in generic reference to a group of identical items, and in subject and object complements with plural nouns as referents. Plural concord is also possible with these, but it is considered less desirable from a normative point of view. Our hypothesis was that plural concord would be more frequent in Hungarian used in bilingual regions, where the language that Hungarian is in contact with would reinforce its use. Sentences 505, 506, 511, 601, 604, 606, 611, and 626 were used to test preferences in number concord. A detailed analysis is presented by Göncz (2001a), so here we present only the most important findings, as summarized in Table 7.19. It provides figures of preference for singular (standard, St) and plural (nonstandard, Nst) forms of eight variables separately and together.

We would like to make a few remarks in connection with Table 7.19.

1. The implicit norm underlying the answers of subjects is in line with how the form is codified in the standard. Hungarian speakers in the Carpathian Basin favor in a 70%: 30% proportion the singular variant in case of all eight variables tested. The form considered more preferable by the literature, that is, the singular form is the dominant one in their language use. Our figures also show the fluctuation 'permitted' by normative grammars, namely, that the plural form cannot be considered nonstandard: in every region plural forms occur in great numbers as well. The approximately 70%: 30% proportion is not valid for both kinds of cases of singular vs. plural use in question: the use of singular forms is more significant in case of nouns (75.18%) than in case of the agreement in subject and object complement adverbs (65.88%). So, our subjects show more standard language use in the case of the former than of the latter. (The difference of 9.3% in favor of more standard noun usage is statistically significant, $\chi^2 = 60.60$, df = 1, p < .01). A possible explanation is that the use of singular and plural nouns is a 'classic' topic of language cultivation manuals and school textbooks, whereas it is quite rare to mention adverb agreement, thus, fewer people know that the singular form is the

Table 7.19. The choice of standard versus nonstandard number concord among speakers in Vojvodina, Prekmurje and Hungary

Tasks	Vojvodina		Prekmurje		Hungary	
	St	Nst	St	Nst	St	Nst
505	119	19	61	5	94	13
	86.2%	13.8%	92.4%	7.6%	87.9%	12.1%
506	103	38	50	15	75	32
	73%	27%	76.9%	23.1%	70.1%	29.9%
511	79	60	38	25	60	47
	56.8%	43.2%	60.9%	39.1%	57.7%	42.3%
601	99	37	48	15	75	32
	72.8%	27.2%	76.2%	23.8%	70.1%	29.9%
604	115	21	52	13	93	14
	84.6%	15.4%	80%	20 %	86.9%	13.1%
606	79	57	35	29	60	47
	58.1%	41.9%	54.7%	45.3%	56.1%	43.9%
611	107	29	47	17	90	16
	78.7%	21.3%	73.4%	26.6%	84.9%	15.1%
626	113	14	53	7	93	5
	89%	11%	88.3%	11.7%	94.9%	5.1%
Total	814	275	385	126	640	206
	74.8%	25.2%	75.3%	24.7%	75.7%	24.3%

* Source: Göncz (2001)

one preferred by language cultivators. The values are $\chi^2 = 3.32$, df = 1, p < .10 for monolinguals, and $\chi^2 = 58.30$, df = 1, p < .01 for bilinguals, demonstrating that the tendency (that, for nouns, a more standard use occurs than in the agreement of adverbs) is only present less saliently for monolinguals but is clearly expressed in the bilingual results.

2. The tendency (in case of all the studied variables) that our subjects use the singular more often is valid in every region. See the last row, "Total", in Table 7.19. The preference for plural is 25.25% in Vojvodina, 24.66% in Prekmurje and 24.35% in Hungary. These three regions show similar results and their differences can be disregarded.

3. In Vojvodina and Prekmurje, the preference for the plural form is only 0.9% and 0.35% higher, respectively than in Hungary. Therefore we cannot uphold the hypothesis that structural differences of number concord of languages in contact *always* affect the use of plural forms in the borrowing language.

3.3.1.9 *Differences of linguistic variables.* Now we are going to compare the results from Vojvodina and Prekmurje with the results from Hungary for every variable, presenting the group average (rounded to two digits) and differences between them (T). T is the value of either the Tukey-Kramer or the Games-Howell paired comparison (depending on whether the results satisfy dispersion homogeneity criteria). Table 7.20 represents results for all universal contact variables.

Vojvodina results differ from those of Hungary in 10 cases: in 9 of these in line with the hypothesis, whereas in one case contrary to it. There are three instances of difference for analytical forms, two for feminization, and one each for word order, diminutives, redundant pronouns, comparison, and placename suffixes.

As for Prekmurje results, they differ from those of Hungary in 9 cases, all in line with the hypotheses except for placename suffixes. There are five instances of difference for analytical forms, and one each for feminization, diminutives, comparison, and placename suffixes.

There are five important differences between Vojvodina and Prekmurje: in the latter, analytical forms are more frequent in 4 cases and word order is less standard in one case.

4.   Conclusion

We had two questions at the start of our research: (1) What is the relationship between actual language use and the codified norm?, and (2) How do speakers of different regions compare to one another? Because of the second question, we formed the general expectation that, due to living in contact situations in the bilingual regions and to their minority status, bilingual Hungarians may not know the linguistic norms and would diverge from standard to nonstandard variants, unlike the members of the control group of monolingual Hungarians from Hungary. Tendencies we have discovered will be presented in terms of these questions and hypotheses.

(1) We claim that the answers of bilingual minority Hungarians differ considerably from those of monolingual Hungarians in Hungary. The former favor less standard variants to more standard ones more frequently.

(2) In the case of the universal contact variables we have chosen 8 linguistic features that are expected to show the effect of language contact through a more salient presence of features characteristic of Indo-European languages. According to our results, contact effects can be identified in the case of the use of analytical forms, feminizing tendencies, and, most likely, in the case of diminutive forms as well, for the whole of the Carpathian Basin since the results of all bilingual regions significantly differ from those of monolingual Hungarians in Hungary, quite in line with our expectations. These contact effects are, however, not as general as to be manifested in the case of every studied variable, since preference for the standard or nonstandard variants is also affected by the type of task in which they appear in the questionnaire, as well as by other linguistic and extra-linguistic factors. The contact effects are not so strong in any of the studied cases as to cause the complete disappearance of the use of the standard variants. This, in our case, also means that the contact effects do not result in a linguistic impoverishment but in changes in the proportions of the use of the standard vs. nonstandard variants, making language use more heterogeneous.

Table 7.20. Differences of averages of universal contact variables in Vojvodina, Prekmurje, and Hungary

Tasks	Vojvodina	Prekmurje	Hungary	Vojvodina vs. Hungary	Prekmurje vs. Hungary	Vojvodina vs. Prekmurje
503 – A	1.28	1.25	1.71	10.33**	9.08**	.66
507 – A	1.73	1.32	1.80	2.10	9.71**	8.13**
514 – A	1.02	1.02	1.03	.47	.81	.42
532 – A	1.42	1.73	1.64	4.88**	1.69	5.87**
536 – A	1.20	1.18	1.19	.44	.28	.67
603 – A	1.75	1.71	1.91	4.73*	4.31*	.83
605 – A	1.83	1.79	1.84	.30	1.28	1.08
607 – A	1.66	1.42	1.58	1.80	2.91	4.59*
613 – A	1.83	1.40	1.80	0.69	7.58**	8.43**
501 – W	1.86	1.83	1.73	3.26	2.23	.56
509 – W	1.99	1.89	1.86	5.08**	.98	3.29
502 – W	1.95	1.75	1.91	1.87	3.55	4.91*
508 – W	1.95	1.95	1.89	2.46	2.31	.17
608 – W	1.90	1.91	1.92	0.44	.30	.06
631 – F	1.64	1.75	1.41	4.98**	6.40**	2.19
632 – F	1.17	1.21	1.18	.12	.84	.96
633 – F	1.29	1.19	1.11	5.28**	1.95	2.32
634 – F	1.12	1.24	1.12	.05	2.33	2.27
504 – D	1.87	1.85	1.84	.92	.16	.62
538 – D	1.88	1.86	1.48	9.87**	8.23**	.36
602 – D	1.60	1.58	1.66	No difference between the regions.		
612 – D	1.96	2.00	1.98	1.61	.91	1.97
510 – R	1.60	1.59	1.66	1.51	1.45	.24
515 – R	1.10	1.09	1.22	3.54	3.30	.22
615 – R	1.07	1.16	1.27	6.05**	2.63	2.52
610 – C	1.83	1.91	1.83	.01	2.04	2.15
621 – C	1.19	1.76	1.03	6.08**	4.08+	.42
512 – S	1.61	1.79	1.20	10.27**	12.95**	3.72
609 – S	1.02	1.03	1.01	1.13	1.30	.52
505 – P	1.86	1.92	1.88	0.53	1.42	1.99
506 – P	1.73	1.77	1.70	0.72	1.40	.85
511 – P	1.43	1.39	1.44	No difference between the regions.		
601 – P	1.73	1.76	1.70	.65	1.23	.72
604 – P	1.85	1.80	1.87	.74	1.64	1.09
606 – P	1.58	1.55	1.56	No difference between the regions.		
611 – P	1.79	1.73	1.85	1.77	2.47	1.12
626 – P	1.11	1.12	1.05	2.34	1.96	.18

A = Analytical forms, W = Word order, F = Feminization, D = Diminutive forms, R = Redundant pronouns, C = Comparison, S = Suffix of place names, P = Plural
** = $p < .01$, * = $p < .05$, + = $p < .10$

From a psychological point of view, the linguistic solutions provided by the bilingual groups are more divergent, whereas monolingual Hungarians tend to be more unified in their answers.

(3) The analysis of universal contact variables shows, beyond the effects of language contact, that changes in people's perception of the world (e.g. what they consider to be "home" vs. "abroad") can be caused by social changes such as modifications of international borders, and these changes, in turn, effect people's language use as well. In our study, the use of case suffixes with placenames is a case in point.

(4) Even though our results do not always support our hypotheses, they do not disprove them either. The only exceptions are the results of variables involving word order and the use of redundant pronouns in some of the bilingual regions studied, since they are, in some cases, more standard than those of monolingual Hungarians. The reasons that we suggest are at the cause of this phenomenon are possible regional dialectal effects as well as the tendency to overfulfill the norm.

(5) The results of our study make it possible to define some characteristics of the (a) Vojvodina and (b) Prekmurje Hungarian contact varieties.

(a) Vojvodina Hungarians define themselves as part of the Hungarian nation. At the same time, they form a bilingual community: in most everyday situations, besides Hungarian they use Serbian as well. That is why their language use is shaped by language contact induced regularities and by other effects of their minority situation. These effects together cause a considerable divergence from a (more) standard language use compared to linguistic practices of monolingual Hungarians in Hungary. Differences between Vojvodina Hungarian and Hungarian spoken in Hungary, however, are not great and are smaller than in the case of other bilingual speech communities, causing no unconquerable communicational difficulties.

As our results show, the contact-induced changes in Vojvodina Hungarian are present in the tendency to use analytical, feminizing forms, and diminutives more frequently. At the same time, in terms of word order and nonuse of redundant pronouns, features of a more normative language use are present, which are results contradicting the expected contact effects. Results concerning the use of sociolinguistic variables which occur in the speech of all Hungarian speakers and which were not discussed in this paper show no significant differences between Vojvodina Hungarians and Hungarians in Hungary.

We would like to emphasize that the Vojvodina and Prekmurje results of the SHOH study show fewer instances of contact induced change and language attrition than are characteristic of the actual language use. This is because, on the one hand, the sample was not representative of the population, overrepresenting professionals, and mainly those volunteered to fill in the questionnaire who knew their language well. On the other hand, some aspects of language use cannot be studied through questionnaire-based data collection. Other studies on Vojvodina Hungarian show more distinct contact induced changes, widespread signs of language attrition and language shift, especially in the case of Hungarians living in communities where they form a minority. It is more useful to interpret data from other sources and from our study as complementary and not contradictory.

(b) Both contact induced changes and signs of language attrition are more salient in the case of Prekmurje Hungarians than in the case of Vojvodina Hungarians. The small size of the population probably plays an important role in this. Divergence from the standard is much stronger here than in Vojvodina. Analytical forms are twice as favored here as by the monolingual Hungarians, and acceptance of feminized profession names and diminutive forms is also widespread. At the same time, there are several parallel characteristics with the Vojvodina region in terms of word order, use of redundant pronouns, comparison, suffixes of placenames and number concord. According to our results, signs of language attrition are the most explicit in this region. Our Prekmurje subjects, having rated their native language proficiency as low, agree with this.

Translated by Eszter Szabó

Notes

* Sections 1, 2.1, 3.1, 3.3, and 4 were written by Lajos Göncz, while Sections 2.2 and 3.2 by Ottó Vörös.

1. Throughout this paper, we refer to towns and villages with their official Serbian or Slovenian names first and their traditional Hungarian names second.

2. The district (*občina* in Slovenian) is the local administrative unit of 20 to 30 smaller settlements. The center is usually a small town of economic or commercial importance in the region. After the independence of Slovenia there has been a new division introduced, so the population belonging to the ethnographic unit of the Őrség became part of the Hodoš-Šalovc district near the Austrian-Hungarian border.

3. In brackets we provide the number(s) of the task(s) containing the variable in the SHOH questionnaire, see Appendix.

CHAPTER 8

Hungarian in Austria

Csanád Bodó

1. Introduction

This chapter discusses a Hungarian-speaking minority which has been, in comparison to those in other countries neighboring Hungary, perhaps the least discriminated against. The relatively favorable position of Hungarians in Austria has to be viewed in the light of the fact that in the second half of the 20th century there was a political division between Austria and the other countries populated by Hungarians in the Carpathian Basin. As described in other chapters of this book, social structure shows relevant differences between Hungarian minorities and their respective majorities. The Hungarian-speaking minority in Austria, however, is more integrated into its German-speaking environment, as I will show through a comparison of the autochthonous Hungarian minority and the German-speaking majority of the same province, Burgenland (Section 2). Although the autochthonous group constitutes only a smaller part of the Hungarian minority in Austria, its sociolinguistic situation is better known than that of nonautochthonous groups. Primarily, it is due to Gal's influential research on language shift in Oberwart/Felsőőr, a small town in Burgenland (Gal 1979, 1984, 1989). In addition to her sociolinguistic work Imre, a Hungarian linguist and native of Oberwart, described the traditional dialect of the same community in a number of studies (e.g. Imre 1971, 1973). More recently, a sociological study has been piggybacked on the 1991 Austrian census, aiming at a comparison of the German-speaking majority and the main minorities, the Hungarians and the Croatians in Burgenland (Holzer & Münz 1993). A comparison of minorities in Burgenland will show that diverse strategies can be employed on language maintenance issues. The sources of data used throughout this chapter will be complemented by my own data from sociolinguistic research in progress within the Oberwart bilingual community.

Immigrant Hungarians in Austria have been studied less extensively; the Sociolinguistics of Hungarian Outside Hungary (SHOH) project included 50 persons from among them in addition to 10 speakers from the autochthonous minority group. (For a description of the project, see Kontra, this volume.) Given the uneven distribution of the two groups in the sample, the results will be mainly discussed in connection with the immigrant group of Hungarians in Austria. In Section 3, I will present linguistic data both from the autochthonous and the immigrant population of Hungarians in the country. Unfortunately, no parallel can be drawn between them in the strict sense due to the differences in the available information. However, I will attempt to make at least some tentative qualitative comparisons of the linguistic behavior of the two groups in Section 4.

2.   Sociolinguistic aspects

2.1 The origin of the contact situation

Historically, the Hungarian-speaking population in Austria forms two distinct groups: the autochthonous minority group in the country's easternmost province of Burgenland, and the immigrants living both in and mainly outside Burgenland. The former group are descendents of a Hungarian population that settled in the Western parts of the Hungarian Kingdom in the 12th century. In the early 13th century, the territory was depopulated except for the settlements of Obere Wart/Őrvidék in Southern Burgenland as well as Oberpullendorf/Felsőpulya and Mitterpullendorf/Középpulya in Central-Burgenland.[1] In the second part of the 13th century, these communities were raised to the rank of collective nobility for defending the Western borders of Hungary. The rank of nobility provided a relative independence against the landowners, but these privileges were not recognized outside Burgenland settlements.

An ethnic stratification of the area was in place already by the late Middle Ages. During the Ottoman Turkish attacks of Western Hungary, a large portion of the population was killed, while others fled to other parts of the country. It is quite understandable that the petty nobility felt strongly tied to the land by the collective privileges and did not want to leave. They formed the core of the continuously present Hungarian population in Burgenland. By the 16th century, settlements of Germans and Croatians, who arrived from Styria or other parts of Austria, surrounded the Hungarian speaking areas of Western Hungary. This is how Hungarian speech islands, with little direct contact with other Hungarian communities came into being. There is a wide zone of 6–18 miles between the enclaves and larger Hungarian populations. To some extent, bilingualism has been present in these communities for the last 400 years.

The autochthonous linguistic area of Burgenland can be divided into two main parts. The first region is the Obere Wart/Őrvidék in the southwest, including the settlements Oberwart/Felsőőr, Unterwart/Alsóőr, and Siget in der Wart/Őrisziget (Rotenturm an der Pinka/Vörösvár community). The second region is central-Burgenland: Oberpullendorf/Felsőpulya and Mitterpullendorf/Középpulya (in 1958, Mittel- and Oberpullendorf were unified under the name of Oberpullendorf).

There are two other ways in which Hungarian speakers came to live in Burgenland. First, agricultural workers came to the Burgenland areas of Seewinkel and Heideboden from other large manors of the landlords in the 18th and 19th centuries. Having undergone language shift, these communities usually broke up during the second half of the

20th century. Second, before Burgenland became a part of Austria in 1921, there was a large number of Hungarians in the towns as well, mainly officials, ecclesiastic functionaries, and merchants. After 1921, the majority of these Hungarian professionals resettled in Hungary.

Besides the mainly indigenous Hungarian-speaking community, the Hungarian population in Austria also consists of immigrants. There have been three main waves of Hungarian immigration: the first, during and after World War II, the second, after the Hungarian revolution in 1956, and the third wave after 1989. In addition, a larger number of ethnic Hungarian immigrants arrived from Romania in the 1980s (Szépfalusi 1991).

2.2 Demographics

According to the 2001 census (Volkszählung 2001; Statistik Austria 2003), of the total population of 8,032,926 (7,322,000 of them Austrian citizens), there were 40,583 persons in Austria who regarded themselves as Hungarian-speaking, but only 63.8% of them (25,884 persons) had Austrian citizenship. Most of the Hungarian-speaking Austrian citizens live in Vienna (15,435 persons), Burgenland (4,704 persons), and Upper Austria (3,849 persons).

Now I will discuss in more detail the autochthonous population of Burgenland and its complete population data. Table 8.1 summarizes the changes that occurred in this province during the last century.

There has been a continuous decrease of the Hungarian speaking population after the end of World War I and the annexation of the western parts of Hungary in 1921

Table 8.1. The number of Hungarians in Burgenland*

Year	N	Percent of the total population of Burgenland
1910	26,225	9.1%
1920	24,930	8.4%
1923	14,931	5.2%
1934	10,442	3.5%
1939	8,346	2.9%
1951	5,251	1.9%
1961	5,629	2.1%
1971	5,447	2.0%
1981	4,025	1.5%
1991	4,973	1.8%
2001	4,704	1.8%

* Sources: 1910 and 1920 – Hungarian census, which asked about mother tongue; 1923–1991 – Austrian censuses, which, between 1923 and 1939, asked about mother tongue, and from 1951 onwards asked about 'Umgangssprache' [colloquial language]. Only data from Austrian citizens are included. Based on Holzer and Münz 1997:18–30 and Bundesanstalt Statistik Österreich 2002.

under the Treaty of Trianon. The decrease was most accentuated in the 1920s, when many officials left for Hungary, and manor workers left for the industrial regions of Upper Austria or immigrated to the United States (Holzer & Münz 1997:1830). After World War II, the size of the population has been more or less constant. An important increase in 1961 can be explained by a wave of emigrants after the Hungarian revolution of 1956, many of whom came to Austria. According to several scholars, the increase in the number of Hungarian-speaking population recorded by the census of 1991 is due to the large-scale political developments in Central and Eastern Europe. After the collapse of communism, social, economical, and political contacts increased between Hungary and the Hungarian-speaking population in Burgenland, and, therefore, the prestige of the Hungarian language most probably also increased (Éger 1994; Holzer & Münz 1997).

The results of the general 1991 census in Austria can be contrasted with the microcensus undertaken in Burgenland in 1990–1991. The latter indicates that 6.1% (16,737 persons) of the total population in the province could speak or understand Hungarian. Within this number, 0.8% (2,276 persons) of the population possessed only passive language skills in Hungarian, while 5.3% (14,461 persons) had active skills. A larger community than the Hungarians, Croatians comprised 9.0% of the population of the province (Holzer & Münz 1993). A comparison of the two censuses, the national and the Burgenland microcensus, reveals important differences regarding the use of Hungarian, while the difference in the case of Burgenland Croatian is minimal. Holzer and Münz (1993:21) argue that these discrepancies can be explained by the difference in the questions used to ask about language use between the general census and the microcensus of Burgenland. The questions of the general census asked about the colloquial language (Umgangssprache) but the microcensus recorded data concerning passive language skills as well. Besides, many of the older generation (over 61) were educated in Hungarian but do not belong to the Hungarian ethnic community. In most cases, this generation does not use Hungarian regularly (they represent 23% of all persons who have knowledge of Hungarian).

Hungarian is known by a number of people higher than the national average in two administrative districts, in Oberwart (6,443 persons, 11.8%) and Neusiedl am See (4,032 persons, 7.8%), as well as in the statuary towns Eisenstadt and Rust (908 persons, 6.8%). This means that approximately 10,500 persons, representing more than 60% of the total population with Hungarian linguistic skills, live in the administrative districts of Oberwart and Neusiedl am See. According to the census, the only settlement with a majority Hungarian population in Austria is Unterwart/Alsóőr.

About 13% of the Burgenland Hungarians, i.e. those who speak or understand Hungarian (henceforth abbreviated as BLH) live in settlements of 5,001–10,000 inhabitants, in contrast with 3.6% of those who speak German only (henceforth referred to as BLG), living mainly in the town Oberwart/Felsőőr (Holzer & Münz 1993:23).

The BLH group is older than the BLG group with only 15% of the former under 15, and almost half (45%) above 60. Table 8.2 summarizes the age structure of both groups.

Table 8.2. Age structure and language proficiency in Burgenland*

Language proficiency	BLG		BLH	
Age group	N	%	N	%
under 15	47,856	20.6	1,595	9.2
16–30	56,110	24.2	2,090	12.5
31–60	86,461	37.3	5,561	33.2
over 61	41,465	17.9	7,490	44.7
Total	231,893	100.0	16,737	100.0

* Based on Holzer and Münz (1993: 24, Table 3).

This means that the BLH group is underrepresented in all generations, except the oldest. However, it is not only the lack of intergenerational language transmission that is responsible for the age-structure of the BLH group. As mentioned above, in the age group of those above 61, we find many people who learned Hungarian in a formal setting (school) and do not speak it regularly.

2.3 Economic standing and social integration

Because of the limited size of the Hungarian-speaking population in Burgenland, Burgenland Hungarians have no economic infrastructure or organizations of their own. After 1989, the economic ties between Austria and Hungary became stronger, and this contributed to an appreciation of the role of Hungarian in commerce and services.

The age structure of the BLH group with its aging population can also be viewed as a reason for the differences with the BLG group in their socioeconomic status. Almost half of the people in the BLH group are retired (43.5%), whereas retirees constitute only 21.7% of the whole population of Burgenland, and 19.4% of the BLG group (see Table 8.3).

Within the group of those actively employed, the BLH group is significantly underrepresented, 9.9% or 516 persons, vs. the BLG group, 16.8%, or 16,353 persons. Nevertheless, the proportion of office clerks within the BLH group is slightly higher (13.3%, or 688 persons) than in the BLG group (11.1%, or 10,825 persons). More accentuated is the difference in the distribution of semi-skilled and unskilled workers in the two groups: 27% (1,401 persons) in the BLH group, and only 21% (20,514 persons) in the BLG group (Holzer & Münz 1993: 25).

The BLH group is better represented, with 56.6% (2,939 persons), among those employed in the service sector, but their proportion is lower both in industry (34%, 1,763 persons) and agriculture (9.4%, 488 persons). The corresponding figures for the BLG group are 45.9% (44,764 persons), 42.3% (41,211 persons), and 11% (10,723 persons), respectively. Regarding the occupational structure of the Hungarian population, it is striking that the proportion of those working in agriculture is relatively low. This is important because the majority of the autochthonous Hungarians worked in agriculture until the 1960s and 1970s (cf. Gal 1979; Imre 1973a). Therefore, the economic

Table 8.3. Language proficiency and socioeconomic status in Burgenland*

Language proficiency Socioeconomic status	BLG		BLH	
	N	%	N	%
employed	97,445	42.0	5,191	31.0
unemployed	4,528	2.0	192	1.1
retirees	44,939	19.4	7,288	43.5
housewives	26,452	11.4	2,001	12.0
students	38,404	16.6	1,796	10.7
pre-school children	18,179	7.8	68	0.4
misc. dependants	935	0.4	31	0.2
not known	1,010	0.4	170	1.0
Total	231,893	100.0%	16,737	100.0%

* Based on Holzer and Münz (1993:25, Table 5).

structure of the Hungarian minority can be described through a shift from agriculture to industry and, even more, to the service sector.

This may be characteristic of the mobility of the young and middle-aged groups. Within the BLH group, the proportion of the persons with a high school degree is higher than the BLG group. Approximately 1,000 persons (21.3%) from the 15–40 age group have a high school degree, in contrast with the 17.4% of the BLG group. Those with a university or college degree are slightly more numerous in the BLH group (5%; 235 persons), as opposed to the BLG group (4.4%; 4,079 persons) (Holzer & Münz 1993:26).

2.4 Domains of minority language use

As there is no official information on the language use of the entire Hungarian minority in Austria, Table 8.4 summarizes data concerning Hungarian language use in Burgenland, based on Holzer and Münz (1993). Naturally, I did not include in the BLH group those who, during the microcensus interviews, did not give an account of their Hungarian language use in any domain. I will be referring to this group as the "restricted BLH group" below.

In Burgenland, Hungarian is used at least in one public domain (workplace, church or community) by 53% of those with a Hungarian background. Almost 45% of the restricted BLH group use Hungarian only in the private domains (family, casual conversations, and travel). Croatians use their minority language in a different way: 75% of the Croatian-speaking population in Burgenland use it in both public and private domains, whereas those who use it only in private domains constitute only 19% (Holzer & Münz 1993:36).

Table 8.4 does not indicate a major difference in the Hungarian language use of different generations. The importance of Hungarian use in the public domains is relatively insignificant in the case of those born before 1930, i.e. those over 61 at the time of data collection. This is mainly due to the situation of the Neusiedl administrative

Table 8.4. Hungarian language use in Burgenland, 1990–1991*

Domains	Generations			Total
	10–35 years	36–60 years	over 61 years	
Workplace	38.1%	35.0%		35.7%
Community	32.7%	47.7%	39.7%	40.3%
Church	28.0%	31.7%	26.0%	28.7%
Family	59.4%	59.6%	41.5%	54.1%
Occasional conversations	82.3%	86.1%	90.9%	86.3%
Travel	77.8%	87.7%	66.2%	77.9%
Total	N = 4,036	N = 4,451	N = 3,691	N = 12,179

* Based on Holzer and Münz (1993:53, Table 28).

district, where the majority of older Hungarian speakers live in a predominantly German environment. In contrast, the BLH group used Hungarian in the public domains both in Oberwart and Oberpullendorf districts, although these had also a monolingual German-speaking majority.

The younger generation, born between 1955 and 1980, uses Hungarian in public domains (i.e. the workplace) to a greater degree than the middle generation (born between 1930 and 1954). This is probably due to the growth of economic relations in the Hungarian-Austrian border region, and, accordingly, to the increasing prestige of Hungarian.

The most important aspect of the private domain is the language of communication used in the family, especially in intergenerational language use. In this respect, German-Hungarian bilingual or German monolingual backgrounds of spouses are one essential factor determining whether parents communicate with their children in the minority language. Mixed marriages constitute 42% within the BLH group. One-third of the people living in mixed marriages do not use Hungarian as the language of communication with their children. In 21% of the cases even if both parents speak Hungarian, they do not use Hungarian with their children (Holzer & Münz 1993:42).

Hungarian is not the intergenerational language of communication in 42% of the older generation, 45% of the middle-aged parents, and 55% of the parents belonging to the young generation (Holzer & Münz 1993:53). Given the low level of intergenerational language use within BLH families, it is important to investigate other sources, especially formal settings, which are available where members of the BLH group can acquire Hungarian, that is, whether Hungarian education is guaranteed in the province.

At the moment, bilingual Hungarian education is only offered in three elementary schools, in Oberwart/Felsőőr, Unterwart/Alsóőr and Siget/Őrisziget. In 1938, however, there were ten schools. In fact, there are no elementary schools with Hungarian as the exclusive language of instruction in Burgenland. Nevertheless, in some schools, Hungarian is available as an optional subject.

In 1987, Hungarian was introduced in the secondary school in Oberpullendorf/Felsőpulya, whereas six other high schools listed it as an optional course. After the collapse of communism in Central Europe in 1989, one of the most significant events in Hungarian education was undoubtedly the establishment, in 1992, of a high school in Oberwart/Felsőőr with Hungarian as a language of instruction. This is a bilingual institution with Hungarian-German and Croatian-German classes where the medium of instruction is German together with the respective minority language. Despite the traditional Hungarian-German bilingual background of the town, there have been more students enrolled in the Croatian-German than in the Hungarian-German classes, however. This is a remarkable sign of the differences concerning language maintenance strategies of the two linguistic groups because, unlike Croatians, Hungarians in Burgenland attribute less importance to the role of schools in maintaining the minority language.

With regard to higher education, one can pursue studies leading to a diploma in Finno-Ugric studies, a Hungarian teacher's diploma, and a diploma in German-Hungarian translation at the University of Vienna. Currently, there is no bilingual teacher training at the teacher training colleges in Burgenland, but a diploma in Hungarian language teaching can be obtained at the nearby western Hungarian teacher training college in Szombathely.

2.5 Language maintenance and shift

From a sociolinguistic point of view, Gal's 1979 book provides the most information on the Hungarian linguistic situation in Austria, more specifically, in the small town of Oberwart/Felsőőr. She puts the initial stage of the language shift process at the late 1950s and early 1960s. During this period the overwhelming majority of the Hungarian inhabitants were already bilingual. The Western European economic boom after World War II reached Austria relatively late, but in this period its effects were already felt even in Burgenland. In the early 1960s, it resulted in the in-migration of a large number of monolingual German workers to the regional center, Oberwart. This was the period when the traditional agricultural Oberwart Hungarian population became differentiated and stratified in sociological terms. Members of the young generation sought other employment opportunities in larger numbers, finding work in industry or the state administration. Many of them became weekly or daily commuters to the more economically developed provinces of Steiermark, Niederösterreich or to Vienna. On the one hand, this led to the dissolution of the previously homogeneous Hungarian-speaking community. On the other hand, this went hand in hand with the economic value loss of the Hungarian language as well as with its symbolic re-evaluation as the language of peasant culture.

Gal's study concentrates on language choice patterns. She argues that the most important factors which predict when bilinguals tend to use Hungarian, or when German is favored, are the speaker's age, peasant status, and social network. This suggests that young people, who are mostly workers with peasant ancestors, speak Hungarian less frequently than older community members. However, the discontinuity between the generations with peasant or non-peasant status can easily be overcome by the speaker's social network. Thus, social identity is not enough to predict the language choice of a speaker who has numerous and intensive ties within the "peasant" social network, i.e. social interactions determined by daily contacts in the traditional community. These speakers' preferences in language choice could be situated at the beginning phase of the language shift continuum. On the other hand, the speech behavior of the individuals with an "industrial" social network has a preference for German in most situations and settings.

2.6 Language attitudes

Similar to the case of language shift, data about the symbolic evaluation of Hungarian and German come from the autochthonous area in Burgenland. Characterizing the socio-psycholinguistic situation of the 1970s and 1980s in Oberwart, Gal writes:

> The current pattern of language attitudes in bilingual Oberwart can be summa-
> rized briefly as the widespread and familiar one in which a language of solidarity
> (Hungarian), identified with the past, with peasant agriculture, with the town's
> minority population and labeled economically "useless", is in symbolic contrast
> with a language of power (German) which is admired, associated with the state,
> with the prestige of education, and with the ability to provide material success in
> the form of mobility out of agriculture into wage labor and skilled occupations.
> (Gal 1989: 317)

However, as mentioned above, the occupational structure of the BLH group (including Oberwart) changed over the last few decades, with the proportion of those working in the agricultural sector significantly decreasing. It can be assumed that accultura-tion from the stigmatized traditional lifestyles of the Hungarian-speaking groups had an effect in the change in attitude towards the minority language. Other factors con-tributing to attitudinal change are regional and local political developments after 1989 (e. g. the emerging economic contact with Hungary and the reinforcement of bilingual education). Nevertheless, the symbolic value of Hungarian is not directly connected to these economic and political developments. Instead, they signal speakers' access to more than one sociolinguistic tradition, and their renegotiation of meaning is con-nected to these traditions. Language attitudes as describes by Gal may have become more diverse in the last decade to also include positive attitudes to Hungarian, as mir-rored in the increased number of those persons who reported the use of Hungarian in the 1991 census.

2.7 Language policy

After the collapse of the Austro-Hungarian Empire, the Austrian Treaty of 1920 de-clared German to be the official language of the state. In Burgenland, this did not affect language use in churches and church schools, but German became mandatory in the institutions and public schools of the province. After the Anschluss, Burgenland became part of the Nazi Germany, and the official use of Hungarian was considerably reduced. Church schools were nationalized, suspending Hungarian education until 1945. After a transitional decade when Austria was occupied by the Allied and Soviet troops, the Austrian Treaty of 1955 did not recognize the Hungarian minority as an ethnic group. It was only the Ethnic Group Law of 1976 which subordinated the promotion of ethnic groups to their demographic status and promoted the application of minority rights, but only inside the autochthonous regions. In other words, when members of the Hungarian or Croatian minority moved to other provinces, they lost their minority rights. The Hungarians of Burgenland are represented in the Consultative Committee of Ethnic Groups, a state organization with an advisory function on minority issues on the government level.

The Hungarian Cultural Alliance of Burgenland (Burgenlandi Magyar Kultúregyesület in Hungarian or Burgenländisch-Ungarische Kulturverein in German), founded in 1968, is the umbrella organization of all Hungarian associations in Burgenland. Its successful political activity is confined by those discourses which question its role as a legitimate representative of the Hungarian-speaking groups. One of the most important outcomes of this debate was that until 1992 the autochthonous Hungarian organization in Burgenland did not admit Hungarian immigrants living in Vienna and other parts of the country as members of the minority group (Holzer & Münz 1997:1833). The immigrants' interests outside of Burgenland are defended by two organizations: the Central Alliance of Hungarian Associations and Organizations in Austria (Ausztriai Magyar Egyesületek és Szervezetek Központi Szövetsége, or Zentralverband Ungarischer Vereine und Organisationen in Österreich), founded in 1980, and the umbrella organization of Austrian Hungarian Associations (Ausztriai Független Magyar Kultúregyesületek Csúcsszervezete, or Ungarische Vereine in Österreich), founded in 1983. Both organizations have their centers in Vienna.

3.   Linguistic aspects

Hungarian in the autochthonous settlements has its roots primarily in the local dialects, although one cannot claim that present-day varieties spoken by younger speakers are identical with traditional varieties. These dialects in Burgenland have been influenced by various linguistic systems: due to the speakers' bilingualism, by Austrian German, its local dialects, and also by Standard Hungarian. All have been part of the communities' linguistic repertoire for several centuries. However, these varieties have not affected the Hungarian dialects of Burgenland to the same extent. The processes in which Hungarian varieties in Burgenland have been involved can be identified as diverging from the traditional dialects in three ways:

–   divergence by means of convergence towards Standard Hungarian and its regional variety spoken in western Hungary (henceforth abbreviated as HH, for Hungarian as spoken in Hungary). The effects of this development are noticeable in the older generations' language use;

- divergence as a result of the effects of language contact. This development can be noticed in all generations; and,
- divergence through language loss. The effects of language loss are particularly prominent in the younger generation's linguistic praxis.

The effects of convergence towards Standard Hungarian (SH) are mainly noticeable on the phonological level. This type of change was identified in Oberwart, where younger speakers of the 1970s did not maintain the phonological style differences between the local dialect forms and SH forms in diverse sociolinguistic settings (Gal 1984). These changes have been crosscut by language contact and loss. The resulting deviations from the traditional dialect concern the phonological, the morphological, the syntactic, and the lexical level as well.

Although this categorization suggests that the three types of divergence are independent of each other, speech communities where language shift and language death are ongoing processes provide a paradigmatic case for the necessity of combining descriptions of structural and functional changes affecting their linguistic repertoires. This suggests that contact induced change in many cases cannot be separated from language-internal processes of change. It also remains a question whether the functional role of these language varieties is mirrored in linguistic change. In other words, it is a general assumption in language loss and maintenance studies that a functional reduction in use and in public domains of the recessive language is accompanied by and correlates with reduction on the level of linguistic structure.

Whereas convergence towards Standard Hungarian can be attributed to sociolectal simplification by means of functional loss of the dialect versus a standard distinction in appropriate sociolinguistic domains of the minority language (cf. Gal 1984), grammatical simplification can also result in similar developments.

In sociolinguistic settings of language shift, it is common for speakers with limited command and use of the minority language to take part in changes which will regularize the resources of the threatened language. For example, both SH and the Hungarian dialect of Oberwart (henceforth: OWH) have several nonproductive nominal classes with stem-internal alternation, but the nouns that form these classes build up different subsets of nouns in the two varieties. These nouns of OWH are heavily influenced in the course of simplification of the nominal class hierarchy. This means that these 'irregular' forms change their class affiliation and get reclassified in one of the productive classes. As an agglutinative language, however, Hungarian has a less complex inflectional class hierarchy in comparison with inflectional languages. Indeed, there are only a few productive classes in Hungarian, and they are identical with each other in both varieties. In this sense, leveling of OWH noun classes results in a convergence towards the standard variety of Hungarian. The morphological alternation with respect to nominal and possessive forms in (1a) contrasts with SH in (1b), where the productive and stable noun class shows no allomorphs.

(1)   a.   OWH (cf. Imre 1971b:70):
          Nom. *cipüö* 'shoe', possessive *cipe-jë* shoe-px3sg 'his/her shoe'
      b.   SH:
          Nom. *cipő* 'shoe', possessive *cipő-je* shoe-px3sg 'his/her shoe'

It is significant that younger BLH speakers use the SH possessive form, i.e. *cipő-je*. Because speakers with incomplete acquisition histories of Hungarian generalize the 'regular' stem at the expense of the one occurring in the possessive construction, this case of grammatical simplification coincides with a convergence towards the more prestigious SH form.

3.1   Borrowing

3.1.1   *Lexical borrowing*
One can distinguish three types of lexical borrowing from German with regard to semantically appropriate expressions in the indigenous language, namely, cultural borrowings, calques, and word substitutions (cf. Jones 1998:81ff.).

3.1.1.1   *Cultural borrowings.* Contacts with speakers of another language result in the adoption of expressions of new concepts, which are often borrowed from the other language. In the Hungarian of Burgenland, German borrowings are widely used, although there is no lexical deficiency in the standard variety of Hungarian. However, the sociolinguistic situation has created isolation from speakers of SH. The lack of access to SH resources has encouraged borrowing terms from German. The dictionary of OWH, for example, reveals numerous instances of cultural borrowings such as *himpiërszoft* 'raspberry juice' (G. *Himbeersaft*), *cimet* 'cinnamon' (G. *Zimmet*), *rëntni* 'pension' (G. *Rente*), *jetráncporál* 'carry off by force' (G. *transportieren*) (Imre 1973b; cf. Imre 1971b:83ff). Although it is easy to recognize their German origin, these borrowings follow the phonotactics of Hungarian.

3.1.1.2   *Calques.* If semantic units are borrowed from another language, it is not obvious that there is a foreign element present since their form is indigenous to the borrowing language. Interestingly, Imre's monograph on OWH (1971b:90) does not report many semantic borrowings from German, and his dictionary of the Oberwart dialect includes only a few instances of loan translations, such as *keriëk* 'wheel; bicycle' (cf. G. *Rad* 'wheel; bicycle' vs. SH *kerék* 'wheel' and *bicikli* 'bicycle') or *toll* 'feather; spring [coiled wire]' (cf. G. *Feder* 'feather; spring [coiled wire]' vs. SH *toll* 'feather' and *rugó* 'spring') (see Imre 1973b).

3.1.1.3   *Word substitutions.* This type of borrowing occurs in bilingual communities despite the existence of an indigenous equivalent and may show a lesser degree of phonotactic assimilation. Examples from Zelliger's material (2001:182) of Upper Austrian immigrant speakers' spontaneous speech samples are *hejcung* 'heating' (cf. G. *Heizung*), *tepih* 'carpet' (G. *Teppich*), *ferlóbung* 'engagement' (G. *Verlobung*).

3.1.2 Structural borrowing

Overt borrowing of grammatical units is extremely rare in language contact, but younger speakers' utterances from Oberwart/Felsőőr illustrate many instances of deviations from the traditional dialect that can be ascribed to the influence of German. Some of these developments are illustrated in sentence (2b).[2]

(2) a. Standard Hungarian:

Sok barát-om-mal ott találkoz-om.
many friend-px1sg-inst there meet-1sg.indef
'I meet many friends there.'

b. Oberwarter younger speaker's speech sample:

Sok barát-ok-at ott találkoz-ok
many friend-pl-acc there meet-1sg.indef
'I meet many friends there.'

There are two phenomena in sentence (2b) that do not occur either in HH or in OWH. First, the nominal phrase of the sentence in (2b) is in the accusative case, although the instrumental case would be appropriate in Hungarian. However, the German equivalent of *találkozik* 'meet', *treffen* requires the accusative case suffix. The use of the accusative, thus, probably stems from the influence of German. Secondly, contrary to German, Hungarian nouns do not require plural agreement after numerals. In sentence (2b), the phrase *sok barátokat* corresponds approximately to the German structure *viele Freunde* (many.PL friend.PL 'many friends').

3.1.3 Simplification 'proper'

In languages with declensional classes, the above example (1a) is a paradigmatic case of analogical leveling or generalization of the unmarked category. Other cases of increase in transparency due to developments from synthetic constructions to analytical ones are discussed in Section 3.3 below.

3.1.4 Sociolectal and/or stylistic simplification

Sociolectal simplification and simplification 'proper' are often indistinguishable, as seen above in analyzing the merger of unproductive and productive patterns of nominal classes. I will return to this in the next section when discussing the distribution of language and style shifting.

3.2 Code-switching

The result of divergence from traditional monolingual norms is overt in pragmatic forms of code-switching in those communities where linguistic purism does not reg-

ulate, at least does not regulate effectively, the use of the language varieties of the linguistic repertoire. The Oberwarter speech community has experienced this attitudinal
change in the course of language shift.

Gal (1979) observes that language shift in Oberwart often leads to asymmetrical
patterns of language use, where parents or grandparents address a child or grandchild
in Hungarian, but the child consistently answers in German. The following is an excerpt from a conversation between two women: A, who was about 30 years old, and
B, in her late sixties, shows an example of this kind of code-switching (Gal 1979:111)
(German is indicated with boldface):

(3)   A: **Un vi get's də Ilse?**
          'And how is Ilse?'
      B: *Annak is ju mëdzs. Mindedzsiknek ju mëdzs, pínz elig, minden.*
          'She's doing fine, they're all doing fine, there's money enough and every-
          thing'.
      A: **Und vos moxt dv, dv Sanyi?**
          'And what is Sanyi doing?'
      B: *Ja, annak is van, már van, már háza neki, ipüt.*
          'He's got too, he's got a house already, he built'.
      A: [Pause] **N'joa, i ge a pissl fek, neni, i ge pissl fuot, nuv in di kirxn.**
          'Well, I'm going away a little, auntie, I'm going out, just to church'.

In such cases, code-switching can be interpreted as a reflection of the dynamics of
intergroup relations among different generations. Naturally, speaker A has no difficulties understanding the answers given by the older interlocutor, but her language choice
represents a change in the traditional assignment of social meaning to the community
languages.

A more usual type is conversational code-switching, as in (4), where the same
speaker switches between German and Hungarian. In the following example, a grandfather tries to order a three-year-old girl and her cousin playing in the shed (Gal
1979:112):

(4)   *Szo! ide dzsüni!* [pause] *Jeszt jerámunyi mind e kettüötök, no hát akkor!* [pause]
      Kumm her! [pause] *Nem koapsz vacsorát!*
      'Well, come here! [pause] Put all this away, both of you, well now! [pause]
      Come here! [pause] You won't get supper!'

Although the children were reported to be Hungarian monolinguals, the grandfather
used German to express more anger and authority according to his communicative intents. This type can be functionally described as metaphorical code-switching
that is used to convey the speaker's attitude toward momentary aspects of the interaction. However, Gal (1979) emphasizes that speakers who practiced this type of
code-switching were not equally distributed through each generation in the community. Rather, the juxtaposition of German and Hungarian utterances in one discourse
is characteristic of middle-aged speakers whose status, life-modes, and values are sit-

uated between the traditional and newly-emerged ones, between those of the older generation with peasant networks and those of the younger speakers with non-peasant networks. Gal (1979: 173) interprets this communicative behavior "as the middle and variable step in the process by which the language choice patterns of the community change from categorical use of one language to categorical use of the other". Furthermore, Gal (1979, 1984) argues that the choice of language by the middle-age group plays a similar function to the choice of style or register between speakers where only one language is habitually used, whether it is the old language (Hungarian), or the new language (German). This suggests that style shifting and language switching are complementary, but, over time, one can replace the other.

Although Gal seems to regard the presence of conversational language switching as an accurate predictor of language shift, there is another possible scenario that stresses life-cycle patterns as affecting the redistribution of language choice functions in contradictory ways. Namely, it is not uncommon in bilingual communities that young people do not follow their parents' linguistic behavior, but later in their lives return to the traditional patterns of language use (McConvell 1991).

This also raises the question whether the above mentioned collapsing distinction of styles or registers in Hungarian can be regarded as a more reliable indicator of language shift than the presence of language switching alone. In this sense, the tendency towards monostylism is a functionally determined type of linguistic change in the context of language shift (cf. Dressler 1996).

3.3 Structural features: analytical and synthetic structures in Hungarian

The SHOH project provides insight into patterns of language use both in immigrant and autochthonous communities in Austria.[3] One of the main issues investigated was the use of synthetic and analytical constructions. The underlying assumption is that bilingual Hungarians outside Hungary may show a tendency to use analytical constructions instead of synthetic ones because of contact with other languages that prefer the former kind of structures. However, this phenomenon can be accounted for by several causes: the replacement of synthetic constructions with analytical ones frequently occurs in the internal language change of monolingual communities; moreover, this morphosyntactic change has often been found in minority languages undergoing language shift and loss (cf. Dressler 1996: 205).

With respect to the relatively divergent Oberwart variety, synthetic word-formation patterns show different degrees of productivity for older and younger generations. Gal (1984) states that such forms are highly productive in the traditional dialect spoken by older speakers, while young members of the speech community, labeled 'narrow-users', introduce non-conservative expressions for these derivational meanings. It should be noted that the younger generation in Oberwart are not what is known as semi-speakers (in the sense of Dorian 1977). Although both types of speakers can appear in speech communities undergoing language shift, the basis for defining the category of 'narrow-user' is the speakers' sociolinguistic practices, i.e. their restricted use of the contracting language, while semi-speakers are recognized by their limited linguistic production. Narrow-users are in this sense similar to another type in Dorian's (1981) categorization on the speakers' continuum model, the 'younger fluent speakers'.

Narrow-users' grammatical competence shows slight divergence from the traditional norm, but it does not influence their productive skills in general. The following discourse from spontaneous speech samples provides alternatives produced by narrow-users to express causative meaning in Hungarian. Causation can be expressed by synthetic constructions both in SH and OWH. In (5a), the causative suffix -tat/-tet is required as semantically and morphologically appropriate. However, example (5b) shows that the synthetic construction is replaced by an analytical one in the speech production of a narrow-user.

(5) a. Standard Hungarian:[4]
         Neki   volt   egy buta szokás-a,   de
         DAT.3SG be.PAST.3SG a   stupid habit-PX3SG but
         le-szok-tat-t-am   róla
         PVB-be.in.habit-CAUS-PAST-1SG.DEF ABL.3SG
         'He had a stupid habit but I got him out of it'

     b. Oberwarter narrow-user's speech sample (Gal 1989:323):
         Neki   buta szokás-a   volt,   de   le
         DAT.3SG stupid habit-PX3SG be.PAST.3SG but PVB
         tud-t-am   neki   szok-ni
         be.able-PAST-1SG.INDEF DAT.3SG be.in.habit-INF
         'He had a stupid habit but I got him out of it'

The second dative construction (5b) expresses the causee (*neki*) that remains covert in the SH sentence. This example does not clearly show a German influence, although it also employs analytical constructions to indicate causation just like German would. Nevertheless, young speakers also produce causation following the German factitive construction with *lassen* 'permit, cause or have done' and infinitive, as in (6b):

(6) a. Standard Hungarian:
         Ő   maga   rajzol-tat-t-a   meg a   szék-ek-et
         s/he her/himself draw-CAUS-PAST-3SG.DEF PVB the chair-PL-ACC
         'S/he had the chairs designed her/himself.'

     b. Oberwarter narrow-user's speech sample (Gal 1989:324):
         Ő   maga   hagy-t-a   a   szék-ek-et   rajzol-ni.
         s/he her/himself permit-PAST-3SG.DEF the chair-PL-ACC draw-INF
         'S/he had the chairs designed her/himself.'

Unfortunately, Gal's data (1989) do not allow us to describe the hierarchy of these developments. Thus, interfering structures of the dominant language might result in loan translation of German *lassen* as Hungarian *hagy* or in periphrastic constructions with overt expression of the causee, as in (5b). It is not only German analytical constructions that influence the narrow-users' speech production; there are also some instances where the causative meaning is lost morphologically:

(7) a. Standard Hungarian:
       Ki   akar-ják   ők-et   éhez-tet-ni
       PVB want-3PL.DEF they-ACC starve-CAUS-INF
       'They want to starve them.'
     b. Oberwarter narrow-user's speech sample (Gal 1989:324):
       Ki   akar-ják   ők-et   éhez-ni
       PVB want-3PL.DEF they-ACC starve-INF
       'They want to starve them.'

The noncausative form in (7b), as opposed to the SH construction, shows that causation, although clear from the context, is not explicitly expressed. Besides the replacement of synthetic constructions with analytical ones, the loss of the grammatical meaning can be traced to a qualitatively different dimension of language contact in a community undergoing language shift. It should be viewed as a sign of language decay which is characteristic of the above mentioned semi-speakers' linguistic competence in general. I will return to this issue in Section 3.4 below.

The SHOH project analyzes, among other things, the use of similar constructions where the Hungarian standard requires synthetic forms, but the nonstandard variant is expressed analytically. One of the variables targeted in the project was the alternate expression of the meaning of potentiality. In SH, the *-hat/-het* suffix for potentiality cannot be replaced by the analytical form with the auxiliary *tud* 'be able to' and infinitive. Attributed to the effect of language contact, the latter construction was expected to occur more often in the speech of bilingual Hungarian speakers.

The project was designed to investigate the use of different linguistic variables by means of a questionnaire to be filled in. (For the parts of the questionnaire that contained the language tasks, see the Appendix.) The informants either had to choose between two sentences on the basis of which one sounded more natural to them, as in (8), or to make metalinguistic statements on the correctness of a given sentence, as well as to correct the form if necessary, see (9).

(8) a. *Tanító néni, fáj   a   fej-em.   Ki   tud-ok*
       teacher aunt ache.3SG the head-PX1SG PVB be.able-1SG.INDEF
       men-ni?
       go-INF
       'Miss, I have a headache. May I go out?'
     b. *Tanító néni, fáj   a   fej-em.   Ki-me-het-ek?*
       teacher aunt ache.3SG the head-PX1SG PVB-go-POT-1SG.INDEF
       'Miss, I have a headache. May I go out?'

(9) *Ha szellőztet-ni akar-ok,   így   kér-ek*
     if   air-INF   want-1SG.INDEF this.way ask.for-1SG.INDEF
     engedély-t: Ki *tud-om*   *nyit-ni*   *az ablak-ot?*
     permission-ACC PVB be.able-1SG.DEF open-INF the window-ACC
     'If I want to air the room, I ask for permission this way: *Can I open the window?*'

Table 8.5 summarizes the results for sentences (8a–b). Contrary to expectations, only a few Hungarian-German bilinguals chose the analytical form, which is similar to the German phrase *kann ich ausgehen* and to the English *may I go out*.

The results for the judgements on sentence (9) are given in Table 8.6. Interestingly, the bilingual Hungarians in Austria corrected the nonstandard form to a slightly greater degree than monolingual Hungarians and the difference was not statistically significant.

In the case of the expression of potentiality, these results do not correspond to the expectations; bilinguals in Austria and monolinguals in Hungary do not differ in their choices of analytical constructions. It should be noted, however, that analytical forms expressing potentiality had a lesser preference in all seven countries involved in the project than other analytic structures (Göncz 2000c: 11f.). This might be the reason why, unlike the preference of other analytical variables, the auxiliary construction is not found in Hungarian as spoken in Austria.

Other variables with analytical and synthetic variants, however, are also used by SH speakers. Thus, these constructions co-exist both in monolingual and bilingual communities. Nevertheless, the synthetic constructions are evaluated by Hungarian language cultivators as the 'more natural' or 'free from the influence of foreign lan-

Table 8.5. The choice of analytical (nonstandard) vs. synthetic (standard) verb forms in Austria and Hungary*

		Austria (n = 60)	Hungary (n = 107)
514:	nonstandard *ki tudok menni*	2 (3.3%)	3 (2.8%)
	standard *kimehetek*	58 (96.7%)	104 (97.2%)

(the difference is not statistically significant according to the Chi-square test)
* Source: Göncz (2000c: 6, Table 1).

Table 8.6. Judging the correctness of and correcting analytical (nonstandard) vs. synthetic (standard) verb forms in Austria and Hungary*

		Austria (n = 59)	Hungary (n = 107)
536:	nonstandard *ki tudom nyitni*	10 (16.9%)	20 (18.7%)
	standard *kinyithatom*	49 (83.1%)	87 (81.3%)

(the difference is not statistically significant according to the Chi-square test)
* Source: Göncz (2000c: 6, Table 1).

Table 8.7. The choice of the "more natural" form: analytical (contact-induced) vs. synthetic (standard) verbal phrase in Austria and Hungary*

		Austria (n = 60)	Hungary (n = 106)
607:	contact induced *ne légy türelmetlen*	34 (56.7%)	45 (42.5%)
	standard *ne türelmetlenkedj*	26 (43.3%)	61 (57.5%)

$\chi^2 = 3.103$, the difference is statistically significant at the p < 0.1 level
* Source: Göncz (2000c: 6, Table 1).

guages'. Whereas synthetic forms express meaning by derivational suffixes, the analytical ones are nominal or verb phrases.

In sentences (10a–b), the subjects had to choose between the analytical verb phrase of (10a) or the synthetic form derived by the active denominal reflexive suffix *-kod/ -ked/ -köd(ik)*. The former construction has a German equivalent with the same structure; cf. *sein ungeduldig* 'be impatient'.

(10) a. *Mindjárt kész az ebéd, ne lé-gy türelmetlen!*
          at.once ready the lunch no be-IMP.2SG.INDEF impatient
          'Lunch is almost ready, don't be impatient!'

      b. *Mindjárt kész az ebéd, ne türelmetlen-ked-j!*
          at.once ready the lunch no impatient-VDER-IMP.2SG.INDEF
          'Lunch is almost ready, don't be impatient!'

As Table 8.7 shows, the bilingual subjects in Austria favored the analytical variant to a greater degree than monolingual Hungarians from Hungary. The results correlated in a statistically significant way with being bilingual. Regarding the use of the synthetic construction in the seven countries, the total proportion was similar to that of Hungary with 54.3% (N = 839) (Göncz 2000c: 17, fn. 17).

When comparing the choice between the nominal form of a derived denominal verb in (11a) and a nominal phrase in (11b), similar results were obtained. Subjects were asked to choose from these sentences containing the derived form *buszozás* 'traveling by bus' or the analytical form *utazás busszal* expressing the same meaning. As in the above examples, the analytical form is supported by the analogous German structure *Bus fahren* of the same meaning.

(11) a. *Un-om már ez-t a sok utazás-t busz-szal.*
          be.tired-1SG.DEF already this-ACC the much travel-ACC bus-INS
          'I'm very tired of all this traveling by bus.'

      b. *Un-om már ez-t a sok busz-oz-ás-t.*
          be.tired-1SG.DEF already this-ACC the much bus-VDER-NDER-ACC
          'I'm very tired of all this traveling by bus.'

The results are summarized in Table 8.8. The analytical construction is less preferred by monolingual subjects (at only 20%), while the Austrian informants chose the two alternatives to the same extent. The Chi-square test shows the difference between the two groups' choices to be significant (Göncz 2000c: 16, fn. 10).

Table 8.8. The choice of the "more natural" form: analytical (contact-induced) vs. synthetic (standard) noun phrase in Austria and Hungary*

		Austria (n = 59)	Hungary (n = 107)
507:	nonstandard *utazást busszal*	30 (50.8%)	21 (19.6%)
	standard *buszozást*	29 (49.2%)	86 (80.4%)

$\chi^2 = 17.417$, the difference is statistically significant at the p < 0.001 level.
* Source: Göncz (2000c:6, Table 1).

When comparing the data of the SHOH project to the above cited constructions from Oberwart, two caveats must be borne in mind. First, the two corpora originate from spontaneous speech samples on the one hand and questionnaires on the other. One should not automatically assume that the Oberwarter narrow-users would have chosen the analytical constructions in an artificial setting such as an interview. Furthermore, the answers of the Austrian subjects of the SHOH project should not lead one to assume that their language variety is not involved in this type of change. For instance, interviews with immigrants in Upper Austria, in Linz and Wels, show several examples of analytical constructions instead of SH compounds, such as *virág-os doboz* (flower-NDER box) vs. SH *virág-láda* (flower-box) 'flower-box' or *baromfi-s ól* (poultry-NDER coop) vs. SH *baromfi-ól* (poultry-coop) 'poultry coop' (see Zelliger 2001:182).

Secondly, the sampling procedures were quite different in the two cases. While the sixty subjects of the Austrian sample of the SHOH project represent a heterogeneous sample, the sentences in (5–7) are produced by members of a relatively homogeneous group from Oberwart, the narrow-users. The choice of some analytical constructions, as in (5–7) or in (8–9), can also be accounted for by these differences in the case of the two groups. Namely, the majority of the Austrian informants of the SHOH project are immigrants who became bilingual only after arriving in their new country. Accordingly, their linguistic deviations from standard Hungarian norms are quite different from those of members of the autochthonous population, who grew up in a bilingual setting.

3.4 Language attrition

So far I have discussed types of linguistic change that occur in "healthy" speech communities, although they can be partially attributed to the influence of the model of the dominant language (e.g. massive and unidirectional lexical interference from German to Hungarian). Other structural losses are not directly affected by the dominant language, whereas language attrition shows some linguistic developments exclusively attributed to the process eventually leading to language death.

It also means that language attrition should not be confused with or reduced to extreme rapid language change, although it is often claimed that the only difference between these two types of change is in its time-span (e.g. Dimmendaal 1992:132; Jones 1998:257). But, by definition, language attrition results, without compensation, in 'pathological' loss of essentials of the recipient language (Dressler 1996). It means that the recessive language becomes dysfunctional, and the lost meanings can only be compensated for by functionally equivalent means of expression from the dominant language. The reduction of possessive structures in OWH will serve as illustration. In Hungarian, possessive meaning is expressed by personal possessive suffixes, as shown in sentence (12a).

(12) a. Standard Hungarian:
                Tizennégy év-es   kor-om-tól   húsz   év-es
                fourteen   year-ADER age-PX3SG-ABL twenty year-ADER
                kor-om-ig,   húsz év-es   kor-om-ban
                age-PX1SG-TER twenty year-ADER age-PX1SG-INE
                hagy-t-am   abba.
                give.up-PAST-1SG.DEF PVB
                'From the age of 14 to 20; I stopped at the age of 20.'
     b. Oberwarter semi-speaker's speech sample:
                tizënnédzs éf   kor-tul husz   év-ig,   husz   iëv-ës
                fourteen   year age-ABL twenty year-TER twenty year-ADER
                kor-á-ban   hat-t-am   abba
                age-PX3SG-INE give.up-PAST-1SG.DEF PVB
                'From the age of 14 to 20; I stopped at the age of 20.'

Besides the lack of possessive suffix on *kor* 'age' in (12b), the possessive suffix -*a* (3rd person singular in HH) is overgeneralized for the appropriate personal suffix -*om* (1st person singular) in the word form *korában*.

Matters are slightly more complex when it comes to the possessed plural form. The plural morph of the possessive form is different in SH and OWH, as can be seen in (13a–b):

(13) a. OWH (cf. Imre 1971b:72):
                dzserëk-ünk-iëk (child-PX1PL-PL) 'our children'
     b. SH:
                gyerek-e-i-nk (child-PX-PL-PX.1PL) 'our children'

However, the plural morphs -*iëk* and -*i* are used only in possessive constructions, the default plural suffix of both varieties being -*k* in all non-possessive nominal forms (e.g. SH *gyerek-ek* 'child-PL'). Semispeakers from Oberwart generalize this form for possessive in many instances: *dzserëk-ëk-ünk* 'child-PL-Px1PL'. Nevertheless, it is more frequent in their speech production that the plural marker does not occur at all in the structure. In other words, several imperfect speakers of OWH are no longer able to express the original distinction of singular and plural meaning in possessive constructions.

Simplification of plural forms means the substitution of a marked form by the more general form. The markedness hierarchy of the Hungarian plural forms is not a result of the effect of the contact language in this case. On the other hand, reduction of the plural meaning might result from the existence of two competing forms both expressing plurality. Whereas simplification and reduction are affected by inherent principles of language change, partially irrespective of the structures of the dominant language, the latter type of change, as seen in the case of possessive constructions, appears to be irreversible in the course of language obsolescence.

4. Conclusion

Broadly speaking, the settlements inhabited by autochthonous or immigrant Hungarians in Austria constitute the second proportionally smallest Hungarian-speaking minority among Hungary's neighboring countries (the smallest being that of neighboring Slovenia). Given the immigrants' lower degree of territorial concentration as well as the controversy of its minority status, efforts of minority language maintenance are only present in the autochthonous speech communities. However, the effectiveness of these language planning strategies to reverse linguistic obsolescence can be questioned at least for two reasons: first, it is worth asking whether school-based efforts compensate for the limitations of intergenerational language transmission. Second, language planning can have more positive results if it develops a cooperative methodology involving indigenous community members in the intervention to reverse language shift. In other words, language maintenance requires the contribution of indigenous speakers in extending the use of the minority language to extra-institutional levels. Nevertheless, it should not pass unnoticed that language maintenance has been supported by political and economic developments since the last decade, which undoubtedly contributed to the emerging economic value and prestige of Hungarian language use, as detectable in the census data showing a slight increase in the numbers of the Hungarian-speaking population.

Obviously, differences between the autochthonous and immigrant minority groups are not only prevalent in their official status and territorial concentration, but in their sociolinguistic history: whereas the BLH groups form linguistic enclaves which have existed in relative isolation from other Hungarian speech communities for several hundred years, the immigrant communities are of discontinuous nature where Hungarian language use is largely maintained by newer immigration movements and not by intergenerational language transmission.

Although the question emerges whether differences in the duration of contact with German have a predictive value for the amount and depth of restructuring in Hungarian as spoken in the autochthonous and immigrant communities, the data discussed here provide only a tentative answer. When comparing the tendency of using analytical forms instead of synthetic ones by younger speakers of Oberwart/Felsőőr and by the Austrian informants of the SHOH project, it has been mentioned that differences between the two groups can partially be accounted for by their different time-span of contact with the majority language. Apart from some intertwining factors in methodology, the analysis of the Hungarian varieties in contact with German, albeit limited in scope, lends further support to the view that qualitative differences in contact effects are correlated with the difference in the length of contact as obvious in the case of Austrian immigrant and autochthonous communities. With regard to the Oberwart/Felsőőr speech community, there is also evidence of linguistic obsolescence, resulting in deviations from traditional norms: the comparison of the less proficient speakers' linguistic production with the traditional dialect shows that there has been a substantial reduction in morphology such as inflectional paradigm leveling, loss of causative derivational forms, and a collapse of the singular vs. plural distinction in possessive constructions. In turn, regarding the sociolinguistic consequences, one should not overlook that these deviations can result in insecurity of performance in the minority language with all its negative implications for language attitudes and, thus, for language choice.

It remains to be seen whether the Hungarian-speaking minority groups, both the autochthonous communities and immigrants, will be able to benefit from Hungary's integration into the European Union and to maintain their language under these politically and economically favorable conditions.

Notes

1. Throughout this paper, names of autochthonous regions and settlements of Hungarians in Austria are referred to by their official German names first, and their traditional Hungarian names second.

2. If not otherwise specified, data are taken from my own corpus collected in Oberwart/Felsőőr during fieldwork conducted between 1997 and 1999.

3. The sixty Austrian subjects of the project were equally selected from three different types of settlements of the Hungarian minority: Vienna, Burgenland, and the diaspora. The subjects were chosen to represent three age groups, two different levels of education, as well as an equal number of men and women and were equally distributed in the sample. The Burgenland sample consisted of 10 subjects each from the autochthonous and immigrant minority groups.

4. OWH has the same grammatical but different phonological structure in these examples.

CHAPTER 9

Hungarian in the United States*

Anna Fenyvesi

1. Introduction

This chapter provides an overview of the Hungarian minority in the United States, the Hungarian-Americans, and their language.

Since no study on the sociolinguistic situation of the entire Hungarian-American population of the United States exists, the description of the sociolinguistic aspects of this community is based on census records and the available comprehensive studies of the sociolinguistic and linguistic aspects of four Hungarian-American communities. These latter are the following: Kontra (1990), the first such study, on Hungarian as spoken in South Bend, Indiana (for a review of it in English, see Kerek 1992); Bartha (1993), on Hungarian in the Delray neighborhood of Detroit, Michigan; Fenyvesi (1995a), on Hungarian in McKeesport, Pennsylvania, a small town just outside Pittsburgh; and Polgár (2001), on the sociolinguistic aspects of Hungarian-Americans in the Birmingham neighborhood of Toledo, Ohio.

2. Sociolinguistic aspects

2.1 The origin of the contact situation

Groups of Hungarian immigrants started arriving in the United States in the mid-19th century.

Before this time, only sporadically did Hungarian individuals resettle in or visit this country. Allegedly, one Hungarian sailed with Leif Ericsson in the 10th century and another with Sir Humphrey Gilbert, one of Elizabethan England's colonists in the New World, in the 16th. Hungarian volunteers fought in the American Revolution and were followed by Hungarian travelers, naturalists and explorers in the 19th century. About 4 thousand Hungarians immigrated to the United States after the failed revolution of 1848–49, and about 800 of them fought as part of the Union Army in the American Civil War (Richmond 1995:126; Benkart 1980:464). They even established a colony of their own, calling it *Új Buda*, 'New Buda', in southern Iowa (Vassady 1979).

Table 9.1. The total number of Hungarian-Americans, 1870–2000, according to censuses*

Years	Born in Hungary	Born in the US of Hungarian or mixed parentage	Total
1870	3,737		3,737
1880	11,526		11,526
1890	62,435		62,435
1900	145,714	81,897	227,611
1910	459,609	215,295	710,904
1920	397,283	538,518	935,801
1930	274,450	316,318	590,768
1940	290,228	371,840	662,068
1950	268,022	437,080	705,102
1960	245,252	456,385	701,637
1970	183,236	420,432	603,668
1980	144,368	582,855	727,223
1990	123,657	873,888	997,545
2000	92,017	848,242	904,662

* Sources: 1870–1960, U.S. Bureau of Census (1960), 1960 Census (quoted in Fishman 1966:4); 1970: U.S. Bureau of Census (1970), quoted in Széplaki 1975:130; 1980–2000: U.S. Bureau of Census, internet data (http://www.census.gov/).

(On this and other Hungarian town and county names in the United States, see Farkas 1971.)

Large scale immigration from Hungary to the United States started in the 1880s, spurred by the failure of agricultural crops and general economic hardship in Hungary, and coinciding with mass immigration from other Eastern and Southern European countries. As Table 9.1 shows, their numbers grew steadily until World War I, resumed after the war, and were significantly cut back in 1924 with the introduction of the Quota System that limited the numbers of Eastern and Southern European immigrants to the United States in general.

This first wave of immigrants was almost exclusively of peasant and working class origin, who came to the United States with the intention of working there for a period of time for much better wages than they could in Hungary, saving as much money as they could, and returning to Hungary to buy their own land and enjoy a better life than before. Known as the sojourners, many, although by far not all of them, did return to Hungary, some even crossing over to the United States more than once. Sojourners complicate the interpretation of census figures since the U.S. authorities did not keep records on them (or on those who came back to the United States after a short visit to the old country) until 1908, although it is estimated that approximately 37% of those who entered the United States until then also returned to Hungary permanently (Benkart 1980:464). For a detailed historical analysis of the causes of this first big wave of emigration, see Boros-Kazai (1981).

How many of the first wave of Hungarian immigrants were actually Hungarian speakers is not very easy to establish either. The interpretation of U.S. census data is complicated by several factors. Pre-1920 data on immigrants born in Hungary include non-Hungarian-speaking minorities in the Greater Hungary before the Treaty of Trianon: the last pre-Trianon census, in 1910, recorded the population of Hungary as comprising only 54% Hungarians, and the rest as minorities (16.1% Romanians, 10.7% Slovaks, 10.4% Germans, 3.6% Serbs and Croats, 2.5% Ruthenians, and 2.2% of other nationalities, Dávid 1988:343). According to various estimates, between 380 and 458 thousand immigrants from Hungary in the peak years of 1899–1913 were Hungarian-speaking (estimates by Benkart 1980:465; Puskás 1982, respectively; Puskás's figure quoted in Tezla 1993:18). Post-1920 census numbers on immigrants from Hungary, in turn, present a different problem: they do not contain all Hungarian-speaking immigrants, since now some of them came from countries with large Hungarian minorities such as Romania. United States censuses had questions on country of birth all throughout the era when Hungarian immigrants have been present in the United States. They did not, however, contain questions about ethnic ancestry and language spoken at home until 1980.

Of the pre-1920 Hungarian-speaking immigrants, about two-thirds were men, most under 30. They went to work in the coal mines and steel mills of the then heavily industrial region south of the Great Lakes, in Pennsylvania, Ohio, West Virginia, northern Illinois and Indiana, as well as to New York, New Jersey, and Connecticut and other northeastern states. Because they originally sought only temporary employment, they typically lived in boardinghouses and were quick to move if better work opportunities presented themselves elsewhere in the region. (For an insightful study of early 20th century boardinghouse life, see Vázsonyi 1978.)

World War I and the 1920 Treaty of Trianon, however, changed the plans of many of the immigrants who had intended to go back to Hungary. Under the treaty, Hungary lost over two-thirds of its territory to Romania, Austria, the newly created Czechoslovakia, and the Kingdom of Serbs, Croats and Slovenes, and, with the territories, also lost was one-third of its Hungarian-speaking population (as well as 90% of its ethnolinguistic minorities). Many of the sojourner type of immigrants in the United States now had their homes and native villages where they had been planning to buy land in foreign countries where they did not want to reside.

In the first two decades of the 20th century, Hungarians settled primarily in the northeast of the United States. The highest concentration of Hungarians, according to the 1920 Census (quoted in Bako 1962:12–13), was in Ohio, Pennsylvania, and New York (between 80 and 100 thousand per state), followed by Illinois (with somewhere between 40 and 50 thousand), Michigan (between 25 and 30 thousand), and Wisconsin and Indiana (10–15 thousand in each). By this time, Hungarians were found in every state of the U.S. Many Hungarian colonies and settlements were formed in and around New York City, Cleveland, Pittsburgh, Philadelphia, Detroit, Chicago, as well as in other places like South Bend and Gary, Indiana; Bridgeport, Connecticut; Youngstown and Akron, Ohio; Newark, Trenton, Passaic, and New Brunswick, New Jersey; and St. Louis, Missouri. (For an ethnographic account of two typical immigrant life stories, see Dégh 1972.) Even after they decided to stay, the formerly mostly peasant Hungarians remained in the industrial regions of the great lakes and the north-east rather than purchase land and take up farming. One notable exception is the strawberry-farming Hungarian community of Árpádhon (later renamed Hammond), Louisiana (see Mocsary 1990 for a historical account, Romero 1989 for a short ethno-graphic description, Dégh 1980 for a gripping folkloric analysis, and Böröcz 1987 for a linguistic analysis of Árpádhon Hungarian-Americans' last names).

After the introduction of the Quota System in 1924, sojourner type immigration ceased to exist, and all East European immigration was severely cut. In the years lead-ing up to World War II, about 15 thousand Hungarians immigrated to the U.S. in all (Benkart 1980:465). They were socially very different from the earlier immigrants: most were middle-class professionals, who, like the professionals of later waves of im-migrants, typically did not settle in the communities of working-class Hungarians but went wherever they found their own livelihood.

Between 1948 and 1952, about 16 thousand Hungarians came to the United States under the Displaced Persons Act of 1948 and as refugees of Hungary's communist regime (Fishman 1966:13). They usually came in family units and were educated pro-fessionals as well as upper class Hungarians. Traditionally, this wave of immigrants is referred to by other Hungarian-Americans as the "D.P.'s". For a detailed, albeit old-fashioned, account of notable Hungarians of this as well as earlier waves of immigrants, see Wass de Czege (1975), whereas for a discussion of designations referring to the various waves of immigrants used by Hungarian-Americans, see Kontra and Nehler (1981a).

After the failed 1956 anti-communist revolution, about 200 thousand people left Hungary – most of them males between the ages of 18 and 25, three-quarters of them urban. About 42 thousand of these "56-ers" (or "freedom-fighters", as they are also called in Hungarian-American communities) immigrated to the United States (Fish-man 1966:14), 3,000 students among them (Széplaki 1975:33). Many of those of working class background and some professionals settled in the traditional Hungarian-American settlements and neighborhoods, while the majority of the professionals and students settled dispersed all around the United States.

Beginning with the late 1950s, immigration from Hungary to the United States (or, for that matter, elsewhere) was minimal because of Hungary's limitations on travel abroad – roughly 5 thousand new immigrants from Hungary came to the U.S. in the 1960s (Széplaki 1975:128). The 1970s and 1980s brought an easing of travel restrictions and larger numbers of immigrants to the United States: 17.5 thousand im-migrants came in the 1980s (*1990 Census*). The collapse of communism in 1989 in Hungary brought an end to the acceptance of political reasons for immigration by US authorities. (The number of Hungarian immigrants in the 1990s is not available yet as Census 2000 figures have not all been released.)

2.2 Demographics and geography[1]

In 2000, of the 281 million population of the United States, slightly under a million and a half (specifically, 1,398,724 people) professed to be of Hungarian ancestry: 904,662 of them specified it as what in the census terminology is defined as "first ancestry", i.e. as the "single ancestry" "Hungarian" or the first part of a "double ancestry" like "Hungarian and Italian" or "Hungarian-Italian", and 494,062 people gave "Hungarian" as their "second ancestry", i.e. as the second part of a double ancestry like "Croatian and Hungarian" or "Croatian-Hungarian". (For definitions of census terms, see Bureau of the Census 1983:6.) These and corresponding figures from 1990 can be seen in Table 9.2.

Table 9.2. People of Hungarian ancestry in the U.S. in 1990 and 2000

Year	Total number of people of Hungarian ancestry	Hungarians of first ancestry (% of total*)	Hungarians of second ancestry (% of total*)
1990	1,582,302	997,545 (63%)	584,757 (37%)
2000	1,398,724	904,662 (65%)	494,062 (35%)

* Percentages are my calculations.

Because sums of figures on various total ancestries in the census contain some people twice (namely, those who reported double ancestries are counted both under their first and second ancestries), most of the detailed figures (e.g. on income, education, etc.) for a given ancestry group are given in the census according to first ancestry. However, some, like figures of the geographical distribution of Hungarians in the United States (see below) are given according to total ancestry.

In 2000, Hungarian-Americans were the 21st largest ancestry group in the United States, out of the total of 106 ancestry designations used in Census 2000, and the 16th largest of the 51 ancestry groups of European origin. They constituted the third largest ethnic population of Eastern European origin after people of Polish and Russian descent (see Table 9.3).

As far as the people who gave "Hungarian" as their language spoken at home, the 2000 census gave their number as almost 118 thousand (specifically, 117,973). (The corresponding figure for 1990 is 147,902.) This is 13.04% of all people of first Hungarian ancestry, i.e. only 13% of people of Hungarian ancestry in the United States actually used Hungarian at home in 2000. (Data on what percentage of foreign-born vs. US-born Hungarians used Hungarian at home in 2000 are not available yet.) The corresponding, 1990 figures for foreign-born vs. US-born Hungarian-Americans are given in Table 9.4: as we can see, 70% of the immigrants and only roughly 7% of US-born (i.e. second- or third-generation) Hungarian-Americans used Hungarian at home in 1990.

At this point, again, census figures have to be interpreted with caution in establishing the true number of Hungarian-speakers. The census figures above show that 70% of all foreign-born immigrants speak Hungarian "at home" and almost 30% of

Table 9.3. Total numbers of people of various Eastern European ancestries in the United States in 2000

Ancestry*	Number of people
Polish	6,290,993
Russian	2,149,673
Hungarian	904,662
Czech	808,825
Ukrainian	622,491
Slovak	514,943
Lithuanian	427,603
Yugoslavian	288,513
Romanian	272,513
Czechoslovakian	268,677
Croatian	258,509
Slovene	124,595
Albanian	109,910
Serbian	98,648
Slavic	74,980
Latvian	74,012
Bulgarian	54,682
Estonian	16,863
Carpatho-Rusyn	7,895
Eastern European	287,040

* Ancestry designations are given as they appear in the census.

Table 9.4. Foreign born vs. US-born Hungarians by first ancestry vs. speaking Hungarian at home, in 1990

	Foreign born	US born	Total
Hungarians who speak Hungarian at home	87,024	60,878	147,902
(% of all Hungarians by first ancestry*)	(70.37%)	(6.97%)	(14.82%)
Total of Hungarians by first ancestry	123,657	873,888	997,545

* Percentages are my calculations.

all the immigrants from Hungary do not. For some of them (especially those who immigrated as very small children with their parents) this might conceivably mean that they actually do not speak Hungarian at all. However, it is probably highly unlikely that all 30% of the immigrants from Hungary do not speak any Hungarian. Thus, it has to be assumed that the number must include Hungarians who use Hungarian but not at home (e.g. those married to non-Hungarian speakers and thus not speaking Hungarian at home but using it, for instance, with friends) and who, thus, simply do not appear in the census as Hungarian-speakers.

   If we compare the population speaking Hungarian at home with other populations speaking Eastern European languages at home, Hungarian is the fourth largest Eastern

Table 9.5. Eastern European languages spoken in the U.S. in 1990 by order among largest 50 languages

Order among 50	Language	Number of speakers	Population by ancestry	% of speakers in ancestry population
7	Polish	723,483	6,542,844	11.06%
15	Russian	241,798	2,114,506	11.44%
16	Yiddish	213,064	*	
22	Hungarian	147,902	997,545	14.83%
27	Ukrainian	96,568	514,085	18.78%
28	Czech	92,485	772,087	11.98%
32	Slovak	80,388	1,210,652	6.64%
34	Serbo-Croatian	70,964	*	
36	Rumanian	65,265	235,774	27.68%
37	Lithuanian	55,781	526,089	10.60%
41	Croatian	45,206	409,458	11.04%

* Data not provided in the 1990 Census.

European language spoken in the United States according to the 1990 Census (Census 2000 figures are not yet available) after Polish, Russian, and Yiddish (see Table 9.5).

Hungarian-Americans, with their 14.83% of home-speakers of Hungarian ranked about average compared to their total population as compared with the other Eastern European language speakers in 1990.

As far as their geographical distribution in the United States is concerned, Hungarian-Americans are found in all 50 states, in various concentrations and numbers. Table 9.6 gives their numbers, by state, as found in Census 2000, together with figures on changes in the Hungarian-American population since 1980 and 1990. (Note that the census takes Hungarian-Americans of both first and second ancestries into account in this case.) Map 9.1 traces them on the map of the United States.

As we can see, most Hungarian-Americans are still found in the states where the immigrants of the early 20th century first settled in great numbers: the top thirteen states contain all nine of the original states with the most Hungarian population, New York, Ohio, Pennsylvania, New Jersey, Illinois, Michigan, Connecticut, Indiana, and Wisconsin. Among these latter are also the six states (Ohio, New York, Pennsylvania, New Jersey, Michigan, and Illinois) that lost most Hungarian-Americans during the 1980s and 1990s – most likely the sign of the aging and dying of the oldest Hungarian-Americans in these states.

Table 9.6. The Hungarian-American population of the United States, by state, 2000

State	2000	Difference since 1990	Difference since 1980	State	2000	Difference since 1990	Difference since 1980
				(continued)			
OH	193,951	−24,194	−49,281	SC	7,953	+1,842	+3,882
NY	137,029	−49,869	−107,643	KY	6,499	+2,439	+872
CA	133,988	−25,133	−30,915	LA	4,625	−1,097	−2,005
PA	132,184	−20,679	−71,101	NM	4,331	−6	+836
NJ	115,615	−26,012	−52,885	AK	3,977	−140	+2,443
MI	98,036	−11,142	−28,783	KS	3,903	−155	−1,219
FL	96,885	−2,937	+7,298	DE	3,886	+418	+484
IL	55,971	−12,468	−28,671	NH	3,784	−309	+394
CT	40,836	−8,672	−12,615	OK	3,626	−171	−965
IN	35,715	−5,113	−8,597	IO	3,366	−344	−1,517
TX	30,234	−1,650	+2,270	UT	3,306	+362	+667
VA	25,783	+605	+3,479	MT	3,250	+500	+121
WI	23,945	−1,440	−9,179	VT	3,058	−44	+484
AZ	23,571	+1,138	+4,372	ME	2,906	−328	+519
MD	22,941	−3,785	−4,960	ND	2,802	−203	−1,489
WA	18,590	+1,793	+2,705	NE	2,740	−578	−1,712
MA	18,427	−1,562	−1,695	ID	2,672	+217	+798
CO	18,411	+1,550	+2,619	AR	2,309	+9	−135
NC	16,100	+3,351	+7,028	AL	2,238	+38	−2,242
GA	15,293	+1,874	+5,416	RI	2,127	−774	−439
MO	13,694	−1,149	−5,123	HI	2,104	−527	−190
MN	12,279	−70	−3,384	DC	2,048	−470	−452
OR	11,265	+489	+357	MS	1,843	+381	+49
NV	10,285	+3,185	+4,359	WY	1,561	+187	+145
WV	7,477	−1,771	−4,080	SD	982	−379	−836
TN	8,323	+974	+2,340	Total	1,398,724	−181,819	−378,178

2.3 Economic standing and social integration

The early 20th century immigrants from Hungary, i.e. the "old-timers", as they were called, were mostly of agricultural and working class background. Várdy (1989b: 222–223) calculates that, for instance, in the peak years of 1905–1907 of immigration, 17% were smallholders, 51.6% landless peasants, 9.5% day laborers, 5.2% household servants of peasant background, and 11.3% unskilled industrial workers, thus totaling 94.6% of all immigrants. These immigrants, as has been mentioned before, started working in mines, steel mills and factories in the United States, that is, became part of the working class.

Later waves of immigrants, such as those immigrating in the second half of the 1920s and in the 1930s, the DP's, and the 56-ers, were of a different economic background than the old-timers. They were predominantly professionals such as lawyers, engineers, teachers, physicians, and business people. The wave of DP's also contained Hungarian aristocrats and other members of the upper class.

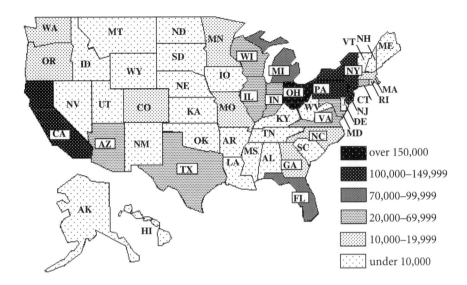

Map 9.1. Hungarian-Americans by state in 2000

By the end of the 20th century, the Hungarian-American population of the United States came to closely resemble the national average as far as occupation, income, and level of education is concerned (see Tables 9.7, 9.8 and 9.9). As reflected in Table 9.7, there is a slightly higher than average percentage of Hungarian-Americans in managerial and professional occupations, and a slightly lower than average percentage in service occupations, in "farming, forestry and fishing", and in "operators, fabricators, and laborers". Income levels (Table 9.8) are somewhat higher among Hungarian-Americans than in the average population. As far as their educational level is concerned, Hungarian-Americans have an overall somewhat higher level of education than the average U.S. population (Table 9.9).

As far as occupation, income and level of education can be treated as indicators of social integration, the above discussed figures show that Hungarian-Americans are fully integrated into mainstream U.S. society.

Linguistic integration into the mainstream society, that is, proficiency in English, is generally considered an important factor of social integration in the United States (cf. Grosjean 1982:66). Census figures show that Hungarian-Americans are linguistically well integrated into English-speaking life in the United States. As I have shown in the discussion of numbers quoted in Table 9.4 above, only 15% of all Hungarian-Americans speak Hungarian at home. In fact, as little as 7% of those born in the United States (that is, the second- and third-generation people) speak Hungarian at home, and we can probably safely assume that a lot of those who do not speak it at home do not speak it at all, i.e. they are monolingual English speakers.

As far as the English proficiency of those Hungarian-Americans is concerned who speak Hungarian in their homes, almost two-thirds (65%) professed to speak English

Table 9.7. Hungarian-Americans and total U.S. population by occupation, 1990

	Hungarian-Americans Numbers	%	Total U.S. population Numbers	%
Employed persons 16 years and over	509,364	100	115,681,202	100
Managerial and professional	177,096	34.8	30,533,582	26.4
Technical, sales, and administrative	170,128	33.4	36,718,398	31.7
Service	48,915	9.6	15,295,917	13.2
Farming, forestry, and fishing	5,044	1	2,839,010	2.5
Production, craft, and repair	56,953	11.2	13,097,963	11.3
Operators, fabricators, and laborers	51,228	10.1	17,196,332	14.9

Table 9.8. Hungarian-Americans and total U.S. population by income, 1990

	Hungarian-Americans	Total U.S. population
Median household income	$35,200	$30,056
Median family income	$42,778	$35,225
Per capita income	$20,606	$14,420

Table 9.9. Hungarian-Americans and total U.S. population by level of education, 1990

	Hungarian-Americans	Total U.S. population
Persons 25 years and over	735,880 (100%)	158,868,436 (100%)
High school graduate or higher	594,720 (80.8%)	119,524,718 (75.2%)
Bachelor's degree or higher	197,114 (26.8%)	32,310,253 (20.3%)
Graduate degree or higher	84,265 (11.5%)	11,477,686 (7.2%)

very well (see Table 9.10) in 1990. As the table shows, Hungarian-speakers rank in English proficiency above the U.S. average population of non-English speakers while ranking exactly in the middle among the eleven Eastern-European languages for which comparable data is available. (Interestingly, Hungarian-speakers have the most similar English-speaking profile to Croatian-speakers – the group that was economically and socially most similar to them among the peoples of the Austro-Hungarian Empire.) Only slightly more than 1,100 people, or 0.77% of the 148 thousand Hungarian-speakers, do not speak English at all.

Supporting evidence concerning these figures is presented in a study on Hungarian immigrants' English proficiency, DeKeyser (2000). He found that 39% of his 57 subjects professed to be more comfortable in Hungarian than in English, 35% said they were more comfortable in English, while 26% said it made no difference.

Other tendencies showing linguistic and social integration of Hungarian-Americans are ways of Anglicizing personal names (through respelling or translation) among immigrants and giving English first names and middle names to their children. For full details, see Kontra (1990–1995).

Table 9.10. Hungarian-speaking Hungarians-Americans compared to speakers of other Eastern European languages and all U.S. non-English speakers according to English proficiency, 1990

Population	Speaks English			
	% very well	% well	% not well	% not at all
All non-English	56.10	22.96	15.16	5.79
Slovak	72.54	20.30	6.85	0.31
Yiddish	71.05	20.75	7.24	0.96
Czech	70.64	23.18	5.86	0.36
Lithuanian	69.51	21.39	8.64	0.46
Croatian	66.34	24.25	8.65	0.75
Hungarian	65.04	25.61	8.58	0.77
Ukrainian	63.12	23.32	12.29	1.28
Polish	62.97	23.43	11.79	1.81
Serbo-Croatian	61.02	25.57	11.79	1.62
Rumanian	51.41	31.15	13.67	3.77
Russian	45.64	27.35	20.83	6.18
Eastern-Europeans, average*	63.57	24.21	10.56	1.66

* My calculations based on the above figures

2.4 Domains of minority language use

Sociolinguistic information on the domains of the use of Hungarian among Hungarian-Americans is available in four detailed linguistic studies on Hungarian-Americans, Kontra (1990), Bartha (1993), Fenyvesi (1995a), and Polgár (2001). All four of these studies targeted communities that were established in the first decades of the 20th century by the "old-timers" and where immigrants of later waves also settled, although somewhat sporadically: these were South Bend, Indiana; Detroit, Michigan; McKeesport, Pennsylvania (just outside of Pittsburgh); and Toledo, Ohio; respectively. The social and sociolinguistic profiles of these communities are very similar, and they present a largely unified picture of the domains of Hungarian language use.

The five domains of language use identified by Greenfield (1968) and used by Fishman (1972b) as basic in the analysis of multilingual speech communities are home, friendship, religion, education, and employment. Of these five, only the first three – home, friendship and religion – are characterized by the use of Hungarian in present-day Hungarian-American communities. The last two – education and employment – typically, involved some use of Hungarian in the earlier days of these communities, but not any more.

As Kontra (1990: 25–27), Bartha (1993: 64–74), Fenyvesi (1995a: 3), and Polgár (2001: 16–28) unanimously report, in the communities studied by them, Hungarian is used primarily with family members and with friends. It is used almost exclusively with parents and grandparents, often with spouses, and rarely with children. Language use with spouses is linguistically mixed, English or Hungarian, due to mixed marriages, but also because earlier second-generation Hungarian-Americans (i.e. the children of old-timers) tend to speak English with their spouses if married to another member of the second generation but Hungarian if married to an immigrant. The children of these marriages nowadays tend to understand a little Hungarian but not speak it fluently. Hungarian-Americans usually use both Hungarian and English with their friends: Hungarian is used especially if the interaction involves two immigrants, less if it occurs between an immigrant and a second-generation person, and typically English is used between second-generation friends. Hungarian language use tends to be absent with neighbors since by the end of the 20th century the once fairly homogeneous Hungarian-American communities have become mixed, and most of the Hungarian-Americans themselves have moved out to other places and are now tied together solely by ethnic institutions like Hungarian churches and clubs rather than a shared neighborhood. Hungarian clubs organize community activities offering an opportunity to speak Hungarian. Favorites are social events like dinners and dances: *szüreti bál* 'grape harvest dance' in McKeesport and Toledo, *disznótoros* 'pig-killing' dinners in Toledo, Hungarian picnics in Detroit and McKeesport, *Szt. Anna bál* 'St. Anne day dinner and dance' and the Ethnic Festival in South Bend, a Hungarian Festival in Detroit and McKeesport, and other such occasions. In comparison, the (more formal) meetings of the William Penn Association (formerly called Verhovay) and the Hungarian Reformed Federation, both fraternal beneficiary associations, are typically run in English in Detroit and McKeesport. No institutions such as Hungarian-speaking restaurants or bars are reported in the four places except for Charley's Tavern in South Bend, run now by the largely English-speaking son of the founder and one unpopular Hungarian restaurant in Toledo. (For an analysis of the role of noodlemaking by older Hungarian-American women in the lives of ethnic communities, see Huseby-Darvas 1991/1992.)

The domain of religion is mixed Hungarian- and English-speaking. Of the South Bend Hungarian churches reported on by Kontra (1990: 125), only one Roman Catholic church offered regular services in Hungarian. Bartha (1993: 66) mentions one Reformed church with regular services. In McKeesport there is one weekly Hungarian service in the Hungarian Reformed Church. In Toledo, the Hungarian Roman Catholic church no longer has a resident Hungarian speaking pastor, only one who visits once every two weeks from Detroit (Polgár 2001: 18).

Education and employment are domains where exclusively English is used now. Education, for the most part, has always been an English-speaking domain for Hungarian-Americans. With the exception of a Hungarian school operated by the Hungarian church from 1907 to 1970 in Detroit (Bartha 1993: 65), the only Hungarian language school experience typically available for Hungarian-American children was in summer schools organized by Hungarian speaking priests and ministers where they taught catechism and basic information about Hungarian history and culture, all in Hungarian. All second-generation speakers in McKeesport, for instance, took part in courses like this as they were growing up in the 1930s and 1940s. These days, however, even in parishes where there is a Hungarian-speaking minister or priest, Sunday school is conducted in English since the attendees typically do not speak Hungarian at all. One existing source of education in Hungarian is provided by Hungarian-speaking Boy Scouts (*cserkészet*), but these, because of the geographic dispersion of Hungarian-Americans, are usually summer programs only. Hungarian as a foreign language courses were offered in a dozen universities in the United States in 1995 (LSA 1995:181), but these usually attract students of non-Hungarian descent interested in the language for academic reasons rather than Hungarian-Americans.

As for the domain of employment, the status quo is very similar to education. Many of the people interviewed for the studies reported at one time or another (typically up until the late 1960s) being able to use Hungarian at the workplace with Hungarian-speaking co-workers at the steel mill or other workplaces. This is, however, no longer the case except for only two of the 24 people interviewed by Polgár in Toledo (2001:27). For a more detailed analysis of the domains of Hungarian language use in the Detroit community, see Bartha 1995/1996; for a comprehensive, anthropologist's account of Hungarian American ethnic life in Michigan, see Huseby-Darvas 2003.

As for the written use of Hungarian, all four studies report on the writing of private letters to relatives in Hungary as the sole domain where Hungarian is used. All four studies also report on the reading of Hungarian language papers (mostly those published in the United States) by Hungarian-Americans. The most recent of the four studies, Polgár (2001:24) also indicates that the internet, specifically, web versions of Hungarian newspapers and magazines might also be becoming a factor supporting language maintenance efforts. She mentions that one of her immigrant subjects is a regular visitor of the homepage of *Nők Lapja* "Women's Magazine", the most popular women's weekly magazine in Hungary.

2.5 Language maintenance and shift, and factors affecting these

Immigrant groups of European origin in the United States are generally regarded as undergoing very rapid language shift, usually complete in three generations (cf. Grosjean 1982:102–107; Paulston 1994:13; Hamp 1994:4838–4839). It seems that Hungarian-Americans present a typical case in this respect: unlike in some other European immigrant groups (such as, for example, Greek-Americans, Seaman 1972:21, and Finnish-Americans, Hirvonen 1998) where third-generation speakers of the immigrant language are found, no studies on Hungarian-Americans to date have found speakers of Hungarian beyond the second generation.

It is generally held that there is no single set of factors that can predict whether minority language maintenance or language shift to the majority language will be the outcome of the bilingualism of a linguistic minority. Summarizing findings of various authors investigating language maintenance and shift, Mesthrie (1994:1989–1990) lists the following groups of factors as influential: demographic factors, economic factors, institutional support, and status of the minority language.

Demographic factors such as the size (the absolute size of a minority community as well as its size relative to the dominant group) and distribution of a minority group have always tilted the maintenance vs. shift equation towards shift in the case of Hungarian-Americans. Even though Hungarians arrived in great numbers in the early decades of the 20th century, they still were relatively small groups: in the peak decades of immigration, the 1910s and 1920s, the 460 thousand and 400 thousand Hungarian immigrants then living in the United States constituted less than 4% of the European immigrants, and less than 3% of all the immigrants (Gibson & Lennon 1999). Also, despite the fact that they settled in large numbers and established immigrant colonies, they lived next to groups of other Eastern-Europeans like Slovaks, Poles, and Serbs. Later, as we have seen, newer immigrants settled even more dispersed. After the 1956 revolution, even though immigration never completely ceased, it never again amounted to a real influx of new immigrants that could have meant a real infusion of Hungarian-speakers into the existing communities.

Economic factors often quoted to support shift are urbanization, industrialization and modernization. Almost exclusively, Hungarian-Americans have always been urban rather than rural, and the early wave almost entirely became industrial workers. The period after World War II, however, was not favorable for the industries that Hungarian-Americans worked in: the coal mines, the steel mills, and many factories (like the Studebaker car factory employing many South Bend Hungarians) closed. Large segments of the ethnic working-class populations from these areas (typically, those in their prime bread-winning years) moved elsewhere – thus further contributing to the dispersion of Hungarian-Americans.

Institutional support has been there in the Hungarian-American communities in the form of ethnic churches since the early decades of the 20th century, and, to a very small extent, in the form of education. In 1966, Fishman was able to report on a rather varied cultural life in the Hungarian-American community: 229 churches, 43 radio stations, 43 periodicals, and 459 other organizations (Fishman 1966:39). By the 1980s and 1990s, Hungarian language media was present only through some Hungarian language newspapers of national distribution, and Hungarian programs in local English-speaking radio stations. The studies referred to mentioned two one-hour programs each in South Bend, Detroit, and McKeesport, broadcasting community news and Hungarian music. (For an anthropological analysis of the role of Hungarian ethnic radio broadcasts in the maintenance of Hungarian-American ethnic identity, see Huseby 1984.)

The status of the language, as a factor in language maintenance or shift, is important in the sense that, everything else being equal, a written language is easier to maintain than an oral one, and, again, a language which constitutes a majority language elsewhere and is held in high esteem has a better chance of being maintained. As much as about 89% of the earliest, peasant immigrants of Hungarian background were literate (Várdy 1989b:232) – a rate actually relatively high for the early 20th century. Later immigrants tended to be of more educated backgrounds.

The picture that emerges is the following. The early decades of the 20th century show communities where language maintenance was possible. However, due to a combination of demographic, economic and institutional reasons, language shift has become dominant in the second half of the 20th century. This is what we see in the available linguistic studies as well: small remnants of communities left over in the old centers of Hungarian-American life, where the only Hungarian speakers left are the aging 56-ers and children of the old-timers, as well as some newer immigrants. At the same time, institutional support has provided an easy access to English through education and the mass media, while economic opportunities have presented upward mobility to all those immigrants assimilating to mainstream English-speaking life, also clearly contributing to language shift.

Official language policy in the United States, or rather the lack of it, has long supported the shift of immigrants to English "without either constitutional or subsequent legal declaration or requirement that English is the official [...] language" (Fishman 1981:517). It has tolerated although did not support immigrant minorities' mother tongue use until the 1960s, and the lack of support for bilingual education meant that the existing education with English as a sole medium of instruction was one of the main forces of linguistic assimilation. The Bilingual Education Act of 1968, providing financial support for bilingual education, came too late for Hungarian-Americans: by this time few if any children of limited English proficiency remained in concentrated numbers in their communities. Similarly, English-Only legislation, which has been instituted in various states since the 1980s, has not affected Hungarian-Americans very much, since, by this time, they have been well on their way to language shift into English.

3.   Linguistic aspects of Hungarian in the United States

3.1   Sources

In the description of the language of Hungarian-Americans I rely on the four detailed studies of Hungarian-American communities and their language discussed above, Kontra (1990), Bartha (1993), Fenyvesi (1995a), and Polgár (2001), as well as on Vázsonyi (1995), a dictionary of American Hungarian. The first three of the studies use the methodology of the sociolinguistic interview and the data they are based on is provided by taped and transcribed interviews with Hungarian-Americans. The interviews done by all three authors included guided conversations about the subjects' life histories, families, history and habits of Hungarian and English language use, and their linguistic attitudes towards the two languages. (For a typescript of a similar kind of interview – one carried out in English – with a Hungarian-American speaker, see Kontra & Nehler 1981b.) In addition to these, Kontra (1990) also used a picture description task aimed at eliciting modern everyday vocabulary in Hungarian, a shortened version of a traditional Hungarian dialectological questionnaire as well as short reading passages and word lists.

The sociolinguistic data concerning the subjects of Kontra's, Bartha's and Fenyvesi's studies thus came from the subject matter of the interviews, while the transcripts of the interviews constituted the corpus for linguistic analysis. Kontra (1990) used 80 hours of recordings with 40 South Bend subjects, Bartha (1993) over 20 hours of recordings with 15 Detroit subjects, and Fenyvesi (1995a) over 13 hours of recordings (or 242 typed pages of transcripts) with 20 McKeesport subjects.

Polgár used the questionnaire of the Sociolinguistics of Hungarian Outside Hungary project (see Kontra, this volume), which she modified very slightly to make it relevant to the situation of Hungarian-Americans. The questionnaire contains both sociolinguistic questions and questions containing language tasks aimed at various linguistic variables of Hungarian (for the translated version of the parts of the original SHOH questionnaire that contains the language tasks, see the Appendix). Polgár (2001) provided a sociolinguistic characterization of the Toledo Hungarians. Even though she elicited the paper-and-pen questionnaire while tape-recording the sessions with 24 subjects, these conversations are not yet transcribed. In the present section I rely on the results of the linguistic questions of her questionnaire, unanalyzed for her thesis.

In describing the lexicon of American Hungarian, I heavily rely on Vázsonyi (1995), a dictionary of this variety. The dictionary is based on the vocabulary used in the ethnographic interviews Andrew Vázsonyi and Hungarian-American ethnographer and folklorist Linda Dégh recorded in the 1960s in the Calumet region, southeast of Chicago.

Even though other large corpuses of recordings have also been collected for linguistic analysis, these never reached the stage of being transcribed and analyzed. About 150 hours of recordings were collected by Elemér Bakó (reported on by Kontra 1985:263; for a description of Bakó's own research agenda, see Bakó 1961, 1962). Kálmán (1970) and Falk-Bánó (1988) are preliminary reports on larger corpuses (of 16 and 54 hours of recordings, respectively), but, again, no studies reporting all of their findings have been published to date. Bartha also collected 180 hours' worth of interviews and about 25 hours' worth of conversation with 45 Hungarian-Americans in New Brunswick, New Jersey, in 1994 (Bartha 1999:46), but her findings of this comprehensive study have yet to be published. For details of pre-1985 linguistic research on Hungarian-Americans, see Kontra (1985).

3.2 A characterization of American Hungarian and its speakers

The fieldwork for the four studies and the dictionary that Section 3 of this paper draws on have all been conducted in traditional Hungarian-American communities, characterized by an interesting socioeconomic and cultural homogeneity. In addition to their social and economic homogeneity, these ethnic communities are surprisingly homogeneous culturally across the Great Lakes states. Because the main masses of the ethnic communities were of the little-educated classes, and because a sense of a national culture, Dégh (1996) argues, is established through education in school, these immigrants carried a loyalty mostly only to their own native local heritage, which, in the 'newly mixed' communities, constituted a diverse mixture of habits and customs from virtually all parts of Hungary. Also, Hungarian immigrants have mostly lived, although geographically close to, but in linguistic isolation from other East European immigrant groups (often retaining natural mistrust with their former ethnic neighbors from the Habsburg monarchy), as well as in cultural and political isolation from the old country. These factors together, Dégh argues, shaped what became the Hungarian-American identity and its new cultural manifestations, which appeared through the suppression of the diverse heritage and the emergence of a set of standardized and homogenized identity symbols as a kind of 'common denominator'.

This cultural and socioeconomic homogeneity permits us to treat Hungarian-Americans in these communities as members of the same community, and their speech from different places as the same variety, which, although it bears traces of different dialects in Hungary, is sociolinguistically unified. In this chapter, therefore, I treat samples of this American variety of Hungarian from South Bend, Indiana, Detroit, the Calumet region, McKeesport, Pennsylvania, and Toledo, Ohio, as belonging to the same variety.

Quite possibly, a study of a Hungarian-American community of a different sociohistorical background would provide different results. Bartha (1999:46–47) provides an indication of a different community in New Brunswick, New Jersey. Here Hungarian-Americans have retained a larger and socially more diverse population, with an educated elite of its own based at Rutgers University, and with several active institutions such as a Hungarian-American athletic club, a heritage center, and an alumni organization. The linguistic results are also different, according to Bartha: Hungarian is maintained to a much higher degree and even supported by purist language ideologies in the community. However, the comprehensive results of the New Brunswick study are not available yet.

In describing the unique features of American Hungarian (abbreviated as AH), I compare them with those of Hungarian as spoken in Hungary (HH), including dialectal and nonstandard features of HH.

Indeed, AH retains several features of specific Hungarian regional dialects (e.g. of the northwestern Győr-Sopron county dialect among South Bend speakers, Kontra 1990:44, 53, 103; and of the northeastern *szabolcs-szatmári* and *abaúji* dialects among McKeesport speakers, Fenyvesi 1995a:19–20, 60, 73).[2]

In addition, nonstandard features which more or less commonly occur in the speech of speakers in Hungary also occur frequently in AH speech.[3] The occurrence of such regional and social linguistic variables in AH has not been systematically studied in any study, and is, therefore, not discussed in this chapter. Their presence is, however, noted in studies of AH whenever the question might arise whether a feature of AH is attributable to the legacy of a dialectal feature of Hungarian.

Variability is present in AH speech in other ways as well, for instance, as intraspeaker variability, when speakers speak Hungarian with AH features sometimes and with HH features other times, depending on the interlocutor, the closeness of American English code-switches in the given discourse segment, or whether something is said early or later on in a Hungarian language conversation. (For an analysis of such variability in AH speech, see Kontra & Gósy 1988.) Despite both intraspeaker and interspeaker variability, however, it is still possible to identify typically AH features on all levels of linguistic structure as well as in the lexicon.

3.3 Borrowing

In identifying a feature of AH as a result of language contact with American English, I use Thomason and Kaufman's (1988:21) notion of borrowing, in the narrow sense of the "incorporation of foreign elements into the speakers' native language". Borrowing, in their framework, is change that occurs when the native language of the speakers (Hungarian, in this case) is influenced by another language. Shift-induced interference plays no role in the AH case because, according to the Thomason-Kaufman model, it comprises the effects of a substrate or adstrate language on a target language (here, American English) through imperfect learning during language shift. Borrowing includes both structural and lexical borrowing, that is, both phonetic, phonological, morphological, syntactic borrowing, and that of lexical items.

3.3.1   *Structural borrowing*
In this subsection I discuss contact-induced features of American-Hungarian phonetics, phonology, morphology, and syntax, relying mostly on Kontra (1990) and Fenyvesi (1995a).[4] What features of AH have been identified in the studies which this discussion is based on is heavily influenced by the methodology of their data collection. Because the South Bend, Detroit and McKeesport studies are based on the transcribed texts of sociolinguistic interviews where speakers provided conversational data, many structural characteristics of their speech went, most likely, undescribed simply because speakers did not produce, or did not have a chance to produce, or, perhaps, chose to avoid them during the interviews. Methodology of transcription has also had an influence on the description of phonological characteristics: for instance, because Kontra used an orthographic transcription of his data, he was not able to investigate the status of assimilation processes in AH speech except for one because most of the assimilation processes are not marked in Hungarian orthography.

   In all of the cases discussed in Subsection 3.2.1, AH borrows structural characteristics of American English.

3.3.1.1 *Phonetic and phonological features.* The presence of several phonetic and phonological features bearing the influence of American English have been documented in studies of AH.

3.3.1.1.1 Subphonemic features.   The most prominently noted subphonemic feature (i.e. one that does not introduce a new phoneme into the phonemic inventory of the language, only a new allophone) is the aspiration of syllable-initial voiceless stops /p, t, k/ in stressed syllables (as in 1 below). (HH has no aspiration at all.)

   (1)   AH [ˌtʰizɛnˈkilɛnts] 'nineteen' (McK, Gen2)[5]

Aspiration is reported primarily in the second-generation speakers' speech: both in South Bend and McKeesport, most of them employ aspiration, with different degrees of frequency among the individual speakers. Some first-generation speakers were found to aspirate some of the time in South Bend, but none were found to do so in McKeesport (Kontra 1990: 41–42; Fenyvesi 1995a: 16). The feature is also noted as present in the speech of Detroit speakers, but no details are given as to its frequency or distribution between speakers of different generations (Bartha 1993: 132).

The velarization of *l* (that is, the use of "dark *l*'s") is also a commonly noted characteristic of AH: in McKeesport, it occurs very rarely in immigrants' speech, but all second-generation subjects use it, some of them most of the time (Fenyvesi 1995a: 19); it occurs in Detroit, too, mostly in the speech of those who immigrated as children and/or went to school in the U.S. (Bartha 1993: 133); and it is also present in South Bend, Kontra 1990: 31):

(2)   AH ['zɛmpłeːn] 'Zemplén [name of a county]' (SB, Gen2)

The realization of the trill *r* as retroflex is noted in Kontra (1990: 45), Bartha (1993: 133), and Fenyvesi (1995a: 18): it occurs some of the time in the speech of about half of the second-generation subjects in McKeesport and only in a few instances in that of immigrants; in Detroit it occurs in the speech of those who also pronounce dark *l*'s; and it is also present in South Bend, e.g.:

(3)   AH ['ɻaːma] 'window pane' (SB, Gen2)

The diphthongization of the three long mid vowels /eː, øː, oː/ of Hungarian as [ej, øÿ, ow] is reported in the speech of South Bend and McKeesport speakers (Kontra 1990: 52–53; Fenyvesi 1995: 19–20, respectively). Diphthongs such as these occur in some regional dialects in Hungary, but the effect of these can be discounted in the case of South Bend speakers since none of the immigrant subjects nor the parents of second-generation subjects came from these dialect areas, but in both groups some speakers have them:

(4)   AH ['søÿłøÿ] 'grape' and [sejk] 'chair' (SB, Gen1 and Gen2, respectively)

In McKeesport, the effect of regional dialects cannot be discounted, since the parents of almost all of the second-generation speakers came from dialect areas with such diphthongs, and these speakers diphthongize these vowels all of the time. Immigrant speakers in McKeesport, however, do not diphthongize at all.

Tapping, the use of a voiced tap [ɾ] intervocalically in post-stress positions as an allophone of /t, d/, occurs occasionally in the speech of some speakers of either generation in South Bend (Kontra 1990: 51), and in that of some second-generation speakers in McKeesport (Fenyvesi 1995a: 17). (The tap only occurs in HH as a very restricted allophone of the trill *r*; Berney 1993: 17).

(5)   AH ['tʰuɾom] 'I know' (McK, Gen2) (vs. HH ['tudom])

Glottalization – specifically, here, the coarticulation of syllable-final *t* or *k* with a glottal stop – is a feature completely missing from HH. It occurs occasionally in the speech of one third of the McKeesport second-generation speakers and does not occur at all in the speech of the first generation:

(6)   AH ['veɪɛʔtɬɛnyɬ] 'accidentally' and ['soʔktak] 'they do [habitually]' (McK, Gen2)

It is important to note that glottalization occurs in the McKeesport data only with *t* and *k*, and not with *p*. The feature is not mentioned at all in Kontra 1990 for South Bend.

Unlike many languages, due to the opposition of short and long vowel phonemes, HH does not have a rule that lengthens short stressed vowels. In the McKeesport data, however, half of the second-generation speakers pronounce phonemically short vowels with a length identical to that of phonemically long vowels in stressed position, i.e. in initial syllables. (HH has initial word stress everywhere without exception, and in AH word-initial stress clearly prevails, although there are some exceptions to this; see Section 3.2.1.1.4 below).

(7)   AH ['tʰuːɾom] 'I know' and ['kʰiːtʃit] 'a little-ACC' (McK, Gen2)

3.3.1.1.2 Phonemic mergers.   AH contains a few cases of phonemic mergers, that is, cases where the realizations of a HH phoneme are identical to the realizations of another, already existing phoneme.

The phoneme /dʒ/ is very rare in HH: it occurs in loanwords, especially of Turkish and English origin, e.g. HH /'laːndʒa/ 'spear' and /dʒɛm/ 'jam', respectively. The phone [dʒ] also occurs as the result of the voicing of /tʃ/, as in /nintʃ##bɛnt/ ['nindʒbɛnt] 's/he is not in'.

In the McKeesport data, [dʒ] also occurs as the realization of /ɟ/ in all environments in the speech of two-thirds of the second-generation speakers (8). It occurs almost exclusively in the speech of half of all second-generation speakers, and alternates with [ɟ] for others. The affricate does not replace the palatal stop with one-third of the second-generation speakers or with any of the first-generation speakers. Kontra (1990:44–45) mentions the realization of /ɟ/ as [dʒ] in the speech of some second-generation speakers in reading word-lists.

(8)   AH ['dʒɛɾɛk] 'child' and ['hodʒ] 'how' (McK, Gen2)

In the McKeesport data there are also a couple of instances of the affricate realization as of /c/, the voiceless counterpart of /ɟ/:

(9)   AH ['kaːrtʃaːkat] 'cards-ACC' (McK, Gen2)

This is, however, very marginal and occurs very rarely in the speech of only two speakers (both of whom pronounce all /ɟ/ sounds [dʒ]).

Bartha (1993:132) also reports the frequent realization of the affricate /ts/ as [s], exclusively in the speech of second-generation speakers:

(10)   AH ['ɑrsɑ] 'his/her face' and ['sipøː] 'shoe' (Dt, Gen2)

3.3.1.1.3 Phonological processes.   The most prominently reported change in phonological processes in AH is degemination.

Geminates occur in HH obligatorily intervocalically, both word-internally and across word boundaries, but they are degeminated next to a consonant. In AH the situation is as follows with regard to geminates and degemination. First-generation speakers mostly retain their geminates (Kontra 1990:43–44; Bartha 1993:133; Fenyvesi 1995a:27–28). Variability is reported for second-generation speakers: some degeminate everywhere, while the rest degeminate most of the time, only occasionally retaining intervocalic geminates. The examples in (11–12) demonstrate degemination:

(11)   AH ['sylɛtɛk] 'they were born' (McK, Gen2) (vs. HH ['sylɛttɛk])

(12)   AH ['mɛni] 'to go' (Detroit and McK, Gen2) (vs. HH ['mɛnni])

According to Imre (1971a:269), the complete lack of geminates can be found in some small Hungarian dialect areas. Because of the rarity of the phenomenon in Hungary, and because none of the subjects or their ancestors come from these areas, the influence of Hungarian dialects in this feature can be discounted.

HH has an obligatory rule of voicing assimilation, according to which all obstruents agree in voicing with a following obstruent (except *v*) or *h*, word-internally or across a word boundary. In the McKeesport corpus all first-generation speakers fully retain this rule, whereas with all second-generation speakers it becomes optional: all of these speakers have variation in that they sometimes assimilate and sometimes do not (Fenyvesi 1995a:22–23):

(13)   ['mɛkhɑɫt] and ['mɛghɑɫt] 's/he died' (McK, Gen2)

A palatalization rule in HH coalesces /t, d, n, c, ɟ, ɲ/ and a following /j/ into the geminated palatalized series of the stops (e.g. /laːt+ja/ → ['laːcca] 's/he sees it'). This process is very common since several suffixes begin with a /j/. Another palatalization process completely assimilates an /l/ to a following /j/ (e.g. /'yl+j/ → ['yjj] 'sit [imperative]'); this assimilation is also very common, because of the frequency of the same /j/-initial endings. There are numerous instances in the McKeesport data where these two assimilation processes do not apply obligatorily in the second-generation speakers' speech. (They occur in the HH-like fashion in the speech of immigrants.) In the second generation, it does not occur at all in the speech of some subjects, occurs optionally in the speech of others, and occurs obligatorily in the speech of yet others. Palatalization does not occur in the following examples:

(14)   AH ['mɛnjynk] 'let's go' (McK, Gen2) (vs. HH ['mɛɲɲynk])

(15)   AH ['fojtatja] 's/he continues it' (McK, Gen2) (vs. HH ['fojtacca])

(16)   AH [ˈdyljøn] 'it should fall' (McK, Gen2) (vs. HH [ˈdyjjøn])

With the exception of some dialect areas (as well as a larger area in eastern Transylvania, Romania), HH has a very restricted obligatory assimilation rule involving *v*: the morpheme-initial *v* of the instrumental suffix *-val/vel* and of the translative suffix *-vá/vé* (but not of other *v*-initial suffixes) completely assimilates to the preceding stem-final consonant. In the McKeesport data (Fenyvesi 1995a:25–26), first-generation speakers assimilate *v*'s fully according to the HH rule. The second-generation speakers' data, however, contains several examples of the lack of *v*-assimilation (17). Only few speakers assimilate in all instances, some assimilate optionally, while the others never do.

(17)   AH [ˈmamaːmval] 'with my mother' and [vaʃval] 'with iron' (McK, Gen2)

This feature is present in the speech of second-generation South Bend speakers (Kontra 1990:73). (It is also reported for the Hungarian Israeli speaker reported to be undergoing language attrition in Vago (1991:247).) The effect of non-assimilating Hungarian dialects can probably be excluded, since none of the immigrant subjects or second-generation subjects' parents came from those areas.

3.3.1.1.4 Suprasegmental features.   As far as suprasegmental features are concerned, AH shows differences from HH in changes in word and phrasal stress as well as in intonation.

In HH stress is not phonemic; on the word level, it always occurs on the first syllable of a word. Both in South Bend and McKeesport there are numerous examples of noninitial stress reported (Kontra 1990:55–57; Fenyvesi 1995a:28–30), although wordinitial stress is definitely prevalent in the speech of all subjects. First-generation speakers have fewer instances of noninitial stress than second-generation speakers. Most of the examples are from compounds (compound numerals, preverb-verb compounds etc.).

Compound numerals receive their primary stress on the first syllable of the compound in HH. In the AH examples that diverge from this pattern, primary stress is placed on the second part of the compound, like it would be in English.

(18)   AH [ˌsaːzˈɛzɛr] 'a hundred thousand' (McK, Gen2)
(19)   AH [ˌhusonˈɛɟ] 'twenty-one' (SB, Gen2)

Verbs preceded by a preverb are – with the exception of cases involving a special kind of emphasis – always pronounced as a phonological word in HH, with the only stress on the first syllable, i.e. on the preverb. In the AH data examples that deviate from this rule, stress is placed on the first syllable of the verb stem in most of the examples, similar to stress placement in a prefixed verb in English (20–21):

(20)   AH [ˌlɛˈiːrni] 'to write it down' (SB, Gen2)
(21)   AH [ˌvisaˈbɛseːlni] 'to talk back' (McK, Gen2)

In a small number of examples, stress is noninitial, but either placed on the second syllable of the preverb (22) or on another syllable which is word-internal for the verb (23 – the preverbs are *alá* 'under' and *fel* 'up', respectively):

(22)   AH [ˌɒlˈaːtɛteːk] 'they put it under it' (McK, Gen2)

(23)   AH [ˌfɛlɛˈmɛltɛ] 's/he lifted it up' (McK, Gen2)

In other compound words where stress was not placed on the first syllable, it occurred on the first syllable of the second half of the compound in all of the cases.

(24)   AH [ˌmɒɟɒrˈorsaːgon] 'in Hungary' [lit. 'in Hungarian-country] (McK, Gen2)

Both in the South Bend and McKeesport data there are numerous examples where the stress within a phrase (noun phrase, verb phrase, or postpositional phrase) is different from what it would be in HH (Kontra 1990: 57–58; Fenyvesi 1995a: 30–32). This feature is found in the speech of all speakers, regardless of generation. The following kinds of phrases show distinctions between HH and AH stress: NPs involving an adjective or quantifier, and phrases with negatives.

Within the HH noun phrase containing a preceding adjective or quantifier, both the adjective or quantifier and the noun receive primary stress (Varga 1975: 32). AH speakers often stress phrases in an English-like manner, placing primary stress on the noun and secondary stress on the preceding adjective or quantifier:

(25)   AH [ˌʃokpʰejnzɛt] 'a lot of money.ACC' (McK, Gen2)

(26)   AH [ˌnɒɟˈɟaːr] 'big factory' (SB, Gen1)

The second kind of phrase, with negation, always receives primary stress on the negative element only, in HH (Varga 1975: 38, 49) (27), unless it is a verb phrase with a tensed verb (usually carrying an auxiliary-like function) and an infinitival complement; in the latter case both the negative element and the infinitive get primary stress, while the tensed verb is unstressed (28).

(27)   HH /nɛm##ɛz##a##vaːroʃ/ → [ˈnɛmɛzavaːroʃ] 'not this city'

(28)   HH /nɛm##tud##iːrni/ → [ˈnɛmtudiːrni] 's/he cannot write'

In the South Bend and McKeesport corpuses these kinds of phrases are the most common source of stress deviation from HH: typically the negative element receives secondary stress and the negated noun, adverbial (29), finite verb, or, the infinitive (30), gets primary stress:

(29)   AH /nɛm##ittɛn/ → [ˌnɛmˈittɛn] 'not here' (SB, Gen2)

(30)   AH / nɛm##tudott##iːrni / → [ˌnɛmtudotˈiːrni] 'she couldn't write'
       (McK, Gen2)

As far as the intonation of AH is concerned, the most prominently noted feature is a different yes/no-question intonation than in HH, although Kontra (1990: 60–67) discusses other intonation features as well, such as an English-like AH mid–high–low statement intonation where HH has falling intonation, and an AH fall–rise intonation in running accounts where, again, HH has falling intonation.

HH yes/no-question intonation rises on the penultimate syllable of the question and falls on the last syllable. AH, on the other hand, has been reported to have widespread English-like rising intonation. In South Bend, Kontra (1990:60) finds it a frequent phenomenon, and in McKeesport it is also reported as present in almost all speakers' speech, regardless of generation (Fenyvesi 1995a:32–33). Typical instances of such intonation are as follows:

(31)   AH *Nem nehéz?* (SB, Gen2) vs. HH *Nem nehéz?*
         'Isn't it hard?'

(32)   AH *Voltál már ott?* (McK, Gen 2) vs. HH *Voltál már ott?*
         'Have you been there yet?'

In 1993 Kontra studied this phenomenon further in South Bend in great detail (playing the game "20 questions" with his subjects as well as having them ask him about Hungary and read out yes/no-questions), but the results of his study have not been published yet (cf. Kontra 1995a).

3.3.1.1.5 Morphophonemic processes: Vowel harmony

As is well known, Hungarian has vowel harmony, i.e. restrictions on what vowels can co-occur within stems and across boundaries between stems and inflectional or derivational suffixes. (Vowel harmony does not operate between stems in compounding or the formation of preverb–verb units.) Basically, the restrictions disallow the mixing of front and back vowels (backness harmony) and require a front rounded suffix after a front rounded vowel in the stem if there is one available (roundness harmony). For a comprehensive description of the rules of Hungarian vowel harmony, see Kenesei et al. (1998:420–425).

AH speech has been reported to violate rules of HH vowel harmony (Kontra 1990:53–55, 69–70; Fenyvesi 1995a:35–39). In a smaller proportion of these cases of violation, disharmonic inflections are used, whereas in a much greater number of cases it is derivational suffixes that are used disharmonically. Disharmonic inflections (33–34) tend to occur in the speech of second-generation speakers, whereas disharmonic derivational suffixes both in their speech and that of immigrants.

(33)   AH *Feri-hoz* (SB, Gen2) (vs. HH *Ferihez*)[6]
         Feri-ALL
         'to Frank'

(34)   AH *ismerős-ek-et* (McK, Gen2) (vs. HH *ismerősöket*)
         acquaintance-PL-ACC
         'acquaintances'

Disharmonic derivational suffixes occur frequently in AH. Both the studies quoted above and Vázsonyi (1995) contain many examples. Kontra (1990:69) quotes examples where the same borrowed English verb is sometimes used with a harmonizing suffix and other times with a disharmonic one: AH *szpell-ez-ik* 's/he spells' ~ *szpell-ol-ni* 'to spell', and AH *missz-ül-öm* 'I miss' ~ *missz-ol-ok* 'I miss'.[7] In the McKeesport data there are some examples of borrowed verbs receiving disharmonic derivational suffixes where the borrowed HH form of the same verb is harmonizing: AH *teszt-ol-ni* vs. HH *teszt-el-ni* 'to test', and AH *print-ol-va* vs. HH *print-el-ve* 'printed [participial form]'. Of the 203 verb entries in Vázsonyi (1995), 77 (38%) contain disharmonic derivational suffixes, e.g. *báderez* 'bother', *cséndzsol* 'change', *elsippol* 'ship', *felpikkol* 'pick up', *felszlejszol* 'slice up', *keccsol* 'catch', *klínol* 'clean', *meridol* 'to marry', *mikszol* 'mix', *misszol* 'miss', *rejdol* 'ride', *rentol* 'rent', *reszpektol* 'respect', *resztol* 'rest', *sévol* 'shave', *szpelol* 'spell', *szpendol* 'spend', *szpréol* 'spray'. The majority of these disharmonic verbs, 73 of the 77, receive disharmonic back suffixes, and only 4 disharmonic front suffixes. Borrowed verbs with disharmonic back suffixes exist in HH, too, but certainly in a much lower proportion than 36% of all borrowed verbs. In comparison, an informal survey of HH speakers in 1994 showed that they used many computer-related verbs borrowed from English in their everyday speech, but only about 6% of these had disharmonic back suffixes (Fenyvesi 1995a:38–39): disharmonic verbs in this survey included *apdétel* 'update' and *csekkol* 'check'. Because for this survey computer-related vocabulary was chosen, the survey also tested the word-formation intuitions of the surveyed HH speakers since most of this vocabulary in 1994 was not used in a standard way in Hungary, so any effect of standardizing tendencies on the speakers could be discounted.

3.3.1.2 *Morphological features*

3.3.1.2.1 Conjugations. Throughout the verbal paradigm HH has a dichotomy of what is called the indefinite (or subjective) and definite (or objective) conjugations: a verb is in the indefinite conjugation if it has no object or if its object is indefinite, and it is in the definite conjugation if it has a definite object. The personal endings on the verb express definiteness/indefiniteness, person and number in one portmanteau morpheme, as in *csinál-unk* '(we) do-1PL.INDEF' vs. *csinál-juk* '(we) do-1PL.DEF'. A complex set of rules determines what constitutes an indefinite object and what a definite object in HH, for instance, an object is indefinite if it is a noun preceded by an indefinite article or no article, or if it is a first or second person pronoun, whereas it is definite if it is a proper noun, or a noun preceded by a definite article, or if it is a possessive noun phrase or a third person pronoun. (For a full description of the conjugations, see Kenesei et al. 1998:321–327.)

In AH a mixing of the two conjugations – i.e. the use of the definite conjugation in place of the indefinite and vice versa – has been reported in Kontra (1990:83–84), Bartha (1993), and Fenyvesi (1995a:40–44). In both South Bend and McKeesport the mixing of the definite and indefinite conjugations occurs rarely in the speech of immigrants and more frequently in the speech of second-generation speakers (only few of the latter do not have this feature at all). Bartha (1993:134) mentions the presence of this feature in Detroit, too.

Some examples of the definite conjugation used instead of indefinite are as follows:

(35) AH *az öreg-ek meg-hal-t-ák* (McK, Gen2)
      the old-PL PVB-die-PAST-3PL.DEF
      'the old people died' (HH: *meg-haltak*)

(36) AH *Akkor ismer-em*   Athens, *Ohio-ba egy Széplaki-t* (SB, Gen2)
      then know-1SG.DEF Athens Ohio-INE a   Széplaki-ACC
      'Then I know a Széplaki in Athens, Ohio' (HH: *ismerek*)

(37) AH *mindég az   hí-t-ák*   engem, igen, *Dani bácsi* (McK, Gen2)
      always that call-PAST-3PL.DEF me   yes   Dani uncle
      'yes, they always called me that, Uncle Dani.' (HH: *hívtak*)

Examples of indefinite conjugation used instead of definite include the following:

(38) AH *és   tud-ott*   az *angol-t* (SB, Gen2)
      and know-PAST.3SG.INDEF the English-ACC
      'and he knew English' (HH: *tudta*)

(39) AH *Ilonká-t   tanít-ott*   de nem *éngemet* (McK, Gen2)
      Ilonka-ACC teach-PAST.3SG.INDEF but not   me
      'he taught Ilonka, but not me' (HH: *tanította*)

(40) AH *össze-szed-t-ünk*   magunk-at* (McK, Gen2)
      PVB-get-PAST-1PL.INDEF ourselves-ACC
      'we got together' (HH: *összeszedtük*)

The examples of mixing of conjugations are many and varied. Even though there are more examples where the indefinite conjugation is used instead of the definite than the other way around, no general tendency in this direction can be clearly established. Certain object types, however, seem to be more likely to cause a breakdown in the definite/indefinite rule: 1st person pronouns, infinitival clauses, objects with definite articles, demonstrative pronoun objects, and sentential objects. For speculations as to why such objects are more problematic, see Fenyvesi (2000:97–99).

One very curious detail about the mixing of the two conjugations in AH – showing that person/number marking is treated separately from marking of the conjugation – is that even when the conjugations are mixed, speakers always seem to choose the suffix corresponding to the right person/number from the other conjugation. No examples of a speaker choosing wrong person/number marking along with the wrong conjugation were found in the South Bend and McKeesport corpuses or among Bartha's examples (1993:134).[8] So, even though the definiteness/indefiniteness marking is undergoing change in AH, the person/number marking is fully retained. This, in effect, means that coding of verbs for person/number/definiteness is splitting in AH to separate person/number and definiteness marking, or, rather, the nonmarking of the latter.

Interestingly, also, many heavily inflectional immigrant languages (such as American Greek, Seaman 1972:165; American Polish, Lyra 1962; American Czech, Henzl 1982; Kučera 1990; American Slovak, Meyerstein 1959; American Serbo-Croatian, Albin & Alexander 1972; and American Russian, Polinsky In press) do not exhibit any change in person/number marking of verbs either while being heavily affected, for instance, in their noun morphology.

3.3.1.2.2 Preverbs.   HH preverbs function, for the most part, similarly to prepositions in verbs with prepositional phrases (e.g. *run up the stairs*) and particles in phrasal verbs (e.g. *blow up the building*) in English. In addition to having a preposition-like meaning like the former or being a noncompositional part of the verb like the latter, they can also have a purely aspectual meaning. Unlike an English preposition and adverbial particle, a HH preverb can occur before, after, or completely separated from the verb it is associated with. Morphological, syntactic, and semantic phenomena associated with preverbs are numerous, and an analysis of them in HH and AH is beyond the scope of this study. For a detailed account of characteristics of HH preverbs see Farkas and Sadock (1989). Instead of aiming for an exhaustive analysis of all aspects of preverb behavior in AH, then, I want to discuss some points that stand out in the McKeesport data (Fenyvesi 1995a:44–48). (Kontra 1990 does not identify AH characteristics in connection with preverbs in the South Bend data although examples involving the phenomena discussed below, do occur in his book.)

There are several examples in the McKeesport data where preverbs are used in a way that differs markedly from HH usage. With few exceptions, all the examples come from second-generation speakers. They can be categorized in the following way: (i) cases where a purely aspectual preverb is lacking, (ii) cases where a preverb-verb construction is replaced by another preverb-verb construction in a simplificatory process, (iii) cases where the preverb of a preverb-verb construction is replaced by another preverb, (iv) cases where the whole preverb-verb construction is replaced by a construction modeled after an English phrasal verb, and (v) miscellaneous cases.

There are cases in the McKeesport data where a preverb is lacking whose meaning in HH would be solely aspectual.[9] In (40), the missing preverb *el* has an inchoative meaning (i.e. signaling the beginning of an action), whereas in (41–42), the missing preverb *meg* is perfective.

(40)   AH *igen   kezd-et   sír-ni* (McK, Gen2)
      rather start-PAST.3SG cry-INF
      'he started to cry very much' (vs. HH *el-kezdett*)

(41)   AH *neki   nehezeb vout tanul-ni   az angol   nyelv-et* (McK, Gen2)
      DAT.3SG harder was learn-INF the English language-ACC
      'it was harder for him to learn the English language' (vs. HH *meg-tanulni*)

(42)   AH *és   ir-ni   magá-tu   tanul-t.* (McK, Gen2)
      and write-INF herself-ABL learn-PAST.3SG
      'And she learned to write by herself.' (vs. HH *tanult meg*)

In other cases the preverb-verb construction is replaced by another construction. In the following examples, a construction comprising the preverbs *be* 'in' and *ki* 'out' and the verbs *megy* 'go' and *jön* 'come', with the meaning 'go somewhere' or 'join' on the one hand, and 'leave' on the other hand, replaces the HH preverb *el* and another verb, where *el* expresses both the adverbial meaning 'away' and a perfective meaning.

(43)   AH *be-men-t*   *a*   *katonaság-ba* (McK, Gen2)
          in-go-PAST.3SG the army-ILL
          'he went to the army' (vs. HH *el-ment*)

(44)   AH *ki-jö-t-em*   *a*   *dzsár-bú* (McK, Gen2)
          out-come-PAST-1SG the factory-ELA
          'I left the factory' (=quit my job) (vs. HH *el-jöttem*)

(45)   AH *be-men-t-ünk*   *Budapest-re* (McK, Gen2)
          in-go-PAST-1PL Budapest-SUB
          'we went to Budapest' (vs. HH *el-mentünk*)

In two other cases not only the preverb, but the whole preverb-verb construction is replaced. In these the HH construction is replaced with *ki-jön*, just like some of the examples above, and they mean 'finish'.

(46)   AH *mikor kí-jö-t-em*   *a*   **high school**-*bú* (McK, Gen2)
          when out-come-PAST-1SG the high-school-ELA
          'when I finished high school' (vs. HH *el-végeztem*)

(47)   AH *május, mikor ki-jö-t-ünk*   *az*   *iskolá-bol* (McK, Gen2)
          May   when out-come-PAST-1PL the school-ELA
          'May, when we finished school' (vs. HH *el-végeztük*)

This feature is simplificatory and does not involve borrowing from English. The latter would probably be manifested in the form of a parallel usage of the preverb with a preposition or an adverbial particle, but since the equivalent English verbs do not have one, this possibility can safely be discounted.

In other cases the preverb is replaced by another preverb. In some of these there is an English construction that is the source of the AH form (48-49), while in others there is none (50–51).

(48)   AH *mikor a   husz   éiv-ed   fel-jár* (McK, Gen2)
          when the twenty year-PX2SG up-go.3SG
          'when your twenty years are up' (vs. HH *le-jár*)

(49)   AH *a   bányá-t   le-zár-t-ák* (McK, Gen2)
          the mine-ACC down-close-PAST-3PL
          'they closed down the mine' (vs. HH *be-zárták*)

Now consider the cases where there is no English source for the construction. In these the AH preverb-verb construction is actually meaningful in HH, but there it cannot

be conjoined with the object in the given sentence: the verb *kimos* in (50) has the HH
meaning 'launder', and *kimagyaráz* in (51) 'explain away' or 'clear up'.

(50) AH *kí-mos-ni   a   géip-et* (McK, Gen2)
      out-wash-INF the car-ACC
      'to wash the car' (vs. HH *meg-mosni*)

(51) AH *angol-ul   joban tud-néi-k   ki-magyaráz-ni* (McK, Gen2)
      English-ESS better be.able-COND-1SG out-explain-INF
      'I could explain better in English' (vs. HH *magyarázni*)

In some cases involving four verbs, an AH preverb-verb construction replaces a HH
verb or preverb-verb construction with which it is not connected in any way, but which
is a syntactic and lexical calque on an English phrasal verb:

(52) AH *rá-tesz-em   a   rádiómüsor-t* (McK, Gen2)
      on-put-1SG the radio.program-ACC
      'I put on the radio program' (vs. HH *bekapcsolom*)

(53) AH *a   kórház-bol   le-te-tt-ek* (McK, Gen1)
      the hospital-ELA down-put-PAST-3PL
      'they laid me off at the hospital' (vs. HH *elbocsátottak*)

(54) AH *joban jön   neki   ki   a   magyar* (McK, Gen1)
      better come.3SG DAT.3SG out the Hungarian
      'for him, Hungarian comes out easier' (vs. HH *megy*)

In some cases the preverb *meg* is lacking where in HH it appears not in its perfective
meaning but rather as a noncompositional part of the verb. Both of these occur in the
speech of the same speaker and involve the same verb, *megismer* 'recognize'; the verb
without the preverb, *ismer*, means 'be familiar with':

(55) AH *vajon   fog-nak ismer-ni?* (McK, Gen2)
      whether FUT-3PL recognize-INF
      'whether they will recognize us' (vs. HH *meg fognak ismerni*)

(56) AH *én fog-om ismer-ni   ő-t* (McK, Gen2)
      I   FUT.1SG recognize.INF he-ACC
      'I will recognize him' (vs. HH *meg fogom ismerni*)

This omission of *meg* probably has to do with the verb *ismer*, which is also problematic
in AH (see below, under the discussion of lexical features): its meaning seems to have
shifted from 'be familiar with' to 'recognize', while the verb *tud*, meaning both 'know'
and 'be able to' in HH, has taken over the meaning 'be familiar with' as well.

Concerning this loss of aspect marking in preverbs in AH, Bartha and Sydorenko
(2000) propose, in an insightful analysis carried out in the Matrix Language Turnover
hypothesis framework, that in AH preverbs gradually lose their function as aspect
markers – an important role assigned to them in HH – and are, instead, used with
a more English-like function of verb modifiers.

3.3.1.2.3 Case. Hungarian, a heavily agglutinative language, has between 17 and 27 cases (the exact number depending on the definition of case by various authors – for details see Kenesei et al. 1998: 191–193). AH shows various differences in case usage as compared to HH, which, as I have demonstrated in detail elsewhere (Fenyvesi 1995/1996), can be grouped as follows: (i) loss of case inflections, (ii) simplification of the system of local cases in locatives, and (iii) replacement of cases. Kontra (1990) discusses differences in case usage with placenames, and Bartha (1993: 135) the loss of accusative suffixes. The majority of both first- and second-generation McKeesport speakers have instances of case usage different from HH in their speech.

About half of the instances where cases are used differently in McKeesport AH than they would be in HH are instances where case suffixes are lost. These instances are probably best seen as a change from the overt morphological case marking of HH to a more English-like system of abstract Case. One of the most often omitted case suffixes in AH is the accusative, as both the McKeesport data and Detroit corpus show (Bartha 1993: 135):

(57)   AH *le-ír-t-am   minden,   ami   kell* (Dt, Gen2)
       down-write-PAST-1SG everything which be.necessary
       'I wrote down everything that's needed.' (vs. HH *mindent*)

(58)   AH *a   magyar   nehezeb   vona   óvas-ni* (McK, Gen2)
       the Hungarian more.difficult be.COND.3SG read-INF
       'it would be more difficult to read the Hungarian [papers]'
       (vs. HH *magyart*)

Bartha (1993: 135) claims that the explanation is most likely phonological. In contrast, Bolonyai (2000), explaining a loss of accusative case suffixes of the same kind among bilingual Hungarian children growing up in the United States in the framework of the 4-M model (Myers-Scotton & Jake 2001), demonstrates that this model's distinction of system vs. content morphemes, where accusative morphemes constitute a class of late system morphemes, predicts that these will be less accurately produced than oblique cases like locative cases.

Other case suffixes – such as the essive, in (59), the instrumental, in (60), the dative, in (61), or the inessive, in (62) – are also sometimes lost in AH:

(59)   AH *az éinek-ek-et   joban tud-om   madzsar-ul   mint*
       the hymn-PL-ACC better know-1SG Hungarian-ESS than
       angol (McK, Gen2)
       English
       'I know the hymns better in Hungarian than English' (vs. HH *angolul*)

(60)   AH *S   ako tanákosz-t-am a   férj-em,   aki   most*
       and then meet-PAST-1SG the husband-PX1SG who now

> *férj-em.* (McK, Gen2)
> husband-px1sg
> 'And then I met my husband who is my present husband.'
> (vs. HH *férjemmel*)

(61) AH *asz hí-t-uk   a   magyar   negyed* (McK, Gen2)
      that call-past.1pl the Hungarian district
      'we called it the Hungarian district' (vs. HH *negyednek*)

(62) AH *egyszer egy hónap* (McK, Gen2)
      once   a   month
      'once a month' (vs. HH *hónapban*)

Using Kontra's corpus of data, Solovyova's (1994) findings about the number of case suffix omissions in South Bend AH are very similar to corresponding results in McKeesport, as Table 9.11 shows.

The other half of the instances where cases are used differently in McKeesport AH than in HH are instances where a different case is used in AH than what would occur in HH. Almost 90% of all case replacements involve a replacement of a local case in McKeesport, whereas the corresponding figure in South Bend (Solovyova 1994) is 80% (Fenyvesi 1995/1996: 390). Some examples are as follows: in (63) ablative is used instead of HH elative and sublative instead of HH illative; in (64) illative is used instead of HH delative; and in (65–67) superessive is used instead of HH sublative, allative, and essive, respectively.

(63) AH *men-t-ek   egy templom-tul a   másik-ra ez-ek   a   népek*
      go-past-3pl one church-abl the other-sub this-pl the people
      'these people went from one church to the other' (vs. HH *templomból, másikba*) (McK, Gen2)

(64) AH *mindenki a   tükör-be   akar-t   egyszere   me-ni*
      everyone the mirror-ill want-past.3sg at.same.time go-inf
      'everyone wanted to go to the mirror at the same time' (vs. HH *tükörhöz*) (McK, Gen2)

Table 9.11. The omission of case suffixes, as percentages of all omissions, in South Bend and McKeesport

Cases	South Bend	McKeesport
All local cases*	39.7%	47.8%
Accusative	29.4%	28.8%
Instrumental	14.7%	7.4%
Dative	10.3%	5.3%
Other cases	5.9%	11.6%

* Sum of percentages for inessive, superessive, allative, inessive, delative, sublative, and elative cases.

(65)   AH *a   kisjány   ki-szalat   az   ut-on*
       the little.girl out-run.PAST.3SG the road-SUP
       'the little girl ran out in the road' (vs. HH *útra*) (McK, Gen2)

(66)   AH *tartoz-t-unk   a   független   egyház-on*
       belong-PAST-1PL the independent church-SUP
       'we belonged to the independent church' (vs. HH *egyházhoz*)
       (McK, Gen2)

(67)   AH ***always** angol-on   beszél-nek ök   is*
       always English-SUP speak-3PL they also
       'they, too, always speak English' (vs. HH *angolul*) (McK, Gen2)

The main findings in connection with the simplification of the locative use of the local cases of AH in comparison with HH are that in AH there seems to be a tendency towards the elimination of the distinction of the in-cases (elative, inessive, and illative), the on-cases (delative, superessive, and sublative) and the at-cases (ablative, adessive, and allative), while the distinction along their direction (movement from vs. static location vs. movement to) distinction is much more fully retained (Fenyvesi 1995/1996: 397–400). For a discussion of case-marking in placenames, see Fenyvesi (1995/1996) as well.

3.3.1.2.4 Possessive suffixes.   Like almost all other Uralic languages, HH has pronominal possessive endings (henceforth referred to as Px in the glosses, following the tradition of Uralic linguistics) on the head noun of the possessed NP (*a könyv-em* the book-Px1SG 'my book'). An overt pronominal for the possessor (in the nominative) is used only when the possessor is specifically emphasized (*az én könyv-em* the I book-Px1SG '*my* book'). The dative is used for the possessor in the construction denoting ownership, *somebody has something*, and the dative possessor phrase in these cases appears overtly only if the possessor is emphasized: ((*nek-em*) *van egy könyv-em* (DAT-Px1SG) is a book-Px1SG 'I have a book').

In AH, the loss of possessive suffixes has been reported for South Bend (Kontra 1990: 72, 85–86) and McKeesport (Fenyvesi 1995a: 66–70), in the speech of both first- and second-generation speakers, although more often in the speech of the latter. They are lost both in simple possessed noun phrases (68) as well as the *somebody has something* construction (69)

(68)   AH *az ö   mama beszél-t...* (vs. HH *mamája*)
       the he mom   speak-PAST.3SG
       'his mom spoke...' (McK, Gen2)

(69)   AH *nincs nek-em dzserek* (vs. HH *gyerekem*)
       not.is DAT-1SG child
       'I have no children.' (McK, Gen2)

3.3.1.2.5 Mood.   Changes in the use of the HH indicative, imperative-subjunctive, and conditional moods have also been reported in AH. For South Bend, a mixing of indicative and imperative-subjunctive mood verb forms as well as conditional forms of nonregular forms have been documented for second-generation speakers (Kontra 1990: 71–72). For McKeesport, a mixing of indicative and imperative forms has been found in the speech of second-generation speakers (Fenyvesi 1995a: 70–71), for instance. An indicative form is used instead of an imperative-subjunctive in (70), and an imperative-subjunctive instead of an indicative in (71):

> (70) AH *az én munká-m   volt, hogy minden   be-megy a   fanesz-ba,*
>   the I   work-px1sg was that everything in-go.3sg the furnace-ill
>   *ami   kell* (vs. HH *bemenjen*) (McK, Gen2)
>   which need
>   'My job was [to make sure] that everything that needs to goes into the furnace'

> (71) AH *de   a   dzserek-ek hamar ért-s-ék   egymás-t*
>   but the child-pl quickly understand-imp-3pl each.other-acc
>   'but children understand each other quickly' (vs. HH *értik*) (McK, Gen2)

In the McKeesport data, all instances of mixing are such that the person/number marking on the verb is correct at the same time, similarly to the cases where the person/number marking is correct while the choice of conjugation is made incorrectly (see Subsection 3.2.1.2.1 above). It is not possible to see whether the same is the case in South Bend, since for the majority of his examples Kontra (1990: 71–72) only provides the form supplied by his subjects but not the context in which they appeared. It would certainly be interesting to investigate this issue further to see if indeed person/number marking is much more intact than the marking of moods just like it is intact while the choice of conjugations is affected.

3.3.1.2.6 Number marking.   Two specific instances of number marking in AH have been tested as part of the Toledo questionnaire study. In both cases, HH requires singular nouns where English has plural forms (these latter occur in HH but are nonstandard). In both instances, standard Hungarian requires the singular form in generic reference to a class of identical items. In the test cases, sentences (505) and (511) of the Sociolinguistics of Hungarian Outside Hungary questionnaire (see the Appendix), subjects had to choose the more natural sounding of two sentences where one contained the standard, the other the nonstandard form. In both cases, AH speakers chose the more English-like, nonstandard Hungarian forms significantly more often than HH speakers did, see Table 9.12.

The AH results can be explained by the fact that in these cases of number marking, the English equivalent sentences reinforce the nonstandard plural forms.

Table 9.12. The choice of standard vs. nonstandard use of number marking in HH vs. AH

		HH*	AH
505:	nonstandard *banánokat*	13 (12.2%)	6 (33.3%)
	standard *banánt*	94 (87.9%)	12 (66.7%)
511:	nonstandard *függönyöket, szőnyegeket*	47 (43.9%)	15 (83.3%)
	standard *függönyt, szőnyeget*	60 (56.1%)	3 (16.7%)

(505): The Chi-square test shows the difference to be significant.
($\chi^2 = 5.364318$; p < .025)
(511): The Chi-square test shows the difference to be significant.
($\chi^2 = 9.57205186$; p < .005)
* HH figures from Csernicskó (1998:257, 260).

3.3.1.3 *Syntactic features*

3.3.1.3.1 Focus.   Focus is a phenomenon in the syntax of HH that is tied in complex ways to many other related issues, such as configurationality, topic-focus relations, and semantics. Since considering this whole range of issues would be well beyond the scope of this paper, I will only deal with focus without regard to the other questions it is closely connected with.

In neutral (i.e. focus-free) sentences all constituents receive primary stress. The focused constituent immediately precedes the finite verb and is accompanied by primary sentential stress, while the other constituents receive secondary stress. HH is a *pro*-drop language; that is, personal pronouns in the subject position appear overtly only if they are emphasized, and in such cases they appear in focus position.

In AH there are numerous violations of focus-related features reported for South Bend (Kontra 1990:75–79, 82), Detroit (Bartha 1993:138), and McKeesport (Fenyvesi 1995a:75–80). Sometimes focus movement is completely lacking; in such examples speakers give emphasis to a constituent through primary sentential stress. Sometimes a phrase other than the phrase the speaker means to emphasize occurs in the pre-verbal position, and the emphasized phrase gets primary stress in a post-verbal position. A great many personal pronouns appear overtly in AH even when they are not emphatic. All these focus-related features of AH are intertwined and cannot be completely separated from each other.

Focus-related features occur in the speech of both generations in South Bend and McKeesport, although more frequently in that of the second generation. (Bartha 1993:138 does not give details of the occurrence of the feature across the generations). Examples of lack of focus and lack of *pro*-drop are given in (72–74); of lack of focus in (75–76); and of lack of *pro*-drop in (77–78):[10]

(72)   AH *Én fizetek   most **eighty-five dollars** egy hónapban.* (SB, Gen2)
       I   pay.1SG now eighty-five dollars a   month.INE
       'I pay 85 dollars a month.'
       (HH: *85 dollárt fizetek most egy hónapban.*)

(73) [What did you do before you retired?]

AH *Én dougosztam a̲ vágóhidon.* (McK, Gen2)
 I worked.1sg the slaughterhouse.sup
 'I worked at the slaughterhouse.'
 (HH: *A vágóhídon dolgoztam.*)

(74) [What language do you pray in?]

AH *Én imádkozok kétszer.* (McK, Gen2)
 I pray.1sg twice.
 'I pray twice.' (3MK2 25:15)
 (HH: *Kétszer imádkozok.*)

(75) AH *mamámnak a neve vout Makai*
 mother.px1sg.dat the name.px3sg was.3sg Makai
 Rouza. (McK, Gen2)
 Róza
 'My mother's name was Róza Makai.'
 (HH: *Mamámnak a neve Makai Róza volt.*)

(76) AH *A Magyar Ház épült 1910-ben.* (SB, Gen1)
 the Hungarian House be.built.3sg 1910-ine
 'The Hungarian House was built in 1910.'
 (HH: *A Magyar Ház 1910-ben épült.*)

(77) AH *miután nyugdijba vonult, ő̲ fojtatta a*
 after retirement.ill proceeded.3sg he continued.3sg the
 lelkészi munkát
 minister work.acc
 'After he retired he continued to work as a minister.'
 (HH: *Miután nyugdíjba vonult, folytatta a lelkészi munkát.*) (McK, Gen2)

(78) AH *De ha magyar istentiszteletre megyek éi̲n joban érzem hogy*
 but if Hungarian service.sub go.1sg I better feel.1sg that
 éi̲n templomba voutam (McK, Gen2)
 I church.iness was.1sg
 'But if I go to the Hungarian service I feel more like I've been to church'
 (HH: *De ha magyar istentiszteletre megyek, jobban érzem, hogy templomban voltam.*)

The AH data from South Bend and McKeesport contain several cases where a phrase occurs in the pre-verbal position in a sentence, but either (a) the focussed phrase receives primary stress, while in accordance with the meaning of the sentence a different phrase should be emphasized and receive phonological stress, or (b) the focussed phrase is the one that should be emphasized and stressed but, instead, another phrase is. In the example sentences below, the AH phrases that are given primary sentential stress in the subjects' speech are marked by a double superscript accent, while the phrase that should be stressed and focussed, according to the meaning, is underlined.

(79)   AH *De   most   ő   már   "háromszor odahaza vót.* (SB, Gen1)
       but   now   he   already   three.times   at.home   was
       'He has been home three times.'
       (HH: *Ő már háromszor volt odahaza.*)

(80)   AH *a   "mi templomunk   vout a   magyar* (McK, Gen2)
       the we   church.px1PL   was   the Hungarian
       'our church was Hungarian'
       (HH: *A mi templomunk "magyar volt.*)

(81)   AH *És   öü huszonedzs dolár   edzs "hounapra   kapot* (McK, Gen2)
       and   he twenty.one dollar   a   month.SUB got.3SG
       'And he was paid twenty-one dollars a month.'
       (HH: *"Huszonegy dollárt kapott egy hónapra.*)

The use of overt pronouns in object positions was tested in the Toledo Hungarian-American community. The questionnaire the linguistic component of which included all the sentences tested in the SHOH project contained two questions where overt object pronouns are nonstandard in HH: in both of these sentences, Toledo Hungarian-Americans provided significantly higher nonstandard results than HH speakers. The two sentences were (515) and (615) of the SHOH questionnaire (see the Appendix). HH speakers provided significantly more standard answers in the case of both questions than AH speakers, as is demonstrated in Table 9.13.

Focusing and constituent order was tested in Toledo with the SHOH questionnaire by sentence (608), where subjects again had to choose the phrase they thought more fitting. Phrase (b) is standard in HH since the infinitival form *menni* 'to go' is in preverbal focused position, whereas in (a) it is not focused, which makes that phrase

Table 9.13. The choice of standard vs. nonstandard use of overt object pronouns in HH vs. AH

		HH*	AH
515:	nonstandard *láttalak téged*	23 (21.9%)	9 (50.0%)
	standard *láttalak*	82 (78.1%)	9 (50.0%)
615:	nonstandard *megkértem őt*	29 (27.4%)	11 (61.1%)
	standard *megkértem*	77 (72.6%)	7 (38.9%)

(515): The Chi-square test shows the difference to be significant.
($\chi^2 = 6.301457$; p < .025)
(615): The Chi-square test shows the difference to be significant.
($\chi^2 = 8.021872$; p < .005)
* HH figures from Csernicskó (1998: 262, 276).

Table 9.14. The choice of standard vs. nonstandard use of focus in HH vs. AH

		HH*	AH
608:	nonstandard *készül menni*	9 (8.4%)	10 (55.6%)
	standard *menni készül*	98 (91.6%)	8 (44.4%)

The Chi-square test shows the difference to be significant.
(χ^2 = 26.56843; p < .001)
* HH figures from Csernicskó (1998:273).

nonstandard. The AH subjects chose the nonstandard, more English-like phrase significantly more often than HH speakers (Table 9.14).

3.3.1.3.2 Agreement. Agreement is another syntactic domain where AH has been reported to be different from HH, in four kinds of cases: (a) between subjects and verbs, (b) between attributive quantifiers and nouns, (c) between nouns and predicative adjectives, and (d) between relative pronouns and their antecedents. In all four of these categories, HH-like agreement is lacking. This has been reported for South Bend (Kontra 1990:80-81) and McKeesport (Fenyvesi 1995a:80–85).

Lack of person and number agreement between subject and verb occurs sometimes in the speech of first-generation speakers in South Bend, and in the speech of almost all second-generation speakers in McKeesport:

(82) AH *És a gyermekei ért magyarul de nem*
and the child.PX3SG.PLP understand.3SG Hungarian.ESS but not
beszél magyarul (HH *értenek, beszélnek*) (SB, Gen1)
speak.3SG Hungarian.ESS
'And his children understand Hungarian but don't speak Hungarian.'

(83) AH *mind a három fijú ud haragusznak* (HH *haragszik*) (McK, Gen2)
all the three boy so be.angry.3PL
'all three boys are so angry'

(84) AH *vót ety kis hibák* (HH *volt egy pár hiba*) (McK, Gen2)
was.3SG a little mistake.PL
'there were a few mistakes'

(85) AH *mindenki meghaltak* (HH *meghalt*) (McK, Gen2)
everyone PVB.died.3PL
'everyone is dead'

The second kind of lack of agreement occurs between quantifiers and countable nouns, where HH requires singular nouns, and English requires plural. This feature also occurs in the speech of both generations.

(86) AH *és azokba voltak sok mesék* (HH *sok mese*) (SB, Gen1)
and that.PL.INE were.3PL many story.PL
'and there were many stories in them'

(87)   AH *tizenédzs éivek* (HH *év*) (McK, Gen2)
        fourteen year.PL
        'fourteen years'

Lack of number agreement between a predicate adjective and its noun occurs in AH phrases involving plural nouns: here, in HH, predicate adjectives are also pluralized:

(88)   HH *A   fiú-k   magas-ak volt-ak.*
        the boy-PL tall-PL   were-3PL
        'The boys were tall.'

Both in South Bend and McKeesport, this kind of lack of HH-like agreement occurs in the speech of second-generation speakers only.

(89)   AH *amikor még fiatal házas   voltunk* (HH *házasok*) (SB, Gen2)
        when   still young married were.1PL
        'when we were newly married'

(90)   AH *ha rosz voltunk, kikaptunk* (HH *rosszak*)
        if bad were.PL be.punished.1PL
        'if we were bad (=misbehaved), we were punished' (McK, Gen2)

HH also has number agreement between a relative pronoun and its antecedent. The lack of such agreement is noted in the speech of second-generation speakers both in South Bend and McKeesport:

(91)   AH *A   leveleket,   ami   jönnek*
        the letter.PL.ACC which come.3PL
        Magyarországról (HH *amik*) (SB, Gen2)
        Hungary.DEL
        'The letters which come from Hungary'

(92)   AH *Klári meg Karcsi azok, aki   ötvenhatba átmentek   Asztriába*
        Klári and Karcsi those who fifty.six.INE over.went.3PL Austria.ILL
        'Klári and Karcsi are those people who left for Austria in '56' (HH *akik*)
        (McK, Gen2)

Two cases of agreement were tested in the questionnaire study carried out in Toledo. In one of them, in HH plural subjects are associated with one thing of the same kind, the noun expressing the thing with which the subjects are associated with receive singular number. (In English, they receive plural agreement.) This was tested with sentence (611) of the SHOH questionnaire, where subjects had to choose the phrase that seemed to them more fitting. As Table 9.15 shows, AH subjects chose significantly more often than HH subjects the more English-like phrase, which is nonstandard in HH.

Another case of agreement was represented by SHOH questionnaire sentence (601), where a singular adjective is required as an object complement in HH, whereas a plural adjective is nonstandard. The AH responses in this case turn out to be significantly more standard than the HH responses (see Table 15), which is most likely

Table 9.15. The choice of standard vs. nonstandard use of agreement in HH vs. AH

		HH*	AH
611:	nonstandard *tűzoltóknak*	16 (15.1%)	8 (44.4%)
	standard *tűzoltónak*	90 (84.9%)	10 (55.6%)
601:	nonstandard *komolyaknak*	32 (29.9%)	1 (5.6%)
	standard *komolynak*	75 (70.1%)	17 (94.4%)

(611): The Chi-square test shows the difference to be significant.
(χ^2 = 8.491963; p < .005)
(601): The Chi-square test shows the difference to be significant.
(χ^2 = 4.702162; p < .05)
* HH figures from Csernicskó (1998:269, 274).

explained by the fact that the adjective in the corresponding English sentence would also be in the singular, so any influence of English reinforces the standard Hungarian variant rather than the nonstandard.

3.3.1.3.3 The *szokott* plus infinitive construction. A change in the meaning of the *szokott* + infinitive construction from habitual present to habitual past tense is also documented for AH (Kontra 1990:114–116; Fenyvesi 1995a:88–89). The verb *szokott* has an auxiliary-like function in HH, although it is marked for past tense and conjugated for the definiteness/indefiniteness distinction, and requires person and number marking. In AH such a change of meaning of this construction occurs mostly in the speech of second-generation speakers. In all of the examples that I have considered it is clear from the context or from details elsewhere in the interview what tense the speakers are referring to (e.g. in the interview where 94 is spoken, the speaker mentions elsewhere that her father is dead).

(93) [Do you have an acquaintance called Sándor?]

    AH *Hát, szoktam   ismerni   egy Sándor bácsit,   de   má*
          well used.to.1SG know.INF a   Sándor uncle.ACC but already
          meghalt. (SB, Gen2)
          PVB.died.3SG
          'Well, I used to know an Uncle Sándor, but he died already.'

(94) [Do you listen to Hungarian radio programs?]

    AH *(: Oh:) igen, a   éidesapám   is   mindig szokta   halgatni*
          oh   yes, the father.PX1SG also always used.to.3SG listen.to.INF
          'Oh, yes, my father also used to listen to it all the time' (McK, Gen2)

3.3.2 *Lexical borrowing*[11]
The best catalog of lexical borrowings in AH is Vázsonyi's (1995) dictionary. It is one of only two existing dictionaries of immigrant languages (the other one being Virtaranta 1992, a dictionary of American Finnish). It contains 900 entries, the part of speech

Table 9.16. The distribution of entries by parts of speech in American Hungarian and American Finnish

Parts of speech	American Hungarian (Vázsonyi 1995)	American Finnish (Virtaranta 1992)
Nouns	640 (71.1%)	3570 (78.1%)
Verbs	202 (22.4%)	593 (13.0%)
Adjectives	72 (8%)	96 (2.1%)
Adverbs	27 (3.0%)	180 (4.0%)
Pronouns	1 (0.1%)	6 (0.1%)
Numerals	1 (0.1%)	–
Postpositions	–	3 (0.05%)
Particles	1 (0.1%)	–
Interjections	9 (1%)	15 (0.3%)
Phrases	20 (2.2%)	89 (2%)

distribution of which are as follows. The greatest number of entries (640) are nouns, followed by verbs (202), adjectives (72) and adverbs (27). There are 20 phrases, frozen in form, which are used as units (e.g. *ájdonó* 'I don't know' or *deccit* 'that's it'), 9 interjections (e.g. *dzsí* 'gee'), one numeral, one pronoun, and one particle. The distribution of entries according to parts of speech is very similar to that in Virtaranta (1992:33), as Table 9.16 demonstrates.[12]

In the subsections below, I will discuss lexical borrowings in three categories: loanwords, loanblends, and calques. I define loanwords as instances of lexical borrowing where the English word form is borrowed with the meaning. Loanblends are typically compounds, one part of which is a borrowed English word whereas the other part is a Hungarian word, and the compound is copied from English. Calques (also sometimes called loan-translations) are words that are modeled on English words but whose forms are Hungarian forms. I regard as calques instances of semantic borrowing as well, i.e. words whose form is Hungarian and which are used in HH as well, but which get a new meaning in AH under the influence of their English equivalent.

Vázsonyi (1995) contains mostly loanwords, some (approximately 30) loanblends, and only three calques. Calques tend to be more difficult to notice in contact varieties than loanwords and loanblends since their forms are native, so this might have influenced Vázsonyi's method of selection of words for the dictionary.

One interesting characteristic of loans in AH – due to the variety not being standardized – is that several words have alternative forms, e.g. *ofisz* ∼ *afisz* ∼ *afic* ∼ *ofic* 'office', *sztrit* ∼ *strit* ∼ *strít* ∼ *stritt* 'street', *basz* ∼ *básx* 'boss', and *bodi* ∼ *badi* ∼ *bádi* 'buddy'.

3.3.2.1 *The phonological adaptation of loans.* Similarly to most borrowing situations, in AH loans undergo phonological adaptation (i.e. nativization).

Most nativization is due to the lack of an exact equivalent of American English phoneme in Hungarian. Some of the most common changes are the following.

/θ, ð/: Hungarian lacks interdental fricatives completely. Loans containing these are adapted with dental stops or, less frequently, with fricatives: /ð/ > /d/ *brader* 'brother', *braderló* 'brother-in-law', *báder* 'bother [n]', *deccit* 'that's it', *deccoké* 'that's OK', *deccól* 'that's all', *deccrájt* 'that's right', and *fader* 'father'; but /ð/ > /z/ *bézingszút* 'bathing suit'; /θ/ > /t/ *ájtinkszó* 'I think so', *bekendfurt* 'back and forth'; /θ/ > /s/ *bászrúm* 'bathroom', *faltísz* 'false teeth', and *szenkszgiving* ~ *tenkszgiving* 'Thanksgiving'.

/ŋ/ > /ng/: Hungarian does not have the velar nasal as a phoneme, only as an allophone of /n/ before velar stops. Words containing this phoneme are nativized with /ng/: *bézingszút* 'bathing suit', *bilding* 'building', *bilongol* 'belong', *bordingház* 'boarding-house', *dájningrúm* 'dining room', *dúing* 'doing; to do', *dresszing* '(salad) dressing', *filingsztésin* 'filling station', *fisingel* 'fish [v]', *gémblingház* 'gambling house', *geng* 'gang', *livingrúm* 'livingroom', *parking míter* 'parking meter', *rangúl* 'wrong [adv]', *szekszgiving* 'Thanksgiving'. In one case, *bólineli* 'bowling alley', the AH word reflects informal, nonstandard English pronunciation with [n] rather than [ŋ].

/w/ > /v/: Since Hungarian lacks /w/, words containing it in the onsets of syllables are nativized into AH with /v/ (for coda /w/'s see discussion of the nativization of diphthongs below). Thus, AH has *drájvé* 'driveway', *hárdversztór* 'hardware store', *halovín* 'Halloween', *hájvé* 'highway', *hómvörk* 'homework', *imbitvín* 'in between', *kvittol* 'quit', *midvájf* 'midwife', *szájdvólk* 'sidewalk', *szvithárt* 'sweetheart', *vasrúm* 'washroom', *vejöldket* 'wildcat', *vell* 'well', *veszt* 'west', *vilbár* 'wheelbarrow', *viszki* 'whiskey'.

In some cases, a word-initial (or, less frequently, word-final) /s/ which is spelled in English with <c> is borrowed with /ts/ (which, in turn, is spelled with <c> in Hungarian): *cent* 'cent', *cigar* 'cigar', *cigárbox* 'cigar box', *címenflór* 'cement floor', *címent* 'cement', *cimentez* 'cement [v]', *cirkulálódik* 'circulate', *cirkulésin* 'circulation', *citi* 'city', but also *cinder* ~ *sinder* 'cinder', *citizen* ~ *szitizen* 'citizen', *fenc* 'fence', *insurenc* ~ *insurensz* 'insurance' *ofic* ~ *afic* ~ *afisz* 'office'. This substitution cannot be explained on phonological grounds, since Hungarian also has /s/ in all positions, and must be, therefore, the result of spelling pronunciation.

/æ/ > /ɛ/ Hungarian lacks a low front vowel, and English words borrowed into AH most often substitute it with its closest equivalent, the lower-mid front /ɛ/ (spelled with <e>). Some examples are as follows: *estré* 'ashtray', *hepi* 'happy', *grencsájd* 'grandchild', *grendmami* 'grandmother', *bólineli* 'bowling alley', *bekporcs* 'back porch', *blekbórd* 'blackboard', *embulenc* 'ambulance', *enimór* 'anymore', *enivé* 'anyway', *ent* 'aunt', *geng* 'gang'. Sometimes, due to spelling pronunciation, it is replaced by /a/ (spelled with <a>: *faktori* (but also ~ *fektri*) 'factory'.

Standard Hungarian and many Hungarian regional dialects completely lack diphthongs. Even though some of the Hungarian immigrants to United States were from dialect areas where diphthongs are present, the vast majority of diphthongs are nativized in loans. The diphthongs /ej, ow/ are usually substituted by long mid vowels /eː, oː/ (spelled with <é> and <ó>, respectively): *bébiszitter* 'baby-sitter', *drájvé* 'driveway', *ekszré* 'X-ray', *estré* 'ashtray', *halidé* 'holiday', *braderló* 'bother-in-law', *hóm* 'home', *ájdonnó* 'I don't know', *bangaló* 'bungalow', *biló* 'below [=subzero temperature]', *bólé* 'bowl', *bólineli* 'bowling alley', *felblóol* 'blow up', *ónol* 'own', *só* 'show [n]', *trektor* 'trac-tor'. The diphthong /aw/ is usually substituted by /aː/, in spelling <á> (*enihá* 'anyhow', *sáor* 'shower', *dántán* 'downtown'), less frequently by two *vowels*, /au/ (*braunsugor* 'brown sugar', *ápszejdaun* 'upside-down', *hausz* 'house'), and at least in one case, with either /aː/ or /oː/, *káboj* ∼ *kóboj* 'cowboy'. The diphthong /aj/ is usually replaced by the closest Hungarian equivalent (long) vowel /aː/ plus /j/: *ájris* 'Irish', *Bájbl* 'Bible', *bájk* 'bike', *dájet* 'diet', *dájetol* 'diet [v]', *juláj* 'July', *lájt* 'light', *midvájf* 'midwife', *múnsájneros* 'moonshiner', *nektáj* 'necktie', *óvertájmoz* 'overtime [v]', *páj* 'pie', *szájdvalk* 'sidewalk'. But, in a few cases, it is substituted by /ɛj/, *átszejdon* 'outside', *felszlejszol* 'slice up', *hejer-men* 'hired man', *loncstejm* 'lunchtime', *nejlán* 'nylon'; and in some cases by either /aːj/ or /ɛj/, *ejdi* ∼ *ájdi* 'idea', *fejn* ∼ *fájn* 'fine', *hejvé* ∼ *hájvé* 'highway', *hejszkúl* ∼ *hájszkúl* 'high school', *lájcensz* ∼ *lejcensz* 'license', *munsájn* ∼ *munsejn* 'moonshine', *ólrájt* ∼ *ólrejt* 'all right', *rájdol* ∼ *rejdol* 'ride', *sztrájk* ∼ *sztrejk* 'strike [n]'.

In at least one type of nativization, not a phoneme but its allophone is what un-dergoes substitution: the American English tap, [ɾ], is nativized as a [d] in AH: for instance, *bader* 'butter', *gódehel* 'go to hell', *hárdetek* 'heart attack', *ráduvé* 'right away'.

Since HH (and, predominantly, AH as well) has word-initial stress, all loans are pronounced with such stress. In some cases, although not always, word-initial un-stressed American English vowels are lost when words containing them are borrowed: *daptol* 'adopt', *daptolás* 'adoption', *genszt* 'against', *lektrik* 'electric', *lörcsik* 'allergic', *mördzsenszi rúm* 'emergency room', *partment* (∼ *apartment*) 'apartment', *pojment* 'ap-pointment'. But, unstressed wordinitial vowels are not always lost. They are sometimes retained in cases when the unstressed syllable contains the vowel only (*akrosz* 'across', *anaunszol* 'announce', *eleksen* 'election'), and always retained when the unstressed syl-lable has a consonant in the coda (*egzeminor* 'examiner', *egzisztál* 'exist', *ekszájtmen* 'excitement', *ekszkjúzol* 'excuse [v]', *ekszpektol* 'expect', *ekszpensz* 'expense', *eksztensen* 'extension', *endzsojol* 'enjoy'). Note that if the initial vowel were deleted these coda consonants could not be resyllabified into the onset of the next syllable, since that would go against the phonotactics of both Hungarian and American English. In some cases noninitial unstressed vowels are also lost, just like in the colloquial spoken Amer-ican English forms of these words: *fektri* (∼ *faktori*) 'factory', *grács* ∼ *grázs* (∼ *garázs*) 'garage'. In at least three cases, the whole unstressed syllable is lost: *gédzsment* 'engage-ment', *kjúzmi* 'excuse me', *tropender* 'interpreter'. Interestingly, one of these examples, *kjúzmi*, contains an onset (*kj*) that does not exist in HH (Siptár & Törkenczy 2000:98), only in American English (cf. *queue* or *cucumber*). This shows that the phonotactic constraints of Hungarian are also affected by contact with English here.

In at least one AH loan a simplification of the word-initial consonant cluster oc-curs, *kacstép* 'scotch tape', although at least one other word, *szkúl* 'school', does not simplify the same cluster. (Another AH example of cluster simplification is *pinkler-szisztem* 'sprinkler-system'; Miklós Kontra personal communication, 1993).

An interesting change occurs in some monosyllabic AH words. Most receive an extra wordfinal vowel, usually /eː/ (<é>): *káré* 'car', *bokszkáré* 'box car', *stritkáré* 'street-car' (but: *puskár* 'push-car'), *báré* 'bar [place]', *hálé* 'hall', *bólé* 'bowling', *háré* 'hair', *sálé* 'shawl'; but also *farma* 'farm', *majna* 'mine [n]', *sifta* 'shift'. In a small number of monosyllabic words, the final consonant is geminated: *stritt* 'street', *blakk* 'block', *trakk* (but also ~ *trok* ~ *trak*) 'truck'. (In connection with this, cf. Nádasdy 1989, observing that in HH monosyllabic loanwords containing short vowels usually also geminate the final consonant.)

3.3.2.2 *The morphological adaptation of loans.* The most regular rule of morphological adaptation of loans in AH is that verbs, just like borrowed verbs in HH, receive a thematizing suffix, *-l* or *-z*, preceded by a connecting vowel if the stem ends in a consonant. I have been able to find only one exception to this rule, in Vázsonyi's dictionary. The verb *fool around* is borrowed in two forms into AH, *fúl araund* and *fularaund*, and the example sentences contain the following inflected forms: *fúlnak araund* 'they fool around' and *fularaundoltak* 'they fooled around', respectively (Vázsonyi 1995:80–81). Of these, the former does not contain the thematizing suffix.

A relatively small number of words receive other derivational suffixes, the most common of which is the very productive suffix *-s* deriving adjectives which, in turn through zero derivation, often form nouns, just like in HH: *galondos* ~ *galandos* 'gallon [adj]', *kannás* 'canned', *bucseros* 'butcher', *drugstóros* 'druggist', *farmeros* 'farmer', *gádneros* 'gardener', *gémbleres* 'gambler', *hólszéles* 'wholesaler', *krénes* 'crane operator', *lamberes* 'lumber dealer', *módlis* 'moulder', *múnsájneros* 'moonshiner', *szalonos* 'saloon keeper'. Some words are further derived with the suffix *-kodik/-kedik/-ködik* to form verbs meaning 'behave in the manner of': *bomoskodik* 'behave like a bum', *butlégereskedik* 'bootleg [v]'.

Other words receiving derivational suffixes include the following. Nominal suffixes (underlined and separated here by hyphens) are found in *dizi-ség* 'dizziness', *drink-ol-ó* 'saloon', *dapt-ol-ás* 'adoption', *hauszklín-ol-ás* 'house cleaning'; *grinór-os-an* 'in the manner of a greenhorn' has an adverbial suffix.

Many verbs are borrowed into AH with preverbs. In some of these the preverbs have an adverbial meaning: *elgémbliz* 'gamble away', *elmuffol* 'move away', *elpussol* 'push away', *felblóol* ~ *felblóoz* 'blow up', *feldzsompol* 'jump up', *felkrenkol* 'crank up', *felmápol* 'mop up', *felpikkol* 'pick up'. In others, the preverbs are purely aspectual: *eldivorszol* 'divorce', *eljúzol* 'use up', *elkenol* 'can', *elkvittol* 'quit', *elmisszol* 'miss', *elsippol* 'ship', *elszeparétol* 'separate', *felhózol* 'hose', *felrézol* 'raise', *felszlejszol* 'slice up', *megbittol* 'beat'.

There is one noun in Vázsonyi (1995) that is borrowed into American Hungarian together with a plural ending and is then reinterpreted as a singular form: *benánesz* 'banana' (cf. *Elloptak egy benáneszt*. 'A banana was stolen', Vázsonyi 1995:38).

In a small number of cases, words change their part of speech affiliation during the borrowing process without any derivation: for instance, *csikihárt* 'chicken-hearted', *akrosz* 'across', and *dánstéz* 'downstairs' are all nouns in AH.

3.3.2.3 *Loanwords.* Loanwords constitute the greatest portion of Vázsonyi (1995), as well as of the lexical borrowings mentioned in Kontra (1990), Bartha (1993) and Fenyvesi (1995a).[13]

Some examples of loanwords from Vázsonyi (1995) are the following.

Nouns: *ájszbokszi* 'ice-box', *aldermány* 'alderman', *balgém* 'ballgame', *bébisóer* 'baby shower', *bigbász* 'big boss', *bodi* 'buddy', *bucser* 'butcher', *csungám* 'chewing-gum', *dipó* 'depot', *faktori* 'factory', *fanesz* 'furnace', *farma* 'farm', *fenc* 'fence', *fórlédi* 'fore-lady', *gréd* 'grade', *hajvé* 'highway', *hálé* 'hall', *hanki* ~ *hunki* 'Hunky', *hómszik* 'homesick', *hómvörk* 'homework', *imigrés* 'immigration', *indzsenér* 'engineer', *insurenc* 'insurance', *kálidzs* 'college', *kársop* 'carshop', *klörk* 'clerk', *majna* 'mine [n]', *mélmen* 'mailman', *múnsájneros* 'moonshiner', *nektáj* 'necktie', *núsz* 'news', *ofisz* 'office', *porcs* 'porch', *rédió* 'radio', *stór* 'stór', *szarokrád* 'sauerkraut', *sztepsz* 'steps', *sztraberi* 'strawberry', *tícser* 'teacher', *vasrúm* 'washroom', *zip* 'zipper'.

Verbs: *ánszerol* 'anwer', *báderoz* 'bother', *bárkol* 'bark', *bászol* 'boss', *bébiszittel* 'babysit', *bettol* 'bet', *börnol* 'burn', *csekkol* 'check', *cséndzsol* 'change', *dempol* 'dump', *diggol* 'dig', *drájvol* 'drive', *ekszkjúzol* 'excuse', *endzsojol* 'enjoy', *faniz* 'be funny', *fikszol* 'fix', *förnicsel* 'furnish', *hanimúnoz* 'go on honeymoon', *hepenol* 'happen', *júzol* 'use', *keccsol* 'catch', *kvittol* 'quit', *misszol* 'miss', *muffol* 'move', *nojzol* 'make noise', *pussol* 'push', *rentol* 'rent', *szpelol* 'spell', *szpendol* 'spend'.

Adjectives: *bizi* 'busy', *bulecprúf* 'bulletproof', *cingel* ~ *szingel* 'single', *csili* 'chilly', *csíp* 'cheap', *dizi* 'dizzy', *fani* 'funny', *dzselesz* 'jealous', *dzsúszi* 'jucy', *fájn* 'fine', *fémes* 'famous', *fenci* 'fancy', *frendli* 'friendly', *hendi* 'handy', *hepi* 'happy', *hómméd* 'home made', *hómszik* 'homesick', *ízi* 'easy', *kúl* 'cool'.

Adverbs: *anesztli* 'honestly', *ápszedaun* 'upside-down', *bekendfurt* 'back and forth', *enimór* 'anymore', *enitájm* 'any time', *imbitvín* 'in-between', *klósz* 'close', *létli* 'lately', *mébi* 'maybe', *nekszdór* 'next door' *ráduvé* 'right away', *rangúl* 'wrong [adv]'.

Interjections: *anesztegád* 'honest-to-God', *dzsí* 'gee', *hajrap* ~ *harjap* 'hurry up!', *helló* 'hallo', *ízi* 'easy!', *máj god* 'my God', *ó* 'oh', *ó boj* 'oh, boy'.

Phrases: *ájdonó* 'I don't know', *ájdunker* 'I don't care', *ájhóp* 'I hope', *ájmín* 'I mean', *ájtinkszó* 'I think so', *deccit* 'that's it', *deccoké* 'that's OK', *decrájt* 'that's right', *dzseszteszém* 'just the same', *fórszél* 'for sale', *gimi* 'give me', *godehel* 'go to hell', *góhet* 'go ahead', *gudbáj* 'good-bye', *haliduszé* 'how do you say?', *hóldap* 'hold-up', *juszí* 'you see', *kjúzmi* 'excuse me', *letszí* 'let's see', *vell* 'well'.

There is one each of numerals (*plenti* 'plenty'), pronouns (*jú* 'you'), and particles (*genszt* 'against').

3.3.2.4 *Loanblends.* The loanblends listed in Vázsonyi's dictionary are the following: *apartment-ház* 'apartment house', *bankház* 'bunk house', *bébiágy* 'baby's bed, child-bed', *betyárburd* 'boarding-house with only men as boarders' (from HH *betyár* 'highwayman, bandit'), *bizniszember* 'businessman', *blakház* 'blockhouse', *borbélysop* 'barbershop', *bordingház* 'boarding-house', *brendúj* (~*brendnyú*) 'brand new', *brikház* 'brick house', *csenszjáték* 'game of chance', *farmaház* 'farm house', *fenc-rózsa* 'fence rose', *fildműves* 'fieldworker', *főbász* 'main boss', *fremház* 'frame house', *frontszoba* 'front room', *fürdőszút* 'bathing-suit', *garázsember* 'garage-man', *gárbicskanna* 'garbage can', *gémblingház* 'gambling house', *gázbill* 'gas bill', *grendmami* 'grandmother', *grendanyuka* 'grandmother', *grédiskola* (∼ *grédszkúl*) 'grade school', *hobóállomás* 'hobo station', *jégbakszi* (∼ *ájszbakszi*) 'ice-box', *kárbiztosítás* 'car insurance', *kompániaház* 'company house', *kórtház* 'courthouse', *kőmajna* 'rock mine', *ókontri* 'old country', *póstaofic* 'post office'. Others, from South Bend, are *fraternális egyesület* 'fraternal association', *kreditkártya* 'credit card', *pártbasz* 'party boss', *virágbakszi* 'flower box' (Kontra 1990: 100); and from Detroit *horszlégy* 'horse fly', *nyaktáj* 'neck tie', *szenes förnesz* 'coal furnace' (Bartha 1993: 113).

In addition, many borrowed verbs also receive Hungarian preverbs and can thus be considered loanblends (see examples in Section 3.2.2.2 above).

3.3.2.5 *Calques.* Vázsonyi (1995) contains only two calques as entries (*asztalfelváró* 'waiter', literally, table-up-waiter, presumably, from the American English verb *wait tables*, and *papír* '(news)paper', which in HH it means 'paper [=material]').

Examples from Kontra (1990: 100–101) include *elcserél* 'change' (HH 'exchange'), *emelet* 'floor' (HH 'nonfirst floor'), *felvesz* 'pick up [e.g. a language]' (HH 'pick up [only physically]'), *valamikor* 'sometimes' (HH 'sometime'), *megüt* 'hit, bump into' (HH 'hit [with hand or instrument]), *les* and *vigyáz* 'watch' (HH 'peep' and 'watch out', respectively); *példát ad* 'give example' (HH only *példát mond* 'say example'), *vonatot cserél* 'change trains' (HH only *átszáll* 'get over'), *fiúbarát* 'boyfriend' (HH *udvarló* 'courter'), *viccet játszik valakin* 'play a trick on' (HH only *megviccel* 'trick [vt]'),

Bartha's (1993: 117–118) list of calques includes *rátesz* 'put on [music]' (HH *bekapcsol* 'turn on'), *moziház* 'movie house' (HH *mozi* 'movie theater'), *dzsélbe tesz* 'put in jail' (HH *bebörtönöz* 'jail'), *tud valakit* 'know somebody' (HH *ismer* 'know'), *megy* 'go, attend' (HH *jár* 'attend').

Fenyvesi (1995a: 92–94) contains *mozi* 'movie' (HH 'movie theater'), *iskola* 'school [=college or university]' (HH *iskola* 'school', *egyetem* 'university', *főiskola* 'college'), *osztály* 'class [time period]' (HH *osztály* 'class [group of people]' vs. *óra* 'class [time period]').

3.3.2.6 *Borrowing of sibling terms.* In HH there are several words denoting female and male siblings. Thus *nővér* 'older sister', *húg* 'younger sister', *bátya* 'older brother', and *öcs* 'younger brother' are used in reference to one's own siblings and whenever the relative age of the sibling of the person in question is known. In addition to these, the words *testvér* 'sibling', *fiútestvér* 'boy sibling', and *lánytestvér* 'girl sibling', *fivér* 'brother', and *nővér* 'sister' are also used either in collectively referring to more than one of the four kinds of siblings, or when referring to siblings whose sex or age relative to the person in question is not known.

The use of terms referring to siblings is very interesting in the McKeesport data as it constitutes a clear example of replacement of marked vocabulary. In the data, sibling words occur almost exclusively in reference to the speakers' own siblings, that is, where HH would use the four basic terms (these are referred to as 'HH sibling terms' from now on). Some AH speakers use the HH sibling terms, in accordance with HH rules. But others who mention sibling terms use only *testvér*, *fiútestvér* and *lánytestvér* in reference to their own siblings (referred to as AH sibling terms below), distinguishing between older and younger siblings with *idősebb* 'older' and *fiatalabb* 'younger':

(95)   AH *egy   fiútesvérem*   *vout* (McK, Gen2)
       one   boy.sibling.px1sg   was.3sg
       'I had one brother'

(96)   AH *éin   vagyok,   meg   a   tesvéirem   Rouza, meg   a   legfiatalab*
       I   am,   and   the   sibling.px1sg   Róza,   and   the   youngest
       tesvéirem,   Albert (McK, Gen2)
       sibling.px1sg   Albert
       'there is me, my sister Róza, and my youngest brother Albert'

(97)   AH *az   időseb   tesvér   ot   születet   Magyarországon* (McK, Gen2)
       the   older   sibling   there   was.born.3sg   Hungary.sup
       'my older sibling was born in Hungary'

There appears to be a tendency among second-generation speakers to use sibling terms paralleling the American English terms instead of the more marked HH vocabulary.[14] Kontra 1990 does not identify this feature, but his data actually contain it. The South Bend corpus shows a more varied picture than the McKeesport data, but it exhibits the same tendencies. In addition to the HH and AH sibling terms, some first-generation South Bend speakers also use the borrowed sibling terms *brader* 'brother' and *sziszter* 'sister'. These borrowings also appear in Vázsonyi's dictionary.

3.4 Code-switching

Code-switching between Hungarian and English is very clearly present in AH according to all the comprehensive studies of it (Kontra 1990: 13–14, 77, 94–96; Bartha 1993: 122–131; Fenyvesi 1995a: 95–96). A detailed analysis of the function and linguistic characteristics of code-switching behavior has, however, not been carried out in any of the studies so far: only rudimentary characterizations and categorizations have been made.

   The interviews that served as the corpus of data mentioned above were not conducive to code-switching on the part of the AH speakers since they knew they were being interviewed by linguists from Hungary, which, as Kontra (1990: 14) observes, elicited more normative (i.e. monolingual Hungarian) speech than an everyday conversation with another AH speaker would have. However, since the subjects knew that the interviewers spoke English fluently and very well, this nevertheless allowed for at least some code-switching. Or, to put it in Grosjean's (1997, 2001) terms, the knowledge that they were conversing with bilingual Hungarian-English speakers activated their English as well, and therefore put them in a "bilingual mode" rather than a "monolingual mode". Being in a bilingual mode, then, they employed code-switching.

Since, as I have mentioned above, the South Bend, Detroit and McKeesport studies did not investigate code-switching in detail, they used basic working definitions of this phenomenon: Kontra (1990:92) and Fenyvesi (1995a:95) considered as code-switching into English any stretch of discourse that was pronounced with the speaker's usual English pronunciation, while considering words and phrases pronounced with Hungarian phonology as borrowings. Bartha (1993:94), in comparison, used frequency of occurrence as a basis of differentiation between one-word switches and lexical borrowing.

AH has been shown to contain word-, phrase-, and clause-level code-switching, as (98–99), (100–101) and (102–103), respectively, demonstrate. (The stretches of discourse that are considered code-switches appear in boldface in the examples below.)

(98) *Nem akarta, hogy híjuk **dad** vagy **father**.* (SB, Gen2)
      'He didn't want us to call him "dad" or "father".'

(99) *Goromba, goromba, **terrible** vout.* (McK, Gen2)
      'He was rought, rough, terrible.'

(100) *Én fizetek most **eighty-five dollars** egy hónapban.* (SB, Gen1)
      'I pay eighty-five dollars a month.'

(101) *Csak magyaról beszélünk **all the time**.* (Dt)
      'We speak only Hungarian all the time.'

(102) *Annyi, annyi minden van itt, **I don't want any gift. All right**.* (Dt)
      'There are so many, so many things here, I don't want any gift. All right.'

(103) *Dougozik öü is, de... **we get along**.* (McK, Gen2)
      'He also works, but... we get along.'

Some instances of AH code-switching involve what can clearly be defined as fixed, often used phrases:

(104) ***See?** Hogy megérti?* (SB, Gen1)
      'See, how he can understand it?'

(105) *Hát, **wait a minute**, aztat kihattad, hogy...* (Dt)
      'Well, wait a minute, you left out that...'

(106) *Nem tudom **for sure**.* (McK, Gen2)
      'I don't know for sure.'

Other instances contain code-switched material necessitated by lexical gaps in the language (107) or in the speaker's vocabulary (108):

(107) [What do you watch on TV?]
      *Többnyire nem **soap opera**. Meg este, mindig a... **the programs, the variety programs**, azt nézem.* (SB, Gen2)
      'Usually not soap operas. And in the evening, always the... the programs, the variety programs, that's what I watch.

(108)   *Nem tudom, angolul... mondani **department**.* (Dt)
        'I don't know, in English, you say department.'

Sometimes code-switched material contains quotations from discourse that was originally said in English:

(109)   *Mondom neki angolú, hogy soha nem hallottam én ezt a nevet magyarul. Ó,
        aszongya: **wait a minute**. Várj. Várj. Beszaladt a szobájába, van neki **dictionary**,
        kigyött, megmondta, hogy mi az magyarul. De igen nevettem. **Boy**, mondom,
        tetőled tanulok meg magyarul.* (SB, Gen1)
        'And I tell him in English that I never heard this word in Hungarian. "Oh", he
        says, "wait a minute". Wait, wait. He ran into his office, he has a dictionary, he
        came out and told me what that was in Hungarian. I laughed. Boy, I said, I'm
        going to learn Hungarian from you.'

(110)   *Múltkor is felhíttam, oszt mondom: **May I speak to George Marton?*** (Dt)
        'The other day I called him and said, "May I speak to George Marton?"'

3.5 Pragmatic features: Address

Address systems, like other aspects of sociolinguistic competence, are seldom mentioned in discussions of immigrant language maintenance and/or shift, although there is ample evidence they too undergo changes. Previous research has revealed changes in the German address system of German New Zealanders (Stoffel 1983).

HH has a system of address based on a dichotomy of formal (V) and informal (T) address, as in many Indo-European languages, with co-occurrence rules among verbs, pronominal address forms, nominal forms, and greetings. V vs. T address is used very much along the lines of Brown and Gilman's (1960) classic article. Some differences are that in Hungarian there is more than one way of expressing V address as far as verb forms and pronominal address forms are concerned. These are the 3rd-person verb forms, on the one hand, and the verb *tetszik* 'to please' followed by infinitival forms on the other. In V address 3rd-person verb forms can co-occur with a pronoun, *ön* or *maga*, where the former is more polite and/or more formal than the latter. The V address *tetszik* does not have a corresponding pronoun – here a nominal address form is used when the interlocutor must be referred to overtly.

The usage of address forms is constant between two members of a dyad, and address changes occur only as a result of change in the relative status of the speakers (e.g. a shift from nonreciprocal address to reciprocal V between a long-acquainted older adult and a younger person just entering adulthood, or a shift from reciprocal V to reciprocal T between a professor and a former student when the latter enters into employment in the same department). Temporary shifts between T and V address documented in Brown and Gilman 1960 and Friedrich 1972, employed to signal sudden changes of attitude, are not acceptable in Hungarian.

In terms of address usage, the McKeesport subjects can be grouped into two very different categories of speakers: first-generation speakers and second-generation speakers who have first-generation speakers of their approximate age or younger in their family – whom I will call 'fluent speakers' in this section – and the rest of the second-generation speakers, whom I will refer to as 'semi-speakers'. Although there is a lot of variation among members of both groups in their usage and perception of rules of address, the two groups stand apart in significant ways.

Fluent speakers actually use Hungarian in everyday conversations, usually with their spouses and one or two friends. They are also aware of the T/V distinction in HH, have rules about using one and the other, and are able to introspect and talk about their usage. Semi-speakers, on the other hand, do not use Hungarian on an everyday basis with anyone (even if their spouse is also a second-generation speaker). They are aware that there are different ways of addressing people in Hungarian, but they usually do not know what these consist of, are not able to introspect about their usage very easily, and also lack the metalinguistic means to talk about it.

In the course of my fieldwork I addressed all my subjects in a way I would have in Hungary. I gave V, *maga*, and first name and honorific kinship title *néni* 'aunt' and *bácsi* 'uncle' to all the speakers one generation older than me (I was 28 years old at the time). The two exceptions were speakers, both of whom insisted that I should address them with T and first names, arguing that 'they weren't so old' to be addressed with V. I addressed the younger speakers with T and first names – some of them because they suggested switching to T during our first meeting, and one because he was younger than I was and we had also met through mutual friends before. I received T and first name address from all the subjects whom I have addressed in the same way, due to mutual agreement with each, mentioned above.

From the members of the semi-speaker group, however, I received more T address than I would have expected according to HH rules. Even though I belonged to the same age group as the children of these subjects, the fact that I was an adult stranger on a somewhat formal mission of research in the community would probably have prompted V, *maga* and first name address in a similar situation among HH speakers. Only some subjects addressed me with V, *maga* and first name address, others addressed me with T and first name, while one speaker addressed me with the T pronoun *te* and V verb forms – an impossible co-occurrence in HH. According to HH rules, nonreciprocal T address towards me would have been especially unusual from older males, and it would have been introduced by a phrase like *'Hope you don't mind if I address you with T'* by the elderly female speakers.

The similarities between HH and AH address concern the use of address forms mostly between parents and their children, children and adults, and lay adults on the one hand and ministers on the other – truly reflecting the scope of Hungarian language use in McKeesport, where most of the speakers spoke Hungarian only in childhood, with their parents, with other immigrant adults, and in church.

All second-generation speakers reported having called their parents just as parents would be addressed in HH. Speakers who remember whether they used T or V verb forms in addressing their parents are divided between those who report having addressed both parents with V, those who addressed their mother with T and their father with V, and those who addressed both parents with T. All speakers remember being addressed by first name and T by their parents. These combinations of address could be perfectly acceptable HH ways of addressing.

All the elderly second-generation speakers remember addressing adults in their childhood (typically, the friends of their parents or the parents of their friends) with first or last name plus honorary kinship title *néni* 'aunt' and *bácsi* 'uncle', and most cite V verbs as examples of how they would have addressed them. One younger second-generation subject reports using T verbs with the same name and title combination in the same situation. Both kinds of address would be acceptable in HH as well.

The speakers unanimously report using reciprocal first name and T verb address with friends, and the two subjects who had Hungarian-speaking co-workers of the same age and rank report the same usage with them as well. In these situations also HH address would be the same. All subjects except the minister and his wife report addressing Hungarian Protestant ministers with the HH-like double title *tiszteletes úr* 'Mr. Reverend'.

The members of the semi-speakers' group exhibit characteristics of address or addressing behavior that are not found in HH. As evidenced by the following facts, these are mostly due to an incomplete learning of and relatively small range of opportunities to use the complete HH address system in general, especially V address.

One such characteristic is the co-occurrence of T pronouns and V verbs in addressing the same person, as has been mentioned above. Another HH co-occurrence violation was occasionally used by one subject, who addressed me with the V pronoun *maga* when she used it in the nominal, but used declined 3rd-person pronouns like *vele* 'with him/her' and *hozzá* 'to him/her' instead of the declined forms of *maga* (e.g. *magával* 'with you.FORMAL' or *magához* 'to you.FORMAL')

Some subjects sometimes had difficulty understanding who my questions referred to when I asked them about themselves with V verbal address (which requires 3rd-person verb forms in HH); they asked me clarification questions, typically referring to their family members who had been mentioned in the interview before. A typical exchange went like the one in (111):

(111)   A: *Hol tetszett születni?* (Where were you.FORMAL born?)
        B: *Apám?* (My father?)
        A: *A Pista bácsi hol született?* (Where was Uncle Pista born?)
        B: *Én?* (Me?)
        A: *Igen.* (Yes.)
        B: *Dukénba.* (In Duquesne.)

For a brief discussion of such and similar communicative failures, see Kontra (1993b).

Other characteristics among the semi-speakers are the following. One subject expressed his belief that the addressing with T or V was a dialectal characteristic of Hungarian. Some openly admitted their inability to tell me what the difference was between two short sentences which were identical except that one contained a T verb and the other a V verb. Others did not seem to have any knowledge about T and V address being different not only in nominal address forms, but also in verb forms, pronominals and greetings. Among the fluent speakers, I found a great tolerance towards being addressed with T forms even by strangers – the American-born subjects all said that they would not mind at all if an adult stranger addressed them with T at the first meeting (while the first-generation speakers all said that they would feel offended if it happened in Hungary, but learned not to mind it in the U.S.).

These second-generation speakers expressed a unanimous uncertainty about when they were supposed to use V address with Hungarians in and/or from Hungary, and all of them claimed to avoid using it with American-Hungarians of approximately their own age or younger. Some second-generation speakers said they believed that V address should be used only with people older than oneself, and to strangers. All fluent speakers except the one who lived a significant portion of her adult life in Hungary (she immigrated when she was 32) admitted that they know they suggest to their interlocutors that they switch from initial V to T more quickly (usually during the very first meeting) than would be usual in Hungary. After all, said one subject, 'a stranger is not a stranger after you've talked to them'. Some subjects said they do not feel any difference in addressing Hungarian-speakers in the U.S. and in Hungary.

Previous research on address in immigrant communities has also shown that the address system in the first language of bilingual immigrant communities may change in relation to the address system of the standard usage in that language in the 'old country'. Stoffel (1983) has demonstrated that there is a marked shift among bilingual Germans in New Zealand towards the use of first names and T forms in situations where a title plus last name and V form address would be predominant in German-speaking countries. She has also shown that in the immigrant community speakers have a higher degree of tolerance towards receiving address forms different from those they would consider appropriate in the given situation (e.g. receiving T address instead of the expected V); she argues that some uncertainty may arise, especially among second-generation speakers, about what address should be used in some situations. In a brief section Kontra (1990: 116–117) also reports that the usage of the AH pronominal and verbal address system is indeed different from that of HH – either lacking V forms or having different rules about when T and V are used.

The findings in McKeesport indicate that, in addition to the above features, the following are also characteristic of AH: a partial lack of V forms and the rules governing their use; a partial lack of metalinguistic ability in talking about address; inability to recall what address was used towards a person the speaker knew well; inability to tell how one is addressed by somebody else in a conversation at the present time; some violations of co-occurrence rules, and significant differences among speakers with respect to these characteristics.

3.6 Language attrition

In addition to characteristics where AH shows the effect of American English, in several features the effect of language attrition can be seen as well, especially in the speech of second-generation speakers. I attribute a linguistic feature to the effect of language attrition if it is a result of simplification and reduction processes (Dorian 1981:8; Mühlhäusler 1977) without compensation elsewhere in the linguistic system. However, it also has to be noted that in many cases borrowing and language attrition effects are inseparable, in what historical linguists (e.g. Campbell & Muntzel 1989) call cases of multiple causation. Thus, I categorize a feature as the result of language attrition if it is a simplification or reduction that did not make the structure more similar to American English. Examples of this from subsections above are the regularization of irregular verb and noun stems, or focus-movement of non-focussed constituents in syntax. Examples of features categorized as a change due to multiple causation, that is, due both to language attrition and to the influence of American English are the loss of gemination, the loss of pronominal possessive suffixes and appearance of non-focussed overt possessor pronoun at the same time, and the frequent lack of focus movement. (As I mentioned in the beginning of Section 3, I attribute a linguistic feature to borrowing if it incorporates elements of the speakers' other language.)

It should be emphasized that I am not claiming to have established with total certainty the cause of any specific change (except, obviously, borrowed words); rather, the claim is that the best available historical explanation – given the nature of the data – is the one I propose. If I categorize all of the 52 features that AH is different from HH in (for all details, see Fenyvesi 1995a, 1998a), the following picture emerges: 20, or less than half of these are due to borrowing alone; 28, or slightly more than half are the result of borrowing and attrition; and only 4 are affected by attrition alone.

Language attrition is, thus, very much present in AH – in most instances, showing its effect together with the influence of borrowing and only in few cases without it.

4.   Conclusion

In this chapter I have provided an overview of the sociolinguistic and linguistic aspects of Hungarian-Americans and their language that information from various studies is available on. As both the sociolinguistic and linguistic evidence demonstrates, Hungarian-Americans as a group are undergoing language shift along the classic three-generation model, similarly to many other immigrant groups of the United States. However, the picture presented in this chapter is incomplete in the sense that the studies it is based on (Kontra 1990; Bartha 1993; Fenyvesi 1995a; Polgár 2001) all target traditional Hungarian-American communities from the oldest, primarily blue-collar settlements, while newer and socioeconomically more diverse communities would very likely present a somewhat different picture – possibly with slightly better chances of language maintenance and linguistically less affected Hungarian as their language. Studies on the latter, however, have not been published to date. Studies such as this would be highly desirable because they would enable us to have a more refined and up-to-date understanding of the state of the Hungarian language in the United States.

Notes

* I want to thank Reverend and Mrs. Daniel Borsay of the Free Hungarian Reformed Church in McKeesport, Pennsylvania, without whose help my research would not have been possible. Thanks are also due to Kati Csoman, my first Hungarian-American friend, who also introduced me to many people in the community. I want to thank István Lanstyák for his ever so detailed and insightful comments on an earlier draft of this paper as well as Helga Arnold F. for her comments on parts of it. Needless to say, any remaining shortcomings are my own responsibility. I am grateful to Miklós Kontra for giving me his South Bend text files on disk.

1. Unless otherwise specified, all data quoted in Sections 2.2 and 2.3 are based on figures from the 1990 Census and Census 2000, released on the internet at http://www.census.gov/.

2. The use of the phoneme /e/ instead of some of the occurrences of /ɛ/ occurs in many regional dialects in Hungary and is also present in the speech of some of the Hungarian-Americans (see Kontra 1990:43–50; Fenyvesi 1995a:15). For a detailed account of this feature, see Kontra (1993a).

3. An example of the former, a very common and nonstigmatized feature of spoken Hungarian, is the deletion of the final *n* in the inessive suffix *-ban* (as in *Washingtonba* 'in Washington' for *Washingtonban*). Another very common feature is the deletion of coda-position *l*'s (as in [boːt] for *bolt* 'shop' or [voːtɑm] 'I was' for *voltam*), which, according to Imre (1971:261), is a general feature of Hungarian regional dialects, but is, most probably, best treated as a sociolinguistic variable.

4. For a detailed assessment of what features are characteristic of only first-generation speakers, second-generation speakers, or both, see Fenyvesi (1998a).

5. In the examples I provide the place (SB=South Bend, Dt=Detroit, and McK=McKeesport) and generation of the speaker from whom the example is given. "Gen1" is used for first-generation, while "Gen2" for second-generation speakers.

6. In examples where morphological structure is of importance, I separate morphemes with hyphens, which, in orthography, would not be used.

7. The thematizing suffixes *-z* and *-l* (preceded by a connecting vowel if the verb stem ends in a consonant) are verbalizing derivational suffixes in Hungarian which are obligatorily used when verbs are borrowed.

8. Interestingly, the same was found for British Hungarian in A. Benkő (2000), a study investigating morphological and syntactic features of Hungarian immigrants and their children in London: while these speakers mixed conjugations here, too, they never used the wrong person/number marking on verbs.

9. The element that fails to receive a preverb is underlined in all of the following examples.

10. In this section all AH examples are accompanied by the HH version of the sentence. In the English glosses of the AH sentences, verbs are supplied in the same tense and without the marking of definiteness/indefiniteness; only the person and number of the subject are marked. In many cases the English translation of the question which the subjects were answering is given in square brackets before the example, in order to supply the necessary context for the AH sentence. The constituents that, according to the context, should be focussed, are underlined in the AH sentences.

11. Unless otherwise marked, all examples in this section are from Vázsonyi (1995).

12. According to these calculations, the sum of the various kinds of entries in Vázsonyi 1995 is 978 rather than 900, due to the fact that some words have two or more meanings which are of different parts of speech, e.g. *bézment* 'basement', *bébi* 'baby' and *itáli* 'Italian' all have nominal as well as adjectival meanings.

13. In my discussion of loanwords, loanblends and calques, examples come mostly from Vázsonyi (1995), since it is more comprehensive than any of the studies of AH, even though some of the borrowings occur both in the dictionary and in one or more of the studies. I include examples from the studies only when they do not also occur in the dictionary.

14. A similar tendency to borrow English words in replacement of marked vocabulary also occurs in American Finnish, where compounds such as *southwest, northeast* etc. are borrowed to replace their Finland Finnish equivalents, which are noncompounded synthetic words (Pekka Hirvonen, personal communication, 1999).

Chapter 10

Hungarian in Australia

Magdolna Kovács

1. Introduction

For centuries Australia was called 'terra incognita australis'. During that time several hundreds of aboriginal languages were spoken in the unknown territory. The arrival of British 'migrants' to Australia threatened multilingualism: the white assimilation policy caused the disappearance of many indigenous languages. By the time of the 1996 census, there were only 48 indigenous languages left in Australia – many of them with only a very small number of speakers. The extensive immigration to Australia from numerous countries after World War II, however, had again increased the diversity of languages in Australia: the total number of languages spoken in 1996 in Australia was 240 (Clyne & Klipp 1999: 10). Hungarian is one of the 'migrant' or, with a more neutral term usually preferred in Australia, 'community' languages.

The variety of the Hungarian language spoken and written in Australia is called Australian Hungarian in this study. Australian Hungarian has developed as a consequence of the migration of Hungarians to this continent. Speakers of Australian Hungarian do not use the term 'Australian Hungarian' for their language but 'Hungarian' or, in some cases, 'Hunglish' which they may have heard being used for the Hungarian language variety spoken in the United States and Canada and applied it together with its negative connotation for their own variety.

Until recently, Australian Hungarian was not a popular research topic. There are a few books concerning the history of the Hungarian migration to Australia (e.g. Kunz 1969, 1997), but these books do not touch upon language issues. The first linguistic analysis of Australian Hungarian was written by Endrődy (1971). His unpublished MA thesis shows English prepositional interference in Australian Hungarian. Ambrosy's (1984) sociolinguistic survey on twelve Hungarian migrants' cultural assimilation also includes information on language use. According to Ambrosy (1984: 24), the main domain of the Hungarian language use in the early 1980s was the home. Clyne (1997) analyzes the code-switching of some trilingual persons in Australia, Australian Hungarians among others.

In my own previous work, I described the proper noun use of Australian Hungarians (1996), characterized in a case study (M. Kovács 1997) the specific features of a second generation Australian Hungarian speaker's speech, discussed morphological features in the code-switching of Australian Hungarians (2001a) and identified links between code-switching and language shift in an immigrant context (2001b).

In this chapter I present an overview of Hungarian in Australia and analyze factors playing a role in the Hungarian language maintenance in Australia. I use my own data, collected among Australian Hungarians, to describe some aspects of the Hungarian language use of this community as well as to provide as insight into the larger context of language maintenance and shift. In the analysis of the sociolinguistic factors, I use Tandefelt's (1988) three-dimensional model of maintenance factors. In the model, time forms one dimension, the different levels of society (societal, group and individual level) the other and sociocultural and linguistic factors the third.

2.   Sociolinguistic aspects

2.1   The historical background of Australian Hungarian

A few Hungarians came to Australia as early as in the first half of the 19th century. These early arrivals were Hungarian Jews; one of them arrived as a convict from England in 1829, the others were mainly goldsmiths and manufacturers (Kunz 1997: 17–25). In the second half of the 19th century, some of the Hungarians who migrated to Australia were political refugees (who fled after the defeat of the 1848–1849 revolution and war of independence), others were in search of adventures and money during the Australian Gold Rush of the 1850s and 1860s (Kunz 1969: 1–160, 1997: 27–114). The number of the earliest migrants was very small. In the 1921 census of Australia only 148 people were listed as having been born in Hungary (Jupp & York 1995: 53).

Between 1936 and 1940 about of 800 people migrated from Hungary to Australia. These people were mostly Hungarian Jews and liberal or social democrats (Kunz 1969: 183, 1997: 115–122) who were afraid of the consequences of the political developments in Europe. Hungarians arrived in Australia in larger numbers only after World War II in two main waves of immigration. The first one started immediately after the war and reached its peak after the so-called 'time of the turn' in Hungary in 1948 when the communists took power. The second wave, the largest one so far, followed the failed anticommunist revolution in 1956. Hungarians arriving in Australia after World War II had different political, cultural and religious backgrounds: they were Jewish survivors of the Holocaust, members of the aristocracy, rightists, as well as social or liberal democrats (Kunz 1969: 185, 1997: 125–150). Most of them left Hungary for political reasons, which was the main reason for emigration after the anticommunist revolution in 1956 as well. Among them there were many young people, tradesmen and factory workers, and also people with university degrees. Almost all social classes except peasants were represented (Kunz 1969: 194, 1997: 155-157): in contrast to the migration to America in the early 20th century, when most of the migrants had an agrarian background, Australian Hungarian migration included only a small number of peasants. After the main wave of migration immediately following the 1956 revolution, people from Hungary arrived in Australia only in small numbers. These latter migrants left Hungary mostly for political or economic reasons. Hungarians migrated to Australia not only from Hungary but also from the neighboring countries (see Section 2.2.2 below concerning demography).

Most Hungarian political refugees wished to migrate to America or to Western Europe, and many of them were not familiar with Australia. Typically, only after waiting for a longer period of time in refugee camps in Austria or Italy did they decide to accept Australia's offer and immigrate to this unfamiliar country. Many of them went through a shock when they arrived to Australia after the exhausting trip on a ship and were placed in refugee camps once again. People emigrating from Budapest experienced culture shock in the beginning even in Sydney in those days.[1] The obligatory two-year contract with the Australian government put many Hungarians, university students and teachers among others, to work on railway constructions in the desert or building power stations, for example, in the Snowy Mountains. Nevertheless, Hungarians soon found their place in Australian society and started to build up their own organizations and societies, as discussed in the following section.

2.2 Factors of Hungarian language maintenance and shift

A number of theories and models have been developed to describe or predict the stages of language maintenance or shift of minority languages. In those models, as pointed out by Clyne (1991:86), the role of the interaction between different minority groups in the society is not taken into account. This interaction can, as it has in the Australian case, lead to the development of a more positive policy, which can further affect language maintenance positively.

The factors playing a role in language maintenance or shift described by Haugen (1953, 1971), Kloss (1966), Fishman (1970, 1972a) and Giles et al. (1977) are further developed by Tandefelt (1988) into a three-dimensional model, in which different levels of society (a societal, a group, and an individual level) form one dimension, while time constitutes the second, and sociocultural and linguistic factors the third dimension. In the following sections most factors listed by Tandefelt are applied to the case of the Australian Hungarian community to describe the current situation of Hungarian in Australia.

2.2.1   *Societal level: Linguistic organization, legislation, and institutions*
Tandefelt (1988:40–48) describes three main factors on the societal level affecting language maintenance and shift: (a) the linguistic organization of the society, (b) legislation affecting the languages used in the society, and (c) institutions (such as school, church, and the media).

Despite the fact that Australia has no official language, English is the national language and the main language of communication, the 'lingua franca' (Clyne & Kipp 1999:16–17). However, with the hundreds of indigenous languages in the past and with the 240 languages in the present, multilingualism has always been represented in the country. The Australian society and language policy did not always accept multilingualism, instead, monoculturalism, monolingualism and assimilation were the leading Australian policies until the 1970s (Romaine 1991: 1–8). The great wave of immigration from non-English speaking European countries after World War II did not change these policies at once. These migrants were expected to speak English in public places, and parents were officially advised to speak English to their children even at home (Ozolins 1991: 331). In the 1970s, a multicultural and multilingual policy began to develop. In 1981, language professionals and ethnic organizations raised the question of the need for an official language policy supporting multilingualism. In 1984, the Australian Senate accepted the idea of multilingualism and outlined the guiding principles of a new language policy. The goal of the language policy was to serve four basic needs: competence in English, maintenance of community languages (that is, minority languages), provision of services in community languages, and opportunities for learning second languages (Ozolins 1991: 344, 1993: 239–242). From the Senate Report, a National Policy on Languages, known as the Lo Bianco Report, was developed in 1987. The main emphasis was placed on the educational level, but the importance of the media was also underlined in the report. The National Language Policy was later followed by state language policies. The federal and state governments began to systematically support multilingual education and community language use in the media (Clyne 1991: 227; Ozolins 1991: 342–348, 1993: 156–249).

Both education and the media have gone through major changes brought about by multiculturalism. Bilingual teaching gradually spread as a government supported part of education. In many schools today children can receive bilingual instruction at primary and secondary levels. Studying certain community languages as second languages at the tertiary level is also available in Australia today. In 1991, the number of community languages available for the Matriculation level exam was 28 (Clyne 1991: 117–131). Hungarian is one of the 28 languages accepted as subjects in the High School Certificate. However, Hungarian does not belong to the most supported and widely taught languages in Australia. It is only taught a few hours per week mainly in Saturday and Sunday schools. The absence of comprehensive, large-scale bilingual education in Hungarian (that is, beyond Saturday and Sunday schools) plays a rather negative role in Hungarian language maintenance.

Broadcasting in community languages was restricted to some rural radio stations until the 1970s. By the 1990s, around 60 community languages were broadcast throughout Australia in 27 radio stations for about 600 hours per week (Clyne 1991: 147). Multicultural TV started in 1980. Broadcasting in Hungarian is available for a few hours per week in the big cities in Australia. Television programs in the Hungarian language are rare.

A telephone interpreting service available since 1973, and the National Accreditation Authority of Translators and Interpreters was created with the establishment of the multicultural era (Ozolins 1991: 340–341). A telephone counseling service, Lifeline, helped people in six languages in 1991 (Clyne 1991: 145), but Hungarian was not

Table 10.1. Language maintenance rates (in percentages) of some community languages in Australia in 1986*

Languages	GEN1	GEN2	GEN2.5**
Chinese	81.9	66.4	22.7
Dutch	48.9	14.7	2.5
Finnish	75.1	59.5	13.3
German	61.1	27.3	3.7
Greek	92.2	88.3	56.6
Hungarian	70.6	49.4	12.8
Italian	88.0	70.0	31.7

* Source: Clyne (1991:66–67).
** "2.5 generation" indicates that one of the parents belongs to the first generation, and the other to the second.

among these. In this study, the role of the media and other institutions (churches and schools) in language maintenance is analyzed at the group level, because they mainly act at that level as maintenance factors in Australian Hungarian.

In summary, the language policy in Australia has substantially changed since 1970s. The policy preferring assimilation, monoculturalism and monolingualism has been revised radically. The current multicultural era supports language maintenance. The policy of multiculturalism, however, came too late for many community and indigenous languages as well. Clyne (1991:66–67) shows that most community languages, including Hungarian, shifted towards English more or less by 1986, a year before the establishment of the National Policy on Languages. The maintenance percentages of a few community languages are shown in Table 10.1.

2.2.2 Group level: Settlement patterns, demography, bilingualism, and cultural characteristics

According to Tandefelt (1988:48–59), factors affecting maintenance and shift on the group level include the following: (a) majority attitudes towards the minority language, (b) the type of minority settlements (isolation or not), (c) the size of the minority, (d) the the number of bilingual members of the minority, and (e) the cultural characteristics of the minority (cultural traditions, ethnic symbols, etc.).

There are no statistics on the exact number of Hungarians living in Australia. Australian censuses list people by the country in which they were born. Figure 10.1 shows the number of Hungarian-born persons living in Australia, according to Australian censuses (Jupp & York 1995:53; *Census 1996*). The number of Hungarian-born people was at its peak in the 1961 census, right after the migration of the refugees of the 1956 revolution.

The number of people of Hungarian language background is not the same as the number of those born in Hungary and living in Australia. Many ethnic Hungarians living as minorities in the countries neighboring post-Trianon Hungary also migrated to Australia, but their number can only be estimated. The main heading of the Australian

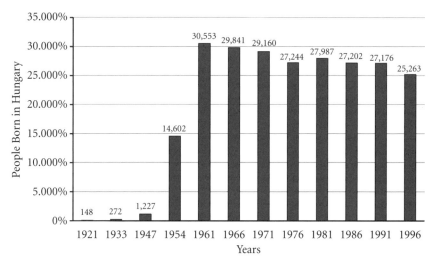

* Source: Jupp and York (1995), and *Census 1996*.

Figure 10.1. Hungarian-born persons in Australia, according to census data*

Hungarian newspaper *Magyar Élet – Hungarian Life* proclaims that it is addressed to 55,000 Hungarians living in Australia. Kunz (1997: 232) estimates the number of Hungarian people who came to Australia from countries other than Hungary as 11,431 and the total number of Hungarians living in Australia as being 74,482. The latter includes first-generation as well as second-generation Hungarians with at least one parent of Hungarian origin. The current Australian censuses (since 1986) also reveal the number of people using community languages at home. Home users of Hungarian numbered 29,789 in 1991. Depending on what we take as the total number of Hungarians, 55,000 or 74,482, half or one third of all first- and second-generation Hungarians are home users of the Hungarian language in Australia. Compared to the most widely spoken minority languages, which, according to Clyne and Kipp (1999: 10), are Italian (375,752 users), Greek (269,770 users) and Cantonese (202,270 users), or compared to the small minority languages, like Finnish with 7,771 users in 1991, Hungarian is a medium sized minority language in Australia.

Hungarians live mainly in big cities; most Hungarian language users live in Sydney and Melbourne (Clyne 1982: 151; also *Census 1991*). This shows a concentration of language users, which may result in better chances of language maintenance. However, in these big cities there are only a few suburbs in which Hungarians live in larger concentrations. Thus, there are not too many Hungarians who have opportunities to use Hungarian in the neighborhood domain.

Hungarians have formed many different groups and associations in Australia, depending on their time of arrival, country of origin, political views and religion. This division into many smaller groups is not conducive to language maintenance. However, Hungarians have many institutions and organizations which are traditionally thought to promote language maintenance. They have associations and societies in different states, social clubs and sports clubs (especially soccer clubs, like "St. George Budapest" in Sydney), political groups, folk music and dance groups as well as scout troops. According to Kunz (1997:174), around 100–200 Hungarian associations have been established and functioned in Australia in the last 50–60 years, many of them only for short periods of time. There are also nursing homes for retired persons (one, in Sydney, is named after St. Elizabeth, and another, in Melbourne, after Árpád, a tribal leader of Hungarians in the 9th century). In Sydney and Melbourne, there are clubs which are visited mainly by Hungarian Jews (Kunz 1997:174). In the bigger cities church services in Hungarian are available for Catholics, Calvinists and occasionally for Lutherans as well. According to Kunz (1997:178–179), the biggest center of Australian Hungarians is in the Wantirna suburb of Melbourne with many Hungarian clubs, a library, five restaurants and cafés, sports fields and playgrounds, and an ecumenical church. The Hungarian nursing home is also in this area. Saturday and Sunday schools for teaching the Hungarian language were originally organized on a volunteer basis. Broadcasting at the community level also relies on volunteers.

Hungarian associations usually organize cultural and political events, such as theater performances, shows, film screening, picnics, markets or celebrations of the Hungarian national holidays. The main cultural and social event of the Australian Hungarians are the Hungarian Days, organized once every three years in one of the big cities.

During the monocultural era, publishing in languages other than English was not encouraged or supported. However, ethnic newspapers, magazines, and church or association bulletins could be published with permission even then. As Kunz (1997:186) points out, the political and religious differences as well as the long distances between the settlements of Hungarians resulted in more than 40 Hungarian journals, magazines, bulletins being published even during the time of assimilatory policies. Most of them survived only for very short periods of time. The only long term newspaper is *Magyar Élet – Hungarian Life* (since 1958). Dezséry's Ethnic Publishing Company in Adelaide has published many Hungarian books.

For a typical example showing that many Hungarian traditions still thrive in Australia in the beginning of the 21st century, part of a forwarded e-mail message dated September 24, 2001, is cited here (1) (translations of Hungarian words in square brackets inserted by me):

(1) Subject: Transylvaniacs events: LAST PUB FOR THE YEAR… and tanchaz ['dance club']!
TANCHAZ: Learn Hungarian folk dancing in one night! Well, some of it anyway – tanchaz feature dance is from the Szatmar region of north-east Hungary. Dances taught for novices and regulars alike by Attila Turcsanyi and Jenni Kovacs of Kengugro, with the opportunity to dance with all kengugro members (some of us have been doing this for more than 20 years…) Special guest: Tim Meyen all the way from Canberra, making szatmari music feel

more like szatmari music with his big black cimbalom ['Hungarian zither']!
(if you've never seen one, here's your opportunity)
BYO palinka ['Hungarian fruit brandy']
Date: Saturday 20th October 2001
Place: Hungarian Community Centre (Melbourne)
Time: 8: 00–10: 30 (set teaching), and then we're open to requests…

The "number of bilingual members of the group" is one of Tandefelt's factors playing a role in language maintenance at the group level. Because linguistic isolation is no longer possible in the current globalized world, most Hungarians know English to some degree. As described above, only half of the Hungarians are home users of the Hungarian language (or only one third of them, by a more conservative count). The language shift into English increases generation after generation.

According to Tandefelt (1988: 48–50), majority attitudes towards the minority language manifest themselves at the group level. During the time of assimilation policies, the attitudes towards minority languages were not very positive. In 1980, according to Rado and Lewis' (1980) study, 67% of monolinguals (and even half of the bilinguals) felt annoyed when hearing minority languages in public places. Attitudes do not change fast. Currently in Australia many people accept the idea of multilingualism, but the old attitudes also survive.

In conclusion, Hungarians have many opportunities to use the Hungarian language at the group level. These are mainly self-supported group events, including a lot of volunteer work. The opportunities for language use at the group level can effect language maintenance positively if the supply meets the demand. However, most Hungarian events and services (except Saturday and Sunday schools and scout troops) are utilized mainly by the first generation. Many second generation Hungarians feel that some of the events and programs are not designed for them but for the older generations.[2] The political and religious differences as well as differences in the time of arrival play a negative role in language maintenance. Partly caused by these differences, many Hungarians do not visit Hungarian events at all. According to Kunz's (1997: 174) estimation, only 5–10% of the Australian Hungarians visit Hungarian associations regularly.

2.2.3   *Individual level: contact-induced changes, attitudes and language use*

The third level of society at which factors play a role in language maintenance is the individual level (Tandefelt 1988: 59–71). The individual level consists of the following factors: (a) competence in the two languages, (b) the (linguistic) consequences of language contact, (c) identification with the language group, and (d) the use of the two languages (domain analysis, language choice and network, and family). These questions will be analyzed in separate sections in more detail below, based on language use questionnaires and interview data I have collected. The common features of the individual language use raise these factors from the individual to the group level.

2.3 The use of Hungarian and English

In M. Kovács (2002) I report on the language use of Australian Hungarians. This pilot study is based on language use questionnaires filled out by 18 Australian Hungarians in 1998 at the Sydney scout club. Young people visiting the club, a few of their relatives, and some organizers of the club answered questions concerning their Hungarian and the English language use. The results of the questionnaire do not, of course, describe the language use of the whole Australian Hungarian community, but only of those who actively take part in some Hungarian events. Presumably, people regularly visiting Hungarian events are expected to pay more attention also to language maintenance than those who are not interested in taking part in Hungarian events at all. The questionnaire was available both in Hungarian and in English. Everyone but one person filled in the questionnaire in Hungarian, which seems, at least to some extent, to prove the above mentioned assumption.

There are both first- (n = 6) and second-generation (n = 12) persons among the subjects. The line between the first and the second generation is drawn based on their age at migration. I placed persons who left Hungary as adults or after the age of 15 among the first generation (GEN1) and counted their Australian-born children and children who left Hungary before the age of 15 as second-generation. Those who left Hungary before the age of 15 are considered to be second generation Hungarians because most of them went to primary school in Australia and not in Hungary, and their linguistic behavior is assumed to be closer to that of the second than the first generation. The second generation is divided into two subgroups, into persons who migrated to Australia as children (6 persons, GEN2A) and Australian-born persons (n = 6, GEN2B).

Figure 10.2 describes the subjects' self-estimated competence in Hungarian and English. Self-estimation does not always correspond to reality but may show the main tendencies of the group the subject belongs to. All the informants except one report themselves as being bilingual at levels ranging from average to perfect, that is, they claim to have a good command in both of their languages. One person (subject 1), who migrated to Australia after the age of 60, reports a fair command of English. There is a difference between the first and second generation in the level of the knowledge of the two languages. All first generation speakers believed that their Hungarian was perfect, and all second generation subjects (both in group A and B) that their English was perfect. Nobody in the first generation stated that their English was perfect, and nobody in the Australian-born generation (GEN2B) claimed that their Hungarian was perfect. Most first-generation informants felt that their English was good. In the group GEN2A most informants' Hungarian was good according to their self-estimation. Two persons in this group, those who went to school in Hungary for 7 or 8 years and migrated to Australia as 13- and 14-year-olds, claimed that their Hungarian was perfect (subjects 7 and 8). Most GEN2B persons' Hungarian was average, and two felt that it was good. There is a statistically significant difference between the three groups in the self-estimated command of Hungarian (after Bonferroni correction, the results

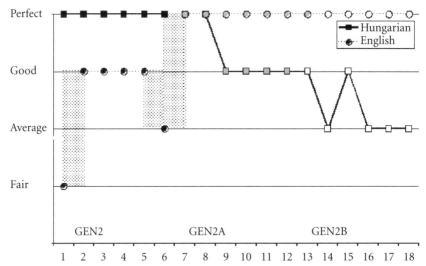

* Subjects in GEN 1 and GEN 2B are arranged in the order of their age (the oldest being #1) and in GEN 2A in the order of their age at migration.

Figure 10.2. Australian Hungarians' self-estimated competence in Hungarian and English*

are significant at the $p < .01$ level between GEN1 and GEN2A, and at the $p < .008$ level between GEN2A and GEN2B). The English of every second-generation person is reported as perfect. Between the first and second generation, there is a statistically significant difference in their English proficiency (at the $p < .001$ level). These results are not surprising: persons in the first generation have a better command of Hungarian than English, and persons in the second generation have a better command of English than Hungarian. The claim of the second-generation persons that their Hungarian is average to perfect, with nobody claiming not to speak any Hungarian, seems to support the presupposition that people visiting Hungarian events are also interested in maintaining the language of their ancestors.

The same persons were also asked about the domains of their language use. The results are shown in Figure 10.3.

The results of the language use questionnaire show that the neighborhood domain, which in some minority communities is the most important bastion of language maintenance, is completely affected by English in all three groups. The people in the study use predominantly English in the work and school domains because there are no Hungarian bilingual schools in Sydney (except for a Saturday school) and only a few persons work together with other Hungarians. The main domains of Hungarian language maintenance are the home, the church and leisure time activities. Four second generation Hungarians do not go to church, and for them this domain is not a maintenance factor.

Leisure time activities show almost equal use of Hungarian and English in the second generation. Taking part in picnics and visiting clubs, organizations, and Hun-

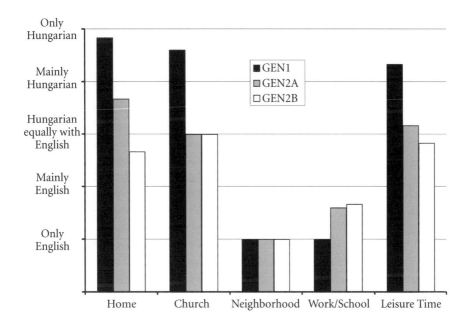

Figure 10.3. The domains of Hungarian and English language use among Australian Hungarians

garian events are listed among these activities. They also include the scout club, which these people attend actively. If, for example, other cultural events or sport activities such as theatre or aerobics classes were included, the results would have been different.

The results show that the use of Hungarian decreases from the first generation to the second. The difference between the first- and second-generation use of Hungarian and English is statistically significant for the home and church domains ($p < .03$) and in leisure time activities ($p < .024$). In the home domain a difference can be pointed out between all three groups ($p < .001$): first-generation subjects almost always use Hungarian at home, group GEN2A mostly Hungarian, and group GEN2B uses slightly more English than Hungarian (the differences between the groups after Bonferrioni correction are significant for GEN1 and GEN2A at the $p < .011$ level; and for GEN2A and GEN2B at the $p < .02$ level).

These results also show a relatively active use of Hungarian in at least three of the five domains (home, church, and leisure time). This seems to prove the presupposition that persons visiting Hungarian events are also interested in actively using the Hungarian language. Bearing in mind Kunz's estimation that only 5–10% of Australian Hungarians visit Hungarian associations and events regularly, the results of the questionnaire are more positive than the reality in the whole Hungarian community. According to Clyne (1991:67), Hungarians had shifted to English already in 1986: then the language maintenance percentage was 70.6% in the first, 49.4% in the second generation, and 12.8% in generation 2.5.

Identification with the language group was not included in the questionnaire concerning language use. Linguistic interview data with 35 Australian Hungarians, collected in 1993–1994 (and described in detail in Section 3.2), give some information about this factor. The interviews were conducted with people who were able to carry out a conversation in Hungarian. Their identification with the Hungarian language group and their attitudes towards the Hungarian language are likely to be positive. To give a glimpse of the complexity of the question concerning identification with the language group, some opinions from the linguistic interviews are cited here. Example (2) contains a part of an interview with a Hungarian Jewish couple who have lived in Australia for many decades. The husband, who migrated to Australia in the 1930s, went back to Hungary before World War II to find a Hungarian-speaking bride in order to maintain his Hungarian background and the Hungarian language. The wife and the husband agree that all migrants who were born in Hungary have ties with the old country. At the same time the wife subtly points to the differences between different migrant groups. The language group for them means the group of their friends. (I have modified the wife's name in the dialog below to protect her identity.)

(2)   Husband: *Hát én má akkor harminc... harmincegy é-... egyedik évembe voltam, gondoltam, hogy itt az ideje letelepedni, én feltétlenül itt akartam élni. És, úgyhogy akkor gondoltam, hogy ha én egy ausztrál nőt veszek el feleségül, akkor, akkor iz-..., ha megélek hetven évet, úgy gondoltam, akkor már rossz akcentussal va-... ha tudok egyáltalán magyarul beszélni, és énnekem nem, szóval engem Magyarország azért kötött.*
Wife: *Mindnyájunkat köt Magyarország, akár zsidók vagyunk, akár keresztények.*
Husband: *Mindnyájunkat. És, úgyhogy akkor gondoltam, hogy a Zsuzsa nagyon szép volt, jópofa nő volt, nem nagyon ismertem, tudott angolul, mikor mondtam neki, azt mondom, hogy elveszem feleségül s megyünk Ausztráliába, aszongya, hogy jaj, milyen szép kaland! Ugyanis meg volt győződve, hogy visszajö-..., hogy visszajövünk.*
[...]
Wife: *A jó barátaink, azok magyarok és magyarul beszélünk velük.* <AusHu1.8 and 9>[3]

Translation:

Husband: 'Well, at that time I was thirty... thirty one-... in the thirty first year of my life, I thought that it was time to settle down because I definitely wanted to live here [in Australia]. And, well, I thought that if I marry an Australian woman then, then er... if I live until I am seventy, I thought then I will speak with a bad accent some-... if I can speak Hungarian at all and I didn't, well, I was attached to Hungary.'
Wife: 'All of us are attached to Hungary, whether we are Jews or Christians.'
Husband: 'All of us. And, well, then I thought that Susan was very beautiful, she was an interesting woman, I did not know her very well, she could speak

English, and when I said to her, I said that I would marry her and we are going to Australia, she said that oh, what a nice adventure! Because, she was convinced that we'll come ba-.. that we'll come back [to Hungary].'

[...]

Wife: 'Our best friends are Hungarians and we speak Hungarian with them.'

Example (3) shows that the language group is not homogeneous, and there are dividing lines, for example political ones, between individuals and groups. Thus, identification with the language group is not obvious in many cases.

(3) *Magyar szervezetbe nem járok, részben politikai okok miatt.* <AusHu1.3>
   'I do not participate in Hungarian associations, partly for political reasons.'

The words of a second generation woman in example (4) shed light on another aspect of the problems of identification. She identifies herself with Hungarians, and her English speaking husband doesn't mind that. This is not the case for all migrants. In some interviews people mention that their spouses (mostly the husbands) do not allow them to be Hungarian but only Australian, and therefore they must speak only English to their children. Yet the husband of this subject also prohibited the wife to speak Hungarian to their children. The earlier assimilation policy in Australia seems to be successfully nestled in people's minds.

(4) *És itt, amennyire tudok magyar lenni, az legalább engemet boldogít. És a férjem hagyja.*
   [...]
   Ausztrál a férjem és a öö nem bánta, hogy táncútam meg ő is táncút, de azér hogy, hogy én beszéljek magyarú otthon a gyerekhöz, azt má meg is tiltotta. Azt mondta, ne gondúd, hogy én arra, meg is mondta, hogy én akarom tudni, hogy mit szósz. Nem tudom, hogy azér vót, mer fél, hogy róla beszélünk vagy nem tudom, de ez egy nagyon normális ausztrál felfogás. Máshol a világon nyomják, hogy mennél több szája, UM... LANG-... nyelven tudjon egy gyerek beszéni, de itt nem olyan. Itt, ezek az ausztrálok olyan furcsák, hogy azér... Talán változni fog, én nem tudom. <AusHu2.1>

Translation:

   'And here [in Australia] as much as I can be Hungarian, it makes me happy. And my husband allows that.
   [...]
   My husband is Australian and he um did not mind that I danced [in a Hungarian dance group], he danced as well, but that, that I would speak Hungarian to our child at home, he forbade me to do that. He said "don't think that I...", he said, "I want to know what you are talking about". I don't know if this was because he was afraid that we would speak about him [in Hungarian] or I don't know but it is a very normal [i.e. common] Australian view. In other

parts of the world they are pushing children to speak more and more mouth, UM... LANG-... languages but here it is not like that. Here, these Australians are so strange that... Maybe it will change, I don't know.'

Most second generation speakers realize that they have a dual identity. They identify themselves with Hungarians as well as with Australians. Examples (5) and (6) are from second generation Hungarians.

(5) *Legérdekesebb benne szerintem az, ha magyarok között vagyok, akkó magyarnak érzem magamat. Ha Magyarországon vagyok, akkor rádöbbenek, hogy én másképp beszélek magyarul, mint a többiek, rájövök, hogy van valami akszentusom vagy van, amikor megakadok a kifejezésekben, viszont arra is rájöttem, ha nagyon akarok, akkor egész folyékonyan tudok beszélni, egész komoly témáról, még akkor is, hogyha egy pár napba telik, míg belezökkenek. ... öm. Ha ausztrálok között vagyok, akkor se érzem magamat másnak, mint az ausztrálok, kivéve talán abban, hogy mondjuk az ausz-... az, az átlag irtó kedves, kellemes és nyugodt ausztrálokkal szemben vagy ausztrálokkal nem tudok olyasmi dolgokról beszélni, amik engem érdekelnek.* <AusHu2.2>

Translation:

'The most interesting part is, in my opinion, that if I am among Hungarians, I feel Hungarian. If I am in Hungary, I suddenly realize that I speak Hungarian differently than the others, I realize that I have some accent or sometimes I get stuck with an expression, but I also discovered that if I really want to, I can speak quite fluently also about quite serious topics, even if I need a few days until I get the swing of it [using the language in Hungary]... um. If I am among Australians, I do not feel different from Australians, except maybe that, let's say, the Aus-, in contrast with the average Australian who is terribly kind, nice and calm, I cannot speak with them about things which I am interested in.'

(6) *Muszáj valahogy, hogy a gyerek tudja, hogy honnan származik. Énszerintem fontos. Hogy valamilyen, nem hogy tartozik a magyar-, magyarokhoz vagy ehhez vagy, de vala-, valahogy neki van valami különleges az é-.. az ő múltja.* <AusHu2.17>

Translation:

'It is necessary that children should know where their roots are. It is important, in my opinion. That to belong to some, not that to belong to Hungarian-, Hungarians or to this or, but some-, somehow that they have something special in their l- in their past.'

In summary, Hungarians in Australia are bilinguals with dominance in Hungarian in the first and dominance in English in the second generation. For the people who visit Hungarian events, associations, churches and clubs, these occasions provide an opportunity to maintain the Hungarian language. However, only a small number of people of Hungarian origin, 5–10%, take advantage of these opportunities. The neighborhood domain is completely dominated by English, because Hungarians do not live in close neighborhood ties with each other. People use mostly English also in the work and school domains. In the school domain Hungarian language use means the use of the opportunity to learn Hungarian at Saturday schools. If Hungarian bilingual schools were organized, this domain could serve as a language maintenance factor much better, as is suggested by Janulf's (1998) study on Swedish-Finnish bilingualism in Sweden, which shows that only people who had had instruction in the minority language (in this case, Finnish) at school used both Finnish and Swedish successfully as adults. The church domain is a maintenance factor among first-generation Australian Hungarians. One third of the second-generation speakers examined in the study do not go to church, and, thus, for them, it is a not a relevant maintenance factor. The shift into English has also reached the home domain: the first generation uses mostly Hungarian at home, but the second generation uses both Hungarian and English in this domain. Leisure time activities serve Hungarian language maintenance both in the first and the second generations, suggesting that, if the Hungarian communities in Australia offered more leisure time activities which could also arouse the interest of the young people, this domain could serve as an important maintenance factor.

3. Linguistic aspects

3.1 Introduction

Hungarian-English language contact has been studied earlier mainly in the context of the United States (e.g. Kontra 1990; Fenyvesi 1995a; Bartha 1995/1996). The results of the studies show that the Hungarian language in the U.S. has changed much over time as a consequence of language contact with English. All subsystems of the Hungarian language show either English interference or intralingual deviation. Intralingual deviations can also mainly be explained as a consequence of language contact, however, not in terms of interference but in terms of extralinguistic factors.

The number of the early migrants to Australia was so low that Hungarian-English language contact in Australian can only be examined in terms of the last 50 to 60 years. Thus, this contact situation is much more recent than Hungarian-English language contact in the U.S. Still, the main tendencies of change remain the same in both the American and Australian varieties of Hungarian. In Australian Hungarian mainly the lexicon and morphology have been investigated (Endrődy 1971; M. Kovács 1996, 1997, 2001a, 2001b, 2001c). The following description of the contact-induced changes in Australian Hungarian is mainly based on my own research, but the main results of Endrődy's (1971) research are also presented. The corpus of data used in the research is described in the following section.

3.2 The data and the subjects

The data I have used in M. Kovács (1996, 1997, 2001a, 2001b, 2001c) to study Australian Hungarian comprises 28 hours' worth of tape-recorded interviews with 35 Hungarians living in Australia. The interviews were collected and transcribed by myself in 1993–94. Most interviews are one-on-one conversations. In four cases married couples or friends were interviewed together (this involved a total of 8 subjects).

The subjects of the interviews were mainly people living in Sydney and other parts of New South Wales. Most subjects were invited to participate in the study at Hungarian events and occasions (Hungarian Days, at church, the scout club, or Saturday school). Other subjects were friends of friends, and some were recruited by an announcement in the Hungarian newspaper *Magyar Élet*.

The subjects were first- and second-generation Hungarian speakers. (The generational affiliation of speakers was defined similarly as in my pilot study, see in the beginning of Section 2.3 above.) The subjects represent relatively equally both first- and second-generation speakers (18 and 17 subjects respectively) and both sexes (19 women and 16 men).

The regional/dialectal background of the subjects is not completely homogeneous but clearly Budapest-dominated: of the 35 interviewees, 22 persons or their parents migrated from Budapest to Australia. Almost all regional parts of Hungary are represented by the interviewees, and, in addition, one person is a Hungarian from Slovakia, and two have a Transylvanian background. The subjects are heterogeneous in their occupations (as Australian Hungarians are): there are workers, tradesmen, high school and university students and teachers, and retirees among them. The average education level of the group is high school.

The data used in Endrődy's (1971:43) study consists of tape recorded interviews and written tests with 55 Hungarian-English bilingual subjects living in the Melbourne area and 18 monolingual Hungarian informants from Budapest.

3.3 Phonology

The phonology of Australian Hungarian has not been studied in detail. Research on American Hungarian, which is the variety closest to Australian Hungarian, shows that many phonetic and phonological features of American Hungarian are different from Hungarian, spoken in Hungary (Kontra 1990:35–67; Fenyvesi 1995a:8–11, 1998a, 1998d). Fenyvesi (1995a:8–9, 14–34) gives an entire list of these features, which she divides into five groups: (1) subphonemic features, (2) phonemic mergers, (3) phonological process, (4) suprasegmental features and (5) borrowing of pronunciation (for details see also the chapter in this volume on American Hungarian).

Many phonological features of Australian Hungarian are the same as those in American Hungarian. Endrődy (1971:186) shows that Hungarian speakers living in Melbourne have two morphophonological features different from Hungarian spoken in Hungary: some informants' speech lacks *v*-assimilation in the instrumental case (like *fiúk-val*⁴ 'with boys' instead of *fiúk-kal* 'with boys') and vowel harmony. In M. Kovács (1997:116–117) I report on three subphonemic features different from Hungarian occurring in a second-generation Australian Hungarian subject's speech: the aspiration of the consonants *p*, *t* and *k* ([kʰɛtøː] vs. HH [kɛttøː] 'two'), a replacement of trilled /r/ by a retroflex vocoid ([haːɻom] vs. HH [haːrom]), and the velarization of the postvocalic lateral approximant (/bɛseɫs/ vs. HH /bɛseːls/). Of the two phonemic mergers listed in Fenyvesi (1995a:8), one can be found in the speech of the same Australian Hungarian subject referred to above: the replacement of /ɟ/ by [dʒ], for example [dʒɛrɛk] vs. HH [ɟɛrɛk] 'child'. The degemination of geminated consonants ([joban] vs. HH [jobban] 'better') and the reduction of the vowel *e* ([tʰøbət] vs. HH [tøbbɛt]) are reported in another of my papers (M. Kovács 1997:116–117) as non-systematically occurring features. All three suprasegmental features discussed by Fenyvesi (1995a:9) in American Hungarian are also found in the speech of the same second generation informant: the change of stress in words and phrases, and the change in intonation in yes/no-questions from rising-falling to English-like rising intonation.

Many other phonological features observed in American Hungarian but not yet reported in Australian Hungarian can also be found in the Australian Hungarian data collected by myself (see Section 3.4). For example, the replacement of word-initial /v/ by [w] under hypercorrection, the diphthongization of vowels, and borrowing of pronunciation, that is, English-like pronunciation in borrowed vocabulary, are observable. Most features occur only in second-generation speech but the replacement of /v/ by [w] as hypercorrection is typical in the speech of the first generation.⁵

In sum, American Hungarian and Australian Hungarian share many phonological features different from the Hungarian spoken in Hungary. Most features show the influence of English, but intralingual deviations also occur as a consequence of incomplete language acquisition. Features which, on the surface, occur as intralingual deviations can be regarded as indirectly influenced by English (because these features, for example, *v*-assimilation, are not present in English, which second-generation informants use predominantly).

3.4 The lexicon of Australian Hungarian

3.4.1 *Borrowing and code-switching*
Contact-induced language changes usually begin with changes in the vocabulary and can later be followed by structural changes (Thomason & Kaufman 1988:65–109). The most visible feature of Australian Hungarian is the number of words borrowed from Australian English.

Different views on how to differentiate between borrowing and one word code-switching and on why such differentiation is important, if it is at all, are discussed by many researchers (for example, Poplack 1980; Grosjean 1982, 1995; Gardner-Chloros 1987; Romaine 1989; Thomason & Kaufman 1988). Some researchers claim that there is no sharp dividing line between the two phenomena and argue for a continuum of switching and borrowing (Gardner-Chloros 1987; Romaine 1989; Auer 1998b).

'Nonce-borrowing' (Weinreich 1953:11; Poplack 1980) is introduced by others as an intermediate category between switches and fully established loans.

In most cases, borrowed words are more integrated than code-switched ones. For that reason, the need to distinguish between borrowing and switching is argued for in this study. The differentiation, however, does not exclude the idea of a continuum: fully integrated borrowed words form one end of the continuum and non-integrated switched words the other, with occasionally occurring borrowed words and morphologically integrated switches in between. Because both borrowed and code-switched words can be integrated morphologically as well as syntactically, but switched words cannot be integrated phonologically, a phonological criterion for distinguishing between borrowing and switching is debatable (di Sciullo et al. 1986; Stenson 1990; Grosjean & Miller 1994; Halmari 1997). Examples (7) and (8) show that even the same word can occur as phonologically integrated or non-integrated in the same data. First-generation speakers (example 7) usually integrate words of English origin more than second-generation speakers do (example 8). The word meaning 'accent' is also found as a borrowed word in Hungarian spoken in Hungary with the form *akcentus*.

(7)   *És imádták az* **akszent***emet.* <AusHu.1.9>
       'And they loved my *accent*.'

(8)   *De elég jól beszélnek, van nekik egy* ACCENT. <AusHu2.28>
       'But they speak quite well, they have an ACCENT.'

On the borrowing side of the continuum, differentiating between nonce-loans and established loans is usually done by using a frequency criterion.[6] For example, Myers-Scotton (1992:35) regards a word as borrowing if it occurs at least three times in at least three informants' speech. In this study, nonce-loans and established loans are not separated from each other, for the following reasons. First, differentiating between nonce loans and established loans has no significance grammatically: both are fully integrated into the borrowing language grammar. Second, many borrowed words used community-wide in a minority group do not necessarily turn up in interviews (cf. Milroy 1987:51). Third, the only larger database of Australian Hungarian until now (see Section 3.2) is not large enough to give reliable results on what is widely used and what is not. For example, the word *fani* (example 9) occurs in the Australian Hungarian data in only one subject's speech (although, six times), despite the fact that it is, according to my observations between 1992 and 1994, widely used in the Australian Hungarian community.

(9)   *Nagyon* **fani***ak vótak.* <AusHu1.23>
       'They were very *funny*.'

Australian Hungarian is a relatively young variety of the Hungarian language and thus cannot yet have developed many established loan words. In comparison, American Hungarian has existed for over a century and the number of loans in it is higher than in Australian Hungarian.

3.4.2   Word classes and semantic areas

In Australian Hungarian, most borrowed words are nouns but verbs and adverbs also occur (M. Kovács 2001c). This is the usual case in other language varieties as well. This result is not surprising because the division of word classes in Hungarian in general gives the same result: the majority of words are nouns. On the whole, the semantic areas of the borrowed nouns follow the topics of the interview questions. For example, they are words connected with work or study (*aktol* 'act [v]', *bariszter* 'barrister', *biznisz* ~ *biznesz* 'business', *csekköl* 'check [v]', *kemiszt* 'chemist', *matéria* 'dress material' etc.), leisure time and hobbies (*dokumentarium* 'documentary', *halidei* 'holiday', *tép* 'tape', *tíví* 'TV', *vidió* 'video', *vikkend* 'week-end' etc.) or with Australian nature, society and the people living there (*aboridzsin* 'aborigine', *aboridzsinal* 'aboriginal', *balt* 'Balt(s)', *lebanéz* ~ *lebanoni* 'Lebanese', *táj* 'Thai'; *dezert* 'desert', *hosztel* 'migrant hostel' etc.). If other topics had been discussed in the interviews, other semantic areas could have also been covered.

The borrowed words are mainly loanwords proper, however, calques and cases of the expansion of the meaning of a Hungarian word under the influence of the corresponding English word also occur. For example, the English word *class* can be translated into Hungarian as used in Hungary with at least three different words when referring to the school environment (*osztály* 'classroom', *óra* 'class period', *tanfolyam* 'course'). In the Australian Hungarian interviews with students, the meaning of the word *osztály* is expanded to cover all the meanings of the three words, *osztály*, *óra* and *tanfolyam*. A few other examples follow. The English word *science*, as a school subject, is *természettudomány* 'natural science' in Hungarian, while Australian Hungarian students use, when referring to this school subject, only the word *tudomány*, which, in the Hungarian of Hungary means any branch of science or the humanities. The Hungarian word *sport* is a cover term for almost all types of motion activities but, as a school subject, the words *testnevelés* or *tornaóra* are used and not the word *sport*, as it is used in Australian Hungarian. The Hungarian word *mozi* has meant only 'movie theater', but the meaning of the word has been expanded in Australian Hungarian to also mean 'movie' or 'film' under the influence of the English word *movie*, which covers both meanings. Because detailed research on Australian Hungarian borrowed nouns has not been done yet, the following Section 3.4.3 only points out the features of borrowing in verbs.

3.4.3   Borrowing in verbs

In this section I analyze direct borrowing on the basis of M. Kovács (2001c). There are 17 verbs (or 21, including all variants of the occurring verbs) in the Australian Hungarian data. Most verbs on the list occur, like nouns, only once in the data, and they are mainly used with medium frequency in Australian Hungarian:[7] *aktol* (1) < E *act* vs. HH *működik*; *apszetol* (1) < E *upset* vs. HH *kizökkent, kihoz a sodrából, felidegesít*; *behoppan* (1) < E *hop in* vs. HH *betoppan, beugrik*; *blaffol* (1) < E *bluff* vs. HH *becsap, rászed, blöfföl*; *csárdzsol* (1) < E *charge* vs. HH *felszámít*; *csekköl* (1) < E *check* vs. HH *ellenőriz*; *diszmisszol* (3) < E *dismiss* vs. HH *elbocsát, felment*; *empenelol* (1) < E *em-*

panel vs. HH *esküdteket felhív, lajstromoz; gemlizik* ~ *gemblizik* (2) < E *gamble* vs. HH *szerencsejátékot űz; hoppingol* (1) < E *hop* vs. HH *emleget; kanuzik* (1) '< E *canoe* vs. HH *kenuzik; komplénol* ~ *komplihol* (5) < E *complain* vs. HH *panaszkodik; menedzsel* (1) < E *manage* vs. HH here: *gépet kezel; nominál* (4) < E *nominate* vs. HH *ajánl, jelöl; sopingol* (1) < E *shopping* vs. HH *bevásárol, vásárolgat; szpellöl* ~ *szpellol* ~ *leszpellingel* (4) < E *spell* vs. HH *betűz; szpotol* (1) < E *spot* vs. HH *foltot kivesz, kitisztít.*

The verbs *komplénol* ~ *komplihol* 'complain' and *szpellöl* ~ *szpellol* ~ *leszpellingel* 'spell' are used with higher frequency in the data, and, in my experience, they are also widely used in the Australian Hungarian community. In contrast, the verbs *gemlizik* ~ *gemblizik* 'gamble' or *sopingol* 'go/do shopping' occur only with low frequency in the data, although they are widely used in the community.

The English origin verbs in the data are supplied with the very productive Hungarian derivational (usually denominal) verbal suffix *-l*,[8] as is mostly the case in American Hungarian (Fenyvesi 1995a: 36; see also Vázsonyi 1995) and, for example, in Burgenland Hungarian in Austria (Gal 1989). The other derivative verbal suffix, the also productive (denominal) *-z(ik)*, occurs in the verbs *gemlizik* ~ *gemblizik* 'gamble' and *kanuzik* 'canoe'. Two verbs are supplied with Hungarian preverbs (*behoppan* 'hop in', *leszpellingel* 'spell').

All borrowed verbs, after having been supplied with a Hungarian derivational verbal suffix, are morphologically and syntactically well integrated into the Hungarian sentences, independent of whether they are occasionally occurring nonce loans or loans used widely in the community. Example (10) shows that after being supplied with the Hungarian derivational verbal suffix *-l*, the English origin verb meaning 'complain' is ready for further suffixation (*-t* is the marker of the past tense and *-ak* marks a third person plural subject). Example (11) contains a verb which occurs only once in the data. In addition to the Hungarian derivational verbal suffix *-l*, it is supplied with the Hungarian infinitive marker *-ni*.

(10)   **Komplénol**tak is érte, hogy mér kő nekik angolul tanulni. <AusHu1.34>
       'They complained about why they had to learn English.'

(11)   Akkor már elkezdtem őket egy kicsit **csárdzsolni**. <AusHu1.11>
       'Then I started to charge them a little bit.'

3.4.4   Unique changes in the lexicon: Neologisms

In connection with Hungarian spoken in Oberwart/Felsőőr, Austria, Gal (1989) raises the issue of taking into account not only the negative but also the positive dimensions of language contact. Borrowed verbs can be seen as a positive dimension in the sense that the speakers use Hungarian verbal suffixes on the verbs of English origin the way Hungarians in Hungary use it on foreign words. Another type of innovation (through the creation of new words which do not exist in Hungarian spoken in Hungary by using Hungarian lexical and grammatical elements or through using existing words in an unusual way) is regarded by Gal (1989: 327–329) as a negative consequence of lexical loss in language contact, on the one hand, and as a creative ability for linguistic innovations on the other. In American Hungarian such changes in lexicon are regarded as intralingual deviations which are explained by Kontra (1990:97) in terms of language attrition in the first generation and incomplete acquisition in the second.

In M. Kovács (2001c) I show that there are more than fifty such neologisms in the verbal category in the Australian Hungarian data. These neologisms are created by mixing up verbs which are close to each other in their meaning or form, and by mixing up verbal preverbs or leaving them off. Because this type of neologism is typical in the second but not in the first generation, I regard the phenomenon as a sign of lexical loss in a contact situation (M. Kovács 2001c). In example (12) the subject mixes up the verbs *gondolkozik* 'think about' and *gondoz* 'take care of'' because the verbs are quite close to each other in their forms.

(12) *Most nehéz nekem, mert mikor gondozok, svédbe gondozok most, nem magyarul.*
     <AusHu2.35>[9]
     'Now it is hard for me because when I *take care about* [meaning: I think], I *take care about* [meaning: I think] in Swedish now, not in Hungarian.

Example (13) shows how complex the question of mixing up verbs is. In the example, the subject uses the verb *ér* 'arrive at, reach; be worth' instead of the verb *elér* in the meaning 'achieve'. This is either a case of leaving out the verbal prefix *el* or a result of the influence of English. Namely, the verb *elér* 'achieve', can, in certain situations, also be used in the meaning 'to reach' which is the meaning of the verb *ér* as well. The informant may have thought that the words are synonymous also in the meaning 'achieve'.

(13) *Gondolom, hogy jobb eredményt fogok érni.* <AusHu2.33>
     I think that I *would reach* /(I *am worth*) [meaning: I would achieve] a better result.'

The number of 'neologisms' is much higher in the nominal category in the Australian Hungarian data, but nouns have not yet been studied comprehensively from this aspect. The number of the lexical items deviating from Hungarian spoken in Hungary totals nearly 1,000 in all in the Australian Hungarian data. This number does not include dialectal or slang words.

3.4.5 A summary of lexical features

The lexicon of Australian Hungarian shows many of the same features which have been identified earlier in American Hungarian. One typical feature of the lexicon in both language varieties is borrowed words. The difference between American and Australian Hungarian borrowing is that Australian Hungarian, being a much younger variety than American Hungarian, does not have very many established borrowings yet. Thomason and Kaufman (1988:65–109) regard lexical change as the first sign of language change in a language contact situation characterized by borrowing. Lexical borrowing alone, however, is not necessarily a sign of ongoing language shift. In a bilingual situation, especially in minority vs. majority language context, lexical borrowing is typical and almost unavoidable.

In addition to borrowing, other lexical changes occur in the speech of Australian Hungarians, especially in the speech of the second generation. Most intralingual deviations can be regarded as consequences of filling lexical gaps, mainly caused by incomplete acquisition of Hungarian in the second generation.

3.5 Australian Hungarian morphology and code-switching

3.5.1   *Morphological features with no code-switching involved*
Being in contact with English, the morphologically very different Hungarian language, undergoes many morphological changes in case marking as well as in verbal conjugation as is shown, for example, in American Hungarian (Kontra 1990:69–74; Fenyvesi 1995a:9–10, 34–75, 1995/1996; Bartha 1996:424–425). So far, English prepositional interference (Endrődy 1971) and the consequences of code-switching in case marking (M. Kovács 2001a, b) have been investigated in Australian Hungarian.

On the basis of written tests and oral interviews, Endrődy (1971) has shown that many case endings undergo changes in Australian Hungarian. He points out (1971:169–238) the semantic transference of English prepositions into Hungarian case endings. Semantic transference is promoted by synonymous diamorphs in English and Hungarian. Endrődy (1971:41) identifies the following synonymous diamorphs, Hungarian endings and English prepositions, which mostly overlap semantically and, thus, are subject to semantic transference: ILL *-bAn* ($\sim$ E *in*), SUP *-On* ($\sim$ E *on*), ALL *-hOz* ($\sim$ E *to*), INST *-vAl* ($\sim$ E *with*), ADE *-nÁl* ($\sim$ E *at* in spatial meaning), TEM *-kor* ($\sim$ E *at* in temporal meaning) and the postposition *alatt* ($\sim$ E *under*). Example (14), cited from Endrődy (1971:170), shows this type of semantic interference. In the example the illative case (*-bAn*), which mostly corresponds to the English preposition *in*, is used. However, in this sentence, the superessive case (*-On*) would be required in Hungarian used in Hungary.

(14)   *Mi-t   lát   a   kép-ben?* <AusHu, Endrődy 1971>
       what-ACC see.3SG the picture-INE
       Mi-t   lát   a   kép-en? <HH>
       what-ACC see.3SG the picture-SUP
       'What do you see in the picture?'[10]

In addition to semantic transference, contact-induced omission of case endings also occurs in Australian Hungarian (Endrődy 1971:177–179, 208–209). The examples of a type of omission in Endrődy's research can be regarded as syntactic calques. An example (15) of this is cited here from Endrődy (1971:177) in a shortened form:

(15)   *A   mult év   Sydney-be   utaz-t-am.* <AusHu, Endrődy 1971>
       the last year Sydney-ILL go-PAST-1SG

> *A múlt év-ben Sydney-be utaz-t-am.* <HH>
> the last year-INE Sydney-ILL go-PAST-1SG
> 'Last year I went to Sydney.'

Endrődy (1971: 183–184, 211–214) also points out that some omissions or substitutions of case marking with another one cannot be regarded as a consequence of English influence (example 16, cited from Endrődy 1971: 212).

(16) *Utána-néz-ek a kávé-hoz.* <AusHu>
       after-look-1SG the coffee-ALL
       Utána-néz-ek a kávé-nak.
       after-look-1SG the coffee-DAT
       'I'll check on the coffee.'

The results of Endrődy's (1971: 195, 235) research show that there is a difference between the use of case endings between the older and younger generations of Hungarians. Higher rates of interference and of deviation without interference can be shown in the younger generation in comparison to the older one.

Because the Hungarian accusative case ending *-t* corresponds to a zero morpheme in English, it is not studied by Endrődy (1971). The morphology of verbs, adjectives and adverbs, except for some aspects of borrowed verbs (see Section 3.4.3), in Australian Hungarian has not yet been studied.

3.5.2 *Morphological features involving code-switching*

In addition to borrowing, code-switching is a very visible phenomenon in bilingual speech. Following Auer (1998b), code-switching is here understood as the alternative use of two (or more) different languages or codes during the same conversational event. Code-switching has often been seen as either a lack of competent knowledge of the languages involved in code-switching or as a 'valuable linguistic strategy' used by bilingual persons (Baker & Jones 1998: 58).[11] Although code-switching is a source of enrichment in the bilingual speech in stable bilingualism, the usage of case marking by Australian Hungarian bilinguals during code-switching suggests a connection between code-switching and language shift in the Australian Hungarian context (M. Kovács 2001a, b). The morphology of code-switching is restricted to intrasentential or, more specifically, intraclausal code-switching.[12] In the Australian Hungarian data, intrasentential code-switching usually involves phrases of one or two words of English inserted into Hungarian speech.

In M. Kovács (2001b) I show that there are differences in the use of case marking in code-switching between different generations. First-generation speakers use switched words in a way similar to borrowing: they supply the switched words with the corresponding Hungarian case endings more often than second-generation subjects. In the speech of the first generation, case marking in different cases, excluding the zero-marked nominative, is supplied in 89.8% of the cases in which code-switching is involved. The corresponding rate of case marking usage in the second generation is

Table 10.2. Generation differences in realizing the matrix case marking in code-switching in Australian Hungarian

Case	GEN1		GEN2	
	Matrix/Total	Percentage	Matrix/Total	Percentage
Nominative	265 / 265	100%	175 / 175	100%
Dative with genitive function	7 / 7	100%	0 / 0	–
Accusative	53 / 60	88%	26 / 50	52%
Dative (nongenitive function)	37 / 37	100%	12 / 13	92%
Inessive	55 / 60	92%	41 / 52	79%
Elative	3 / 4	75%	2 / 6	33%
Illative	43 / 47	91%	13 / 20	65%
Superessive	22 / 23	96%	8 / 14	57%
Delative	2 / 2	100%	1 / 1	100%
Sublative	17 / 19	89%	2 / 9	22%
Adessive	2 / 2	100%	0 / 0	–
Ablative	6 / 7	86%	1 / 4	25%
Allative	7 / 7	100%	1 / 4	25%
Essive-Formal	0 / 0	–	0 / 1	0%
Instrumental	13 / 14	93%	5 / 5	100%
Temporal	0 / 0	–	1 / 1	100%
Causal-Final	3 / 4	75%	0 / 0	–
Terminative	1 / 1	100%	1 / 1	100%

much lower, 57.5%. The χ^2 test shows the generational differences in case marking in switching are statistically significant ($p < .001$).

In second-generation speech, code-switching morphology seems to shift away from L1 morphology mostly into the direction of L2 morphology. Figure 10.4 and Table 10.2 show that the most often omitted case in code-switching is the accusative, the case of the direct object: it comprises 52.0% of the cases omitted by the second generation. This can be explained in terms of transference from English, in which the direct object is unmarked. In the locative cases, the inessive is well maintained even when switched: in 80.4% of the cases even by the second generation. The dative is also strongly maintained by the second generation, at the rate of 92.3%. Other locative cases are realized less by the second generation, for example, the illative is present in 65.0% and the superessive in 57.1% of the cases. If a case ending required by Hungarian grammar is not realized, zero-marking is the most common substitution in both generations. The nominative is unmarked both in Hungarian and English, thus it does not cause a conflict between the two languages in code-switching.

Nagy (1994) examines Hungarian-English code-switching in the United States. Her 11 informants are first-generation speakers who have only lived in the US for about 4–5 years or less and their goal is to go back to Hungary. Her results are very different from the results shown above: almost all switched words are supplied with the required Hungarian morphology.

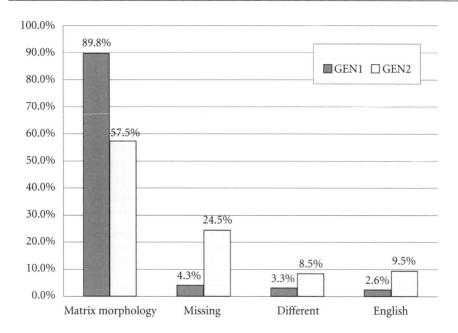

Figure 10.4. Case marking usage in different generations in Hungarian-English code-switching in Australian Hungarian

On the basis of the morphological analyses of case marking in code-switching in Australian Hungarian and Australian Finnish, I suggest a distance-based contin- uum model to describe the shift away from the matrix language, that is, the L1 of the speakers, in code-switching (M. Kovács 2001b).[13]

There are two paths in the distance-based continuum model. The first path is the following:

Path 1:

> (borrowing) > smooth switching > flagged switching > transferred codes > bare forms

Smooth switching refers to a switch with no signs of hesitation and with full matrix morphology. The switch is likely to be of the 'borrowing type', that is, all matrix mor- phology necessary according to the rules of Hungarian spoken in Hungary is provided, as in example (17): the Hungarian 3rd singular possessive suffix is attached to the noun *girlfriend*, and the English verb *break up* has the Hungarian verbal suffix *-ol*, the marker of the past tense *-t* and third person plural subject marker *-ak*. The English adverb *up* in the phrasal verb is translated into Hungarian as a verbal prefix *föl* 'up' and placed before the verb, as required by the matrix language rule. The second subject personal pronoun is left out because Hungarian is a *pro*-drop language and personal pronoun subjects are used only under focus.

(17) *Nek-i   vót   GIRLFRIEND-je   és*
      DAT-3SG   be.PAST.3SG girlfriend-PX3SG   and
      föl-BREAK-ol-t-ak. <AusHu2.21>
      up-break-VDER-PAST-3PL
      'He had a GIRLFRIEND and [they] BROKE up.'

Flagged switches (cf. Poplack 1980) involve either a sign of hesitation or words such as the Hungarian *ilyen* 'kind of, such a' or *olyan* 'kind of, like' or demonstrative pronouns like *ez* 'this' or *az* 'that'. In addition to flagged switches, flagging can occur also in other kinds of switches. The morphology of flagged switches occurs either with full congruence with the matrix language (example 18), with half-congruence (example 19) or with no congruence at all. Half-congruence means that the case ending is provided on the flag word but not on the switched word. In example (19), the demonstrative pronoun *ez* is supplied with the illative case ending but the switched word, *lifestyle*, is not.

(18) *Csinál-t-am   ilyen   SPOT CHECK-ek-et.*   <AusHu1.23>
      do-PAST-1SG   kind.of spot check-PL-ACC
      'I did [kind of] SPOT CHECKS.'

(19) *Azok   nem, nincsen-ek olyan, el-vesz-ve   eb-be   a,   eb-be   a*
      that-PL not   be.NEG-PL   like   PVB-lose-PART   this-ILL the   this-ILL the
      nagy   BUSY LIFESTYLE.
      big   busy lifestyle.
      'They are not, like, aren't lost in this, in this big BUSY LIFESTYLE.' <AusHu2.1>

Transferred codes have no congruence with the matrix language but are transferred from the embedded language.[14] In example (20), the switched phrase is supplied with the sublative case ending *-re,* which is the closest translation of the English preposition *for,* although the Hungarian matrix requires the adessive case *-nál.* Transferred codes can also produce what is called bare forms (cf. Myers-Scotton 1993: 92–93, 95–97, 112–116) in which no matrix marking occurs. This is a transition form into the next group in which only bare forms occur. Example (21) shows that by leaving out the accusative case marking *-t,* a bare form is produced. Because English has no overt marker of accusative, the zero marking is here regarded as a transfer from English.

(20) *Egy repülő UM COMPANY-re   akar-ok   dolgoz-ni.* <AusHu2.32>
      a   air   UM company-SUB   want-1SG   work-INF
      'I want to work for an air UM COMPANY.'

(21) *Apu kap   egy, egy, egy MAGAZINE.* <AusHu2.35>
      Dad get.3SG a   a   a   magazine
      'Dad gets a, a, a MAGAZINE.'

Bare forms can also occur without transference from the embedded language. In this case, either the conflict between the matrix and the embedded language grammars causes a more 'neutral' bare form, or the bare form is a consequence of the speaker searching for the right word. In example (22) the illative case governed by the verb *megy* 'go' is not provided, but a bare form is produced in connection with the switched noun.

(22) *És   men-t   a,   a,   IMMIGRATION.* <AusHu2.35>
      and go-PAST-3SG the the immigration
      'And he went to the IMMIGRATION [office].'

The second path also begins with full congruence with the matrix language. This congruence decreases left to right. This path of the model involves smaller or longer chunks of the embedded language, what are called 'embedded language islands' (cf. Myers-Scotton 1993:137–148) and ends with a mixed matrix in which a joint grammar of the two (or more) languages develops:

> Path 2:
>
> > (borrowing >) smooth switching > double marking > small switched islands > longer switches > mixed matrix

The first two steps in the path are the same as in path 1. Double marking (cf. Myers-Scotton 1993:110–112) which involves the use of both matrix and embedded language marking in the same switched word, is shown in example (23). The word *refugee* is provided with the English plural marker as well as its Hungarian equivalent (-*k*). In the Australian Hungarian data, double marking occurs rarely and when it does, it involves plural marking.

(23) *Amikor össze-szed-t-ék   a   REFUGEES-ok-at.* <AusHu2.24>
      when   PVB-collect-PAST-3PL the refugees-PL-ACC
      'When they collected the REFUGEES.'

Example (24) involves a small switched island in which a whole phrase is switched with the English preposition. The sentence includes a strong repair phenomenon. Example (25) contains a longer chunk of English which increases the distance from Hungarian, the matrix language.

(24) *Az ásv-   ...   hogy mond-j-am, az ásv-   ...   -v- ...   az*
      the miner- PAUSE how say-IMP-1SG the miner- PAUSE -r- PAUSE the
      ás-   ...   IN THE MINES.
      min- PAUSE IN THE MINES
      'He worked the minera- ..., how shall I say it, the minera- -r-... the min- ...
      IN THE MINES. <AusHu2.1>

(25) *Anyu most is   tud*
      Mom now also be-able.3SG
      csinál-ni YEAH, OH GOSH, CHINESE COOKING. <AusHu2.35>
      do-INF YEAH, OH GOSH, CHINESE COOKING
      'Mom can still do YEAH, OH GOSH, CHINESE COOKING.'

The following step of the continuum involves sentences in which a clear matrix language is not distinguishable, but the sentences are made up by involving the grammars of both languages, that is, the case of a composite matrix language occurs. In example (26), the Hungarian definite article precedes the switched subject *periods* and the copula is left out from the first part of the sentence as it would be the case in the Hungarian matrix language. However, the subject does not use the Hungarian but the English plural marker, and the predicative adjective agrees with English and not with Hungarian grammar (the latter would require the plural also on the predicative adjective if the subject is in the plural). The second part of the sentence contains the Hungarian copula, but the main information is in English. Thus, the sentence is a case of a composite matrix language in a sentence involving code-switching.

(26) *És   nagyon... a   PERIODS nagyon LONG és   van*
      and   very   the periods very   long and be.3SG
      MATHEMATICS EVERY DAY. <AusHu2.29>
      mathematics every day
      'And very, the PERIODS are very LONG and there is MATHEMATICS EVERY DAY.'

Myers-Scotton's (1993:208–228, 1998, 2001) Matrix Language Turnover Hypothesis describes situations in which a composite matrix language or a complete turnover of the matrix language can develop as a consequence of frequent intrasentential code-switching. Whether the turnover will lead to the development of a pidgin and, further, of a creole language or to language death mainly depends on extralinguistic factors.[15]

Australian Hungarian code-switching involves, in most cases, a clear matrix language. However, examples of shifting into the direction of the embedded language can also be found. Especially in the speech of the second generation, the tendency towards a composite matrix language in connection with switches is observable. If extralinguistic factors (described in Section 2.2) point to the direction of language maintenance and not to that of a complete shift to English in the whole community, Hungarian in Australia can develop in a more English-like direction and some special morphological phenomena used in code-switching can be grammaticalized (cf. Auer 1998b, 1999). Especially the frequency of the unmarked object in code-switching points towards the direction of grammaticalization.

3.6 Syntax

The syntactic changes occurring in American Hungarian (Kontra 1990:75-87; Fenyvesi 1995a:10–11, 75–90) can also be observed in the Australian Hungarian data. A shift towards English-like word order, the presence of syntactic calques, the lack of *pro*-drop, the lack of agreement between subjects and verbs, between predicative adjectives and verbs, between attributive quantifiers and nouns, and between relative pronouns and the antecedent nouns, among other things, can be found in some subjects' speech. Interspeaker variability in syntax seems to be high, with more English-like syntax in the speech of the second than that of the first generation.

In the data, syntactic calques clearly stand out. Example (27) shows a syntactic calque in which the whole sentence said with Hungarian words is actually a word-by-word translation of the corresponding English sentence, except for the omitted copula, which follows the rules of Hungarian syntax.

(27) *Ez nem egy ig-..., nem egy rossz hely lak-ni.* <AusHu2.12>
     this not a   rea-.., not a   bad   place live-INF.
     'This is not a rea-, not a bad place to live.'

The overuse of the indefinite article *egy* 'a(n)' is also a consequence of the syntactic calques mirrored from English (example (28)). The indefinite article *egy* 'a(n)' is not required in standard Hungarian in the second part of this sentence.

(28) *Van   egy rokon-om,   aki egy matektanár* <AusHu2.17>
     be.3SG a   relative- PX.1SG who a   math.teacher
     'I have a relative who is a math teacher.'

The sentence in example (29) lacks agreement between the subject (in plural) and the verb (in singular). The verb form would also require the third person plural (*születtek*) in standard Hungarian. Example (30) shows a lack of agreement between the quantifier and its noun. Hungarian quantifiers are not followed by plural but singular nouns. Morphological deviation, or, convergence with English, can also be identified in this sentence: in standard Hungarian, the verb governs the ablative and not the accusative case in the noun *szó* 'word'.

(29) [...] *itt szület-ett   a   szüle-i-d.* <AusHu2.28>
     here be.born-PAST.3SG the parent-PL-PX.2SG
     'your parents were born here'

(30) *Pár szav-ak-at   nem tud-om, hogy mi-t   jelent.* <AusHu2.16>
     few word-PL-ACC no   know.1SG that what-ACC mean.3SG
     'A few words, I don't know what they mean.'

The syntax of Australian Hungarian has not yet been studied systematically, and no statistics are available on the frequency of different syntactic features of Australian Hungarian. The few examples provided in the present study show only a very narrow selection of the syntactic changes occurring in Australian Hungarian.

4. Conclusion

As this chapter's overview of Hungarian in Australia and the analysis of factors playing a role in the Hungarian language maintenance in Australia have shown, time is a very important dimension in language maintenance. Factors playing a role in maintenance can change during time. In the Australian context, the societal level has gone through major changes from a monocultural, monolingual and assimilationist policy into the direction of one supporting multiculturalism and multilingualism. A new language policy, the National Policy on Languages, favoring multilingualism, was established in 1987. It provides better chances for minority languages to survive in Australia. However, the consequences of the earlier policy reach far into the future: the era when minority people were asked to speak English even at home already produced major language shifting in most of the community languages in Australia, and the process is not reversible in all cases. The new language policy supports, for example, bilingual teaching. However, the main support is usually given to the main minority languages with most speakers. In the case of Hungarian, a medium sized minority language, language teaching continues to be largely limited to Saturday and Sunday schools and depends partly on volunteer work. It is possible to choose Hungarian as a High School Certificate subject, which may encourage the second generation to maintain the language more. Media, especially radio stations, also support Hungarian language maintenance. In many cases, however, broadcasting as a maintenance factor is restricted to the first generation: the members of the second generation do not feel the programs are aimed at them.

At the group level, Hungarians in Australia have actively organized many language maintenance supporting associations, societies, clubs, parishes, scout troops, nursing homes and so on. Newspapers and other publications are also published in Hungarian. The facts that only 5–10% of the Australian Hungarian population regularly visit Hungarian associations and events and that the first generation is more actively taking part than the second show that the effectiveness of the maintenance factors is reduced over time at the group level. The size of the minority, the settlement type and the number of bilingual speakers can also act as maintenance or shift factors (Tandefelt 1988: 48–56). Hungarian is a medium sized minority language in Australia with no isolation and with large-scale bilingualism. These factors promote shift rather than maintenance in the Australian Hungarian context. According to Tandefelt (1988: 48–50), majority attitudes also act at the group level. During the years of assimilation policy, majority attitudes (and even minority attitudes towards other minority languages) were negative. With the official turn to multiculturalism, majority attitudes also began to change in a more positive direction. However, the process takes time.

In Tandefelt's model (1988: 59–71), the actual language use, attitudes and the linguistic consequences of language contact are factors acting at the individual level. However, as I see it, the language use of individuals also acts at the group level when the dimension of time is taken into account. A domain analysis of Hungarian language use among Australian Hungarians has showed that most Hungarians who visit Hungarian events use both Hungarian and English. The use of the English language significantly increases from the first to the second generation. With the time dimension in mind, this fact also points into the direction of language shift.

The linguistic consequences of Hungarian-English language contact in Australia are also described in this chapter. Changes in Australian Hungarian with regard to Hungarian spoken in Hungary are observable at all levels of the language (phonology, morphology, syntax, and the lexicon). English interference and simplification induced by contacts as well as intralingual deviation can be found in Australian Hungarian. The role of code-switching in the process of language change is shown in a distance based model. It is argued, for example, that losing the accusative ending in code-switching or using case endings which are influenced by English prepositions in code-switching create a greater and greater distance from the agglutinative morphology of Hungarian and draws the Australian Hungarian variety closer to English, i.e. convergence is taking place. Generational differences with the second generation using more English-like grammar point into the direction of language shift also at the level of the grammar.

Because sudden factors like war can also play an important role in language maintenance or shift, as Haugen (1953) outlined already in the 1950s, no exact prediction for Hungarian language maintenance in Australia can be given. Minority language speakers do not like their language to be proclaimed doomed to death by researchers in any case. However, the importance of one maintenance factor, the role of real bilingual education at school, missing in the case of Australian Hungarians, must be emphasized here (cf. Janulf's 1998 results on Finnish in Sweden).

Furthermore, maintaining the language of the ancestors is not always a necessary condition for keeping a minority group identity alive. A second-generation Australian Hungarian summarizes this fact as follows: '*Hát mer efektív akármennyire rosszul beszélek magyarul vagy, vagy ausztrál vagyok vagy itt élünk, valahogy magyarnak érzem magamat.*' <AusHu 2.17> That is: 'Well, effectively, no matter how poorly I speak Hungarian or, or that I am Australian or, or that we live here, I feel that I am somehow Hungarian.'

Notes

1. These experiences have been described by many Australian Hungarians in the 35 interviews I did in 1993-94 (see the data in Section 3.2).

2. This was a view often expressed to me in personal communication and interviews with Australian Hungarians in 1993-94.

3. After the examples, the information in angle brackets refers to the corpus of data (AusHu = Australian Hungarian), while the first number refers to generation, and the second to the number assigned to the subject. In the following examples, borrowing is marked with boldface, code-switching with small caps, pauses with three dots, and omitted text with three dots in brackets. "HH" refers to Hungarian forms as used in Hungary.

4. This feature can also be found in some Hungarian dialects.

5. Loss of some other phonological features, like voicing assimilation or palatal assimilation, is reported occurring in American Hungarian. Whether they also occur in Australian Hungarian has not been studied to date.

6. I use the term 'nonce-loan' in a way different from how it is used in code-switching research (Poplack 1980). I regard a word a 'nonce-loan' if it is morphologically and syntactically as well as phonologically integrated but occurs in the data only with low frequency.

7. The numbers in brackets given after each verb refer to how many times the word occurs in the data.

8. The vowel in the suffix can be /o/, /ø/ or /ɛ/, as required by vowel harmony.

9. The informant also knows the Swedish language and had been in Sweden before the interview, but no Swedish influence can be traced in the mixing of the two verbs.

10. The third person singular verb form indicates formal (*vous*) address of the second person addressee.

11. In this article, the term bilingualism also covers multilingualism.

12. Many researchers call this type of code-switching "mixing" (see, for example, Muysken 2000). Because the term intrasentential switching is used in the meaning of intraclausal switching in code-switching research, intrasentential switching is here used to refer to intraclausal code-switching as well.

13. Matrix language here refers to L1, that is, Hungarian versus English, which is L2. Some researchers argue against the existence of a matrix language in code-switching (Meeuwis & Blommaert 1998), however, in the Australian Hungarian data a matrix language can be positively established.

14. Embedded language refers to the language from which words or phrases are inserted into the matrix language. Here the embedded language refers to L2, the English language.

15. The hypothesis is tested, for example, for Pennsylvania German (Fuller 1996) and Karelian (Sarhimaa 1999).

CHAPTER 11

The grammars of Hungarian outside Hungary from a linguistic-typological perspective

Casper de Groot

1. Methodological remarks

1.1 Introduction

Chapters 3 through 10 of this volume give ample examples of differences which hold between Hungarian spoken in Hungary (HH) and a number of varieties of Hungarian spoken outside Hungary (HO). Most differences – if not all – between HH and HO can be explained in terms of language contact where HO takes over features from adjacent languages, which all happen to belong to the Indo-European language family. In this chapter I evaluate a number of the differences observed from a linguistic typological point of view and examine whether the changes in the HO varieties follow or violate linguistic universals and implicational hierarchies, and whether co-occurrences of changes can be explained in terms of universals or hierarchies.

The reader of the former chapters will have noticed that the differences between HH and the HO varieties are mainly in phonological and morphological aspects of grammar, and not in syntactic aspects. We do not witness dramatic changes in word order, for instance. Still, a lot can be said about other typological changes, such as number marking, copula support, person marking and morphological complexity. That is what I will do in this chapter after a brief introduction to linguistic typology.

1.2 Linguistic typology

Linguistic universals are statements which hold for all natural languages. Since Greenberg (1963) four main types of universals have been distinguished on the basis of the parameters: absolute and statistical on the one hand, and unconditional and implicational on the other. Consider the following (cf. Comrie 1981):

(1) absolute unconditional All languages have property P.
statistical unconditional Almost all languages have property P.
absolute implicational For all languages, if a language has P, then it also has Q.
statistical implicational If a language has P, then it will probably also have Q.

Many implications relevant to the universals follow from hierarchies, e.g.:

(2) R > Q > P

The hierarchy tells us that if a language has P, it will also have Q, and from Q we can predict that the language will also have R. If a language has Q, it will also have R. Languages may have R only. There are no languages that have P and R but not Q, or only Q or P but not R.

Let us now see what type of universals will be relevant to a comparison of HH with HO. Absolute unconditional universals hold for all languages, thus language change will not effect these universals. Statistical unconditional universals do not offer typologically motivated explanations for language change by language contact. The last two types, the implicational universals, however, are of particular interest for the comparison. If the value for P has changed in HO we may then expect the value for Q to be changed as well. In comparing HO with HH, I will therefore focus on phenomena for which hierarchies are established.

2.   Number marking

2.1 Typology: Set nouns versus singular object nouns

For the discussion of number marking I will make use of the very insightful typological study on nouns and the noun phrase by Rijkhoff (2002). Rijkhoff shows that on the basis of morphosyntactic and semantic properties the 'noun' can be divided into six sub-types (or nominal subcategories). Rijkhoff refers to them as *Seinsarten* ('modes of being'). Two of these *Seinsarten* are of particular interest for the understanding of some of the differences which hold between HH and HO. The differentiation between the subcategories is based on the observation that first order nouns, i.e. nouns that are used for (discrete) spatial objects in the real world, do not all have the same semantic and morphosyntactic properties. The morphosyntactic properties are established on the basis of the following criteria:

– Do first order nouns appear in the plural form when modified by a numeral (where n > 1)?
– Are first order nouns in a direct construction with a numeral?
– Must the numeral combine with a classifier?

Logically speaking there are four possibilities (disregarding the differences in word and morpheme order):

1. numeral + noun + plural (no classifier)
2. numeral + noun (no plural, no classifier)
3. numeral + classifier + noun (no plural)
4. numeral + classifier + noun + plural

We will here focus on types 1 and 2. An example of a language of type 1 is, for instance, Dutch, whereas an example of a type 2 language is Hungarian. Both languages are contained in Rijkhoff's language sample. Consider the following examples from the two languages:

(3)   Dutch

    a.   *twee boek-en*
       two   book-PL
       'two books'

    b.   **twee boek*
       two   book

    c.   *een   boek*
       a/one book
       'a/one book'

    d.   *de boek-en*
       the book-PL
       'the books'

(4)   Hungarian (HH)

    a.   *két   könyv*
       two   book
       'two books'

    b.   **két   könyv-ek*
       two   book-COLL

    c.   *egy   könyv*
       a/one book
       'a/one book'

    d.   *a   könyv-ek*
       the book-COLL
       'the books'

Both in Dutch and Hungarian the numeral is in a direct construction with the noun (cf. 1 and 2 above in contrast to 3 and 4), but only in Dutch does the noun appear in the plural form. Rijkhoff notes that from a cross-linguistic perspective, number marking (with or without an attributive numeral) seems to be the exception (Dutch) rather than the rule (Hungarian). When comparing Dutch with Hungarian, we see that in Dutch an NP headed by a *bare* noun must refer to a single individual. When reference is made to more than one individual object, the noun must be suffixed with a plural marker. In other words, plural marking is obligatory, both with and without a numeral modifier (see 3a and d). Rijkhoff calls such nouns (which are typically found in the Indo-European languages) *singular object nouns*. Hungarian, on the other hand, has nouns that seem to denote a set of individuals. These nouns are called *set nouns*. A set can have any cardinality: it may contain just one individual (singleton set 4c) or it may consist or more individuals (multiple set 4a). The marker -*k* in Hungarian (4d) is considered a collective marker rather than a plural marker (cf. Rijkhoff 2002:51f.).

A reinforcement of Rijkhoff's claim may be found in the following examples, where Dutch employs the plural form and Hungarian the singular:

(5)   Dutch

    a.   *Zijn   er   appel-s?*
        COP.PL   there   apple-PL
        'Do you have apples?' (at the greengrocer's)

    b.   *Marie   kocht   appels.*
        Mary   bought   apple-PL
        'Mary bought apples.'

(6)   Hungarian

    a.   *Alma   van-e?*
        apple   COP.3SG-QM
        'Are there apples?'

    b.   *Mari   almá-t   vett*
        Mary   apple-ACC   bought
        'Mary bought apples.'

What I will claim in the following section is that HO does not merely take over the plural marking on nouns, but rather that, due to language contact, HO develops from a *set noun*-type language into a *singular object noun*-type language. Consequently, the collective marker -*k* is in the state of reinterpretation as a plural marker.

2.2   Typology: Number discord versus number concord

Rijkhoff (2002:107) observes that most of the 33 languages with set nouns in his sample have some sort of 'number' discord. The discord between the subject and the verb may take the following form (in pseudo-English):

(7)   a.   *Three boy walks.*   Not: 'Three boy walk.'
    b.   *Boys (collective) walks.*   Not: 'The boys walk.'

Rijkhoff suggests that if a language has 'number' discord, then it has set nouns. In Section 2.1 above we have seen that HH has set nouns. The following examples in (8) show that HH also has 'number' discord.

(8)   a.   *Három   fiú   sétál.*
        Three   boy   walk.3SG
        'Three boys walk.'

    b.   *Péter   és   Mary sétál.*
        Peter   and   Mary walk.3SG
        'Péter and Mary walk.'

HH does not show 'number' discord if the Subject is specified by a noun with the collective marker:

(9) A   fiú-k   sétál-nak.
     the boy-COLL walk-3PL
     'The boys walk.'

2.3 HO versus HH

When we look at -*k* marking of the noun in HO, we can observe that the many of the speakers of most varieties use the Indo-European system as exemplified by Dutch in Section 2.1 above, i.e. -*k* is used as a plural marker. In the following examples I will contrast HH with HO and Dutch (DU). Note that Dutch represents the type of languages which have singular object nouns, and that Dutch is not in contact with Hungarian or any varieties thereof.

(10) a. HH   *sok   ember*
               many   people
      b. HO   *sok   ember-ek*
               many   people-PL
      c. DU   *veel   mens-en*
               many   people-PL
               'Many people.'

(11) a. HH   *János almá-t   vett.*
               John apple-ACC bought
               'John bought apples.'
      b. HO   *János almá-k-at   vett.*
               John apple-PL-ACC bought
               'John bought apples.'
      c. DU   *Jan   kocht   appel-s.*
               John   bought   apple-PL
               'John bought apples.'

The examples (10) and (11) convincingly show that HO uses -*k* as a plural marker, which is different from HH and, in its distribution, similar to plural marking in Dutch.

Even in certain possessives where HH employs the singular/set form, HO uses the collective. Note that the collective in possessives in Hungarian is marked by -*i*. Consider the following example:

(12) a. HH   *Fáj   a   láb-am.*
               ache.3SG the leg-PX1SG
               'My legs are aching.'
      b. HO   *Fáj-nak   a   láb-ai-m.*
               ache-3PL the leg-PL-PX1SG
               'My legs are aching.'

    c. DU   *Mijn benen doen pijn.*
               my   leg.PL do   ache
               'My legs are aching.'

Let us now have a look at concord in HO. As Rijkhoff (2002) suggests, languages which show 'number' discord, have set nouns. As shown above, HO does not have set nouns but rather singular object nouns. Therefore, by implication, HO should not have 'number' discord. The data of the different HO varieties does indeed show that the majority of speakers prefer the number concord over 'number' discord. Consider for instance the following example from Vojvodina (Göncz & Vörös, this volume):

(13) HO *Feri és   Mari sétál-ni   men-nek.*   concord
           Feri and Mary walk-INF go-3PL
           'Feri and Mary go out for a walk.'
      HH *Feri és   Mari sétál-ni   megy*   discord
           Feri and Mary walk-INF go.3SG
           'Feri and Mary go out for a walk.'

The following example comes from American Hungarian (AH) (Fenyvesi, this volume):

(14) AH *Mind a   három fijú ud haragusz-nak.*   concord
           all   the three boy so be.angry-3PL
           'All three boys are so angry.'
      HH *Mind a   három fiú   úgy haragszik*   discord
           all   the three boy so be.angry.3SG
           'All three boys are so angry.'

Interestingly, if one would take (14 HH) to be the standard, (14 AH) would count as a mistake. However, from a typological point of view, both utterances are all right if AH can be considered to be a language with singular object nouns, and HH a language with set nouns.

    In conclusion, if HO is considered a 'singular object noun'-type language and not a set noun-type language as HH, the parameter of *Seinsarten* 'modes of being', neatly accounts for the following phenomena: the plural marking of nouns after a numeral, the use of plural forms of the noun in some other cases, and plural agreement with the verb in a number of cases.[1]

3. Copula support

3.1 Typology

The typological study of non-verbal predication by Hengeveld (1992) will provide a good framework for the discussion of the occurrences of copula *van* 'be' in HH and HO. Non-verbal predications are predications in which a predicate other than a verbal one applies. Consider, for instance, the following examples in pseudo English, where the predicates are in bold:

(15) a. *Mary **clever**.*   'Mary is clever.'
      b. *Peter **student**.*   'Peter is a student.'
      c. *John **the teacher***   'John is the teacher.'
      d. *The cat **in the garden**.* 'The cat is in the garden.'
      e. ***To Tom** a book.*   'Tom has a book.'

The predicates in (15) are all non-verbal but an adjectival, a nominal, a locational and a possessive predicate, respectively. Languages may allow none, some, or all of the types of non-verbal predicates. Many languages in the world do not employ any supportive element like a copula or some other device in one or more of the examples in (15). Hengeveld (1992) argues that languages choose between two strategies to mark their predicates. In the first, markings on the non-verbal predicates pattern along with intransitive verbs. In the second, markings on the non-verbal predicates are different from those on intransitive verbs. Hengeveld refers to the first type as the Zero1 strategy and the second as the Zero2 strategy (where 'Zero' indicates the absence of a copula or verbal element). Together with languages such as Egyptian Arabic, Abkhaz, Ket, Turkish, Ngalakan, Mam, Nasioi, Pipil, Lango, and Guaraní, Hungarian is classified a Zero1 type language, as can be witnessed from the following examples:

(16) a. *János sétál-Ø.*
        John walk-3sg
        'John walks.'
      b. *János lusta Ø.*
        John lazy
        'John is lazy.'

Now let us have a look at the occurrences of copula in Hungarian. When we render the examples of (15) into Hungarian, we get (17). Note that HH employs a copula in (17d) and (17e) but not in (17a) through (17c):

(17) a. *Mari okos.*
        Mary clever
        'Mary is clever.'
      b. *Péter diák.*
        Peter student
        'Peter is a student.'
      c. *János a   tanár.*
        John the teacher
        'John is the teacher.'
      d. *A   macska a   kert-ben   van.*
        The cat   the garden-ine cop.3sg
        'The cat is in the garden.'

e. *Tamás-nak könyv-e   van.*
    Tom-DAT   book-PX3SG.POSS COP.3SG
    'Tom has a book.'

Hengeveld (1992:199) argues that the distribution of copulas over non-verbal predications in Zero1 type languages can be accounted for on the basis of the following
hierarchy:

(18)   PREDICATIVITY HIERARCHY
       Bare > Referential > Relational
                        Non-presentative > Presentative

HH does indeed follow this hierarchy. The cut-off point in the hierarchy for HH is
between 'Referential' and 'Relational', i.e. Bare (17a, b) and Referential (17c) predicates
do not require a copula, whereas Relational (17d, e) predicates do. The sub-hierarchy
Non-presentative – Presentative does not seem to be relevant to Hungarian.
     The distribution of the copula *van* 'be' in non-finite constructions, i.e. in em-
bedded constructions, follows the same pattern (cf. De Groot 1989:190f.) as in finite
constructions, as exemplified in (17). Examples of embedded constructions are given
in (19), where the embedded predicate is in bold:

(19) a. *az **okos** lány*
          the clever girl
          'the clever girl' [lit. "the clever being girl"]
      b. *a **kert-ben** levő   macska*
          the garden-INES COP.PRES.PART cat
          'the cat in the garden' [lit. "the in the garden being cat"]

HH does not allow Bare nominal or referential predicates in non-finite constructions. Embedded bare nominal and referential predicates must be expressed in finite
embedded clauses, as in:

(20) a. *Péter, aki diák*   . . . .
          Peter REL student
          'Peter, who is a student, ...'
      b. *János, aki a   tanár*   . . . .
          John REL the teacher
          'John, who is the teacher, ...'

Hengeveld (1992) claims the validity of the hierarchy in (18) only for finite (main)
predications and not for embedded constructions. Embedded non-verbal predications
are beyond the scope of his study. On the basis of the examples in (19) and (20) we
may, however, suggest that the hierarchy in (18) applies both to main and embedded
(non-finite) predications and that the cut-off point for HH is between 'Referential'
and 'Relational' for both domains.

When we take a look at the use of copula in the Hungarian varieties outside Hungary, we see the following. The distribution of copula *van* in main predications in HO is the same as in HH. The distribution of the copula in embedded non-finite constructions, however, differs in the sense that many speakers of HO do not use a copula in embedded relational expressions. Consider the following example from Vojvodina and Prekmurje (Göncz & Vörös, this volume):

(21) HH *a   fal-on   levő   kép*
          the wall-SUP COP.PRES.PART picture
          'the picture on the wall' [lit. "the on the wall being picture"]
     HO *a   kép   a   fal-on*
          the picture the wall-SUP
          'the picture on the wall'

Note that no copula has been applied in (21 HO). The tendency to use constructions without a copula in embedded constructions in HO may now be explained on the basis of the hierarchy in (18): the cut-off point for copula support in embedded non-finite constructions in HO moves from before Relational to after Relational. Consider the following hierarchies, where // indicates the cut-off point within a hierarchy:

(22) Copula support in HH
     finite constructions: Bare > Referential // Relational
     non-finite constructions: Bare > Referential // Relational

(23) Copula support in HO
     finite constructions: Bare > Referential // Relational
     non-finite constructions: Bare > Referential > Relational //

Typological studies on language variation based on hierarchies clearly indicate that variation is typically found at the cut-off points in hierarchies (cf. Dik 1997). This now also holds for the variation in the use of a copula in HO. In other words, the change in the use of the copula between HH and HO clearly follows typological principles.

Together with the change in the use of the copula, there is also a change in the order of the head and the dependent in the constructions involved, as can be seen in the examples in (21). Note that HO does not allow the following type of constructions:

(24) HO **a   fal-on   kép*
          the wall-SUP picture
          'the picture on the wall'

I have not found any typological study in the linguistic literature that explains the change in word order when copula is not used. An explanation may be found along the following lines. Relative constructions in languages with basic SOV word order can take two positions in the noun phrase, before or after the head. The position is conditioned by the nature of the relative clause, being non-finite or finite (cf. Dik 1997). Non-finite relative clauses precede the head, whereas finite relative clauses follow the head:

(25) a. *az éneklő   lány*
         the sing.PRES.PART girl
         'the singing girl'
     b. *a lány aki énekel*
         the girl REL sing.3SG
         'the girl who sings'

Constructions with copula in Hungarian pattern along with the relative constructions as in (25):

(26) a. *a fal-on   levő   kép*
         the wall-SUP COP.PRES.PART picture
         'the picture on the wall'
     b. *a kép   amely a fal-on   van*
         the picture REL   the wall-SUP COP.3SG
         'the picture which is on the wall'

Further typological research may reveal a systematic correspondence between relative constructions and copula constructions, or, possibly even a unifying hierarchy may be established.

4.   Person marking

4.1 Typology

Languages have different systems of referential person markers. The three main types are the following:

(27) a. Free Pronouns
     b. Free Pronouns and NPs, together with person marking elements (weak pronouns or clitics) on the Head (where the Head is a Verb, Noun, or Adposition)
     c. Person marking elements (bound morphemes) on the Head with optional Pronouns and NPs

Along the lines proposed by Givón (1976), De Groot and Limburg (1986) presented a diachronic, typological account for the relation between the three systems which includes a number of morphological, syntactic, semantic and pragmatic aspects. De Groot and Limburg (1986) argue that languages can be characterized as (i) Free Pronoun type, (ii) Clitic type, or (iii) Appositional type for the level of the sentence, the NP and the PP, as illustrated by the frequent co-occurrences of the hypothetical constructions in (28)–(30):

(28) A. FREE PRONOUN TYPE LANGUAGE
    a. me , I see him , John
    b. house him , John
    c. behind him , John

(29) B. CLITIC TYPE LANGUAGE
    a. (me ,) I=see=him (, John)
    b. house=him (, John)
    c. behind=him (, John)

(30) C. APPOSITIONAL TYPE LANGUAGE
    a. (me) a-see-m (John)
    b. house-m (John)
    c. behind-m (John)

In construction (28) *me* and *John* are presented as extra-clausal constituents (indicated by the commas) which have the pragmatic function of theme/topic and tail/coda respectively. The constructions in (29) illustrate the cliticization of the pronouns (indicated by =) and the intermediate stage of internalization of the theme/topic and tail/coda constituents into the clause, NP, or PP. The constructions in (30) represent the stage in which the theme/topic and tail/coda constituents are internalized but still optional, and the former pronouns occur as referential affixes (indicated by –) on the verbal, nominal, or adpositional stems. There is a great amount of evidence that points in the direction of a general diachronic process where languages of type A develop into languages of type B, type B into type C, and type C into type A.

In addition to discussing the diachronic process, De Groot and Limburg (1986) show that within type C languages some hierarchical relations can be established. Two of them are as follows:

(31) a. Verb > Noun > Adposition
    b. Subject > Object

Hierarchy (31a) states that if a language has person marking on just one category, it will be the Verb; if on two, it will be on the Verb and the Noun. Hierarchy (31b) predicts that if a language has person marking of one participant on the verb it will be the Subject. If a language has person marking of the Object, it will also have person marking of the Subject on the verb.

4.2 HO versus HH

HH is claimed to be an Appositional type language for the categories Verb and Noun (cf. De Groot 1989, 2000), as seen in (32) and (33):

(32) Person marking on Verb

    a. *énekel-nek*
       sing-3PL
       'they sing'

    b. *ők   énekel-nek*
       they sing-3PL
       'they sing'

    c. *a   gyerekek énekel-nek*
       the children sing-3PL
       'the children sing'

(33) Person marking on Noun

    a. *a   kabát-ja*
       the coat-3SG
       'his/her coat'

    b. *az ő   kabát-ja*
       the s/he coat-3SG
       'his/her coat'

    c. *a   gyerek kabát-ja*
       the child   coat-3SG
       'the child's coat'

Note that the free pronouns and NPs are optional extensions, they are in a kind of appositional relation with the person marking element on the Verb and Noun. Free pronouns are generally used to express Topic of Focus status of a participant. The Adposition behaves differently. Person marking on Adpositions is possible, it is not possible, however, to extend these forms with a free pronoun or an NP. Consider:

(34) Person marking on Adposition

    a. *mellett-e*
       beside-3SG
       'beside hem/her/it'

    b. **ő   mellett-e*[2]
       s/he beside-3SG
       'beside hem/her/it'

    c. **Péter mellett-e*
       Peter beside-3SG
       'beside Peter'

Constructions such as (34b–c) still existed in Middle Hungarian but are obsolete in Modern Hungarian. The grammatical counterpart of (34c) is (35):

(35) *Péter mellett*
     Peter beside
     'beside Peter'

HH has appositional type constructions with Subjects only and not with Objects, i.e. Subjects are marked by a person marker on the verb and Objects are not. There is, however, agreement in definiteness between Verb and Object. The agreement is fused with the Subject person marker:

(36) a. *Lát-ok egy virág-ot.*
    see-1SG.INDEF a flower-ACC
    'I see a flower.'
  b. *Lát-om a virág-ot.*
    see-1SG.DEF the flower-ACC
    'I see the flower.'

HH has one particular form used if the Subject is first person singular and the Object is second person (singular or plural). See, for an example, (38) below. The suffix, historically, originates from two person markers: *l* '2SG' and *k* '1SG'. In present-day Hungarian, however, the form does not distinguish between singular or plural Object. Therefore the use of the form could also be considered an instance of object agreement and not of Object person marking.

The location of HH in the three typological scales is then as follows:

(37) a. HH is a type C language which develops into a type A language: Adpositional constructions are of type A
  b. The cut-off point in hierarchy (31a) is between Noun and Adposition: Verb > Noun // Adposition
  c. The cut-off point in hierarchy (31b) is between Subject and Object: Subject // Object

There is Subject person marking and Object agreement. The former belongs to a type C language, whereas the latter is a property of type A languages

Let us now have a look at HO. There are three typologically remarkable facts to consider, namely (i) the preference for overt pronouns, (ii) the loss of possessive suffixes, and (iii) the loss of the distinction between the indefinite and definite conjugation of the verb, and, therefore the loss of Object agreement.

4.2.1 *Overt pronouns*

All varieties of Hungarian outside Hungary show some preference for the use of overt pronouns. In those cases in which HH would not use a free pronoun (because there is no pragmatic relevancy), HO often does use a free pronoun, as for instance in (38), from task (515) of the Sociolinguistics of Hungarian Outside Hungary questionnaire:

(38) HH
    Tegnap lát-t-alak a tévé-ben.
    yesterday see-PAST-1SS.2OBJ the TV-INE
    'I saw you on TV yesterday.'

HO

Tegnap   lát-t-alak   téged   a   tévé-ben.
yesterday see-PAST-1SS.2OBJ you.ACC the TV-INE
'I saw you on TV yesterday.'

The use of *téged* in HH would be redundant, since the second person object is already marked in the suffix *-lak* on the verb. We may, thus, conclude the following. The use of overt pronouns in HO is a step in the development of HO, an Appositional type language, towards HO being a Free pronoun type language, as predicted in Section 4.1. In the diachronic process, the use of overt pronouns is the first step. The second step will be that the person marking elements on Heads will wear down, first, to agreement markers and then, ultimately, to zero.

4.2.2   Loss of possessive suffixes

Fenyvesi (this volume) reports that possessive suffixes on nouns of American Hungarian are becoming lost. For instance:

(39)   AH

a.   *Az ő   mama beszélt* ... (HH *mamá-ja*)
     the s/he mom spoke   mom-PX3SG
     'His mom spoke ...'

b.   *Nek-ik   vout templom* (HH *templom-uk*)
     DAT-3PL was church   church-PX3PL
     'They had a church.'

4.2.3   Loss of Object agreement

Fenyvesi (this volume) also reports that AH uses person marking elements on verbs, however, the indefinite and definite conjugations are often used inconsistently. In other words, the distinction between the two conjugations in AH is neutralized. Hence, the Object agreement has become obsolete.

We may now conclude that some varieties of HO can typologically be characterized in the following fashion:

(40)   a.   HO is a type C language which develops into a type A language:
           Nominal and Adpositional constructions are of type A
           The preference for the use of overt pronouns

b.   The cut-off point in hierarchy (31a) is between Verb and Noun:
     Verb // Noun > Adposition

c.   The cut-off point in hierarchy (31b) is between Subject and Object:
     Subject // Object
     There is Subject person marking and there is no Object agreement. The former belongs to a type C language, whereas the latter is a property of type A languages

By comparing the typological features of HH with HO we can see that HO is some steps ahead in the development in the cyclic process of person marking systems.[3] Note that in the development HO strictly follows that predicted path. Also note that the co-occurrence of three apparent by unrelated phenomena, (i) the use of overt pronouns, (ii) the loss of person markers on the Noun but not the Verb, and (iii) the loss of Object agreement, all correlate with the transition of a language from a type C language into a type A language. A straightforward explanation for HO being ahead of HH lies in language contact: all contact languages belong to the type A.

5.   Morphology

A comparison of HH and the HO varieties reveals very interesting morphological differences. Where HH uses morphologically complex, synthetic forms, HO shows a preference for the use of morphologically simplex, analytical forms. Unfortunately, there is no typological study available that could form the basis for an explanation of the systematic change from synthetic to analytical expressions of the languages involved. Therefore, I will limit the discussion of typological morphological aspects to some general observations here.

The authors of the preceding chapters all report the use of analytical expressions in their varieties of Hungarian outside Hungary, where HH would use synthetic forms. The application of the different morphological patterns is not limited to just one or two categories. It seems that the different patterns spread over a large section of grammar. The following table presents the different types discussed in the earlier chapters:

Table 11.1. Synthetic versus analytical expressions in HH and HO

	HH (synthetic)	HO (analytical)
Modality	Ki-me-*het*-ek? out-go-MOD-1SG 'May I go out?'	Ki *tud*-ok men-ni? out be.able-1SG go-INF 'May I go out?' (Ukraine)
Reflexive	Szépít-*kez*-ett beautify-REFL-PAST.3SG.INDEF 'She beautified herself.'	Szépít-ette *magá*-t beautify-PAST.3SG.DEF oneself-ACC 'She beautified herself.' (Ukraine)
Causative	Meg-rajzol-*tat*-ta PVB-draw-CAUS-PAST.3SG.DEF a szék-et. the chair-ACC 'S/he had the chair designed.'	*Hagy*-ta a szék-et permit-PAST.3SG.DEF the chair-ACC rajzol-ni. draw-INF 'S/he had the chair designed.' (Austria)
Compounding	tag-létszám member-number 'number of members'	tag-ok létszám-a member-PL number-3SG.POSS 'number of members'

Table 11.1 shows that a contrast between synthetic and analytical expressions in HH and HO occurs in all three main domains of morphology: (i) inflection (modality), (ii) derivation (verbal reflexives and causatives), and (iii) compounding. A change from synthetic to analytical expression is in itself a quite common phenomenon. However, it is far from common that such a development occurs in all three morphological domains at the same time, and, moreover, that such a development skips a natural intermediate stage, that of inflection. I will return to the co-occurrence of phenomena in Section 5.2 below.

5.1   Morphological change

For the general view on morphological change consider the following quotation from Hock and Joseph (1996:183):

> The fate of morphology from Sanskrit to its modern descendants gives credence to the common belief that languages tend to develop in cycles: from isolating to agglutinating, from agglutinating to inflectional (through amalgamation of different affixes into one), from inflectional to isolating (through sound change and analogy), and so on.

Note that the suffixes -*het*, -*kez*, and -*tat* in the examples in Table 11.1 are clear by agglutinating suffixes which do not show any fusion with other suffixes. Note also that HO can neither be considered an inflectional language nor an isolating language. It still contains the morphological properties of an agglutinating language, as can be witnessed in forms such as *szépítette*, *széket*, and *létszáma* in Table 11.1. In other words, the change from HH to HO does not follow the chain of gradual changes attested in many languages, but rather seems to be a change from morphologically complex to morphologically simplex, i.e. from an agglutinating language with multi-morphemic words to an agglutinating language with less-multi-morphemic words. It would be interesting to know whether this type of change is limited to contact induced language change or whether such change may also occur without language contact. If the latter were the case, the traditional view on morphological change (cf. Hock & Joseph 1996) would then not be sufficient. If we take complex and simplex to be the typological parameters, the two types of development are two different realizations:

(41)   complex →simplex
   (i)   agglutinating → inflectional → isolating
   (ii)   multi-morphemic → less-multi-morphemic

Indo-European languages exhibit a development as in (i), where HH and the HO varieties show a development as in (ii).

5.2 Co-occurrence of phenomena

Let us now take a look at the co-occurrence of change in the different morphological domains as set out in Table 11.1. I will briefly describe the relevant properties of the constructions involved.

5.2.1 *Modality: -hat versus tud*

In HH, the inflectional suffix -*hat* is the marker of objective modality. The periphrastic construction with *tud* is also widely used, however rather as the expression of some other modality, i.e. the person oriented modality ('be able'). HO now tends to use the periphrastic construction to express both types of modality.

5.2.2 *Reflexive: -kezik versus magát*

Verbal reflexive formation in HH takes two-place (transitive) verbs as its input and derives one-place (intransitive) verbs as its output. This type of formation rule changes the argument structure of the verbs, it is an argument reduction rule. HO does not apply the argument reduction rule. It takes a two-place verb and marks the second argument by the reflexive pronoun *maga*. This strategy also applies in HH, as for instance in the case of the verb *lát* 'see':

(42) *Lát-ja   magá-t   a   tükör-ben.*
      see-3SG.DEF oneself-ACC the mirror-INE
      'S/he sees him/herself in the mirror.'

The use of the reflexive pronoun instead of the verbal reflexives may be viewed as an overextension of the use of the transitive pattern in (42).

5.2.3 *Causative: -tat versus hagy*

Causative formation is an argument extension rule. Both HH and HO employ such a rule. Instead of the formative suffix, HO uses the verb *hagy* 'let', 'permit', which is a transitive verb. In HH, it has, however, also a limited use as an auxiliary element in a causative construction, as for instance in (43):

(43) *Hagy-ja   a   terv-et   fejlőd-ni.*
      let-3SG.DEF the plan-ACC develop-INF
      'S/he lets the plan develop.'

The use of *hagy* in causative constructions in HO could also be considered an example of overextension.

5.2.4 *Compounding: taglétszám versus tagok létszáma*

The use of disjunct expressions instead of compounds widely differs from the other three above-mentioned types. There are two strategies. In the first one, the modifying noun, i.e. the first noun in the compound, receives an attributive marker. This marker may be -*i*, as in example (44a), or -*s*, as in (44b). Compare:

(44) a. HH   Ukraine, Vojvodina
          lég-tér   *lég-i   tér*
          air-space   air-ADER space
          'air space'   'air space'
      b. HH   Austria
          baromfi-ól   *baromfi-s   ól*
          poultry-coop   poultry-ADER coop
          'poultry coop'   'poultry coop'

The formation of attributes from nouns by means of the suffixes -*i* and -*s* is very common in HH, as for instance in:

(45) a. *az   erkély-es   ház*
          the balcon-ADER house
          'the balconied house'
      b. *a   kert-i   ház*
          the garden-ADER house
          'the garden house'

In the case of the expressions of (44), however, HH uses the compound and not the disjunct expression.

The second strategy as an alternative disjunct expression for a compound is the possessive construction. Compare:

(46) HH *tag-létszám*   HO *tagok   létszám-a*
          member-number   members number-3SG.POSS
          'number of members'   'number of members'

Note that *létszám* 'number' in HH is the head of the compound, whereas *tagok* in HO counts as the head of the construction. Again, HH would not use the disjunct expression is this case. The structure, however, is in itself a correct structure and employed in many other cases.

The following example illustrates the urge to split up morphological complex words into smaller units. The form in HH is the nominalization of a denominal verb, whereas the form in HO is a nominalization followed by a specifying element marked by the instrumental case. Note that the form in HH is not a compound and that it contains just one lexical stem, whereas the form in HO has two lexical stems. Compare

(47) HH *busz-oz-ás*   HH *utaz-ás   bus-szal*
          bus-VDER-NDER   travel-NDER bus-INS
          'bus trip'   'bus trip'

5.2.5   *Conclusions of this section*

On the basis of the brief discussion of the four types of synthetic versus analytical expressions we may conclude the following. In the case of four unrelated morphological complex expressions, HO prefers to use analytic or disjunct expressions. The syntactic patterns of these expressions are available and are in use for similar or related categories. In HH these patterns have a limited use, while in HO they have a wide use (overextension). The availability of analytical or disjunct expression patterns makes a change from complex to simplex expressions possible. Consequently, in other cases where there are no alternative patterns available, complex expressions will remain as they are and will not derive into less complex expressions.

6.   Conclusions

The aim of this chapter has been to evaluate a number of differences which occur between HH and HO from a linguistic typological point of view and see whether the changes in the HO varieties follow or violate linguistic universals and implicational hierarchies, and whether co-occurrences of changes can be explained in terms of universals or hierarchies. The conclusions are the following:

(i)   Changes from HH into HO can indeed be explained in terms of linguistic hierarchies and universals. In this chapter I have shown that a number of the changes follow paths or cyclic processes which are also found in the diachrony of individual languages. These paths and processes are typologically captured in linguistic hierarchies. In some other cases, the co-occurrence of several changes can be explained on the basis of linguistic universals and their implications.

(ii) The change of several different phenomena can in four cases be explained on the basis of just one parameter each.

    a.   The parameter of *Seinsarten* 'modes of being', i.e. HO is a 'singular object noun'-type language accounts for the following phenomena: the plural marking of nouns after a numeral, the use of plural forms of the noun in some other cases, and plural agreement on the verb in a number of cases.

    b.   The parameter of Predicativity accounts for the use or absence of a copula in relational expressions.

    c.   The parameter of Person Marking Type Language accounts for the use of overt pronouns, the loss of possessive markers on nouns, and the loss of object agreement.

    d.   The parameter of Morphological Complexity accounts for the use of analytic or disjunct expressions in the morphological domains of inflection, derivation, and compounding.

(iii) The study of language change through language contact offers new insights in linguistic typology. In this chapter, it appears that in all cases but one linguistic hierarchies and universals established on synchronic descriptions of a sample of languages also account for the type of changes from HH to HO. In the case of the development of synthetic to analytic expressions, however, there does not seem to be a counterpart in universal typology. The development of synthetic to analytic expressions similar to the one in HH to HO is not attested in the development of languages, which are not in contact with other languages. In other words, the data and the analysis in Section 5 suggest that language change through language contact may be subsidiary to a unique set of universals.

Notes

1. Data from Basque in contact with Spanish support this conclusion. Note that Basque, like Hungarian, is a set noun language and Spanish a singular object noun language. Young native speakers of Spanish who acquire Basque as a second language treat Basque as a singular object noun language. Consequently, they apply number marking and number agreement similar to the Spanish system and different from the Basque system (W. Jansen, p.c.)

2. For emphatics, HH employs pronominal forms as clitics and not as free pronouns, as in (i):

(i)   ő=mellett-e
      (s)he=beside-3sg
      'beside HIM/HER'

Ömellette is one phonological word with main stress on the first syllable, which clearly shows that *ő* in forms such as (i) is not a free pronoun.

3. Varieties of a language may show different states in the cyclic process described in this paragraph. One such example is found in Berber, where two varieties, Shluh and Kabyle, clearly represent two different but adjacent stages (De Groot & Limburg 1986:37ff.).

Bibliography

1960 Census: 1960 Census of Population, Supplementary Reports, PC(S1)-28, December 10, 1962.

1990 Census: U. S. Bureau of Census internet data. http://www.census.gov/. Date of access: October 1, 2001.

Ágoston, Mihály (1990a). *Rendszerbomlás? (Nyelvhasználatunk zavarai)* [The collapse of a system? Problems in our language use]. Újvidék: Forum.

Ágoston, Mihály (1990b). "A jugoszláviai magyarság anyanyelvéről [On the native language of Vojvodina Hungarians]. In Nándor Burányi (Ed.), *Magyarok Vajdaságban. A "Magyar Szó" tematikai különkiadása* [Hungarians in Vojvodina: A special issue of *Magyar Szó*] (pp. 18–19). Újvidék: Forum.

Ágoston, Mihály (1994). "Hogyan hová? Kiépíteni magunkba életképes anyanyelvet, hogy anyanyelvünkben (is) megmaradhassunk [How and where to? Developing a vital mother tongue so we can survive in our mother tongue (too)]." *Híd, 58*(1–4), 202–215.

Albin, Alexander & Alexander, Ronelle (1972). *The Speech of Yugoslav Immigrants in San Pedro, California*. The Hague: Nijhoff.

Alexics, György (1913). "Csángó [The Csángós]." *Magyar Nyelv, 9*, 349–352.

Ambrosy, Anna (1984). *New Lease on Life. Hungarian Immigrants in Victoria. Assimilation in Australia*. Adelaide: Dezsery Ethnic Publications.

Andrić, Edit (1995). "A szerb nyelvnek a vajdasági magyar nyelvre gyakorolt hatása [The influence of Serbian on Hungarian in Vojvodina]." In Ilona Kassai (Ed.), *Kétnyelvűség és magyar nyelvhasználat* [Bilingualism and Hungarian language use] (pp. 235–243). Budapest: MTA Nyelvtudományi Intézete.

Antal, László G. (1993). *Situaţia Minorităţii Etnice Maghiare în România* [The situation of the Hungarian ethnic minority in Romania]. Odorheiu Secuiesc: A.C.H.R.

Anuarul Statistic al RSR [Romanian Statistical Yearbook]. Bucureşti: Institutul National de Statistica.

Arany, A. László (1998[1939–40]). "A kétnyelvűség jelenségeinek pszichológiai alapjai [Psychological aspects of bilingual phenomena]." In István Lanstyák & Szabolcs Simon (Eds.), *Tanulmányok a magyar–szlovák kétnyelvűségről* [Studies in Hungarian–Slovak bilingualism] (pp. 7–31). Pozsony: Kalligram.

Arel, Dominique (1995). "Language politics in independent Ukraine: Towards one or two state languages." *Nationalities Papers, 23*(3), 597–622.

Auer, Peter (1988). "A conversation analytic approach to code-switching and transfer." In Monica Heller (Ed.), *Codeswitching: Anthropological and Sociolinguistic Perspectives* (pp. 187–214). Berlin: Mouton de Gruyter.

Auer, Peter (1998). "Introduction: Bilingual conversation revisited." In Peter Auer (Ed.), *Code-switching in Conversation: Language, Interaction and Identity* (pp. 1–24). London/New York: Routledge.

Auer, Peter (1999). "From code-switching via language mixing to fused lects: Towards a dynamic typology of bilingual speech." *International Journal of Bilingualism, 3*(4), 309–332.

B. Lőrinczy, Éva (Ed.). (1992). *Új magyar tájszótár* [A new dialect dictionary of Hungarian]. Vol. 3. Budapest: Akadémiai Kiadó.

Baker, Robin (1997). "On the origin of the Moldavian Csángós." *The Slavonic and East European Review, 75*, 658–680.

Baker, Colin & Prys Jones, Sylvia (Eds.). (1998). *Encyclopaedia of Bilingualism and Bilingual Education.* Clevedon: Multilingual Matters.

Bako, Elemer (1961). "Hungarian dialectology in the USA." *Hungarian Quarterly, 1*, 48–53.

Bakó, Elemer (1962). *American Hungarian Dialect Notes: Goals and Methods of Hungarian Dialectology in America.* New Brunswick, NJ: American Hungarian Studies Foundation.

Bakos, Ferenc (1982). *A magyar szókészlet román elemeinek története* [The history of the Romanian elements of the Hungarian lexicon]. Budapest: Akadémiai Kiadó.

Bakos, Ferenc (1984). "Román jövevényszavaink legújabb rétegéhez" [On the newest layer of Romanian loanwords in Hungarian]. In Béla Nagy (Ed.), *Magyar–román filológiai tanulmányok* [Studies in Hungarian–Romanian philology] (pp. 179–185). Budapest: ELTE Román Filológia Tanszék.

Bartha, Csilla (1993). *Egy amerikai magyar közösség nyelvhasználatának szociolingvisztikai megközelítései* [Sociolinguistic approaches to the language use of a Hungarian American community]. Budapest: *Kandidátusi* dissertation.

Bartha, Csilla (1995/1996). "Social and linguistic characteristics of immigrant language shift: The case of Hungarian in Detroit." *Acta Linguistica Hungarica, 43*(3–4), 405–431.

Bartha, Csilla (1996). "A társadalmi kétnyelvűség típusai és főbb vizsgálati kérdései [The types and main research issues of societal bilingualism]." *Magyar Nyelvőr, 120*, 263–282.

Bartha, Csilla (1997). "Helységneveink ragozása határainkon innen és túl [The inflection of placenames inside and outside Hungary]." In Gábor Kiss & Gábor Zaicz (Eds.), *Szavak–nevek–szótárak: Írások Kiss Lajos 75. születésnapjára* [Words, names, and dictionaries: A festschrift for Lajos Kiss on the occasion of his 75th birthday] (pp. 49–61). Budapest: A Magyar Tudományos Akadémia Nyelvtudományi Intézete.

Bartha, Csilla (1999). "A purista nyelvideológiák szerepe a nyelvcsere folyamatában [The role of purist language ideologies in the process of language shift]." In Nóra Kugler & Klára Lengyel (Eds.), *Ember és nyelv: Tanulmánykötet Keszler Borbála tiszteletére* [Humans and language: Studies in honor of Borbála Keszler] (pp. 44–54). Budapest: ELTE BTK Mai Magyar Nyelvi Tanszék.

Bartha, Csilla & Sydorenko, Olena (2000). "Changing verb usage patterns in first and second generation Hungarian-American discourse." In Anna Fenyvesi & Klára Sándor (Eds.), *Language Contact and the Verbal Complex of Dutch and Hungarian: Working Papers from the 1st Bilingual Language Use Theme Meeting of the Study Centre on Language Contact, November 11–13, 1999, Szeged, Hungary* (pp. 31–48). Szeged: Teacher Training College.

Baugh, John (1999). *Out of the Mouths of Slaves: African American Language and Educational Malpractice.* Austin: University of Texas Press.

Bencze, Lajos (1994). *Írott szóval a megmaradásért. A szlovéniai magyarság 70 éve* [Written words for survival: 70 years in the life of Hungarians in Slovenia]. Győr: Hazánk.

Benda, Kálmán (1989). *Moldvai csángó-magyar okmánytár, 1467–1706. I–II* [Moldavian Csángó Hungarian collection of documents, 1467–1706, vols I and II]. Budapest: Magyarságkutató Intézet.

Benedek, H. János (1997a). "Csángó falvak gazdasági problémái [Economic problems of Csángó villages]." In Ferenc Pozsony (Ed.), *Dolgozatok a moldvai csángók népi kultúrájáról* [Studies on the folk culture of Moldavian Csángós] (pp. 195–209). Kolozsvár: Kriza János Néprajzi Társaság.

Benedek, H. János (1997b). "Egy moldvai magyar parasztcsalád gazdálkodása [The management of a Moldavian peasant household]." In Ferenc Pozsony (Ed.), *Dolgozatok a moldvai csángók népi kultúrájáról* [Studies on the folk culture of Moldavian Csángós] (pp. 210–223). Kolozsvár: Kriza János Néprajzi Társaság.

Benkart, Paula (1980). "Hungarians." In Stephan Thernstrom (Ed.), *Harvard Encyclopedia of American Ethnic Groups* (pp. 462–471). Cambridge: Belknap Press.

Benkő, Loránd (1989). "A csángók eredete és települése a nyelvtudomány szemszögéből [The origin and settlement of the Csángós from a linguistic point of view]." *Magyar Nyelv, 85*, 271–287, 385–405.

Benkő, Annamária (2000). *An Analysis of British Hungarian: Some Morphological Features of Hungarian as Used by Hungarian Immigrants and their Descendants in London.* Szeged: University of Szeged MA thesis.

Benő, Attila (1999). *A vizualitás szerepe a szókölcsönzésben* [The role of visuality in lexical borrowing]. In Vilmos Keszeg (Ed.), *Kriza János Néprajzi Társaság Évkönyve 7* [The yearbook of the János Kriza Ethnographic Society, Vol. 7] (pp. 266–280). Kolozsvár: Kriza János Néprajzi Társaság.

Benő, Attila (2000). *A magyar–román nyelvi érintkezés jelentéstani kérdései* [Semantic interferences in Hungarian–Romanian language contact]. Kolozsvár: Babeş-Bolyai University MS.

Beregszászi, Anikó (1995/1996). "Language planning issues of Hungarian place-names in Subcarpathia." *Acta Linguistica Hungarica, 43*(3–4), 373–380.

Beregszászi, Anikó (1997). "Kárpátaljai szavak a Magyar Értelmező Kéziszótárban? [Subcarpathian words in the Concise Defining Dictionary of Hungarian?]." *Pánsíp, 5*(2), 24–27.

Beregszászi, Anikó, Csernicskó, István, & Orosz, Ildikó (2001). *Nyelv, oktatás, politika* [Language, education, and politics]. Beregszász: Kárpátaljai Magyar Tanárképző Főiskola.

Berney, Dorothy (1993). *A Phonetic and Phonemic Analysis of Standard Hungarian.* Pittsburgh: University of Pittsburgh MS.

Biacsi, Antal (1994). *Kis délvidéki demográfia* [A short demographics of Vojvodina]. Szabadka: Magyarságkutató Tudományos Társaság and Szabadkai Szabadegyetem.

Bihari, László (1994). "Szőcs Anna – egy csángó Budapesten [Anna Szőcs, a Csángó in Budapest]." *Magyar Hírlap.* August 27, 1994, 4.

Bjulleten' statistiki [Bulletin of statistics]. 1990/10, 76–79. Moskva.

Bokor, József (1990). "A tájszókincsek vizsgálata egy családon belül [A study of regional dialectal vocabulary in one family]." In Géza Szabó (Ed.), *II. Dialektológiai szimpozion* [2nd Symposium on Dialectology] (pp. 163–169). Veszprém: Veszprémi Akadémiai Bizottság.

Bolonyai, Agnes (2000). ""Elective affinities": Language contact in the abstract lexicon and its structural consequences." *International Journal of Bilingualism, 4*(1), 81–106.

Borbáth, Erzsébet (1993). "A moldvai csángó gyermekek kétnyelvűsége [The bilingualism of Moldavian Csángó children]." *Új Horizont, 23*, 92–95.

Borbáth, Erzsébet (1994). "A kétnyelvű oktatás lehetőségei a moldvai csángó magyar falvakban [The possibilities of bilingual education in Moldavian Csángó Hungarian villages]." *Folia Practico-Linguistica, 24*, 216–220.

Borbáth, Erzsébet (1996). "A moldvai csángó gyermekek székelyföldi iskoláztatásának tapasztalatai [The experiences of educating Moldavian Csángó children in Székelyföld]." In István Csernicskó & Tamás Váradi (Eds.), *Kisebbségi magyar iskolai nyelvhasználat* [Minority Hungarian language use in schools] (pp. 69–74). Budapest: Tinta.

Borbély, Anna (1995/1996). "Attitudes as a factor of language choice: A sociolinguistic investigation in a bilingual community of Romanian-Hungarians." *Acta Linguistica Hungarica, 43*, 311–321.

Böröcz, József (1987). "Name language shift in Árpádhon, Louisiana." *Hungarian Studies, 3*, 227–241.

Boros-Kazai, Mary (1981). "The emigration problem and Hungary's lawmakers, 1880–1910." *Hungarian Studies Review, 8*, 25–44.

Botlik, József & Dupka, György (1991). *Ez hát a hon...*: Tények, adatok, dokumentumok a kárpátaljai magyarság életéből: 1918–1991 [So this is our land...: Facts, data and documents about the life of Subcarpathia Hungarians, 1918–1991]. Budapest/Szeged: Mandátum and Universum.

Botlik, József & Dupka, György (1993). *Magyarlakta települések ezredéve Kárpátalján* [A thousand years of the Hungarian populated settlements in Subcarpathia]. Budapest/Ungvár: Intermix and Patent.

Botlik, József, Csorba, Béla, & Dudás, Károly (1994). *Eltévedt mezsgyekövek. Adalékok a délvidéki magyarság történetéhez 1918–1993* [Boundary posts that lost their way: Additional details about Hungarians in the Vojvodina, 1918–1993]. Budapest: Hatodik Síp Alapítvány – Új Mandátum.

Brown, Roger W. & Gilman, Albert (1960). "The pronouns of power and solidarity." In Thomas A. Sebeok (Ed.), *Style in Language* (pp. 253–276). Cambridge, MA: MIT Press.

Brunner, Georg (1995). *Nemzetiségi kérdés és kisebbségi konfliktusok Kelet-Európában* [The minority issue and minority conflicts in Eastern Europe]. Budapest: Teleki László Alapítvány.

Bundesanstalt Statistik Österreich (2002). *Volkszahlungen 1981–2001*. Umgangssprache Burgenland. Gemeinden und Ortschaften. Wien, im August 2002. http:// www.volkszaehlung.at/

Bureau of the Census (1983). *1980 Census of Population: Ancestry of the Population by State, 1980*. Supplementary report PC80-S1-10. http://www.census.gov/. Date of access: October 10, 2001.

Campbell, Lyle (1989). "Finno-Ugric prehistory in the light of recent developments." Paper presented at the Symposium on Linguistic Prehistory at the annual meeting of the American Anthropological Association, Washington, DC.

Campbell, Lyle & Muntzel, Martha C. (1989). "The structural consequences of language death." In Nancy C. Dorian (Ed.), *Investigating Obsolescence: Studies in Language Contraction and Death* (pp. 181–196). Cambridge: Cambridge University Press.

Census 1991: CLIB 91. Census of Population and Housing. Australian Bureau of Statistics.

Census 1996: CLIB 96. Census of Population and Housing. Australian Bureau of Statistics.

Census 2000: U. S. Bureau of Census internet data. http://www.census.gov/. Date of access: October 1, 2004.

Chambers, J. K. (2003). Sociolinguistics of immigration. In David Britain & Jenny Cheshire (Eds.), *Social Dialectology: In honour of Peter Trudgill* (pp. 97–113). Amsterdam/Philadelphia: John Benjamins.

Chambers, J. K. & Trudgill, Peter (1998). *Dialectology* (2nd edition). Cambridge: Cambridge University Press.

Clyne, Michael G. (1982). *Multilingual Australia: Resources, Needs, Policies.* Melbourne: River Seine Publications.

Clyne, Michael G. (1991). *Community Languages: The Australian Experience.* Cambridge: Cambridge University Press.

Clyne, Michael G. (1997). "Some of the things trilinguals do." *International Journal of Bilingualism, 1,* 95–116.

Clyne, Michael & Kipp, Sandra (1999). *Pluricentric Languages in an Immigrant Context: Spanish, Arabic and Chinese.* Berlin: Mouton de Gruyter.

Comrie, Bernard (1981). *Language Universals and Linguistic Typology.* Oxford: Blackwell.

Constitution of Romania (1991). Second Edition. The Self-Managed Public Company "Monitorul Oficial", Bucureşti, 1995.

Convention (1997). Framework Convention for the protection for national minorities and explanatory report. Strasbourg: Council of Europe.

Csango Minority Culture in Romania. Rapporteur: Mrs Tytti Isohookana-Asunmaa, Finland. Doc. 9078. 4 May 2001. Council of Europe Parliamentary Assembly, Committee on Culture, Science and Education.

Csapo, Marg (1983). "Slide-rule instead of sheepskin coat: Language maintenance among post-second-World-War Hungarian immigrants." *Canadian Ethnic Studies, 15,* 83–92.

Csapó, György (1994). "Hogyan ásta alá Fehér Kati az államrendet... [How Kati Fehér undermined the political system]." *Erdélyi Napló* 1994/2.

Csepeli, György, Örkény, Antal, & Székely, Mária (2000). "The steadiness and transformation of national-ethnic identity." *Minorities Research: A Collection of Studies by Hungarian Authors, 2,* 46–63.

Cserján, Károly, Győri, Vilmos, & Szabó, Mátyás (1999). *Demographische und sozioökonomische Merkmale der Bevölkerung mit Ungarisch als Umgangssprache. Sonderauswertung der Volkszählung 1991 durch das Österreichische Statistische Zentralamt* [Demographic and Socioeconomic Features of the Hungarian-speaking population: A Special Interpretation of the 1991 Census by the Austrian Central Office of Statistics]. Wien: Kerkai Jenő Egyházszociológiai Intézet.

Csernicskó, István (1995). "A kárpátaljai magyarság és a kétnyelvűség (1945–1993) [Hungarians in Subcarpathia and their bilingualism, 1945–1993]." In Ilona Kassai (Ed.), *Kétnyelvűség és magyar nyelvhasználat* [Bilingualism and Hungarian language use] (pp. 129–145). Budapest: MTA Nyelvtudományi Intézete.

Csernicskó, István (1997). "Kárpátaljai szójegyzék [A list of Subcarpathian vocabulary]." *Pánsíp, 5*(2), 28–29.

Csernicskó, István (1998). *A magyar nyelv Ukrajnában (Kárpátalján)* [The Hungarian language in Ukraine (Subcarpathia)]. Budapest: Osiris Kiadó and MTA Kisebbségkutató Műhely.

Csernicskó, István & Fenyvesi, Anna (2000). "The sociolinguistic stratification of Hungarian in Subcarpathia." *Multilingua, 19*(1–2), 95–122.

Csoma, Gergely & Bogdánfalvy, János (1993). "Népszámlálás a moldvai csángó falvakban [Census in Moldavian Csángó villages]." In Péter Halász (Ed.), *Megfog vala apóm szokcor kezemtül... Tanulmányok Domokos Pál Péter emlékére* ["My father would take my hand...": Studies in memory of Pál Péter Domonkos] (pp. 165–167). Budapest: Lakatos Demeter Egyesület.

Daftary, Farimah & Gál, Kinga (2000). *The new Slovak language law: Internal or external politics?* ECMI Working Papers # 8. http://www.ecmi.de/publications/

Dávid, Zoltán (1988). "The Hungarians and their neighbors, 1851–2000." In Steven Borsody (Ed.), *The Hungarians: A Divided Nation* (pp. 333–345). New Haven: Yale University Press.

Dégh, Linda (1972). "Two Hungarian-American stereotypes." *New York Folklore Quarterly, 28*, 3–14.

Dégh, Linda (1980). "Grape-harvest festival of strawberry farmers: Folklore or fake?" *Ethnologia Europaea, 14*, 114–131.

Dégh, Linda (1996). "Hungarians." In Robert M. Taylor, Jr. & Connie A. McBirney, (Eds.), *Peopling Indiana: The Ethnic Experience* (pp. 224–242). Indianapolis: Indiana Historical Society.

De Groot, Casper (1989). *Predicate Structure in a Functional Grammar of Hungarian.* Dordrecht: Foris.

De Groot, Casper (2000). "Minor word classes." In Geert Booij, Christian Lehmann, & Joachim Mugdan (Eds.), *Morphology: An International Handbook on Inflection and Word-Formation,* Vol. 1, Chapter 79 (pp. 820–831). Berlin: Walter de Gruyter.

De Groot, Casper & Machiel J. Limburg (1986). "Pronominal elements: Diachrony, typology, and formalization in Functional Grammar." *Working Papers in Functional Grammar, 12.*

DeKeyser, Robert M. (2000). "The robustness of critical period effects in second language acquisition." *Studies in Second Language Acquisition, 22*(4), 499–533.

Deme, László (1970). *Nyelvi és nyelvhasználati gondjainkról* [On our problems with language and language use]. Pozsony: Madách-Posonium.

Dik, Simon (1997). *The theory of functional grammar. Part 2: Complex and Derived Constructions.* Berlin: Mouton de Gruyter.

Dimmendaal, Gerrit (1992). "Reduction in Kore recondisered." In Matthias Brenzinger (Ed.), *Language Death: Factual and Theoretical Explorations with Special Reference to East Africa* (pp. 117–135). Berlin/New York: Mouton de Gruyter.

Di Sciuollo, Anne-Marie, Muysken, Pieter, & Singh, Rajendra (1986). "Government and code-mixing." *Journal of Linguistics, 22*, 1–24.

Domonkos, László (1992). *Magyarok a Délvidéken* [Hungarians in Vojvodina]. Budapest: Zrínyi Kiadó.

Domokos, Pál Péter (1987). *A moldvai magyarság* [Moldavian Hungarians]. Budapest: Magvető.

Dorian, Nancy C. (1977). "The problem of the semi-speaker in language death." *International Journal of the Sociology of Language, 12*, 23–32.

Dorian, Nancy C. (1981). *Language Death: The Life Cycle of a Scottish Gaelic Dialect.* Philadelphia: University of Pennsylvania Press.

Drávai, Gizella (1969). "Nyelvrosta. Így mondjuk, de mondjuk így [A linguistic sieve: This is how we say it, but let's say it this way]." In *Kárpáti Kalendárium* 1969: 65, 91, and 135. Uzshorod: Kárpáti Könyvkiadó.

Dressler, Wolfgang U. (1996). "Language death." In Rajendra Singh (Ed.), *Towards a Critical Sociolinguistics* (pp. 195–210). Amsterdam/Philadelphia: John Benjamins.

Dupka, György (Ed.). (1993). *'Sötét napok jöttek...': Koncepciós perek magyar elítéltjeinek emlékkönyve: 1944–1955'* [Dark days followed: Reminiscences of Hungarian convicts of show trials, 1944–1955]. Budapest/Ungvár: Intermix and Patent.

Dupka, György (Ed.). (1993). *Egyetlen bűnük magyarságuk volt: Emlékkönyv a sztálinizmus kárpátaljai áldozatairól (1944–1946)* [Their only sin was that they were Hungarians: White book on the victims of Stalinism in Subcarpathia, 1944–1946]. Budapest/Ungvár: Intermix and Patent.

Dupka, György (1994). "A magyarság számának, összetételének és települési területeinek változása Kárpátalján (1910-től napjainkig) [The change in the number, composition and settlement areas of the Hungarians in Subcarpathia (from 1910 to the present)]." In József Kovacsics (Ed.), *Magyarország nemzetiségeinek és a szomszédos államok magyarságának statisztikája (1910–1990)* [Statistics on Hungary's minorities and the Hungarians of the neighboring states, 1910–1990] (pp. 164–174). Budapest: Központi Statisztikai Hivatal.

Éger, György (1991). *A burgenlandi magyarság rövid története* [A short history of the Hungarians in Burgenland]. Budapest: Anonymus.

Endrődy, Tibor (1971). *"Prepositional" Interference and Deviation in Migrant German and Migrant Hungarian in Australia.* Clayton, Victoria: Monash University M.A. thesis.

Ètnični menšini v Ukraini [Ethnic minorities in Ukraine]. Kiiv: Institut sociologii NAN Ukraini u spravax nacional'nostej ta migracii.

Eysenck, Michael W. & Keane, Mark T. (1990). *Cognitive Psychology.* Mahwah, NJ: Lawrence Earlbaum.

Falk-Bánó, Klára (1988). "Characteristics of language shift in two American Hungarian bilingual communities." *Papers and Studies in Contrastive Linguistics, 24,* 161–170.

Farkas, Donka & Sadock, Jerrold (1989). "Preverb climbing in Hungarian." *Language, 65,* 318–338.

Farkas, Zoltan J. (1971). "Hungarian city and county names in the United States." *Names, 19,* 141–143.

Fekete, Réka (2000). "I. Csángó Oktatási Konferencia [The First Csángó Education Conference]." *Moldvai Magyarság* June 6–7, 2000.

Fenyvesi, Anna (1995a). "Language contact and language death in an immigrant language: The case of Hungarian." *University of Pittsburgh Working Papers in Linguistics, 3,* 1–117.

Fenyvesi, Anna (1995b). Hungarian diglossia in Slovakia: A new linguistic approach. *Budapest Review of Books, 5*(2), 37–39.

Fenyvesi, Anna (1995c). *Lovári Borrowings in Hungarian Slang.* Pittsburgh: University of Pittsburgh MS.

Fenyvesi, Anna (1995/1996). "The case of American Hungarian case: Morphological change in McKeesport, PA." *Acta Linguistica Hungarica, 43,* 381–404.

Fenyvesi, Anna (1998a). "Patterns of Borrowing and Language Attrition: American Hungarian in McKeesport, Pennsylvania." In Casper de Groot & István Kenesei (Eds.), *Approaches to Hungarian, Vol. 6: Papers from the Amsterdam Conference* (pp. 229–249). Szeged: JATE Press.

Fenyvesi, Anna (1998b). "Linguistic minorities in Hungary." In Christina Bratt Paulston & Donald Peckham (Eds.), *Linguistic Minorities in Eastern and Central Europe* (pp. 135–159). Clevedon: Multilingual Matters.

Fenyvesi, Anna (1998c). Inflectional morphology. In István Kenesei, Robert M. Vago, & Anna Fenyvesi (Eds.), *Hungarian* (Descriptive Grammars) (pp. 191–381). London: Routledge.

Fenyvesi, Anna (1998d). "Nyelvkontaktus és nyelvvesztés az amerikai magyarban: A hasonulások sorsa a mckeesporti beszélők nyelvében [The role of language contact and language attrition in American Hungarian: The fate of phonological assimilation in McKeesport speakers' speech]." In Klára Sándor (Ed.), *Nyelvi változó nyelvi változás. A 9. Élőnyelvi Konferencia előadásai (Szeged, 1996. augusztus 22–24.)* [Linguistic variables and language change: Papers from the 9th Sociolinguistics Conference, August 22–24, 1996, Szeged] (pp. 85–98). Szeged: JGYF Kiadó.

Fenyvesi, Anna (2000). "The affectedness of the verbal complex in American Hungarian." In Anna Fenyvesi & Klára Sándor (Eds.), *Language Contact and the Verbal Complex of Dutch and Hungarian: Working Papers from the 1st Bilingual Language Use Theme Meeting of the Study Centre on Language Contact, November 11–13, 1999, Szeged, Hungary* (pp. 94–107). Szeged: Teacher Training College.

Ferguson, Charles A. (1959). "Diglossia." *Word, 15,* 325–340.

Fishman, Joshua A. (1965). "Who speaks what language to whom and when." *La Linguistique, 2,* 67–88.

Fishman, Joshua A. (1966). *Hungarian Language Maintenance in the United States.* Bloomington: Indiana University.

Fishman, Joshua A. (1967). "Bilingualism with and without diglossia; diglossia with and without bilingualism." *Journal of Social issues, 23*(2), 29–38.

Fishman, Joshua A. (1970). *Sociolinguistics: A Brief Introduction.* Rowley, MA: Newbury House.

Fishman, Joshua A. (1972a). *The Sociology of Language: An Interdisciplinary Social Science Approach to Language in Society.* Rowley, MA: Newbury House.

Fishman, Joshua A. (1972b). "The relationship between micro- and macro-sociolinguistics in the study of who speaks what language to whom and when." In J. B. Pride & Janet Holmes (Eds.), *Sociolinguistics: Selected Readings* (pp. 15–32). Hammondsworth: Penguin.

Fishman, Joshua A. (1981). "Language policy: Past, present, and future." In Charles A. Ferguson & Shirley Brice Heath (Eds.), *Language in the USA* (pp. 516–526). Cambridge: Cambridge University Press.

Fodó, Sándor (1973). "Szláv jövevényszók a kárpátaljai magyar nyelvjárásokban [Slavic loanwords in Subcarpathian Hungarian dialects]." *Magyar Nyelvjárások, 19,* 41–52.

Fodor, Katalin (1995). "A csángók identitásproblémájának nyelvi és nyelven kívüli okairól [The linguistic and extralinguistic causes of the Csángós' identity problem]." In Ilona Kassai (Ed.), *Kétnyelvűség és magyar nyelvhasználat* [Bilingualism and Hungarian language use] (pp. 121–127). Budapest: MTA Nyelvtudományi Intézet.

Forrai, Ibolya (1989). *Népi írásbeliség a bukovinai székelyeknél* [Folk literacy among Bukovina Szeklers]. Budapest: Múzsák.

Foucher, Michel (1994). *Minorities in Central and Eastern Europe.* Strasbourg: Council of Europe Press.

Friedrich, Paul (1972). "Social context and semantic feature: The Russian pronominal usage." In John J. Gumperz & Dell Hymes (Eds.), *Directions in Sociolinguistics* (pp. 270–300). New York: Holt, Reinhart and Winston.

Fuller, Janet M. (1996). "When cultural maintenance means linguistic convergence: Pennsylvania German evidence for the matrix language turnover hypothesis." *Language in Society, 25,* 493–514.

Gajdoš, Peter & Pašiak, Ján (1995). *Vývoj sociálno-ekonomickej situácie slovenskej spoločnosti* [The development of the socio-ecological situation of Slovak society]. Bratislava: Veda.

Gal, Susan (1979). *Language Shift: Social Determinants of Linguistic Change in Bilingual Austria.* New York: Academic.

Gal, Susan (1984). "Phonological style in bilingualism: The interaction of structure and use." In Deborah Schiffrin (Ed.), *Meaning, Form and Use in Context: Linguistic Applications* (pp. 290–302). Washington, DC: Georgetown University Press.

Gal, Susan (1987). "Codeswithing and consciousness in the European periphery." *American Ethnologist, 14,* 637–653.

Gal, Susan (1988). "The political economy of code choice". In Monica Heller (Ed.), *Codeswitching: Anthropological and Sociolinguistic Perspectives* (pp. 245–264). Berlin: Mouton de Gruyter.

Gal, Susan (1989). "Lexical innovation and loss: The use and value of restricted Hungarian." In Nancy C. Dorian (Ed.), *Investigating Obsolescence: Studies in Language Contraction and Death* (pp. 313–331). Cambridge: Cambridge University Press.

Gáldi, László (1947). *A Dunatáj nyelvi alkata* [A linguistic characterization of Dunatáj]. Budapest: Gergely.

Gálffy, Mózes, Márton, Gyula, & Szabó T., Attila (Eds.). (1991). *A moldvai csángó nyelvjárás atlasza I–II* [The atlas of the Moldavian Csángó dialect, Vols. 1 and 2]. Budapest: Magyar Nyelvtudományi Társaság.

Gardner-Chloros, Penelope (1987). "Code-switching in relation to language contact and convergence." In Georges Lüdi (Ed.), *Devenir bilingue – parler bilingue* [Becoming bilingual – speaking bilingually]. *Actes du 2e colloque sur le bilinguisme, Univesité de Neuchâtel, 20–22 septembre 1984* (pp. 99–113). Tübingen: Niemeyer.

Gazda, József (1994). "A nyelv és a magyarságtudat szintjei a moldvai csángóknál [Levels of language and Hungarian identity among Moldavian Csángós]." *Néprajzi látóhatár, 3*(1–2), 269–281.

Gereben, Ferenc (1999). *Identitás, kultúra, kisebbség. Felmérés a közép-európai magyar népesség körében* [Identity, culture, and minorities: A survey of the Hungarian population in Central Europe]. Budapest: Osiris and MTA Kisebbségkutató Műhely.

Gibson, Campbell J. & Lennon, Emily (1999). "Historical Census Statistics on the Foreign-born Population of the United States: 1850–1990." Washington, DC: The Bureau of the Census. *Population Division Working Paper No. 29.* http://www.census.gov/population/ www/documentation/twps0029/twps0029.html. Date of access: October 10, 2001.

Giles, Howard, Bourhis, Richard Y., & Taylor, Donald M. (1977). "Towards a theory of language in ethnic group relations." In Howard Giles (Ed.), *Language, Ethnicity and Intergroup Relations* (pp. 307–348). New York: Academic Press.

Givón, Talmi (1976). "Topic, pronoun, and grammatical agreement." In Charles N. Li (Ed.), *Subject and Topic* (pp. 146–188). New York: Academic Press.

Goebl, Hans, Nelde, Peter H., Starý, Zdeněk, & Wölck, Wolfgang (Eds.). (1997). *Kontaktlinguistik/Contact Linguistics/Linguistique de contact 2.* Halbband/Volume 2/Tome 2. Berlin/New York: Walter de Gruyter.

Göncz, Lajos (1985). *A kétnyelvűség pszichológiája. A magyar–szerbhorvát kétnyelvűség lélektani vizsgálata* [The psychology of bilingualism: A psychological study of Hungarian–Serbo-Croatian bilingualism]. Újvidék: Forum.

Göncz, Lajos (1998). "A kisebbségi oktatás néhány kérdéséről a tannyelv tükrében [On minority education from the perspective of the language of instruction]." In Éva Hódi (Ed.), *Szarvas Gábor Nyelvművelő Napok 1998* [Gábor Szarvas Language Cultivation Days, 1988] (pp. 39–53). Ada: Szarvas Gábor Nyelvművelő Egyesület.

Göncz, Lajos (1999). *A magyar nyelv Jugoszláviában (Vajdaságban)* [The Hungarian language in Yugoslavia (Vojvodina)]. Budapest/Újvidék: Osiris, Forum and MTA Kisebbségkutató Műhely.

Göncz, Lajos (2000a). "Hol beszélnek legszebben magyarul? A kárpát-medencei magyar beszélőközösségek anyanyelvi sztereotípiái [Where is the most beautiful Hungarian spoken? Linguistic stereotypes of Hungarian speech communities in the Carpathian Basin]." *Hungarológiai Közlemények, 1,* 147–154.

Göncz, Lajos (2000b). "A vajdasági magyarság területi és nemzeti kötődése [The attachment of Vojvodina Hungarians to their region and nation]." In Anna Borbély (Ed.), *Nyelvek és kultúrák érintkezése a Kárpát-medencében* [Language and culture contact in the Carpathian Basin] (pp. 79–87). Budapest: MTA Nyelvtudományi Intézete.

Göncz, Lajos (2000c). "Analitizáló és szintetizáló nyelvi megoldások Kárpát-medencei magyar beszélőközösségek nyelvhasználatában [Analytical and synthetic forms in Hungarian speech communities of the Carpathian Basin]." *Fórum Társadalomtudományi Szemle, 3,* 3–18.

Göncz, Lajos (2001a). "Nyelvi és szociológiai változók összefüggése a Kárpát-medencei magyar beszélőközösségeknél kisebbségi és többségi helyzetben [Correlations between linguistic and sociological variables in Carpathian Basin Hungarian speech communities in minority and majority situations]." *Magyar Nyelv, 97,* 152–171.

Göncz, Lajos (2001b). "Az egyes és a többes szám használata Kárpát-medencei magyar beszélőközösségeknél [The use of the singular and plural in Hungarian speech communities in the Carpathian Basin]." *Pszichológia, 4,* 371–391.

Göncz, Lajos & Kodžopeljić, Jasmina (1991). "Exposure to two languages in the preschool period, metalinguistic development and the acquisition of reading." *Journal of Multilingual and Multicultural Development, 12,* 65–81.

Göncz, Lajos & Kontra, Miklós (2000). ""Feminizálás" a kárpát-medencei magyar beszélőközösségek nyelvhasználatában ["Feminization" in the language use of Carpathian Basin Hungarian speech communities]." *Modern Filológiai Közlemények, 2,* 83–96.

Greenberg, Joseph (1963). *Universals of Language.* Cambridge, MA: MIT Press.

Greenberg, Marc L. (1999). *Uralic Influences in South Slavic.* Lawrence: University of Kansas, MS.

Greenfield, L. (1968). "Spanish and English usage self-ratings in various situational contexts." In Joshua A. Fishman (Ed.), *The Measurement and Description of Language Dominance in Bilinguals,* Seventh progress report. New York: Yeshiva University.

Grétsy, László (Ed.). (1976). *Mai magyar nyelvünk* [Our Hungarian language today]. Budapest: Akadémiai Kiadó.

Grétsy, László & Kovalovszky, Miklós, (Eds.). (1983 and 1985). *Nyelvművelő kézikönyv I. és II.* [Language cultivation handbook, Vols 1 and 2]. Budapest: Akadémiai Kiadó.

Grétsy, László & Kemény, Gábor (Eds.). (1996). *Nyelvművelő kéziszótár* [Concise handbook of language cultivation]. Budapest: Auktor.

Grimes, Barbara F. (2002). *Ethnologue: Languages of the World.* On-line edn. at http://www.ethnologue.com/. Dallas, TX: Summer Institute of Linguistics.

Grosjean, François (1982). *Life with Two Languages: An Introduction to Bilingualism.* Cambridge, MA: Harvard University Press.

Grosjean, François (1995). "A psycholinguistic approach to code-switching: The recognition of guest words by bilinguals." In Lesley Milroy & Pieter Muysken (Eds.), *One Speaker, Two Languages: Cross-disciplinary Perspectives on Code-switching* (pp. 259–275). Cambridge: Cambridge University Press.

Grosjean, François (1997). "Processing mixed language: Issues, findings, and models." In Annette M. B. de Groot & Judith F. Kroll (Eds.), *Tutorials in Bilingualism: Psychological Perspectives* (pp. 225–254). Mahwah, NJ: Lawrence Erlbaum Associates.

Grosjean, François (2001). "The bilingual's language modes." In Janet L. Nicol (Ed.), *One Mind, Two Languages: Bilingual Language Processing* (pp. 1–22). Oxford: Blackwell.

Grosjean, François & Miller, Joanne L. (1994). "Going in and out of languages: An example of bilingual flexibility." *Psychological Science, 5*(4), 201–206.

Grozdova, I. N. (1971). "Etnokulturális folyamatok napjainkban a kárpátaljai magyar lakosság körében [Present-day ethnocultural tendencies among Subcarpathian Hungarians]." In Gyula Ortutay (Ed.), *Népi kultúra – népi társadalom*. Az MTA Néprajzi Kutatóintézetének évkönyve V–VI. [A people's culture, a people's society: The yearbook of the Ethnography Institute of the Hungarian Academy of Sciences, Vols. 5–6] (pp. 457–466). Budapest: Akadémiai.

Gumperz, John J. (1982). *Discourse Strategies*. Cambridge: Cambridge University Press.

Gyönyör, József (1993). *Közel a jog asztalához* [Close to the table of law]. Pozsony: Madách-Posonium.

Gyönyör, József (1994). *Terhes örökség: A magyarság lélekszámának és sorsának alakulása Csehszlovákiában* [Burdensome heritage: The demographics and fate of Hungarians in Czechoslovakia]. Pozsony: Madách-Posonium.

Gyurgyík, László (1994). *Magyar mérleg. A szlovákiai magyarság a népszámlálási és népmozgalmi adatok tükrében* [Measuring Hungarians: The Hungarians of Slovakia, as reflected in census and migration data]. Pozsony: Kalligram.

Gyurgyík, László (1999). *Changes in the Demographic, Settlement, and Social Structure of the Minority in (Czecho)-Slovakia between 1918–1998*. Budapest: Institute for Central European Studies.

Gyurgyík, László (2002). "Népszámlálás 2001. A szlovákiai magyarság településszerkezetének, valamint a szlovákiai magyarlakta területek etnikai jellegének változásai az 1990-es években [Census 2001: Changes in the settlement structure of Hungarian settlements and in the ethnic character of Hungarian areas in Slovakia]". *Új Szó* September 6, 2002, 9–12.

Gyurgyík, László & Sebők, László (2003). *Népszámlálási körkép Közép-Európából 1989–2002* [An overview of Central European censuses, 1989–2002]. Budapest: Teleki László Alapítvány.

Habsburg, József (1888). *Czigány nyelvtan (Románo csibákero sziklaribe)* [Gypsy grammar]. Budapest: Akadémiai Kiadó.

Hadrovics, László (1985). *Ungarische Elemente im Serbokroatischen* [Hungarian elements in Serbo-Croatian]. Budapest: Akadémiai Kiadó.

Halász, Péter (1993). "A Lakatos Demeter Egyesület [The Lakatos Demeter Society]." In Péter Halász (Ed.), *"Megfog vala apóm szokcor kezemtül..." Tanulmányok Domokos Pál Péter emlékére* ["My father would take my hand...": Studies in memory of Pál Péter Domonkos] (pp. 169–173). Budapest: Lakatos Demeter Egyesület.

Halász, Péter (1994). "Eredmények és feladatok a moldvai csángók néprajzi kutatásában [Results and tasks of ethnographic research among Moldavian Csángós]." *Néprajzi látóhatár, 3*(1–2), 1–37.

Halász, Péter (1997). "Új szempontok a moldvai magyarok táji-etnikai tagozódásának vizsgálatához [New aspects of analyzing the geographic and ethnic stratification of Moldavian Csángós]." In Ferenc Pozsony (Ed.), *Dolgozatok a moldvai csángók népi kultúrájáról* [Studies on the folk culture of Moldavian Csángós] (pp. 7–26). Kolozsvár: Kriza János Néprajzi Társaság.

Halmari, Helena (1997). *Government and Codeswitching: Explaining American Finnish*. Amsterdam: John Benjamins.

Hamp, E. P. (1994). "United States of America: The language situation." In R. E. Asher & J. M. Y. Simpson (Eds.), *The Encyclopedia of Language and Linguistics* (pp. 4838–4839). Oxford: Pergamon.

Harlig, Jeffrey (1995a). "Sociolinguistics (real and imagined) in Eastern Europe: An introduction." In Jeffrey Harlig & Csaba Pléh (Eds.), *When East Met West: Sociolinguistics in the Former Socialist Bloc* (pp. 1–24). Berlin/New York: Mouton de Gruyter.

Harlig, Jeffrey (1995b). "Socialism and sociolinguistics in the eastern bloc." In Jeffrey Harlig & Csaba Pléh (Eds.), *When East Met West: Sociolinguistics in the Former Socialist Bloc* (pp. 25–44). Berlin/New York: Mouton de Gruyter.

Harlig, Jeffrey & Csaba Pléh (Eds.). (1995). *When East Met West: Sociolinguistics in the Former Socialist Bloc.* Berlin/New York: Mouton de Gruyter.

Haugen, Einar (1949). "Problems of bilingualism." *Lingua, 2,* 271–290.

Haugen, Einar (1953). *The Norwegian Language in America: A Study in Bilingual Behavior.* Philadelphia: University of Pennsylvania Press.

Haugen, Einar (1971). "The ecology of language." *The Linguistic Reporter Supplement, 25,* 19–26.

Haugen, Einar (1972). "The analysis of linguistic borrowing." In Anwar S. Dil (Ed.), *The Ecology of Language: Essays by Einar Haugen* (pp. 79–109). Stanford, CA: Stanford University Press.

Hengeveld, Kees (1992). *Non-verbal Predication: Theory, Typology, Diachrony.* Berlin: Mouton de Gruyter.

Henzl, Vera (1982). "American Czech: A comparative study of linguistic modifications in immigrant and young children speech." In Roland Sussex (Ed.), *The Slavic Languages in Emigré Communities* (pp. 33–46). Edmonton: Linguistic Research Inc.

Herman, József & Imre, Samu (1987). "Nyelvi változás – nyelvi tervezés Magyarországon [Language change and language planning in Hungary]." *Magyar Tudomány, 32*(4), 513–531.

Hirvonen, Pekka (1998). "The Finnish-American language shift." In Jussi Niemi, Terence Odlin, & Janne Heikkinen (Eds.), *Language Contact, Variation, and Change* (pp. 135–150). Joensuu: University of Joensuu.

Hock, Hans H. & Joseph, Brian D. (1996). *Language History, Language Change, and Language Relationship: An Introduction to Historical and Comparative Linguistics.* Berlin: Mouton de Gruyter.

Hódi, Sándor (1989). "A pszichózisok és öngyilkosságok területi és etnikai megoszlása a Vajdaságban [Geographic and ethnic distribution of cases of psychosis and suicide in Vojvodina]." *Magyar Pszichológiai Szemle, 6,* 547–566.

Hódi, Sándor (1990a). "A VMDK és a "Hétfejű sárkány" [The Democratic Community of Vojvodina Hungarians and the "Seven-headed dragon"]." In Zoltán Kalapis (Ed.), *Magyarok Jugoszláviában '90* [Hungarians in Yugoslavia, 1990] (pp. 25–31). Újvidék: A Vajdasági Magyarok Demokratikus Közösségének Évkönyve.

Hódi, Sándor (1990b). "Nemzeti identitásunk zavarairól." In Nándor Burányi (Ed.), *Magyarok Vajdaságban. A "Magyar Szó" tematikai különkiadása* [Hungarians in Vojvodina: A special issue of Magyar Szó] 6. Újvidék: Forum.

Hódi, Sándor (1992). *A nemzeti identitás zavarai* [Problems of national identity]. Újvidék: Forum.

Holzer, Werner & Münz, Rainer (1993). "Landessprachen: Deutsch, Kroatisch und Ungarisch im Burgenland [Languages of Burgenland: German, Croation, and Hungarian]." In Werner Holzer & Rainer Münz (Eds.), *Trendwende? Sprache und Ethnizität im Burgenland* [Change of trends? Language and ethnicity in Burgenland] (pp. 19–85). Wien: Passagen.

Holzer, Werner & Münz, Rainer (1997). "Deutsch – Ungarisch [German – Hungarian]." In Hans Goebl, Peter H. Nelde, Zdeněk Starý, & Wolfgang Wölck (Eds.), *Kontaktlinguistik/Contact Linguistics/Linguistique de contact* 2. Halbband/Volume 2/Tome 2 (pp. 1828–1835). Berlin: Walter de Gruyter.

Horger, Antal (1913). "A *csángó* név eredetéhez [About the origin of the name *Csángó*]." *Magyar Nyelv, 9,* 418–421.

Horváth, Katalin (1976). *A kárpátontúli magyar nyelvjárások magánhangzórendszere* [The vowel system of the Hungarian regional dialects in Subcarpathia]. Uzshorod: Ungvári Állami Egyetem.

Horváth, Katalin (1991). "Szebben beszélünk, mint Magyarországon? [Do we speak a more beautiful Hungarian than people in Hungary?]." *Kárpáti Igaz Szó* November 13, 1991: 8.

Horváth, Katalin (1992). "Vengerskije govory Zakarpat'ja [Regional dialects of Hungarian in Subcarpathia]." *Acta Hungarica, 1*, 20–21.

Horváth, Katalin (1998). "Újabb keletű szláv átvételeink [Our recent Slavic loanwords]." *Kárpáti Igaz Szó* February 14, 1998: 13.

Horváth, Katalin & Lizanec, Péter (1993). "A kárpátaljai magyar nyelvjárások főbb sajátosságairól [On the most important characteristics of regional dialects of Hungarian in Subcarpathia]." In Péter Lizanec and Katalin Horváth (Eds.), *Az Ungvári Hungarológiai Intézet tudományos gyűjteménye* [A scholarly collection of the Užhorod Hungarian Studies Institute] (pp. 57–74). Budapest/Ungvár: Intermix.

Horváth, István & Scacco, Alexandra (2001). "From the unitary to the pluralistic: Fine-tuning minority policy in Romania." In Anna-Mária Bíró & Petra Kovács (Eds.), *Diversity in Action: Local Public Management of Multi-Ethnic Communities in Central and Eastern Europe* (pp. 241–272). Budapest: Local Government and Public Service Reform Initiative, Open Society Institute.

Huseby, Éva Veronika (1984). "Ethnic radio: A study of Hungarian radio programs in Detroit and Windsor." In William Lockwood (Ed.), *Michigan Discussions in Anthropology No. 7: Beyond Ethnic Boundaries* (pp. 51–84). Ann Arbor: University of Michigan.

Huseby-Darvas, Éva V. (1991/1992). "Handmade Hungarianness: The construction of ethnic identity among elderly noodlemakers in Michigan." *Hungarian Studies, 7*, 188–196.

Huseby-Darvas, Éva V. (2003). *Hungarians in Michigan*. East Lansing: Michigan State University Press.

Hutterer, Miklós & György Mészáros (1967). *A lovári cigány dialektus leíró nyelvtana: Hangtan, szóképzés, alaktan, szótár* [A descriptive grammar of the Lovári dialect of Romani: Phonology, derivational and inflectional morphology, and a dictionary]. Budapest: Magyar Nyelvtudományi Társaság.

Imre, Samu (1971a). *A mai magyar nyelvjárások rendszere*. [The system of the dialects of modern Hungarian] Budapest: Akadémiai Kiadó.

Imre, Samu (1971b). *A felsőőri nyelvjárás* [The Hungarian dialect of Felsőőr (Oberwart)]. Budapest: Akadémiai Kiadó.

Imre, Samu (1973a). "Az ausztriai (burgenlandi) magyar szórványok [Hungarian diaspora in Austria (Burgenland)]." *Népi kultúra – népi társadalom, 7*, 119–135.

Imre, Samu (1973b). *Felsőőri tájszótár* [Dialect dictionary of Felsőőr (Oberwart)]. Budapest: Akadémiai Kiadó.

Ivić, Pavle (1964). *Balkan Linguistics*. Lecture course taught at the summer Linguistic Institute of the Linguistic Society of America, Indiana University.

Janhunen, Juha (1981). On the structure of Proto-Uralic. *Finnisch-Ugrische Forschungen, 44*(1–3), 23–42.

Janulf, Pirjo (1998). *Kommer finskan i Sverige att fortleva? En studie av språkkunskaper och språkanvändning hos andragenerationens sverigefinnar i Botkyrka och hos finlandssvenskar i Åbo* [Will Finnish survive in Sweden? A study of the language competence and language use of second-generation Finns living in Botkyrka, Sweden and of Finland Swedes in Turku, Finland]. Stockholm: Almqvist and Wiksell International.

Jemec, Grigorij S. & Djačenko, B. I. (1993). *Ciganskie naselennja Zakarpattja* [The Gypsy population of Subcarpathia]. Užhorod: Vidavnictvo Karpati.

Jones, Mari C. (1998). *Language Obsolescence and Revitalization: Linguistic Change in Two Sociolinguistically Contrasting Welsh Communities.* Oxford: Clarendon.

Jordan, Peter (1998). "Romania." In Christina Bratt Paulston & Donald Peckham (Eds.), *Linguistic Minorities in Central and Eastern Europe* (pp. 184–223). Clevedon: Multilingual Matters.

Jupp, James & York, Barry (1995). *Birthplaces of the Australian People: Colonial and Commonwealth Censuses, 1828–1991.* Canberra: Australian National University.

Kallós, Zoltán (1993). "Gyűjtési élményeim Moldvában [My field experiences in Moldavia]." In Anikó Péterbencze (Ed.), *"Moldvának szíp tájaind születem...": Magyarországi Csángó Fesztivál és Konferencia, Jászberény* ["I was born in beautiful Moldavia": Hungary's Csángó Festival and Conference, Jászberény] (pp. 95–109). Jászberény: Jászberényi Múzeum.

Kálmán, Béla (1970). "Amerikai magyarok [Hungarian-Americans]." *Magyar Nyelvőr, 94,* 377–385.

Kapaló, James (1994). "Közelebb a csángókhoz [Closer to the Csángós]." *Művelődés, 22*(3), 30–31.

Katona, Edit (1995). "Interferencia-jelenségek mérése a vajdasági magyar nyelvhasználatban [Measuring interference phenomena in Vojvodina Hungarian language use]." In Ilona Kassai (Ed.), *Kétnyelvűség és magyar nyelvhasználat* [Bilingualism and Hungarian language use] (pp. 225–233). Budapest: MTA Nyelvtudományi Intézete.

Kellogg, Ronald T. (1995). *Cognitive Psychology.* Thousand Oaks, CA: Sage Publications.

Kemp, Walter A. (Ed.). (2001). *Quiet Diplomacy in Action: The OSCE High Commissioner on National Minorities.* The Hague/London/Boston: Kluwer Law International.

Kenesei, István (1996). "Képző vagy nem képző? [Derivational suffix or not?]." In István Terts (Ed.), *Nyelv, nyelvész, társadalom: Emlékkönyv Szépe György 65. születésnapjára barátaitól, kollégáitól, tanítványaitól* [Language, linguist, and society: Festschrift for György Szépe on the occasion of his 65th birthday, from his friends, colleagues, and students] (pp. 92–95). Pécs: JPTE PSZM Projekt Programiroda.

Kenesei, István (1998a). Syntax; derivational morphology; ideophones and interjections; lexicon. In István Kenesei, Robert M. Vago, & Anna Fenyvesi, *Hungarian. (Descriptive Grammars)* (pp. 1–190, 351–81, 454–455, 456–467). London: Routledge.

Kenesei, István (1998b). "A toldalékmorfémák meghatározásáról [On the definition of inflectional morphemes]." *Magyar Nyelvőr, 122,* 67–80.

Kenesei, István, Vago, Robert M., & Fenyvesi, Anna (1998). *Hungarian. (Descriptive Grammars).* London: Routledge.

Kepecs, József (Ed.). (1996). *Kárpátalja településeinek nemzetiségi (anyanyelvi) adatai (1880–1941).* [Ethnic (mother tongue) data of Subcarpathia's settlements, 1880–1941]. Budapest: Központi Statisztikai Hivatal.

Kerecsényi, Edit (1994). "Radamos benépesedése, gazdasági és társadalmi viszonyai a XVIII–XIX. században [The settlement of and economic and social relations in Radamos in the 18th–19th centuries]." In Imre Gráfik (Ed.), *Tanulmányok a szlovéniai magyarság köréből* [Studies on Hungarians in Slovenia] (pp. 19–83). Budapest: Teleki László Alapítvány.

Kerek, Andrew (1992). "Hunglish in Ohio: Review of Miklós Kontra, "Fejezetek a South Bend-i magyar nyelvhasználatból"." *The New Hungarian Quarterly, 33,* 140–143.

Keszler, Borbála (1997). "Képző-e a -hat, -het? [Is *-hat/-het* a derivational morpheme?]." *Magyar Nyelvőr, 121,* 86–90.

Kiefer, Ferenc (1997). "Verbal prefixation in the Ugric languages from a typological-areal perspective." In Stig Eliasson & Ernst Håkon Jahr (Eds.), *Language and Its Ecology: Essays In Memory of Einar Haugen* (pp. 323–341). Berlin: Mouton de Gruyter.

Kiefer, Ferenc (1998). "Alaktan [Morphology]." In Katalin É. Kiss, Ferenc Kiefer, & Péter Siptár (Eds.), *Új magyar nyelvtan* [A new grammar of Hungarian] (pp. 187–289). Budapest: Osiris.

Kis, Emese (1975). *Încadrarea substantivelor de origine maghiară în sistemul morfologic a limbii române* [The adaptation of nouns of Hungarian origin to the morphological system of the Romanian language]. București: Editura Academiei Republicii Socialiste România.

Kiss, Jenő (1994). *Magyar anyanyelvűek – magyar nyelvhasználat* [Hungarian speakers and Hungarian language use]. Budapest: Nemzeti Tankönyvkiadó.

Kiss, Lajos (1976). *Szláv tükörszók és tükörjelentések a magyarban* [Slavic calqued words and semantic calques in Hungarian]. Budapest: Akadémiai Kiadó.

Khazanarov, K. H. (1982). *Rešenie nacional'no-jazykovoj problemy v SSSR* [The solution of the minority-linguistic issue in the USSR]. Moskva: Izdatel'stvo političeskoj literatury.

Kloss, Heinz (1966). "German American language maintenance efforts." In Joshua A. Fishman (Ed.), *Language Loyalty in the United States: The Maintenance and Perpetuation of Non-English Mother Tongues by American Ethnic and Religious Groups* (pp. 206–252). The Hague: Mouton.

Kloss, Heinz (1967). "Types of multilingual communities: A discussion of ten variables." In Stanley Lieberson (Ed.), *Explorations in Sociolinguistics* (pp. 7–17). Bloomington: Indiana University.

Kniezsa, István (1955). *A magyar nyelv szláv jövevényszavai* [Slavic lexical borrowings in Hungarian]. Budapest: Akadémiai Kiadó.

Kocsis, Károly & Kocsis-Hodosi, Eszter (1998). *Ethnic Geography of the Hungarian Minorities in the Carpathian Basin*. Budapest: Geographical Research Institute and Minority Studies Programme, Hungarian Academy of Sciences.

Kontra, Miklós (1985). "Hungarian-American bilingualism: A bibliographic essay." *Hungarian Studies, 1*, 257–282.

Kontra, Miklós (1990). *Fejezetek a South Bend-i magyar nyelvhasználatból* [The Hungarian language as spoken in South Bend, Indiana]. Budapest: MTA Nyelvtudományi Intézete.

Kontra, Miklós, Ringen, Catherine O., & Stemberger, Joseph P. (1990). "The effect of context on suffix vowel choice in Hungarian vowel harmony." In Werner Bahner, Joachim Schildt, & Dieter Vieweger (Eds.), *Proceedings of the 14th International Congress of Linguistics, Berlin/GDR, August 10–15, 1987* (pp. 450–453). Berlin: Akademie Verlag.

Kontra, Miklós (1990–1995). "Changing names: Onomastic remarks on Hungarian-Americans." *Journal of English Linguistics, 23*(1–2), 114–122.

Kontra, Miklós (1993a). "The messy phonology of Hungarians in South Bend: A contribution to the study of near-mergers." *Language Variation and Change, 5*, 225–231.

Kontra, Miklós (1993b). "Communicative interference and failure: A classification with examples from Hungarian Americans." *I.T.L. Review of Applied Linguistics, 101–102*, 79–88.

Kontra, Miklós (1995a). "Módszertani megjegyzések az amerikai magyar eldöntendő kérdőintonáció kapcsán [Methodological remarks in connection with the American-Hungarian yes/no-question intonation]." In Ilona Kassai (Ed.), *Kétnyelvűség és magyar nyelvhasználat* [Bilingualism and Hungarian language use] (pp. 271–285). Budapest: MTA Nyelvtudományi Intézetének Élőnyelvi Osztálya.

Kontra, Miklós (1995b). "Magyar nyelvhasználat határainkon túl [Hungarian language use outside Hungary]." In László Diószegi (Ed.), *Magyarságkutatás 1995–96* [Hungarian studies 1995–1996] (pp. 113–123). Budapest: Teleki László Alapítvány.

Kontra, Miklós (1995/1996). "English Only's Cousin: Slovak Only." *Acta Linguistica Hungarica, 43*, 345–372.

Kontra, Miklós (1997). "Hungarian linguistic traitors champion the cause of contact dialects." In Wolfgang Wölck & Annick de Houwer (Eds.), *Recent Studies in Contact Linguistics* (pp. 181–187). Bonn: Dümmler.

Kontra, Miklós (1998). *The Sociolinguistics of Hungarian Outside Hungary* (Final Report to the Research Support Scheme) Budapest: Linguistics Institute, Hungarian Academy of Sciences MS. http: //e-lib.rss.cz/diglib/pdf/22.pdf

Kontra, Miklós (1999). ""Don't speak Hungarian in public!" – A documentation and analysis of folk linguistic rights". In Miklós Kontra, Robert Phillipson, Tove Skutnabb-Kangas, & Tibor Várady (Eds.), *Language: A Right and a Resource. Approaching Linguistic Human Rights* (pp. 81–97). Budapest: Central European University Press.

Kontra, Miklós (2000). "Towards intercultural competence in Europe." *Sociolinguistica, 14*, 168–173.

Kontra, Miklós (2001a). "Hungarian verbal puzzles and the intensity of language contact." *Journal of Sociolinguistics, 5*, 163–179.

Kontra, Miklós (2001b). "A nyelvi kontaktus intenzitása vagy új divergens változás? Mi okozza a felvidéki és délvidéki kontaktusváltozatok egyes különbségeit? [The intensity of language contact or a new divergent change? What causes some differences in the contact varieties of Slovakia and Vojvodina Hungarian?]." In József Andor, Tibor Szűcs, & István Terts (Eds.), *Színes eszmék nem alszanak... Szépe György 70. születésnapjára I* [Colorful ideas do not sleep: Festschrift for György Szépe on the occasion of his 70th birthday] (pp. 698–705). Pécs: Lingua Franca Csoport.

Kontra, Miklós (2003). "Changing mental maps and morphology: Divergence caused by international border changes." In David Britain & Jenny Cheshire (Eds.), *Social Dialectology: In Honour of Peter Trudgill* (pp. 173–190). Amsterdam/Philadelphia: John Benjamins.

Kontra, Miklós & Nehler, Gregory L. (1981a). "Ethnic designations used by Hungarian-Americans in South Bend, Indiana." *Ural-Altaic Yearbook, 53*, 105–111.

Kontra, Miklós & Nehler, Gregory L. (1981b). "Language usage: An interview with a Hungarian American." *Hungarian Studies Review, 8*, 99–118.

Kontra, Miklós & Gósy, Mária (1988). "Approximation of the standard: A form of variability in bilingual speech." In Alan R. Thomas (Ed.), *Methods in Dialectology* (pp. 442–455). Philadelphia: Multilingual Matters.

Kontra, Miklós, Ringen, Catherine O., & Stemberger, Joseph P. (1990). "The effect of context on suffix vowel choice in Hungarian vowel harmony." In Werner Bahner, Joachim Schildt, & Dieter Vieweger (Eds.), *Proceedings of the 14th International Congress of Linguistics Berlin / GDR, August 10–15. 1987* (pp. 450–453). Berlin: Akademie Verlag.

Kontra, Miklós & Saly, Noémi (Eds.). (1998). *Nyelvmentés vagy nyelvárulás? Vita a határon túli magyar nyelvhasználatról* [Language rescue or language treason: A debate about the use of Hungarian outside Hungary]. Budapest: Osiris.

Kontra, Miklós, Phillipson, Robert, Skutnabb-Kangas, Tove, & Várady, Tibor (1999). "Conceptualising and implementing linguistic human rights." In Miklós Kontra, Robert Phillipson, Tove Skutnabb-Kangas, & Tibor Várady (Eds.), *Language: A Right and a Resource. Approaching Linguistic Human Rights* (pp. 1–21). Budapest: Central European University Press.

Köpeczi, Béla (1994). *History of Transylvania*. Budapest: Akadémiai Kiadó.

Kossa, János (1978). *A mi nyelvünk* [Our language]. Újvidék: Forum.

Kotics, József (1997). "Erkölcsi értékrend és társadalmi kontroll néhány moldvai csángó faluban [The system of moral values and societal control in some Moldavian Csángó villages]." In Ferenc Pozsony (Ed.), *Dolgozatok a moldvai csángók népi kultúrájáról* [Studies on the folk culture of Moldavian Csángós] (pp. 36–55). Kolozsvár: Kriza János Néprajzi Társaság.

Kótyuk, István (1973). *Ukrainizmy v vengerskom govore nizovja reki Už Zakarpatskoj oblasti Ukrainiskoy SSR* [Ukrainianisms in the Hungarian of the lower Už river area of the Subcarpathian Region of the Ukrainian SSR]. Uzsgorod: Uzsgorodi Állami Egyetem, *Kandidátusi* dissertation.

Kótyuk, István (1991). "A kétnyelvűség és a kárpátaljai magyar köznyelv [Bilingualism and the colloquial Hungarian of Subcarpathia]." In Sándor Győri-Nagy & Janka Kelemen (Eds.), *Kétnyelvűség a Kárpát-medencében* [Bilingualism in the Carpathian Basin] (pp. 66–69). Budapest: Széchenyi Társaság.

Kótyuk, István (1995). *Anyanyelvünk peremén* [On the outskirts of our mother tongue]. Ungvár/Budapest: Intermix.

Kovács, Andor (1999). *A világ magyarsága: Történeti áttekintés és címtár. Európa I.* [Hungarians in the world: An historical overview and address list. Europe, Vol. 1]. Budapest: Magyarok Világszövetsége.

Kovács, Elemér (1996). "Így látjuk mi. A kárpátaljai magyarság értékrendje [We see it in this way: The scale of values of Subcarpathia Hungarians]." *Kárpátaljai Szemle, 4*(6), 18–19.

Kovács, Magdolna (1996). "Tulajdonnevek használata az ausztráliai magyar nyelvben [The use of proper nouns in Australian Hungarian]." In Edit Mészáros (Ed.), *Ünnepi könyv Mikola Tibor tiszteletére* [Festschrift to celebrate Tibor Mikola] (pp. 198–201). Szeged: JATE.

Kovács, Magdolna (1997). "Language attrition in Australian Hungarian: A case study." In László Borsányi & Edit Szőke (Eds.), *International Conference of PhD Students: University of Miskolc, Hungary, August 11–17, 1997. Section Proceedings. Humanities* (pp. 114–121). Miskolc: Miskolci Egyetem.

Kovács, Magdolna (2001a). "Code-switching and case marking in Australian Finnish and Australian Hungarian." In Tõnu Seilenthal, Anu Nurk, & Triinu Palo (Eds.), *Congressus Nonus Internationalis Fenno-Ugristarum* (pp. 139–144). 7.-13.8.2000 Tartu. Pars V. Tartu: Eesti Fennougristide Komitee.

Kovács, Magdolna (2001b). *Code-switching and Language Shift in Australian Finnish in Comparison with Australian Hungarian*. Åbo: Åbo Akademi Förlag.

Kovács, Magdolna (2001c). ""A szókincs az nekem nem annyira bő": Az ausztráliai magyarság nyelvének néhány lexikai sajátossága a nyelvfenntartás szempontjából ["Vocabulary is not that wide for me": Lexical characteristics of the language of Australian Hungarians from the perspective of language maintenance]." *Néprajz és Nyelvtudomány, 41*(1), 135–148.

Kovács, Magdolna (2002). "Hatalom és nyelv: Fokozatos nyelvváltás az ausztráliai magyarok körében [Power and language: A gradual language shift among Australian Hungarians]." In István Hoffmann, Dezső Juhász, & János Péntek (Eds.), *Hungarológia és dimenzionális nyelvszemlélet. Előadások az V. Nemzetközi Hungarológiai Kongresszuson* [Hungarian studies and a dimensional view of language: Publications of the 5th International Congress on Hungarian Studies] (pp. 339–349). Debrecen/Jyväskylä.

Kučera, Karel (1990). *Česky jazyk v USA* [The Czech language in the USA]. Praha: Univerzita Karlova.

Kunz, Egon (1969). *"Blood and Gold": Hungarians in Australia*. Melbourne: Cheshire.

Kunz, Egon (1997). *Magyarok Ausztráliában* [Hungarians in Australia]. Budapest: Teleki László Alapítvány.

Labov, William (1966). "Hypercorrection by the lower middle class as a factor in linguistic change." In William Bright (Ed.), *Sociolinguistics* (pp. 84–113). The Hague: Mouton.

Lampl, Zsuzsanna (1999). *A saját útját járó gyermek. Három szociológiai tanulmány a szlovákiai magyarokról* [The child that goes his own way: Three sociological studies on Hungarians in Slovakia]. Pozsony: Madách-Posonium.

Lampl, Zsuzsanna & Sorbán, Angéla (1999). "A szlovákiai és az erdélyi magyarok médiapreferenciái és fogyasztói szokásai [The media preferences and consumer habits of Hungarians in Slovakia and Transylvania]." *Fórum Társadalomtudományi Szemle, 1*(1), 19–34.

Langman, Juliet (2002). "Mother-tongue education versus bilingual education: Shifting ideologies and policies in the Republic of Slovakia." *International Journal of the Sociology of Language, 154*, 47–64.

Langman, Juliet & Lanstyák, István (2000). "Language negotiations in Slovakia: Views from the Hungarian minority." *Multilingua, 19*(1–2), 55–72.

Lanstyák, István (1991). "A szlovák nyelv árnyékában. A magyar nyelv helyzete Csehszlovákiában 1918–1991 [In the shadow of the Slovak language: The situation of the Hungarian language in Czechoslovakia, 1918–1991]." In Miklós Kontra (Ed.), *Tanulmányok a határainkon túli kétnyelvűségről* [Studies on Hungarian bilingualism outside Hungary] (pp. 11–72). Budapest: Magyarságkutató Intézet.

Lanstyák István (1993). Kétnyelvűség és nyelvművelés [Bilingualism and language cultivation]. *Magyar Nyelvőr, 117*, 475–479.

Lanstyák, István (1994a). *A magyar nyelv szlovákiai változatainak nyelvkörnyezettani és kontaktusnyelvészeti kérdései* [Sociolinguistic and contact linguistic aspects of the varieties of Hungarian spoken in Slovakia]. Bratislava: Comenius University PhD Dissertation.

Lanstyák, István (1994b). "Kétnyelvűség és nemzeti nyelv (Néhány gondolat a standard nyelvváltozatnak kétnyelvűségi helyzetben való elsajátításáról) [Bilingualism and national language: Some thoughts on the acquisition of the standard variety in bilingual situations]." *Irodalmi Szemle, 37*(2), 63–75.

Lanstyák, István (1994c). "Az anyanyelv és a többségi nyelv oktatása a kisebbségi kétnyelvűség körülményei között [Mother tongue and majority language instruction under the circumstances of minority bilingualism]." *Regio, 5*(4), 90–116.

Lanstyák, István (1995). "Kétnyelvű egyén – kétnyelvű közösség – kétnyelvű iskola. Identitásunk alapja az anyanyelvű oktatás [The bilingual individual, the bilingual community, and the bilingual school: Mother tongue instruction is the base of our identity]." In István Lanstyák & László Szigeti (Eds.), *Érveink az alternatív – kétnyelvű oktatással szemben* [Our arguments against alternative bilingual education] (pp. 7–20). Pozsony: Mécs László Alapítvány Kiskönyvtára.

Lanstyák, István (1998). *A magyar nyelv szlovákiai változatainak sajátosságai* [Characteristics of the varieties of Hungarian spoken in Slovakia]. Dunaszerdahely: Lilium Aurum.

Lanstyák, István (1999/2000). "Types of loanwords in the varieties of Hungarian in Slovakia." *Philologia Fenno-Ugrica, 5–6*, 15–48.

Lanstyák, István (2000a). *A magyar nyelv Szlovákiában* [The Hungarian language in Slovakia]. Budapest/Pozsony: Osiris, Kalligram, and MTA Kisebbségkutató Műhely.

Lanstyák, István (2000b). "K otázke striedania kódov (mad'arského a slovenského jazyka) v komunite Mad'arov na Slovensku [On the question of code-switching in the Hungarian community in Slovakia]." *Slovo a slovesnost, 61*(1), 1–17.

Lanstyák, István (2000c). "Bilingual versus bilingual education: The case of Slovakia." In Robert Phillipson (Ed.), *Rights to Language: Equity, Power, and Education* (pp. 227–233). Mahwah, NJ/London: Lawrence Erlbaum Associates.

Lanstyák, István (2001). *A magyar nyelv szlovákiai változataiban található szlovák kölcsönszavak rendszerezéséről* [On the classification of Slovak loanwords in the varieties of Hungarian spoken in Slovakia]. Bratislava: Comenius University manuscript.

Lanstyák, István & Szabómihály, Gizella (1996a). "Contact varieties of Hungarian in Slovakia: A contribution to their description." *International Journal of the Sociology of Language, 120*, 111–130.

Lanstyák, István & Szabómihály, Gizella (1996b). "Kódváltás és nemzeti azonosságtudat. [Code-switching and national identity]." In Károly Gadányi, József Bokor, & Miklós Guttmann (Eds.), *Nyelvi tudat, identitástudat, nyelvhasználat* [Language awareness, identity and language use] (pp. 163–174). Szombathely: Berzsenyi Dániel Tanárképző Főiskola.

Lanstyák, István & Szabómihály, Gizella (1997). *Magyar nyelvhasználat – iskola – kétnyelvűség* [Hungarian language use, education, and bilingualism]. Pozsony: Kalligram.

Lanstyák, István & Szabómihály, Gizella (1998). "Nyelviváltozó-típusok a magyar nyelv szlovákiai változataiban [Types of linguistic variables in the varieties of the Hungarian language spoken in Slovakia]." In Klára Sándor (Ed.), *Nyelvi változó – nyelvi változás. A 9. Élőnyelvi Konferencia előadásai (Szeged, 1996. augusztus 22–24.)* [Linguistic variables and language change: Papers from the 9th Sociolinguistics Conference, August 22–24, 1996, Szeged] (pp. 99–112). Szeged: JGYF Kiadó.

Le Page, Robert & Tabouret-Keller, Andree (1985). *Acts of Identity: Creole-Based Approaches to Language and Ethnicity*. Cambridge: Cambridge University Press.

Ligeti, Lajos (1976). "A magyar nyelv török kapcsolatai és ami körülöttük van [The Turkic connections of Hungarian and what surrounds them]." *Magyar Nyelv, 72*, 11–27 and 129–136.

Ligeti, Lajos (1986). *A magyar nyelv török kapcsolatai a honfoglalás előtt és az Árpád-korban* [The Turkic connections of Hungarian before the Hungarian conquest and during the Árpád era]. Budapest: Akadémiai Kiadó.

Liszka, József (1996). "Etnikai és kulturális folyamatok a pannon térség északi határvidékén. [Ethnic and cultural processes in the Northern borderland of the Pannonian area]." In Judit Katona & Gyula Viga (Eds.), *Az interetnikus kapcsolatok kutatásának újabb eredményei* [Recent findings in interethnic studies] (pp. 201–207). Miskolc: Herman Ottó Múzeum.

Lizanec, Petro (1972). *Ukrainsko-vengerskie jazykovyje kontakty* [Ukrainian-Hungarian language contact]. Lvov: Doctor of Science dissertation.

Lizanec, Petro (1970). *Magyar–ukrán nyelvi kapcsolatok (A kárpátontúli ukrán nyelvjárások anyagai alapján)* [Hungarian-Ukrainian language contact (Studied on the basis of Ukrainian dialects spoken in Subcarpathia)]. Uzshorod: Uzshorodi Állami Egyetem.

Lizanec, Petro (1976). *Vengerskije zaimstrovania v ukrainskix govorax Zakarpat'ja: Vengersko-ukrainskije mežjazykovyje svjazi* [Hungarian loanwords in Ukrainian dialects of Subcarpathia: Hungarian-Ukrainian language contacts]. Budapest: Akadémiai Kiadó.

Lizanec, Petro (1992). *A kárpátaljai magyar nyelvjárások atlasza I. kötet.* [Atlas of Hungarian dialects in Subcarpathia, Vol. 1] Budapest: Akadémiai Kiadó.

Lizanec, Petro (1993a). "Ukrán valamint orosz elemek a kárpátaljai magyar nyelvjárásokban [Ukrainian and Russian elements in Subcarpathian Hungarian dialects]." *Hungarológia, 3,* 169–179.

Lizanec, Petro (1993b). "Ukrán valamint orosz elemek a kárpátaljai magyar nyelvjárásokban." In Péter Lizanec & Katalin Horváth (Eds.), *Az Ungvári Hungarológiai Intézet tudományos gyűjteménye* [A scholarly collection of the Užhorod Hungarian Studies Institute] (pp. 50–56). Budapest/Ungvár: Intermix.

Lizanec, Petro (1996). *A kárpátaljai magyar nyelvjárások atlasza II. kötet.* [Atlas of Hungarian dialects in Subcarpathia, Vol. 2] Uzshorod: Patent.

Lizanyec, Petro & Horváth, Katalin (1981). "A kárpátontúli magyar nyelvjárások főbb sajátosságairól [On the most important characteristics of regional dialects of Hungarian in Subcarpathia]." *Magyar Nyelvjárások, 24,* 3–18.

LSA (1995). *Directory of Programs in Linguistics in the United States and Canada.* Washington, DC: Linguistic Society of America.

Lükő, Gábor (1935). "Havaselve és Moldva népei a X–XII. században [The peoples of Havaselve and Moldavia in the 10th to 12th centuries]." *Ethnographia, 46,* 90–105.

Lükő, Gábor (1936). *A moldvai csángók. I: A csángók kapcsolatai az erdélyi magyarsággal* [The Moldavian Csángós, Vol. 1: Relations between Csángó and Transylvania Hungarians]. Budapest: published by the author.

Lyra, Franciszek (1962). *English and Polish in Contact.* Bloomington, IN: Indiana University PhD dissertation.

Maco, N. O. & Luc, O. M. (1997). "Nacional'nij sklad naselennja Zakarpatskoj oblasti (zgidno perepisu 1989 r.) [Nationality composition of the Subcarpathian territory (According to the 1989 Census)]." In *Materiali naukovo-praktičnoj konferencii "Deržavne reguljuvannja mižetničnix vidnosin v Zakarpatti"* [Papers from the scholarly and practical conference on 'The national settlement of interethnic relations in Subcarpathia'] (pp. 214–234). Užhorod: UžDU.

Magocsi, Paul Robert (1996). "The Hungarians in Subcarpathia (Subcarpathian Rus')." *Nationalities Papers, 24*(3), 525–534.

Magyar, Zoltán (1994). "Vallás és etnikum kapcsolata egy moldvai csángó faluban [The connection between religion and ethnicity in a Moldavian Csángó village]." *Néprajzi látóhatár, 3*(1–2), 75–88.

Magyar törvénytár (1918). *évi törvénycikkek* [The Hungarian Code of Laws. Articles of 1918]. 1919. Budapest: Franklin Társaság.

Márton, Gyula (1972). *A moldvai csángó nyelvjárás román kölcsönszavai* [Romanian loanwords in the Moldavian Csángó dialect]. Bukarest: Kriterion.

Márton, Gyula, Péntek, János, & Vöő, István (1977). *A magyar nyelvjárások román kölcsönszavai* [The Romanian loanwords of Hungarian regional dialects]. Bukarest: Kriterion.

Marshall, David (1986). "The question of an official language: Language rights and the English Language Amendment." *International Journal of the Sociology of Language, 60,* 7–75.

Meeuwis, Michael & Blommaert, Jan (1998). "A monolectal view of code-switching. Layered code-switching among Zairians in Belgium." In Peter Auer (Ed.), *Code-switching in Conversation: Language, Interaction and Identity* (pp. 76–98). London/New York: Routledge.

Menges, Karl H. (1945). "Indo-European influences on Ural-Altaic languages." *Word, 1*, 188–193.

Mervis, Carolyn B. & Rosch, Eleanor (1981). "Categorization of natural objects." *Annual Review of Psychology, 32*, 89–116.

Mesaroš, Šandor (1981). *Položaj Madjara u Vojvodini 1918–1929* [The situation of Hungarians in Vojvodina, 1918–1929]. Novi Sad: Filozofski fakultet and Institut za istoriju.

Mesaroš, Šandor (1989). *Madjari u Vojvodini 1929–1941* [Hungarians in Vojvodina, 1929–1941]. Novi Sad: Filozofski fakultet and Institut za istoriju.

Mesthrie, Rajend (1994). "Language maintenance, shift, and death." In R. E. Asher & J. M. Y. Simpson (Eds.), *The Encyclopedia of Language and Linguistics* (pp. 1988–1993). Oxford: Pergamon.

Meyerstein, Goldie Piroch (1959). *Selected Problems of Bilingualism among Immigrant Slovaks.* Ann Arbor, MI: University of Michigan PhD dissertation.

McConvell, Patrick (1991). "Understanding language shift: A step towards language maintenance." In Suzanne Romaine (Ed.), *Language in Australia* (pp. 143–186). Cambridge: Cambridge University Press.

Mikecs, László (1989). *Csángók (Az 1941-es kiadás reprintje kiegészítésekkel.)* [The Csángós (A reprint of the 1941 edition with addenda)]. Budapest: Optimum.

Mikeš, Melanija (1974). *Glasovni razvoj dvojezične dece* [The linguistic development of bilingual children]. Novi Sad: Pokrajinska zajednica za naueni rad.

Milroy, Lesley (1987). *Observing and Analysing Natural Language: A Critical Account of Sociolinguistic Method.* Oxford: Blackwell.

Mirnics, Károly (1990a). "Magyarok Jugoszláviában a számok tükrében [Statistics on Hungarians in Vojvodina]." In Nándor Burányi (Ed.), *Magyarok Vajdaságban, A "Magyar Szó" tematikai különkiadása* [Hungarians in Vojvodina: A thematic issue of "Magyar Szó"] (p. 20). Újvidék: Forum.

Mirnics, Károly (1990b). Egy asszimilálódó nemzeti kisebbség jelene és jövője [The present and future of an assimilating national minority]. In Zoltán Kalapis (Ed.), *Magyarok Jugoszláviában '90* [Hungarians in Yugoslavia, 1990] (pp. 181–190). Újvidék: A Vajdasági Magyarok Demokratikus Közösségének Évkönyve.

Mirnics, Károly (1994). "Módszertani nehézségek a vajdasági magyarság identitásának tanulmányozásában [Methodological difficulties of the study of Vojvodina Hungarians' sense of identity]." In József Kovacsics (Ed.), *Magyarország nemzetiségeinek és a szomszédos államok magyarságának statisztikája (1910–1990)* [Statistics on Hungary's minorities and on Hungarians in neighboring states, 1910–1990] (pp. 141–153). Budapest: Központi Statisztikai Hivatal.

Mocsary, Victoria Ann (1990). *Árpádhon: The Largest Rural Hungarian Settlement in the United States.* Hammond: Southeastern Louisiana University.

Mollay, Károly (1982). *Német–magyar nyelvi érintkezések a XVI. század végéig* [German-Hungarian linguistic contacts up until the end of the 16th century]. Budapest: Akadémiai Kiadó.

Molnár Csikós, László (1989). "A magyar nyelv helyzete Jugoszláviában [The situation of the Hungarian language in Yugoslavia]." *Magyar Nyelvőr, 113*, 162–175.

Molnár Csikós, László (1993). "A délszláv országokban élő magyarok nyelvi és nyelvhasználati problémái [Linguistic and language use problems of Hungarians living in the former Yugoslavia]." *Magyar Nyelvőr, 117*, 479–482.

Mühlhäusler, Peter (1977). *Pidginisation and Simplification in Language.* Canberra: Pacific linguistics.

Murádin, László (1994). "A kétnyelvűség sajátos megnyilvánulása a moldvai csángó magyarok nyelvi tudatában [A unique manifestation of bilingualism in the linguistic consciousness of Moldavian Csángó Hungarians]." *Néprajzi látóhatár, 3*(1–2), 307–310.

Murádin, László (1995). "A magyar–román kétnyelvűség zavarai a közigazgatásban [The problems of Hungarian-Romanian bilingualism in administration]." *Kétnyelvűség, 2*, 21–24.

Murvai, László (1996). *Fekete fehér könyv* [The black and white book]. Cluj-Napoca: Stúdium.

Murvai, László (2000). "Magyar nyelvű oktatás Romániában 1989–1999 között [Hungarian language education in Romania, 1989–1999]." *Nyelvünk és Kultúránk, 112*, 119–134.

Muysken, Pieter (2000). *Bilingual Speech: A Typology of Code-mixing.* Cambridge: Cambridge University Press.

Myers-Scotton, Carol (1992). "Comparing codeswitching and borrowing." *Journal of Multilingual and Multicultural Development, 13*(1–2), 19–39.

Myers-Scotton, Carol (1993). *Duelling Languages: Grammatical Structure in Codeswitching.* Oxford: Clarendon.

Myers-Scotton, Carol (1998). "A way to dusty death: The Matrix Language turnover hypothesis." In Lenore A. Grenoble & Lindsay J. Whaley (Eds.), *Endangered Languages: Language Loss and Community Response* (pp. 289–316). Cambridge: Cambridge University Press.

Myers-Scotton, Carol & Jake, Janice L. (2001). "Explaining aspects of code-switching and their implications." In Janet L. Nicol (Ed.), *One Mind, Two Languages: Bilingual Language Processing* (pp. 84–116). Oxford: Blackwell.

Myhovych, I. I. (1997). "Problemi socializacii osnovnyx etnosocial'nyx spil'not Zakarpattja [The problems of socialization of essential ethno-social groups of Subcarpathia]." In *Materiali naukovo-praktičnoj konferencii "Deržavne reguljuvannja mižetničnix vidnosin v Zakarpatti"* [Papers from the scholarly and practical conference on 'The national settlement of interethnic relations in Subcarpathia'] (pp. 46–57). Užhorod: UžDU.

Nádasdy, Ádám (1989). "Consonant length in recent borrowings into Hungarian." *Acta Linguistica Hungarica, 39*, 195–213.

Nagy, Edit (1994). *A Study of Borrowing and Code-switching in the Speech of Hungarians Living in Columbia, South Carolina.* Columbia: University of South Carolina MA thesis.

Németh, Andrea (2002). "A kódváltás pragmatikai kérdései egy kétnyelvű közösségben [Pragmatic aspects of code-switching in a bilingual community]." In István Lanstyák & Szabolcs Simon (Eds.), *Tanulmányok a kétnyelvűségről* [Studies in bilingualism] (pp. 127–168). Pozsony: Kalligram.

Némethová, Andrea (2001). *A kódváltás grammatikája és pragmatikája (Egy baráti közösség kódváltási szokásainak vizsgálata)* [The grammar and pragmatics of code-switching: An investigation of the code-switching practices of a group of friends]. Bratislava: Comenius University MA thesis.

Niedzielski, Nancy A. & Preston, Dennis R. (2000). *Folk Linguistics.* Berlin/New York: Mouton de Gruyter.

Novak, Franc (1985). *Slovar beltinskega prekmurskega govora* [The dictionary of the Prekmurje Belatinci language]. Murska Sobota: Pomurska založba.

Nyisztor, Tinka (1997). "A gyertya használata mindenszentek és halottak napján Pusztinában [The use of candles on All Saints' Day and the Day of the Dead in Pusztina]." In Ferenc Pozsony (Ed.), *Dolgozatok a moldvai csángók népi kultúrájáról* [Studies on the folk culture of Moldavian Csángós] (pp. 113–122). Kolozsvár: Kriza János Néprajzi Társaság.

Očovský, Štefan (1992). "Interpretation of statistical data on nationalities." In Jana Plichtová (Ed.), *Minorities in politics: Cultural and language rights* (pp. 94–100). Bratislava: Czechoslovak Committee of the ECF.

Orosz, Ildikó & Csernicskó, István (1998). *The Hungarians in Subcarpathia.* Budapest: Tinta.

Ozolins, Uldis (1991). "National language policy and planning: migrant languages." In Suzanne Romaine (Ed.), *Language in Australia* (pp. 329–348). Cambridge: Cambridge University Press.

Ozolins, Uldis (1993). *The Politics of Language in Australia.* Cambridge: Cambridge University Press.

Pálffy M., Zoltán (1997). "Moldvai csángó diákok erdélyi iskolákban [Moldavian Csángó students in Transylvanian schools]." *Regio, 8*(3–4), 58–79.

Papp, György (1992). A vajdasági magyar hivatalos és közéleti nyelvhasználat a nyelvtörvény után [Vojvodina Hungarian official and public language use after the language law]. In Sándor Győri-Nagy and Janka Kelemen (Eds.), *Kétnyelvűség a Kárpát-medencében II* [Bilingualism in the Carpathian Basin, Vol. 2] (pp. 96–102). Budapest: Pszicholingva Nyelviskola and Széchenyi Társaság.

Papp, György (1995). "Beszédhelyzeti kötődésű kölcsönszavak és közlési interferenciák a jugoszláviai magyarság nyelvében [Situational attachment, loanwords and communicational interference in the language of Vojvodina Hungarians]. In Ilona Kassai (Ed.), *Kétnyelvűség és magyar nyelvhasználat* [Bilingualism and Hungarian language use] (pp. 215–223). Budapest: MTA Nyelvtudományi Intézete.

Paulston, Christina Bratt (1994). *Linguistic Minorities in Multilingual Settings.* Amsterdam: John Benjamins.

Pávai, István (1995). "A moldvai magyarok megnevezései [Designations of Moldavian Hungarians]." *Regio, 6*(4), 149–164.

P. Csige, Katalin (1993). "Lexikai és grammatikai russzicizmusok a kárpátaljai magyar nyelvhasználatban [Lexical and structural Russicisms in the Subcarpathian Hungarian language use]." In Kinga Klaudy (Ed.), *Harmadik Magyar Alkalmazott Nyelvészeti Konferencia* [The 3rd Hungarian Applied Linguistics Conference] (pp. 379–382). Miskolc: Miskolci Egyetem.

Péntek, János (1981). "A román–magyar nyelvi kölcsönhatás néhány szemantikai vonatkozása [Semantic aspects of Romanian-Hungarian language contact]." *Nyelv- és Irodalomtudományi Közlemények, 25,* 77–81.

Péntek, János (1994). Normagondok Erdélyben [Problems with the norm in Transylvania]. *Magyar Nyelvőr, 116,* 133–146.

Péntek, János (1999). *Az anyanyelv mítosza és valósága* [The myth and reality of the mother tongue]. Kolozsvár: Anyanyelvápolók Erdélyi Szövetsége.

Péntek, János (2001). Kontaktusjelenségek és folyamatok a magyar nyelv kisebbségi változataiban [Contact phenomena and processes in minority varieties of the Hungarian language]. In *A nyelv ritkuló légköre: Szociolingvisztikai dolgozatok* [The thinning air of language: Papers on sociolinguistics] (pp. 151–169). Kolozsvár: Korunk Baráti Társaság.

Petition, I. (1991). In József Botlik & György Dupka (Eds.), *Ez hát a hon...: Tények, adatok, dokumentumok a kárpátaljai magyarság életéből: 1918–1991* [So this is our land...: Facts, data and documents about the life of Subcarpathia Hungarians, 1918–1991] (pp. 160–166). Budapest/Szeged: Mandátum and Universum.

Petition, II. (1991.) In József Botlik & György Dupka (Eds.), *Ez hát a hon...: Tények, adatok, dokumentumok a kárpátaljai magyarság életéből: 1918–1991* [So this is our land...: Facts, data and documents about the life of Subcarpathia Hungarians, 1918–1991] (pp. 167–175). Budapest/Szeged: Mandátum and Universum.

Pivar, Ella (1994). "Kót, a legkisebb szlovéniai magyar falu [Kót, the smallest Hungarian village in Slovenia]." In Imre Gráfik (Ed.), *Tanulmányok a szlovéniai magyarság köréből* [Studies on Hungarians in Slovenia] (pp. 115–141). Budapest: Teleki László Alapítvány.

Polgár, Etelka (2001). *Language Maintenance and Language Shift: A Sociolinguistic Analysis of a Hungarian-American Community*. Szeged: University of Szeged MA Thesis.

Polinsky, Maria (In press). "Russian in the US: An endangered language." In Evgeny Golovko (Ed.), *Russian in Contact with Other Languages*. Oxford: Oxford: University Press.

Popis 2002 [Census 2002]. Beograd: Republički zavod za statistiku.

Poplack, Shana (1980). ""Sometimes I'll start a sentence in English Y TERMINO EN ESPAÑOL": Towards a typology of code-switching." *Linguistics, 18*, 581–618.

Pozsony, Ferenc (1994). "Újesztendőhöz kapcsolódó szokások a moldvai csángóknál [New Year's traditions among Moldavian Csángós]." *Néprajzi látóhatár, 3*(1–2), 151–166.

Pozsony, Ferenc (1997a). "Egy moldvai csángó család vallásos tárgyai [The religious objects of a Moldavian Csángó family]." In Ferenc Pozsony (Ed.), *Dolgozatok a moldvai csángók népi kultúrájáról* [Studies on the folk culture of Moldavian Csángós] (pp. 240–247). Kolozsvár: Kriza János Néprajzi Társaság.

Pozsony, Ferenc (1997b). "Látomások a moldvai csángó falvakban [Apparitions in Moldavian Csángó villages]." In Ferenc Pozsony (Ed.), *Dolgozatok a moldvai csángók népi kultúrájáról* [Studies on the folk culture of Moldavian Csángós] (pp. 248–258). Kolozsvár: Kriza János Néprajzi Társaság.

Puskás, Julianna (1982). *Kivándorló magyarok az Egyesült Államokban. 1880–1940.* [Immigrant Hungarians in the United States, 1880–1940]. Budapest: Akadémiai Kiadó.

Rácz, Endre (Ed.). (1971). *A mai magyar nyelv* [Present-day Hungarian]. Budapest: Tankönyvkiadó.

Rado, Marta & Lewis, Ramon (1980). "Exploring student attitudes in Australia towards ethnic language maintenance." *I.T.L. Review of Applied Linguistics, 49–50*, 117–136.

Recensămîntul populaţiai şi locuinţelor din 7 ianuarie 1992 Vol. IV. Structura etnică şi confesională a populaţiei. [Census of population and localities, 7 January, 1992. Vol. 4. Ethnic and denominational structure of the population]. Comisia Naţională pentru Statistică, [Bucureşti] 1995.

Recensămîntul populaţiai şi locuinţelor 2002 – Tabele, date preliminare. [2002 census of population and localities: Tables and preliminary data]. 2002. Bucureşti: Insitutul Naţional de Statistica.

Réger, Zita (1979). "Bilingual Gypsy Children in Hungary: Explorations in "Natural" Second Language Acquisition at an Early Age." *International Journal of the Sociology of Language, 19*, 59–82.

Report on the Situation of Hungarians in the Ukraine. http://www.htmh.hu/dokumentumok.

Richmond, Yale (1995). "Hungarians." In Yale Richmond (Ed.), *From Da to Yes: Understanding the East Europeans* (pp. 105–124). Yarmouth: Intercultural Press.

Rijkhoff, Jan (2002). *The Noun Phrase: A Typological Study of Its Form and Structure*. Oxford: Oxford University Press

Romaine, Suzanne (1989). *Bilingualism*. Oxford: Blackwell.

Romaine, Suzanne (1991). "Introduction." In Suzanne Romaine (Ed.), *Language in Australia* (pp. 1–24). Cambridge: Cambridge University Press.

Romero, Virginia (1989). "Hungarian folklife in the Florida parishes of Louisiana." In Louisiana Folklife Program (Ed.), *Folklife in the Florida Parishes* (pp. 68–76). Hammond: Southern Louisiana University.

Rosetti, Alexandru (1964). *Istoria limbii române* [The history of the Romanian language]. București: Editura Academiei R.S.R.

Rosová, Tatiana & Bútorová, Zora (1992). "Slovaks and Hungarians in Slovakia." In Jana Plichtová (Ed.), *Minorities in politics: Cultural and language rights* (pp. 174–181). Bratislava: Czechoslovak Committee of the ECF.

Rot, Sándor (1967). "Magyar–ukrán és ukrán–magyar kétnyelvűség Kárpát-Ukrajnában [Hungarian-Ukrainian and Ukrainian-Hungarian bilingualism in Subcarpathian Ukraine]." *Magyar Nyelvőr, 91*, 185–191.

Rot, Sándor (1968). *A magyar nyelv fejlődése. A magyar–keleti szláv nyelvi kapcsolatok* [The development of the Hungarian language: Language contact between Hungarian and Eastern Slavic languages]. Kiev/Užgorod: Rad'anska Skola.

Sammallahti, Pekka (1988). "Historical phonology of the Uralic languages: With special reference to Samoyed, Ugric, and Permic." In Denis Sinor (Ed.), *The Uralic Languages: Description, History, and Foreign Influences* (pp. 478–554). Leiden: E.J. Brill.

Sándor, Anna (2000). *Anyanyelvhasználat és kétnyelvűség egy kisebbségi magyar beszélőközösségben, Kolonban* [The use of mother tongue and bilingualism in a minority Hungarian speech community in Kolíňany, Slovakia]. Pozsony: Kalligram.

Sándor, Klára (1995). "Az élőnyelvi vizsgálatok és az iskola: a kisebbségi kétnyelvűség [Sociolinguistic research and school: Minority bilingualism]." *Regio, 6*(4), 121–148.

Sándor, Klára (1996a). "Apró Ábécé – apró esély: A csángók "nyelvélesztésének" lehetőségei és esélyei [A "Small Reader", a small chance: The chances and possibilities of Csángó language revitalization]." In István Csernicskó & Tamás Váradi (Eds.), *Kisebbségi magyar iskolai nyelvhasználat* [Minority Hungarian language use in schools] (pp. 51–67). Budapest: Tinta.

Sándor, Klára (1996b). "A nyelvcsere és a vallás összefüggése a csángóknál [The connection between language shift and religion among the Csángós]." *Korunk, 1996*(1), 60–75.

Sándor, Klára (1996c). Dialectology and language planning: The Changos and speakers of "Pure Hungarian". Paper presented at the 9th International Conference of Methods in Dialectology, Bangor (Wales), July 29, 1996.

Sándor, Klára (1998). "A magyar–török kétnyelvűség és ami körülötte van [Hungarian-Turkish bilingualism, and all that is around it]." In István Lanstyák & Gizella Szabómihály (Eds.), *Nyelvi érintkezések a Kárpát-medencében különös tekintettel a magyarpárú kétnyelvűségre* [Linguistic contacts in the Carpathian-basin, with special attention to bilingualism involving Hungarian] (pp. 7–26). Pozsony: Kalligram Könyvkiadó and A Magyar Köztársaság Kulturális Intézete.

Sándor, Klára (1999). "Contempt for linguistic human rights in the service of the Catholic Church: The case of the Csángós." In Miklós Kontra, Robert Phillipson, Tove Skutnabb-Kangas, & Tibor Várady (Eds.), *Language: A Right and a Resource. Approaching Linguistic Human Rights* (pp. 317–331). Budapest: Central European University Press.

Sándor, Klára (2000). "National feeling or responsibility: The case of the Csángó language revitalization." *Multilingua, 19*(1–2), 141–168.

Sándor, Klára (In press). "A csángókat megmentik ugye? [They save Csángós, don't they?]." In Ferenc Pozsony (Ed.), *Csángó-tanulmányok* [Studies on the Csángós]. Kolozsvár.

Sarhimaa, Anneli (1999). *Syntactic Transfer, Contact-induced Change, and the Evolution of Bilingual Mixed Codes: Focus on Karelian-Russian Language Alternation.* Helsinki: Finnish Literature Society.

Seaman, David P. (1972). *Modern Greek and American English in contact.* The Hague: Mouton.

Seres, András (1994). "Moldvai magyar lakodalmi szokások [Moldavian Hungarian wedding customs]." *Néprajzi látóhatár, 3*(1–2), 89–114.

Simon, Szabolcs & Kontra, Miklós (2000). "Slovak linguists and Slovak language laws: An analysis of Slovak language policy." *Multilingua, 19*, 73–94.

Siptár, Péter & Törkenczy, Miklós (2000). *The Phonology of Hungarian.* Oxford: Oxford University Press.

Škiljan, Dubravko (1992). "Standard languages in Yugoslavia." In Ranko Bugarski & Celia Hawkesworth (Eds.), *Language Planning in Yugoslavia* (pp. 27–42). Columbus, OH: Slavica.

Sklad nasalennja po okremix nacional'nostjax i ridnij movi za dannimi perepisi naselennja 1989 roku [The composition of population according to separate nationalities and mother-tongue in accordance with the 1989 Census] (1990). Užhorod: Zakarpatske oblasne upravlinnja statistiki.

Skutnabb-Kangas, Tove (1984). *Bilingualism or Not: The Education of Minorities.* Clevedon: Multilingual Matters.

Skutnabb-Kangas, Tove (2000a). *Linguistic Genocide in Education – Or Worldwide Diversity and Human Rights?* Mahwah, NJ: Lawrence Erlbaum Associates.

Skutnabb-Kangas, Tove (2000b). "Nyelvi emberi jogok [Linguistic human rights]." In Klára Sándor (Ed.), *Nyelv és hatalom, nyelvi jogok és oktatás* [Linguistic human rights: Language and power, language rights and education] (pp. 111–123). Csíkszereda: Apáczai Csere János Pedagógusok Háza Kiadója.

Slovenija. Karta Slovenskih Narečij [Slovenia: A map of Slovenian dialects] (1990). Geodetski zavod Slovenije Kartografski oddelek.

Solchanyk, Roman (1993). "The politics of language in Ukraine." *RFE/RL Research Report, 2*(10), 1–4.

Solovyova, Ariadna (1994). *Morphological Peculiarities in a Corpus of American Hungarian Speech.* Bloomington, IN: Indiana University MS.

Sorbán, Angella (2000). ""Tanuljon románul a gyermek, hogy jobban érvényesülessen." Az asszimiláció természetrajzához ["The child should study in Romanian to succeed better in life": On the nature of assimilation]." *Magyar Kisebbség, 3*, 167–180.

Solso, Robert L. (1995). *Cognitive Psychology.* 4th edition. Boston: Allyn and Bacon.

Spasovski, Milena (1994). *Teritorijalni razmeštaj naroda i nacionalnih manjina u SR Jugoslaviji* [The geographic location of peoples and ethnic minorities in the Federal Republic of Yugoslavia]. *Jugoslovenski Pregled, 38*(1), 31–64.

Statistični urad Republika Slovenije [The Statistics Office to the Republic of Slovenia]. *Neobjavljeni podatki po naselji za leto 1981* [Unpublished population data from 1981]. Ljubljana: MS, 1982.

Statistik Austria 2003. Volkszählung 2001: Demographische Hauptergebnisse. http://www.statistik.at/gz/vz_tab3.shtml

Stenson, Nancy (1990). "Phrase structure congruence, governement, and Irish-English code-switching." In Randall Hendrick (Ed.), *The Syntax of the Modern Celtic Languages* (pp. 167–197). New York: Academic.

Stenson, Nancy (1991). "Code-switching vs. borrowing in Modern Irish." In Peter Sture Ureland & George Broderick (Eds.), *Language Contact in the British Isles* (pp. 559–579). Tübingen: Niemeyer.

Stewart, Susan (1993). "Ukraine's policy toward its ethnic minorities." *RFE/RL Research Report, 2*(36), 55–62.

Stoffel, G. M. (1983). "Forms of address amongst German-English bilinguals in New Zealand." *General Linguistics, 23*(2), 79–93.

Šutaj, Štefan & Olejník, Milan (1998). "Slovak report." In Jerzy Kranz (Ed.), *Law and Practice of Central European Countries in the Field of National Minorities Protection after 1989* (pp. 269–317). Warszawa: Center for International Relations.

Szabó, Zoltán (1968). "Studiul funcţional al împrumuturilor de originea românească ale limbii maghiare literare vechi [The functional search of the borrowings of Romanian origin in Old Hungarian]." *Studii şi Cercetări Lingvistice,* 553–559.

Szabó, Zoltán (1975). "Stylistic remarks on the Romanian loanwords of Old Hungarian." *Revue Roumaine de Linguistique, 20*(6), 41–46.

Szabó, Attila T. (1962). "Eredmények és hiányosságok a magyar szókincs román eredetű feudalizmuskori elemeinek vizsgálatában [Results and shortcomings in the study of Romanian loanwords in Hungarian in the age of feudalism]." *Studia Universitatis Babeş-Bolyai, 1,* 19–34.

Szabómihály, Gizella (1993). "Nyelvhasználat és szociális háttér [Language use and social background]." *Hungarológia, 3,* 59–72.

Szántó, Miklós (2001). *Tengerentúli magyarok* [Hungarians overseas]. Budapest: Akadémiai Kiadó.

Szarka, László (1998). "A (cseh)szlovákiai közösség nyolc évtizede 1918–1998. Történeti vázlat [Eight decades of Hungarians in (Czecho)Slovakia, 1918–1998: A historical sketch]." In László Tóth (Ed.), *A (cseh)szlovákiai magyar művelődés története 1918–1998. I. rész* [An intellectual history of Hungarians in (Czecho)Slovakia, 1918–1998, Part I] (pp. 9–80). Budapest: Ister.

Szathmári, István (1988). "Nyelvi változások – nyelvi norma [Linguistic changes and linguistic norm]." In Jenő Kiss & László Szűts (Eds.), *A magyar nyelv rétegződése* [The stratification of the Hungarian language] (pp. 38–49). Budapest: Akadémiai Kiadó.

Székely, András Bertalan (1983). "A magyar nyelvű oktatás és közművelődés a jugoszláviai Mura-vidéken [Hungarian education and culture in Prekmurje in Yugoslavia]." *Nyelvünk és Kultúránk, 53,* 54–60.

Szeli, István (1983). *A magyar kultúra útjai Jugoszláviában* [Hungarian culture in Yugoslavia]. Budapest: Kossuth.

Szépfalusi, István (1991). "Magyarul beszélők a mai Ausztriában [Speakers of Hungarian in Austria today]." In Miklós Kontra (Ed.), *Tanulmányok a határainkon túli kétnyelvűségről* [Studies on Hungarian bilingualism outside Hungary] (pp. 73–121). Budapest: Magyarságkutató Intézet.

Széplaki, Joseph (1975). *The Hungarians in America 1583–1975: A chronology and fact book.* Dobbs Ferry, NY: Oceana.

Szilágyi, N. Sándor (1994). *Szociálpszichológiai tényezők a szókölcsönzésben* [Sociopsychological factors in lexical borrowing]. Kolozsvár: Babeş-Bolyai University MS.

Szilágyi, N. Sándor (1998). "De ce nu-şi pot însuşi copiii maghiari limba română în şcoală? []" *Altera, 7,* 131–148.

Szilágyi, N. Sándor (2002a). "A magyar nyelv a Magyarországgal szomszédos országokban [The Hungarian language in countries neighboring Hungary]." Lecture delivered at the Hungarian Academy of Sciences, Budapest, May 2, 2002.

Szilágyi, N. Sándor (2002b). "About the Csángó dialects in Moldavia (Romania)." Paper presented at the Conference on Endangered Minority Cultures in Europe, Budapest, February 15–16, 2002.

Szőcs, Anna (1993). "A Moldvai Csángómagyarok Szövetsége [The Association of Moldavian Csángó Hungarians]." In Péter Halász (Ed.), "Megfog vala apóm szokcor kezemtül..." Tanulmányok Domokos Pál Péter emlékére ["My father would take my hand...": Studies in Memory of Pál Péter Domonkos] (pp. 163–164). Budapest: Lakatos Demeter Egyesület.

Tamás, Lajos (1966). Etymologisch-historiches Wörterbuch der ungarischen Elemente im Rumänischen [Etymological-historical dictionary of Hungarian elements in Romanian]. Budapest: Akadémiai Kiadó.

Tánczos, Vilmos (1995a). Gyöngyökkel gyökereztél. Gyimesi és moldvai archaikus imádságok [Your roots are pearls: Archaic prayers from Gyimes and Moldavia]. Csíkszereda: Pro-Print.

Tánczos, Vilmos (1995b). "A nyelvváltás jelensége a moldvai csángók egyéni imarepertoárjában [The phenomenon of codeswitching in the individual prayer repertoire of Moldavian Csángós]." Kétnyelvűség, 3, 51–68.

Tánczos, Vilmos (1996). Keletnek megnyílt kapuja [The gate to the East has opened]. Kolozsvár: Korunk Baráti Társaság.

Tánczos, Vilmos (1999). "A moldvai csángók lélekszámáról [On the number of Moldavian Csángós]." In Ferenc Pozsony (Ed.), Csángósors: A molvai csángók a változó időkben [The fate of Csángós: The Csángós of Moldavia at times of change] (pp. 7–32). Budapest: Teleki László Alapítvány.

Tandefelt, Marika (1988). Mellan två språk. En fallstudie om språkbevarande och språkbyte i Finland [Between two languages: A case study of language maintenance and language shift in Finland]. Uppsala: Uppsala universitetet.

Tátrai, Nóra (2000). "What does a holistic view reveal about the language use of a bilingual group?". In Anna Fenyvesi & Klára Sándor (Eds.), Language Contact and the Verbal Complex of Dutch and Hungarian: Working Papers from the 1st Bilingual Language Use Theme Meeting of the Study Centre on Language Contact, November 11–13, 1999, Szeged, Hungary (pp. 177–188). Szeged: Teacher Training College.

Tezla, Albert (1993). The Hazardous Quest: Hungarian Immigrants in the United States 1895–1920: A Documentary. Budapest: Corvina.

The Hague Recommendations Regarding the Education Rights of National Minorities & Explanatory Note (1996). The Hague: Foundation on Inter-Ethnic Relations.

The Hungarians in Slovakia (1997). The Hungarians in Slovakia. Bratislava (Pozsony): Information Centre of the Hungarian Coalition in Slovakia.

The Oslo Recommendations Regarding the Linguistic Rights of National Minorities & Explanatory Note (1998). The Hague: Foundation on Inter-Ethnic Relations.

The Situation (2002). The Situation of Hungarians in Slovakia. http://www.htmh.hu/reports2002/slovakia2002.htm

Thomason, Sarah Grey (2001). Language Contact: An Introduction. Washington, DC: Georgetown University Press.

Thomason, Sarah Grey & Kaufman, Terrence (1988). Language Contact, Creolization, and Genetic Linguistics. Berkeley: University of California Press.

Tompa, József (Ed.). (1969–1970). A mai magyar nyelv rendszere I., II [The structure of present day Hungarian, Vols 1 and 2]. Budapest: Akadémiai Kiadó.

Tóth, Lajos (1994). *Magyar nyelvű oktatás a Vajdaságban 1944-től napjainkig* [Hungarian language education in Vojvodina from 1944 to the present]. Szabadka: Szabadkai Szabadegyetem.

Törkenczy, Miklós (1994). "A szótag" [The syllable]. In Ferenc Kiefer (Ed.), *Strukturális magyar nyelvtan II: Fonológia* [A structural grammar of Hungarian II: Phonology] (pp. 273–392). Budapest: Akadémiai Kiadó.

Trudgill, Peter (1992). *Introducing Language and Society.* Hammondsworth: Penguin.

Trudgill, Peter (1996). "Az olvasókönyvek és a nyelvészeti ideológia – szociolingvisztikai nézőpontból. [School readers and linguistic ideology from a sociolinguistic perspective]" In István Csernicskó & Tamás Váradi (Eds.), *Kisebbségi magyar iskolai nyelvhasználat* [Minority Hungarian language use in schools] (pp. 1–10). Budapest: Tinta.

Tur, Yevgenyi (1996). *Karta nacional'nostej Ukrainy ili nacional'naja karta* [The map of nationalities of Ukraine or the national chart]. *Region* January 16, 1996: 17.

U.S. Bureau of the Census (1960). *Historical Statistics of the United States: Colonial Times to 1957.* Washington, DC: U.S. Bureau of the Census.

Vadkerty, Katalin (1994). "Hungarians in postwar Slovakia." *The Hungarian Quarterly, 35,* 115–127.

Vago, Robert M. (1991). "Paradigmatic regularity in first language attrition." In Herbert Seliger & Robert M. Vago (Eds.), *First Language Attrition* (pp. 241–251). Cambridge: Cambridge University Press.

Vago, Robert M. (1998). "Phonology." In István Kenesei, Robert M. Vago, & Anna Fenyvesi, *Hungarian. (Descriptive Grammars)* (pp. 382–453). London: Routledge.

Váradi, Tamás (1995/1996). "Stylistic variation and the (bVn) variable in the Budapest Sociolinguistic Interview." *Acta Linguistica Hungarica, 43*(3–4), 295–309.

Váradi, Tamás & Kontra, Miklós (1995). "Degrees of stigmatization: *t*-final verbs in Hungarian." In Wolfgang Viereck (Ed.), *Proceedings of the International Congress of Dialectologists,* Bamberg, 29.7.-4.8. 1990, Vol. 4. *Zeitschrift für Dialektologie und Linguistic.* Beiheft 77 (pp. 132–142). Stuttgart: Franz Steiner.

Várdy, Steven Béla (1989a). "Soviet nationality policy in Carpatho-Ukraine since World War II: The Hungarians of Sub-Carpathia." *Hungarian Studies Review, 16*(1–2), 67–91.

Várdy, Steven Béla (1989b). "The great economic immigration from Hungary: 1880–1920." In Steven Béla Várdy & Ágnes Huszár Várdy (Eds.), *The Austro-Hungarian Mind: At Home and Abroad* (pp. 215–239). New York: Columbia University Press.

Varga, József (1990). "Élő nyelvjárási elemek a Muravidéken [Current regional dialectal elements in Prekmurje]." In Géza Szabó (Ed.), *II. Dialektológiai Szimpozion* [2nd Symposium on Dialectology] (pp. 157–162). Veszprém: Veszprémi Akadémiai Bizottság.

Varga, László (1975). *A Contrastive Analysis of English and Hungarian Sentence Prosody.* Budapest: Linguistics Institute of the Hungarian Academy of Sciences.

Vassady, Béla (1979). "Kossuth and Újházi on establishing a colony of Hungarian 48-ers in America, 1849–1852." *Canadian-American Review of Hungarian Studies, 6,* 21–46.

Vázsonyi, Andrew (1978). "The Cicisbeo and the Magnificent Cuckold: Boardinghouse life and lore in immigrant communities." *Journal of American Folklore, 91,* 641–656.

Vázsonyi, Endre (1995). *Túl a Kecegárdán: Calumet-vidéki amerikai magyar szótár* [Beyond Castle Garden: An American Hungarian dictionary of the Calumet region]. Budapest: Teleki László Alapítvány.

Vinnai, Győző (1995). *Délvidék. Bevezetés. Magyarok kisebbségben és szórványban* [Vojvodina: An introduction – Hungarians in minority and dispersed situations]. Budapest: A Magyar Miniszterelnökség Nemzetiségi és Kisebbségi Osztályának válogatott iratai, 1919–1944.

Virt, István (1994). "Halál és emlékezés (Halottak napi szokások a Bákó megyei Pusztinában) [Death and remembering: Day of the dead customs in Pusztina, Bákó county]." *Néprajzi látóhatár, 3*(1–2), 125–134.

Virtaranta, Pertti (1992). *Amerikansuomen sanakirja: A Dictionary of American Finnish.* Turku: Institute of Migration.

Volkszählung 2001 – Hauptergebnisse II – Österreich.
http://www.statistik.at/neuerscheinungen/vzaustria/shtml

Votruba, Martin (1998). "Linguistic Minorities in Slovakia." In Christina Bratt Paulston & Donald Peckham (Eds.), *Linguistic Minorities in Central and Eastern Europe* (pp. 255–279). Clevedon: Multilingual Matters.

Wass de Czege, Albert (1975). *Our Hungarian Heritage.* Astor, FL: Danubian Press.

Weinreich, Uriel (1953). *Languages in Contact: Findings and Problems.* The Hague: Mouton.

Zelliger, Erzsébet (2001). "Nyelvi és nyelvhasználati kérdések a felső-ausztriai magyar diaszpórában [Issues of language and language use in the Hungarian diaspora of Upper Austria]." *Magyar Nyelv, 97,* 171–184.

Zel'ová, Alena (1992). "The integration of the Hungarian minority in Slovakia: The language problem." In Jana Plichtová (Ed.), *Minorities in Politics: Cultural and Language Rights* (pp. 155–158). Bratislava: Czechoslovak Committee of the ECF.

Zgodovina Slovencev [The history of Slovenes] (1979). Ljubljana: Cankarjeva založba.

Zsemlyei, János (1979). *A Kis-Szamos vidéki magyar tájszólás román kölcsönszavai* [Romanian loanwords in the Kis-Szamos regional dialect of Hungarian]. Bukarest: Kriterion Könyvkiadó.

Zsemlyei, János (1995). "Román tükörszavak, tükörkifejezések és hibridszavak a romániai magyarság nyelvhasználatában [Romanian calques, calqued expressions and hybrid words in the language use of Romania Hungarians]." In Ilona Kassai (Ed.), *Kétnyelvűség és magyar nyelvhasználat* [Bilingualism and Hungarian language use] (pp. 245–252). Budapest: MTA Nyelvtudományi Intézete.

APPENDIX

The linguistic questions
of the SHOH questionnaire

Below is presented the list of questions that target linguistic variables from the questionnaire used in the Sociolinguistics of Hunngarian Outside Hungary project. The instructions and the task sentences are provided with their English translations, and morpheme-by-morpheme glosses are also given for the task sentences. (The abbreviations used in the glosses can be found in the *List of abbreviations* in this volume.)

* * *

AZ ALÁBBI MONDATOK KÖZÜL KARIKÁZZA BE AZ EGYIKET, AZT, AMELYIKET
TERMÉSZETESEBBNEK ÉRZI.

Out of the following pairs of sentences, circle the letter corresponding to the sentences you consider to be more natural sounding.

501 (1) *A   találkozás-t   Péter-rel   jó   jel-nek   tart-ott-a.*
       the meeting-ACC Peter-INS good sign-DAT consider-PAST-3SG

    (2) *A   Péter-rel   való   találkozás-t   jó   jel-nek*
       the meeting-ACC be.APRT meeting-ACC good sign-DAT

       tart-ott-a.
       consider-PAST-3SG
       'S/He considered meeting Peter a good sign.'

502 (1) *Valószínűleg fog-ok   kés-ni   egy kicsi-t,   vár-j-anak   meg!*
       probably   FUT-1SG be.late-INF a   little-ACC wait-IMP-3PL PVB

    (2) *Valószínűleg kés-ni   fog-ok   egy kicsi-t,   vár-j-anak   meg!*
       probably   be.late-INF FUT-1SG a   little-ACC wait-IMP-3PL PVB
       'I'll probably be a little late, please wait for me.'

503 (1) *Be-fizet-t-ed   már   az idei   tagság-i   díj-at?*
       PVB-pay-PAST-2SG already the this.year membership-ADER fee-ACC

    (2) *Be-fizet-t-ed   már   az idei   tag-díj-at?*
       PVB-pay-PAST-2SG already the this.year member-fee-ACC
       'Have you paid this year's membership fee yet?'

504 (1) *Éhes   vagy, kis   bogar-am? Ad-j-ak   egy kis   kenyér-ké-t?*
       hungry be.2SG little bug-PX1SG give-IMP-1SG a   little bread-DIM-ACC

(2) *Éhes   vagy,   kis   bogar-am? Ad-j-ak   egy kis   kenyer-et?*
hungry be.2sg little bug-px1sg give-imp-1sg a little bread-acc
'Are you hungry, my sweetie? Shall I give you a little bread?'

505 (1) *Néz-d,   milyen   szép   banán-ok-at   árul-nak az*
look-imp.2sg what.kind beautiful banana-pl-acc sell-3pl the
üzlet-ben!
store-ine

(2) *Néz-d,   milyen   szép   banán-t   árul-nak az üzlet-ben!*
look-imp.2sg what.kind beautiful banana-acc sell-3pl the store-ine
'Look, what beautiful bananas are being sold in the store.'

506 (1) *A   ma-i   gyerek-ek at-tól   vál-nak   önző-k-ké,   hogy*
the today-ader child-pl that-abl become-3pl selfish-pl-tra that
minden-t   meg-kap-nak.
everythin-acc pvb-get-3pl

(2) *A   ma-i   gyerek-ek at-tól   vál-nak   önző-vé,   hogy*
the today-ader child-pl that-abl become-3pl selfish-tra that
minden-t   meg-kap-nak.
everythin-acc pvb-get-3pl
'Modern children become selfish because they get everything [that they
want].'

507 (1) *Un-om   már   ez-t   a   sok   utazás-t   busz-szal.*
be.tired-1sg emph this-acc the much traveling-acc bus-ins

(2) *Un-om   már   ez-t   a   sok   busz-oz-ás-t.*
be.tired-1sg emph this-acc the much bus-vder-ader-acc
'I am very tired of all this traveling by bus.'

508 (1) *Ez-zel   az eshetőség-gel   is   kell számol-ni.*
this-ins the possibililty-ins also must count-inf

(2) *Ez-zel   az eshetőség-gel   is   számol-ni kell.*
this-ins the possibililty-ins also count-inf must
'This possibility has to be taken into account, too.'

509 (1) *A   bejárat   az épület-be   a   másik oldal-on van.*
the entrance the building-ill the other side-sup be.3sg

(2) *Az épület   bejárat-a   a   másik oldal-on van.*
the building entrance-px3sg the other side-sup be.3sg
'The entrance of the building is on the other side.'

510 (1) *Hahó, itt   vagy-ok! Lát-sz?*
hello here be-1sg see-2sg

(2) *Hahó, itt   vagy-ok! Lát-sz engem?*
hello here be-1sg see-2sg me
'Hello, I'm here! Can you see me?'

511 (1) *Eb-ben   az   üzlet-ben nemcsak függöny-t,   hanem szőnyeg-et is*
     this-INE the store-INE not.only curtain-ACC but   rug-ACC   also
     lehet   vásárol-ni.
     possible buy-INF

   (2) *Eb-ben   az   üzlet-ben nemcsak függöny-ök-et, hanem szőnyeg-ek-et*
     this-INE the store-INE not.only curtain-PL-ACC but   rug-PL-ACC
     is   lehet   vásárol-ni.
     also possible buy-INF
     'In this store not only curtains but rugs are sold, too.'

512 (1) *Koszovó-ban folytatód-nak a   tárgyalás-ok   az albán-ok   és*
     Kosovo-INE continue-3PL the negotiation-PL the Albanian-PL and
     a   szerb-ek között.
     the Serb-PL between

   (2) *Koszovó-n   folytatód-nak a   tárgyalás-ok   az albán-ok   és*
     Kosovo-SUP continue-3PL the negotiation-PL the Albanian-PL and
     a   szerb-ek között.
     the Serb-PL between
     'Negotiations continue between Albanians and Serbs in Kosovo.'

513 (1) *Valószínűleg külföld-re   fog-nak költöz-ni.*
     probably   abroad-SUB FUT-3PL move-INF

   (2) *Valószínűleg, hogy külföld-re   fog-nak költöz-ni.*
     probably   that abroad-SUB FUT-3PL move-INF
     'They will probably move abroad.'

514 (1) *Tanító   néni, fáj   a   fej-em.   Ki-me-het-ek?*
     teacher aunt ache.3SG the head-PX1SG PVB-go-POT-1SG

   (2) *Tanító   néni, fáj   a   fej-em.   Ki   tud-ok   men-ni?*
     teacher aunt ache.3SG the head-PX1SG PVB be.able-1SG go-INF
     'Miss, I have a headache. May I go out?'

515 (1) *Tegnap   lát-t-alak   a   tévé-ben.*
     yesterday see-PAST-1SG.2OBJ the TV-INE

   (2) *Tegnap   lát-t-alak   téged   a   tévé-ben.*
     yesterday see-PAST-1SG.2OBJ you.ACC the TV-INE
     'I saw you on TV yesterday.'

UGYANAZT A MONDANIVALÓT KÜLÖNFÉLEKÉPPEN FEJEZHETJÜK KI. OLVAS-
SA EL AZ ALÁBBI 4 MONDATOT, UTÁNA PEDIG ÉRTÉKELJE ŐKET KARIKÁZÁS-
SAL!

The same thing can be expressed in different ways. Read the following four sentences and judge them by circling the most suitable characterization.

521 *Mari-nak is   meg kell old-ani-a   a   saját problémá-i-t.*
    Mary-DAT also PVB must solve-INF-3SG the own problem-PX3SG.PL-ACC

(1) nagyon jó (2) elfogadható (3) elég rossz (4) nagyon rossz
very good   acceptable   quite bad   very bad

522 *Mari-nak   is   meg kell   old-ani   a   saját problémá-i-t.*
Mary-DAT also PVB must solve-INF the own problem-PX3SG.PL-ACC

(1) nagyon jó (2) elfogadható (3) elég rossz (4) nagyon rossz
very good   acceptable   quite bad   very bad

523 *Mari   is   meg kell, hogy old-ja   a   saját problémá-i-t.*
Mary also PVB must that solve-IMP.3SG the own problem-PX3SG.PL-ACC

(1) nagyon jó (2) elfogadható (3) elég rossz (4) *nagyon rossz*
very good   acceptable   quite bad   very bad

524 *Mari   is   meg kell   old-ja   a   saját problémá-i-t.*
Mary also PVB must solve-IMP.3SG the own problem-PX3SG.PL-ACC

(1) nagyon jó (2) elfogadható (3) elég rossz (4) nagyon rossz
very good   acceptable   quite bad   very bad
'Mary has to solve her own problems, too.'

JÓNAK TARTJA-E A KÖVETKEZŐ MONDATOKAT?
Do you consider the following sentences good?

531 *Ott   van   a   szék   a   szoba sark-á-ba.*
there be.3SG the chair the room corner-PX3SG-ILL
'The chair is in the corner of the room.'

(a) jónak tartom
I consider it good
(b) rossznak tartom, jobb így: . . . .
I consider it bad; it is better like this: . . . .

532 *Nem tud-om,   a   bank-i   számlá-já-n   mennyi   pénz*
not   know-1SG the bank-ADER account-PX3SG-SUP how.much money
van.
be.3SG
'I don't know how much money there is in his/her bank account.'

(a) jónak tartom
I consider it good
(b) rossznak tartom, jobb így: . . . .
I consider it bad; it is better like this: . . . .

533 *Ha meg-ír-t-a   volna is   a   level-et, nem men-t   volna*
if   PVB-write-PAST-3SG COND also the letter-ACC not go-PAST.3SG COND
semmi-re.
nothing-SUB
'S/He wouldn't have achieved anything even if s/he had written the letter.'

(a) jónak tartom
    I consider it good
(b) rossznak tartom, jobb így: ....
    I consider it bad; it is better like this: ....

534 *Az ilyen dolg-ok-at   mindig a barát-ok-kal beszél-em meg, felnőtt*
    the such thing-PL-ACC always the friend-PL-INS speak-1SG PVB adult
    ember-ek-kel   soha.
    person-PL-INS never
    'I discuss such matters with my friends, never with adults.'

    (a) jónak tartom
        I consider it good
    (b) rossznak tartom, jobb így: ....
        I consider it bad; it is better like this: ....

535 *A szerződő   fel-ek   a megállapodás-t közjegyző előtt írás-ban*
    the contracting party-PL the agreement-ACC notary   before writing-INE
    foglal-t-ák.
    contain-PAST-3PL
    'The contracting parties have put the agreement in writing before the notary public.'

    (a) jónak tartom
        I consider it good
    (b) rossznak tartom, jobb így: ....
        I consider it bad; it is better like this: ....

536 *Ha szellőztet-ni akar-ok, így   kér-ek   engedély-t: Ki*
    if air-INF   want-1SG like.this ask-1SG permission-ACC PVB
    tud-om   nyit-ni   az ablak-ot?
    be.able-1SG open-INF the window-ACC
    'When I want to air the room, I ask for permission like this: May I open the window?'

    (a) jónak tartom
        I consider it good
    (b) rossznak tartom, jobb így: ....
        I consider it bad; it is better like this: ....

537 *Már   dél   lesz,   mi-re   meg-érkez-ünk a*
    already noon be.FUT.3SG what-SUB PVB-arrive-1PL the
    szülőváros-om-ban   a család-om-hoz.
    native.town-PX1SG-INE the family-PX1SG-ALL
    'It'll be noon by the time we arrive at my family's house in my native town.'

    (a) jónak tartom
        I consider it good

(b) rossznak tartom, jobb így: . . . .
I consider it bad; it is better like this: . . . .

538 *Tájékoztat-juk ügyfel-ei-nk-et,*   *hogy a*   *bankkönyv-ecské-k-et*
inform-1PL   customer-PL-PX1PL-ACC   that   the   bank.book-DIM-PL-ACC
a   *jövő hónap-ban cserél-jük*   *ki.*
the   next   month-INE   exchange-1PL   PVB
'We want to inform our customers that we'll be exchanging the bank booklets next month.'

(a) jónak tartom
I consider it good
(b) rossznak tartom, jobb így: . . . .
I consider it bad; it is better like this: . . . .

KARIKÁZZA BE AZ (1)-T VAGY A (2)-T ASZERINT, HOGY MELYIK ILLIK BELE JOBBAN A MONDATBA!
Circle (1) or (2), depending on which one fits into the sentence better.

601 *A*   *képviselő-k*   *az ok-ok-at*   . . .   *tart-ott-ák.*
the   representative-PL   the   reason-PL-ACC   {...}   consider-PAST-3PL

(1) *komoly-ak-nak* (2) *komoly-nak*
serious-PL-DAT   serious-DAT
'The representatives considered the reasons serious.'

602 *Miért sír-sz,*   *kis*   *bogar-am? Meg-üt-ött-ed*   *a*   ...?
why   cry-2SG   little   bug-PX1SG   PVB-hit-PAST-2SG   the   {...}?

(1) *kez-ecské-d-et?*   (2) *kis*   *kez-ed-et?*
hand-DIM-PX2SG-ACC   little   hand-PX2SG-ACC
'Why are you crying, sweetie? Have you hurt you little hand?'

603 *A*   *repülőgép-ek meg-sért-ett-ék*   *Svájc*   ... .
the   airplane-PL   PVB-violate-PAST-3PL   Switzerland   {...}.

(1) *lég-i*   *ter-é-t*   (2) *lég-ter-é-t*
air-ADER   space-PX3SG-ACC   air-space-PX3SG-ACC
'The airplanes violated Switzerland's air space.'

604 *Az*   *autó-s*   *mozi-ban az utas-ok*   ...   *ül-ve*   *néz-het-ik*
the   car-ADER   movie-INE   the   passanger-PL   {...}   sit-PCVB   watch-POT-3PL
a   *film-et.*
the   film-ACC

(1) *autó-k-ban* (2) *autó-ban*
car-PL-INE   car-INE
'In drive-in movies the passangers watch the movie sitting in their cars.'

605 *Fáj*   *a*   *fej-em,*   *mert*   *a*   *szomszéd egész délután*   ... .
ache.3SG the   head-PX1SG because   the   neighbor   whole   afternoon   {...}

(1) *hegedű-n   játsz-ott*   (2) *hegedül-t*
violin-SUP play-PAST.3SG   play.violin-PAST.3SG
'I have a headache because the neighbor played the violin all afternoon.'

606 *Fiú-k, nem at-tól   vál-tok   …   hogy el-végz-itek   az*
boy-PL not that-ABL become-2PL {…} that PVB-finish-2PL the
iskolá-t,   hanem at-tól, ha tüz-et   olt-otok.
school-ACC but   that-ABL if fire-ACC put.out-2PL

(1) *tűzoltó-k-ká*   (2) *tűzoltó-vá*
fireman-PL-TRA   fireman-TRA
'Guys, you will become firemen not by finishing the school but by putting out fires.'

607 *Mindjárt kész   az   ebéd,   … .*
at.once   ready the lunch, {…}

(1) *ne   légy   türelmetlen!* (2) *ne   türelmetlenked-j!*
not be.IMP.2SG impatient   not be.impatient-IMP.2SG
'Lunch is almost ready, don't be impatient.'

608 *Itt   van   még Péter? – Itt,   de   már   … .*
here be.3SG still Peter – here but already {…}

(1) *készül   men-ni* (2) *men-ni készül*
prepare.3SG go-INF   go-INF prepare.3SG
"Is Peter here?" "Yes, but he is preparing to go."

609 *Az egyik ismerős-öm   fi-a   …   volt   katona.*
the one   acquaintance-PX1SG son-PX3SG {…} be.PAST.3SG soldier

(1) *Craiová-n*   (2) *Craiová-ban*
Craiova-SUP   Craiova-INE
'A friend of mine's son served in the army in Craiova.'

610 *Az osztály-ban senki   sem … .*
the class-INE   nobody not {…}.

(1) *magas-abb, mint ő*   (2) *magas-abb nál-a*
tall-CMP   than s/he   tall-CMP   ADE-PX3SG
'Nobody in the class is taller than him/her.'

611 *A   fiú-k   még tavaly   jelentkez-t-ek   … .*
the boy-PL still last.year sign.up-PAST-3PL {…}.

(1) *tűzoltó-k-nak*   (2) *tűzoltó-nak*
fireman-PL-DAT   fireman-DAT
'The boys signed up to be firemen last year.'

612 *Az-t hisz-em, ebéd után mindenki-nek jól es-ik egy … –*
that-ACC believe lunch after everyone-DAT well fall-3SG a {…} –
mond-t-a a háziasszony kedves mosoly-lyal.
say-PAST-3SG the hostess nice smile-INS

 (1) *kávé-cska* (2) *kávé*
  coffee-DIM   coffee
  "'I think after lunch everyone feels like having a little coffee", said the hostess
  with a nice smile.'

613 *A tükör előtt hosszan … .*
the mirror before for.long {…}

 (1) *szépít-ett-e   magá-t* (2) *szépítkez-ett*
  beautify-PAST-3SG self-ACC beautify.REFL-PAST.3SG
  'She beautified herself in front of the mirror for a long time.'

614 *Kár, hogy már nem megy a mozi-ban a Superman, mert*
pity that already not go.3SG the movies-INE the Superman because
szívesen … .
gladly {…}.

 (1) *meg-néz-né-nk* (2) *meg-néz-nők*
  PVB-see-COND-1PL   PVB-see-COND.1PL
  'It's a pity "Superman" is not playing in the movies any more, we would see
  it gladly.'

615 *Találkoz-t-am Hedvig-gel, s … hogy ve-gy-en nek-em egy*
meet-PAST-1SG Hedvig-INS and {…} that buy-IMP-3SG DAT-1SG a
kifli-t.
croissant-ACC

 (1) *meg-kér-t-em* (2) *meg-kér-t-em ő-t*
  PVB-ask-PAST-1SG   PVB-ask-PAST-1SG s/he-ACC
  'I met Hedvig and asked her to buy me a croissant.'

**ÍRJON A PONTOK HELYÉRE (HA SZÜKSÉGESNEK ÉRZI!) EGY ODAILLŐ
VÉGZŐDÉST VAGY SZÓT!**
 Fill in the blanks with a suitable ending or word (if you feel that one is missing).

621 *Patrícia magas-abb Klaudiá…, pedig egy év-vel fiatal-abb.*
Patricia tall-CMP Claudia although a year-INS young-CMP
'Patricia is taller than Claudia, even though she is a year younger.'

622 *Az-t akar-om, hogy ő nyi… ki az ajtó-t.*
that-ACC want-1SG that s/he open PVB the door-ACC
'I want him/her to open the door.'

623 *Középiskolá-nk... sok szakképzetlen pedagógus tanít.*
high.school-PX1PL many unqualified teacher teach.3SG
'Several teachers teach without qualifications in our high school.'

624 *Jó nap-ot kíván-ok, a főnök... jö-tt-em, panasz-t*
good day-ACC wish-1SG the boss come-PAST-1SG complaint-ACC
szeret-né-k te-nni.
like-COND-1SG put-INF
'Hi, I came to the boss, I'd like to file a complaint.'

625 *Kovács János az-t kér-te, hogy a jelölő bizottság*
Kovács John that-ACC ask-PAST-3SG that the nominating committee
tekint-s-en el at-tól, hogy ő-t titkár-rá
exclude-IMP-3SG PVB that-ABL that s/he-ACC secretary-TRA
jelöl-j-e és .... (meg-választ-ani).
nominate-IMP-3SG and .... PVB-elect-INF
'John Kovács requested that the nominating committee exclude nominating and appointing him as secretary.'

626 *Erzsi néni-nek fáj... a szív..., Kati néni-nek meg a láb... is*
Liz aunt-DAT ache the heart Kathy aunt-DAT and the foot also
fáj....
ache
'Aunt Liz has a pain in her heart [lit. her heart aches] and Aunt Kathy has aching feet [lit. her feet ache] too.'

627 *Mi is meg-ven... az-t a malac-ot, de egy kicsit drágán*
we also PVB-buy that-ACC the piglet-ACC but a little expensively
ad-ják.
give-3PL
'We would buy that piglet, too, but they're overcharging it a bit.'

628 *Ha Péter rossz-ul válogat... meg a barát-a-i-t, pórul*
if Peter bad-ESS choose PVB the friend-PX3SG-PL-ACC discomfited
jár.
go.3SG
'If Peter chooses his friends badly, he'll soon be discomfited.'

629 *Mi-nek ez a halogatás?! Nem szeret-em, ha valaki*
what-DAT this the delay? not like-1SG if somebody
el-hala... a döntés-ek-et.
PVB-postpone the decision-PL-ACC
'Why this delay? I don't like it when somebody postpones making decisions.'

ÍRJON A PONTOK HELYÉRE EGY ODAILLŐ FOGLALKOZÁSNEVET!
Fill in the blanks with a suitable profession name.

631–632.

Anyá-m   *egy középiskolá-ban tanít,*   *ő*   *tehát* ……….
mother-PX1SG   a   highschool-INE teach.3SG s/he thus ……….
'My mother teaches in a high school, so she is a …… ?'

Tavaly ki-nevez-t-ék   *az iskola él-é-re,*   *most tehát*
last.year PVB-appoint-PAST-3PL the school top-PX3SG-SUB now thus
már ………. *is.*
already ………. also
'Last year she was appointed to run the school, so now she is also the ………. ?'

633   *Kovács Juli-t*   *már*   *régóta*   *ismer-em. Mióta ide-költöz-t-ünk,*
Kovács Julie-ACC already for.long know-1SG since PVB-move-PAST-1PL
nál-a   *csinál-tat-om a*   *frizurá-m-at,*   *vagyis ő*   *a* ……….
ADE-3SG do-CAUS-1SG the hairdo-PX1SG-ACC so   s/he the ……….
'I have known Julie Kovács for a long time. Since we moved here, I have been having my hair done by her, so she is [my] ………. ?'

634   *A*   *legutóbbi választás-ok-on számos nő*   *kerül-t*   *a falv-ak*
the latest   election-PL-SUP several woman get-PAST.3SG the village-PL
és város-ok él-é-re.   *A mi város-unk-ban Nagy Ilona*
and town-PL top-PX3SG-SUB the we town-PX1PL-INE Nagy Helen
le-tt   *a* ……….
become-PAST.3SG the ……….
'In the latest elections, many women came to head villages and towns. In our town, Helen Nagy became ………. .'

UGYANAZT A MONDANIVALÓT KÜLÖNFÉLEKÉPPEN FEJEZHETJÜK KI. OLVAS-SA EL AZ ALÁBBI 4 MONDATOT, UTÁNA PEDIG ÉRTÉKELJE ŐKET KARIKÁZÁS-SAL!

The same thing can be expressed in different ways. Read the following four sentences and judge them by circling the most suitable characterization.

641   *A*   *menekültügyi főbiztos-nak*   *meg kell old-ani-a*   *a*
the refugee.matter high.commissioner-DAT PVB must solve-INF-PX3SG the
menekült-ek elhelyezés-é-vel   *kapcsolatos problémá-k-at.*
refugee-PL placement-PX3SG-INS connected problem-PL-ACC

    (1) nagyon jó (2) elfogadható (3) elég rossz (4) nagyon rossz
      very good   acceptable   quite bad   very bad

642   *A*   *menekültügyi főbiztos-nak*   *meg kell old-ani a*
the refugee.matter high.commissioner-DAT PVB must solve-INF the
menekült-ek elhelyezés-é-vel   *kapcsolatos problémá-k-at.*
refugee-PL placement-PX3SG-INS connected problem-PL-ACC

(1) nagyon jó (2) elfogadható (3) elég rossz (4) nagyon rossz
   very good   acceptable   quite bad   very bad

643 *A   menekültügyi   főbiztos   meg kell   hogy old-j-a   a*
   the refugee.matter high.commissioner PVB must that solve-IMP-3SG the
   menekült-ek elhelyezés-é-vel   kapcsolatos problémá-k-at.
   refugee-PL placement-PX3SG-INS connected problem-PL-ACC

   (1) nagyon jó (2) elfogadható (3) elég rossz (4) nagyon rossz
      very good   acceptable   quite bad   very bad

641 *A   menekültügyi   főbiztos   meg kell   old-j-a   a*
   the refugee.matter high.commissioner PVB must solve-IMP-3SG the
   menekült-ek elhelyezés-é-vel   kapcsolatos problémá-k-at.
   refugee-PL placement-PX3SG-INS connected problem-PL-ACC

   (1) nagyon jó (2) elfogadható (3) elég rossz (4) nagyon rossz
      very good   acceptable   quite bad   very bad
   'The high commissioner for refugees has to solve the problems related to
   the housing of the refugees.'

Index

In the series *IMPACT: Studies in language and society* the following titles have been published thus far or are scheduled for publication: